THE TWENTIETH-CENTURY NEWSPAPER PRESS IN BRITAIN

AN ANNOTATED BIBLIOGRAPHY

THE
Twentieth-Century Newspaper Press in Britain

AN ANNOTATED BIBLIOGRAPHY

DAVID LINTON

INTRODUCTION BY RAY BOSTON

MANSELL

First published 1994 by
Mansell Publishing Limited, *A Cassell imprint*
Villiers House, 41/47 Strand, London WC2N 5JE, England
387 Park Avenue South, New York, New York 10016–8810, USA

British Library Cataloguing-in-Publication Data
A catalogue record for this book is available from the British Library.

Library of Congress Cataloging-in-Publication Data
Linton, David, 1916–
    The twentieth-century newspaper press in Britain: an annotated
bibliography / David Linton.
        p.   cm.
    Includes bibliographical references and index.
    ISBN 0–7201–2159–0
    1. British newspapers–History–20th century–Bibliography.
I. Title.
Z6956.G6L58   1994
[PN5114]
015.41035–dc20   93–42784
                                                                    CIP

Typeset by Colset Private Ltd, Singapore
Printed and bound in Great Britain by Biddles Ltd,
Guildford and King's Lynn

CONTENTS

PREFACE

As I write, more than seven years have passed since the publication of my own and Ray Boston's *The newspaper press in Britain: an annotated bibliography*. In the Introduction that follows, very aware of the ever-accelerating pace of change in the newspaper industry, Ray makes a strong case for a new work that reflects recent history and makes its own contribution in recording it. So that is what the reader is now offered: not only a revision, an updating and a re-packaging, but also a thorough re-assessment of the twentieth century with a new line of readers in mind.

Perhaps surprisingly at first glance (with virtually all trace of previous centuries removed), the result has been a great increase in entries, from some 2,900 to over 3,700. This is explained in part by the decision to widen the range of authors considered for inclusion. 'News' journalists were the criterion in 1987: this time a selection of other writers such as essayists, dramatic critics, sports reporters and media academics join the lists as being contributors in their own special fields to newspaper history. 'Registered as a newspaper at the Post Office' embraces news magazines etc. And new formats have qualified for inclusion: CD-ROM makes its bow alongside the microform entries that were included before.

'Britain' in the title is shorthand for the full name of the United Kingdom of Great Britain and Northern Ireland. The press in the present-day Republic of Ireland is therefore only covered when the content of a publication covers the entire island. Newspapers published for the British Forces, serving overseas and/or in the UK, have been included, as have the subject of ships' newspapers and – reverting to geographical qualification – the press published in Britain to cater for the growing ethnic population.

As explained in 'Arrangement of Material' on a later page, the main text is preceded by a section entitled 'Reference Works'. New readers in particular may be at a loss as to where to begin; now they should turn first to the Reference Works section, which like the main Bibliography section is annotated, providing the flavour as well as indicating the value of reference materials (some of it historical and no longer published).

Selection of these significant 'signposts' has been an arbitrary matter, but the opportunity has been taken to include some works that are not primarily 'press' titles (for example, writers' dictionaries, general bibliographies, etc.). Publications sought in the main Bibliography may be found instead in Reference Works.

The Chronology that follows the Bibliography is a 'twentieth-century-to-date' version of a popular feature of our original book. It is intended as a supplementary aid – British press history in a nutshell – unlike the Index, which is absolutely central to the work. This Index has been greatly expanded and subdivided, and reflects several areas which have received special attention in this new compilation.

Press freedom, ethics, media studies, advertising, training of journalists, photo-journalists and cartoonists – all these and many more aspects of the British newspaper press have found inclusion in both the Bibliography and the Index.

The twentieth century has not quite run its course: there may well be dramatic events ahead. But here is the story to date, as chronicled by journalists or about journalism, 'frozen in time'.

ACKNOWLEDGEMENTS

First and foremost, I acknowledge most readily the continued and extremely valued close association of Ray Boston, who was my co-author on the earlier (1987) bibliography. This time he contributes a challenging Introduction, based on exceptional scholarship.

Many others have given generous help and advice, especially Ms Jill Allbrooke and Stephen Lester, British Library Newspaper Library; Miss Melanie Aspey (former Manager) and Eamon Dyas (Manager), Group Records, News International; Dr Joseph O. Baylen, Regent's Professor of History Emeritus, Georgia State University; Michael Bromley and Henry Clother, Graduate Centre for Journalism, City University, London; John Frost, Historical Newspaper Service; Dr Dennis Griffiths, Editor, *The Encyclopedia of the British Press*; Dr Nicholas Hiley; Roger Holland and colleagues, Newspaper Society; Bob James; John le Neve Johnson, Honorary Secretary, London Press Club; Barrie MacDonald, Librarian, Independent Television Commission; Mrs Sally Mellis, National Council for the Training of Journalists; James Mosley and colleagues, St Bride Printing Library, London; Donald Munro, Assistant Librarian, Institute of Historical Research, London; George Newkey-Burden, *The Daily Telegraph*; Steve Peak, Editor, *The Media Guide*; Gordon Phillips; Dr Chris Pond, Head of Information, House of Commons; Jonathan Purday, National Bibliographic Service, British Library; Andrew Saint, English Heritage; David Simmonds, of L. Simmonds (Fleet Street booksellers); Philip Spink, Head of Information, Advertising Association; Miss Justine Taylor, former Archivist, Reuters; Chris Underwood, General Secretary, Chartered Institute of Journalists; Tony Weller, Monopolies and Mergers Commission.

Last, but certainly not least, may I express warm appreciation of the co-operation and professionalism of those closely concerned at Mansell Publishing and Cassell: notably Veronica Higgs, Sandra Margolies and Catherine Johnston, and Colin Hutchens.

INTRODUCTION: FROM INKWELLS TO DIRECT INPUT

A bibliography which tries to focus attention on one very small section of a vast historical canvas might seem to many to be straining at a gnat and hardly worth the effort. It might even seem to some to be obsessional and positively obscurantist. Nevertheless, so many incredible things have happened to that evolved chronicle, the newspaper, during the twentieth century, it was thought desirable as well as useful to devote a whole book to this subject: one that would offer to students and researchers a considered distillation of the heavy tonnage of material relating to the British newspaper press which has accrued since 1900.

After almost four hundred years of snail's pace evolution that was more of a struggle against reaction than a progress towards democracy, the physical appearance and the general purpose of the British newspaper changed fundamentally during the closing years of the nineteenth century. To put it more bluntly, Fleet Street finally settled for profitability rather than respectability, after striving hopelessly to become a 'moral workshop', addressing the entire British nation at home and abroad, for most of Victoria's reign. The popular, twentieth-century British press was ushered in amid a flurry of sceptical bankers and sizeable bank loans. The new, irresponsibly sensationalist newspaper momentum from the USA was permitted to express itself in Britain through the halfpenny *Daily Mail*, which was produced imitatively and not, as might have been expected, innovatively by the House of Northcliffe.

The revolution began in 1889, with the arrival in Britain from New York of Ottmar Mergenthaler's brilliant invention, the Linotype machine. Using this, and many more like it over the next few years, proprietors of the sage and sober British 'class' press (or most of them) quickly transformed their products into a bright and breezy 'mass' press. The rest, as they say, is printing history, which, decoded, means the revolution was far more important commercially than it was journalistically.

When we come to consider the second major printing revolution of the twentieth century, computerization, it is important to note that old, pre-Wapping Fleet Street also holds the memory of the near-death in 1986 of almost the entire British industrial newspaper product as it had been made each day since the early 1890s. This near-disaster was only narrowly averted by the quick thinking (and forward planning) of an industrial prince from Adelaide, Rupert Murdoch, owner of *The Sun, News of the World, The Times,* and *The Sunday Times.*

The printers had created a situation of near-bankruptcy by their repeated strike actions against direct input. Murdoch responded with an Australian-style, moonlight flit, or quick overnight exit from Fleet Street, to less expensive, less troublesome and fully manned computerized factories in Wapping. His example was copied by the remaining Fleet Street proprietors, as soon as they could find alternative accommodation. They were able to finance most of the cost of their exodus with money from the sale of buildings left behind (derived booty estimated at £1 billion), thus creating one of the most profitable resurrections since the raising of Lazarus.

It also seems to be generally agreed among contemporary historians that the end of Fleet Street as 'a habitation of the mind' (to quote a sorrowing Liberal Party guru of the late Victorian era) dates from the arrival there of the New Journalism and of Alfred Harmsworth in the 1880s and 1890s, rather than from the bold outwitting of the Luddite trade unions in the 1980s by Eddy Shah and Rupert Murdoch.

Nobody seems to be entirely clear just what H. W. Massingham, the Liberal guru, meant by his élitist phrase, even though it is easy enough to gather his drift. A Victorian version of 'a centre of excellence' is all that may have been intended. But it is much more likely that Massingham was making the same point as his close friend, the Liberal historian G. M. Trevelyan, in his revivalist outburst of 1901: 'The Philistines have captured the Ark of the Covenant [i.e. the printing press] and have learnt how to work their own miracles through its terrible power.'

Trevelyan was referring to the demise of what he considered to be the 'essential' Fleet Street – the old, Dickensian Fleet Street, dominated for most of the nineteenth century by the free and independent *Times*. This centrally placed, Liberal-inclined, national media powerhouse had operated on the assumption that the main aim of any *serious* newspaper should be to look like *The Times* typographically, and to mould public opinion politically in the social reform image of the Liberal Party.

It had depended on subsidies rather than sales to do this (Tories, then as now, were contemptuous of anyone who had to buy a newspaper to find out what was going on in Whitehall). It had also relied on paternalism rather than prostitution to ensure brand loyalty. The result, in Trevelyan's eyes, had been a late Victorian Golden Age of quality journalism or, as it was termed in those days, 'literature in a hurry'. This carefully sustained 'peak of journalistic performance', he went on, had been much more beneficial to the nation as a whole than could be said of 'the tawdry New Journalism from America'. It was also in sharp contrast to 'the dreary, leaden prospect which now stretches before us'. This, he said, can only bring forth meretricious formula-writing and attention-grabbing sensationalism, 'as the new, profit-seeking Tory newspaper proprietors – those arrogant grocers who would sell news like soap – set out to exploit public ignorance and moral weakness in the shameless manner of disorderly houses'. With hindsight, it must be said, Trevelyan was remarkably prescient!

But how and why did it become so vitally necessary to transform a 'class' press into a 'mass' press? And why was it that only the tawdrier aspects of US newspaper practice, such as sensational 'stunts' and 'circus' page-layouts with screaming headlines, were preferred in Fleet Street, and the better ones, such as investigative and campaigning journalism, were ignored? The short answer seems to be that paternalism had become very expensive, uphill work, producing small thanks in the way of votes and circulation. Pandering to popular prejudice against 'rich toffs' seemed to many advertisers and businessmen to be a much easier way of gathering mass votes as well as mass circulations.

It was also much easier to fill the pages of those recently Americanized, 'human interest story' newspapers (such as *The Daily Telegraph* and *The Daily News*) if you hired some impoverished, agency-trained journalists from the provinces instead of arrogant, 'belletrist' amateurs from Oxford. 'To be a writer for a news-paper today [i.e. 1850] requires more knowledge, genius, readiness and scholarship than ever you may want in St Stephen's [i.e. in an MP]', wrote that impatient, hard-working, old school journalist and fashionable man-of-letters, William Makepeace Thackeray. By the 1880s, however, most of the geniuses had left Fleet Street in disgust, to produce – or to teach others how to produce – unbridled literary creations of their own. They were replaced by professionals (i.e. formula-writers) who, according to H. W. Massingham, operated 'more like engineers', and were much more willing to compose 'the hasty judgements, distorted truths and elastic morality' that the new proprietors required.

In short, the huge capital outlay required to industrialize the old-fashioned family newspaper business (and, among other things, enable the boldest of the industrializers to pick up a peerage for so doing) was of such magnitude that only the most single-minded proprietors were likely to succeed. Overnight, or so it seemed, Fleet Street ceased to be an arena for gentlemen. It became a bear-garden or, if you prefer, a snake pit restricted to those 'new men' from the world of com-merce who could combine the talents of J. P. Morgan with those of Joseph Pulitzer and William Randolph Hearst.

Initially, mass production of newspapers was thought to be impossible without large bank loans and plenty of cash-rich investors to cover the cost of specially designed Hoe printing presses imported from the USA, capable of producing more than a million copies a day. It was also deemed essential (especially by the listening banks) to provide a new kind of newspaper language which would attract rather than deter a mass readership, thus encouraging American-style business practices based on advertising.

The same kind of buccaneering enterprise would later be used to empower computerization in the 1980s, when ever-rising costs were suddenly brought down tenfold by removing most of the expensive human labour involved in production and replacing it with a much cheaper worker fashioned out of the applied science of robotics. One of the most simple and vivid illustrations of the revolutionary effect of computerization – put about by propagandists on both sides during the early 1980s (i.e. among trade unionists as well as employers) – claimed that if it had taken 6,000 men and women each working day up to 1986 to produce one single copy of the *Daily Mirror*, it would require only some 600 after computerization had been reluctantly accepted by the defeated print unions. It was a simplistic argument but sufficiently accurate to be memorable.

There were, however, one or two eccentric behaviourists to be found in Fleet Street during its earliest and most noticeable period of moral decline, the outstanding one being William Thomas Stead, editor of *The Pall Mall Gazette* from 1883 to 1889. He was amazingly successful at demonstrating the need for a 'radiant, radical and rebellious' campaigner for social reform and political freedom in the manner of his American counterpart and role model, Horace Greeley, founding editor of the *New York Tribune*. Stead was deeply impressed by Greeley's messianic campaigning style and said so most firmly when he wrote about him in *The Northern Echo*, shortly after Greeley's death in 1878. Much later, it was said of Stead (by his friend, T. P. O'Connor) that 'he was too much of a fanatic to be a good journalist and too much of a journalist to make a good fanatic'.

But when Stead died on board the *Titanic* in 1912, the *New York Sun* stated, in all seriousness, that 'in the years between 1884 and 1888, Stead came closer to governing Great Britain (through his campaigning journalism) than anyone else'. This belated tribute to Stead's audacious 'Government by Journalism' proposal, written in Holloway Gaol in 1886 during his brief imprisonment there for breaking the law, was almost the only reference to a uniquely populist political stance made during his editorship. Repeatedly, Stead urged that a public watchdog role should be played, fearlessly and continuously, by all newspapers and magazines regardless of their political affiliations. Like Noam Chomsky in the 1960s, Stead made it his job to subject all political institutions to a severely critical analysis, and concluded that 'a new representative method is needed, not to supersede but to supplement that which exists'.

Businessmen like George Newnes and Alfred Harmsworth were much more interested in the personal fortunes that could be made out of fast-looking, fast-talking, irresponsibly sensational newspapers, produced in the style of their millionaire American counterpart, Scots-born James Gordon Bennett Sr, founder of the *New York Herald*. Harmsworth declared he was able to judge good journalism 'more naturally than Stead', by reference to his pocket-book and 'the real needs of the public'. He openly admitted that he had looked to the USA for a populist, non-élitist kind of newspaper language that could be reproduced 'by office boys for office boys'. He found it in the mid-Western states of America, where the halfpenny press had been directed to capture the attention of the thousands of non-English-speaking immigrants of humble origin who seemed most anxious to become Americans. This political, as well as literary, aim was easily achieved, first and most profitably, by Joseph Pulitzer of St Louis, Missouri, and then, outrageously, by that Californian 'Citizen Kane', William Randolph Hearst, of San Francisco. Not surprisingly, their names became watchwords among newspapermen on both sides of the Atlantic.

By the turn of the century, sociologists and political philosophers, students of urbanization and of the new, rabble-rousing power of the press, were beginning – like Matthew Arnold some years earlier – to brood publicly over the implications of mediated experience. What, they asked themselves, was going on here: was it simply the good-natured creation of consensus in a representative democracy, or 'the manufacturing of consent' in an increasingly cynical, profit-oriented oligarchy? Everybody that mattered dismissed the 'manufacturing of consent' notion (a phrase first used in 1922 by Walter Lippmann in his *Public opinion*) because it sounded like socialist paranoia, opting instead for the 'creation of consensus', which seemed more Arnoldian and British. But very few commentators were able to deny that excessive and vindictive press censorship during World War I, followed by the setting up of the deferential British Broadcasting Company in 1922, had meant a sad end to that essential democratic exercise – the Right to Know.

The broadcasting of news for the first time immediately affected not only the newspaper interests but also the powerful agencies which supplied news to the newspapers. All were jealous of the BBC's powers or wished to share in them. However, in an agreement made later in 1922, the news agencies reluctantly agreed to supply John Reith's BBC with a daily summary of the world's news. The summary, they insisted, should be long enough 'to constitute a broadcasted message of half-an-hour's duration, and approximately between 1,200 and 2,400 words'. Thus began the compression of the world's news, scarce or plentiful, dramatic or dull, significant or insignificant, into the regular daily mould that we in Britain have been conditioned to accept right down to the present day – or, perhaps it would be fairer to say, up to the autumn of 1955 when the BBC's monopoly over broadcasting came to an end.

But how do we know all this? Where are the archives? How was it recorded for posterity? Not, regrettably, in carefully researched historical works based on primary sources (i.e. archival materials; Asa Briggs's 4-volume *History of broadcasting in the UK*, 1961–79, being an exception). More often than not, newspaper history has been assigned to very 'low' levels of historical recording – of anecdote and polemic, of local monograph and oral tradition, or occasional essays which pass quickly and spiritedly over the frozen tundra with a media studies bias. Historians of all kinds have been emphasizing the value of the newspaper as an historical source ever since the French Revolution. But, as a subject for historical study beyond the trivial, the newspaper has been carefully and snobbishly avoided by most academic historians. Result: newspaper history has been left almost entirely to the enthusiasm of individual journalists as they neared retirement, or when they felt themselves to be in the prime of their anecdotage (e.g. Charles Lamb's essay, 'Newspapers thirty-five years ago', written and published in

1831, says very little about newspapers and far too much about his day-dreams in the Fleet Street of the 1790s).

With one notable exception (Stephen Koss), all the major histories of the British press have been written by professional journalists: F. Knight Hunt, *The Fourth Estate* (1850); Alexander Andrews, *The history of British journalism* (1859); James Grant, *The newspaper press* (1871); Charles Pebody, *English journalism* (1882); H. R. Fox Bourne, *English newspapers* (1887). These commentaries are not without value, but the chief concern of their authors was to record the story of individual institutions and not to interpret them for posterity. They may, perhaps, be forgiven for having been less than critical, and for having taken a rather narrow, partisan perspective. It must also be remembered they were writing in the heyday of the 'Whig interpretation of history', according to which there had been a steady march towards 'democracy' from 1688 to the Victorian era – a progress mirrored faithfully in the striving towards maturity of a uniquely 'free' press, reckoned to be absolutely free intellectually if not constitutionally.

From the days of Defoe and Wilkes to the triumphant repeal of the so-called 'taxes on knowledge' in 1855, the newspaper, it was claimed, had won for itself the confident, middle-class status of 'the Fourth Estate' in a nation which had only ever needed three Estates, or semi-feudal, tripartite guardianship (Altar, Throne and Cottage) from time immemorial. After 1855, it seems, the newspaper went from strength to strength (despite growing misgivings as to quality) by extolling the greater virtues of cheapness, popularity and liveliness. J. D. Symon, *The press and its story* (1914), Henry Simonis, *The street of ink* (1917), and even T. H. S. Escott, *Masters of English journalism* (1911), with its cautious, ponderous, literary style, still looked back on a history that was a simple linear progression to their own time.

General histories were rarer between the wars. If we except Stanley Morison, *The English newspaper* (1932) as being concerned mainly with typography, the most substantial and scholarly work is by the German, Karl von Stutterheim, *The press in England* (translated 1935). There are also the first three volumes of *The history of The Times* to be considered, covering the period 1785–1912 (publication starting in 1935). They are among the best researched, best written and least partisan 'house' histories published in English. The anonymous editor of these volumes (now known to be Morison) was uniquely placed to make use of private archival material relating to *The Times* as a publishing phenomenon, which others, historians as well as journalists, could only envy.

But the most impressive press history of the twentieth century so far is Stephen Koss, *The rise and fall of the political press in Britain* (two volumes, 1981 and 1984). Researching privately but networking most successfully, as only an American at Oxford could be expected to do, Koss made constructive use of hitherto unknown family archive material covering both the nineteenth and the twentieth centuries up to 1983. He did all this stylishly and with almost effortless ease. Regrettably, within a few months of the publication of the second volume, Koss died after an operation for a heart transplant.

The traditional Whig approach to press history, so beloved by the cheeky tabloid press during the timid and repressed 1930s, was continued unthinkingly after 1945 by Harold Herd, in *The march of journalism* (1952), and by Francis Williams's *Dangerous estate* (1957). These very popular works added very little, apart from updating and readability, to their more prolix predecessors. It is true, Williams's book was rather more critical than most, but only in a somewhat knock-about, left-wing manner, implying that the British press was little more than a Tory-led, capitalistic swindle. New and important questions were avoided; new perspectives were most certainly not given; and even Michael Leapman's *Treacherous estate* (1992) and Raymond Snoddy's *The good, the bad and the unacceptable* (1992) should be seen as little more than extended magazine articles perpetuating the same old-fashioned genre. Their concern is ever with personalities ('all history is biography'), of journalists, proprietors and individual newspapers. Nowhere, in these gossipy books, does that concern for people extend to an analysis of the social effect that tabloid journalism was having on the overall quality of British journalism.

Suddenly, everybody seemed to be writing up the news in tabloid newspaper style – an infection which hit the 'qualipops' like a nervous reflex action. But nobody bothered to draw attention to this damaging, semi-Australianization of Fleet Street. 'Ouch! Gotcha! Well done, boy!' and 'Watch it, Mac!' – this was the newspaper language of the 1980s. But only the *Columbia Journalism Review* (alarmed by the spread of the infection) was brave enough to point the finger at Rupert Murdoch and his ilk and describe them as a social as well as a newspaper problem. As for the economic, political and social structure within which the British press operates, this was virtually ignored. For honourable exceptions, see R. A. Scott-James, *The influence of the press* (1913); Lord Camrose, *British newspapers and their controllers* (1947); H. A. Innis, *The press: a neglected factor in the economic history of the twentieth century* (1949); Charles Wintour, *Pressures on the press: an editor looks at Fleet Street* (1972); and James Curran, ed. *The British press: a manifesto* (1978).

Unfortunately, between the repeal of the newspaper stamp in 1855 and the advent of the Audit Bureau of Circulations in the 1930s, there were no official records of newspaper circulations. A valuable unofficial listing is to be found in A. P. Wadsworth's 'Newspaper circulations, 1800–1954', in the *Transactions of the Manchester Statistical Society* (1955). But those well-laid-out lists in the advertising trade directories, often estimated only through publishers' claims, are highly suspect. The directories themselves are a mine of information about other aspects of the press. But circulation was not alone in its commercial neglect.

There have been one or two 'authorized' histories of the big news agencies – for example, Graham Storey's *Reuters' century* (1951); Donald Read's *The power of news: the history of Reuters* (1992); and George Scott's *Reporter anonymous* (1968) on the Press Association. There have also been a few indifferent accounts of the profession of journalism: F. J. Mansfield, *Gentlemen! The press* (1943); Cyril Bainbridge, *One hundred years of journalism* (centenary of the Institute of

Journalists, 1984); C. J. Bundock, *The National Union of Journalists* (1957); and former journalist Harry Christian's *The development of trade unionism and profes-sionalism among British journalists: a sociological enquiry* (1976). But none of these, apart from Dr Christian's thesis, and perhaps Bainbridge with his long experience, placed journalism in the larger, national setting of the development of the profes-sions, or of white-collar employment as a whole.

Advertising too received some measure of academic attention, but the economics of the industry were very much a secondary concern of both E. S. Turner's *The shocking history of advertising* (1953) and Terry Nevett's *Advertising in Britain* (1982). The development of economic, and later of labour, history after 1945 meant that it was the technical side of the press which was the first to benefit from fresh work and some new questionings. (See J. L. Kieve, *The electric telegraph*, 1973.) However, it is with the cheap, post-1855 press that the much more difficult task of discovering what really went on in the Victorian era still lies. For instance, it is a paradox that, in proportion as the later Victorian papers grew in social accep-tance, being no longer taxed or suspected by central government, they declined markedly in critical vigour. For a partial explanation of this softening-up process, see Lucy Brown, *Victorian news and newspapers* (1985), pp. 56–7, on the political use of government advertising.

Again, for most of the more famous defunct national newspapers (e.g. *The Morning Post, Daily Herald* and *News Chronicle*) very few historical records now exist, and even for the survivors the situation is little better. *The Daily Telegraph*, for example, can come up with scant archival evidence to show it even existed before 1911, having lost most of its earlier records in the bombing of its London repository during World War II. Nevertheless, increasing numbers of critical studies have appeared during the last thirty years which will form the building blocks of any new general history. David Ayerst's *Guardian: biography of a newspaper* (1971) has been the most notable single study. Moreover, the story of that particular newspaper is carried on to 1988, most satisfactorily, in Geoffrey Taylor's *Changing faces* (1993). David Kynaston's *The Financial Times* (1988) is also much more than a mere centenary history, charting its progress from inkwells to direct input and from setting by hand to printing in New Jersey by satellite, in more than five hundred very readable pages.

A. M. Gollin's *The Observer and J. L. Garvin* (1960) and Ayerst's *Garvin of The Observer* (1985) are both more concerned with the journalist than with the journal. For posterity and *The Sunday Times*, Hobson, Knightley and Russell's *The pearl of days* (1972) is much more of a soft-sell for Thomson Newspapers, or a self-serving celebration of success, than a worthwhile history. Again, A. J. P. Taylor's *Beaverbrook* (1972) is only concerned generally with the *Daily Express* and the *Sunday Express*, being more of a sycophantic eulogy of 'a little old devil' than an in-depth biography. Fortunately, Anne Chisholm and Michael Davie's *Beaverbrook* (1992) gives a much more acceptable account of the man and his times. Reginald Pound and Geoffrey Harmsworth's *Northcliffe* (1959), while making much new material available for consideration, still suffers from being an 'official' history –

unlike Richard Bourne's *Lords of Fleet Street: the Harmsworth dynasty* (1990), which is a well-balanced re-assessment of Northcliffe and the other Harmsworths. Reverting to *The Guardian* once more, it is important to note there is still much to be gleaned from the archives deposited in the John Rylands Library of Manchester University.

But the Whigs were right, of course: a large part of the history of the press *is* to be found in the lives of journalists and proprietors. Arthur Pearson, George Newnes, Glenesk, Lawson and Northcliffe – the financial activities of all of these exceedingly clever businessmen could be usefully examined under the aegis of LSE's Business History Unit or the Business Archives Council. Major journalists, on the other hand, have been fully and generously treated in recent years, with excellent studies by Gollin and Ayerst of Garvin (above); Stephen Koss of A. G. Gardiner in *Fleet Street radical* (1973); and A. F. Havighurst's *Radical journalist: H. W. Massingham* (1974). In addition, J. O. Baylen is preparing a full biography of W. T. Stead, and Lawrence Brady a study of T. P. O'Connor. This still leaves Robert Donald, C. E. Montague and J. A. Spender of the Fleet Street 'greats', as well as the major editors of the 1920s and 1930s (e.g. Ralph Blumenfeld, Kennedy Jones, Arthur Christiansen and Guy Bartholomew) to be examined further, using materials uncovered by television researchers and others. But the biographical side of the re-writing of the history of the press is already well advanced. And for those with access to CD-ROM (Compact Disc–Read Only Memory), the British Library's *Bibliography of Biography* (1992–) is a valuable new tool.

The study of journalism itself, or of journalistic writing as a special form of literature, remains somewhat more backward. The journalist poseur, the 'belletrist' or literateur, has long commanded attention (e.g. John Gross, *The rise and fall of the man of letters*, 1969). But the working journalist has not been so often noticed and needs to be carefully re-examined today in terms of aims, special rewards and increased social status. Meanwhile, Jeremy Tunstall's *Journalists at work* (1971), Alan Lee's *The origins of the popular press in England, 1855–1914* (1976), and essays by Philip Elliott and Anthony Smith in Boyce, Curran and Wingate, *Newspaper history* (1978) are perhaps dust-covered but still useful references. Another neglected area has been the training of journalists, which has remained a matter of dispute within the craft or industry, from the eighteenth century to the present day. 'Journalists may be born and not made. But they can still be trained to be better', is a neat summary of this dispute put about as recently as 1979, by the now-defunct Printing and Publishing Industry Training Board. (See also A. J. Lee, 'Early schools of journalism', *Journalism Studies Review*, 1976, and Fred Hunter, *Grub Street and academia*, 1982.)

Inroads of a tentative nature have been made recently into some age-old journalistic problems (e.g. 'Can we trust what the papers say' plus 'Who will criticise the critics?', *Journalism Studies Review*, 1976; and 'Who was Junius? The computer says it knows', *Journalism Studies Review*, 1977). Foundations have also been laid for a new and systematic history of the English newspaper from 1620 to the present day (edited by Dr Michael Harris of Birkbeck College, London University). In fact, the last decade has seen something of a revolution in the historiography of the press. Detailed studies on the one hand (e.g. *William Camrose: giant of Fleet Street*, by his son, Lord Hartwell, 1992) and comprehensive reference works on the other (e.g. Linton and Boston, *The newspaper press in Britain: an annotated bibliography*, 1987, and Dennis Griffiths, *The encyclopedia of the British press*, 1992) have improved updating possibilities for general analyses, popular histories and surveys.

But what of the future? The age of the operative, as distinct from the artisan historian, is already upon us. There are important parts of the opaque history of the twentieth-century British press which will, if wanted, become easily visible to all on computer through database retrieval (e.g. the press coverage of the Falklands War). But, as we approach the end of the twentieth century and continue to exploit the new technology, there are at least two factors which must be borne in mind: first, the possible untrustworthiness of our existing records and second, the ability of the operator to understand the history of the press in terms of contemporary society. Much press history is in danger of being clouded forever, as papers die or are taken over (e.g. Britain's senior Sunday newspaper, *The Observer*, was acquired by *The Guardian* in 1993 and swallowed whole). Most proprietors have little interest in keeping records for the benefit of posterity. But this, surely, is what they must be encouraged and even enticed to do. Many newspapers have much archival material stored away somewhere which must not be destroyed thoughtlessly in some Monday-morning, spring-cleaning exercise. A systematic appeal to all extant newspapers for information about their records would be a step forward. It would also help if database compilers generally made more checks than they seem to do at present on the quality and reliability of so-called facts contained in newspaper cuttings. If they do not, then all their mistakes will be preserved in amber (i.e. in databases) from here to eternity.

Mercifully, the history of the British press has never been the monopoly of specialist press historians – nor should it ever become so. The drive and motivation of the press stem from the observed needs of society at large. All things are grist to its mill, even gossipy Fleet Street anecdotes and self-indulgent memoirs. It is also important to recognize that the twentieth-century British press peaked very early indeed – politically, commercially and as a common carrier of functional information in a representative democracy.

It was at its most confident, worthwhile and profitable during the 1914–18 war, despite heavy-handed military censorship and clumsy attempts by the coalition Government to manipulate official news. When *The Globe*, an influential London evening newspaper, published a Cabinet-leaked, stop press item on 5 November 1915 saying 'Lord Kitchener resigns', it was immediately closed down (after a police raid) and put out of business for two whole weeks, simply because its editor, Charles Palmer, had ignored an official 'D' (for Defence) notice requesting the press 'to refrain from any reference to the movements of Lord Kitchener till further notice'.

For most Arnoldians and Reithians, however, it was downhill all the way, from the end of World War I and the commercial prurience of post-war sensationalists to the outbreak of World War II, when official manipulators were able once more to take a firm hold of the 'half-free' British press in the hallowed name of national security. The space given to 'hard' news in most of the popular dailies (and especially in the *Daily Mirror*, after it was re-launched as a tabloid in 1934) seemed to grow smaller and smaller, steadily and annually, squeezed out in most cases by more and more public offerings of ripe 'info-tainment' or 'human interest' stories. By 1939, in the eyes of the mature generation, there was very little of the old public service tradition left, except in *The Times* and *The Daily Telegraph*. Market forces were dominant almost everywhere except, most noticeably, in Manchester, where that articulate voice of Liberalism, *The Manchester Guardian*, was just managing to survive honourably on the fat profits of its rabble-rousing sister paper, the *Manchester Evening News*.

Sadly, the British press became an emaciated casualty of World War II, taking a very long time to recover its former energy and strength. Paradoxically, the press was freer under strict wartime controls than under certain inescapable peacetime pressures, such as advertising and the need to keep up an increasingly profitable circulation. Matters of principle could still be discussed with information-starved readers, but not when they were in conflict with the State or with profitability. The development of television in the 1950s was not the sole reason for the failure of the press to regain its pre-war popularity. The retention of newsprint rationing until the end of 1958; the extraordinary growth in the political muscle-power of the print unions; and the utter spinelessness of collective management when faced with union demands – all these, we can now see, were as damaging to society as the antics of a few unruly tabloids.

As for the British journalist, opinion polls recorded that, up to the 1960s and beyond, the general public had no more respect for the average journalist than for the average door-to-door salesman. After the 'Flight to Wapping' in 1986, however, his (and her) image changed very much for the better. Computerization, in itself, did very little to improve the quality of journalism (though it certainly brought financial prosperity to those journalists able to cope with the changes); neither did Australianization which, in the early 1990s, became a serious social problem as well as a journalistic one, when 'sledging', a form of gamesmanship used by Australian cricketers to unsettle the opposition, was transferred to the political arena by the tabloids led by *The Sun*.

On the other hand, recent research suggests that all-graduate recruitment (many with direct input experience as well as shorthand and tape recorders) helped to raise overall standards in Fleet Street. Even the sweatier tabloids became drier, sharper and generally more acceptable during the early 1990s, and the greatly improved 'qualipops' (i.e. *The Guardian*, *The Daily Telegraph*, and *The Independent*) demonstrated that serious 'think' pieces (on the economy or the Royal Family, for example) need not be as dull and circumspect as most broadsheet editors had decreed hitherto. The 'qualipops' also managed to look alike, each choosing to imitate the pace-setting *Guardian* in literariness and layout, which was yet another life-saving move dictated by television.

Currently, newspaper readers in Britain with serious informational needs can consider themselves thrice blessed (at the very least) every day of the year. Radio, it has been said, is the *alerting* medium. It tends to be the first medium that tells us something newsworthy has happened. Television is clearly the *involving* medium. It engages the emotions more completely than the others. Yet the printed press is still the best *informing* medium. It alone is capable of handling complexity and providing details for future historians. But for how much longer?

Ray Boston
Cardiff
June 1994

ARRANGEMENT
OF THE MATERIAL

Entries are arranged alphabetically by author, where the term 'author' includes corporate entities such as newspapers and other publications, or any organization responsible for the text of a book, commemorative issue etc. A word-by-word alphabetical sequence is used, not letter by letter – hence 'de Vries' precedes 'Deacon' and Thomson, George, precedes Thomson Foundation, The.

Among an author's works, books and theses take priority over articles, and in each category the order of entries is chronological.

The main Bibliography is preceded by a section on Reference Works. Readers are advised to study this – and the Introduction – carefully before detailed examination of the remainder, as the information on these basic publications is not repeated in the main sequence. Late entries appear on pages 353–8.

Many of the annotations, as well as commenting critically on the work concerned, provide information on the author or content of the work.

An appendix in the form of a Chronology of British newspaper history, 1900–1994, provides a signpost to the significant events, principal personalities and newspapers themselves that have made the news during the century to date.

The Index is an integral and essential element, with subject entries as well as comprehensive cross-references. References are to item numbers.

REFERENCE WORKS

REFERENCE WORKS

1   *Advertisers Annual*. London: Kelly's Directories, 1925–77; East Grinstead (W Sussex): Kelly's, later Thomas Skinner, now Reed Information Services, 1978–.
The 'Blue Book' of the advertising industry. Now three vols, Vol 2 (UK Media) including newspapers.

2   *Advertisers Weekly*. 21st anniversary number. 19 Apr 1934. 138pp.

3   – – –.   40th anniversary number. 16 Apr 1953. 134pp.

4   – – –.   Golden Jubilee number. 28 Apr 1963.
'1913–1963: a half-century in the service of advertising'.
Founded by John C. Akerman, the title was changed to *Ad Weekly* in 1969 and to *Adweek* in 1972; absorbed into *Campaign* 1975. Concerned with all aspects of the press – not only advertising.

5   *Advertising World, The*. London: 1901–40: thereafter (1941–3) a supplement to *World's Press News*.
Monthly founded by William and Gomer Berry – their first publication. In 1902 featured a series 'Notable media', including *Daily Express*, *The Daily News*, *News of the World*.

6   *Benn's Press Directory*. Tonbridge (intermittently Tunbridge Wells) (Kent): 1978–86. Annual. Continuation of *The Newspaper Press Directory* (q.v.), and itself continued as *Benn's Media Directory* (1981–92, 2–3 vols), and as *Benn's Media* (1993–, 3 vols).
The first volume of this major reference guide includes the UK newspaper press, with individual titles listed in detail, and a separate listing of publishers and their titles.

7   *Bibliography of Biography*. London, later Boston Spa (W Yorks): British Library, 1970–.
Originally available as hardcopy and in microfiche; from 1992 on CD-ROM, with single disc updated annually. *BoB* affords comprehensive access to biographical works, memoirs, diaries etc recorded by the BL and the US Library of Congress.

8   *Bibliography of British newspapers.* Series of vols, gen ed Charles Alpin Toase: *Wiltshire.* Ed Robin K. Bluhm. London: Library Association, 1975. 28pp. (Revised edn in preparation); *Kent.* Eds Winifred F. Bergess, Barbara R.M. Riddell and John Whyman. London: British Library, 1982. xviii + 139pp; *Durham and Northumberland.* Ed Frank W.D. Manders. London: British Library, 1982. xvi + 65pp; *Derbyshire.* Eds Anne Mellors and Jean Radford. London: British Library, 1987. xiii + 74pp; *Nottinghamshire.* Ed Michael Brook. London: British Library, 1987. xvii + 62pp; *Cornwall and Devon.* Eds Jean Rowles and Ian Maxted. London: British Library, 1991. xiv + 37 + 123pp.

This series, edited by the Reference, Special and Information Section (now Information Group) of the Library Association, provides complete lists of titles under place of publication, with dates and changes and locations in the county concernd and elsewhere.

9   Blum, Eleanor. *Basic books in the mass media.* Urbana (IL): University of Illinois Press, 1972, 1980. 426pp.

The extensive British content can easily be picked out from the index. This bibliography was developed from the same author's (and publisher's) *Reference books in the mass media* (1962–3).

10   Blum, Eleanor, and Frances Goins Wilhoit. *Mass media bibliography: an annotated guide to books and journals for research and reference.* Urbana: University of Illinois Press, 1990. 344pp.

Further establishes Ms Blum's eminence as a media bibliographer, with a total of 1,947 entries.

11   *BookBank.* London: Whitaker, 1988–. Monthly, bimonthly and annual series on CD-ROM.

Provides access to Whitaker's comprehensive database of English-language books in print, out of print back to 1970, forthcoming titles, and publishers. The databases of Bowker (USA) and Thorpe (Australia/New Zealand) are also now accessible.

12   *Books in English.* London, later Boston Spa (W Yorks): British Library, 1971–. A cumulation on microfiche bimonthly and then annually; cumulations of annual listings are also available (the latest covering 1981–92).

Lists all English-language books held by the BL and the US Library of Congress.

13   *British Editor, The.* Birmingham: Association of British Editors, 1989–. Quarterly newsletter.

14   *British Journalism Review.* London: (latterly Cassell), 1989–. Initally quarterly, then twice annually.

In-depth articles, with an academic approach, mainly on current issues. Founder-ed Geoffrey Goodman.

15   British Library, *Catalogue of the Newspaper Library, Colindale,* comp P.E. Allen. 8 vols. Vols 1–4, *Newspapers, magazines and journals by place,* Vols 5–8: *Newspapers, magazines and journals by title.* (Holdings as at 1971.)

The BL is the national library for the UK, established in 1973, incorporating (*inter alia*) the library departments of the British Museum. Outside the BL, copies of this catalogue are held in London by the Westminster and Guildhall (City) Libraries.

The entire holdings of the Newspaper Library will eventually be included in the BL's Online Catalogue. This will be available in the new building at St Pancras as well in the existing reading rooms. Supplements (2 vols) to Nov 1993 were published in 1994.

16 *British Library Newspaper Library Newsletter*. London: British Library, 1980–. Latterly twice annually.

The August 1982 issue was devoted to the Golden Jubilee of the library at Colindale.

17 *British National Bibliography*. London: Council of the British National Bibliography, 1950–74; thereafter London, and later Boston Spa (W Yorks): British Library, 1974–. Weekly, with interim and annual cumulations and some five-year vols; since 1981 available on microfiche and from 1989 also on CD-ROM (two discs covering 1950–85, one 1986–). Online availability via BLAISE-LINE (British Library Automated Information Service); the latter also holds the file of the National Serials Data Centre, which covers (*inter alia*) all British newspapers.

BNB is primarily a classified catalogue to all new and forthcoming books with British imprints – including first issues of serials and any changes in their titles. Separate vols in the hardback version for author, title and subject indexes.

18 *British Newspaper Index*. Reading: Research Publications (International), 1990–. Quarterly.

A cumulation on a single CD-ROM of the recent indexes of *The Times*, *The Sunday Times*, three *Times Supplements*, *Financial Times*, *The Independent* and *Independent on Sunday*.

19 *British Rate and Data (BRAD)*. London (latterly Cockfosters (Herts)): Maclean Hunter, 1954–. Monthly. From Sep 1994, additional Newspapers vol.

Comprehensive listing, with current rates, circulation data etc, of media – including all newspapers – that carry advertising: the standard serial reference in the field.

20 *Cambridge bibliography of English literature, The*. Cambridge: Cambridge University Press, 1940; New York, 1941.

Lists all forms of literature (including newspapers and related works) up to 1900. Superseded by *The new Cambridge bibliograghy of English literature*. 1969–77. 5 vols. Each of these has a large sections devoted to 'Newspapers and magazines', Vol 4 covering 1900–50, ed Peter Davison (Vol 5 is the index to the previous four). This is the most comprehensive and authoritative of all listings by date. Short (one-vol) edn, 1981. In preparation is *The Cambridge bibliography of English literature*, 3rd edn, with Davison again editing 'Newspapers' in the twentieth-century vol (to be Vol 5), it will be available in both printed and CD-ROM format.

21 *Campaign*. London: Haymarket Press, 1968–. Weekly.

Campaign is a continuation – in a larger format – of *World's Press News* (q.v.) as a leading trade medium. From the start it has followed a more critical, investigative line.

22   – – –.   'Blockbuster no. 1': The press. 28 Nov 1986. 24pp.
Special report on national and regional newspapers.

23   – – –.   Silver Jubilee issue. 17 Sep 1993.

23A   – – –.   1968–1993 (Silver Jubilee). 27 Sep 1993.
Singles out Eddy Shah and Rupert Murdoch as the principal newspaper innovators of
the period. In an interview, Shah recalls the dramatic changes stemming from his
successful battle against the pickets at Warrington in 1983.

24   Camrose, William Ewert Berry, *1st Viscount. British newspapers and their
controllers.* London: Cassell, 1947; revised edn, 1948. xix + 178pp.
Valuable source-book not only on national and provincial newspapers but also six
'political periodicals', from the authoritative standpoint of the chairman and editor-in-
chief of *The Daily Telegraph,* and former chief proprietor of both *The Sunday Times* and
the *Financial Times.* It was designed to pre-empt the deliberations of the first Royal
Commission on the Press.

25   *Clover Newspaper Index.* Biggleswade (Beds): 1986–. Weekly/fortnightly.
Subject index to the 'quality' nationals.

26   *CPU News.* London: Commonwealth Press Union, 1988–. Bimonthly.
This members' publication was launched as *News-letter* by the Empire Press Union in
1929; later became *Bulletin,* and then *CPU Quarterly* (1968–88).

27   Desmond, Robert William. *The information process: world news reporting
of the twentieth century.* Iowa City (IA): University of Iowa Press, 1978.
xiv + 495pp.

28   – – –.   *Windows on the world: world news reporting, 1900–1920.* Iowa City:
University of Iowa Press, 1980. xii + 608pp.

29   – – –.   *Crisis and conflict: world news reporting between two wars, 1920–40.*
Iowa City: University of Iowa Press, 1982. xii + 502pp.

30   – – –.   *Tides of war: world news reporting, 1931–1945.* Iowa City: University of Iowa Press, 1984. xi + 544pp. In imprint and on original title-page:
1940–1945.
This and the above books by Dr Desmond form a unique series on a global scale, with
the fullest parade published anywhere of reporters of the Western world and the
newspapers and agencies they served. The early bibliographies are meagre, but the
indexes are excellent throughout.

31   *Dictionary of business biography.* London: Butterworth (for Business History
Unit, London School of Economics), 1984–6. 5 vols (and supplement), ed David
J. Jeremy.
Each volume contains extensive and fully documented treatment of outstanding indiv-
iduals engaged in newspaper ownership or management. The contributors are Richard

Davenport-Hines, Jeremy, Rachel Lawrence, Gordon Phillips, Christine Shaw, and Patricia Storey (qq. v. in main Bibliography).

32 *Editors.* London: PR Newslink.
Media guides: series of six vols. Vol 1 (monthly) covers national newspapers and Vol 3 (every four months) regional dailies and weeklies.

33 Evans, Harold [Matthew]. *Editing and design: a five-volume manual of English, typography and layout.* London: Heinemann; New York: Holt, Rinehart & Winston. 1, *Newsman's English.* 1972, 1986. xiii + 224pp. 2, *Handling newspaper text.* 1974, 1986. ix + 366pp. 3, *News headlines* 1974. ix + 150pp. 4, *Pictures on a page (photo-journalism, graphics and picture editing).* 1978, 1987. xiv + 332pp. 5, *Newspaper design.* In association with Edwin Taylor. 1973. ix + 214pp. Series published under the auspices of the National Council for the Training of Journalists.
Despite his weight of responsibilities at the time (he edited *The Sunday Times* from 1967 to 1981), Evans here distils his outstanding editorial expertise; the series constitutes a guide to every aspect of its subject in a most engaging as well as practical manner.

34 Ferguson, Joan Primrose S. *Scottish newspapers held in Scottish libraries.* Edinburgh: Scottish Central Library, 1956. Revised edn, *Directory of Scottish newspapers.* Edinburgh: National Library of Scotland, 1984. 155pp.
The original covered 380 papers, in forty-one libraries. In the new edition coverage was extended to 1,178 titles.

35 *Glasgow Herald index.* Glasgow: 1906–68. Annual. Extended as Glasgow Herald Index Project by Department of Information Science, University of Strathclyde, to cover 1969–84. 8 vols (each covering two years). Continuing as *The Herald index.*

36 Griffiths, Dennis Morgan, ed. *The encyclopedia of the British press, 1422–1992.* Basingstoke (Hants): Macmillan, 1992. x + 694pp.
The first comprehensive reference work of its kind. The biographies/histories of newspapers and people are preceded by seven episodic surveys. Those covering the twentieth century are 'The British press, 1861–1918', by Joseph O. Baylen; '. . . 1919–1945', by Aled Jones; and 'The post-war years', by Louis Heren. 'Fleet Street editors' (present-day and recent newspapers) is one of several useful appendices.

37 *Guardian index, The.* Ann Arbor (MI): UMI, 1986–. Monthly, in print, with quarterly and annual cumulations.

38 – – –. *1929–1972.* Marlborough (Wilts): Adam Matthew Publications, 1993–. 5 parts on microfiche, with user's guide: Part 1: 1927–1935; Part 2: 1936–1945, with listing and guide, publ 1993. The three remaining parts in preparation.
Arranged by subject, this index is based on the original records in the John Rylands University Library of Manchester.

39 *Guild Journal.* London: Guild of (British Newspaper) Editors, 1948–. Quarterly.

40 *Hart's rules for compositors and readers at the University Press, Oxford.* First printed for in-house use, 1893; first published ('15th edn'), Oxford: OUP, 1904; 39th edn, 1983, rptd 1991.
A standard work since it was made available to all. (*See also Oxford writers' dictionary.*)

41 *Headlines.* London: Newspaper Society, 1968–. Monthly, later bimonthly. Replaced *Newstime* as the Society's principal mouthpiece: 'Britain's regional press in focus'.

42 Hoffmann, Ann. *Research for writers.* London: A. & C. Black, 1986, 1992. Previous edns under title *Research: a handbook for writers and journalists.* Speldhurst (Kent): Midas Books, 1975; London: Black, 1975, 1979.
All-round practical reference source, with a section on Newspapers and periodicals (including 'indexes available').

43 *Hollis Press and Public Relations Annual.* Sunbury-on-Thames (Middx): 1969–.
Not only is 'the press' a target readership of *Hollis*, but also sections are devoted to listings of British publications (including newspapers and publishers).

44 *Index to the Financial Times.* London: from 1981 (published from 1982). Monthly, with annual cumulation. From 1987, continued from Reading: Research Publications (International).

45 *Index to The Independent.* Reading: Research Publications (International), 1991–. Monthly, with annual cumulation on CD-ROM.

46 *Index to The Scotsman.* Edinburgh: Unit for the Study of Government in Scotland, 1983–. Monthly, with annual cumulation.

47 *IPI Report.* Zürich, now London: International Press Institute, 1952–. Monthly.
The journal of the Institute, the headquarters of which are now in Vienna. It publishes an annual World Press Freedom Review.

48 Journal, The. *Diamond Jubilee Journal, 1912–1972.* London: Institute of Journalists, Nov 1972. 36pp.
Commemorating the sixtieth anniversary of the foundation of the publication. It is now a quarterly distributed to members of both the Chartered Institute of Journalists (the professional body) and the Institute of Journalists (Trade Union).

49 *Journal of Newspaper and Periodical History.* London: World Microfilms Publications, 1984–90. 3 per year; then Westport (CT): Meckler, 1990–1; Greenwood, 1992. 2 per year; thereafter (1994–) *Studies in Newspaper and Periodical History.* Annual. Ed Dr Michael Harris (London).
'A focus for all those with a professional or academic interest in press history from the 17th to the 20th century'.

50 *Journalism Studies Review.* Cardiff: Centre for Journalism Studies (University College, University of Wales), 1976–83. Annual. Founder-eds (Sir) Tom Hopkinson and Ray Boston.

51 *Journalist.* 75th birthday edition. London: Nov–Dec 1983.
A sixteen-page pull-out, edited by Tony Craig, tracing the history of the 'organ of the National Union of Journalists', founded in Manchester in 1908 as the *National Union Journal*, this being the year after the union itself had been founded after a meeting in Birmingham. Due honour is given to Henry Marriott Richardson, editor (1908–19) and first general secretary of the NUJ (1918–36). *Journalist* is now published bimonthly.

52 *Journalist, The.* London: 1886–1909. Weekly (later monthly to 1912, as *The Journalist and Newspaper Proprietor*).
'A newspaper for all newspaper producers'.

53 *Journalist's Handbook, The.* Ayr, later Irvine (Strathclyde): Carrick, 1984–. Quarterly.
Contemporary commentary, reviews etc.

54 *Journalist's Week.* London: Maxwell Business Communications, 1990–1.

55 Linton, [George] David [Hough], and Raymond (Jack) Boston, eds. *The newspaper press in Britain: an annotated bibliography.* London: Mansell, 1987. xvii + 361pp.
The pioneer work in this field in modern times, this has the same structure as the present volume, but covers all eras up to 1986. There is an additional appendix: 'Location of papers and other archives'.

56 McCoy, Ralph Edward. *Freedom of the press: an annotated bibliography.* Carbondale (IL): Southern Illinois Press; London: Feffer & Simons, 1968. 576pp.
Covers a period from the fifteenth century to the mid-1960s. There are 8,000 entries including books, pamphlets, articles, films, from all English-speaking countries.

57 – – –. *Freedom of the press: a bibliocyclopedia: ten year supplement (1967-1977).* Carbondale (IL): Southern Illinois Press, 1979. xix + 559pp.
'A third as many again in only ten years': heresy, blasphemy and sedition have now given place to obscenity, the 'right to know' and the 'right to privacy'.

58 *Media Guide, The.* London: Fourth Estate/Guardian Books, 1992. Ed Steve Peak.
First edition of new quick-reference book, dated 1993. Includes 'A Media Library' section. The 1994 edition is expanded, with useful commentary on current issues.

59 *Media Reporter, The.* Sale (Cheshire), later Derby: Brennan Publications; then London: Bouverie Publishing Co.
'Britain's quarterly journalism review', founded 1976 by James Brennan; absorbed into *UK Press Gazette*, 1985.

60   *Media Week.* London: Patey Doyle, 1985–8; then Maxwell Business Communications, 1988–92; EMAP, 1992–.

61   *Media Yearbook, The.* Ayr, later Irvine (Strathclyde): Carrick, 1992, 1993. The first edition had a 'Who's who in British journalism'.

62   Morison, Stanley (Edward). *The English newspaper: some account of the physical development of journals printed in London between 1622 and the present day.* Cambridge: Cambridge University, Press, 1932; New York: Macmillan. xii + 335pp. Based on six lectures for the Sandars Readership in Bibliography. A commendably accurate and splendidly attractive historical panorama, concentrating on typographical aspects – not surprisingly in view of the author's distinction in that field; moreover, Morison at that time also had *The Times* official history in hand. More than three hundred newspapers are represented, with 150-plus line blocks.

63   *Newspaper Focus.* London, later Teddington (Middx): Haymarket Press, 1989–. Monthly.
For newspaper publishers and managers.

64   *Newspaper Press Directory, The.* London: Mitchell (1846–1948), London, then Tonbridge (Kent): Benn (1949–76). Annual but *not* published in 1848–50, 1852–3, 1855, 1941–4, 1950). Mitchell and Benn published, respectively, a Diamond Jubilee edition in 1905, and a Centennial edition in 1951. Until 1953 the Benn issues were published in parallel with their weekly, *The Newspaper World.*
The world's oldest press guide, founded by Charles Mitchell, a leading pioneer London advertising agent. Valuable source material can be derived from not only the editorial lists and publishers' notices, but also the annual surveys of the British press with obituaries etc. Moreover, a newspaper map of the UK was included as a supplement from 1860 until the end of Mitchell's ownership. From 1978, the work first appeared as *Benn's Press Directory* (q.v.).

65   Newspaper World, The. *The press, 1898–1948.* With an introduction by Richard Woolley (editor). London: Benn, 1948. 160pp.
'By distinguished contributors from all sections of the press', this publication marked the fiftieth birthday of *The Newspaper World*, a weekly founded by Charles Baker under the title *Newspaper Owner and Manager*. It took its eventual title in 1913 and was acquired by Benn in 1933. Publication ceased in 1953.

66   *NEWSPLAN.* London: British Library (series). *Report of the pilot project in the South-West.* By Rosemary Wells. 1986. x + 218pp (pp 113–214 in microfiche form.
The initial research for the national scheme for the preservation of local newspapers on archival microfilm. Includes summary history of English newspaper publishing. Followed by: *Reports of the NEWSPLAN project: in the East Midlands.* By Ruth Gordon. 1989. 412pp; *in the Northern Region.* By David Parry. 1989. 352pp; *in Yorkshire and Humberside.* By Andrew Parkes. 1990. vii + 352pp; updates pub 1991 and 1992; *in the*

North Western Region. By Ruth Cowley. 1990. xxxviii + 306pp; *in the West Midlands.* By Tracey J. Watkins. 1990. viii + 313pp (revised edition in preparation); *in Ireland.* By James O'Toole. 1992. Publ with the National Library of Ireland (Dublin), and embracing Northern Ireland as well as the Irish Republic. xxiii + 283pp; *in Wales/ Cymru.* By Beti Jones. 1994. Publ (bilingual) with Welsh Regional Library System (Aberystwyth). xi + 303pp; *in Scotland.* By Alice Mackenzie (in preparation); *in London and the South-East.* By Selwyn Eagle (in preparation).

67 *Newstime.* London: Newspaper Society, 1982–8. Monthly.
Replacing two existing titles, this contained current news and views from the Society. It celebrated the 150th anniversary of the latter's foundation with a souvenir issue (April/May 1986). Succeeded in turn by *Headlines.*

68 *Northern Ireland newspapers: a checklist with locations.* Belfast: Library Association (Northern Ireland), 1979. Ed J.R.R. Adams; checklist of microfilm held in 1983; expanded 2nd edn publ 1987. 63pp.

69 *Oxford writers' dictionary, The.* Oxford: Oxford University Press, 1990 (paperback).
Content is indentical to *The Oxford dictionary for writers and editors.* Oxford: Clarendon Press, latest edn 1989 (hardback). This derives from *The authors' and printers' dictionary,* ed F. Howard Collins (first publ 1905). (*See also Hart's rules* . . .)

70 *Palmer's Index to The Times Newspaper.* London: later Shepperton-on-Thames (Middx), Hampton Wick (Middx), Corsham (Wilts). Vols covering (Oct) 1790 to (June) 1941 were published between 1868 and 1943. Available on microfilm from H. Pordes, Cockfosters (Herts). A reprint to 1905 has been published – Nendeln (Liechtenstein): Kraus Reprint, 1965. The same period published on CD-ROM: Cambridge: Chadwyck-Healey, 1994–5.
'Containing an index to everything in the various numbers issued during the month': valuable material, even if decidedly eccentric by modern standards of indexing. In 1891, Samuel Palmer, a bookseller, began issuing retrospective as well as current indexes. He died in 1899, but the Palmer family continued publication; after the 1905 index, *Palmer's* appeared in parallel with *The Annual (later) Official Index to The Times* (q.v.).

71 Peet, Hubert William. *A bibliography of journalism: a guide to the books about the press and pressmen.* London: Sell, 1915. 11pp. Reprint of a contribution to *Sell's World's Press, 1915.*
Still valuable as an annotated reference, by the then editor of *Sell's*; based on 'The world's press bibliography', with lengthy surveys appearing in three parts: 1907, 1910, 1912.

72 *PIMS UK Media Directory.* London: PIMS International, 1980–. Founded (as *PRADS Directory*) 1973.
Named editorial contacts; continually updated and indexed, and available online.

73 *PR Planner United Kingdom.* London: Romeike Group, 1966–. Loose-leaf contacts guide, updated monthly. Also available on disc.

74   *Press, The.* London: Central Office of Information, 1979. 6pp reference pamphlet in Fact Sheets on Britain series (ref 16/FSB/79).
This replaced a 44pp 1976 booklet *The British press* (ref R5572/76), used 'in preparing articles, speeches, broadcasts etc' and was itself replaced by *The press in Britain*, an 8–16pp pamphlet (1982, 1988, 1993) for the Foreign and Commonwealth Office. 'The press' is also a section of *Britain: An Official Handbook*. London: HMSO (for FCO), annual. 1994 edn is the 45th, with ten pages devoted to the subject.
    A book-length COI production (for publication by HMSO), and also entitled *The press*, is in preparation in The Aspects of Britain series. This is intended for 'factual briefing on Government policy'.

75   Press Council, The. *The press and the people.* London: Annual report, series published 1954–91.
In addition to summarizing cases considered by the Council during the year, and its adjudication, each of the later reports has useful current 'facts in figures' on the British newspaper and periodical industries, and (from the 1965/6 report onwards) examination of leading publishing houses. The 1980/1 report (published 1984) featured 'Then there was one: London's evenings'. That for 1982/3 (published 1985) featured 'The Monopolies Commission, and the press . . . "an independent examination of the legislation, and how it has worked in practice"'. The 1984 report (also published 1985) included 'The growth of the freesheets', while those for 1985 and 1986 (both publ 1987) featured 'Fleet Street revolution' (q.v.).
    'A regional revolution' appeared in the 1987 report (publ 1988). The report for 1989 (publ 1990) contained 'Readers' representatives: Ombudsmen en masse' – a first list of those appointed by national newspapers to deal with complaints and alleged breaches of the Council's Code of Practice. The Council's last report (for 1990, publ 1991) had a foreword by the retiring chairman, Louis Blom-Cooper, entitled 'Epitaph – critique on Calcutt'.

76   Price, Warren C. *The literature of journalism: an annotated bibliography.* Minneapolis: University of Minnesota Press; London: Oxford University Press, 1959, 1960. xiii + 489pp.
Contains 3,147 annotated entries, many of them for British works, under such headings as history, biography, newspapers – appraisals, techniques, education, periodicals, management, public opinion, propaganda and public relations, radio and television, foreign press – plus subject and author indexes.

77   Price, Warren C., and Calder M. Pickett. *An annotated journalism bibliography, 1958–1968.* Minneapolis: University of Minnesota Press; London: Oxford University Press, 1970. x + 285pp.
After the death of Price in 1967, Pickett (of the University of Kansas) finalized this follow-up. It contains a further 2,172 entries, now in a straight alphabetical sequence since so many books defy easy categorization.

78   *Printers' Ink.* UK edition: London: 1909–18. Monthly.
The first London editor was Thomas Russell, later the first advertisement manager of

The Times, who on his retirement described *Printers' Ink* as 'the great formative influence of the period.' A pioneer of pocket-size publication, it was the leading journal for the US advertising industry at the turn of the century.

79 *Royal Commission on the Press report, 1947–1949* (the 'Ross report'). London: Her Majesty's Stationery Office, Cmd 7700, 1949. 370pp. Evidence, Cmd 7317 etc, 1948.

80 *Royal Commission on the Press report, 1961–1962* (the 'Shawcross report'). HMSO, Cmnd 1811, 1962. 239pp (1 vol); minutes of evidence, Cmnd 1812, 1962 (9 vols).

81 *Royal Commission on the Press report 1974–1977* (the 'McGregor report'). HMSO. Interim report: The national newspaper industry, Cmnd 6433, 1976. 128pp: Final report, Cmnd 6810, 1977. 318pp. Appendices, Cmnd 6810-1, 1977. 166pp.

Other publications from this Commission were: Research Series: No 1, 'Industrial relations in the national newspaper industry' (by ACAS), Cmnd 6680, 1976. 358pp. 2, 'Industrial relations in the provincial newspaper and periodical industries' (by ACAS), Cmnd 6810-2, 1977. x + 158pp. 3, 'Attitudes to the press' (by Social and Community Planning Research), Cmnd 6810-3, 1977. xviii + 382pp. 4, 'Analysis of newspaper content' (by Professor Denis McQuail), Cmnd 6810-4, 1977. xii + 364pp. 5, 'Concentration of ownership in the provincial press' (by Nicholas Hartley, Peter Gudgeon, Rosemary Crafts), Cmnd 6810-5, 1977. x + 124pp. 6, 'Periodicals and the alternative press'. Cmnd 6810-6, 1977. x + 74pp.

Working Papers: No. 1, 'New technology and the press' (by Rex Winsbury), 1975, 60pp. 2, 'Review of sociological writing on the press' (by Professor McQuail), 1976. 99pp. (Includes an extensive and valuable bibliography.) 3, 'Studies on the press' (by Oliver Boyd-Barrett, Colin Seymour-Ure, Jeremy Tunstall), 1977. 400pp. 4, 'The women's periodical press in Britain, 1946–76' (by Cynthia L. White), 1977. 88pp.

Minority report by Geoffrey Goodman and David Basnett, reprinted as *The press.* London: Labour Party, 1977. 18pp.

82 *Scotmedia.* Glasgow: Scotmedia Magazine, monthly.
Covers the Scottish media scene – including newspapers.

83 *Sell's Dictionary of the World Press.* London: Sell, annually 1883/4–1911/12 incl (1899 in 2 vols); continued as *Sell's World's Press,* 1914, 1915, 1919, 1921. Preceded by *The Philosophy of Advertising,* 1881, 1882. Incorporated a Who's who from 1913 to 1921 incl.
The value of *Sell's* to present-day press researchers lies not so much in the directory sections (matched as they were by competitors) as in the annual editorial features. *A bibliography of journalism* (*see* Peet, H.W.) was reprinted from the issue of 1915.

84 *Serials in the British Library.* London, later Boston Spa (W Yorks): British Library, 1981–. Quarterly, with annual cumulations.
Replaced the *British Union Catalogue of Periodicals (BUCOP)*; original 4 vols thereof (1955–8) listed *c.* 140,000 titles – including newspapers – in *c.* 400 libraries.

85   *Sources for newspaper history.* London: National Register of Archives, 1994. Information sheet no 10.

86   Times, The. *The Times Index*, covering 1785–90 (single-year vols). Reading: Newspaper Archive Developments (later Research Publications), 1978–84.
Palmer's Index to The Times Newspaper (q.v.) covered 1790–1941.
   The Annual Index to The Times (from 1906) and its quarterly successor, *The Official Index to The Times* (from 1914) – published London: The Times – first appeared in parallel with *Palmer's*, but after the latter's end continued on its own. The title was *Index to The Times* from 1957 to 1972; in the latter year publication moved to Reading: Newspaper Archive Developments.
   In 1973, the title was changed again (to *The Times Index*), the publishers being renamed Research Publications (International) in 1982. Latterly, frequency has been monthly with annual cumulations. Rptd New York: Kraus. Years from 1906 available on microfilm, and (in preparation) from 1906 to 1940 on CD-ROM from Cambridge: Chadwyck-Healey.

87   – – –.   *Tercentenary handlist of English and Welsh newspapers, magazines and reviews, 1620–1920.* London: The Times, 1920; facsimile reprint, London: Dawson, 1966. 324pp + indexes (1 + xxxv). Introduction: 'Early press laws' (in fact, a brief early history). Section I: London and suburban; Section II: Provincial. Although his name does not appear in the book, J.G. Muddiman as compiler was applauded by Lord Northcliffe, as well as by a reviewer, in a major '300th birthday of journalism' feature in *The Times* of 2 December 1920, publication marking the tercentenary of the presumed first English-language coranto. An occasionally acrimonious exchange between Muddiman and others pointed to several omissions and errors, no doubt due in part to the haste in which the *Handlist* was compiled; but it remains a standard reference.

88   *Two-Ten Communications UK Media Directory.* London: Two-Ten Communications. Est 1976 as *Editorial Media Analysis (EMA)*.
Covers all British newspapers; updated bimonthly.

89   *UK Media Yearbook.* London: Zenith Media/Campaign, annual, 1988–9.
Statistical analysis, including newspaper circulations and readership – costly, but the most comprehensive of surveys.

90   *UK Press Gazette.* Souvenir issue, ed Joseph Grizzard. London: publ with no 1,000 (same date, i.e. 3 Jun 1985). 148pp.
Charles Wintour, then editor of 'journalism's newspaper', leads off with a masterly review of the preceding twenty years in the national press. He is followed, in an article 'How it all began', by Colin Valdar, founder of *UKPG* in 1965 and publisher of the weekly until 1983, when Bouverie Publishing Co was acquired by Timothy Benn Publishing.

91   – – –.   25th anniversary issue. Cockfosters (Herts): Maclean Hunter, 3 Dec 1990.

92 *Warwick guide to British labour periodicals, The, 1790–1970: a checklist,* ed Royden Harrison, Gillian B. Woolven, and Robert Duncan. Hassocks (W Sussex): Harvester Press; Atlantic Highlands (NJ): Humanities Press, 1977. 702pp.

Two of the editors were from the Centre for the Study of Social History at the University of Warwick. The 4,125 entries (which include labour *newspapers*) are given three broad categories: publications by wage-earners' organization; those in the interests of the working class; and those for the 'betterment' thereof. Relevant entries have detailed annotations on origins, aims etc.

93 *Willings Press Guide.* London: Willing; later Thomas Skinner; now East Grinstead (W Sussex): Reed Information Services. Annual.

Established in 1871 as *Frederick May's London Press Dictionary and Advertiser's Handbook*; 1874–89, *May's British and Irish Press Guide*; present title since 1890. Now a two-volume work, Vol 1 covering the UK.

94 *World's Press News.* Coronation souvenir, ed Ernest A. Goodey. London: 1 May 1953. 96pp.

'An historical document tracing the progress of British advertising and the British press and ancillary trades during the reigns of six monarchs'.

95 – – –. 25th birthday number. 5 Mar 1954. lxxiipp. A supplement 'reflecting every facet of advertising and the press'. With an introduction by the editor, W.W. Weal.

The weekly *World's Press News* – 'the national newspaper for the press, advertising, paper and printing' – was founded by Tibor Korda in 1929 and later acquired by Haymarket Press. Its title was changed to *Campaign* in 1968.

96 *Writers' and Artists' Yearbook.* London: A. & C. Black, 1902–. Annual.

Includes a section 'National and regional newspapers and magazines'; and (in recent edns) 'Writing for newspapers', by Jill Dick.

97 *Writer's Handbook, The.* London: Macmillan; 1987–. Annual. Ed Barry Turner.

Includes a section 'National and regional newspapers'.

The media in today's nationals

Several national newspapers now have specialist media coverage. *The Guardian* launched *Media Guardian* (originally as a single page) in 1984, and *The Times, The Independent* and (London) *Evening Standard* also devote regular space to the subject. The *Financial Times*, although with no set allocation, presents news and influential comment, while the national Sundays have occasional informed contributions.

THE BIBLIOGRAPHY

THE BIBLIOGRAPHY

98 Abdullahi, A. *A one world one voice?: Libyan affairs coverage by one European and three African newspapers, 1970–1986.* Leicester: University of Leicester, 1990 (PhD thesis).
The European newspaper is *The Times*; no fundamental differences in attitude were apparent.

99 *Abergavenny Chronicle.* Centenary supplement. Abergavenny (Gwent): 12 Aug 1971.
A Tindle Newspaper title since 1983.

100 Abrahams, Gerald. *The law for writers and journalists.* London: Herbert Jenkins, 1958.
Still of practical value, although inevitably dated.

101 Abrams, Mark. *The newspaper reading public of tomorrow.* London: Odhams, 1964.
Research used as the basis for the launch of *The Sun* by IPC in 1963.

102 *Accrington Observer and Times.* Centenary supplement. Accrington (Lancs): 27 Mar 1987.

103 Adam, George. *Behind the scenes at the Front.* London: Chapman & Hall, 1915. viii + 239pp.
The Paris correspondent of *The Times*.

104 Adams, Valerie. *The media and the Falklands campaign.* Basingstoke (Hants): Macmillan, 1986. x + 224pp.
The author wrote with long personal experience at the Ministry of Defence.

105 Adams, W.J. 'Giles' cartoon annuals'. *Book and Magazine Collector,* Jan 1985.
Informative summary of the selections of the work of Giles the cartoonist first published by Express Newspapers in 1946.

106 Adamthwaite, Anthony. 'The British Government and the media, 1937–1938'. *Journal of Contemporary History,* 18, 1, 1983.

107   Adcock, A. '*Stamford Mercury*: earliest provincial newspaper'. *Notes and Queries*, 14 Jun 1913.
More recent research suggests that the designation 'earliest', based on the probable year of 1713, belongs elsewhere.

108   Addison, Paul. 'Politicians under pressure: Lord Rothermere and British foreign policy'. *In* G. Peele and C. Cook, eds. *The politics of re-appraisal, 1918–1935.* London: Macmillan, 1975.

109   *Admap*. Monthly magazine. London: 1964–91; Henley-on-Thames (Oxon): NTC Publications, 1991–.
'Analysis and views rather than people and news'; with frequent informed expositions of advertising and marketing through the medium of newspapers.

110   – – –.   'Floodlight on the nationals'. Sep 1982.
A series of signed contributions on current issues.

111   – – –.   'Looking at newspapers'. Sep 1987.
Five state-of-the-art articles.

112   – – –.   Silver Jubilee edition. Nov 1989.

113   *AFN News*. Gloucester: 1982–91. Quarterly, later bimonthly.
Newsletter of the Association of Free Newspapers (and latterly also of the Association of Free Magazines and Periodicals).
   The first-named organization finally became the Association of Free and Weekly Newspapers, which was wound up in 1991.

114   Agate, James (Evershed). *Ego: the autobiography of James Agate.* London: Hamish Hamilton. 9 parts, 1935–46. Publ abridged as *A shorter ego.* London: Harrap. 3 vols, 1945–9.
The serial diary of the most influential dramatic critic of his time – a unique record of contemporary literary, theatrical and social London. During that time, Agate was dramatic critic of *The Sunday Times*; he had cut his teeth with *The Manchester Guardian*.

115   Aguirre, P.G. *The coverage of Central America by the British press.* London: City University, 1985 (PhD thesis), 1985. 422pp.

116   Aitchison, James. *Writing for the press: an introduction.* London: Hutchinson, 1988. x + 124pp.
An up-to-date training manual, intended for students e.g. on National Council for the Training of Journalists courses.

117   Aitken, Ian (Levack). 'On the outside, spitting in'. *The Guardian*, 14 Oct 1992.
The newspaper's political editor on his journalistic career – hired by Beaverbrook for the *Daily Express* before joining *The Guardian*.

118   Aitken, Jonathan (William Patrick). *Officially secret.* London: Weidenfeld & Nicolson, 1971. x + 236pp.

The author (great-nephew of Lord Beaverbrook) was with *The Sunday Telegraph* in 1970 when, together with his editor Brian Roberts, he was prosecuted for his Nigerian Civil War reports, which allegedly made use of secret information emanating from the British High Commission in Lagos. (Both of the accused were acquitted.) He reviews the historical background to the Official Secrets Act.

119   Albert, Tim. *Medical journalism*. Oxford: Radcliffe Medical Press, 1992. Provides useful general, as well as specialized, advice.

120   *Alderley, Wilmslow and Knutsford Advertiser*. Centenary supplement. Alderley Edge (Cheshire): 8 Aug 1974.

121   Alderson, Andrew. 'At the court of King David'. *The Sunday Times*, 12 Jul 1992.
Sir David English becomes chairman and editor-in-chief of Associated Newspapers in the latest 'musical chairs' among the editors of the nationals.

122   Alexander, John, ed. *Central government for journalists*. London: LGC Communications, 1988.
Commissioned as a students' textbook by the National Council for the Training of Journalists.

123   Alioua, F. *Analysis of linguistic factors in reports of a political event: the Falklands War as a case study*. Sheffield: University of Sheffield, 1990 (PhD thesis).
The main factor is shown to be the predominance of patriotic sentiment.

124   Allaun, Frank. *Spreading the news: a guide to media reform*. Nottingham: Spokesman Press (for Campaign for Press and Broadcasting Freedom), 1988. 112pp.
By a leading left-wing Labour MP.

125   Allbrooke, Jill. *Guide to family history sources at the Newspaper Library*. British Library/Federation of Family History Societies (in preparation).
By the information officer at Colindale.

126   Alldridge, John. *Special assignment*. With a foreword by Sir William Haley. London: Bell, 1960. 191pp.
Staffer with the *Manchester Evening News* selects sixteen reporters and their assignments – most in print although a few from radio (the book is based on a BBC radio series).

127   Alldritt, Keith. *Churchill the writer: his life as a man of letters*. London: Hutchinson, 1992. viii + 168pp.
Journalism was Winston Churchill's main source of income when he was out of office; he was for example the principal outside contributor to the *News of the World*. However, that was only one period during his long career when he made masterly use of the written word. This treatise is summary in treatment.

128   Allen, A.L. *Bristol and its newspapers*. Bristol: 1934.

129   Allen, Gertrude M. 'The women's page specialist'. *The Writer*, Aug 1925.

130   Allen, J.E. 'Modern newspaper make-up'. *Typography*, 5, 1938.

131   Allen, Margaret. 'Up-market porn'. *British Journalism Review*, Summer 1990.
Bemoans the values of 'women's interest' pages in the up-market national press (with
no women editors in sight), and equally those encouraged by the tabloids where women
editors *have* emerged. Margaret Allen had been a features editor of *The Times*, and a
prolific writer on financial affairs.

132   Allen, Peter. '*Socialist Worker* – paper with a purpose'. *Media, Culture and
Society*, 7, 1985.
On the Socialist Workers Party's weekly.

133   Allen, Robert. *Voice of Britain: the inside story of the Daily Express*.
Cambridge: Patrick Stephens, 1983. 192pp.
Extensively illustrated from the John Frost Historical Newspaper Collection. Traces in
popular style the vicissitudes of the *Express* and its outstanding personalities, from its
foundation in 1900 by Arthur Pearson and its great Beaverbrook years (1916–64) to
the Fleet Holdings of the 1980s.

134   No entry.

135   Allen, Robert, and John Frost. *Daily Mirror*. Cambridge: Patrick Stephens,
1981. 90pp.
Appropriately for a picture paper with the *Mirror*'s unique pedigree, this selection
of facsimile front pages, photos and cartoons reflects the great events and *Mirror* personalities over nearly eighty years.

136   Alleyne, Mark D., and Janet Wagner. 'Stability and change at the "big five"
news agencies'. *Journalism Quarterly*, 70, 1, Spring 1993.
Statistical comparisons as at 1990, including Reuters.

137   Allott, Serena. 'A hungry paper tiger'. *The Daily Telegraph*, 9 Jan 1987.
On Robert Heron, collector of historic newspapers and founder of the Press Archives
business.

138   Amery, Colin. 'Keep the flavour of Fleet Street'. *Financial Times*, 15 Feb
1988.
A plea to preserve the area's architectural style.

139   Amery, Leopold Charles Maurice Stennett. *My political life*. London:
Hutchinson, 1953–5. 3 vols. Vol 1, *England before the storm, 1896–1914*;
Vol 2, *War and peace, 1914–1929*; Vol 3, *The war years, 1929–1940*.

140   – – –. *The Leo Amery diaries*. Vol 1, *1896–1929*, ed John Barnes and
David Nicholson. London: Hutchinson, 1980; Vol 2, *The Empire at bay: the
Leo Amery diaries 1929–1945*, ed Barnes and Nicholson. Hutchinson, 1988.
Before becoming a leading politician, Amery (1873–1955) was colonial editor and
military correspondent of *The Times*.

141 Amory, Mark, ed. *The collected and recollected Marc*. London: Fourth Estate, 1993. Introduction by Craig Brown.
Tribute in words and pictures to the multi-talented Mark Boxer, who was the first editor of *The Sunday Times Magazine* and later edited both *Tatler* and *Vogue*. As 'Marc', his cartoons enlivened *The Guardian, The Times, The Daily Telegraph* among others.

142 Andrews, *Sir* [William] Linton. *Problems of an editor: a study in newspaper trends*. London: Oxford University Press, 1962. x + 181pp.
A tersely written but heavily didactic memoir that has the sole merit of being founded on much first-class editorial experience.

143 – – –. *Linton Andrews: the autobiography of a journalist*. London: Benn, 1964. 262pp.
Andrews (1886–1972) writes after retirement from the editorship of the *Yorkshire Post*, which he had held from 1939 to 1960. The knighthood bestowed during that period was a recognition of his standing as one of the most influential regional editors of his time.

144 – – –. 'Editorship'. In *The press, 1898–1948. (The Newspaper World* Golden Jubilee.) London: Benn, 1948.

145 – – –. 'The press over six reigns: 50 years of journalistic revolution'. *The Journal*, Jun 1953.

146 – – –. 'Salute the old guard'. *World's Press News* (21st birthday no), 5 Mar 1954.

147 Andrews, *Sir* [William] Linton, and H(enry) A(rchibald) Taylor. *Lords and laborers of the press: men who fashioned the modern British newspaper*. Carbondale (IL): Southern Illinois University Press, 1970. xx + 330pp.
Unusual in being essays on British journalists by two leading British practitioners but published in the USA. Has chapters devoted to Stead, Scott, Donald, Northcliffe, J.A. Spender, Garvin, Camrose, Mann, Blumenfeld, Beaverbrook, Haley, 'King, Cudlipp and others', Cummings, (George) Murray, Thomson (of Fleet), and 'viceroys of a press empire': Hamilton, Dunnett, Sayers and Giddings – all of the Thomson group.

148 Angell, *Sir* Norman (formerly Ralph Norman Angell Lane). *The press and the organisation of society*. London: Labour Publishing Co, 1922. 123pp. 2nd (revised) edn, Cambridge: Gordon Fraser, 1933. vii + 70pp.
Angell (1874–1967) was first associated with Northcliffe before World War I, becoming manager of the *Continental Daily Mail* in Paris. This early post-war study foreshadowed the first Labour government.

149 Anglo, Michael. *Service newspapers of the Second World War*. London: Jupiter Books, 1977. 139pp.

150 Anstey, Joanna, comp. *Echoes: twenty-five years of the Telegraph Magazine*. London: W.H. Allen (for Daily Telegraph), 1990.
Anthology of contributions since *The Daily Telegraph* launched its magazine in September 1964.

151   Anstey, Joanna, and John Silverlight, eds. *The Observer observed: 200 years of distinguished writing from one of the world's great newspapers*. London: Barrie & Jenkins, 1991. 304pp.
Distillation – in pictures as well as words – of outstanding items from the two hundred years' history of *The Observer*.

152   *Anywhere for a news story*. London: John Lane The Bodley Head, 1934.
Introduction by H.W. Nevinson, who as one of the thirteen contributors related the story of the siege and relief of Ladysmith.

153   Appleton, Tony, comp. *The writings of Stanley Morison: a handlist*. Brighton: Appleton, 1976. 117pp.
A splendid memorial to Morison, listing in detail every publication in his unique professional career as print and newspaper designer, historian and essayist.

154   Appleyard, S. '*The Lincoln, Rutland and Stamford Mercury*'. *Lincolnshire Life*, Jun/Jul 1965.
It has now been established that the *Lincoln, Rutland and Stamford Mercury* – the oldest published by the EMAP group – is directly descended from the *Stamford Mercury* founded by the printers Thomas Bailey and William Thompson in 1713. Francis Howgrave, who started a rival *Stamford Mercury* in 1732, carried on the title so that it has had an unbroken sequence – second only to *Berrow's Worcester Journal* among British newspapers.

155   Armstrong, George Gilbert. *Memories of George Gilbert Armstrong, journalist, politician, author, preacher*. London (printed by Unwin): 1944.
Armstrong was Northern editor of *The Daily News*, and then the *News Chronicle*.

156   Article 19. *Information freedom and censorship: Article 19 world report*. 1988, Harlow (Essex): Longman, 1988. 340pp; 1991, London: Library Association/ Article 19, 1991. 471pp.
The first report covered media in fifty countries, the second seventy-seven – including the UK in both.

157   – – –. *No comment: censorship, secrecy and the Irish Troubles*. London: Article 19, 1989. 110pp.

158   – – –. *Freedom of expression and information in the United Kingdom*. London: Article 19, 1991. 32pp.
A Country Commentary.

159   – – –. *Press law and practice: a comparative study of press freedom in European and other democracies*. London: Article 19 (for Unesco), 1993. 307pp.
This detailed comparative study analyses the press laws of eleven contrasting democracies; these include the UK, by Andrew Nicol.

160   – – –. *The Article 19 freedom of expression handbook: international and comparative law, standards and procedure*. London: Article 19, 1993. xxix + 288pp.

Topics include press freedom and editorial independence; protection of journalists' sources; and licensing of newspapers and journalists. Article 19, the International Centre Against Censorship, takes its title from that Article of the United Nations Universal Declaration of Human Rights.

161   Arundale, Justin. 'The library, *Today*'. *Library Association Record*, Mar 1986. Setting up, from scratch, the library at the then new national newspaper *Today* with an all-professional staff of librarians.

162   Ashmead-Bartlett, Ellis. *With the Turks in Thrace*. London: Heinemann; New York: 1913. x + 335pp.

163   – – –.   *Some of my experiences in the Great War*. London: Newnes, 1918. 287pp.
Although primarily associated with *The Daily Telegraph* through his long and distinguished career as a special correspondent, Ashmead-Bartlett was sent to cover the Dardanelles campaign in 1915 as the representative of all the London press. He was forced by censorship to depict this as a splendid Allied success, and a letter to the British prime minister he attempted to smuggle out via the Australian Keith Murdoch was intercepted, and he was expelled. But back in London, and still with Murdoch's support, he wrote a stinging indictment in *The Times*, and Sir Ian Hamilton, the expedition commander, was dismissed.

164   Ashton, Harold. *First from the Front*. London: Pearson, 1914. 167pp.
Ashton represented *The Daily News* in Flanders during World War I. But he was no exception to the general rule, which was to be unquestionably supportive and submissive to the will of the General Staff, in order to receive accreditation as a war correspondent.

165   Askew, Barry. 'The last barricade in the war against the electronic media'. *UK Press Gazette*, 28 Sep 1987. (In The Tabloids series.)
By a former editor of the *News of the World*.

166   Aspden, Hartley. *Fifty years a journalist: reflections of an old Clitheronian*. Clitheroe (Lancs): Advertiser and Times, [1930]. 63pp.
Eventually, Aspden became a long-service director of Northcliffe's Amalgamated Press.

167   *Assignments: the (British) Press Photographers' Association Yearbook*. Oxford: Phaidon, 1987–9.
The first yearbook, ed Anna Tait, was illustrated by a selection of work over the years by members of the then newly formed professional body; *Assignments 2* (ed Michael Young, foreword by Mark Haworth-Booth, afterword by George Hill) covered outstanding work since *Assignments 1*; similarly *Assignments 3* (ed Sir Tom Hopkinson), which covered a further year's selection.

168   Associated Newspapers. *The great adventure, 1896–1936: presenting in permanent form the commemorative articles and tributes published in the Daily Mail on the occasion of the 40th anniversary of this pioneer newspaper, May 4th 1936*. London: 1936. 73pp.

Associated Newspapers Ltd was formed in 1905, to publish the *Daily Mail, Evening News, Weekly Dispatch* etc.

169   Astor, *Hon* John Jacob (later *1st Baron* Astor of Hever). 'The future of *The Times*'. *Empire Review*, Sep 1923.
J.J. Astor, younger son of William Waldorf, had become chairman and co-proprietor of *The Times* in the previous year.

170   Atienza, T. 'What the papers said'. *In* J. Fyrth, ed. *Britain, Fascism and the Popular Front*. London: Lawrence & Wishart, 1985.

171   Atkins, John Black. *The life of Sir William Howard Russell, the first special correspondent*. London: John Murray; New York: Dutton, 1911. 2 vols: total 804pp.
Until recent years, this was the only full biography of Russell, the most famous of war correspondents. The campaigns he covered were all in the nineteenth century, but he lived until 1907. There is a memorial in St Paul's Cathedral (London).

172   – – –.   *Incidents and reflections*. London: Christophers, 1947. 262pp.

173   – – –.   'The work and future of war correspondents'. *The Monthly Review*, Sep 1901.
Atkins was himself a distinguished 'special' for *The Manchester Guardian*, his work culminating in South Africa, 1899–1900. (Later he became the paper's London editor.)

174   – – –.   'C.P. Scott: a great editor'. *The Spectator*, 40, 1932.

175   Atkinson, B.M.C. *Reporting ecological issues: steps towards new news values*. Cardiff: University of Wales, 1991 (MPhil thesis).

176   Atkinson, Frank. *The English newspaper since 1900*. London: Library Association, 1960. 34pp. (LA Special Subject List no 32.)
A classified bibliography, listing 367 works; within its limits, accurate and useful.

177   Atlay, James Beresford. *The Globe centenary: a sketch of its history*. London: 1903.
The story of the famous London evening, told only eighteen years before its demise.

178   Aubrey, Crispin, John Berry, and Duncan Campbell. 'The eavesdroppers'. *Time Out*, May 1976.
This exposé of Government Communications Headquarters at Cheltenham led to all three authors being tried in 1978 under the Official Secrets Act (the so-called 'ABC Trial'); all were acquitted.

179   Aubrey, Crispin, Charles Landry, and David Morley. *Here is the other news: challenges to the local commercial press*. London: Minority Press Group (later Comedia), 1980. 80pp.
A co-operative production, tracing the varying fortunes of the community and local radical press in Britain during the previous decade.

180 Audit Bureau of Circulations. *A commemorative book to mark the occasion of the Golden Jubilee of the Audit Bureau of Circulations: 20th October 1931 to 20th October 1981.* London: ABC, 1981.
A souvenir consisting of 'then and now' facsimile news pages and advertisements from leading publications in membership with the ABC.

181 Auld, John A.M. 'They never close'. *The Media Reporter*, 2, 3, 1978.
The story of the Press Association in brief thumb-nail sketch form.

182 Austin, A[lexander] B[erry]. *We landed at dawn: the story of the Dieppe raid.* London: Gollancz, 1943. 127pp; Sydney: Angus & Robertson, 1943. xii + 153pp.

183 – – –. *Birth of an army.* London: Gollancz, 1943.
The Allied landings and operations in Tunisia, 1942–3. Austin, a highly literate *Daily Herald* war correspondent, was later killed in Italy.

184 Austin, Roland. '*Gloucester Journal*, 1722–1922'. *Notes and Queries*, 12th ser, 10, 1922.

185 *Author's and Writer's Who's Who, 1934, The.* London: Shaw Publishing Co [1934]. Ed Edward Martell.
The only known issue of this reference book, useful for the sheer quantity of biographical entries for journalists prominent at the time.

186 Averis, Ernest, ed. *Hold the front page.* Bristol: Bristol United Press, 1984.
An account of the success story of the *Bristol Evening Post*, started in 1932 in opposition to Rothermere's newly launched *Bristol Evening World* (the latter ceased publication in 1962). This well-illustrated booklet also traces the complex fortunes of Bristol's other morning and evening papers.

187 Ayerst, David George Ogilvy. *The Guardian: biography of a newspaper.* London: Collins; Ithaca (NY): Cornell University Press, 1971. 702pp.
Celebrating the 150th anniversary of the foundation of *The Manchester Guardian*, this in fact chronicles the fortunes of the newspaper up to 1956 (when A.P. Wadsworth, long-serving editor, died in office). Written by a former staffer, it is particularly good on the early years; but it does not do justice to the part played by C.E. Montague, who ran the paper almost single-handed in the years before World War I when C.P. Scott, his father-in-law and proprietor/editor, was striving to become a political *éminence grise* in London; nor does it explain adequately the failure to back staff correspondents reporting the Russian Revolution.

188 – – –. *Garvin of The Observer.* London (Beckenham): Croom Helm; and Dover (NH), 1985. viii + 314pp.
'Garvin came from the bottom drawer, the son of an immigrant Irish labourer . . . It was the breadth as well as the depth of his interests that made *The Observer* the newspaper without which no English Sunday was complete.' Garvin also edited *The Pall Mall Gazette* for more than three years in tandem with *The Observer*: 'Its faded files are still a delight to the eye of a journalist or book-lover.'

189   – – –, ed. *The Guardian omnibus, 1821–1971: an anthology of 150 years of Guardian writing.* London: Collins, 1973. 768pp.
'By the *Guardian* about its own times – and not a history of the paper'; as such, it admirably complements Ayerst's biography.

190   – – –. ' "Garve": the emergence of an editor'. *Library Chronicle* (Texas), new series, 9, 1975.
Full-length study of Garvin's career.

191   *Ayr Advertiser.* Centenary number. Ayr: 6 Aug 1903.

192   – – –. 'Our 150th anniversary'. 6 Aug 1953.
From 1803 to 1839 the *Air Advertiser*, this Clyde and Forth Newspapers title is the oldest Scottish weekly with a continuous history.

193   *A–Z of Britain's free newspapers and magazines.* Gloucester: Association of Free Newspapers/Association of Free Magazines and Periodicals, 1990, 1991.
A directory that covered all the 'frees', not just those in Association membership.

194   Aziz, Qutubuddin. *Pakistan and the British media.* Karachi: Royal Book Co, 1989. 281pp.
Surveys British coverage in the critical period 1978–85.

195   Badsey, Stephen D. *British official photography in the First World War.* Monograph (unpublished) for Imperial War Museum, 1981.
Includes detail of the photo agencies that served the newspapers at home.

196   Bagilhole, Barbara. 'Merger and monopoly in the provincial local press: a case study from Nottingham'. *Bulletin of Local History East Midlands Region*, 1984.
Examines the Nottingham newspapers then published by T. Bailey Forman.

197   Bagnall, Nicholas. *Newspaper language.* Oxford: Butterworth-Heinemann (Focal Press), 1993. vii + 221pp.
Advice, with copious examples, by a *Sunday Telegraph* man.

198   Bailey, Eleanor. 'Whiter than white knight'. *Journalist's Week*, 15 Mar 1991.
On Sir Nicholas Lloyd, editor of the *Daily Express*.

199   Bailey, Herbert. 'Reuters' monopoly in foreign news'. *The Nation and Athenaeum*, 8 Dec 1923.
A critical study of the war-stretched resources of Reuters.

200   Baily, Francis Edward. *Twenty-nine years' hard labour.* London: Hutchinson, [1934]. 287pp.
Life as seen from the 'coal-face' of daily reporting in Fleet Street.

201   Bainbridge, Cyril, ed. *One hundred years of journalism: social aspects of the press.* London: Macmillan (for the Institute of Journalists), 1984. xvii + 166pp.

Celebrating the centenary of the foundation of the National Association of Journalists, which was chartered as the Institute of Journalists in 1890. Part I consists of appraisals by outside authorities of the role of the press in modern society; Part II is a history of the IOJ, emphasizing its role as a professional body rather than a trade union.

202 Bainbridge, Cyril, and Roy Stockdill. *The News of the World story: 150 years of the world's bestselling newspaper*. London: HarperCollins, 1993. 351pp.
A surprisingly sober narrative of an undoubtedly successful but often controversial progress. The historians repeat with reason R.D. Blumenfeld's generous dictum: 'An unusually good newspaper', and rightly point to its technical and other qualities.

203 Baird, Patricia. 'The *Glasgow Herald* index project'. *British Library Newspaper Library Newsletter*, 8, Jun 1987.
The project was started by the University of Strathclyde in 1984.

204 'Baird's: the *Belfast Telegraph*'. *The Newspaper World*, 4 Mar 1939. (In The Oldest Newspapers series.)

205 Baistow, Tom. *Fourth-rate estate: an anatomy of Fleet Street*. London: Comedia, 1985. 115pp.
A professional media analyst (formerly foreign editor of the *News Chronicle* etc) makes his overall opinion clear in his title.

206 – – –. 'Hope lies in diversity'. *The Listener*, Press issue, 24 Apr 1986.
Current upheavals could 'herald a return to the diverse press essential to an informed, socially balanced and politically literate democracy'.

207 Baker, Alfred. *Pitman's practical journalism*. London: Pitman, 1915. With note on newspaper law by Edward A. Cope; 2nd edn, ed Cope, 1931.
'An introduction to every description of literary effort in connection with newspaper production'.

208 Baldwin, Herbert F. *A war photographer in Thrace: an account of personal experiences during the Turco-Balkan War, 1912*. London: T. Fisher Unwin, 1913.

209 *Ballad of Captain Bob, The, or The man in the Mirror*. London: Infotext Manuscripts, 1992. 30pp.
'The strange life and mysterious death of Robert Maxwell, composed and illustrated by the I.T.M.A. team'.

210 *Banffshire Advertiser*. Centenary supplement. Buckie (Grampian): 17 Nov 1981.

211 *Banffshire Journal*. Centenary number. Banff (Grampian): 4 Sep 1945.
Now in Scottish Provincial Press group.

212 Bankes, Caroline. '*The Guardian* toasts a quiet maverick'. *Journalist's Week*, 15 Jun 1990.
Assessing Peter Preston's record after fifteen years as editor of *The Guardian* – and the development of the paper itself in various directions.

213 – – –. 'Glitz, glamour, Royals and soap'. *Journalist's Week*, 3 Aug 1990.
Interview with Eve Pollard, then editor of the *Sunday Mirror*.

214 – – –. 'The Mac factor'. *Journalist's Week*, 9 Nov 1990.
On Lord McGregor of Durris, to head the Press Complaints Commission on its formation in January 1991. McGregor chaired the Royal Commission on the Press that
reported in 1977.

215 Banks, Elizabeth L. *The autobiography of a 'newspaper girl'.* London:
Methuen, 1902. viii + 319pp.
Records 'stunts' carried out for the popular press of the day, in a most readable and
idiosyncratic style.

216 Barber, [John Lysberg] Noel. *The natives were friendly . . . so we stayed the
night.* London: Macmillan, 1977. 226pp. Milton Keynes: Robin Clark, 1979.
Rattling tales of journalistic derring-do by a past master of a dying art: the popular,
'follow-me-around' style of personal reporting. Barber was formerly editor of the *Continental Daily Mail* in Paris.

217 Barber, Lynn. *Mostly men.* London: Viking, 1991, 288pp. Harmondsworth:
Penguin, 1992.
Barbed journalistic profiles from *Sunday Express, Independent on Sunday* etc.

218 – – –. 'The most mysterious millionaire'. *Sunday Express (Magazine)*,
Jul 1987; rptd *UK Press Gazette*, Classics of Journalism series, 21/8 Dec 1987.
On J.P. Getty III.

219 – – –. 'There are no gays in Auchtermuchty . . . and never trust a man
with a beard'. *Independent on Sunday (The Sunday Review)*, 4 Feb 1990.
Profile of Sir John Junor, later a columnist for *The Mail on Sunday* but no longer the
Sunday Express (which he edited for 32 years). Auchtermuchty (in Fife) often figured
in Junor's highly opionated 'JJ' column as a town upholding high moral standards.

220 Barclay, *Sir* Thomas. *Thirty years: Anglo-French reminiscences (1876–1906).*
London: Constable, 1914. viii + 389pp.
Barclay was a leading *Times* correspondent: 'I was soon lost in the intellectual omni-
science the *Times* correspondents in those days affected to possess.' He was closely
associated with the genesis and fulfilment of the Entente Cordiale between Britain
and France.

221 Bardgett, Suzanne. '"No braver companion . . . no finer reporter": the
writings of A.B. Austin, *Daily Herald* war correspondent, 1940–42'. *Imperial
War Museum Review*, 6, 1991.
Austin began the war as an RAF press officer, but switched to front-line reporting. The
tribute in the title of this article comes from his follow-correspondent, Christopher
Buckley. Austin's papers are held in the Imperial War Museum.

222 – – –. 'Dieppe: a disaster beyond words'. *Financial Times (Weekend FT)*,
15–16 Aug 1992.

Fifty years back: what really happened during the raid on Dieppe, and the quandary caused for the press who were anticipating a famous victory.

223   Barker, A. *Government and the mass media: an examination of the role of Government press officers and specialist journalists.* Imperial College of Science and Technology, 1987 (PhD thesis).

224   Barker, Dudley (Raymond). *The young man's guide to journalism.* London: Hamish Hamilton, 1963. 160pp.
Kindly advice remarkably free of the usual tired cynicism. The book also includes an outline history of the British press and a view of Fleet Street in the 1960s.

225   Barker, Nicolas (John). *Stanley Morison.* London: Macmillan, 1972. 566pp.
The first major biography of Morison (1889–1963), who 'found typography without organized history or principles; he left it with both'. In his thirty years at *The Times*, Morison possibly had wider influence there than anyone other than the owner and editors (in fact, he himself edited *The Times Literary Supplement* from 1945 to 1948). Barrington-Ward, when editing *The Times*, referred to Morison as 'the conscience' and 'the sage' of the newspaper.

226   Barkley, William. *William Barkley's notebook.* London: Daily Express, 1948. 200pp. Reprinted as *Reporter's notebook.* London: Oldbourne (Daily Express), [1959]. 178pp.
Barkley made his name as an authoritative parliamentary reporter for the *Daily Express* and political editor of the *Sunday Express*. His working life in the 1930s is well portrayed in this *Notebook*.

227   Barman, Thomas Gustav. *Diplomatic correspondent.* London: Hamish Hamilton, 1968.
Barman was with *The Times* as its Stockholm and Paris correspondent before World War II. He later became the BBC's diplomatic voice.

228   Barnes, F., and J.L. Hobbes. *Handlist of newspapers published in Cumberland, Westmorland and north Lancashire.* Kendal: Titus Wilson, 1951. Reprinted from *Cumberland and Westmorland Antiquarian and Archaeological Society Tract*, ser 14, [1951].

229   Barnes, Simon. *A sportswriter's year.* London: Heinemann, 1989. xi + 196pp.
The Times is the author's platform.

230   Barnetson, William Denholm (*Baron*). *The economics of newspapers and news agencies.* Edinburgh: Scottish Academic Press, 1973. 45pp.
An essay based on a lecture Barnetson gave at Edinburgh University, examining 'the great pruning' that took place during the late 1950s and early 1960s among British newspapers, and blaming the broadcasting media for most of the 'deaths'.

231   – – –. 'Sir William Barnetson on Reuters'. (Interview by A.G. McBain.) *Accountants Magazine*, Jun 1973.

A rare public pronouncement by one of the most successful and admired pressmen of recent times (1917–81). Barnetson's chairmanships of Reuters and United Newspapers were only two of his manifold high offices on both the British and the international scene.

232   Barnett, Anthony. 'Some notes on media coverage of the Falklands'. *In* Francis Barker etc, eds. *Confronting the crisis: war, politics and culture in the eighties.* Colchester (Essex): University of Essex, 1984.

233   Barnett, Steve. 'You can have anything they want'. *The Guardian*, Jun 1989.
A study, supported by tabulation of the eight major national groups, of the concentration of media.

234   'Barnsley newspapers'. *Barnsley Chronicle*, 27 Dec 1974.

235   Barrington-Ward, Mark. 'Garvin, James Louis'. In *Dictionary of national biography, 1941–1950.* Oxford: Oxford University Press, 1959.
By the son of R.M. Barrington-Ward (then editor of *The Times*, and a close associate of Garvin).

236   Barron, E.H., ed. *A Highland editor: selected writings of James Barron of the Inverness Courier.* Inverness: 1927.
The *Courier* is now a Scottish Provincial Press weekly.

237   Barrow, Logie J.W. *The socialism of Robert Blatchford and The Clarion newspaper (1889–1918).* London: University of London, 1975 (PhD thesis).

238   Barson, Susie, and Andrew Saint. *A farewell to Fleet Street.* London: Historic Buildings and Monuments Division (with Allison & Busby), 1988. 60pp.
Illustrated booklet to accompany the retrospective exhibition staged by English Heritage at the Museum of London: first-class and authoritative on the whole area of Fleet Street (and beyond) and its long connection with printing and publishing.

239   Bartlett, [Charles] Vernon [Oldfield]. *Mud and khaki: sketches from Flanders and France.* London: Simpkin, 1917. 187pp.
War reporting, extracted from various British publications.

240   – – –.   *This is my life.* London: Chatto & Windus, 1937. 330pp.
Published in the USA as *Intermission in Europe: the life of a journalist and broadcaster.* New York: Oxford University Press, 1938. 296pp.

241   – – –.   *Tomorrow always comes.* New York: Knopf, 1944. 159pp.
About World War II.

242   – – –.   *And now, tomorrow.* London: Chatto & Windus, 1960. 255pp.

243   – – –.   *I know what I liked.* London: Chatto & Windus, 1974. 210pp.
Bartlett (1894–1983) made his name with Reuters at the Versailles Peace Conference of 1919. He later reported for the *Daily Herald* and *The Times* from various European capitals, and attracted international attention as the *News Chronicle*'s diplomatic correspondent in the 1930s.

244   Bateman, Mary. 'A lady correspondent in South Africa'. *Pearson's Magazine*, Jul 1902.
Describes her work for the *Daily Express* in the Boer War.

245   *Batley News*. Centenary number. Batley (W Yorks): 1 Sep 1976.
Weekly in the United Provincial Newspapers groups.

246   *Battle of Britain, The*. Verplanck (NJ): Historic Briefs, 1992. Vol 1.
Large-format work, introduced by John Frost, whose newspaper collection is drawn on extensively: 'As seen by the people and press of Britain during World War II'.

247   Bauermann, Werner. *Die Times und die Abwendung Englands von Deutschland um 1900*. Cologne: Orthen, 1939. 78pp.
A polemical essay decrying the influence of *The Times* in dividing Britain from Germany in 1900.

248   Bawtree, Angela. *Newspaper publishing: the inside story*. London: Crédit Suisse, Buckmaster & Moore, 1986.
A business survey.

249   Baxter, *Sir* [Arthur] Beverley. *Strange street: an autobiography*. London: Hutchinson; New York: Appleton-Century, 1935. 286pp.
The *Daily Express* is central to Baxter's story, especially the years 1929–33 when, as editor, he formed a notable Canadian triumvirate with Beaverbrook (his chairman) and E.J. Robertson, the general manager.

250   – – –.   'Britain and propaganda'. *The Strand Magazine*, Feb 1940.
Contributed as 'Beverley Baxter, MP', Baxter having become a Member of Parliament after leaving Fleet Street.

251   Baylen, Joseph O[scar]. *'God's junior partner': the life and times of W.T. Stead*. (In preparation.)

252   – – –.   'W.T. Stead and the Boer War: the irony of idealism'. *Canadian Historical Review*, 40, Dec 1959.
Stead was a strong anti-Boer War protagonist, and hence out of step on this score with popular sentiment.

253   – – –.   'W.T. Stead as publisher and editor of the *Review of Reviews*'. *Victorian Periodicals Review*, 12, Sep 1979.

254   – – –.   'W.T. Stead'. *In* W.F. Kuehl, ed. *Biographical dictionary of internationalists*. Westport (CT): Greenwood Press, 1983.

255   – – –.   'The Review of Reviews'. *In* A. Sullivan, ed. *British literary magazines. Vol 3: The Victorian and Edwardian age*. Westport (CT): Greenwood Press, 1984.

256   – – –.   'Review of Reviews Office/Stead's Publishing House'. *In* J. Rose and P.J. Anderson, eds. *Dictionary of literary biography, Vol 112: British literary publishing houses, 1881–1965*. Detroit: Gale Research, 1991.

Although Stead's greatest fame came from his editorship of *The Pall Mall Gazette* in the 1880s, he was still a towering figure in journalistic and public life in the early 1900s, in particular as editor of his own monthly *Review of Reviews*.

The above is a selection of Prof Baylen's extensive 'Stead' canon, with particular reference to the final years.

257   Baylen, Joseph O[scar], and Beryl Isaac Diamond. 'A journalist's quest for recognition: Frederick Greenwood and the purchase of the Suez Canal Company shares, 1875–1909'. *Journal of Newspaper and Periodical History*, Spring 1986.

258   Baylen, Joseph O[scar], and Norbert J. Gossman, eds. *Biographical dictionary of modern British radicals*. 3 vols. Vol 3, 1870–1914. Hemel Hempstead (Herts): Harvester Wheatsheaf, 1988 (2 parts).
The biographies include extensive treatment of those prominent in using the press in support of their cause – including Baylen on Stead.

259   Baynes, Ken, ed. *Scoop, scandal and strife: a study of photography in newspapers*. With an introduction by (Sir) Tom Hopkinson, contributions from Derrick Knight and Allen Hutt, and reproductions from papers in the John Frost Collection. London: Lund Humphries, 1971. 172pp.
This fascinating work was published in association with a Welsh Arts Council travelling exhibition.

260   Beach, *General Sir* Hugh. 'News management in conventional war – a review article'. *British Army Review*, Dec 1987.

261   Bean, John Malcolm William, ed. *The political culture of modern Britain: studies in memory of Stephen Koss*. London: Hamish Hamilton, 1987. xi + 306pp. Foreword by John Gross.
The sixteen contributors include R.K. Webb on Unitarian journalism, and Alfred Gollin on Northcliffe's support of the aviation pioneers.

262   Beare, Geraldine. 'Local newspaper indexing projects and products', *The Indexer*, Oct 1989.
Especially on *The Glasgow Herald Index* and *The Index to The Scotsman*.

263   Beaufort, J.M. de. *Behind the German veil: a record of a journalistic war pilgrimage*. New York: Dodd, Mead, 1917. xix + 403pp.
World War I analysis by a *Daily Telegraph* reporter.

264   Beaverbrook, William Maxwell Aitken, *1st Baron*. *Politicians and the press*. London: Hutchinson, [1925]. 127pp.
Born in Canada in 1879, Aitken was already a successful industrialist and prominent politician when he took control of the *Daily Express* in 1916. Soon raised to the peerage, launching the *Sunday Express*, and later acquiring the *Evening Standard*, Beaverbrook was well established when he wrote this slight but typically direct and unvarnished slice of journalism.

265 – – –. 'Death of Northcliffe: "creator of newspapers" '. *Daily Express*, 15 Aug 1922.

266 – – –. 'The press of the future'. *Sunday Express*, 24 Feb 1924.

267 – – –. 'Newspaper finance'. *Evening Standard*, 10 Sep 1926.
Beaverbrook had acquired the *Evening Standard* in 1923.

268 – – –. 'A bold newspaper enterprise'. *Daily Express*, 14 Mar 1927.

269 – – –. '*Daily Express* aims'. *Daily Express*, 16 Mar 1927.

270 – – –. 'The policy of the *Daily Express*'. *Daily Express*, 3 Dec 1927.

271 – – –. 'A new epoch in journalism: the story of the *Daily Express*'. *Daily Express*, 8 Nov 1928.

272 'Beaverbrook Newspapers'. In *The press and the people, 1971/1972*. (Press Council Annual Report.)

273 Beavin, H. '*Hinckley Journal, South Leicestershire Advertiser*'. *Hinckley Historian*, 22, 1988.

274 *Beckenham Journal*. Centenary number. Beckenham (Greater London): 1 Sep 1976.
Then a weekly in the Westminster Press group.

275 Beckles, Gordon [Gordon Beckles Willson]. 'Not for nonentities: how much are you worth to the press-cutting agencies'. *The Strand Magazine*, Feb 1946.
Describes the operation of cuttings agencies in London and features one of the pioneers, Henry (not John, as here) Romeike, a Polish-born immigrant from Paris. He joined forces with Edward Curtice, already running a cuttings agency in London; the Romeike & Curtice agency survives to this day. The author of this article, professional name Gordon Beckles, had been a *Daily Express* staffer for ten years and deputy editor of the *Daily Mail* for two.

276 *Bedford Record*. Centenary souvenir. 15 Oct 1974.
Then a weekly in the Westminster Press group.

277 Begley, George. *Keep mum!: advertising goes to war*. London: Lemon Tree Books, 1975.
Subject to the strict rationing of newsprint, newspapers were of course a major medium for the Government's campaigns.

278 Behr, Edward. *Anyone here been raped and speaks English?: a foreign correspondent's life behind the lines*. New York: Viking, 1978. London: Hamish Hamilton, 1981. New English Library, 1982. xvii + 316pp; with a new epilogue. Harmondsworth: Penguin, 1992. xiv + 345pp.
Dashing narrative by a reporter for US journals and Reuters, summing up the determinedly 'bright' Anglo-American journalistic tradition with awful clarity.

279   Beith, A.J. *The press and English local government.* Oxford: University of Oxford, 1968–9 (BLitt thesis).

280   *Belfast News-Letter.* 'Our 200th year begins' (bicentenary supplement). 1 Sep 1936.
One of the world's oldest newspapers, founded by Francis Joy in September 1737; later, ownership passed to the Henderson family until 1989, when it was sold to an Ulster-based consortium. The *Belfast News Letter* is now published (in the Tindle Newspaper group) four days a week, as a free newspaper, with the *Ulster News Letter* remaining a paid title circulating throughout the province six days a week.

281   Belfast Telegraph. *Jubilee: fifty years today, 1870–1920.* Belfast: 7 Sep 1920.

282   – – –.   *The sign of the popinjay: the history of its new office at 112 Fleet Street.* Belfast: [1928].
Today a Thomson Regional title, the *Belfast Telegraph* (weekday evenings) has by far the largest circulation of any Northern Ireland newspaper.

283   Belfield, Richard, Christopher Bird, and Sharon Kelly. *Murdoch: the decline of an empire.* London: Macdonald, 1991. viii + 336pp; with sub-title: *the great escape.* London: Warner, 1994. viii + 376pp.
A largely financial exposé of News Corporation, following on a Channel 4 TV documentary. The paperback has two new chapters admitting a 'corporate recovery'.

284   Bell, Allan. *The language of the news media.* Oxford: Oxford University Press, 1991. xv + 277pp.

285   Bell, Bell R. *The complete press photographer.* London: Pitman, 1927.

286   Bell, Enid (Hester Chataway) Moberly. *The life and times of C.F. Moberly Bell, by his daughter.* With an introduction by Sir Valentine Chirol. London: Richards Press, 1927. 326pp.
Moberly Bell (1847–1911) first came to prominence as the *Times* correspondent in Egypt, but it was in later executive roles that he became outstanding: assistant manager in the critical years running up to Northcliffe's acquisition in 1908, then managing director until his death.

287   – – –.   *Flora Shaw – Lady Lugard, D.B.E.* London: Constable, 1947. 310pp.
The remarkable story of a pioneer woman foreign correspondent who also reached managerial heights: Flora Shaw served *The Times* in various areas, but it was her work in South Africa, where her political influence became as significant as her journalism, that led to her appointment as head of the Colonial Department. In this complementary biography, the author describes Flora Shaw's close association with Moberly Bell.

288   Bell, Robert. 'Directory of Northern Ireland political periodicals'. *Fortnight*, 18 Nov 1985.

289 Bell, Robert, Robert Johnstone, and Robin Wilson. *Troubled times: Fortnight magazine and the Troubles in Northern Ireland, 1970–91*. Belfast: Blackstaff Press, 1991.
An anthology from on the spot.

290 Bell, Thomas. 'First two months of the ABC'. *World's Press News*, 15 Sep 1932.
Report as chairman on the initial work of the Audit Bureau of Circulations.

291 Bell, Walter George. *Fleet Street in seven centuries*. London: Pitman, 1912. xiv + 608pp.
'Being a history of the growth of London beyond the walls into the Western Liberty, and of Fleet Street to our time'. The last two chapters of this informative but rambling treatise deal with the advent of newspapers into the area. Bell was a night editor of *The Daily Telegraph*.

292 – – –. 'New buildings for the *Daily Telegraph*'. *The Daily Telegraph*, 28 Jun 1929.
Feature on the transformation of 135 Fleet Street.

293 Belloc, [Joseph] Hilaire [Pierre René]. *The free press*. London: Allen & Unwin, 1918. vii + 102pp.
Belloc (1870–1953) was literary editor of *The Morning Post* earlier in his long and varied career, 'when Fleet Street was more or less a habitation of the mind'.

294 Beloff, Nora. *Freedom under Foot: the battle over the closed shop in British journalism*. London: Temple Smith, 1976. 143pp.
By a former political correspondent of *The Observer*, taking the side of the editors against the more militant members of the National Union of Journalists.

295 Belsey, Andrew, and Ruth Chadwick, eds. *Ethical issues in journalism and the media*. London: Routledge, 1992. 179pp. (In Professional Ethics Series.)
'Journalism is centred on a set of essentially ethical concepts: freedom, democracy, truth, objectivity, honesty, privacy' – so aver these editors.

296 Benfield, Chris. 'A very good bet'. *UK Press Gazette*, 26 Sep 1988.
On *North West Times*, a daily newly launched from Manchester – alas, shortlived.

297 Bennett, Catherine. 'The ivory towers of Docklands'. *The Guardian*, 22 Oct 1990.
Lighthearted piece on Peregrine Worsthorne (former editor) and his colleagues planning the Comment pages of *The Sunday Telegraph*.

298 – – –. 'La crème de la scum'. *The Guardian*, 4 May 1992.
On the 'Royal ratpack' – the journalists like Harry Arnold (*Daily Mirror*, later *The Sun*), James Whitaker (also *Daily Mirror*), and Richard Kay (*Daily Mail*), who thrive on gossip about the Royal Family.

299   Bennett, [Enoch] Arnold. *Hilda Lessways*. London: Methuen, 1911.
In this second novel in the Clayhanger series, the heroine joins George Cannon, who starts the *Five Towns Chronicle* in opposition to the *Staffordshire Signal* – which proves too well-entrenched to be supplanted. These are based on the real-life *Staffordshire Knot* (which lasted ten years) and *Staffordshire Sentinel*.

300   – – –.   *The card*. London: Methuen, 1911; Penguin, 1973.
The fictional 'card' himself, Denry Machin, likewise gets involved in 'The Great Newspaper War' by pitting the upstart *Five Towns Daily* against (again) the *Signal*.

301   – – –.   *The title*. London: Chatto & Windus, 1918.
A comedy in which a title is offered to a journalist: 'Journalists say a thing that they know isn't true, in the hope that if they keep on saying it long enough it *will* be true.'

302   – – –.   *The Evening Standard years: Books and Persons, 1926–1931*. London: Chatto & Windus, 1974. xviii + 481pp. Ed Anthony Mylett.
Every one of Bennett's Books and Persons reviews from the newspaper is reprinted.

303   Bennett, *Sir* Ernest Nathaniel. *With the Turks in Tripoli: being some experiences in the Turco-Italian War of 1911*. London: Methuen, 1912. xii + 319pp.
Late exploits in the career of a notable *Westminster Gazette* 'special' correspondent.

304   Bennett, John. 'The *Scotsman* index project'. *British Library Newspaper Library Newsletter*, 8 Jun 1987.
This was launched by the Unit for the Study of Government in Scotland in 1983.

305   Bennett-England, Rodney Charles, ed. *Inside journalism*. London: Peter Owen, 1967. 240pp.
A symposium of essays by working journalists compiled for student trainees by a long-serving officer of the National Council for the Training of Journalists.

306   Bentley, Edmund Clerihew. *Those days: an autobiography*. London: Constable, 1940. xv + 327pp.
Although remembered more widely as a detective novelist and poet, Bentley here portrays London journalism from 1880s to World War I from the standpoint of *Daily News* (and later *Daily Telegraph*) staff man.

307   *'Berkshire Chronicle'*. *The Newspaper World*, 6 Aug 1939. (In The Oldest Newspapers series.)
The *Berkshire Chronicle*, now the *Reading Chronicle*, was established in 1825.

308   *Berkshire Mercury*. 250th anniversary supplement. Reading: 12 Jul 1973.
This paper was founded as the *Reading Mercury* 1723; it finally became *The Mercury*, ceasing publication in 1987.

309   Bermant, Chaim. 'The *Jewish Chronicle*: 150 not out'. *British Library Newspaper Library Newsletter*, 13, Autumn/Winter 1991.
The oldest Jewish newspaper in the world, established in 1841.

310 Bernays, Robert. *Special correspondent*. London: Gollancz; New York: Putnam, 1934. 352pp.

The title refers to Bernays' work for the *News Chronicle*, from India, Germany, Austria etc.

311 Berrey, R. Power. *The romance of a great newspaper*. London: News of the World, 1933. 57pp.

A slim, promotional, 'official' history that fails to fulfil its promise to tell the 'full' story of that Sunday phenomenon, the *News of the World* – a paper actually founded in 1843, but here claimed to date back to 1796.

312 *Berrow's Worcester Journal*. No 12,888: 250th anniversary number. Worcester: 28 Dec 1940.

313 Berrow's Worcester Journal. *Berrow's Coronation souvenir, 1690–1953*. May 1953. 'A link in the chain through thirteen reigns'.

The '1690' claim for *Berrow's* (indisputably the 'oldest surviving British newspaper') was not itself seriously disputed until J.G Muddiman ('J.B. Williams') initiated discussion in the pages of *Notes and Queries* (1914 and 1916). Certainly Stephen Bryan's *The Worcester Post-Man* appeared weekly from 1709, Hervey Berrow – his successor as publisher – adding his name to the title of *The Worcester Journal* in 1753. *Berrow's Journal*, now a title under Reed ownership, has been a free newspaper since 1987.

314 – – –. *Tercentenary souvenir*. Supplement, 1990.

'300 years in the life of the journal'.

315 – – –. *Tercentenary, 1690–1990*. Reed Midland Newspapers, 1990. 48pp.

'A step back in time with the world's oldest newspaper'. Neither the supplement nor the booklet, fascinating as they are, provides any fresh evidence for the 1690 date, while 'world's oldest' is an unfortunate over-statement.

316 Berry, Adrian. *Ice with your evolution*. London: Harrap, with Daily Telegraph, 1986.

By *The Daily Telegraph*'s science correspondent: collected pieces.

317 Berry, David (Dave), Liz Cooper, and Charles Landry. *Where is the other news?: the news trade and the radical press*. London: Minority Press Group (later Comedia), 1980. 80pp.

The theme of this co-operative production is that the commercial distribution system prevents some of the more radical publications from reaching their intended audience.

318 Berry, Paul, and Alan Bishop, eds. *Testament of a generation: the journalism of Vera Brittain and Winifred Holtby*. London: Virago, 1985. x + 390pp.

Brittain and Holtby met at Oxford University after World War I, as recorded in the former's *Testament of friendship*. Their articles and reviews appeared in more than twenty newspapers and periodicals, notably *The Manchester Guardian* and *Time and Tide*.

319   Bertram, James A. 'The editors of *The Scotsman*'. *Scots Magazine*, 1, 1924.

320   Bertrand, Claude-Jean, ed. *The British press: an historical survey*. With a foreword by Lord Francis-Williams. Paris: OCDL, 1969. 208pp.
A brief but useful anthology (in English) in the *Documents anglo-américains*. A table of 'landmarks' in the history of the British press forms a valuable prologue.

321   *Best of Granta reportage, The*. London: Viking, 1993; Penguin, 1994.
Selected from journalism published in *Granta* magazines over the previous twelve years: only a minority of the contributions are immediate reports, and even they are not from newspapers; but their enduring quality qualifies the work for inclusion.

322   Betjeman, (*Sir*) John. 'The local paper'. *The Strand Magazine*, Mar 1948.
The future Poet Laureate contributed this (illustrated) tribute to his local paper, the *Newbury Weekly News* (established 1867).

323   Bevins, Anthony. 'The crippling of the scribes'. *British Journalism Review*, Winter 1990.
The political editor of *The Independent* points the finger at editorial interference by certain national proprietors.

324   Bezzant, Reginald. *Newspaper carriage and parcels traffic on British railways*. London: Dawson [1951]. xi + 140pp.
The author was then the circulation manager of the *News of the World*.

325   *Bicester Advertiser*. Centenary special. Bicester (Oxon): 10 Jan 1979.
A Westminster Press weekly.

326   Biddle, Deborah, ed. *Using newspaper in the classroom*. London: Newspaper Society, 1990.
Joint project between Kirklees Metropolitan Borough Council and *Huddersfield Daily Examiner* for the Newspapers in Education series.

327   Bignami, Marialuisa. *Le origini del giornalismo inglesi*. Bari: Adriatica, 1968. 351pp. (In the Biblioteca di Studi Inglesi series.)

328   Bilainkin, George. *Diary of a diplomatic correspondent*. London: Allen & Unwin, 1942.
Bilainkin was a diplomatic writer for Allied Newspapers.

329   Billington, M[ary] F[rances]. *Journalism for women*. London: London School of Journalism, 1918. Lecture series.

330   – – –. 'Women and journalism'. In *The woman's library in six volumes: education and professions*. Vol 1. London: Chapman & Hall, 1903.
Already experienced on other national newspapers, Mary Billington was on *The Daily Telegraph* staff from 1897, establishing a high reputation for descriptive writing; she became president of the Society of Women Journalists.

331 Billington, Michael. *One night stands*. London: Nick Hern Books, 1993.
A selection of the theatre notices by the doyen of drama critics – for *The Guardian* since 1971 (and previously *The Times*).

332 Bird, R.K. *The news interview: its historic origins and present-day expressions*. Cardiff: University of Wales, 1980 (MEd thesis).

333 Birkinshaw, Patrick J. *Freedom of information: the law, the practice, and the ideal*. London: Weidenfeld & Nicolson, 1989. xxii + 291pp.

334 *Birmingham Daily Post, The*. Jubilee number. 4 Dec 1907.
Tracing back its ancestry to the *Birmingham Journal* of 1732, the *Daily Post* was founded in 1857 by John Frederick Feeney and John Jaffray. It quickly became, and remained, a major force in provincial journalism. 'Daily' was dropped from its title in 1918.

335 *Birmingham Gazette*. 175th anniversary number. 16 Nov 1916.

336 Birmingham Gazette. *Progress, 1741–1929*. 1929.

337 – – –.   *Two hundred years of the Birmingham Gazette*. 17 Nov 1941.
The paper was founded as *Aris's Birmingham Gazette*; later it became the *Birmingham Daily Gazette*, then the *Birmingham Gazette*. It had a mass circulation before being absorbed into the *Birmingham Post*.

338 *Birmingham Post, The*. Centenary supplement. 4 Dec 1957.
One hundred years since the foundation of *The Birmingham Daily Post*. (*See also* Whates, H.R.G.)

339 – – –.   125th anniversary supplement. Dec 1982.
By 1982 the paper, along with the *Birmingham Evening Mail*, was in the Birmingham Post and Mail group. In 1991, it was bought out by management and became part of Midland Independent Newspapers.

340 'Birmingham Post, The'. (Histories of Birmingham no 8.) In *Birmingham Sketch*, 1958.

341 *Birmingham Press Club, The: 125th anniversary*. Birmingham: 1900. 20pp.
Booklet celebrating the history of what was founded as the Junior Pickwick Club in 1865 (name changed in 1875).

342 'Birmingham's oldest newspaper'. *The Newspaper World*, 5 Aug 1939. (In The Oldest Newspapers series.)
Refers to the *Birmingham Gazette*.

343 Birt, John. *Decent media*. Fleming Memorial Lecture to Royal Television Society, Apr 1988, reported in *The Times*, 8 Apr, and abridged in *UK Press Gazette*, 11 Apr.
The BBC's then deputy director-general recommends *inter alia* a Council of the Media – 'a quorum of quangos'.

344 Bishku, Michael B. 'The British press and the future of Egypt, 1912–1922'. *International Historical Review*, 8, 1986.

345   – – –.   'Intrigue, propaganda and the press: British perceptions of and reactions to the 1919 Egyptian uprising'. *Journal of Newspaper and Periodical History*, Winter 1987–8.

346   Bishop, Patrick. *Famous victory: the Gulf War*. London: Sinclair-Stevenson, 1992.
Acclaimed first-hand report by *The Daily Telegraph*'s Middle East correspondent.

347   – – –.   'Reporting the Falklands'. *Index on Censorship*, 6, 1982.
Bishop was *The Observer*'s correspondent in the Falklands campaign.

348   Bishop, Patrick, and John Witherow. *The winter war*. London: Quartet, 1982. 153pp.
Witherow reported the Falklands campaign for *The Times*. Published soon after the event, it is most revealing on shipboard life with the Task Force.

349   Bishop, Robert L. 'The decline of national newspapers in the UK'. *Gazette*, 31, 1983.
An American academic's view.

350   Black, Conrad (Moffat). *A life in progress*. Toronto: Key Porter, 1993; London: Weidenfeld & Nicolson (revision in preparation).
Revealing autobiography of the Canadian proprietor of *The Daily* and *Sunday Telegraphs* etc.

351   – – –.   'Hello sweetheart, get me a peerage'. *Saturday Night* (Toronto), Dec 1992.
Outspoken if light-hearted piece by the Canadian owner (through Hollinger) of the Telegraph group.

352   – – –.   'Why the best newspapers are ahead of the times'. *The Daily Telegraph*, 8 Sep 1993.
In the immediate aftermath of News International's drastic price cut of *The Times*, the owner of the *Telegraph* avers that 'quality newspapers will be able to carry their readers and advertisers into electronic forms of delivery'.

353   Blackburn, P. *The 'social' nature of technological change: an analysis of production technology, with special reference to changes in the national newspaper industry*. Manchester: University of Manchester, 1980 (MSc thesis).

354   *Blackburn Times*. Jubilee number. Blackburn: 3 Jun 1905.

355   – – –.   Centenary number. 1955.
Now a free paper in the United Provincial Newspapers group.

356   Blackman, Victor. *Naff off!: confessions of a Fleet Street photographer*. London: BFP Books, 1987. 176pp.
Blackman was with the *Daily Express* for thirty years. His title derives from an inelegant Royal riposte.

357   Blackwell, Trevor. *A study of the popular press: readings in the Daily Mirror and the Daily Express, 1945–1969.* Birmingham: University of Birmingham, 1971–2 (PhD thesis).

358   Blagden, Cyprian. *The Stationers' Company: a history, 1403–1959.* London: Allen & Unwin, 1960. 321pp.
The licensing and control of printing – and by extension, the dissemination of news – is a major theme in this scholarly account. The Company was incorporated by Royal Charter in 1557, and still occupies the historic Stationers' Hall (London EC).

359   Blain, Neil, Raymond Boyle, and Hugh O'Donnell. *Sport and national identity in the European media.* Leicester: Leicester University Press, 1993. 256pp.
Comprehensive analysis of coverage by TV and press of major sporting events across Europe.

360   Blain, Virginia, Patricia Clements, and Isobel Grundy. *The feminist companion to writers in English.* London: Batsford, 1990.
Women writers from the Middle Ages to the present: includes biographies of journalists who have espoused the feminist cause.

361   Blake, George. *The press and the public.* London: Faber, 1930. 36pp. A Criterion Miscellany.

362   Blatchford, Robert Peel Glanville. *My eighty years.* London: Cassell, 1931. xix + 284pp.
Blatchford concentrates in this memoir on his foundation (in 1891) of *The Clarion.* He gave up a highly paid Fleet Street career to start what became the first mass-circulation socialist weekly. It was also significant in its typographical innovation, promotion of Blatchford's own individual views, and appeal to such specialist groups as the cycling club movement.

363   Blom-Cooper, (*Sir*) Louis. 'The last days of the Press Council'. *British Journalism Review*, Spring 1991.
Chronicle by the last chairman of the Council before it was transmogrified into the Press Complaints Commission.

364   Blowitz, Henri (Georges Stefan Adolphe Opper) de. *My memoirs.* London: Edward Arnold, 1903. vi + 358pp. Published in the USA as *Recollections of M. de Blowitz* (Philadelphia: 1902). and as *Memoirs of M. de Blowitz* (New York: Doubleday, Page, 1905. x + 321pp).
The classic autobiography of the Bohemia-born *Times* correspondent in Paris who achieved unparalleled influence in diplomatic circles. An unrepentant egotist, Blowitz (1832–1903) must in some instances be taken with a pinch of salt.

365   Blumenfeld, R[alph] D[avid]. *R.D.B.'s diary, 1887–1914.* London: Heinemann, 1930. viii + 248pp. Published in the USA as *In the days of bicycles and bustles.* New York: Brewer & Warren, 1930.

Extracts over a twenty-seven-year period from the diary of the London correspondent of the *New York Herald*, who was destined to become editor of the *Daily Express* from 1904 to 1932. (Blumenfeld (1864–1948) was born in the USA.)

366   – – –.   *What is a journalist?: do's and don'ts*. London: [1930]. 22pp.

367   – – –.   *All in a lifetime*. London: Benn, 1931. x + 276pp.

368   – – –.   *The press in my time*. London: Rich & Cowan, 1933. 253pp. (In the In My Time series.)
This and the above are valuable, wide-ranging reminiscences published soon after 'R.D.B.' retired from the full-time *Express* editorship. (He was followed as editor by Beverley Baxter, but Blumenfeld recounts how he was soon able to secure the succession for Arthur Christiansen, a brilliant 'sub' and layout man whom he had been grooming in the paper's Manchester office.)

369   – – –.   'Lord Northcliffe'. In *The Post Victorians*. London: Nicholson & Watson, 1933.

370   Boardman, Harry. *The glory of Parliament*, ed (Sir) Francis Boyd. London: Allen & Unwin, 1960. 208pp.
Parliamentary writing by a leading correspondent for *The Manchester Guardian*.

371   *Bognor Regis Observer*. 100 years souvenir issue. Bognor Regis (W Sussex): 5 May 1972.
Weekly today in the Portsmouth and Sunderland Newspapers group.

372   'Bolton's newspaper family'. *The Newspaper World*, 14 Jan 1939. (In The Oldest Newspapers series.)
The Tillotsons established the *Bolton Evening News* (now a Reed Publishing title) in 1867, and also have a special niche in national press history as founders in 1873 of the Tillotson Newspaper Fiction Bureau, largest and most successful syndicate of its kind.

373   Bone, Frederick Dorling. 'The history of the Central News'. *World's Press News*, 6 Jun 1929. (In the Pillars of the Press series.)
At the time of publication of this article, Central News was a competitor to the Press Association on the home front, and to Reuters for overseas news.

374   – – –.   'The romantic history of the "Topical"'. *World's Press News*, 20 Jun 1929.
In the inter-war years, Topical was a prominent Fleet Street news as well as picture agency.

375   – – –.   'Reuters are always right'. *World's Press News*, 4 Jul 1929.

376   – – –.   'The birth of the picture paper: early days of the *Illustrated London News*'. *World's Press News*, 25 Jul 1929.

377   Bone, James. 'Fleet Street in the twentieth century'. In *Fleet Street Annual*, 1951.

A Glaswegian Scot, James Bone joined *The Manchester Guardian* in 1902, and was its distinguished London editor from 1912 to 1945.

378   Boon, John. *Victorians, Edwardians and Georgians: the impressions of a veteran journalist extending over forty years*. London: Hutchinson, 1928. 2 vols.
Includes the author's work for the Exchange Telegraph agency, and reports as a war correspondent for *The Times* (1914–21).

379   Boorman, (Henry) Roy Pratt. *Kent Messenger centenary*. Maidstone: Kent Messenger, 1959. 203pp.
An illustrated history.

380   – – –, comp. *The Newspaper Society: 125 years of progress*. Maidstone (Kent): Kent Messenger, for the Newspaper Society, 1961. 190pp.
The then Provincial Newspaper Society was founded in 1836. This profusely illustrated account of its day-to-day history was compiled by a former chairman.

381   – – –. *Your family newspaper*. Maidstone: Kent Messenger, 1968. 176pp.
Published to mark the golden jubilee of the Home and Southern Counties Newspaper Proprietors' Federation. Boorman was then chairman of the Kent Messenger group.

382   Boorman, (Henry) Roy Pratt, and Eric Maskell. *Tonbridge Free Press centenary*. Tonbridge: Free Press, 1969. 147pp.

383   Bose, Mihir. 'Fallen stars of the City page'. *Business*, Mar 1988.
The City editors: how the 'insiders' ousted the 'share-tippers'.

384   Boseley, Sarah. 'A tabloid hero in black and white'. *The Guardian*, 16 Oct 1989.
On John Pilger, campaigning journalist par excellence – highlighting his acrimonious departure from the *Daily Mirror*.

385   Boston, Ray(mond) (Jack). *The essential Fleet Street: its history and influence*. London: Blandford, 1990. 192pp.
The evolution of news journalism. Profusely illustrated; pictures researched by David Linton.

386   – – –. Cudlipp, Lord (Hugh); Hopkinson, Sir (Henry) Tom; Martin, (Basil) Kingsley; Scott, Charles Prestwich: biographies in *The Fontana biographical companion to modern thought*, ed Alan Bullock and R.B. Woodings. London: Collins, 1983.

387   – – –. 'The "by appointment" royal reporters'. *UK Press Gazette: souvenir issue*, 3 Jun 1985.
From the first Court Newsman – Joseph Doane (from 1806) – to the current Palace Press Secretary, Michael Shea.

388   Boston, Richard. *Osbert: a portrait of Osbert Lancaster*. London: Collins, 1989. 256pp.
How pocket cartoonist was only one of Lancaster's many talents.

389   – – –, ed. *The press we deserve*. London: Routledge & Kegan Paul, 1970. vii + 158pp.
A collection of essays.

390   Bosworth, Richard J.B. 'The British press, Conservatives, and Mussolini'. *Journal of Contemporary History*, 5, 2, 1970.

391   Bottomley, Ted, and Anthony Loftus. *A journalist's guide to the use of English*. Wolverhampton (Staffs): Star Publications (for Express and Star), 1971; revd 1972, rptd 1974.
A training manual.

392   Bourne, Richard. *Lords of Fleet Street: the Harmsworth dynasty*. London: Unwin Hyman, 1990. xi + 258pp.
The basis of the book are biographies of Northcliffe and the three Rothermere generations. A valuable corrective to some earlier 'histories'.

393   Bowen, David. 'Rupert Murdoch's debt-defying high wire act'. *Business*, Sep 1986.
Appraisal of Murdoch's international financial activity, based on an interview; now inevitably somewhat dated.

394   Bower, Tom. *Maxwell: the outsider*. London: Aurum Press, 1988. 374pp. Revd edn: Mandarin pbk; New York: Viking, 1991. 539pp.
An 'unauthorized' version – serialized in *The Sunday Times* from 28 Feb 1988. After Maxwell's death, Bower was able to be even more outspoken in his revision.

395   – – –. *Tiny Rowland: a rebel tycoon*. London: Heinemann, 1993. ix + 659pp.
The first full-length (and again entirely unauthorized) biography of the chief of the Lonrho empire – including *The Observer* until May 1993. An epitome of dogged detective work.

396   – – –. 'Maxwell House: bad to the last drop'. *New Republic* (Washington), Apr 1991.
Robert Maxwell issued one of his many writs for this.

397   Bowman, William Dodgson. *The story of The Times*. London: Routledge; New York: Lincoln McVeagh (Dial Press), 1931. x + 342pp.
Covers the years to 1922 (the death of Northcliffe) in a respectful manner.

398   Bown, Jane. *Portraits*. London: Chatto & Windus, 1990.
Outstanding studies from *The Observer*'s famed photographer.

399   Boxer, [Charles] Mark [Edward]. 'On being there first'. *The Sunday Times Magazine*, 22 Feb 1987.
By the first of the Magazine's editors. Boxer is also fondly remembered as the cartoonist 'Marc'.

400   Boyce, [David] George. 'Crusaders without chains: power and the press barons, 1896–1951'. In James Curran *et al.*, eds. *Impacts and influences: essays on media power in the twentieth century*. London: Methuen, 1987.

401   Boyce, [David] George, James Curran, and Pauline Wingate, eds. *Newspaper history: from the seventeenth century to the present day*. London: Constable, for the Acton Society Press Group; Beverly Hills (CA): Sage Publications, 1978. 423pp. (In the Communication and Society series.)
As well as the three editors, eighteen other authorities contribute to this revisionary academic history, which re-examines the factors that affected the early development and subsequent political influence of the British press. Has an extensive bibliography and chronology.

402   Boyd-Barrett, [J.] Oliver. *The international news agencies*. London: Constable; Beverly Hills (CA): Sage, 1980. 284pp. (In the Communication and Society series.)
Deals with the four big agencies critically and in great detail.

403   – – –.   'The international news agencies'. *The Media Reporter*, 1, 3, 1977.
A sketchy article published long before this author's book on the same topic.

404   – – –.   'Market control and wholesale news: the case of Reuters'. In *Newspaper history . . .*, ed G. Boyce *et al* (q.v.).

405   – – –.   'The Big Four news agencies'. *The Media Reporter*, 4, 3, 1980.

406   – – –, joint ed. *Studies on the press*. Royal Commission on the Press, Working Paper 3. London: HMSO, 1977.

407   Boyd-Barrett, [J.] Oliver, and Michael (Beaussenat) Palmer. *Le trafic des nouvelles: les agences mondiales d'information*. Paris: Alain Moreau, 1981. 712pp.
A major study of the international agencies, containing much new material regarding their financial background, and a forward look. It also examines the new agencies created especially to serve the Third World.

408   Boyle, Andrew (Philip More). *Poor, dear Bracken: the quest for Brendan Bracken*. London: Hutchinson, 1974. 377pp.
The title is taken from Churchill's reported comment on hearing of the death of his close friend and political associate. Bracken was a most successful Minister of Information during World War II, as well as chief proprietor of *The Financial News* and then *Financial Times*.

409   Boyle, Paul, comp. *Cassandra at his finest and funniest*. London: Paul Hamlyn, for the *Daily Mirror*, 1967; New York: Crown, 1967. 254pp.
A collection from the Cassandra column in the *Daily Mirror*, written by (Sir) William Connor. The leading polemicist of the era, he was appointed by H.G. Bartholomew in 1935, and continued to hit hard – without fear or favour – for thirty-two years,

interrupted only by war service. Returning therefrom, he started his first column with the immortal words: 'As I was saying when I was interrupted . . .'

410 Boyne, (*Sir*) Harry [Henry Brian]. *The Houses of Parliament*. London: Batsford, 1980. 96pp.
By *The Daily Telegraph*'s chief lobby correspondent for twenty years. Includes a section on Parliament and the press.

411 Braddon, Russell. *Roy Thomson of Fleet Street; and how he got there*. London: Collins, 1965. 376pp. Fontana, 1968.
A notable biography using, as its climax, the first twelve years of Thomson's unpretentious but highly effective 'invasion' of the British media. Braddon's book was published before *The Times* became the comparatively short-lived 'jewel' in the Thomson crown. It contains few revelations, but leaves no doubt that the subject was well liked by almost everyone who worked for him.

412 Bradley, (Henry) James, ed. *Fifty great years, 1897–1947*. Manchester: Kemsley Newspapers, 1947.
On the *Evening Chronicle*, founded by Edward Hulton as *Manchester Evening Chronicle* and with title shortened from 1914. Bradley was himself a columnist and leader writer on the *Evening Chronicle*. He was an outstanding secretary of the National Union of Journalists (1951–69) and president of the International Federation of Journalists for six years.

413 Brandon, [Oscar] Henry. *Special relationships: a foreign correspondent's memoirs*. London: Macmillan, 1989. 436pp.
The Czech-born Brandon writes with all his massive authority as chief *Sunday Times* representative in Washington (1950–83) – the doyen of such correspondents and friend of Presidents.

414 'Brave boost by the weeklies, A'. (Scotland survey). *Headlines* (The Newspaper Society), Spring 1990.
Highlights the advent of Thomson Regional Newspapers' *Scotland on Sunday* and *The Glaswegian*, which soon claimed the largest circulation of any free newspaper in Britain.

415 Brendon, Piers. *Eminent Edwardians*. London: Secker & Warburg, 1979. xvi + 255pp. Harmondsworth (Middx): Penguin, 1981.
The four notables covered include Northcliffe.

416 – – –. *The life and death of the press barons*. London: Secker & Warburg, 1982. xii + 288pp. New York: Atheneum, 1983.
Some twenty-four press 'barons' and one 'baroness' are here entertainingly viewed and sagely considered. Most are Americans who tend to be more capricious and more crazed than their British equivalents, and thus have most of the best tunes in this slickly orchestrated, highly selective piece of Anglo-American history. The British 'barons' included are Barnes, Delane, Burnham, Stead, O'Connor, Northcliffe, Rothermere, Beaverbrook, King, plus the Australian-in-London (and elsewhere) Murdoch.

417 – – –. *Our own dear Queen*. London: Secker & Warburg, 1986.
Frank assessment of the Royal Household – including its press relations.

418 Brennan, [A.] James [S.] '*The Guardian* on the move'. *The Media Reporter*, Autumn 1976.
By the editor/publisher in the first issue of this quarterly.

419 – – –. 'Battling for 150 years and still fighting on'. *UK Press Gazette*, 21 Apr 1986.
Celebrating the 150th anniversary of the Newspaper Society (originally the Provincial Newspaper Society).

420 Brenton, Howard, and David Hare. *Pravda: a Fleet Street comedy*. London: Methuen, 1985. 124pp.
The book of the play; *Pravda* (Russian for 'truth'), billed as 'a reader's revenge' because it puts modern Fleet Street 'on the stand' for the first time, had its successful première at the National Theatre (London) in May 1985. Includes some sharp dialogue; for example: 'The press and politicians: a delicate relationship. Too close and danger ensues. Too far apart, and democracy itself cannot function'.

421 Brewer, Roy, comp. *Newspapers: past, present, future*. London: Newspaper Society, 1985. 10pp.
A booklet on newspaper production and (briefly) on the history of the Newspaper Society to mark the occasion of the latter's 150th anniversary (which in fact occurred in 1986).

422 Brex, Twells, comp. '*Scaremongerings' from the Daily Mail, 1896–1914: the paper that foretold the war*. London: Daily Mail, [1914].
An anthology to support the newspaper's contention that it had made 'unremitting effort, in the face of intense opposition, to urge that the British Navy and Army should be kept in a condition to meet the present crisis'.

423 *Brighouse Echo*. Centenary supplement. Brighouse (W Yorks): 26 Jun 1987.
In Johnston Press ownership.

424 *Brighton and Hove Gazette*. '150 years ago – the first *Gazette*'. 26 Feb 1971.
This paper was the weekly associate of the *Evening Argus*, in the Westminster Press group, until its end in 1985.

425 *Brighton and Hove Herald*. 150th anniversary issue. 8 Feb 1956.

426 *Britain's newspaper and magazine industry*. Bristol: Jordan & Sons, 1989, 1990. Introductory commentary by Norman Bleetman.

427 'Britain's oldest weekly: *The Worcester Post-Man* and *Berrow's Worcester Journal*'. *The Newspaper World*, 18 Mar 1939. (In The Oldest Newspapers series.)

428 '*British Chronicle – Hereford Times*'. *The Newspaper World*, 6 May 1939. (In The Oldest Newspapers series.)

The *British Chronicle* became the *Hereford Journal*, and subsequently in 1932 merged into the *Hereford Times*.

429   *British Gazette, The.* 'The birth and life of *The British Gazette*'. London: 13 May 1926.
From the last of the eight issues of the government's emergency newspaper published during the General Strike. It contains the dictum, almost certainly by the editor, Winston Churchill, that 'It becomes a memory: but it remains a monument'.

430   British Library, The. *Newspapers in the British Library.*
A pamphlet on the newspaper collections in the BL's Reference Division: at Colindale (London NW9) – principally nineteenth- and twentieth-century newspapers and periodicals – and Bloomsbury (London WC1), the main depository for pre-nineteenth-century newspapers as well as books of all eras. The accessions at both are constantly growing, because of the BL's function as a library of legal deposit under the Copyright Act of 1911 (as amended by the British Library Act 1972).

431   – – –. *Newspaper Library: an introduction to the collections and services.*
Leaflet for visitors to Colindale.

432   – – –. *The plan for the newspaper collections.* 1979.
Sets out the policy of microfilming provincial as well as national titles received (the Legal Deposit Office for newspapers has been at Colindale since 1991).

433   – – –. *Microfilms of newspapers and journals for sale.* Latest edn, 1985–6. 85pp.

   – – –. *Bibliography of Biography; Bibliography of British newspapers; Books in Britain;* British Library: *Catalogue of the Newspaper Library; British Library Newspaper Library Newsletter; British National Bibliography; NEWSPLAN; Serials in the British Library: see Reference Works section.*

434   Brittain, *Sir* Harry Ernest. *Pilgrims and pioneers.* London: Hutchinson, [1946]. 276pp.

435   – – –. *Happy pilgrimage.* London: Hutchinson, [1949]. 355pp.
Includes a chapter on parliamentary reporting.

436   – – –. 'The first Imperial Press Conference'. In *The Newspaper Press Directory, 1910.* London: Mitchell, 1910.
Brittain was the principal founder of the Empire Press Union (later the Commonwealth Press Union). He was a leading international as well as national figure in journalism during his long life (1873–1974).

437   Brittain, Victoria, ed. *The gulf between us.* London: Virago, 1991.
The 'gulf' here is both metaphorical, as between the media and the military, and the Gulf War, when much was kept from the media.

438   Brittain, William James. *This man Beaverbrook.* London: Hutchinson, [1941]. 63pp. (In the Leaders of Britain series.)
In 1941 Beaverbrook was Minister of Aircraft Production, and doing his utmost to

galvanize the British war effort for his friend and colleague Winston Churchill, at a time when the country stood alone against the Axis powers. W.J. Brittain himself had a varied career in the press, editing the *Sunday Dispatch* 1934–6 and launching the short-lived *Recorder* in the 1950s.

439 Broackes, (*Sir*) Nigel. *A growing concern*. London: Weidenfeld & Nicolson, 1979.
The growth of Trafalgar House (including at one time Express Newspapers) by its chairman.

440 Brodzky, Vivian, *et al*, eds. *Fleet Street: the inside story of journalism*. London: Macdonald, 1966. 219pp.
Fifty prominent figures on the Fleet Street scene of the 1960s contributed brief articles to this work, produced for the benefit of the Press Club's restoration appeal. The editor was a former labour correspondent for the *Daily Herald*, who later moved to the *News of the World*.

441 Brogan, Hugh. *The life of Arthur Ransome*. London: Jonathan Cape, 1984. 472pp. Also publ Hamish Hamilton, 1985. 456pp.
A most readable as well as scholarly study of Ransome (1884–1967), who, following his reporting adventures in Russia, became famous as a writer for children.

442 Bromhead, Peter. 'Parliament and the press'. *Parliamentary Affairs*, 16, 1962–3.

443 Bromley, Michael. 'War of words: the *Belfast Telegraph* and loyalist populism'. *In* Alan O'Day and Yonah Alexander, eds. *Ireland's terrorist trauma: interdisciplinary perspectives*. Hemel Hempstead (Herts): Harvester Wheatsheaf, 1988.
A study of Northern Ireland's largest-circulation newspaper during the 1974 Ulster Workers' Council strike.

443A – – –. 'From conciliation to confrontation: industrial relations, government and the Fourth Estate, 1896–1986'. *In* Alan O'Day, ed. *Government and institutions in post-1832 Britain*. Lampeter (Dyfed): Edwin Mellen Press (in preparation).

444 Brooke, Leslie Ernest John. *Somerset newspapers, 1725-1960*. Yeovil: 1960.
A first-class bibliography, with historical annotations.

445 Brookes, Christopher. *His own man: the life of Neville Cardus*. London: Methuen, 1985.
A well-rounded biography of a multi-talented writer.

446 Brooks, Peter. 'Science, the press and Empire: Pearson's publications, 1890–1914'. *In* John MacKenzie, ed. *Imperialism in the natural world*. Manchester: Manchester University Press, 1990.

447 Brooks, [William] Collin. *Devil's decade: portraits of the nineteen-thirties*. London: Macdonald, 1948. 208pp.

The well-known editor of *Truth* turns his hand successfully to biography: he includes two newspaper controllers, Beaverbrook and Rothermere.

448　　Brothers, Caroline. 'The anthropology of civilian life: French and British press photography of civilian life in the Spanish Civil War'. *Journal of Newspaper and Periodical History*, 8, 2, 1992.
How the camera can be made to lie – or at least pervert the truth.

449　　Brown, A.W. '*Dumfries and Galloway Courier and Herald*: short study of its origin and history'. *In Gallovidian Annual*, 20, 1940.
This weekly was founded in 1809.

450　　Brown, Ivor (John Carnegie). *Old and young: a personal summing up.* London: Bodley Head, 1971. 242pp.

451　　– – –.　'C.P. Scott'. In *The Post Victorians*. London: Nicholson & Watson, 1933.
Unusually, Brown himself moved from dramatic criticism – notably for *The Manchester Guardian* and *The Observer* – to the editorship of the latter (1942–8).

452　　– – –.　'Who are the editors?' *The Strand Magazine*, Mar 1947.
Provides summarized information on other leading editors of the day, seven being featured in excellent photos as well as in Brown's written assessment.

453　　Brown, Maggie. 'Reuters: Fleet Street's El Dorado'. *IPI Report*, Oct 1982.
How Britain's national newspapers found they were part-owners of a 'goldmine'.

454　　– – –.　'Rough seas for D-Notices'. *The Independent*, 9 Dec 1987.
Interview with Rear-Admiral William Higgins, secretary of the Defence, Press and Broadcasting Committee.

455　　– – –.　'The family firm'. *The Independent*, 15 Feb 1989.
On the Rothermere dynasty.

456　　Brown, Percy. *Round the corner.* London: Faber, 1934. 336pp.

457　　– – –.　*Almost in camera.* London: Hollis & Carter, 1944. 238pp.
A photojournalist of the highest class.

458　　Brown, Stephen J.M. *The press in Ireland.* Dublin: Brown & Nolan, 1937; New York: Lemma Publishing Corporation, 1971. 304pp.
Dated, but still valuable from a historical point of view. Provides useful summaries of the background of a wide range of Irish newspapers and periodicals.

459　　[Browne, T.B.]. *The Advertiser's ABC.* London: Browne, 1886–1918, 1920–31/2.
This sizeable press guide, first appearing as from 'The London Central Agency for Advertisements', was published by the largest such business at the turn of the century.

460　　Bruce, Brendan. *Images of power: how the image makers shape our leaders.* London: Kogan Page, 1992. 192pp.
Public relations and advertising in the political sphere.

461 Bruce, Colin, and Terry Charman. 'The British Pacific Fleet of 1944–45, and its newspaper, *Pacific Post*'. *Imperial War Museum Review*, 8, 1993.

462 Bruce Lockhart, Robin. 'Brendan Bracken – founding father'. *History Today*, Apr 1991.
A close-up view of the enigmatic Bracken, both as founder of *History Today* and chairman of the *Financial Times* in post-World War II days. Bruce Lockhart was himself foreign manager, then also promotion manager of the *FT*, and was concerned with its early development into a general business newspaper.

463 Bruttini, Adriano. *La stampa inglese: monopoli e fusioni, 1890–1972*. Parma: Guanda, 1973. 265pp. (In the Studi e Ricerche nel Giornalismo series.)

464 Bryant, Mark. *World War II in cartoons*. Swindon (Wilts): W.H. Smiths 1989. 160pp.
First-class selection of the 'cartoon war' from both sides, accompanied by a most informative commentary

465 – – –, ed. *The complete Colonel Blimp*. London: Bellew Publishing, 1991. 190pp. Foreword by Michael Foot; introduction by Colin Seymour-Ure.
David Low's creation from every aspect – with copious examples of the Blimp cartoons.

466 Bryant, Mark, and Simon Heneage, comps. *Dictionary of British cartoonists and caricaturists, 1730–1980*. Aldershot (Hants): Scolar Press, 1994.
Those who have contributed to national newspapers and leading periodicals – notably *Punch* – are well represented and illustrated.

467 Bryson, Bill. *The Penguin dictionary for writers and editors*. London: Viking, 1991.

468 Buchan, Norman, and Tricia Sumner, eds. *Glasnost in Britain?: against censorship and in defence of the word*. London: Macmillan, 1989.
Essays on the obstacles to real open government in this country. Includes Tom Baistow on 'The predators' press'.

469 Buckley, Christopher. *Road to Rome*. London: Hodder & Stoughton, 1945. 334pp.
Military operations in Italy, 1943–4 – where Buckley, known as 'The Bishop', first made his name as *The Daily Telegraph*'s correspondent. Later he took part in the Normandy landings, witnessed the Japanese surrender in Burma, and was killed covering the Korean War in 1950. Buckley was also the posthumous author of three volumes of official 'popular' war history.

470 *Bucks Herald*. 150th anniversary supplement. Buckingham: 7 Jan 1982.
A weekly in EMAP ownership.

471 Budd, Ernest. *A printer goes to war*. London: Howard Baker, 1978. 182pp.
The 'father of desert newspapers' was Captain Warwick Charlton, who founded *Tripoli Times* in 1943 – but it was Major Budd, a printer in civilian life, who had responsibility

for its production, in the most testing circumstances. Charlton later edited *Eighth Army News* and *Crusader*.

472   Bullard, F. Lauriston. *Famous war correspondents*. Boston: Little, Brown; Bath: Pitman, 1914. xii + 437pp.
Something of a classic in its field; covers a remarkable panorama, with more than adequate treatment of the British pioneer 'specials'. Steevens and Forbes died early in 1900, but Burleigh, Villiers and of course Churchill lived on to report battles in the new century.

473   Bullmore, Jeremy J.D., and Michael J. Waterson, eds. *The Advertising Association handbook*. Eastbourne (E Sussex): Holt, Rinehart & Winston, 1983.
Includes Ron Carpenter, 'National daily and Sunday newspapers'; and Douglas Lowndes, 'Regional newspaper'.

474   Bundock, Clement J. *The National Union of Journalists: a jubilee history, 1907–1957*. London: Oxford University Press, 1957. x + 254pp.
Bundock was the first national organizer of the NUJ, and later the national secretary. His history is based largely on Mansfield's *Gentlemen, the press!* (1943), but he also draws on official union records.

475   Burchett, Wilfred Graham. *Burchett reporting the other side of the world, 1939–1983*, ed Ben Kiernan; with a preface by John Pilger. London: Quartet Books, 1986. xxix + 315pp.
An assessment – mainly by fellow-journalists – of an 'unconforming' correspondent (for the *Daily Express* etc) who reported from the front line in World War II (including Hiroshima), Korea, Vietnam etc. His increasingly radical views caused his native Australia to disown him.

476   Burchill, Julie. *Ambition*. London: The Bodley Head, 1989. 263pp.
Fiction – at least one hopes it is fiction – about a woman's drive to become the world's youngest national newspaper editor. In 1993, the real-life Julie Burchill moved from columnist on *The Mail on Sunday* to lead film critic on *The Sunday Times*.

477   Burgen, Stephen. 'High wire act: losing friends in far-flung places'. *The Guardian (Media Guardian)*, 25 May 1992.
The effect of the new pricing structure at Reuters, and the reduction of stringers – particularly for *The Independent* – in covering overseas news.

478   Burke, Roger. *The murky cloak: local authority–press relations*. London: Charles Knight, 1970. xiii + 141pp.
Deals with the sometimes fraught relations between councils and the press, both serving the same local community.

479   Burleigh, Bennet. *Empire of the East: or, Japan and Russia at war, 1904–5*. London: Chapman & Hall, 1905. xii + 458pp.
The last of the prolific output of a star *Daily Telegraph* war correspondent.

480 Burnet, *Sir* Alastair [James William Alexander]. *America 1843–1993: 150 years of reporting the American connection.* London: Hamish Hamilton (Economist Books). 1993. 274pp.
Distillation of transatlantic coverage in the columns of *The Economist,* with retrospective comment by Burnet, who as editor (1965–74) was firmly in favour of the US Government's prosecution of the war in Vietnam. He moved to the *Daily Express* as editor (1974–6) before becoming a leading figure in national television.

481 Burnham, [Edward] Frederick Lawson, *4th Baron. Peterborough Court: the story of the Daily Telegraph.* London: Cassell, 1955. x + 225pp.
A family saga, written up rather mistily by a great-grandson of the printer and second owner of the paper (Joseph Moses Levy). It jogs along without reference to archival material, from the foundation year (1855) – when the *Daily Telegraph* was saved from bankruptcy by Levy – through to its sale to the Berry brothers in 1928. The author touches lightly on the taking over of sole control by Camrose in 1937, and concludes just after the latter's death in 1954.

482 Burroughs Wellcome & Co. *The evolution of journalism etcetera: souvenir of the International Press Conference, London, 1909.* London: Burroughs Wellcome, [1909]. 352pp.
Incorporates a remarkable collection of portraits (and potted biographies) of eighty-two editors, proprietors, contributors and war correspondents. With an introduction by (Sir) Henry Solomon Wellcome, American-born co-founder of the firm. The conference was held by the International Union of Associations of the Press.

483 Burrowes, John. *Frontline report: a journalist's notebook.* Edinburgh: Mainstream, [1984]. 196pp.
The author's main experience derives from the the *Sunday Mail* (Glasgow).

484 Burton, G.H. 'Lincolnshire newspapers and journalists'. *Stamford Mercury,* 24 Apr 1914.

485 Bury and Norwich Post. *The Post.* Bury St Edmunds (Suffolk): 25 Dec 1931.

486 *Bury Free Press.* 'Our jubilee'. Bury St Edmunds (Suffolk): 15 Jul 1905.

487 – – –. Centenary supplement, 1855–1955. 2 Sep 1955.

488 – – –. 125th anniversary special supplement. 1 Aug 1980.

489 *Bury Times.* Jubilee number. Bury (Lancs): 8 Jul 1905.
This weekly was established in 1855.

490 Bussey, Harry Findlater. *Sixty years of journalism: anecdotes and reminiscences.* Bristol: J.W. Arrowsmith, 1906. 303pp.
Bussey looks back over no fewer than seventeen appointments during his long career, culminating in eighteen years with the Press Association in London.

491 Busvine, Richard. *Gullible travels.* London: Constable, 1945.
War correspondent, including in the Western Desert.

492   Butler, Arthur. 'The history and practice of lobby journalism'. *Parliamentary Affairs*, 13, 1959.

493   Butler, Nancy. *Newspapers*. London: Hodder & Stoughton, 1989. (An Introducing Media Studies book.)

494   Buxton, G.H. *Notes on newspapers*. Stamford (then Rutland): Stamford Mercury, 20 Mar 1914.

495   *Caernarfon and Denbigh Herald, The*. 150th anniversary supplement. Caernarfon: 2 Jan 1981.
In North Wales Weekly News group (Welsh title: *Yr Herald Cymraeg*).

496   Calder, [*Hon*] Angus [Lindsay Ritchie]. *The people's war: Britain, 1939–45*. London: Cape; New York, 1969; London: Pimlico, 1993.
Lord Ritchie-Calder's second son provides useful material on wartime newspapers and the public reaction. Includes extracts from *The Newpaper Press Directory, 1945*.

497   Calder, [Peter] Ritchie (*Baron* Ritchie-Calder). *The lesson of London*. London: Secker & Warburg, 1941. 127pp. In Searchlight Books series.

498   – – –.   *Carry on, London*. London: English Universities Press, 1941. 163pp.
In the 1930s, Calder established his reputation as both a political commentator and a science specialist for the *Daily Herald*. These early works have endured as a critical view of the reactions to and the social implications of the German Blitz on London. Calder later moved to the *News Chronicle*.

499   Callender Smith, Robin. *Press law*. London: Sweet & Maxwell, 1978. xvi + 303pp.
Obsolete in some detail.

500   Calvet, Henri. 'L' action politique d'un grand journaliste, Geoffrey Dawson'. *Revue d'Histoire 2ème Guerre Mondiale*, 7, 28, 1957.
Examines the pre-war role of Dawson, editor of *The Times*, in supporting the policy of appeasement towards Germany.

501   *Cambrian News*. 125th anniversary number. Aberystwyth (Dyfed): 23 Nov 1985.
Established in 1860 in Bala as the *Merionethshire Herald*. It adopted its present title in 1869, and has been published weekly by the Read family for the past fifty years.

502   *Cambridge Evening News: inside story*. Cambridge: 1971.
The paper was established in 1888, as the *Cambridge Daily News*.

503   *Cambridge Evening News*. Centenary number. Jan 1988.

504   *Cambridge Independent Press and Chronicle*. Bicentenary number. Cambridge: 25 Feb 1944.
Later became the *Cambridge Chronicle*.

505 'Cambridge's weekly newspapers: the *Independent Press and Chronicle* and its predecessors'. *The Newspaper World*, 12 Aug 1939. (In The Oldest Newspapers series.)

506 Cameron, Alan, and Roy Farndon. *Scenes from sea and city: Lloyd's List, 1734–1984* (250th anniversary supplement). Colchester: Lloyd's of London Press, (17 Apr) 1984. 288pp.
A sumptuous celebration of the 250 years since the first publication of the original *Lloyd's List*. The first long chapter, 'From coffee-house to the computer', deals in text and pictorially with the history of the paper itself in its various manifestations.

507 Cameron, [Mark] James [Walter]. *Touch of the sun.* London: Witherby, 1950. 310pp.
Reports on Asia, notably the Bikini atom bomb tests and Korea, respectively for the *Daily Express* and *Picture Post*.

508 – – –. *Mandarin red: a journey behind the Bamboo Curtain.* London: Michael Joseph, 1955; New York: Rinehart, 1955. 288pp.
Communist China in 1954, covered for the *News Chronicle*.

509 – – –. *Witness.* London: Gollancz; Toronto: Doubleday, 1966. Published in the USA as *Here is your enemy: complete report from North Vietnam.* New York: Holt, Rinehart & Winston, 1966. 144pp.
By the time of this book's publication, Cameron was freelancing for the *Daily Mail, Daily Herald,* and *Evening Standard.*

510 – – –. *Point of departure: experiment in biography.* London: Arthur Barker, [1967]. 318pp. Published in the USA as *Point of departure: an attempt at autobiography.* New York: McGraw-Hill, 1967. Rptd London: Panther, 1969. 319pp. With new foreword, Stocksfield (Northd): Oriel Press, 1978. 318pp. Panther, 1980.
A memoir that describes most readably the early life of this Fleet Street 'star' (1911–85) from his harsh schooldays in Brittany, where he lived with his writer-father 'simply because it was cheaper than Glasgow in the late '20s', to his radical, 'have-pen-will-travel' years through the immediate post-war decade. By the 1970s, Cameron had also become a television personality (e.g. the Cameron Country series), as a result of his dry, laconic reflections as a foreign correspondent-cum-war reporter.

511 – – –. *What a way to run the tribe: selected articles, 1948–67.* London: Macmillan, 1968; New York: McGraw-Hill, 1968. 347pp.
Covering – first hand – Algeria, Germany, Spain, Cuba, India, Vietnam, Africa, the Middle East etc.

512 – – –. *An Indian summer: a personal experience of India.* London: Macmillan, 1974; Harmondsworth (Middx): Penguin, 1987. 224pp.
Fine and enduring writing in love of India.

513 – – –. *The best of Cameron.* London: Hodder & Stoughton, 1981; pbk 1983. xiv + 349pp. (In the New English Library.)

Cameron's work for *The Guardian* and *The Observer* is also represented here, among fourteen newspapers and periodicals.

514   – – –.   *Cameron in The Guardian, 1974–1984*, comp Martin Woollacott. London: Hutchinson, 1985. 216pp.
A collection of essays from Cameron's weekly column in *The Guardian* after his travelling days were over.

515   – – –.   'Wars and corrs'. In *100 years of Fleet Street*. London: Press Club, 1982.

516   – – –, ed. *Vicky: a memorial volume*. London: Allen Lane The Penguin Press, 1967. 160pp.
Victor Weisz (professional name Vicky) was born in Berlin in 1911, but came to London as a young man and became one of the greatest political caricaturists of his time. He made his name with the *News Chronicle*, then moved to the *Daily Mirror*, and his genius came to full flower in London's *Evening Standard*. Cameron was a close colleague and friend, and makes his tribute here after Vicky's death in 1966.

517   Campaign. *Who's Who in Journalism*. 1969.
Despite its title, this was a direct successor to *World's Press News' Directory of Newspaper and Magazine Personnel and Data*, and contained no biographical information. *See also Reference Works section.*

518   Campaign for Free Speech on Ireland. *The British media and Ireland*. London: Information on Ireland, 1979. 55pp.
An occasionally tendentious but well-documented and pugnacious analysis of British media coverage of the Northern Ireland conflict.

519   Campaign for Press and Broadcasting Freedom. *A manifesto for the media*. *Free Press* (special issue), 37, Oct 1986.

520   – – –.   *A manifesto for the nineties: towards media freedom*. *Free Press* (special issue), 65, Jul 1991.

521   – – –.   *Report of the special parliamentary hearings on the Freedom and Responsibility of the Press Bill*. London: CPBF, 1993. 178pp. Ed Mike Jempson.
The full record of the hearings of the Bill introduced by Clive Soley MP early in 1993, which if enacted would have set up a statutory independent press authority.

522   Campbell, A. Albert. *Belfast newspapers, past and present*. Belfast: Baird, 1921. 21pp.
From the publishers of the *Belfast Telegraph*.

523   Campbell, [Archibald] Doon, ed. *The British press: a look ahead*. London: Commonwealth Press Union, 1978. 90pp.
Thirty-five brief but illuminating contributions from Fleet Street on the state of Fleet Street (and the regional press) in 1978, with – as it has turned out – over-optimistic hopes for the immediate future. Includes interviews by the editor with Vere Harmsworth

(later 3rd Viscount Rothermere) of Associated Newspapers and (Sir) Larry Lamb, then of *The Sun.*

524   Campbell, Duncan. *Reminiscences and reflections of an octogenarian Highlander.* Inverness: 1910.
Campbell was for over twenty-six years editor of the *Northern Chronicle,* Inverness.

525   *Campbeltown Courier and Argyllshire Advertiser.* Centenary supplement, 1873–1973. Campbeltown (Strathclyde): 5 Jul 1973.
Weekly in Oban Times group.

526   Campion, Sidney Ronald. *Only the stars remain.* London: Rich & Cowan, 1946. 224pp.
The fourth and final book of memoirs by a journalist, notably as parliamentary correspondent for Allied Newspapers, who later became a leading public relations officer.

527   Camrose, William Ewert Berry, *1st Viscount. London newspapers, their owners and controllers: the Daily Telegraph's three-quarters of a million sale.* London: Daily Telegraph & Morning Post, 1939. 19pp.
Based on an article on 13 June 1939, this satisfactorily refuted rumours that the British press as a whole was 'largely controlled by Jews and international financiers'.

   – – –.   *British newspapers and their controllers: see Reference Works section.*

528   – – –.   'The proprietor's part of greatest benefit to press and public'. In *The press, 1898–1948* (*Newspaper World* Golden Jubilee). London: Benn, 1948.
William Berry (1879–1954) was the elder brother of Gomer Berry (later Lord Kemsley), and was raised to the peerage in 1929.

529   Cannell, J.C. *When Fleet Street calls: being the experiences of a London journalist.* London: Jarrolds, 1932. 286pp.

530   Cannon, Carl Leslie, comp. *Journalism: a bibliography.* New York: New York Public Library, 1924. vi + 360pp. Rptd, with additions, from *Bulletin of the New York Public Library,* Feb-Jul 1923.
Still a valuable aid, although now dated, concentrating largely on publications, and offering few annotations.

531   Cardus, *Sir* [John Frederick] Neville. *Autobiography.* London: Collins, 1947. 252pp. John Calder, 1984.
Singled out by Hetherington in his *Guardian years* (1981) as an outstanding book for students of journalism. Cardus (1889–1975) joined *The Manchester Guardian* in 1917, first writing on cricket in 1919. Thereafter, up to 1939, he wrote an average of eight thousand words a week on that subject and on music.

532   Carey, John. *Original copy: selected reviews and journalism, 1969–1986.* London: Faber, 1987.

533　– – –, ed. *The Faber book of reportage*. London: Faber, 1987. xxxviii + 706pp.
Anthology, including in the later pages such British journalists as Cameron, Pilger, Fenton, Gavin Young, Jan Morris, Fisk. The selection is excellent (if warlike in the majority), but there is regrettably little about the authors and their work.

534　Carmichael, J.H. 'Manchester as a newspaper centre: city of eighty publications'. *World's Press News*, 24 Mar 1932.

535　Carmichael, Jane. *First World War photographers*. London: Routledge, 1989. xi + 167pp.
Authoritative survey of the work – on the Western, Home and other Fronts – of those who covered the 1914-18 war. Some of the few photographers, like Ernest Brooks (formerly of the *Daily Mirror*), were well represented in the press, although the true horrors of the war were largely avoided in the cause of patriotism.

536　– – –. 'Army photographers in North West Europe'. *Imperial War Museum Review*, 7, 1992.
The work of the Army Film and Photographic Unit, particularly on and after the D-Day landings.

537　Carnie, William. *Reporting reminiscences*. Aberdeen: Aberdeen University Press, 1902–6. 3 vols: vi + 433pp.

538　Carr, Clarence Firbank, and Frederick Edward Stevens. *Modern journalism: complete guide to the newspaper craft*. London: Pitman, 1931.

539　Carr, E[dward] H[allett]. *The twenty years' crisis, 1919–1939*. London: Macmillan, 1939. xv + 312pp.
Later (1941–6) to be assistant editor of *The Times* and a major proponent of appeasement.

540　Carr, *Sir* Emsley. 'The Sunday press through the centuries'. *World's Press News*, 12 Mar 1931.
Carr had then achieved forty of his fifty years as editor of the *News of the World*.

541　Carrington, Charles Edmund. *Rudyard Kipling: his life and work*. London: Macmillan, 1955. xxii + 549pp. Revised Harmondsworth (Middx): Penguin, 1986. 634pp.
Until Angus Wilson's 1977 book, this was the standard biography of Kipling. One little-known (and brief) episode in Kipling's journalistic career after he left India was his work on the staff of *The Friend of the Free State*, published for the British Army in Bloemfontein.

542　Carter, Albert Charles Robinson. 'The role of war artists in South Africa'. In *Art Annual, 1900*. London.

543　Carter, Ernestine. *With tongue in chic*. London: Michael Joseph, 1974. 197pp.

Autobiography of the women's editor of *The Sunday Times* from 1955 to 1968, then associate editor for a further four years. High fashion was her special field, bringing her international fame.

544 Carter, Frederick W.P. *Secrets of your daily paper: the veil off Fleet Street.* London: Cassell, 1929. 109pp.

545 Carter, John. *A handlist of the writings of Stanley Morison.* Cambridge: Cambridge University Press, 1950. Supplemented by Phyllis M. Handover, in *Motif 3*, 1959 (covering 1950–9).
A standard reference until updated by Appleton (q.v.).

546 – – –. *Stanley Morison.* London: Hart-Davis, 1956.

547 Carter, Martin. *The Midlands: communication media.* Hove (E Sussex): Wayland, 1973. 96pp. (In Wayland Regional Studies series.)

548 'Case for the *Daily Worker*, The'. London: 1941. 20pp. By four members of the former editorial board: J.B.S. Haldane, Sean O'Casey, J. Owen, and R. Page Arnot.
The Communist *Daily Worker* was suppressed by government order from January 1941 to September 1942.

549 Casey, John. 'Bad times: how a newspaper lost its unique authority through its populist delusions'. *The Spectator*, 21 Mar 1987.
A critique of the change of readership sought by *The Times*.

550 Castlerosse, Valentine Edward Charles Browne, *Viscount* (later Earl of Kenmare). *Valentine's day.* London: Methuen, 1934. 271pp.
Distilling the author's hugely successful Londoner's Log column in the *Sunday Express*. He was recruited in this capacity overnight by his close friend Beaverbrook.

551 Catling, Thomas. *My life's pilgrimage.* With an introduction by Lord Burnham. London: John Murray, 1911. xviii + 384pp.
The author worked on *Lloyd's Weekly News(paper)* for over fifty years – latterly as its editor.

551A – – –, ed. *The press album.* London: John Murray, 1909. 224pp.
Articles, illustrations, autographs – and many advertisements for newspapers of the day. Publ in aid of the Journalists' Orphan Fund.

551B – – –. 'The founder of *Lloyd's*'. *Lloyd's Weekly News*, 30 Nov 1902.
A tribute to Edward Lloyd, the pioneer of popular Sunday journalism, who had died in 1890, but his paper was still riding high.

552 Catt, Jonathan Charles. 'Sources for local newspaper history'. *Local Historian*, Nov 1985.

553 Catterall, Peter. *British history, 1945–1987: an annotated bibliography.* Oxford: Blackwell (for Institute of Contemporary British History), 1990.
Includes, at length, 'The press' in a section 'Media and communications'.

554   Caulkin, Simon. 'The inside story'. *The Observer*, 6 Jun 1993.
Narrative of the 'battle' for *The Observer*, won by *The Guardian*.

555   Cave, Albert. 'The newest journalism'. *The Contemporary Review*, 91, 1907.

556   Cayford, Joanne M. *The Western Mail, 1869–1914: the politics and management of a provincial newspaper*. Cardiff: University of Wales, 1992 (PhD thesis).

556A   – – –.   'The national newspaper of Wales'. *Planet: The Welsh Internationalist*, 98, Apr/May 1993.
On the *Western Mail*.

557   'Centenary of the *News of the World*: Sunday newspaper with the largest circulation in the world'. *World's Press News*, 30 Sep 1943.

558   Central News. *Jubilee: a record of the celebrations*. London: 1921.
Established in 1893 as Central Press to provide domestic news in the Conservative interest, the service was reorganized from 1871 as Central News to offer also a foreign telegraphic link. It remained a significant force until its acquisition by the Press Association and Exchange Telegraph after World War II. The founder was William Saunders, also a leading provincial newspaper proprietor.

559   Centre for the Study of Cartoons and Caricature. *E.H. Shepard: exhibition of political cartoons*. Canterbury: University of Kent, 1974.
Published before the official opening of the Centre. Contains one hundred drawings for *Punch*, to which Shepard began contributing in 1907.

559A   – – –.   *Getting them in line: an exhibition of caricature in cartoons.* Canterbury: University of Kent, 1975. 48pp.
To mark the opening of the Centre, 'the National Archive for published political and social cartoons'. Contains three essays including Colin Seymour-Ure on 'How special are cartoonists?'; and Stephen Bann on 'Cartoons, art and politics'.

559B   – – –.   *Beaverbrook's England, 1940–1965: an exhibition of cartoon originals by Michael Cummings, David Low, Vicky, and Sidney 'George' Strube* . . . 96pp. Canterbury: University of Kent, [1981].

560   Cesarani, David. *The Jewish Chronicle and Anglo-Jewry, 1841–1991*. Cambridge: Cambridge University Press, 1994.

561   Chalfont, (Alun) Arthur Gwynne Jones, *Baron. Communication and international security*. London: Stationers' Company, 1987. Annual Livery Lecture.
Gwynne Jones was defence correspondent of *The Times*, then minister of state at the Foreign and Commonwealth Office, but returned to journalism as foreign editor of *The New Statesman*.

562   Chaloner, S.R. *Die britische Presse vom Standpunkt der Zeitungsindustrie und ihrer Finanzierung*. Münster: 1929. 52pp.

563 'Champion of reform, A – the *Leeds Mercury*'. *The Newspaper World*, 27 May 1939. (In The Oldest Newspapers series.)
Later in 1939 the *Mercury* was merged into today's *Yorkshire Post*.

564 Chance, H. Gordon, ed. *Bicentenary: Gloucester Journal, 9 April 1722– 8 April 1922*. Gloucester: Chance & Blond, 1922. 143pp.
Includes history by Roland Austin. Founded by Robert Raikes (father of the founder of Sunday Schools) and William Dicey. Latterly a Northcliffe title, it is no longer published separately. The early files of the *Journal* are preserved in Gloucester Library.

565 Chancellor, (*Sir*) Christopher (John Howard). *Reuters in wartime, 1939–45*. London: Reuters, [1945].
Chancellor's own service as general manager of Reuters began at the height of the war (1944) and continued until 1959.

566 Chancellor, Edwin Beresford. *The annals of Fleet Street: its traditions and associations*. London: Chapman & Hall, 1912. xi + 344pp.

567 Chapman, Colin R. *An introduction to using newspapers and periodicals*. Birmingham: Federation of Family History Societies, 1993. 30pp.

568 *Chard and Ilminster News*. Centenary supplement. Taunton (Somerset): 9 May 1974.
Weekly in South West Counties Newspapers group.

569 Chater, Tony. 'Sixty socialist years, 1930–1990'. *Morning Star*, 2 Jan 1990.
Illustrated centenary article by the editor, harking back to the launch of the *Daily Worker* in 1930 and before.

570 *Chatham, Rochester and Gillingham News*. Centenary supplement, 1859– 1959. Chatham (Kent): 14 Aug 1959.

571 – – –. 125th anniversary number. Chatham: 6 Jul 1984.
Special issue containing a facsimile of *Chatham News* no 1 (2 July 1859). The *Chatham, Rochester and Gillingham News* of today is owned by EMAP.

572 Cheshire, A.G. 'Press photography at the Front: some Belgian experiences of a *Daily Sketch* man'. In *Sell's World's Press, 1915*. London: Sell, 1915.

573 Chesshyre, Robert. *The return of a native reporter*. London: Viking, 1987. 384pp; Harmondsworth (Middx): Penguin, 1988. 352pp.
Britain observed after four years away as *The Observer*'s correspondent in Washington. Earlier he was the paper's Northern Ireland correspondent and a columnist.

574 Chester, Lewis. 'The press breaks free'. *The Illustrated London News*, Nov 1986.
The pictorial element adds to the impact of this story of the move from Fleet Street.

575   Chester, Lewis, Stephen Aris, Cal McCrystal, and William Shawcross. *Watergate*. London: André Deutsch, 1973.
The US presidential scandal by the *Sunday Times* Insight team.

576   Chester, Lewis, and Jonathan Fenby. *The fall of the house of Beaverbrook*. London: André Deutsch, 1979.
How Trafalgar House moved in to acquire the failing Beaverbrook newspapers.

577   Chester, Lewis, Magnus Linklater, and David May. *Jeremy Thorpe: a secret life*. London: André Deutsch; Fontana, 1979.
Insight Team from *The Sunday Times* investigates the private affairs of the Liberal Party's leader.

578   *Chester Chronicle*. 150th birthday number. Chester: 2 May 1925.

579   – – –.   Bicentenary supplement. 2 May 1975.

580   *Chester Courant*. Bicentenary souvenir edition, 1730–1930. Chester: 26 Nov 1930.
Established by 'country gentlemen' as *Adam's Weekly Courant*. It merged in 1982 with the *Chester Express*, as a free weekly within the Chester Observer group.

581   Chester Public Library. *Chester newspaper index*. Chester: City Council. 2 vols (covering 1955–9 and 1960–4).

582   Chesterton, G[ilbert] K[eith]. *The wisdom of Father Brown*. London: Cassell, 1914.
Contains, in 'The purple wig', the splendid affirmation: 'Journalism consists largely in saying "Lord Jones Dead" to people who never knew Lord Jones was alive.'

583   – – –.   *Autobiography*. London: Hutchinson, 1936. 347pp. Rptd 1969, with an introduction by Anthony Burgess; Hamish Hamilton, 1986, with an introduction by Richard Ingrams.
Includes a chapter 'Figures in Fleet Street', in which Chesterton wrote that 'Journalism is now conducted like any other business. It is conducted as quietly, as sensibly, as the office of any moderately fraudulent financier.' 'G.K.C.' (1874–1936), a remarkable personality as well as a prolific author, started his journalism on *The Daily News* in pre-World War I days; his essays in *The Illustrated London News* continued until his death.

584   – – –.   *Chesterton: an anthology, selected with an introduction by D.B. Wyndham Lewis*. London: Oxford University Press, 1957. xxi + 235pp. (In the World's Classics series.)
'G.K.C. worked as a journalist in the flourishing, romantic days of Fleet Street.'

585   Chibnall, Stephen J. *Law-and-order news: an analysis of crime reporting in the British press*. London: Tavistock Publications, 1977. xiv + 288pp.
Chibnall's thesis – that 'much of what we read in law-and-order news does not necessarily

correspond with the reality of events' – is developed from the viewpoint of a teaching sociologist rather than from that of a journalist. His thought-provoking essay contains some useful examples of instructions to police on the use of falsehood and propaganda in the war on crime.

586 – – –. *Crime reporting in the British press: a sociological examination of its historical development and current practice.* Colchester: University of Essex, 1981 (PhD thesis).

587 – – –. *Chronicles of the gallows: the social history of crime reporting.* Keele (Staff): University of Keele Sociological Review Monograph, 29, 1984.

588 *Chichester Observer.* Centenary, 1887–1987: Supplement. Chichester (W Sussex): 18 Jun 1987. 48pp.
Now a Portsmouth and Sunderland Newspapers title.

589 Chipp, David. 'PA gets the message'. *UK Press Gazette*: souvenir issue, 3 Jun 1985.
'Meeting the challenge of computerised information'; an article by the 1971–85 editor-in-chief of the Press Association.

590 Chippindale, Peter, and Chris Horrie. *Disaster!: the rise and fall of the News on Sunday.* London: Sphere, 1988.
'An anatomy of business failure'.

591 – – –. *Stick it up your punter!: the rise and fall of The Sun.* London: Heinemann, 1990; Mandarin, 1992. 372pp.
Close-up view of the workings of Britain's most popular daily paper – and in particular of its controversial editor, Kelvin MacKenzie. (In terms of sales, the 'fall' in the title has yet to come to pass.)

592 Chirol, *Sir* [Ignatius] Valentine. *Fifty years in a changing world.* London: Jonathan Cape, 1927. 351pp. New York: 1928.
Chirol (1852–1929) was an influential and perceptive correspondent in Berlin for *The Times* before becoming its foreign editor (1899–1912).

593 Chisholm, Anne, and Michael Davie. *Beaverbrook: a life.* London: Hutchinson, 1992. ix + 589pp; Pimlico 1993.
Full-scale biography – astute, absorbing and entertaining – written by a husband-and-wife team with the aid of the Aitken family. Davie was with *The Observer* from 1950 to 1977, and again from 1981 to 1988.

594 Christian, Harry. *The development of trade unionism and professionalism among British journalists: a sociological enquiry.* London: University of London (London School of Economics), 1976 (PhD thesis).

595 – – –, ed. *The sociology of journalism and the press.* Keele (Staffs): University of Keele, 1980.
This sociological review monograph is a valuable anthology.

596   – – –.   'Professional man or wage earner?'. *Journalism Studies Review*, 1976.
Deals with the rival claims of the National Union of Journalists and the Institute of Journalists to represent the best interests of journalists.

597   Christiansen, Arthur. *Headlines all my life*. London: Heinemann, 1961. xi + 295pp. New York: Harper.
One of Fleet Street's most successful editors (*Daily Express*, 1933–57) gives a fascinating account of non-stop day-to-day work in harness with his demanding proprietor, Beaverbrook. Christiansen (born in 1904, died at the age of fifty-nine), the technician-editor *par excellence*, openly admits that 'the policies were Lord Beaverbrook's job, the presentation mine'.

598   Christie-Miller, John, ed. *The development of Stockport, 1922–1972, and the history of the Stockport Advertiser*. Stockport (Cheshire): Stockport Advertiser, 1972.

599   Christoph, James B. 'The press and politics in Britain and America'. *Political Quarterly*, 34, 1963.
A useful corrective to the erroneous idea that the press in Britain enjoys privileged protection, as in the USA.

600   *Chronicle and Echo*. Golden Jubilee souvenir supplement. Northampton: 2 Nov 1981.
An evening transferred from United Provincial Newpapers to EMAP in 1992.

601   'Chronicler of Derby, The'. *The Newspaper World*, 8 Jul 1939. (In The Oldest Newspapers series.)
Refers to *The Derby Mercury*, established in 1789.

602   Churchill, Randolph (Frederick Edward Spencer). *What I said about the press*. London: Weidenfeld & Nicolson; New York: World Publishing, 1957. 112pp.
About Churchill's successful libel action against Odhams Press Ltd (and *The People*) in 1956 . . . and three critical speeches.

603   – – –.   *Twenty-one years*. London: Weidenfeld & Nicolson, 1965. 135pp.
A deliberately rumbustious autobiographical sketch, harking back to the author's student days plus impressive examples of his early journalism (e.g. personal interviews with Hitler and Mussolini).

604   Churchill, (*Sir*) Winston (Leonard Spencer). *Thoughts and adventures*. London: Thornton Butterworth, 1932; MacMillan, 1942. Publ in USA as *Amid these storms*. New York: Scribner, 1932. Rptd from *The Daily Telegraph* etc.

605   – – –.   *Step by step, 1936–1939*. London: Thornton Butterworth, 1939; New York: Pitman, 1939. Reprints from *The Daily Telegraph* and *Evening Standard*.

When in the political wilderness, Churchill expressed his warning voice – and made a livelihood – in every available newspaper and periodical. More than five hundred articles have been traced; such books as the above have themselves achieved classic status.

606 – – –. *Frontiers and wars*. London: Eyre & Spottiswoode, 1962. 567pp; Harmondsworth (Middx): Penguin, 1972. 605pp.
Abridged reprint of (a) *The story of the Malakand Field Force*; (b) *The river war*; (c) *London to Ladysmith via Pretoria*; and (d) *Ian Hamilton's march*. Lieutenant Churchill served in the Army in India and at the age of twenty-three sent despatches to *The Daily Telegraph*, which were edited for (a), first published in 1897; (b) was 'an historic account of the reconquest of the Soudan' based on despatches to *The Morning Post* and published in 1899; (c) and (d) appeared in 1900, and are collections of Churchill's Boer War despatches to *The Morning Post*.

607 *Churchill and the press*. Plaistow (Essex): Plaistow Pictorial, 1974.
Historic pages, drawn from the John Frost Collection, celebrating the centenary of Winston Churchill's birth.

608 *Citizen, The*. Centenary supplement: 1876–1976. Gloucester: 1 May 1976.
Today an evening title in the Northcliffe Newspapers group.

609 *City Press*. 75th anniversary number. London: 22 Jul 1932.
A specialized newspaper for the City of London.

610 Clark, Peter A. *Sixteen million readers: evening newspapers in the UK*. Eastbourne (E Sussex): Holt, Rinehart & Winston (with the Advertising Association), 1981. 97pp.
By the secretary-general of the Market Research Society, this is a unique source book of statistics on the evenings. London and Glasgow have chapters of their own. Supplemented by four loose tabulated appendixes.

611 – – –. 'The national press: a personal scrutiny'. *Admap*, Nov 1976.

612 – – –. 'Fleet Street figures that recount a story of change'. *Campaign*, 16 Oct 1981.
To mark the golden jubilee of the Audit Bureau of Circulations. This eight-page feature has most valuable text and tabulated matter, showing fluctuations of circulation and advertising expenditure of all Britain's current nationals.

613 – – –. 'The newspapers that came in from the cold'. *Admap*, Sep 1988.
On the revival of free titles.

614 Clark, William. *Hugh Redwood: with God in Fleet Street*. London: Hodder & Stoughton, 1976.
Redwood was religious editor of the *News Chronicle*.

615 Clark, William Donaldson. *From three worlds: memoirs*. London: Sidgwick & Jackson, 1986. 304pp.

Clark's journalistic career included, notably, diplomatic correspondent for *The Observer* (1950–5), returning to that paper (as editor of The Week column) after serving the Prime Minister (Anthony Eden) as public relations adviser.

616   Clarke, *(Sir)* Basil. *My round of the war*. London: Heinemann, 1917.

617   – – –.   *How the progress of the war was chronicled by pen and camera*. London: Amalgamated Press, 1919.
Clarke was on the Western Front as correspondent for the *Daily Mail* 1914–16, then with Reuters. After the war he edited the *Sheffield Independent* and latterly was a pioneer government information officer.

618   Clarke, Neville, and Edwin Riddell. *The sky barons: the men who control the global media*. London: Methuen, 1991. ix + 246pp.
Features, *inter alia*, Rupert Murdoch, Conrad Black, and Robert Maxwell.

619   Clarke, Peter Frederick. *Lancashire and the new Liberalism*. Cambridge: Cambridge University Press, 1971. x + 472pp.
Features C.P. Scott and *The Manchester Guardian*.

620   Clarke, Thomas. *Producer co-operatives in market systems: a case study of the Scottish Daily News in the context of the political economy of the press*. Coventry: University of Warwick, 1983 (PhD thesis).
On the 'workers' co-operative' which launched, unsuccessfully, the *Scottish Daily News*.

621   Clarke, Thomas. 'The descent of Robert Maxwell'. *Media, Culture and Society*, 14, 3, Jul 1992.

622   Clarke, Tom. *My Northcliffe diary*. London: Gollancz; New York: Cosmopolitan Book Corporation, 1931. xiii + 304pp.
Covers the years 1910–22 (the year of Northcliffe's death); for half of this period Clarke was news editor of the *Daily Mail*, and particularly close to 'the Chief'.

623   – – –.   *My Lloyd George diary*. London: Methuen, 1939. vii + 248pp.
Covers 1926–33, when Clarke was editor of the *News Chronicle*.

624   – – –.   *Journalism*. London: R. Ross, 1945. 63pp. (In the Ross Careers Books series.)
Based on lectures given to students of London University between 1936 and 1939.

625   – – –.   *Northcliffe in history: an intimate story of press power*. London and New York: Hutchinson, [1950]. 216pp.
A full-length, and more outspoken, memoir published long after its subject's death.

626   Clarkson, Wensley. *Dog eat dog: confessions of a tabloid journalist*. London: Fourth Estate, 1990. 205pp.
By a former *Sunday Mirror* man.

627   'Classics of journalism'. *UK Press Gazette*, from 23 Nov 1987 (occasional series). *See also* Barber, Lynn; Coleman, Terry; Colvin, Marie; Lloyd, John; *Sunday Times* (Insight Team).

628 Clayson, Sir Eric (Maurice). *The place of the provincial newspaper in the British press*. London: Stationers' Company, 1965. Annual Livery Lecture.
Clayson was then chairman of the *Birmingham Post*; he was a former president of the Newspaper Society and a founder of the Press Council.

629 Clayton, Joan. *Journalism for beginners*. London: Piatkus, 1992.

630 'Cleaning up the 4th Estate: the way ahead'. *UK Press Gazette* (ser) 30 May–4 Jul 1988. *See also* Edwards, Robert; Goodman, *Baron*; Loynes, Tony; Morgan, Kenneth; Stephenson, Hugh; Trelford, Donald.

631 Cleverley, Graham A.W. *The Fleet Street disaster: British national newspapers as a study in mismanagement*. With a preface by Rex Winsbury. London: Constable; Beverly Hills (CA): Sage, 1976. 175pp. (In the Communication and Society series.)
A detailed and devastating broadside, with no discernible improving effect.

632 Clifford, Alex[ander] [Graeme]. *'Crusader'*. London: Harrap, 1941. 190pp.
About Britain's Eighth Army in the Western Desert in 1940. Clifford, pre-war Berlin correspondent for Reuters, and 'eyewitness' for the whole Allied press at Allied HQ in France after war broke out, had now begun his most distinguished service for the *Daily Mail*.

633 – – –. *Three against Rommel: the campaigns of Wavell, Auchinleck and Alexander*. London: Harrap, 1943. 427pp. Publ in USA as *Conquest in North Africa*. Boston (MA), 1943.

634 Clive, Eric M, and George A. Watt. *Scots law for journalists*. Edinburgh: W. Green & Sons (for National Council for the Training of Journalists), 1965; 4th edn, with Bruce McKain as additional author, 1984.

635 Clough, Robert. *A public eye*. London: Hamish Hamilton, 1981. 201pp.
Memoirs of a leading journalist on Tyneside: for Newcastle's *North Mail*, the *Evening Chronicle* and *The Journal* (of which Clough became editor after World War II). (He later stepped up to become local managing director of what became Thomson Regional Newspapers.) Discursive in style, and unhappily no index.

636 Clutterbuck, Richard. *The media and political violence*. London: Macmillan, 1981.
Includes several case studies and an annotated bibliography.

637 Coates, John. 'The Fleet Street context and the development of Chesterton's prose style'. *Prose Studies*, 6, 1983.
G.K. Chesterton became a notable writer for national newspapers in the immediate pre-World War I years.

638 Cobbett, William Willson, and Sidney Dark, eds. *Fleet Street: an anthology of modern journalism*. London: Eyre & Spottiswoode, 1932. xxiii + 426pp.

Wide-ranging extracts from British newspapers from the 1890s to the 1930s, with no obvious pattern or *raison d'être*.

639   Cochrane, R. 'The centenary of *The Scotsman*'. *Bookman*, 51, 1917.

640   Cock, Frederick William. 'The *Kentish Post or Canterbury News Letter*'. *The Library*, Jul 1913. Rptd as a booklet.

641   Cockburn, Cynthia. *Brothers: male dominance and technological advance.* London: Pluto Press, 1983. 264pp.
Detailed study of photocomposition in newspaper offices.

642   Cockburn, [Francis] Claud. *Reporter in Spain*. London: Lawrence & Wishart, 1936. 141pp.
Despatches, written under the pseudonym Frank Pitcairn, from the Spanish Civil War, when the author was correspondent for the *Daily Worker*.

643   – – –.   *Nine bald men*. London: Hart-Davis, 1956. 203pp.
Tongue-in-cheek essays for *Punch*, one of the best being on the Press Council, entitled 'Council of perfection'.

644   – – –.   *In time of trouble: an autobiography*. London: Hart-Davis, 1956. 264pp. Publ in the USA as *A discord of trumpets: an autobiography*. New York: Simon & Schuster, 1956. 314pp.
Cockburn, ex-*Times* correspondent in New York, was founder-editor of *The Week* when he went out to Spain in 1936. This left-wing gossip-sheet, like the *Daily Worker*, was suppressed under Defence Regulations (1941–2), but survived, still under Cockburn, until 1946. It had an influence quite out of proportion to its tiny circulation.

645   – – –.   *The devil's decade: the thirties*. London: Sidgwick & Jackson; New York: Mason & Lipscomb, 1973. 256pp.
Describes vividly that 'little moment between the crisis and the catastrophe' (i.e. between the New York stock-market crash of 1929 and the outbreak of World War II), when the press on both sides of the Atlantic seemed to be caught unawares. It includes sharply observed essays on the failure of most press campaigns in the 1930s and the bowdleriza-tion of news – especially political news – by the popular press.

646   – – –.   *Cockburn sums up: an autobiography*. London: Quartet Books, 1981, 1984. 269pp.
In his foreword, Graham Greene describes Cockburn (1904–81) as 'one of the two greatest journalists of the twentieth century' (the other being Chesterton).

647   Cockburn, Patricia. *The years of The Week*. London: Macdonald, 1968. 287pp. Harmondsworth (Middx): Penguin, 1971. 293pp. London: Comedia, 1985. 288pp. With an introduction by Richard Ingrams.
A record by Claud Cockburn's widow.

648   Cockerell, Michael, Peter Hennessy, and David Walker. *Sources close to the Prime Minister: inside the hidden world of the news manipulators.* London: Macmillan, 1984. 255pp. Expanded edn (Papermac), 1985.

A critical analysis of the lobby system by Cockerell from the BBC and two journalists. Describing it as 'one of the most secretive administrative systems in the democratic world', they call for abolition of all 'non-attributable' briefing.

649 Cockett, Richard B. *The Government, the press and politics in Britain, 1937–1945*. London: University of London, 1988 (PhD thesis).

650 – – –. *Twilight of truth: Chamberlain, appeasement and the manipulation of truth*. London: Weidenfeld & Nicolson, 1989. 229pp.
Among the major British newspapers, only *The Daily Telegraph, Daily Mirror, Reynolds' News* and *Yorkshire Post* challenged Chamberlain's appeasement policy.

651 – – –. *David Astor and The Observer*. London: André Deutsch, 1991. xi + 315pp.
A tribute to a great editorship.

652 – – –. ' "In wartime every objective reporter should be shot": the experience of British press correspondents in Moscow, 1941–1945'. *Journal of Contemporary History*, 23, 4. 1988.

653 – – –. 'The Foreign Office news department and struggle against appeasement'. *Historical Research*, 63, 1990.
Highlights in particular the campaign by Reginald (Rex) Leeper, head of the news department 1935–8, against the Government's official policy.

654 – – –. 'Sir Joseph Ball, Neville Chamberlain and the secret control of *Truth*'. *Historical Journal*, Mar 1989.
Another strand in the manipulation of political opinion in the immediately pre-war period; Ball was director of the Conservative research department when Chamberlain was prime minister; the weekly *Truth* was then owned by Lord Luke.

655 – – –, ed. *My dear Max: the letters of Brendan Bracken to Lord Beaverbrook, 1925–1958*. London: Historians' Press, 1990. viii + 215pp.

655A Cockett, Richard B., and Brian Brivati, eds. *The political journalism of Peter Jenkins*. London: Cassell (in preparation).
Largely from *The Guardian*, where Jenkins was political commentator, 1974–85.

656 Cohen, Phil, and Carl Gardner, eds. *It ain't half racist, mum: fighting racism in the media*. London: Comedia/Campaign Against Racism in the Media, 1982. vi + 119pp.

657 Cohen, Stanley, and Jock Young, eds. *The manufacture of news: social problems, deviance and the mass media*. London: Constable, 1973; revised 1981; Beverly Hills (CA): Sage. 383pp.

658 Cohen, Yoel Michael. *British foreign policy-making and the news media*. London: City University, 1981 (PhD thesis).

659   – – –.   *Media diplomacy: the Foreign Office in the mass communications age*. London: Cass, 1986.

660   Cole, Peter. 'The ageing of an editor'. *British Journalism Review*, Autumn 1990.
Describes the 'seven ages' of his time as the first editor of *The Sunday Correspondent*.

661   No entry.

662   – – –.   'Guardian angel'. *The Sunday Times*, 2 May 1993.
On *The Observer* – with its future decided. Cole now writes as professor of journalism at the University of Central Lancashire.

663   Coleman, Terry. *The scented brawl: selected articles and interviews*. London: Elm Tree, 1978. xii + 191pp.
Consists mainly of profiles and special assignments for *The Guardian*.

664   – – –.   *Movers and shakers*. London: André Deutsch, 1987.
Further interviews for *The Guardian*. Introduction by Alistair Cooke.

665   – – –.   'The certainties of two nations'. *The Guardian*, 1987, rptd *UK Press Gazette*, 30 Nov 1987 (Classics of Journalism series).
Reporting on the General Election campaigns in Scotland and the North of England.

666   Coleridge, Nicholas. *Paper tigers*. London: Heinemann, 1993. xvi + 592pp. Mandarin, 1994.
'The carnivorous world of the twenty-five most powerful newspaper tycoons' . . . the rather long-winded result of several hundred interviews. Lord Rothermere comes across with particular effect.

667   Coles, Joanna. 'How *Today* greets the dawn'. *The Guardian*, 22 Oct 1990.
A day with David Montgomery (then editor) and others.

668   – – –.   'Scorpio's rising star'. *The Guardian (Media Guardian)*, 1 Feb 1993.
On Amanda Platell, newly appointed managing editor at Mirror Group Newspapers.

669   Colgate, W. 'Death at 164: the portrait of a newspaper'. *Queen's Quarterly*, 45, 1938.
On *The Morning Post*: 'b. 1772; d. 1937'.

670   'Colindale Newspaper Library'. *Au Courant* (journal of the NKTV–European Newspaper Collectors' Club), 3, 4, Winter 1988/9.

671   Colley, William. *News hunter*. London: Hutchinson, 1936. 317pp.
Colley was with the *Daily Mail*, and also had a long period at the *Evening Standard*.

672   Collier, Richard. *The warcos: the war correspondents of World War II*. London: Weidenfeld & Nicolson, 1989. x + 230pp.
A splendidly balanced narrative, highlighting all the leading reporters – and many of the photographers – with the Allied forces and on the British Home Front. Supplemented by an excellent bibliography. Collier writes from first-hand experience.

673 Collins, Henry Michael. *From pigeon post to wireless*. With an introduction by Sir Roderick Jones. London: Hodder & Stoughton, 1925. xiii + 312pp.
An authoritative personal account of the launching of an intercontinental news service for Reuters, particularly the setting up of offices in the Far East and Australia, negotiations in Persia, and South Africa in the immediate aftermath of the Boer War. Published long after Collins' retirement.

674 *Colne Times*. Centenary number. Burnley (Lancs): 22 Mar 1974.
Weekly in United Provincial Newspapers ownership.

675 Colquhoun, Iain H. *A prosperous press*. London: Barrie & Rockliff, for the Institute of Economic Affairs, 1961. 48pp.

676 Colvin, Marie. 'War on women'. *The Sunday Times*, Mar 1987, rptd *UK Press Gazette*, 23 Nov 1987 (Classics of Journalism series).
Reporting on a refugee camp in The Lebanon.

677 – – –. 'My future – by heroine of the camps'. *The Sunday Times*, rptd *UK Press Gazette*, 1 Feb 1988 (Classics of Journalism series).
Interview with Dr Cutting in Beirut.

678 Comedia. 'The alternative press: the development of underdevelopment'. *Media, Culture and Society*, Apr 1984.
Comedia was a co-operative publisher; authors of the article are Charles Landry, David Morley, and Russell Southwood. Explains how 'alternative' means the non-established, non-capitalistic order; instances *New Socialist* and *New Internationalist* as current alternative titles.

679 *Committee of Privy Counsellors appointed to inquire into 'D' Notice matters: report*. London: 1967. Cmnd 3309. 28pp.
This report arose from the 'Chapman Pincher' case, in which the defence correspondent of the *Daily Express* was arraigned for ignoring the 'D' Notice system of censorship. The committee, headed by Lord Radcliffe, completely exonerated the paper and the journalist, in a report that was most revealing on the Fleet Street practices of the day. The government riposted with a White Paper (*see* 'D' Notice).

680 *Committee on privacy and related matters: report*. London: HMSO (for Home Office), 1990. Cm 1102.
The committee, under the chairmanship of David Calcutt QC, recommended the institution of a Press Complaints Commission (replacing the Press Council), to adjudicate on cases of alleged malpractice.

681 Committee on Scottish Newspapers. *A programme for microfilming Scottish newspapers*. Edinburgh: National Library of Scotland, 1986.

682 'Compact group in family ownership, A'. In *The press and the people, 1973/1974*. (Press Council Annual Report.)
'The *Daily Telegraph* group is the simplest of all Britain's major press groups'.

683 *Company of Newspaper Makers, The: inaugural banquet at the Mansion House on 26th February 1932.* Souvenir programme, incl foreword by the Company's first master, R.D. Blumenfeld.
It was merged into the Stationers' Company in 1937.

684 Compton, H. *Newspapers.* London: Educational Supply Association, 1954. 116pp. (In How Things Are Made series).

685 *Congleton Chronicle.* Centenary supplement, 1893–1993. Congleton (Cheshire): 14 Oct 1993.
An independent weekly.

686 Connor, Robert. *Cassandra: reflections in a mirror.* London: Cassell, 1969.
A posthumous tribute by his son to (Sir) William Connor, the *Daily Mirror* columnist who called himself 'Cassandra'.

687 Connor, (*Sir*) William Neil. *The English at war.* London: Secker & Warburg, 1941. 127pp. (In the Searchlight Books series.)
Connor, here writing under his pseudonym 'Cassandra', was *the* polemic journalist of his day. The attacks in this booklet are direct and personal in the extreme.

688 'Contemporary British press, The'. *The Economist,* Nov 1928 (ser).
These controversial articles deplore, *inter alia,* 'the growing trivialization' and the seeming abandonment of 'boring but functional' public service journalism.

689 Cook, Arthur. *Story unused: a correspondent in the Far East, 1963–67.* London: Allen & Unwin, 1971.
For the *Daily Mail.*

690 Cook, Chris, and Jeffrey Weeks, eds. *Sources in British political history, Vol 5: guide to the private papers of leading writers, intellectuals and publicists.* London: Macmillan, 1978.
Valuable for archival research into the careers and publications of (*inter alia*) journalists in the political arena.

691 Cook, *Sir* Edward Tyas. *The press in war-time, with some account of the Official Press Bureau: an essay.* London: Macmillan, 1920. xv + 200pp. Ed A.M. Cook.
Written with the further authority of one who had been joint director of the Bureau from 1915 to 1919.

692 Cook, Fred. 'Manchester as second Fleet Street: northern headquarters of London papers'. *World's Press News,* 2 Jan 1930.

693 Cooke, [Alfred] Alistair. *America observed: the newspaper years of Alistair Cooke.* London: Reinhardt Books/Viking Press; New York: Knopf, 1988. xiv + 235pp. Ed Ronald A. Wells.
The wide public acclaim for Cooke as an outstanding exponent of radio and television, especially in interpreting America to his native Britain, is reflected in the professional

respect for his fluency as a journalist. Born in Manchester in 1908, he was *The Manchester Guardian*'s United Nations correspondent from 1945 to 1948 and the paper's chief US correspondent from 1948 to 1972. By then a naturalized US citizen, Cooke was created an Hon KBE (1973).

694   Cooper, Charles Alfred. *An editor's retrospect: fifty years of newspaper work.* London: Macmillan, 1896. xv + 430pp.
'From wood press to rotary web' . . . Dr Cooper had the difficult task in 1876 of taking over the editorship of *The Scotsman* from Alexander Russel; he was able to consolidate the paper's pre-eminence, remaining in office until 1905.

695   Cooper, George Henry. *Fifty years' journalistic experience and chronicles of a typical industrial area.* Cleckheaton (Yorks): John Siddall, 1938. 99pp.
The area concerned is the then West Riding.

696   Cooper, Liz, Charles Landry, and Dave Berry. *The other secret service: press distribution and press censorship.* London: Minority Press Group/Campaign for Press Freedom, 1980.
The principal criticism expressed is the 'closed shop' policy of such major newspaper and magazine distributors as W.H. Smith & Son.

697   Coopers & Lybrand. *The provincial newspaper industry.* London: 1975.
Accountants' submission to the (third) Royal Commission on the Press.

698   Coote, *Sir* Colin (Reith). *Editorial: the memoirs of Colin R. Coote.* London: Eyre & Spottiswoode, 1965. x + 332pp.
Published after the author's retirement from the managing editorship of *The Daily Telegraph*; previously he was with *The Times*, where the atmosphere, he writes, was 'just horrible'; his views on Nazi Germany were utterly opposed to those of his editor, Dawson.

699   Coote, John (Oldham). *Altering course: a submariner in Fleet Street.* Barnsley (S Yorks): Pen & Sword Books (Leo Cooper), 1992. 160pp.
After a distinguished naval career, the author joined Beaverbrook Newspapers (*Daily Express* etc) and was group vice-chairman and managing director 1968–74. Much close-up material on Beaverbrook and his other close associates.

700   Coppard, Kit. *IPI – the defence of press freedom: Part 2. 1976–1988.* London: International Press Institute, 1988.
Sequel to Rosemary Righter's survey of the Institute's first twenty-five years.

701   Corbett, Howard. 'The secret of Northcliffe'. *World's Press News*, 7 Apr–20 Oct 1932.
Nostalgic speculation, in a long series of articles (twenty-three instalments). Corbett was manager of *The Times* during World War I and until shortly before Northcliffe's death in 1922.

702   Cormack, Alexandar Allan. *The Chalmers family and Aberdeen newspapers.* Peterculter: 1958. 39pp.
Includes an outline history of the *Aberdeen Journal* and its contemporaries.

703   Cosgrove, S. *The living newspaper: history, production and form*. Hull: University of Hull, 1982 (PhD thesis). 270pp.

704   Coster, Ian. 'The conversion of Swaff'. In *His friends in aspic*. London: John Miles, 1939.
Interview with Hannen Swaffer, then the most famous of Fleet Street journalists, having foresworn alcohol but espoused spiritualism (and certain that Northcliffe's spirit was suffering purgatory by attending every conference at Northcliffe House but unable to assert his presence!).

705   *County Echo*. Centenary number. Fishguard (Dyfed): 6 Aug 1993.
A Tindle group weekly.

706   Courlander, Alphonse. *Mightier than the sword*. London: T. Fisher Unwin, 1912. 352pp.
Courlander's pen was wielded with particular effect from Paris on behalf of the *Daily Express* in the pre-World War I era. But this is a work of fiction – of derring-do in and around a mythical national paper called *The Day*.

707   Courtenay, William. *Airman Friday*. London: Hutchinson, [1937].
Air correspondent, *Evening Standard*, 1932–6, and simultaneously 'publicist' for a variety of flying enterprises: circuses, record attempts, airport openings etc. Furnishes useful information on the air correspondents of the pre-World War II period.

708   Courtney, Janet Elizabeth (*née* Hogarth), ed. *The making of an editor: W.L. Courtney, 1850–1928*. London: Macmillan, 1930. vii + 233pp.
A stepping-stone towards William Leonard Courtney's long and influential editorship of *The Fortnightly Review* was his years as dramatic and literary critic of *The Daily Telegraph*. But this biography is also interesting on his time at Newcastle upon Tyne with the short-lived *Northern Tribune*.

709   Courtney of Penwith, Leonard Henry, *1st Baron*. 'The making and reading of newspapers'. *The Contemporary Review*, 79, 1901.
Lecture to the Social and Political Education League. It was estimated that Courtney penned some three thousand leaders for *The Times* in his long career with that paper.

710   Courtney, William Leonard. *The passing hour*. London: Hutchinson, 1925.

711   *Coventry Evening Telegraph: inside story*. Coventry: 1972. 39pp.
Established in 1891 by Edward Iliffe as the *Midland Daily Telegraph*: it is now in the Midland Independent Newspapers group.

712   *Coventry Mercury and Standard. The Newspaper World*, 29 Jul 1939. (In The Oldest Newspapers series.)

713   *Coventry Standard*. Bicentenary number. Coventry: 19 Jul 1941.
Jopson's Coventry Mercury began on 20 July 1741; became *Jopson's Coventry and Northampton Mercury* briefly in 1743; then the *Coventry Mercury*, 1787, and *Coventry Standard*, 1836. The *Coventry Independent* (1873) became the *Coventry Mercury* in 1888; the two were later merged.

714 'Cowdray interests, The'. In *The press and the people, 1968–1969.* (Press Council Annual Report.)
A useful summary of a complex financial structure, which now includes the *Financial Times*, Westminster Press, Longman and Penguin.

715 Cowing, Gwyneth. 'The story of the Barnet press'. *In* W.H. Golder, *Historic Barnet*, 1984.

716 Cox, (*Sir*) Geoffrey (Sandford). *Defence of Madrid.* London: Gollancz, 1937.
This was the year when, as a reporter, Cox moved from the *News Chronicle* to the *Daily Express*.

717 – – –. *The Red Army moves.* London: Gollancz, 1941.
Still with the *Express*, having transferred from France to the Finnish Front etc.

718 – – –. *The road to Trieste.* London: Heinemann, 1947. 249pp.
Covers the Trieste campaign of Spring 1945, when Cox had returned to the *News Chronicle* as a political correspondent. He later became a television chief.

719 – – –. *Countdown to war: a personal memoir of Europe, 1938–1940.* London: Kimber, 1988. 229pp.
From his youthful days as foreign correspondent, ranging Europe for the *Daily Express*; affords much close-up material on Beaverbrook's treatment of his staff.

720 Cox, Harold. 'The power of the press'. *Edinburgh Review*, Aug 1918.

721 Cox, Sarah, and Robert Golden. *Newspaperworker.* Harmondsworth (Middx): Penguin Books (Kestrel), 1978. (In People Working series.)

722 Cox, W., ed. *Government publishing and bookselling.* London: HMSO, 1963. 148pp.
Includes a section on the *London, Edinburgh* and *Belfast Gazettes*, and *Hansard*.

723 Cox, [William] Harvey, and David Morgan. *City politics and the press: journalists and the governing of Merseyside.* London: Cambridge University Press, 1973, 1974. viii + 159pp.
A critical treatise based particularly on relations between the (*Liverpool*) *Daily Post* and its evening associate, the *Liverpool Echo*, and the local community.

724 Cozens-Hardy, Harry Theobald. *The glorious years: random recollections of prominent persons in Parliament, in literature, on and off the platform, on the playing fields, and in the pulpit, the prize ring and the press – recaptured in London, Paris and New York between 1897 and 1952.* London: Robert Hale, 1953. 255pp.
The author's own press 'pedigree' included the *Norfolk News* (leaving for London 1897), *The Daily News* (US correspondent, 1904–14; he was one of the first on the Western Front), and the *News Chronicle*.

725 Craig, Charles. *The British documentary photograph as a medium of information and propaganda during the Second World War, 1939–45.* London: Imperial War Museum (unpubl MPhil thesis).

726   Cranfield, Geoffrey Alan. *The press and society: from Caxton to Northcliffe*. London and New York: Longman, 1978. 242pp. (In the Themes in British Social History series.)
A brave attempt to survey the whole history of the press in relation to the development of British society, managing to minimize the usual academic vagueness about working journalism while maximizing more controversial, socio-economic implications of the daily demands. It reaches the Northcliffe era rather too soon.

727   Crawley, Aidan Merivale. *Leap before you look*. London: Collins, 1988.
Autobiography of a politician and media personality, recounting how in his early days as a journalist he attended the 1st and 2nd Lords Rothermere as well as reporting for the *Daily Mail* and *Sunday Dispatch*.

728   Crawshay, Myfanwy I. *Journalism for women*. London: Fleet Publications, 1932. 77pp. (In The Writer's Library.)

729   *Creative Camera*. 'Fifty years of picture magazines'. London: Jul/Aug 1982.
Valuable material on the origins of modern photojournalism, and its development in Britain e.g. in (*Weekly*) *Illustrated*, *Picture Post*, and *Lilliput*. Also article on the first twenty years of *The Sunday Times Magazine* (first of the 'Sunday supplements').

730   – – –.   'Information and propaganda'. Jul/Aug 1985.
Includes Colin Osman, 'The foundation of *Parade*'. This was the first overseas magazine for the British Army: founded in Cairo in August 1940, and continuing right through weekly to February 1948. The article also puts into context the daily *Eighth Army News* and its weekly supplement, *Crusader* (both edited by Captain Warwick Charlton – 'one of the most original journalists and editors of all time'), and their more 'official' daily counterpart, *Union Jack*. Also deals with the Army Film and Photographic Unit.

731   Crewe, Quentin (Hugh). *Well, I forget the rest: autobiography of an optimist*. London: Hutchinson, 1991.
Deals notably with Beaverbrook's *Evening Standard* as film critic etc; also worked as columnist for the *Daily Mail* and *Sunday Mirror*.

732   *Crewe and Nantwich Chronicle*. Centenary supplement. Chester: 21 Mar 1974.
A Thomson Regional newspaper.

733   Crone, Tom. *The law and the media: an everyday guide for professionals*. London: Heinemann, 1989; Oxford: Butterworth-Heinemann, 1991, 1994.

734   Crosland, [Charles] Anthony [Raven]. 'The mass media'. *Encounter*, 19, Nov 1962.
An incisive examination of political journalism by a Labour politician of Cabinet rank.

735   Crosland, Susan (née Barnes). *Ruling passions*. London: Weidenfeld & Nicolson, 1989; Futura, 1990. 460pp.
Novel with a Sunday newspaper setting – a field familiar from her real-life interviews for *The Sunday Times*, collected in two books.

736 Cross, *Brigadier* Lionel L., comp. *The 9th Commonwealth Press Conference (India and Pakistan), 1961.* London: Commonwealth Press Union. vi + 160pp.

737 – – –. *The 10th Commonwealth Press Conference (West Indies Area), 1965.* London: CPU. v + 144pp.
The compiler of these proceedings was then secretary of the CPU.

738 *Croydon Advertiser.* Jubilee supplement. Croydon (then Surrey): 15 Feb 1919.

739 – – –. *1869–1969.* Centenary number. 14 Feb 1969. 48pp. Incorporating a facsimile of the first issue (*The Croydon Advertiser and East Surrey Reporter*). Also issued as a hardback volume (Feb 1969) with the same title. Jesse Ward's pioneer foundation has grown into one of the largest newspaper series in the southern boroughs of Greater London, and Surrey. (The paper is now in the Portsmouth and Sunderland Newspapers group.)

740 *Croydon Times, The.* Centenary souvenir, 1861–1961. 30 Jun 1961.
The sizeable Croydon Times group of weeklies was eventually absorbed into the rival Croydon Advertiser group.

741 Crozier, Michael. *The making of The Independent.* London: Gordon Fraser, 1988; Coronet, 1989. 128pp.
An insider's view of the successful launch (with the aid of £18 million venture capital) of the new national 'quality' daily, conceived by Andreas Whittam Smith.

742 Crozier, S.F. 'The press and the Army'. *Army Quarterly,* 68, 2, Jul 1954.

743 Cruikshank, Robert James (Robin). *Roaring century, 1846–1946.* London: Hamish Hamilton, 1946. xi + 280pp.
Described as a 'reverie', this attractive work – published to mark the centenary of the foundation of *The Daily News* – compares the England of 1846 with that one hundred years later, commenting on the intervening scene. Cruikshank, from 1948 editor of the *News Chronicle* (as a result of the merging of *The Daily News* and *The Daily Chronicle*), was the ideal author for this task.

744 – – –. 'A revolution in Fleet Street over the past 50 years'. In *The press, 1898–1948* (Newspaper World Golden Jubilee). London: Benn, 1948.

745 Cudlipp, Hugh (*Baron*). *Publish and be damned!: the astonishing story of the Daily Mirror.* London: Andrew Dakers, 1953. xi + 292pp. Publ in West Germany as *Sensationen für Millionen.* Munich, 1955.
This celebration of fifty years of the *Daily Mirror* is also the author's own punchy personal account of a career in the Mirror group in which he began as features editor of the *Mirror* in 1932 (when only twenty-two) and was promoted to the editorship of the *Sunday Pictorial* in 1937. The title is typical of Cudlipp's (highly successful) approach to tabloid journalism.

746 – – –. *At your peril.* London: Weidenfeld & Nicolson, 1962. 400pp.

'A mid-century view of the exciting changes of the press in Britain, and a press view of the exciting changes of mid-century' . . . in other words, a wider view of Fleet Street, nine years on. Cudlipp, in his day, could elicit more reader interest in fewer words than almost any other working editor in Fleet Street.

747 − − −. *Walking on the water*. London: Bodley Head, 1976. 428p
The story of Cudlipp's hectic years in the top echelons of the Mirror group, later part of the International Publishing Corporation. It culminates in his replacement of Cecil King as chairman in 1968. King – 'lonely, self-tortured' – is described as seeing himself, mistakenly, as 'a man of destiny'. Of his own brief interlude in the Beaverbrook group, Cudlipp comments: 'The editors of the *Daily Express*, the *Sunday Express*, the London *Evening Standard* and the Glasgow *Evening Ciitizen* enjoyed absolute freedom to agree wholeheartedly with their master's voice.'

748 − − −. *The prerogative of the harlot: press barons and power*. London: Bodley Head, 1980; Lawrence (MA): 1981. 304pp.
Hears, Northcliffe, the first Rothermere, Luce, Beaverbrook: all, according to Cudlipp, pursued personal vendettas. The title is taken from Prime Minister Baldwin's famous anti-press speech of 1931.

749 − − −. 'Oh yes, Fleet Street has a beating heart'. In *100 years of Fleet Street*. London: Press Club, 1982.
A tribute to W.N. Connor ('Cassandra') and Peter Wilson, colleagues and friends of Cudlipp on the *Daily Mirror* since 1935.

750 − − −. 'The deathbed repentance'. *British Journalism Review*, 1, 2, 1990.
'The current proprietors or publishers of the British national newspapers are a motley lot with little in common beyond a fascination with the balance sheet and a distaste for each other . . . it is to the editors I look for reform, rating their self-respect and the standing of their profession above their salaries and perks.'

751 − − −. 'Laughter in court'. *British Journalism Review*, 3, 2, 1992.
Records by a major protagonist – Cudlipp was then in charge of the *Daily Mirror* – of the famous libel case brought against the paper by the American entertainer Liberace. The comment at issue appeared in September 1956; the case did not come to court until June 1959.

752 Culf, Andrew. 'News that's getting lost in the selling'. *The Guardian (Media Guardian)*, 2 Dec 1991.
How the Press Association, Britain's national news agency, could lose its monopoly.

753 *Cumberland and Westmorland Herald, 1860–1960*. Penrith (then Cumberland): 1960.
The centenary number of an independent weekly.

754 *Cumberland and Westmorland Herald*. 125th birthday supplement. Penrith (Cumbria): 16 Nov 1985. Ed G.I. Hodgson.

755 *Cumberland News.* 175th anniversary number. Carlisle: 1990.
Published today as a weekly by Cumbrian Newspapers, this began as the *Carlisle Patriot* in 1815.

756 Cummings, A(rthur) J(ohn). *The Moscow trial.* London: Gollancz, 1933. 287pp.
A notable *News Chronicle* commentator writing on the 'spy trial' in Moscow of British engineers.

757 – – –. *The press and a changing civilisation.* London: John Lane The Bodley Head, 1936. xv + 139pp. (In the 20th Century Library.)
'The press in society: American, German and Russian as well as British'. Cummings, of the *News Chronicle*, matched Kingsley Martin as an influential commentator on the press as well as a distinguished contributor. Here he sees his 'beloved' world of journalism 'evolving into a simple dichotomy of socialists and anti-socialists'. He clearly feared the Right more than the fragmented Left, as World War II approached and his own Liberal Party dithered in the middle.

758 Cummings, Michael. *On the point of my pen: the best of Cummings.* Horndean (Hants): Milestone Publications, 1985. 240pp, incl 220 page-size cartoons.
A cartoon history from 1961. Comments on the current scene as depicted by Cummings of the *Daily Express* and *Sunday Express*. (The author is the son of A.J. Cummings.)

759 Cunningham, John. 'National daily newspapers and their circulations in the UK, 1908–1978'. *Journal of Advertising History*, 4, Feb 1981.
Marked the Golden Jubilee of the Audit Bureau of Circulations. A brief introduction, but with an excellent table of national mornings and London evenings.

760 – – –. 'Frees are jolly good business'. *The Guardian*, 1 Aug 1988.
On the *Daily News* (Birmingham), in particular, then in the vanguard of the success of the local free papers.

761 Curran, James. *Media, power and politics.* London: Routledge (in preparation). 240pp. (In Communication and Society series.)
Considers the radically new concerns of media research, under three main headings: media influence, media organizations, and media and society.

762 – – –, ed. *The British press: a manifesto.* London: Macmiilan, for Acton Society Press Group, 1978. viii + 339pp.
Essays, mainly critical of the Royal Commission on the Press, from a left-wing viewpoint. Curran's own contribution, 'Advertising and the press', argues that advertising pressures have increasingly shaped business news sections and similar features.

763 – – –. 'The press as an agency of social control: an historical perspective'. In *Newspaper history . . .*, G. Boyce *et al.* (q.v.).

764 – – –. 'Press freedom as a property right: the crisis of press legitimacy'. *Media, Culture and Society*, 1, 1, 1979.

765 – – –. 'The impact of advertising on the British mass media'. *Media, Culture and Society*, 3, 1, 1981.

766 – – –. 'Communications, power and social order'. In *Culture, media and society*, ed M. Gurevitch *et al.* London: Methuen, 1982.
Inter alia, covers the rise of the commercial press in the eighteenth and nineteenth centuries, and its role in the 'making of the middle class'.

767 Curran, James, and Michael Gurevitch, eds. *Mass media and society.* London: Edward Arnold, 1991.
Updated version of the following title. 3rd edn: Routledge, 1988. xi + 372pp; 4th edn: Routledge, 1991. 428pp.

768 Curran, James, Michael Gurevitch, and Janet Woollacott, eds. *Mass communication and society.* London: Edward Arnold, with the Open University, 1977; Beverly Hills (CA): Sage. 479pp.
Curran, in 'Capitalism and control of the press, 1800–1975', examines the changes in press structure which, he claims, led to a right-wing bias overall.

769 Curran, James, and Jane Seaton. *Power without responsibility: the press and broadcasting in Britain.* London: Fontana, 1981. 382pp. Revised edn: Methuen, 1985. xii + 396pp. 3rd edn: Routledge 1988. xi + 372pp; 4th edn: Routledge, 1991. 428pp.
Contains sections by Curran on the history of the press, press policy, the liberal theory of press freedom, and sociology. Extensive, with a detailed bibliography, but not remarkable for political balance.

770 Curran, James, Anthony Smith, and Pauline Wingate, eds. *Impacts and influences: essays on media power in the twentieth century.* London: Methuen, 1987.
Collection of essays on a wide variety of related topics – including the press barons then in the ascendant.

771 Curran, James, and Colin Sparks. 'Press and popular culture'. *Media, Culture and Society*, Apr 1991.
Major treatise on the entertainment factor – as opposed to news content – in the British press. Extensive bibliography.

772 Curtis, Liz. *Ireland: the propaganda war: the media and the 'battle for hearts and minds'.* London: Pluto, 1984. vii + 335pp.
'A damning indictment of a servile press': a polemic.

773 Curtis, Michael Howard. *The press.* London: News Chronicle, 1951. 68pp. (In the Background to the News series.)
By a future editor of the *News Chronicle*. A summary of useful general knowledge intended to accompany a reading of the daily news to schools and debating societies.

774 – – –. 'The fascinating story of the British press'. *World's Press News* (Coronation souvenir), 1 May 1953.

775 'D.C. Thomson'. *The Observer*, 18 May 1952.
Profile of the autocratic Scots publisher two years before his death, aged ninety-three:

'The citizens of Dundee have for long been as conscious of his existence as Edinburgh people are of the Castle looming over them.'

776 *'D' Notice System,* The. London: HMSO, 1967. Cmnd 3312.
A government White Paper, which dissents from the report published by the Committee of Privy Counsellors (q.v.). It continues to denounce the *Daily Express* for potential damage to the public interest when the paper ignored this advisory note system, issued periodically by the Government of the day.

777 Dahlgren, Peter, and Colin Sparks, eds. *Communication and citizenship: journalism and the public sphere.* London: Routledge, 1991; pbk, 1993. 256pp. (In Communication and Society series.)
How responsible (and successful) have been the press and television in educating the public on real issues?

778 *Daily Chronicle, The.* 20,000th issue. London: 12 Apr 1926.
The *Clerkenwell News and General Advertiser* was founded (as a weekly) in 1856, becoming in turn *The Clerkenwell News and London Times; The London Daily Chronicle and Clerkenwell News*; and *The Daily Chronicle*, 1872. Its national status stemmed from its purchase by Edward Lloyd in 1876, and thence the transfer to United Newspapers (Henry Dalziel, Lloyd George etc) in the Liberal interest in 1918. (Eventually in 1930 it merged with *The Daily News* to become the *News Chronicle*.)

779 *Daily Citizen: being the story of a great Labour newspaper.* London, [1915].
The *Daily Citizen* was launched with Trades Union Congress backing in 1912; it ceased three years later. The editor was Frank Dilnot.

780 Daily Express. *The end of the story, and other leaderettes from the Daily Express.* London: [1921]. 110pp.

781 – – –. *These tremendous years, 1919–1938.* London: Daily Express, 1938. 272pp.
While not marking any particular milestone in the eventful history of the *Express* itself, this is a popular survey of the inter-war years in typical *Express* style. (With Beaverbrook retaining the American-born editor, R.D. Blumenfeld, on his acquisition of the paper in 1916, it prospered under his very personal style of proprietorship and achieved its pinnacle with world record sales in the late 1930s under a youthful editor, Christiansen.)

782 – – –. *Twenty tremendous years, 1939–1961,* ed Paul Tabori. London: Express Books, 1961. 288pp.
An equally striking *'Express* treatment' of the next two decades.

783 *'Daily Express, The*: an interview with its editor, Mr D. Marks'. *Admap*, Apr 1970.
Derek Marks, the paper's outstanding parliamentary correspondent in the 1950s, was editor from 1965 to 1971.

784 Daily Graphic. *Twenty-one years' progress of the pioneer illustrated daily newspaper.* London: 4 Jan 1911 (supplement).
The *Daily Graphic* was established in 1890 by W.L. Thomas as the first successful

illustrated daily newspaper. It merged with the *Daily Sketch* in 1926, but the original title was revived by Kemsley (Gomer Berry) in 1946. The paper was then sold to Associated Newspapers (Rothermere) in 1952, in the following year reverting to the title *Daily Sketch.*

785   *Daily Jang, The.* Report on opening of new offices. London: 17 Jul 1992.
In 1992, *The Daily Jang* (in Urdu, 'Struggle') celebrated the twenty-first anniversary of publication of its London edition – the pioneer ethnic-language UK daily, with a weekly English section. The paper was founded in Delhi in 1937, but its head office has since moved to Karachi.

786   *Daily Mail.* 20th birthday number. London: 4 May 1916.
Includes 'The rise of the *Daily Mail*', by Lord Northcliffe (Alfred Harmsworth had become a peer in 1905). Preliminary issues of the *Daily Mail* started in February 1896, but the official launch of Harmsworth's 'penny newspaper for one halfpenny' was on 4 May. It has remained Associated Newspapers' 'flagship' ever since.

787   – – –.   25th birthday number. London: 4 May 1921. *See also* McKenzie, F.A.
Seven thousand guests attended Northcliffe's anniversary luncheon in Olympia, London.

788   – – –.   'Death of Viscount Northcliffe, the founder of the *Daily Mail*'. 15 Aug 1922.
(Northcliffe's brother Harold, 1st Viscount Rothermere, succeeded him as chief proprietor.)

789   Daily Mail. *Northcliffe House,* ed H.W. Wilson. 1927, 53pp.

790   *Daily Mail.* 10,000th issue. 12 May 1928.
Including an article by Rothermere.

791   – – –.   40th birthday number. 4 May 1936.

792   – – –.   Jubilee edn, 1896–1946. 4 May 1946.

793   Daily Mail. *News in our time, 1896–1947: Golden Jubilee book of the Daily Mail.* London: Associated Newspapers, [1946]. 176pp.
The most considerable 'spin-off' of the many excellent commemoratives from the *Daily Mail,* this graphically portrays the march of British and world history.

794   – – –.   *Turn of the century: 1900–1950: the story of fifty tremendous years,* ed Frank Owen. 1950. 48pp.

795   Daily Mail & General Trust/Associated Newspapers. In *The press and the people, 1967/1968.* Press Council Annual Report.

796   'Daily Mail starts colour'. *World's Press News,* 1 Jun 1933.

797   Daily Mirror. *The romance of the Daily Mirror (1903–1924).* London: 1924.
'An illustrated record of the enterprise of the *Daily Mirror* in the twenty-one years of

its eventful career'. That career had begun with a nearly disastrous start, when Alfred Harmsworth (later Northcliffe) launched 'the first daily newspaper for gentlewomen' on 2 November 1903. The first Lord Rothermere – who provided the foreword to this publication – took over control from his brother in 1914. (Eventually, in 1984, Mirror Group Newspapers – also comprising the *Sunday Mirror, Sunday People, Daily Record* (Glasgow) etc – was acquired from Reed International by Robert Maxwell; after his death, a major reconstruction took place.)

798 *Daily Mirror.* '90 years young'. 2 Nov 1993.
Souvenir supplement, featuring historic front pages.

799 Daily News, The. *Strike fortnight: a diary.* 1926. 32pp.
Editorial leaders that did not appear during the General Strike.

800 *Daily News, The.* 25,000th issue. 26 May 1926.

801 – – –. Special amalgamation issue (*Daily News* and *Westminster Gazette*). 1 Feb 1928.
The Daily News was born on 21 January 1846 under the very short-lived editorship of Charles Dickens. After this faltering start, it became and remained a popular national paper in the Liberal tradition until merged into the *News Chronicle* in 1930.

802 *Daily Telegraph, The.* Jubilee number. 17 Sep 1905.
In the late nineteenth century and at the time of this fiftieth anniversary, the *Telegraph* was directed by Edward Levy-Lawson (1st Baron Burnham).

803 Daily Telegraph, The. *An Englishman looks at his newspapers.* [1930].
A promotion item.

804 *Daily Telegraph, The.* '75 years of progress' (supplement). 5 Nov 1930.

805 – – –. 'A century in Fleet Street'. 29 Jun 1955.

806 Daily Telegraph, The. *Our first 100 years.* 1955. 96pp.
Recounts an outstanding event in each year of the paper's history. Illustrated.

807 – – –. *125 years in words and pictures as described in contemporary reports in The Daily Telegraph,* 1855–1980. 1980. 111pp.
Updated and more elaborate than the centenary 'special' of twenty-five years previously.

808 *Daily Telegraph, The. Telegraph*: on the move to a great future. (Extra: 8pp). 3 Mar 1986.
'Trailer' for the fully photocomposed paper to emerge from London's Docklands as well as Manchester.

809 – – –. (Souvenir of 47 years in Manchester). Manchester: 14 Sep 1987.
With reminiscences by Michael Kennedy, Northern editor, 1960–86.

810 – – –. '50 years ago: *The Morning Post*'. London: 30 Sep 1987.
Reprint of H.A. Gwynne's 'Farewell and hail!' published in the last issue of that newspaper before its absorption in *The Daily Telegraph.*

811   Daily Telegraph, The. *The Daily Telegraph record of the Second World War: month by month from 1939 to 1945.* London: Sidgwick & Jackson, in association with The Daily Telegraph, 1989. 208pp. Introduction by Max Hastings; afterword by John Keegan. Ed Hugh (Montgomery-) Massingberd.

812   *Daily Telegraph, The/The Sunday Telegraph.* The Telegraph plc, 1993. 28pp. 'The Telegraph information pack' booklet, outlining both history and the current scene.

813   Daily Worker. *The Daily Worker at war.* London: 1941.
Established in 1930, the Communist *Daily Worker* was suppressed under Defence Regulations in the year of this publication.

813A   *Daily Worker.* '25 fighting years'. Silver Jubilee number, 1955.

814   Dalrymple, James, and Alan Ruddock. 'Blood on the Mirror'. *The Sunday Times*, 22 Nov 1992.
The upheaval in the management and editors at Mirror Group Newspapers.

815   Darby, John. *Dressed to kill: cartoonists and the Northern Ireland conflict.* Belfast: Appletree Press, 1983.

816   Dark, Sidney Ernest. *The life of Sir Arthur Pearson Bt., G.B.E.* London: Hodder & Stoughton, 1922. vii + 228pp.
'Newspaper proprietor, and founder of the St. Dunstan's hostel for soldiers and sailors blinded in the Great War 1914–1918'. This standard biography relates how in the former capacity (Cyril) Arthur Pearson (1866–1921) launched the highly successful *Pearson's Weekly* – 'to interest, to elevate, to amuse' – in 1890. He followed it with *Pearson's Magazine* and a string of other periodicals, and entered national newspapers by purchasing the *Morning Herald*, which in 1900 developed into the *Daily Express*.

817   – – –.   *Not such a bad life.* London: Eyre & Spottiswoode, 1941. 317pp.
Dark worked mainly for the *Daily Mail*, then *Daily Express*.

818   *Darlington and Stockton Times.* Centenary, 1847–1947. Darlington (Co Durham): 1947.

819   Darlow, Thomas Herbert. *William Robertson Nicoll: life and letters.* London: Hodder & Stoughton, 1925. iv + 475pp.
Concentrates largely on Nicoll's editorship of the *British Weekly*, although it has some mention of his long-running gossip column for *The Sketch*.

820   Darracott, Joseph, comp. A *cartoon war.* London: Leo Cooper, 1989.
Traces the major cartoonists' work in World War II, covering each theatre in turn.

821   Darwin, Bernard (Richard Meirion). *Mostly golf: a Bernard Darwin anthology.* London: A. & C. Black, 1976. xv + 198pp. Ed Peter Ryde.
'There were writers on sport before him whom he was the first to acknowledge, but no writer for a daily paper had noticeably trodden the path of eminence before.' Darwin was golf correspondent for *The Times* for forty-six years.

822   Davenport, Nicholas. *Memoirs of a City radical*. London: Weidenfeld & Nicolson, 1974.
Much here on financial journalism.

823   Davenport-Hines, Richard P.T. 'Dalziel, Davison Alexander, 1st Lord Dalziel of Wooler'. *In* David J. Jeremy, ed. *Dictionary of business biography*, Vol 2. London: Butterworth, for the Business History Unit, London School of Economics, 1984.
Davison Dalziel founded Dalziel's News Agency (1895), and in the Unionist interest acquired *The Standard* (1910) and *The Pall Mall Gazette* (1915).

824   – – –.   'Getting away with Murdoch'. *The Tatler*, Jul 1992.

825   'David Low'. *Picture Post*, 22 Oct 1938.
A tribute to the cartoonist, then at the height of his powers and fame.

826   Davids, James. 'Sunday goliaths beware'. *UK Press Gazette*, 13 Mar 1989.
The attractive design of the new *Wales on Sunday*.

827   Davidson, Andrew, 'Conrad goes global'. *The Sunday Times*, 22 Dec 1991.
How Conrad Black, the latest in the line of Canadian media moguls, took control of the ailing *Daily Telegraph* and *Sunday Telegraph* at a bargain price – and has since extended his interests internationally.

828   Davidson, John. *Fleet Street, and other poems*. London: Grant Richards, 1909. 148pp.

829   Davidson, Michael. *The world, the flesh and myself*. London: Arthur Barker, [1962]. 354pp.
The journalism is to a degree secondary in this memoir – but there is valuable material on his time as a correspondent for *The Observer* etc in the Middle and Far East in the early post-World War II years.

830   Davie, Michael. 'Shah of Pimlico takes on Fleet Street'. *The Observer*, 24 Nov 1985.
Profile of Eddy Shah – preparing to launch his national newspaper, *Today* – and his background.

831   Davies, Dido. *William Gerhardie: a biography*. Oxford: Oxford University Press, 1990. 384pp.
Gerhardi – then without the final 'e' – was a literary protégé of Beaverbrook; this book provides excellent source-material.

832   [Davies, Edward W.] *Newspaper Society, 1836–1936: a centenary retrospect: See entry 2439.*

833   Davies, Edward W. 'The Press Association in action'. *In The press, 1898–1948. (The Newspaper World Golden Jubilee)*. London: Benn, 1948.
Davies was then general manager of the PA.

834   Davies, Nicholas. *The unknown Maxwell.* London: Sidgwick & Jackson, 1992; Pan, 1993. vi + 346pp.
On the man rather than his business affairs or publications. Davies includes much on the planning, and eventual launch in 1990, of *The European.* 'The weekly newspaper for Europe' was indeed 'Maxwell's greatest project' and, although restricted in international readership because of being entirely in English, is a continuing memorial to his more admirable ambitions.

835   Davies, Picton. *Atgofiom dyn papyr newydd.* Liverpool: Hugh Evans, 1962.
The author's experience covered the conservative English-language *Western Mail* in Cardiff and the radical Welsh-language *Y Genedl (The Nation)* in Caernarfon.

836   Davies, Russell, and Liz Ottaway. *Vicky.* London: Seeker & Warburg, 1987. xxii + 197pp.
A sumptuous biography, published to coincide with a memorial exhibition to 'Vicky' (real name, Victor Weisz, 1913–66), 'the best-loved and most fiercely-hated cartoonist of his time'. Ottaway writes from the Centre for Cartoons and Caricature (University of Kent), holding about 3,400 Vicky originals. Michael Foot contributes a personal memoir.

837   Davis, Anthony. *Working in journalism.* London: Batsford, 1979.

838   Davis, Richard. 'Northern Ireland political papers and the Troubles, 1966–1990'. *In* Alan O'Day and Yonah Alexander, eds. *Ireland's terrorist experience.* Aldershot (Hants): Avebury, 1991.

839   Dawn, A.F. *A history of freedom of speech and the press in England since 1900.* London: University of London (London School of Economics), 1933 (MSc Econ thesis).

840   Dawson, John D'Arcy. *Tunisian battle.* London: Macdonald, 1943. 251pp.

841   – – –.   *European victory.* London: Macdonald, [1945]. 259pp.
By a war correspondent for Kemsley Newspapers.

842   Dawson, Thomas. *The law of the press.* London: Staples, 1927, 1947. xxiii + 222pp.

843   Day, Kenneth. *The typography of press advertising: a practical survey of principles and their application.* London: Benn, 1956. 304pp.

844   'Day in two centuries, A'. *The Times,* 24 Jun 1974.
Described in *The Times* official history as 'an Olympian leader' – published in the first issue from Gray's Inn Road.

845   *D-Day to victory.* With an introduction by Wynford Vaughan-Thomas. London: Collins, 1984.
Marking the fortieth anniversary of the D-Day landings in France. Facsimiles of British, US and Services newspapers of June 1944, selected from the John Frost Collection.

846   de Vries, Leonard, ed. *Panorama 1842–1865: the world of the early Victorians through the eyes of The Illustrated London News*. London: John Murray, 1967.

847   *Deacon's Newspaper Handbook and Advertisers' Guide*. London: Samuel Deacon & Co, 1863-1904 (intermittent).
'London, provincial, colonial, and foreign'. Useful source for circulation figures.

848   Deakin, Phyllis. *Press on*. Worthing (W Sussex): H.E. Walter, 1984. 124pp.
Retrospective history of the Women's Press Club of London, set up in the war (1944) with the author as first chairman. It continued until 1972.
   Deakin was a pioneer woman reporter on *The Times* – serving as a war correspondent in World War II – and remains a vice-president of the Society of Woman Writers and Journalists.

849   Dean, Brenda *(Baroness)*. 'Reflecting on fighting impossible odds'. *The New Statesman*, 19 Feb 1987.
As general secretary of SOGAT (the first woman to hold such a position in a major trade union), Dean played a leading role in the eventually unsuccessful battle by the printing unions against News International when that company moved to Wapping (1986–7).

850   Dean, Edward J. *Lucky Dean: reminiscences of a press photographer*. London: Robert Hale, 1944. 208pp.
The author was 'Dixie' Dean of the *Daily Mirror*.

851   *Dean Forest Guardian*. Centenary number. Coleford (Glos): 5 Jul 1974.

852   Deedes, William Francis *(Baron)*. 'A chapter of excellence'. *The Daily Telegraph*, 1 Sep 1987.
Tribute to Lord Hartwell on his retirement as editor-in-chief, by the former editor.

853   – – –.   'Is there still a point in keeping a watchdog with no teeth?'. *The Daily Telegraph*, 26 Oct 1988.
On the Press Council: he answers the question with a firm affirmative: there is, he avers, no alternative.

854   Deeley, Peter, and Christopher Walker. *Murder in the Fourth Estate: an investigation into the roles of the press and police in the McKay case*. London: Gollancz, 1971.
The full story by two *Observer* reporters of the tragic case in 1969–70 when Mrs McKay, wife of the deputy to Rupert Murdoch, was kidnapped (by mistake for Mrs Murdoch); arrests were made and sentence passed, but the body was never found. Deeley and Walker offer some possibly unjustified criticism of the part played by the press during the search and fruitless negotiations.

855   Delano, Anthony. *Slip-up: how Fleet Street caught Ronnie Biggs and Scotland Yard lost him: the story behind the scoop*. London: André Deutsch; New York: Quadrangle/New York Times, 1977. 174pp; revised London: Coronet, 1986.
Biggs, one of the ringleaders in the 'Great Train Robbery', was hunted down in Brazil by reporters of the *Daily Express*, with the *Daily Mail* also on the spot.

856   Deli, P. 'The image of the Russian purges in the *Daily Herald* and the *New Statesman*'. *Journal of Contemporary History*, 20, 1985.

857   Delmer, [Denis] Sefton. *Trail sinister* (an autobiography, Vol 1). London: Secker & Warburg, 1961. 423pp.

858   – – –.   *Black boomerang* (an autobiography, Vol 2). London: Secker & Warburg, 1962. 320pp.
Delmer was a notable *Daily Express* correspondent from the 1930s, who returned to Berlin after having been engaged in wartime 'black' propaganda – hence the title of his second volume.

859   Demarest, Kathy K. 'Royal Press Office – public service or public relations?'. *Journalism Studies Review*, 1980.

860   'Demon barber of Devil's Island'. *The Guardian*, 9 Oct 1989.
Profile of Conrad Black, new owner of the Telegraph group.

861   Dempster, Nigel, and Peter Evans. *Behind palace doors*. London: Orion, 1993.
Cashing in on the current troubles of the Royal Family, and public fascination, the *Daily Mail's* ace diarist (Dempster) collaborates in disclosures that owe much to invented dialogue.

862   *Denbighshire Free Press*. Special centenary edition. Denbigh (Clywd): 24 Jun 1981.
Weekly in the North Wales Newspapers group: originally *Vale of Clywd Free Press*.

863   Denison, Guy Melville. *The Evening Post: the story of a newspaper and a family*. Nottingham: T. Bailey Forman, 1978.
The centenary of a leading regional evening, which remained in family ownership until (subject to Monopolies and Mergers Commission approval) joining Northcliffe Newspapers in 1994.

864   Denniston, Robin Alastair, and (*Sir*) Denis Hamilton. 'Thomson, Roy Herbert, 1st Baron Thomson of Fleet'. In *Dictionary of national biography, 1971–1980*. Oxford: Oxford University Press, 1986.

865   Department of National Heritage. *Press regulation and privacy*. White Paper; publication expected 1994.

866   *Derby Evening Telegraph*. Centenary supplement. Jul 1979.
Today, a title in the Northcliffe Newspapers group. It was the result of a merger in 1932 between the *Derby Daily Telegraph* and the *Derby Daily Express*.

867   Derbyshire County Council. *Local newspapers in Derbyshire*. Derby: Derbyshire Library Service, 1984.

868   *Dereham and Fakenham Times*. Centenary issue. North Dereham (Norfolk): 8 Feb 1980.
An Eastern Counties Newspapers group weekly.

869 Desmond, Raymond George Coulter. *Our local press.* Walthamstow (London): Walthamstow Antiquarian Society, 1955. 82pp.
Detail on the newspapers of south-west Essex.

870 Devon, Stanley. *'Glorious': the life-story of Stanley Devon.* London: Harrap, 1957. 233pp.
Illustrated with some of the outstanding pictures by the Kemsley group's chief photographer; many appeared in Kemsley's national pictorial 'flagship', the *Daily Sketch* (intermittently, *Daily Graphic*).

871 *Devon and Exeter Daily Gazette.* Anniversary number. Exeter: 5 Mar 1910.
The paper at this time claimed '138 years' uninterrupted existence, 25 years in the present ownership'. The traditional date for the foundation of the original *Exeter Gazette* is 1772; it became *Woolmer's Exeter and Plymouth Gazette*.

872 *'Devon and Exeter Gazette'.* The Newspaper World, 9 Sep 1939. (In The Oldest Newspapers series.)

873 Diamond, John. 'This editor is dressed to kill'. *The Guardian (Media Guardian)*, 8 Mar 1993.
On Eve Pollard – as editor of the hitherto moribund *Sunday Express* fighting off, spiritedly and professionally, the challenge of *The Mail on Sunday*.

874 Dibblee, G. Binney. *The newspaper.* London: Williams & Norgate, 1912. 256pp. New York: Henry Holt, 1913. 256pp. (In the Home University Library of Modern Knowledge.)
Covers the UK, the USA and continental Europe. By the one-time manager of *The Manchester Guardian*.

875 – – –. 'The printing trades and the crisis in British industry'. *The Economic Journal*, Mar 1902.
Refers to an important article in *The Times*, 1 Dec 1901.

876 Dicey, Edward James Stephen. 'Journalism new and old'. *The Fortnightly Review*, 83, 1905.
Dicey (1832–1911), in tracing a century of the British press, was able to call on experience also of two national editorships: *The Daily News* (briefly) and *The Observer* (for nineteen years). He also became a recognized authority on the British Constitution.

877 Dick, Jill. *Freelance writing for newspapers.* London: A. & C. Black, 1991. 166pp.

878 Dickens, Monica (Enid). *My turn to make the tea.* London: Michael Joseph, 1953. 224pp. Harmondsworth (Middx): Penguin (with Joseph), 1962. 221pp. London: Heinemann, 1978.
This humorously embellished account of the author's early days as a provincial reporter is just one of the several bestsellers from this great-granddaughter of Charles Dickens; her principal employer was the *Sunday Chronicle*.

879   Dickinson, Mark. *To break a union: the Messenger, the State and the NGA*. Manchester: Booklist, 1984. 208pp.
Critical account of the success of Eddy Shah of the Messenger group in publishing at Warrington against violent opposition from the National Graphical Association and other trade union elements; this led to the largest fine in legal history.

880   Dillon, Emile Joseph. *Leaves from life*. London: Dent, 1932. ix + 243pp.
By the mystery-enshrouded correspondent in Russia (etc) for *The Daily Telegraph* from 1887 to 1914, described by Stead as 'far and away the ablest, most cultured and most adventurous newspaperman I have ever met'. Dillon could speak twenty-six languages and write leaders in five.

881   Dilnot, Frank Buckland. *The adventures of a newspaper man*. London: Smith, Elder, 1913. 315pp.
The author is primarily remembered as editor of the first Labour daily, the *Daily Citizen* (1912–15). He was also war correspondent for the *Daily Chronicle*, and a 'special' for the *Daily Express* and *Daily Mail*. The book provides many anecdotes as he wanders over Europe in that Edwardian sunset before World War I.

882   *Directory of British Journalism, The*. London: Strand Publications, 1971, 1972; Industrial Newspapers, 1974.

883   *District Advertiser*. 5,000th issue. Cheadle (Cheshire): 12 Feb 1993.
Weekly, now free, which was founded in 1889.

884   Divine, A[rthur] D[urham]. *Road to Tunis*. London: Collins, 1944; New York: 1944 (under the pseudonym of David Rame).

885   – – –.   *Divine truth*. London: Faber, 1945.
The author was a South African-born war correspondent, later defence correspondent, for *The Sunday Times* and other papers in the then Kemsley group.

886   Dixey, John. 'How new technology is transforming Fleet Street'. *Admap*, Oct 1984.
A good state-of-the-art survey.

887   Dobson, Christopher. *The freelance journalist: how to survive and succeed*. Oxford: Butterworth-Heinemann, 1992. 180pp.

888   Dobson, Robert M.H. *Final night: a record of the last days of the Morning Post as a separate journal*. Uxbridge (Middx): King & Hutchings, 1938. 58pp.

889   Dodge, John, and George Viner, eds. *The practice of journalism*. London: Heinemann, 1963. 351pp.
A now dated textbook, produced under the auspices of both the National Council for the Training of Journalists and the National Union of Journalists; sixteen anecdotal contributions.

890   Donald, *Sir* Robert, comp. *The Imperial Press Conference in Canada*. With a foreword by Viscount Burnham. xvi + 296pp. London: Hodder & Stoughton, 1921.

Staged at Ottawa in 1920, the conference referred to in the title was the Empire Press Union's first post-World War I conference: Donald, a leading press figure of the period, was chairman.

891 – – –. 'New forces in journalism'. In *Sell's World's Press, 1921*. London: Sell, 1921.

892 *Doncaster Gazette*. 150th birthday. Doncaster (now S Yorks): 15 Oct 1936.

893 *Dorking Advertiser*. Centenary souvenir. Dorking (Surrey): Feb 1987.
Today a Trinity International weekly.

894 Douglas, James. *Down Shoe Lane*. London: Herbert Joseph, 1930.
An ex-editor of both *The Star* and the *Sunday Express* tells his story.

895 Douglas, Roy. *The World War, 1939–1945: the cartoonists' vision*. London: Routledge, 1990.
Black-and-white reproductions from the press – mainly on the Allied side.

896 – – –. *Between the wars, 1919–1939: the cartoonists' vision*. London Routledge, 1992. xi + 353pp.
Two uneasy decades in international affairs, as illustrated by a generation of outstanding political cartoonists (but about whom, regrettably, little is vouchsafed).

897 – – –. *'Great nations still enchained': the cartoonists' view of empire, 1848–1914*. London: Routledge, 1993. ix + 221pp.
Like its predecessors, strong on history and commentary; but on the cartoonists themselves, weak – in fact, quite silent.

898 Douglas, Torin. 'Free sheets shed their Cinderella status'. *The Times*, 7 Jun 1983.

899 Douglas-Home, (*Hon*) Charles (Cospatrick). *No end of a lesson*. London: Alliance Publishers (for the Institute for European Defence and Strategic Studies), 1986. Foreword by Rupert Murdoch.
Leaders from the editor of *The Times*.

900 Doull, Matthew. 'Nightmare on Fleet Street: price war threatens profits and jobs at national newspapers as *Times* slashes cover price'. *The Daily Telegraph*, 4 Sep 1993.
Early comments on the effect of the drastic reductions by Murdoch's News International.

901 *Down Recorder*. 150th anniversary supplement. Downpatrick (Northern Ireland): 1986.
The then *Downpatrick Recorder* was founded in 1836.

902 Downing, J.D.H. *Some aspects of the presentation of industrial relations and race relations in some major British news media*. London: University of London, 1975 (PhD thesis).

903   Downing, John. 'The final chapter'. *UK Press Gazette*, 10 Apr 1989.
A senior photographer's nostalgic retrospect over twenty-five years in Fleet Street, as his newspaper, the *Daily Express*, joins the exodus. The article is illustrated by a group photo of the sixty staff photographers with the *Express* in April 1960 – sixty years after the paper's launch under that title.

904   Drake, P. 'The *Town Crier*, Birmingham's labour weekly, 1919–1951'. *In* A. Wright and R. Shackleton, eds. *Worlds of labour: essays in Birmingham labour history*. Birmingham: University of Birmingham/WEA, 1983.

905   Draper, Alfred. *Scoops and swindles: memoirs of a Fleet Street journalist*. London: Buchan & Enright, 1987. 310pp.
Crime reporter with the *Daily Express* etc who eventually left the field when the end of capital punishment destroyed much of the drama in murder cases.

906   Drawbell, James Wedgwood. *James Drawbell, an autobiography*. New York: Pantheon, 1964. 383pp. Published in the UK as *Time on my hands*. London: Macdonald, 1968.
Covers, in somewhat egoistical terms, the author's career as editor of *The Sunday Chronicle* and managing editor and consultant for the George Newnes group – notably *Woman's Own*. Drawbell describes his happy youth in Scotland, army service in World War I, and life as a working journalist in Scotland, Canada, the USA and Britain.

907   – – –.   'How the press caters for women's interests'. In *The press: 1898–1948* (*The Newspaper World* Golden Jubilee). London: Benn, 1948.

908   Dreyfus, John. 'The impact of Stanley Morison'. In *The Penrose Annual, 1969*.
Illustrates his work, not only for *The Times* but also for four other nationals.

909   Driberg, Tom (Thomas Edward Neil Driberg, *Baron* Bradwell). *Colonnade*. London: Pilot Press, 1949.
A collection of Driberg's contributions as the first 'William Hickey' columnist of the *Daily Express*.

910   – – –.   *The best of both worlds: a personal diary*. London: Phoenix House, 1953.
The 'two worlds' of the title are politics and journalism; in the former capacity, Driberg was a leading Member of Parliament.

911   – – –.   *Beaverbrook: a study in power and frustration*. London: Weidenfeld & Nicolson, 1956. viii + 323pp.
A close-up – and far from flattering – pen-portrait.

912   – – –.   *'Swaff': the life and times of Hannen Swaffer*. London: Macdonald, 1974. xi + 284pp.
A focal Fleet Street personality of this century, Swaffer (1879–1962) was with Northcliffe in the early days of the *Daily Mirror* and *Daily Mail*, then with the *Daily Sketch*, *Daily*

Graphic, Daily Express (where he was drama critic), *Weekly Dispatch* and *The People* (he was editor of both), and most notably gossip columnist of the *Daily Herald* for thirty years. Driberg immediately brings Swaffer to life: 'Any day or evening in the 1930s, 1940s, or 1950s a tall, cadaverous elderly man could be seen strolling, or rather stalking meditatively . . . His antiquated black clothes, a floppy black tie or stock, a black hat as rusty as the rest of his gear, a fag-end, nearly finished, drooping from his mouth . . .'

913 Drogheda, (Charles) Garrett (Ponsonby) Moore, *11th Earl of. Double harness: memoirs*. London: Weidenfeld & Nicolson, 1978. xi + 387pp.
The 'press' part of the author's 'double' career led to his chairmanship of the *Financial Times*.

914 Duguid, Charles. *How to read the money article*. London: Effingham Wilson, 1901; 6th edn revised F.W.H. Caudwell, 1931; 7th edn, by W. Collin Brooks. London: Pitman, 1936. xiv + 144pp.
Duguid was a pioneer financial writer, and when he wrote this book was City editor of *The Westminster Gazette*; he later had similar appointments with *The Morning Post* and the *Daily Mail* (and simultaneously for *The Observer*). In his interesting preface to the 1936 edition, Brooks (himself then the City editor of the *Sunday Dispatch*) pays tribute both to Duguid's 'talent for simple exposition of tangled subjects' and to 'this unassuming little book' as 'a standard elementary work'.

915 *Dumfries and Galloway Standard*. 150th anniversary supplement. Dumfries: Apr 1993.
A weekly in the Trinity International group.

916 Duncan, P.D. *Newspaper science: the presentation of science in four British newspapers during the interwar years, 1919–1939*. Brighton: University of Sussex, 1980 (thesis). 260pp.

917 Duncum, A. Philip, ed. *The Westminster Press provincial newspapers*. London: Westminster Press, 1952. ix + 84pp.
Originally known as the Starmer Group (Sir Charles Starmer being chairman at the time), the Westminster Press group took its new title from *The Westminster Gazette* when that became a morning paper (in 1921). Since the latter was merged into *The Daily News*, the Westminster Press has had no nationals, but has developed a large list of regionals. It is a subsidiary today of the Pearson enterprise. Duncum has since written an (unpublished) history to 1973.

918 Dunfermline Press. *Centenary souvenir 1859–1959: one hundred years of news in Dunfermline and West Fife*, ed J.A. Romanes. Dunfermline: 21 Apr 1959.
Today, a weekly in the Clyde and Forth group.

919 Dunlop, Andrew. *Fifty years of Irish journalism*. Dublin: Hanna & Neale, 1911. 304pp.

920 Dunn, Cyril, comp. *Shouts and murmurs: a selection from The Observer*, 1962–3. London: Hodder & Stoughton, 1963. 319pp.

921 — — —. *The Observer revisited, 1963-4.* London: Hodder & Stoughton, 1964. 256pp.

922 Dunn, James. *Paperchase: adventures in and out of Fleet Street.* London: Selwyn & Blount, [1938]. 279pp; Ryerson Press, 1939.
'Jimmie' Dunn was a popular columnist for the *Daily Mail.*

923 Dunn, Philip. *Press photography.* Sparkford (Somerset): Oxford Illustrated Press, 1988.
With contributions on most aspects of the 'state of the art'.

924 Dunnett, Alastair (MacTavish). *Among friends: an autobiography.* London: Century Press, 1984. 234pp.
'I have a covenant with Scotland' . . . the prevailing sentiment of this success story by the former editor of Glasgow's *Daily Record* (1946–55) and *The Scotsman* (1956–72).

925 Dunnett, Peter J.S. *The world newspaper industry.* New York and London (Beckenham): Croom Helm, 1987. xi + 275pp.
This Canadian academic author includes a forty-page chapter on the industry in the UK, with copious statistics.

926 *Dunstable Gazette.* 125th anniversary souvenir. Dunstable (Beds): Feb 1990.
In the Home Counties Newspapers group.

927 *Durham County Advertiser.* 150th birthday number, 1814–1964. Durham: 11 Sep 1964.
The paper became the *Durham Advertiser* – a weekly in the Westminster Press group.

928 Dutt, R(ajani) Palme. *The rise and fall of the Daily Herald.* London: Labour Monthly/Daily Worker, 1964. 17pp.
Palme Dutt was the editor of *Labour Monthly* and *Workers' Weekly* twenty years and more before.

929 Dyas, Eamon. 'The early development of the Newspaper Library'. *British Library Newspaper Library Newsletter*, 10, Jun 1989.

930 — — —. 'Hidden collections at the Newspaper Library'. *British Library Newspaper Library Newsletter*, 11, Jul 1990.
Both based on a talk at the British Library, 29 Mar 1988. The second instalment ventilates the problem of defining a newspaper.

931 — — —. 'Newspapers as source material for women's studies, 1830s–1930s'. In *Women's Studies.* London: British Library, 1990.

932 — — —. 'Variant editions of the national press'. *British Library Newspaper Library Newsletter*, 14, Autumn 1992; 15, Spring 1993.
Valuable material on weekly, regional and other versions of the nationals.

933 Dyfed County Council. *A guide to local newspapers in Dyfed.* Haverfordwest: Dyfed CC, [n.d.].
Covers the area of the former Cardiganshire, Carmarthenshire and Pembrokeshire.

934   'Dynamic days in Fleet Street's Royal Family'. *The Times*, 20 Feb 1981.
To mark Cecil King's eightieth birthday.

935   Dyson, Will [William Henry]. *Cartoons*. London: Daily Herald, 1913, 1914.
Dyson, Australian-born, was chief cartoonist for the *Daily Herald* 1913–25 and 1931–8.
Although therefore the examples published here are from early in his career, they are
representative of his remarkable genius in expressing an angry radical viewpoint.

936   – – –.   *Willl Dyson's war cartoons*. London: Hodder & Stoughton, 1916.

937   Eade, Charles, ed. *Churchill, by his contemporaries*. London: Hutchinson,
1953. 528pp.
Includes essays on Winston Churchill as war correspondent (by G. Ward Price), journalist (by Colin Coote), biographer and historian (by Malcolm Muggeridge), broadcaster
(by Richard Dimbleby), and editor (by Beric Holt). The last-named recounts how
Churchill has his place in newspaper history as editor of *The British Gazette* during the
General Strike (1926).

938   Eagle, Selwyn, ed. *Information sources for the press and broadcast media*.
Borough Green (Kent): Bowker-Saur, 1991.
International content.

939   *East Anglian Daily Times*. Jubilee souvenir, 1874–1924. Ipswich: 13 Oct
1924.
Originally this paper was the *Ipswich Times*. It is now in the Eastern Counties
Newspapers group.

940   East Anglian Daily Times. *Souvenir of the inauguration of the new press*. 28
Feb 1936.
Includes an article entitled 'Some early provincial newspapers'.

941   *East Anglian Daily Times*. Centenary supplement, 1874–1974. 14 Oct 1974.

942   *East Hampshire Post*. Centenary issue, 1883–1983. Petersfield (Hants): 7
Sep 1983.
Weekly in Portsmouth and Sunderland Newspapers group – originally *Petersfield Weekly
News*.

943   *East Kent Times*. Centenary supplement, 1866–1966. Ramsgate: 1966.

944   *Eastbourne Gazette*. 125th anniversary supplement. Eastbourne (E Sussex):
11 Jul 1984.
Now a Johnston Press title.

945   *Eastern Evening News*. Centenary supplement. Norwich: 4 Jan 1982.
History of the first evening paper in East Anglia, now part of the Eastern Counties group.

946   *Eccles and Patricroft Journal*. Centenary supplement, 1874–1974.
Eccles (Greater Manchester): 31 Jan 1974.

947   No entry.

948   Eckert, Vera. *Sisters doing it for themselves?: women in the national press.* London: City University, 1987 (MA thesis).

949   Economist, The. *Echoes: 150 Economist years.* London: 1993. Promotion booklet.

950   *Economist, The.* 150th anniversary number. 5 Sep 1993.
Covering a world stage from their London base, two editors of this weekly journal are seen to have dominated its twentieth-century history: Walter Layton and Geoffrey Crowther. Both became chairman (and were raised to the peerage).

951   – – –. The future surveyed: an anniversary supplement. 11–17 Sep 1993.
Unusually, an anniversary marked by distinguished contributors being commissioned to look *forward* 150 years.

952   Economist Intelligence Unit. *The national newspaper industry: a survey.* With an introduction by Lord Devlin (as chairman of the Joint Board for the National Newspaper Industry). London: EIU, 1966.
Sections of this major commissioned publication – commonly known as the Devlin Report – are devoted to management, production, finance, trade unions, social benefits, newsprint. It is detailed, and pulls no punches.

953   *Economist Pocket Style Book, The.* London: Economist Publications, 1986. Reissued as *The Economist Style Guide.* Economist, 1991; Hamish Hamilton, 1993.
A staff style book published for an interested outside readership also.

954   Eddy, Paul, Magnus Linklater, and Peter Gillman. *The Falklands War.* London: André Deutsch, 1982. 274pp.
Reportage by *The Sunday Times* Insight Team, including interviews after the event. Analyses the political factors very acutely.

955   Eddy, Paul, Elaine Potter, and Bruce Page. *Deadline disaster.* London: Hart-Davis, 1976. x + 435pp.
The Sunday Times Insight Team investigates the DC-10 crash near Paris in 1974.

956   Edelman, [Israel] Maurice. *The Mirror: a political history.* London: Hamish Hamilton, 1966. 221pp.
Edelman was a Fleet Street journalist and war correspondent before entering Parliament and writing several successful novels with a parliamentary background. However, this is a disappointing 'official' treatment by an ex-*Mirror* man, narrow as well as superficial. It almost completely ignores the early experimental days of the famous tabloid.

957   Edgar, Donald. *Express '56: a year in the life of a Beaverbrook journalist.* London: John Clare, 1981. 179pp.

Published long after Edgar had experienced the year in question (Christiansen's final year as editor.)

958 – – –. *My years of fame as William Hickey.* London: John Clare, 1989. Extracts from his Hickey column in the *Daily Express* in 1953–4.

959 'Edgar Wallace, reporter'. *World's Press News*, 18 Feb 1932. An obituary tribute.

960 *Edinburgh Evening News, The. 1873–1923.* Edinburgh: 1923. 33pp. An associate of *The Scotsman* in the Thomson Regional group since 1963.

961 Edwards, Robert (John). *Goodbye Fleet Street.* London: Cape, 1988; Coronet, 1989. xi + 260pp. By the former editor of the *Daily Express* (twice), *Sunday People*, and *Sunday Mirror* (for a record thirteen years). Edwards ranks as a great survivor of the Beaverbrook era, but opted out when the Mirror group was taken over by Maxwell: 'a character, and at least that is in the best and worst traditions of Fleet Street'.

962 – – –. 'Tabloid responsibility put in perspective'. *UK Press Gazette*, 27 Jun 1988. (Cleaning Up the 4th Estate series.)

963 Edwards, Ruth Dudley. *The pursuit of reason: The Economist, 1843–1993.* London: Hamish Hamilton, 1993. xix + 1,020pp. Finely crafted history to mark the 150th anniversary. The author has made the best of a rich interwoven tapestry of characters and journalism – not least during an eventful twentieth century.

964 Einzig, Paul. *In the centre of things: the autobiography of Paul Einzig.* London: Hutchinson, 1960. 319pp. Einzig was not only foreign editor of *The Financial News* (1922–45), but also was closely concerned with the negotiations that led to its merger with the *Financial Times*. This memoir is a valuable source-book on the financial journalism of the time.

965 Eldridge, John, ed. *Getting the message: news, truth and power.* London: Routledge, 1993. 368pp. (In Communication and Society series). A collection of essays representative of the latest work by eleven members of the Glasgow University Media Group, critical as always of the role of the press and broadcasting in interpreting current issues.

966 Elliot, *Sir* John. 'Aitken, William Maxwell, Baron Beaverbrook'. In *Dictionary of national biography, 1961–1970.* Oxford: Oxford University Press, 1981. By R.D. Blumenfeld's son (who changed his name at Beaverbrook's instigation, and later himself had a distinguished career on the railways).

967 Elliott, Blanche (Beatrice). *A history of English advertising.* London: Business Publications/Batsford, 1962. xvi + 231pp. A readable survey of a complex topic, harking back to pre-press days.

968   Elliott, Brendan John, ed. *The Stirling Journal and Advertiser: a local index.* Stirling: University of Stirling. Vol 2, 1870–1919. Publ 1979.

969   Elliott, *Brigadier* C.L. 'The impact of the media in the prosecution of contemporary warfare'. *British Army Review*, 103, Apr 1993.
'Television has become the primary source of reporting now . . . newspapers have been forced into other areas, such as analysis or investigation, but also downwards to the trivial.'

970   – – –.   'The impact of the media on modern warfare'. *Despatches* (Ministry of Defence), 4, Autumn 1993.
'War has ceased to be a distant thing on a foreign field.'

971   Elliott, Philip (Ross Courtney). *Reporting Northern Ireland: a study of news in Britain, Ulster and the Irish Republic.* Leicester: Centre for Mass Communication Research, 1972. Rptd in *Ethnicity and the media.* Paris: Unesco, 1978.

972   – – –.   'Professional ideology and organisational change: the journalist since 1800'. *In* [D.]G. Boyce *et al*, eds *Newspaper history* . . . (q.v.).

973   Ellis, Elizabeth. *The British Library Newspaper Library, 1973–1986.* Lougborough (Leics): Loughborough University of Technology, 1986 (MA thesis).

974   Ellis, Walter. 'Back with a vengeance'. *The Sunday Times (Magazine)*, 24 Jan 1993.
On David Montgomery, appointed chief executive of Mirror Group Newspapers – returning to the *Daily Mirror* to which he had been recruited twenty years before. He had moved in 1980 to *The Sun*, then *The People*; to the *News of the World* as editor aged thirty-seven (in 1985), and to *Today* also as editor (1987).

975   Elton, Oliver. *C.E. Montague: a memoir.* London: Chatto & Windus; Garden City (NY): Doubleday, 1929. xiii + 335pp.
Especially valuable on the history of *The Manchester Guardian* when Montague was its dramatic critic (and later its deputy editor).

976   Engel, Matthew. 'An unmanageable surfeit of sport'. *British Journalism Review*, 5, 1, 1994.
A *Guardian* sports writer bemoans the ever-increasing coverage in this sphere – especially in the Sundays ('quantity in the qualities').

977   – – –, ed. *The Guardian book of cricket.* London: Michael Joseph (Pavilion Books), 1986.
From the files of *The (Manchester) Guardian*.

978   Engen, Rodney. *Sir John Tenniel: 'Alice's White Knight'.* London: Scolar Press, 1991. 234pp.
A major – and lavishly illustrated – biography of not only the artist of *Alice in Wonderland*, but even more significantly the editor of *Punch* from 1864 to 1902.

979 Englefield, Dermot, ed. *Workings of Westminster*. Aldershot (Hants) and Brookfield (VT): Dartmouth, 1991.
Essays in honour of David Menhennet, librarian of the House of Commons. Includes 'Compiling the record: the making of *Hansard*', by Ian Church; and 'Parliament informs: the work of the Public Information Office', by Chris Pond.

980 English, *Sir* David. 'The English lesson on saving the dailies'. Address to Press '84 Conference, Berlin. Rptd in *UK Press Gazette*, 16 Apr 1984.
By the editor-in-chief of the *Daily Mail* and *Mail on Sunday*.

981 English, *Sir* David, *et al. Divided they stand*. London: Michael Joseph, 1969. x + 428pp.
Written by David English (then foreign editor) and other *Daily Express* staff about the US presidential election of 1968. English later became editor first of the *Daily Sketch* and, when that paper was merged into the *Daily Mail*, of the latter (from 1971).

982 Ensor, *(Sir)* R(obert) C(harles) K(irkwood). *England, 1870–1914*. Oxford: Clarendon Press, 1936; (pbk), 1985. 672pp.
Two chapters describe the Harmsworth revolution in the character of newspapers ('from paternalism to commercialism'). Ensor was a prominent leader-writer for several national newspapers in the 1900s, and was the columnist 'Scrutator' in *The Sunday Times* from 1940 to 1953.

983 – – –. 'The press'. *In* Sir Ernest Barker, ed. *The character of England*. Oxford: Clarendon Press, 1947.

984 Ervine, St John Greer. *The future of the press*. London: World's Press News, [1933]. 32pp.
As well as being a playwright of note, Ervine was the highly respected drama critic of *The Observer* and other publications.

985 Escott, T(homas) H(ay) S(weet). *Masters of English journalism: a study of personal forces*. London: T. Fisher Unwin, 1911. 368pp. Rptd Westport (CT): Greenwood Press, 1970.
Extolling the newspaper virtues of cheapness, popularity and liveliness, Escott looks back on the history of journalism, which he views as a simple linear progression to his own day, and largely a matter of potted biographies. He is at his most informative on that second generation of builders of the penny paper: Greenwood, Labouchere, and the Harmsworths.

986 – – –. 'The evolution of the leader'. *Living Age*, 236, 1903.

987 – – –. 'Behind the scenes in Fleet Street'. *The London Quarterly Review*. 119, 1913.

988 – – –. 'Old and new in the daily press'. *The Quarterly Review*, 227, 1917.

989 – – –. 'What the newspaper owes to the magazine'. *The London Quarterly Review*, 128, 1917.

The Times under Delane comes again under Escott's scrutiny in this essay and that listed immediately above. One of the most prolific of press historians, Escott (1844–1924) is today recognized more as a source of private information than of extended analysis.

990   Essery, John, ed. *Gotcha: classic headlines from The Sun.* Harmondsworth (Middx): Penguin (Signet), 1993. With foreword by Kelvin MacKenzie, editor of *The Sun.*
GOTCHA!, trumpeting the sinking of the Argentine cruiser *Belgrano* in the Falklands War, has been one of the more notorious front-page headlines in the paper.

991   *Essex Chronicle.* 225th anniversary. Chelmsford: 1989.
Series on a long history of reporting on national and local events. Founded as *Chelmsford and Colchester Chronicle*, 1764.

992   *Essex County Standard.* Centenary supplement. Colchester: 10 Jan 1931.
A weekly, now in the Reed Regional newspaper group.

993   Euromedia Research Group. *The media in Western Europe: the Euromedia handbook.* London: Sage, 1991. 28pp.

994   European Community. *The daily press of the European Community.* Brussels: EC, [n.d]. 44pp. Introduction by Jacques Keyser (International Centre for Higher Education in Journalism).
'How the daily newspapers of the European Community [including the UK] . . . welcomed the Brussels Agreement of January 24, 1962'.

995   *European Society for News Design News.* London: ESND, 1990–. Quarterly newsletter for members, with news and views of the world of design.

996   Evans, Beriah Gwynfe. 'The Welsh press'. In *Sell's World's Press, 1921.* London: Sell, 1921.

997   Evans, F.H. *Brief sketch of the career of the Lincoln, Rutland and Stamford Mercury.* Stamford (Lincs): 1938.

998   No entry.

999   Evans, Harold [Matthew]. *The Suez crisis: a study of press performance.* Durham: University of Durham, 1966 (MA thesis).
Published in the year that Evans left *The Northern Echo* for Fleet Street and *The Sunday Times* (editor, 1967–81).

        – – –.   *Editing and design: see Reference Works section.*

1000   – – –.   *Newspaper publishing: is the freedom of the press in danger?* London: Stationers' Company, 1979. Annual Livery Lecture.

1001   – – –.   *Good times, bad times.* London: Weidenfeld & Nicolson, 1983. Coronet, 1984; New York: Atheneum, 1984; London: Phoenix, 1994: xxviii + 498pp.
Evans dwells with justification on his outstandingly successful years as a campaigning editor of *The Sunday Times*, and with barbed directness on his year (1981–2) editing

The Times. Most of his preface to the third edition is a renewed diatribe against his erstwhile proprietor: 'The secret of Murdoch's power over the politicians is . . . that he is prepared to use his newspapers to reward them for favours given and destroy them for favours denied.'

1002   – – –.   *Front page history.* Research by Hugh Barty-King. London: Quiller Press, 1984; Harmondsworth (Middx): Penguin, 1985. 192pp.
'Events of our century that shook the world': front-page facsimiles and photos. Nearly all the illustrations come from the files of The Photo Source (combining the libraries of Keystone Press, Fox Photos and Central Press).

1003   – – –.   'Is the press too powerful?'. *Columbia Journalism Review*, Jan–Feb 1972.

1004   – – –.   'The half-free press'. *New Society*, 8 Mar 1974. Rptd in *The freedom of the press*, by Harold Evans *et al.* With an introduction by Sir William Haley. London: Hart-Davis, MacGibbon, 1974. 94pp. (Granada Guildhall Lectures.)

1005   – – –.   'Privacy and journalism – striking the balance'. *The Sunday Times*, 10 Jun 1973.
An important statement of editorial principle at a time of considerable public (and press) debate on newspaper ethics.

1006   – – –.   'The future of *The Sunday Times*'. In D. Campbell, ed. *The British press.* London: Commonwealth Press Union, 1978.

1007   – – –.   'British press less than half-free'. *The Media Reporter*, Mar 1979.

1008   – – –.   'On newspapers'. Ser in *The Listener*, 22, 29 Jan, 5, 12 Feb 1981.

1009   – – –.   'Six of the best'. In *100 years of Fleet Street.* London: Press Club, 1982.
A selection of six historic press pictures.

1010   Evans, *Sir* [Sidney] Harold. *Downing Street diary: the Macmillan years, 1957–1963.* London: Hodder & Stoughton, 1981. 318pp.
A well-respected official spokesman at 10 Downing Street – 'within the Establishment but not of it' – appends to his diary a chapter on 'The Fourth Estate', i.e. the lobby system at close quarters.

1011   Evans, *(Sir)* Trevor (Maldwyn), ed. *The Great Bohunkus: tributes to Ian Mackay.* London: W.H. Allen, 1953. 208pp.
Salute to a larger-than-life *News Chronicle* stalwart by his opposite number at the *Daily Express* as industrial correspondent, and by other contemporaries. Evans later became a director of Beaverbrook Newspapers.

1012   – – –.   'The evolution of industrial news reporting'. In *The press, 1898–1948 (The Newspaper World* Golden Jubilee). London: Benn, 1948.

1013 *Evening Argus*. Centenary supplement. Brighton: 31 Mar 1980.
Today, a title in the Westminster Press group.

1014 Evening Chronicle. *Fifty great years, 1897–1947 . . . to mark the Golden Jubilee of the Evening Chronicle*. Manchester: Kemsley Newspapers, 1947. 124pp.
Launched in Manchester by (Sir) Edward Hulton, the *Evening Chronicle* lasted under the Kemsley banner until 1963. This Jubilee publication was edited by H.J. Bradley (then editor of the paper).

1015 *Evening Chronicle*. Centenary. Newcastle upon Tyne: Nov 1985.
Established in 1885. Today, it is an associate of *The Journal* in Thomson Regional Newspapers.

1016 *Evening Chronicle*. Centenary special. Oldham (Lancs): 17 Mar 1980.

1017 *Evening Despatch*. Final-day commemorative supplement. Darlington (Co Durham): 18 Apr 1986.
Founded in 1914 as the *Northern Despatch*, this changed title in 1969; it ceased publication as part of Westminster Press's rationalization of its regional chain.

1018 *Evening News*. 'Fifty years, 1873–1923'. Edinburgh: 1923.

1019 – – –. Centenary special souvenir. 22–4 May 1973.
The evening associate of *The Scotsman* (in the Thomson Regional group).

1020 *Evening News, The*. 10,000th issue. London: 21 Nov 1913.

1021 – – –. Jubilee number: 1881–1931. 27 Jul 1931.

1022 – – –. 'Our fifty years of leadership'. 31 Aug 1944.
Established in 1881, *The Evening News* had its fortunes transformed as a result of its purchase by Alfred Harmsworth (later Northcliffe) in 1894, reaching the highest circulation of any evening paper in the world. After Northcliffe's death, it passed to his brother Harold (1st Lord Rothermere); it was merged by Associated Newspapers into *The (Evening) Standard* in 1980.

1023 *Evening Post, The*. Centenary supplement. Nottingham: 2 May 1978.
Published by T. Bailey Forman until 1994. In the face of union confrontation, it became in 1976 the first British newspaper to introduce direct computer input by journalists. An unusual event in earlier history (1905) was the renaming of the street in which the newspaper was (and is) based as Forman Street, 'honouring and perpetuating the name of the founder' (John Forman).

1024 *Evening Post, The, 1890–1965*, ed R.A. Rumfitt. St Helier (Jersey): 1965.
Imposing and most informative seventy-page commemorative issue of the oldest surviving (and widest-selling) newspaper in the Channel Islands (now titled *Jersey Evening Post*). Contributions include '179 years of Jersey newspapers', by W.J. Job; and a brief separate article on its sister paper, the *Jersey Weekly Post* (established 1910). The history

of both is largely centred on one personality, W.E. Guiton (proprietor and editor of *The Evening Post,* 1891–1927).

1025 *Evening Sentinel.* Centenary supplement, 1873–1973. Stoke-on-Trent: 16 Apr 1973.
Formerly the *Staffordshire Daily Sentinel.* It is now in the Northcliffe Newspapers group.

1026 *Evening Standard.* Centenary number. London: 1 May 1927.
The anniversary commemorated here is the passage of exactly one hundred years since the first publication of *The Standard.* It was originally an evening paper, later a morning which from 1860 was joined by the *Evening Standard.* It was acquired successively by Pearson (1904), Dalziel (1910), Hulton (1915), and Beaverbrook (1923).

1027 – – –. 'The first footstep. "Moonday", 21 July 1969'.
'Moon landing souvenir', marking the first landing earlier that day. There is a colour reconstruction of the event. Eleven editions were run off.

1028 – – –. 150th anniversary number. 20 May 1977.
Printed on distinctive pink paper. (The *Evening Standard* later merged with *The Evening News* in 1980. Its title was successively change to *New Standard, The Standard, The London Standard,* and (temporarily) *The London Evening Standard.* A weekly media section was introduced in 1992.

1029 Evening Standard and Daily Mail. *The London Blitz.* London: Chapmans Publishers, 1990.
Selection from the *Evening Standard,* September 1940–May 1941 – sixty pages and more than two hundred photographs.

1030 *Evening Star.* Centenary special. Ipswich (Suffolk): 16 Feb 1985; supplement, 18 Feb 1985.
Eastern Counties title: originally *Star of the East.*

1031 *Evening Telegraph and Post.* Souvenir centenary supplement. Dundee: 15 Mar 1977.
The present-day paper, one of the D.C. Thomson group, incorporates the *Dundee Evening Telegraph* (established 1877) and *Dundee Evening Post* (established 1900).

1032 Ewart, Andrew, and Vernon Leonard, eds. *100 years of Fleet Street: as seen through the eyes of the Press Club.* London: Brant Wright Associates, for the Press Club, 1982. 76pp.
Contains brief contributions as a centenary tribute, including: 'Cogito, ergo Press Club', by Alec Harrison; 'In the worst possible taste' (cartoons), by Peter Johnson; 'Wars and corrs', by James Cameron; 'Six of the best' (selected press photos), by Harold Evans; 'The rise and rise of a qualipop' (*The Guardian*), by Peter Preston; 'Tip for tap in the City', by Patrick Sergeant (City editor, *Daily Mail,* for more than twenty-two years); 'Mothering the Gauloise set' (the Foreign Press Association), by Roland Hill; 'Gone, gone, gone' (papers that have disappeared), by Tom Baistow.

1033   Ewing, Alexander McLean. *A history of the Glasgow Herald, 1783–1948.* *Glasgow: Outram, 1949.*

1034   *Exchange Telegraph Group of companies.* London: Extel, [1957]. 24pp.
The Exchange Telegraph Company was founded in 1872, primarily to report prices and other news from the Stock Exchange, where it acquired exclusive rights. The present-day Extel is still based in the financial world.

1035   *Express and Star.* Centenary souvenir. Wolverhampton (Staffs): 2 Nov 1974.
Celebrates the one hundred years since the launch of the *Midland Counties Evening Express*, which was merged with the *Evening Star* in 1884. Today, this highly successful title is the 'flagship' of the Midland News Association group, built up by the Graham family.

1036   *Eyewitness: 25 years through world press photos.* London: Quiller Press; New York: William Morrow (both for World Press Foundation), 1981; Harmondsworth (Middx): Penguin, 1981. Ed Harold Evans. Extended and revised as *Eye witness 2: three decades through world press photos.* London: Quiller Press, 1985. Series continued by *Eyewitness 88.* Amsterdam: Agon (for World Press Foundation), 1988; and *Eyewitness: world press photo: 1990.* Oxford: Phaidon Press; from 1991 London: Thames & Hudson. The latest in the series (for 1993) presents the prizewinners and others selected from the 22,475 entries from 2,429 photographers in 93 countries – including the UK.

1037   Ezard, John. 'Keith Waterhouse is very well'. *The Guardian*, 12 Mar 1990.
Profile of the prolific columnist and author.

1038   'Facts about free publishing'. *PR Week*, 13 Nov 1986 (supplement).
Produced by the Association of Free Newspapers when the 'frees' were a fast-developing market.

1039   'Fair name, A'. *The Newspaper World*, 21 Jan 1939.
The story of the *Huddersfield Daily Examiner*.

1040   Fairfax, James. *My regards to Broadway.* Sydney: Angus & Robertson, 1992.
Largely Australian-oriented, but has useful material on Rupert Murdoch, Conrad Black, and their British interests.

1041   Fairhead, Mike. *Latest developments in newspaper technology.* Leatherhead (Surrey): Pira International (in preparation).
All aspects from prepress to distribution, with financial aspects considered as well as the significance of continuous technical change.

1042   Fairley, D. 'D Notices, Official Secrets and the law'. *Oxford Journal of Legal Studies*, 10, 1990.

1043   Fairlie, Henry. 'Brilliance skin deep: the case of the *Daily Mirror*'. *Encounter*, July 1957.

By an incisive, deeply conservative political commentator who began his professional life as a leader-writer on the *Manchester Evening News,* moved to *The Times,* became freelance, and left Britain in 1970 to work permanently in Washington.

1044   Falk, Bernard. *Bouquets for Fleet Street: memories and musings over fifty years.* London: Hutchinson, 1951. 427pp.
Falk, a Fleet Streeter via the *Daily Mail* and the editing of *Reynolds's News* and several other papers, conveys a picture of Fleet Street in the 1930s redolent of Evelyn Waugh's Lord Copper.

1045   *Falkirk Herald.* Centenary number. 18 Aug 1945.
This weekly is now in the Johnston group.

1046   Fallon, Ivan (Gregory). *Billionaire: the life and times of Sir James Goldsmith.* London: Little, 1991; Arrow, 1992.
The deputy editor of *The Sunday Times* tells, *inter alia,* the inside story of Goldsmith's ambitious but short-lived weekly news magazine *Now!.*

1047   Fallon, Ivan (Gregory), and Maurice Chittenden. 'Cap'n Bob at bay'. *The Sunday Times,* 29 Sep 1991.
The fortunes of Maxwell and his media empire – a commentary as full as could be published before the tycoon's death and his empire's disintegration.

1048   Farago, Peter Joseph. *Science and the media.* London: Oxford University Press, 1976.
In writing this polemical essay Dr Farago drew on his years of press experience in gathering science news and interpreting it for a general audience.

1049   *Farnham Herald.* Centenary number. Farnham (Surrey): 3 Jul 1992.
The 'flagship' of the Tindle Newspaper group.

1050   Farnsworth, Gordon B. *A study of consumer journalism in British newspapers up to 1978.* Cardiff: University of Wales, 1983 (PhD thesis).
The press as a watchdog on consumer issues.

1051   Farnworth, Keith. *The Turner story: bringing the news to Sheffield.* London: Henry Melland, 1991. 204pp.
The centenary of H. Turner & Sons, newsagents and distributors in and around Sheffield. Includes an informative chapter on the history of the city's newspapers, notably the enduring *Sheffield (Daily) Telegraph.*

1052   *Farnworth and Worsley Journal.* Centenary special. Bolton (Lancs): 6 Sep 1973.
Incorporates *Farnworth Observer.*

1053   Farrer, David. *G – for God Almighty: a personal memoir of Lord Beaverbrook (1940–1946).* London: Weidenfeld & Nicolson; New York: Stein & Day, 1969.
Farrer was one of Beaverbrook's political secretaries.

1054 Faulks, Sebastian. 'The rule of reckless rectitude'. *The Guardian (Media Guardian)*, 3 Feb 1992.
Profile of William (Lord) Rees-Mogg, with a generally favourable estimate of his period as editor of *The Times* and more recent journalism as a columnist for *The Independent*.

1055 Fay, Gerard Francis Arthur. *Passenger to London*. London: Hutchinson; New York: Macmillan, 1961. 221pp.
An elegant essay in traditional style, by the last London editor of *The Guardian* before the editor himself moved there from Manchester.

1056 Fayle, C(harles) Ernest. *Lloyd's List and Shipping Gazette, 1734–1934: 200 years of shipping news*. London: Lloyd's, 1934. 48pp.

1057 Featherstone, S. *The role of newspaper editorials in the reproduction of community*. Leeds: University of Leeds, 1986 (thesis).

1058 Feinstein, Adam. 'Foreign correspondents' haven is 100 – and going strong'. *IPI Report*, Mar 1988.
The story of the centenary of the Foreign Press Association in London.

1059 Felstead, Sidney Theodore. *In search of sensation: being thirty years of a London journalist's life*. London: Robert Hale, 1945. 304pp.

1060 Fenby, Charles. 'For new openings see local press'. *In The Penrose Annual, 1984.*
The neglected significance of the provincials in advertising.

1061 Fenby, Jonathan. *The international news services*. New York: Schocken Books, 1986. xii + 275pp.
A Twentieth Century Fund report which surveys the 'big four' international 'wire' agencies, including of course Reuters. This is not the first of its kind, but does bring an up-to-date and balanced view to the agencies' record in serving the Third World countries against Unesco's controversial bid for a 'New World Information Order'.

1062 – – –. 'Revolution that hit the rocks'. *UK Press Gazette*, 16 Sep 1991.
Surveys the new era in national newspapers that so far has only produced *The Independent* as an undoubted success – and even that is not as planned. In May 1993, Fenby himself became the editor of a national: *The Observer*.

1063 Fenton, James (Martin). *All the wrong places: adrift in the politics of Asia*. New York: Atlantic Monthly Press, 1988; London: Viking, 1989; Harmondsworth (Middx): Penguin, 1990. 269pp.
A collection of extended press reports, some from *The Independent*.

1064 – – –. 'The fall of Saigon'. *Granta*, 15, 1985.
This is a development of Fenton's highly regarded reportage from Indo-China (1973–5). He later figured in various staff capacities at *The New Statesman*, *The Guardian*, *The Times*, and *The Independent*, and made a considerable reputation as a poet.

1065 Ferguson, Duncan. *The Scottish newspaper press.* Edinburgh: Oliver & Boyd, 1946. 40pp. (A Saltire pamphlet.)

1066 Ferris, Paul. *The house of Northcliffe: the Harmsworths of Fleet Street.* London: Weidenfeld & Nicolson, 1971; New York: World Books, 1972. 340pp. A very readable reassessment of Northcliffe and other members of the Harmsworth family. Well balanced as between their journalism, business affairs, and the private lives behind their very public façades.

1067 ffolliott, Rosemary. 'Matched and despatched'. *The Irish Genealogist,* 3, 7. Useful pointers to the use of newspapers in tracing family history.

1068 Field, Eric. *Advertising – the forgotten years.* London: Benn, 1959. A top-ranking advertising man himself – notably in the initiation of government campaigns in World War I – Field gives in a small compass a most useful factual account of the significant people, practices and publications in his profession. Includes a chapter 'How the newspapers woke up'.

1069 Fienburgh, Wilfred. *Twenty-five momentous years: a 25th anniversary in the history of the Daily Herald.* London: Odhams, 1955. 208pp. Established in 1911 as a printers' lock-out sheet, *(The) Daily Herald* was launched on 15 April 1912 as a national, socialist newspaper. Temporarily a weekly in World War I (as *The Herald*), it revived from 1919 under the continued editorship of George Lansbury. It became the official Labour/TUC organ in 1922, with Hamilton Fyfe as editor, and came under the control of J.S. Elias (Lord Southwood) of Odhams Press in 1929. After a major face-lift and an aggressive sales drive, it claimed for a brief period in 1933 the world's biggest circulation (over 2 million). Odhams were eventually forced, through lack of advertising, to sell to the Mirror group in 1961, and in 1964 the *Daily Herald* was reborn as *The Sun*.

1070 *Fife Herald.* 150th anniversary supplement. Cupar (Fife): 15 Mar 1972. Established in 1822, today this paper is the *Fife Herald News*, in the Johnston Press group.

1071 'Fifty years of *The People*'. *World's Press News,* 8 Oct 1931. This famous Sunday paper (founded in 1881) was intermittently *The Sunday People* (from 1972 to 1986).

1072 *Financial News, The.* 20th anniversary number. London: 23 Jan 1904.

1073 – – –. 50th anniversary number. 22 Jan 1934. Includes a supplement, 'The City 1884–1934', by (Sir) Oscar Hobson, in the last of his five years of editorship. *The Financial News* was founded by the financier–MP Harry H. Marks as London's first financial daily. Acquired by Brendan Bracken in 1927, it was merged into *The Financial Times* in 1945.

1074 Financial Times. *The Financial Times index: a complete record of references in the Financial Times to companies and matters of financial interest.* London: 92 (monthly) parts, covering May 1913 to Dec 1920. For current *Index to the Financial Times*, see *Reference Works Section*.

1075   *Financial Times.* Golden Jubilee supplement, 1888–1938. 14 Feb 1938. 88pp.

1076   – – –.   25,000th issue. 11 Nov 1969.
The *FT* came under the control of William Berry (Camrose) in 1919; after World War II, it absorbed its rival, *The Financial News*, with Brendan Bracken (hitherto chairman of the latter) taking control. Acquired in 1957 by the Cowdray interests, the paper became part of the Pearson group. Still printed from London on the pink newsprint adopted in 1893, it also has international editions from Frankfurt and New York.

1077   – – –.   'The building of a newspaper: Lord Drogheda and the *Financial Times*'. 1 Apr 1975.
After being managing director from 1945 to 1970, Drogheda became chairman of the *FT* in 1971.

1078   Financial Times. *Financial Times survey of British readership research.* 1980.

1079   *Financial Times.* 30,000th issue. 7 Aug 1986.

1080   – – –.   The newspaper industry. Survey, ed Raymond Snoddy. 27 Jul 1987.

1081   – – –.   Centenary: facsimile of first issue. 12 Feb 1988.

1082   – – –.   'A century for the *FT*'. 13 Feb 1988 (leader).

1083   – – –.   'The first 100 years'. Special report. 15 Feb 1988. 84pp.
It includes three pages on the newspaper itself by its historian, David Kynaston. This issue was claimed to be 'the largest national daily newspaper in history'.

1084   Financial Times. *The Newspaper Industry Conference: speakers' papers.* 1988. Proceedings of the conference held in London, 12–13 Apr 1988.
The papers include: Bill O'Neill (News International), 'How the UK industry is changing'; Andrew Knight (chief executive), 'How *The Daily Telegraph* was saved'; Andreas Whittam Smith (editor and chief executive), 'Carving out a quality circulation – the *Independent* experience'; Ralph Ingersoll (chairman, Ingersoll Publications) and Howard Green (Yellow Advertiser Group), 'The outlook for the regional market: the battle between paid-for and free newspapers'; Alec Kenny (Saatchi & Saatchi), 'What are the prospects for growth in newspaper advertising'; Derek H. Terrington (Phillips & Drew), 'An analyst's view of the industry'.

1085   *Financial Times.* Centenary of first pink *Financial Times.* 4 Jan 1993.
Facsimile of 3 Jan 1893; and 'The *Financial Times* looks back to the world of 1893'. The paper itself appeared on this one day on *white* newsprint.

1086   Fincher, Judith. *The Clarion movement.* Manchester: University of Manchester, 1973 (MA thesis).

1087   Fincher, Terry. *Creative techniques in photojournalism.* London: Batsford, 1980. 168pp.

Drawn from experience notably for Keystone Press, *Daily Herald, Daily Express* – and illustrated from Fincher's outstanding portfolio.

1088   Fincher, Terry, and Tony Lynch. *The Fincher file*. London: Quartet Books, 1981. 197pp.
Selected from photography notably for the *Daily Herald* and *Daily Express.*

1089   Finney, Angus. 'Rhino in a glasshouse'. *Journalist's Week*, 14 Sep 1990.
On Stewart Steven, editor of *The Mail on Sunday* – and later *Evening Standard.*

1090   Firmin, Stanley. *Crime man*. London: Hutchinson, 1950. 184pp.

1091   *First World War, The: a documentary record*. Marlborough (Wilts): Adam Matthew Publications. From the War Reserve Collection in Cambridge University Library.
Series One: European War, 1914–1919. Listings and guides accompanying microfilm series. Six parts: Part 2 (published 1993) includes Trench journals; Part 3 (forthcoming) Allied propaganda.

1092   Firth, John B. 'Traditions that have built up the *Daily Telegraph*'. *The Daily Telegraph*, 1 Oct 1937.
This leader marked the acquisition of *The Morning Post.*

1093   Fischer, Heinz-Dietrich. '*The Times*'. In *Die grossen Zeitungen: Porträts der Weltpresse*. [Munich]: 1966.

1094   Fisher, John Oswald Hamilton, ed. *Eye-witness: an anthology of British reporting*. London: Cassell, 1960. xv + 284pp.
One of the few British collections of its kind; good reading for aspiring recruits. The sixty-one reports – published between 1815 and 1960 – are embellished by Fisher's informed commentary.

1095   Fishlock, Trevor. *Out of red darkness: reports from the collapsing Soviet empire*. London: John Murray, 1992.
First-hand history from the Moscow correspondent of *The Sunday Telegraph.*

1096   Fisk, Nicholas. *Look at newspapers*. London: Hamish Hamilton, 1962. 96pp. (In the Look Books series).

1097   Fisk, Robert. *The point of no return: the strike which broke the British in Ulster*. London: Times Books/André Deutsch, 1975.

1098   – – –.   *In time of war: Ireland, Ulster and the price of neutrality, 1939–45*. London: André Deutsch, 1983; Paladin, 1985.

1099   – – –.   *Pity the nation: Lebanon at war*. London: André Deutsch, 1990. xix + 662pp. Revised edn, Oxford: Oxford University Press, 1992. xv + 703pp.
Books by the notable reporter for, successively, *The Sunday Times, The Times*, and *The Independent*. In *Pity the nation*, Fisk makes clear that his account of the agonies of

Lebanon in retrospect often differs markedly from the political stance of *The Times* when his reports were published therein.

1100   – – –.   'Free to report what we're told'. *The Independent*, 6 Feb 1991.

1101   Fleet, Kenneth George. *The influence of the financial press*. London: Stationers' Company, 1983. Annual Livery Lecture.
Fleet's own influence began when he was City editor for *The Sunday Telegraph* in 1963–6; he moved to *The Daily Telegraph* (until 1977), and here relates how Lord Hartwell, on engaging him, remarked: 'Your job is to make our readers richer.' Fleet, who explains how the takeover battles in the 1950s first moved 'the City' to the front page, was City editor-in-chief of Express Newspapers at the time of this lecture.

1102   *Fleet Street Annual, The*, ed Harold Herd. London: Fleet Publications, 1930–1959.
The 1950 and 1951 editions contain particularly valuable chronologies and articles on British journalism of the half-century.

1103   'Fleet Street revolution – Part 1'. In *The press and the people* (Press Council Annual Report 1985). London: Press Council, 1987.
This first – anonymous, and impartially written – narrative deals with Mirror Group Newspapers, Fleet Holdings, and The Telegraph Group.

1104   'Fleet Street revolution – Part 2'. In *The press and the people* (Press Council Annual Report 1986). London: Press Council, 1987.
'Mr Shah's total revolution; Mr Murdoch's triumph; *Independent* achievement'.

1105   Fletcher, Ian. 'The growth of the free-distribution newspaper'. *Admap*, May 1982.
By one of the most successful entrepreneurs in this new field.

1106   Fletcher, Leonard. *They never failed: the story of the provincial press in wartime*. London: Newspaper Society, [1946]. 80pp.
A tribute to unremitting publication locally during World War II.

1107   Fletcher, Richard J. 'British propaganda and World War II – a case study'. *Media, Culture and Society*, Apr 1982.

1108   Flintham, David, and [Dennis] Nicholas Herbert (*3rd Baron* Hemingford). *Press freedom in Britain*. London: Newspaper Society, 1991.
The perceived threat implicit in the move for the Press Complaints Commission to be given statutory backing.

1109   *Follow my leader: commentaries from The Times*. With an introduction by Sir John Squire. London: Edward Arnold, 1934. 256pp.

1110   'Foot, David' [Anthony Fouracre]. *The country reporter*. Newton Abbot (Devon): David & Charles, 1990; Fontana, 1993. 176pp.
Two years with the *Western Gazette*.

1111   Foot, Michael [Mackintosh]. *Debts of honour*. London: Davis Poynter, 1980. x + 240pp. Pan (Picador), 1981. 222pp.

Just before he began his four-year stint as leader of the Labour Party, Foot relaxed sufficiently to pay tribute to such varied personal inspirations as Hazlitt, Beaverbrook, H.N. Brailsford – 'the greatest socialist journalist of the century' – 'Vicky' the cartoonist, Randolph Churchill, Defoe and Swift.

1112   – – –.   *Another heart and other pulses: the alternative in the Thatcher society*. London: Collins, 1984. 220pp.

The story of Labour's disastrous election campaign in 1983 – blamed here in part on the influence of the largely Tory-owned national press.

1113   – – –.   'On editors'. *Tribune*, 31 Jan 1947.

Foot was himself editor of the socialist *Tribune* for several years.

1114   – – –.   'Cameron, (Mark) James (Walter)'. In *Dictionary of national biography, 1981–1985*. Oxford: Oxford University Press, 1990.

1115   – – –.   (under the pseudonym of Cassius). *Brendan and Beverley: an extravaganza*. London: Gollancz, 1944. 78pp.

Written when Foot was acting editor of the *Evening Standard* (1942–5), about Brendan (later Viscount) Bracken and (Sir) Beverley Baxter. They are given the names (and characters) of the Tories Mr Tape and Mr Tadpole, revived from Disraeli's *Coningsby*.

1116   Foot, M[ichael] R[ichard] D[aniel]. 'History at Printing House Square'. In *The Penrose Annual, 1950*.

A historian's view of *The Times*.

1117   Foot, Paul [Mackintosh]. 'Strenuous liberty . . . a nervous revival?'. *British Journalism Review*, Summer 1991.

Applauding the apparent revival of trade union activities in the national press. Foot, an outspoken columnist with the paper until the upsets of 1993, began with the *Daily Mirror* in 1979.

1118   *Forres, Elgin and Nairn Gazette*. 150th anniversary edition. Elgin (now Grampian): Jul 1987.

In Scottish Provincial Press group.

1119   Forster, Peter. *The spike*. London: Hutchinson, 1969; Harmondsworth (Middx): Penguin. 251pp.

A good Fleet Street novel.

1120   Fortescue, Granville. *At the front with three armies: my adventures in the Great War*. London: Melrose, 1915. 271pp.

The author was a correspondent for *The Daily Telegraph*. The book mainly constitutes Fortescue's reports in that paper in the early 'death or glory' days, when truth about the 'war to end wars' was not simply the first casualty but also a ghost to haunt war correspondents generally.

1121   Foster, Alan J. 'The politicians, public opinion and the press: the storm over British military intervention in Greece in December 1944'. *Journal of Contemporary History*, 19, 1984.

1122   – – –. 'The Beaverbrook press, Eastern Europe, the Soviet Union and the coming of the Cold War: "independent conservatism" and foreign policy'. *Media, Culture and Society*, Jan 1986.
Traces the consistent pro-Soviet attitude of Beaverbrook (as expressed in the *Daily Express* etc) throughout the 1930s and 1940s.

1123   – – –. 'The British press and the coming of the Cold War'. *In* Anne Deighton, ed., *Britain and the first Cold War*. London: Macmillan, 1990.

1124   – – –. 'An unequal guarantee: Fleet Street and the British guarantee to Poland, 31 March 1939'. *Journal of Contemporary History*, 26, 1991.

1125   – – –. 'The Beaverbrook press and appeasement: the second phase'. *European History Quarterly*, 1, 1992.

1126   Foster, Reginald. *Dover front*. London: Secker & Warburg, 1941.
Correspondent for the *Daily Herald* at Dover, 1940-1. In 1963, when with the *Daily Sketch*, was imprisoned for refusing to divulge his sources to the Vassall Tribunal.

1127   Fowler, Eric. 'Norwich newspapers and their editors'. *East Anglian Magazine*, 22, 1963.

1128   Fowler, Roger. *Language in the news: discourse and ideology in the press*. London: Routledge, 1991. 254pp.
Fowler argues that the presentation of news is circumscribed by the social and political environment.

1129   Fox, Celina. 'Images of the people: the example of *The Graphic*'. *Society for the Study of Labour History Bulletin*, 44, Spring 1982.

1130   Fox, W.E. *Printers, press and profits*. London: Labour Research Department, [1932]. 30pp.

1131   Fox Bourne, Henry Richard. '*Newspapers of the new century*'. In *Sell's Dictionary of the World's Press, 1901*.

1132   Fraenkel, Josef, ed. *The Jewish press of the world*. London: World Jewish Congress, 1955, 1961.
Includes a 'Great Britain' section.

1133   Francis, John. *The thunderer of South Wales*. Carmarthen (Dyfed): Carmarthen Journal, 1992.
The history of the oldest newspaper in Wales surviving under its original title; now in the Northcliffe Newspapers group.

1134   Francis, John Collins. 'The *Globe* centenary'. *Notes and Queries*, ser 9, 11:41–3, 17 Jan 1903.

1135 – – –. 'Diamond Jubilee of the *Newspaper Press Directory*'. *Notes and Queries*, ser 10, 3:241, 22 Apr 1905; 261, 8 Apr 1905.

1136 – – –. 'Jubilee of the *Daily Telegraph*'. *Notes and Queries*, ser 10, 4:243, 23 Sep 1905.

1137 – – –. 'The Times'. *Notes and Queries*, ser 11, 9:421, 30 May 1914; original prospectus and average daily circulation; 502, 27 Jun 1914.

1138 – – –. 'The Standard'. *Notes and Queries*, ser 12, 1:341, 29 Apr 1916; 363, 6 May 1916; 381, 13 May 1916.

1139 – – –. 'The Observer, 1791–1916'. *Notes and Queries*, ser 12, 2:124, 12 Aug 1916.

1140 – – –. 'The Morning Post, 1772–1916', *Notes and Queries*, ser 12:301, 14 Oct 1916; 322, 21 Oct 1916; 342, 28 Oct 1916.

1141 Franklin, Bob, and David Murphy. *What news?: the market, politics and the local press*. London: Routledge, 1991. vii + 229pp.
Local newspapers in Britain – some 1,800 at the last count – afford a useful political platform to balance the preponderantly right-wing nationals, but all too many – in the authors' opinion – have their comment dictated from the centre. This is an important treatise in an under-estimated section of the press.

1142 Franklin, Olga (Rose). *Born twice*. London: P. Garnett, 1951. 180pp.

1143 – – –. *Oh! That spike*. London: Hammond, [1957]. 218pp.

1144 – – –. *Steppes to Fleet Street*. London: Gollancz, 1968.
Franklin, of Russian descent, was a woman's writer for the *Daily Mail* etc.

1145 Fraser, Alastair. 'This sporting strife'. *Evening Standard*, May 1993.
On *Daily Sport* (principal director: David Sullivan) and its niche in the national scene.

1146 Fraser, David. *A modern campaign: or, war and wireless telegraphy in the Far East*. London: Methuen, 1905. 356pp.
Reporting from the Russo-Turkish War, notably the Battle of the Yalu (1904).

1147 – – –. *Persia and Turkey in revolt*. Edinburgh: Blackwood, 1910. xii + 440pp.
Wide-ranging correspondence as a 'special' for *The Times*.

1148 Fraser, George, and Ken Peters. *The Northern Lights*. London: Hamish Hamilton, 1978. 143pp.
A close-up history of the *Press and Journal* and *Evening Express* (Aberdeen), published on the latter's centenary. Both authors had been editors of the *Evening Express*, and Peters of the *Press and Journal* also. Today the two titles are Thomson Regional Newspapers.

1149 *Fraserburgh Herald*. Centenary edition. Fraserburgh (Grampian): 23 Mar 1984.
Includes a history by Tom Fowler.

1150   Frayn, Michael. *The tin men*. London: Collins, 1965. 191pp.

1151   – – –.   *Towards the end of the morning*. London: Collins; Harmondsworth (Middx): Penguin, 1967. 255pp. London: Fontana, 1984; Harvill, 1985. US title: *Against entropy*.
This and the above are novels based on the author's intimate knowledge of Fleet Street. *Towards the end of the morning* (dramatized by Geoffrey M. Matthews) was shown on BBC television in 1983.

1152   – – –.   *Alphabetical order.* London: French, 1975.
Play with a provincial newspaper library setting.

1153   – – –.   *Clouds*. London: Eyre Methuen, 1977.
Play about two journalists, male and female, sent to Cuba by rival Sunday magazines; includes such aphorisms as: 'There is a painful difference, often obscured by popular prejudice, between reporting something and making it up.'

1154   – – –.   *The original Frayn*. Edinburgh: Salamander Press, 1983. 203pp. Ed and introduced by James Fenton.
Reverentially chosen reprints from *The Guardian* and *The Observer*; Frayn was a columnist for these nationals in the 1960s.

1155   Free Communications Group. *Free the press: the case for democratic control*. London: FCG, 1971. (In the Place of Management series, no 1.)
Published by a short-lived but influential pressure group set up by professional journalists. The FCG also had its own journal: *The Open Secret*.

1156   *Free Media Digest*. Northampton: WP Publications, 1982–.
'The independent voice of the free newspaper and magazine industry'.

1157   *Free Press*. London: Campaign for Press (and Broadcasting) Freedom.
Established in 1979 as the organization's bulletin; now a bimonthly journal.

1158   *Free press in the world, The*. Naples: Federazione Italiana Editori Giornali (Italian Federation of Newspaper Editors), for the 10th Congress of FIEJ (the international body), 1957. 293pp.
An imposing work, including 'Great Britain', a survey compiled by the Newspaper Society.

1159   *Free Press of Monmouthshire*. Henry Hughes newspapers celebrate 100 years: supplement. Pontypool (Gwent): 23 Sep 1977.

1160   – – –.   125th anniversary supplement. 16 Mar 1984.
Features the founder of the *Pontypool Free Press*: David Walkinshaw.

1161   Freeman, W. *The London Gazette*: 'Britain's queerest periodical'. *Chambers's Journal*, 8th ser, 10, 1941.

1162   French, Philip, and Deac Rossell, eds. *The press observed and projected*. London: British Film Institute/Observer, 1991. 136pp. (NFT Dossier No 6.)

Critical booklet, to accompany the National Film Theatre's season of films concerning the press, both fictional and factual. Many important British movies are featured. Chapter on 'The journalist in British films' by Jeffrey Richards.

1163 Fresco, Monty. *Pictures all my life*. Tunbridge Wells (Kent): Midas Books, 1982.
A selection of the best work of the *Daily Mail*'s leading photographer.

1164 Freund, Gisèle. *Photography and society*. London: Gordon Fraser, 1980. 231pp. Translation from the French of *Photographie et société*.
Includes a brief historical survey of photography in the press.

1165 Friederichs, Hulda. *The life of Sir George Newnes, Bart*. London: Hodder & Stoughton, 1911, xi + 304pp.
Newnes (1851–1910), the pioneer of the cheap modern periodical and magazine, launched *Tit-Bits* in 1881. That stroke of genius led to a succession of new titles carefully planned to meet demand. On an individual basis, Newnes also successfully entered the daily newspaper business with *The Westminster Gazette*; by the turn of the century, his only rivals were Harmsworth and Pearson.

   Friederichs was herself a formidable pioneer woman journalist. She was 'chief interviewer' on *The Pall Mall Gazette*, *The Westminster Budget* (a weekly), and the Saturday edition of *The Westminster Gazette*.

1166 'From visitors' list to daily paper'. *The Newspaper World*, 17 Dec 1938. (In The Oldest Newspapers series.)
John Grime founded the *Blackpool Gazette* in 1873; his descendants today still have immediate control of that paper (a weekly) and the *West Lancashire Evening Gazette*. (Both these papers are in the United Provincial Newspapers group).

1167 *Front page Scotland*. Glasgow: Scottish Daily Record & Sunday Mail, 1988. A large-format volume.
'The news of this century as seen through the pages of Scotland's national newspapers, the *Daily Record* and *Sunday Mail*', major elements of Mirror Group Newspapers.

1168 Fuller, John G. *Troop morale and popular culture in the British and Dominion armies, 1914–1918*. Oxford: Clarendon Press, 1991. 218pp.
Covers extensively (with both a chapter and a list in appendix form) the little-examined field of Army newspapers.

1169 Furlong, Monica. 'The press gang – a series of Fleet Street profiles'. *Punch* (ser of 12), 21 Feb–20 Jun 1962.
Illustrated by caricatures of the current editors.

1170 Furneaux, Rupert. *News of war: stories and adventures of the great correspondents*. London: Max Parrish, 1964.

1171 Fyfe, [Henry] Hamilton. *Behind the scenes of the General Strike*. London: Labour Publishing Co, 1926. 88pp.

The traumatic events of the Strike week marked the end of Fyfe's editorship of Labour's *Daily Herald*. From Victoria's Jubilee of 1887 to the end of World War II, Hamilton Fyfe (1869–1951) had one of the longest and widest careers in Fleet Street history. He was editor of the *Daily Mirror* from 1903 to 1907; special correspondent, for the *Daily Mail*, then he reported from Mexico and the Western Front for *The Times*; he edited the *Daily Herald* from 1922 to 1926.

1172   – – –.   *Northcliffe: an intimate biography*. London: Allen & Unwin, 1930; New York: Macmillan, 1930; rptd 1969. ix + 357pp.
A sympathetic study, discussing *inter alia* Northcliffe's beliefs on press ownership.

1173   – – –.   *T.P. O'Connor*. London: Allen & Unwin, 1934. 351pp.
As a highly experienced journalist with a gift for popular exposition, Fyfe on 'T.P.' was a 'natural'. O'Connor (1848–1929) ranks of course as much more than an editor – although his identification with *The Sun*, *The Star*, and his own *T.P.'s Weekly* is an indelible chapter in British press history; he was also a considerable figure in the complex web of Irish politics in the late Victorian era, and as a Member of Parliament at Westminster.

1174   – – –.   *My seven selves*. London: Allen & Unwin, 1935. 320pp.
From 'foolish young fellow' of fourteen to 'poor and content' at sixty-three.

1175   – – –.   *Press parade: behind the scenes of the newspaper racket and the millionaires' attempt at dictatorship*. London: Watts, 1936. 154pp.

1176   – – –.   *Britain's war-time revolution*. London: Gollancz, 1944. 248pp.
The author's diary from September 1939 to December 1942.

1177   – – –.   *Sixty years of Fleet Street*. London: W.H. Allen, 1949. 227pp.

1178   'Gabriel' [James Friell]. *Cartoons by Gabriel*. London: Daily Worker, 1938. Commentary by Phillip Bolsover.
'Gabriel' was staff cartoonist for the Communist *Daily Worker* from 1936 for twenty years (with a five-year interval serving in the Army).

1179   Gale, John Mackinnon. *Clean young Englishman*. London: Hodder & Stoughton, 1965. 192pp; Harmondsworth (Middx): Penguin, 1969. 203pp.
A journalist's autobiography.

1180   Gall, Sandy [Henderson Alexander]. *Don't worry about the money now*. London: Hamish Hamilton, 1983. 343pp; Hodder & Stoughton (NEL), 1984. 464pp.
Latterly Gall became a notable television presenter, but this book covers adventures on behalf of Reuters.

1181   Gallagher, O.D. [E. O'Dowd]. *Retreat in the East*. London: Harrap, 1944. 190pp. Publ in the USA as *Action in the East*.
Gallagher was a South African-born correspondent for the *Daily Express* in Abyssinia, Spain (throughout the Civil War), Palestine, China, France and the UK in 1939–40, and then in the Western Desert with the Eighth Army. This, his only book, is devoted

to a graphic account of his experience of early British wartime disasters in Malaya and Burma: 'I have told the truth, so far as I am able.'

1182 Gallagher, Tom. 'The press and Protestant popular culture: a case study of the *Scottish Daily Express*'. *In* Graham Walker and Tom Gallagher, eds. *Sermons and battle hymns: Protestant popular culture in modern Scotland.* Edinburgh: Edinburgh University Press, 1991.

1183 Gamble, William. 'Newspaper illustration of today'. In *Penrose's Pictorial Annual, 1913–14.* London: Lund Humphries, 1914.

1184 Gammage, M.T. '*The Birmingham Daily Gazette*: a case history of the conservative provincial press, 1862–1914'. *West Midland Studies,* 13, 1980.

1185 Gander, L[eonard] Marsland. *After these many quests.* London: Macdonald, 1949. 367pp.
Gander was *The Daily Telegraph*'s pioneer radio correspondent from 1926 and the paper's (and indeed the world's) first television critic from 1935. He returned to cover radio and television after distinguished service as a war correspondent.

1186 Gannon, Franklin Reid. *The British press and Germany, 1936–1939.* Oxford: Clarendon Press, 1971. xiv + 314pp.
Surveys seven national dailies, plus the *Manchester Guardian, Sunday Times* and *Observer,* giving special attention to the policy of appeasement urged on the nation by *The Times* under Geoffrey Dawson.

1187 Gardiner, A(lfred) G(eorge). *Prophets, priests and kings.* London: Alston Rivers, 1908.

1188 – – –. *Pillars of society.* London: Nisbet, 1913. 354pp. New York, 1914.
First reprints from the influential profiles written by Gardiner (1865–1946) as editor of *The Daily News.*

1189 – – –. *The Daily Mail and the Liberal press: a reply to 'Scaremongerings' and an open letter to Lord Northcliffe.* London, [1914]. 16pp.
As editor of *The Daily News,* Gardiner rebuts the *Daily Mail*'s claim to be 'the paper that foretold the war'. Signed A.G.G.

1190 – – –. *Life of George Cadbury.* London: Cassell, 1923. ix + 324pp.
After his enforced 'retirement' from the editorship, Gardiner wrote this important biography of the chocolate magnate (1839–1922) who had acquired *The Daily News,* initially as the front man of Lloyd George's syndicate; its successor, the *News Chronicle,* remained in Cadbury control until its end in 1960.

1191 – – –. 'The press and the State'. *The Nation,* 15 Sep 1923.

1192 – – –. 'Two journalists: C.P. Scott and Lord Northcliffe: a contrast'. *The Nineteenth Century and After,* Feb 1932.

1193 Gardiner, Juliet. *Picture Post women*. London: Collins & Brown, 1993. 144pp.
Not only women as portrayed in the magazine, but also those (such as Grace Robertson) who took many of the outstanding photographs, or assisted in the editing.

1194 Garland, Nicholas. *Not many dead: journal of a year in Fleet Street*. London: Hutchinson, 1990. xv + 299pp.
The year concerned was 1986, when Garland (a notable political cartoonist) was agonizing as to whether to join the about-to-be launched *Independent*. In very outspoken diary style, he covers *The Daily* and *Sunday Telegraphs* also in close-up.

1195 Garlick, Vera F.M. *News*. London: Longmans, 1965.

1196 Garner, William. *Paper chase*. London: Grafton, 1988. [256pp.]
Fleet Street thriller.

1197 Garret, Alexander. 'Battle of the books'. *Journalist's Week*, 21 Sep 1990.
On the Newspaper Library at Colindale, leading up to the problems of preservation of a 'crumbling' collection.

1198 Garside, Patricia L. 'Reporting the metropolis – the changing relationship between London and the press, 1870–1939'. *London Journal*, 16, 1991.

1199 Garth, Alan. 'A day in the life of regional and local daily papers'. *Newstime* (Newspaper Society), Sep 1983.
The day in question was 8 June 1982: 108 dailies were analysed for both editorial and advertising coverage. Garth carried out a similar exercise on 5 June 1984; the results were summarized in *Admap*, April 1985.

1200 – – –. 'The regional giant awakes'. *Campaign*, 30 Mar 1984.
The current scene: the Newspaper Society, the Regional Newspaper Advertising Bureau, and the upsurge of free papers.

1201 – – –. 'Selling the regionals nationally'. *Newstime*, Apr 1984.

1202 – – –.   'A marriage of opportunity'. *Newstime*, Jan 1988.
On the controlling interest in Iliffe in Birmingham (notably the *Birmingham Post*) and Coventry then secured by Ingersoll of the USA.

1203 – – –. 'The free concept which paid off'. *UK Press Gazette*, 15 Aug 1988.
The then booming regional press scene, showing how the free sector grew by nearly 30 per cent in 1987 – and how the major groups had all established a large stake among the 'frees'.

1204 – – –. 'The giants get it together'. *Admap*, Jan 1990.
On the major regional groups.

1205 – – –. 'Another country'. *Media Week*, 22 Feb 1991.
The media scene in Scotland.

1206 Garvin, [Hilda] Katharine ('Kit'). *J.L. Garvin: a memoir*. London: Heinemann, 1948. ix + 215pp.

A daughter's personal view of a famous father (1868–1947), who edited an evening daily, *The Pall Mall Gazette* (1912–15), but whose appointment to *The Observer* by Northcliffe in 1908 continued under the Astor dynasty until 1942; this memoir also traces Garvin's editorship of the *Encyclopaedia Britannica* in the late 1920s.

Going against contemporary practice with editors at *The Times*, Garvin signed his weekly 'Articles' and was therefore a much more public figure. After parting from *The Observer*, he wrote weekly for the *Sunday Express* and *The Daily Telegraph* (where he had begun his London career).

1207 Gascoigne, Bamber. *Encyclopedia of Britain*. Basingstoke (Hants): Macmillan, 1993.

New one-volume compendium, with copious entries on journalists, newspapers etc contributed by Dennis Griffiths.

1208 Gaunt, Philip. 'The training of journalists in France, Britain and the US'. *Journalism Quarterly*, Fall 1988.

Makes the point that law is given special attention in British journalism schools; but regrettably out of date with regard to courses at university level.

1209 – – –. 'Distributing the news'. *Media, Culture and Society*, 14, 1, Jan 1992.

Systems in the USA, France and Britain – 'pre- and post-Wapping'.

1210 Gavin, Kent, and William (Bill) Hagerty. *Flash bang wallop!: the intimate experiences of Fleet Street's top press photographer*. Newton Abbot (Devon): David & Charles (Westbridge Books), 1978. 128pp.

Gavin's work was with the *Daily Mirror* etc.

1211 Gedye, G[eorge] E[ric] R[owe]. *Fallen bastions: the Central European tragedy*. London: Gollancz, 1939. 513pp. Publ in the USA as *Betrayal in Central Europe*.

Gedye was correspondent in Central Europe for several newspapers, notably *The Daily Telegraph* (1929–38), from which he was dismissed for the anti-appeasement attitudes of this book.

1212 Gennard, John. *A history of the National Graphical Association*. London: Unwin Hyman, 1990. xx + 590pp.

A full-length exposition of the NGA and its predecessors, associates and rivals as printing trade unions. Detailed rather than analytical.

1213 – – –. 'The implications of the Messenger group dispute'. *Industrial Relations Journal*, 15, 3, 1984.

This was the notorious 1983 confrontation between Eddy Shah and the National Graphical Association operatives who demanded a closed shop at his Messenger Newspapers printworks at Warrington.

1214   – – –.   'The NGA and the importance of new technology'. *New Technology, Work and Employment*, 2, 2, 1987.

1215   Gennard, John, and Stephen Dunn. 'The impact of new technology on the structure and organization of craft unions and the printing industry'. *British Journal of Industrial Relations*, 21, 1983.

1216   'Gentleman warrior behind "the Thunderer"'. In *Now!*, 28 Nov 1980.
About Rees-Mogg, then in what turned out to be the last months of his editorship of *The Times*.

1217   Geraghty, Cecil. *The road to Madrid*. London: Hutchinson, 1937.
A correspondent for the *Daily Mail* writing from a convinced pro-Nationalist stance.

1218   Gerald, (James) Edward. *The British press under government economic controls*. Minneapolis: University of Minnesota Press, 1956; New York: Greenwood Press, 1977. xiv + 235pp.
A well-documented study of the British press from 1939 to 1955, which proves that the wartime imposition of controls such as those on newsprint and advertising had paradoxically a liberating effect on Fleet Street, enabling it to concentrate on news-gathering and ignore the usual pressure from commercial interests.

1219   – – –.   *The social responsibility of the press*. Minneapolis: University of Minnesota Press, 1963.

1220   Gerhardie (originally Gerhardi), William Alexander. *Jazz and Jasper*. London: Duckworth, [1928]. Republ as *Doom*. London: Macdonald, 1974.
The story of Adams and Eva: a novel of fantasy with a thinly disguised parody of Beaverbrook (in the shape of Lord Ottercove).

1221   Geyer, Curt. 'Die *Times* repräsentiert Englands Oberschicht'. *Süddeutsche Zeitung* (Munich), 26–7 Feb 1955.
'Oberschicht' means 'upper class'.

1222   Gibb, D(avid) E(ric) W(ilson). *Lloyd's of London: a study in individuality*. London: Lloyd's. 1959, 1972. ix + 587pp.
An official history which distils the research to that date on (the 17th–18th-century) Edward Lloyd's *Lloyd's News* and *Lloyd's List* – and the rival *New Lloyd's List*.

1223   Gibb, Ian P., ed. *Newspaper preservation and access*. Munich and London: K.G. Saur, 1988. 2 vols. Total 449pp.
Proceedings of the symposium held in London, August 1987, by the International Federation of Library Associations. Contains the opening address by Sir Denis Hamilton, on the importance of the press to the historian.

1224   Gibb, Mildred Anne, and Frank Beckwith. *The Yorkshire Post: two centuries*. Leeds: Yorkshire Conservative Newspaper Co, 1954. xii + 112pp.
Other members of the editorial staff also contributed, in celebration of the bicentenary of the *Leeds Intelligencer*.

1225 Gibbard, Les. *Gibbard's double decade omnibus*. London: Bellew Publishing, 1991. Foreword by John Cole.
Political history, 1969–81, in four hundred cartoons from *The Guardian*.

1226 Gibberd, Kathleen. *Our own affairs: a guide to the intelligent reading of the newspaper*. London: Dent, 1939. xiii + 252pp.

1227 – – –. *Citizenship through the newspaper*. London: Dent, 1939. xi + 267pp; revised 1944. xi + 186pp.
Two books written for a wartime British public to reassure those who might have doubted it that the national press was a vital component in a healthy democracy.

1228 Gibbs, (*Sir*) Philip (Armand Hamilton). *The street of adventure*. London: Heinemann, 1909. 460pp. New York: 1919.
Gibbs (1877–1962) was literary editor in turn of the *Daily Mail, Daily Chronicle*, and *Tribune* in the early 1900s; *The street of adventure* is a famous work of fiction based on the Fleet Street of that era. Several characters were based on real-life journalists; for example, Benjamin Harrison on Franklin Thomasson, proprietor of the *Tribune*, and the heroine Katherine Halstead on Emilie Hawkes Peacocke, who first came to Gibbs's notice as a reporter on *The Northern Echo*. No doubt Gibbs's experience on the shortlived *Tribune* contributed to his jaundiced condemnation of 'The Street of Adventure': 'Its atmosphere . . . produced something of the same symptoms as the drug habit. The victim loathes the poison, but craves for it.'

1229 – – –. *The soul of the war*. London: Heinemann, 1915. 362pp. Revised edn, Hutchinson, [1929]. 318pp.
The first of Gibbs's classic examples of reportage from the Western Front in World War I. The only correspondent to report during the whole length of the war, he was afterwards knighted.

1230 – – –. *The battles of the Somme*. London: Heinemann, 1917. vi + 336pp.
Gibbs's elegant but periphrastic reports to the *Daily Telegraph* and *Daily Chronicle* between 1 July and 8 October 1916 describe better than most the feelings of the front-line infantry soldier – the British 'Tommy'.

1231 – – –. *From Bapaume to Passchendaele: on the Western Front, 1917*. London: Heinemann, 1918. vii + 384pp. New York: Doran, 1918. ix + 462pp.

1232 – – –. *Realities of war*. London: Heinemann, 1920. vii + 455pp. Revised edn, Hutchinson, [1929]. 352pp. Publ in the USA as *Now it can be told*. New York: 1920.
Definitive first-hand reporting on World War I, free at last of censorship.

1233 – – –. *Adventures in journalism*. London: Heinemann, 1923. 336pp. New York: Harper. 363pp.
Covers twenty years of its author's career (but not World War I).

1234   – – –.   *The pageant of the years: an autobiography.* London: Heinemann, 1946. vii + 530pp.

1235   – – –.   *The journalist's London.* London: Alan Wingate, 1952. vii + 175pp. (In Londoner's Library series.)
Chatty, but informative.

1236   – – –.   *The war dispatches*, ed Catherine Prigg. Douglas (Isle of Man): Anthony Gibbs & Phillips/Times Press, 1964. ix + 409pp.
Combines extracts from five of Sir Philip Gibbs's books of World War I vintage. Anthony Gibbs, himself a war correspondent in World War II, contributes a most appealing introduction.

1237   Gibbs, (*Sir*) Philip, and Bernard Grant. *Adventures of war with Cross and Crescent.* London: Methuen, 1912. viii + 241pp. Publ in the USA as *The Balkan War.* Boston: [1913].
The Balkan League of four nations fought under the Cross against the Turks under the sign of the Crescent in 1912–13. This was Gibbs's first book of war reporting; Grant accompanied him as front-line photographer.

1238   Giblett, Pamela, Dorothy Henderson *et al.*, eds. *Newspapers – the living textbook.* London: Newspaper Society, 1988.
London and Essex Guardian Newspapers cooperated in the production of this Newspapers in Education publication.

1239   Gibson, Jeremy S.W., comp. *Local newspapers 1750–1920: England and Wales; Channel Islands; Isle of Man; a select location list.* Birmingham: Federation of Family History Societies, 1987. 65pp.

1240   Gifford, Denis. *Stap me!: the British newspaper strip.* Aylesbury (Bucks): Shire Publications, 1971. 96pp.

1241   – – –.   'Sidney Strube, 1891–1936'. *In* Maurice Horn, ed. *The world encyclopedia of cartoons.* New York: Chelsea House, 1980.
Tribute to the cartoonist of the 'Little Man' for the *Daily Express.*

1242   Gilbert, Bentley Brinkerhoff. *David Lloyd George: a political life: the architect of change, 1863–1912.* London. Batsford, 1972. 546pp.
Covers Lloyd George's surprise move into *The Daily News* in 1901, replacing E.T. Cook as editor.

1243   Gilbert, Martin. *Winston Churchill: a life.* London: Macmillan, 1991. xxii + 1066pp.
This massive single-volume biography embraces Churchill's journalistic oeuvre.

1244   Giles, Frank (Thomas Robertson). *Sundry times.* London: John Murray, 1986. x + 262pp.
An autobiography of some courage, modest in approach yet authoritative in judgement. Giles had been editor of *The Sunday Times* from 1981 to 1983, and had published a biography of Henri de Blowitz in 1962.

1245 Giles, Vic(tor). 'Newspaper design and its impact'. *In* Dennis Griffiths, ed. *Encyclopedia of the British press, 1422–1992*. Basingstoke (Hants): Macmillan, 1992.
By the designer of several national newspapers.

1246 Giles, Vic(tor), and F(rederick) W(est) Hodgson. *Creative newspaper design*. Oxford: Heinemann, 1990. 291pp.
Aimed at students: 'the techniques and principles governing newspaper design in today's hi-tech environment'. Includes a historical summary.

1247 Gill, Crispin. 'The *Western Morning News*, 1860–1985.' *Devonshire Association Reports and Transactions*, 117, 1985.

1248 Given, John La Porte. *Making a newspaper*. London: Williams & Norgate, 1913. iii + 325pp.

1249 Glandon, Virginia E. *Arthur Griffiths and the advanced-rationalist press, Ireland, 1900–1922*. New York: P. Lang, [1985]. xi + 323pp.
Irish periodicals – some in the vernacular – with an appendix listing newspapers.

1250 Glasgow Herald. *The Glasgow Herald, 1783–1911*, ed W. Stewart. Glasgow: Outram, [1911?]. 48pp.
John Mennons founded the *Glasgow Advertiser* (a twice-weekly paper) in 1783; its title became *Glasgow Herald* (*and Advertiser*) nine years later, but it did not become a daily until 1859, by which time it was under the control of George Outram and his family. Ownership passed to the Lonrho group in 1979, but Caledonian Newspaper Publishing achieved a management buy-out in 1992. The title was changed to simply *The Herald* earlier in the same year.

1251 – – –. *At the sign of the Green Dragon*. Glasgow: Outram, 1927.

1252 *Glasgow Herald*. 150th anniversary number. 27 Jan 1933.

1253 Glasgow Herald. *Casual columns: the Glasgow Herald miscellany*, ed R.N. Biles. [1955]. 317pp.
Extracts from The Week-end Page over twenty years.

1254 – – –. *The Glasgow Herald*, 1783–1958. 27 Jan 1958. 96pp.

1255 – – –. *The pick of the Herald*. Glasgow: Richard Drew. Vol 1, 1982.

1256 *Glasgow Herald. Glasgow Herald: Scotland's newspaper, 1783–1983*. 200th anniversary number: special colour supplement. 27 Jan 1983.

– – –. *Glasgow Herald index: see Reference Works section*.

1257 No entry.

1258 *Glasgow newspapers 1715 to 1979: a chronological guide*. Glasgow: Mitchell Library; 2nd edn, 1979. (A Glasgow Room publication.)

1259 Glendinning, Matthew. 'Is sport writing as sick as a parrot?'. *British Journalism Review*, 3, 4, 1992.
'In the tabloid market sport is now the major factor in selling newspapers.'

1260   Glendinning, Victoria. *Rebecca West: a life*. London: Weidenfeld & Nicolson, 1987. xv + 288pp.

1261   Glenton, George, and William Pattinson. *The last Chronicle of Bouverie Street*. London: Allen & Unwin, 1963. 218pp.
All the sadness and bitterness provoked by the merger of the *News Chronicle* – itself a composite – and *The Star* (one of London's three post-World War II evenings) into the *Daily Mail* and *Evening News* respectively is expressed here by two ex-*News Chronicle* reporters.

1262   Gliserman, Susan. 'Mitchell's *Newspaper Press Directory*: 1846–1907'. *Victorian Periodicals Newsletter*, 4, Apr 1969.
A comprehensive bibliography of the first sixty-two years (fifty-six issues) of the world's oldest press guide.

1263   *Globe, The*. Centenary number. 1 Jan 1903.
A London evening, *The Globe* was published until 1921. (It was owned briefly by Beaverbrook in pre-war days.)

1264   *Gloucester Journal*. 1722–1972. Gloucester: 8 Apr 1972.
Founded by Robert Raikes (the elder), the *Journal* was used by his son – the founder of Sunday Schools – as a medium to press for prison reform. The paper was revived (as a weekly) by Northcliffe Newspapers in 1990.

1265   *Gloucestershire Gazette*. Centenary supplement. Dursley (Glos): 28 Oct 1978.
Published weekly by the Bailey Newspaper group; originally *Dursley, Berkeley and Sharpness Gazette and West Gloucestershire Advertiser*.

1266   Glover, Stephen. *Paper dreams*. London: Jonathan Cape, 1993; pbk, 1994.
The story of *The Independent* and *Independent on Sunday* by one of the three founders. The business side is a more permanent record than the (very) personal touch.

1267   – – –.   'Black's magic'. *Evening Standard*, 17 Mar 1993.
Since Conrad Black took control of *The Daily Telegraph*, the profits have greatly improved – and so, says Glover, has the editorial content, although circulation still causes anxiety.

1268   – – –.   'The dead hand of Lonrho'. *Evening Standard*, 28 Apr 1993.
Decrying Lonrho and its record as publisher of *The Observer*.

1269   – – –.   'A defeatist survivor'. *The Spectator*, 29 May 1993.
Celebrates Lord Deedes' eightieth birthday with an affectionate assessment of his sixty-two years in journalism – the only pre-war 'Fleet Street' editor still practising his craft.

1270   – – –.   'The colour of money'. *Evening Standard*, 7 Jul 1993.
Doubting the benefit of the use of colour every day in the nationals: *The Guardian* was then planning to make this move.

1271   Godfrey, Michael. 'Why I'm delighted it's the end of Fleet Street EC4'. *UK Press Gazette*, 4 Jun 1988.
Interview with Lord Marsh as chairman of the Newspaper Publishers Association.

1272   Goldenberg, Susan. *The Thomson empire*. Agincourt (Ont): Methuen, 1984; London: Sidgwick & Jackson, 1985. 296pp.
Traces in detail, with a chronology and copious other appendices, the birth and growth of the Thomson Corporation and in particular, of course, the life and business career of Roy Thomson (the 1st Baron Thomson of Fleet).

1273   Goldman, Aaron L. 'Claud Cockburn, *The Week* and the "Cliveden set"'. *Journalism Quarterly*, 1972, 721–8.

1274   Goldsmith, Sam, ed. *Britain in the eye of the world: the Foreign Press Association in London, 1888–1988*. London: FPA, 1987. 96pp. 27 contributors.
'Normally the foreign correspondent is largely left to his own devices, to make what he can of the British. Official Britain extends a cautious hand to him but not much more. The British are not very good at explaining themselves. Take us or leave us, they seem to say' (Roland Hill, a former FPA president).

1275   Gollin, Alfred Manuel. *The Observer and J.L. Garvin, 1908–1914: a study in a great editorship*. London: Oxford University Press, 1960. xiii + 444pp.
A detailed analysis of Garvin's first six eventful – and very political – years at *The Observer*. More about the journalist than his newspaper, this tells the story of how an ambitious First Lord of the Admiralty deliberately 'leaked' Cabinet secrets to the newly appointed editor in order to provoke a public outcry in favour of his own policy of an arms race with Germany.

1276   Goodbody, John. *The Star: its place in the rise of London evening newspapers, 1888–1914*. University of London (Birkbeck College), 1985 (MA thesis).

1277   – – –. '*The Star*: its role in the rise of popular newspapers, 1888–1914'. *Journal of Newspaper and Periodical History*, Spring 1985.

1278   Goodhart, David. 'Inside the industrial relations jungle'. *UK Press Gazette*: souvenir issue. 3 Jun 1985.
By a contributor to the *Financial Times*'s industrial column.

1279   Goodhart, David, and Patrick Wintour. *Eddie Shah and the newspaper revolution*. London: Coronet, 1986. 303pp.
Shah had moved from Warrington to the national big-time. The book covers the eve of the launch of *Today* and has much useful material on developments elsewhere.

1280   Goodman, Arnold Abraham, *Baron*. *Tell them I'm on my way*. London: Chapmans, 1993. xiii + 464pp.
Outspoken memoirs, with a chapter devoted to 'The newspapers'. Of the Newspaper Publishers Association (of which he was at one chairman), Lord Goodman comments: 'The NPA was in the main composed of the most impossible body of men that could

have been assembled outside of the United Nations'. He also held the chairmanship of *The Observer*.

1281   – – –.   'Tradition and talent in an age of transition'. *UK Press Gazette*, 13 Jun 1988. (In Cleaning Up the 4th Estate series.)

1282   Goodman, Geoffrey (George). *The miners' strike*. London: Pluto Press, 1985. 213pp.
By the then industrial editor of the *Daily Mirror*; later founder-editor, *British Journalism Review*.

1283   Gordon, Harold Sidney, and Rodney Bennett, comps. *Through the eyes of The Times*. London: University of London Press, 1937. 182pp.

1284   Gordon, Nick. 'Women's war daily'. *The Sunday Times*, 27 Jun 1993.
On the front-line women in the bloody war in the former Yugoslavia – featuring Maggie O'Kane of *The Guardian* and Janine di Giovanni of *The Sunday Times*.

1285   Gordon, Paul, and David Rosenberg. *Daily racism: the press and black people in Britain*. London: Runnymede Trust, 1989. 73pp.
Critical of the press in general in its racist attitudes.

1286   Gore, John (Francis). *The ghosts of Fleet Street*, illustrated by Joseph Pike. London: Eyre & Spottiswoode, [1928]. viii + 114pp.
'A street of hasty judgment, of distorted truth, of elastic morality, of easy conviction'.

1287   Gould, Ann, ed. *Masters of caricature: from Hogarth and Gillray to Scarfe and Levine*. London: Weidenfeld & Nicolson, 1981. 240pp.
Introduction by William Feaver.

1288   – – –.   'The newspaper cartoon'. In *The Penrose Annual, 1971*. London: Lund Humphries, 1971.
A long and profusely illustrated article.

1289   – – –.   'The picture-politics of Francis Carruthers Gould'. In *Politics in cartoon and caricature*, special issue of *20th Century Studies*, 13/14, Dec 1975.
The author writes with the authority of F.C. Gould's granddaughter.

1290   Gould, *Sir* Francis Carruthers. *Political caricatures*. London: Edward Arnold, 1903, 1904, 1905, 1906.
Classic drawings stemming from the regular contributions by Gould (1844–1925) to *The Westminster Gazette*. The first staff caricaturist on a daily British paper (*The Pall Mall Gazette*), he eventually became assistant editor at *The Westminster* to J.A. Spender, being equally skilled with words and the artist's pencil. The MS of an unpublished auto-biography is in the House of Lords.

1291   Goulden, John Frank. *Newspaper management*. London: Heinemann, for the National Council for the Training of Journalists, 1967. xi + 92pp.
Based on the author's experience with the Kemsley, Thomson and United Newspapers groups – notably for the *Sheffield Telegraph*.

1292   Goulden, Mark. *Mark my words!: the memoir of a journalist/publisher*. London: W.H. Allen, 1978, vii + 256pp.
The climax of Goulden's career was in fact his chairmanship of W.H. Allen; but there is much of interest here about his pre-war provincial and national newspaper and magazine journalism, notably as editor-in-chief of *The Sunday Referee*.

1293   Gourlay, [Jack] Logan, ed. *The Beaverbrook I knew*. London: Quartet Books, 1984. xi + 272pp.
A former *Daily Express* man puts together thirty-three essays (and an extract from a television documentary) that serve to illustrate the widely differing views of Beaverbrook held by his contemporaries. The Centre for Cartoons and Caricature provides an evocative selection from its Beaverbrook collection.

1294   Grace, Tony. 'The trade-union press in Britain'. *Media, Culture and Society*, Apr 1985.
One of the four journals examined in detail is *Journalist* (the organ of the National Union of Journalists).

1295   Graham, Harry Joscelyn Clive. *The Mother of Parliaments*. London: Methuen, 1910. xii + 314pp.
Including parliamentary reporting, pre-World War I style.

1296   Graham, Michael. '*The Standard*: evening paper'. *Notes and Queries*, ser 12, 1, 20 May 1916.

1297   Graham-Yooll, Andrew. *Point of arrival*. London: Pluto Press, 1992.
Critical of the lack of freedom enjoyed by Britain's newspapers: by the editor of *Index on censorship*.

1298   Grant, Bernard. *To the four corners: the memories of a news photographer*. London: Hutchinson, [1933]. 287pp.
Daily Mirror/Sunday Pictorial assignments. *See also under* Gibbs, *Sir* P.

1299   Grant, John. 'Every newsman's editor'. *The Times*, 8 Sep 1987.
The former deputy editor pays tribute to Sir William Haley, and portrays life in Printing House Square during his editorship.

1300   *Graphic, The*. Jubilee number. 6 Dec 1919.
The 'illustrated weekly newspaper' founded in 1869 by W.L. Thomas was quick to cover the Franco-Prussian War and thus establish its reputation. *The Graphic* was incorporated into *The Sphere* in 1932 (after a brief period as *The National Graphic*).

1301   Graves, Robert [von Ranke], and Alan Hodge. *The long weekend: a social history of Great Britain, 1918–1939*. London: Faber, 1940; Hutchinson, 1985; New York: Macmillan, 1941. 472pp.
Commercial considerations prompted the famous poet/novelist to team up with a leading social historian to produce this untypical work – but it still reads well, not least the plentiful quotations from the contemporary press.

1302   *Gravesend Reporter.* Centenary number. Gravesend (Kent): 4 Feb 1956.

1303   Gray, Bernard. *War reporter.* London: Robert Hale, 1942. 183pp.
'The first reporter to see bombs dropped on the Germans', claimed Gray's newspaper, the *Sunday Pictorial.* Gray went missing in the Mediterranean before this book was published.

1304   Gray, Robert. 'And now for some words for a sponsor'. *PR Week*, 4 Nov 1993.
Developing from the controversial 'advortorial' (advertising matter within the editorial pages) most nationals will now accept 'sponsorial' (the sponsorship of feature pages and whole supplements on almost any topic bar news reporting). A tabulation of existing opportunities is appended to this article.

1305   Gray, Tony. *The real professionals.* London: Heinemann, [1967]. 218pp.
A Fleet Street novel.

1306   – – –.   *Fleet Street remembered.* London: Heinemann, 1990. 328pp.
'An anthology of memories': forty-three contributors in all, preceded by the author's own survey of the Fleet Street story. Unhappily error-strewn.

1307   *Great front pages, D-Day to victory, 1944–1945.* With an introduction by Wynford Vaughan-Thomas and illustrated from the John Frost Collection. London: Collins, 1984. 128pp.

1308   *Great newspapers reprinted*, ed Brian Lake. With illustrations from the John Frost Collection. London: Peter Way, 1971–5. Monthly.

1309   'Great press wars, The, 1929–1933: five years of births, marriages and deaths'. *World's Press News*, 14 Dec 1933.

1310   *Great Royal front pages.* With an introduction by Anthony Holden; illustrations from the John Frost Collection. London: Collins, 1983. 128pp.
A sumptuous large-format 'scrapbook of historic Royal events'.

1311   *Great sporting headlines.* With an introduction by Ian Wooldridge; facsimile illustrations from the John Frost Collection: 'from W.G. Grace to Zola Budd', in large format. London: Collins, 1984. 121pp.

1312   *Great Yarmouth Mercury.* Centenary supplement. Great Yarmouth (Norfolk): 22 Feb 1980.
An Eastern Counties group weekly.

1313   Green, A.P. *Thirty thousand and one Fleet Street nights.* Frome (Somerset): [1937]. 136pp.

1314   Green, Geoffrey. *Pardon me for living: an autobiography.* London: Allen & Unwin, 1985. x + 207pp.
By the football correspondent (and one-time sports editor) of *The Times*, after thirty-one years in the job.

1315 Green, Michael. *Nobody hurt in small earthquake.* London: Heinemann, 1990. 246pp.
Professional humorist recalls his provincial reporting origins (on the Northampton *Chronicle and Echo*), and early days in Fleet Street. (His title is an adaptation of the 'classic' but unsubstantiated headline: 'Small earthquake in Chile: not many dead').

1316 Green, Stephen. 'The British Library's Newspaper Library in a new era'. *Journal of Newspaper and Periodical History*, Winter 1984.
The then head of the Newspaper Library relates how it is meeting the problems of an ever-increasing collection and growing reader demand.

1317 Green, Walter. *No better 'ole.* Braunton (Devon): Merlin Books, 1982. 204pp.
By a journalist who became owner of the *Daventry Weekly Express.*

1318 Greenberg, Susan, and Graham Smith. *Rejoice!: media freedom and the Falklands.* London: Campaign for Press and Broadcasting Freedom, 1983. 40pp.
Very critical survey of Government–media relations during the Falklands conflict, taking its title from the Prime Minister's exclamation on the re-taking of South Georgia.

1319 Greene, [Henry] Graham. *A sort of life.* London: Bodley Head, 1971. 216pp. New York: Simon & Schuster, 1971. 220pp.
Rather a thin first slice of autobiography, but Greene does comment interestingly on his days on *The Times* editorial staff (1926–30), and mentions his subsequent film and literary criticism for *The Spectator* and *Night and Day.*

1320 Greene, *(Sir)* Hugh (Carleton), and Thomas Barman. 'Warsaw, September, 1939'. *The Listener*, 22 Jul 1969.
Thirty-year memories as *Daily Telegraph* correspondent in Warsaw at the outbreak of World War II. Hugh Greene, elder brother of Graham, contributed this to the BBC's magazine in the year he stepped down as the Corporation's director-general.

1321 Greene, Thomas R. 'Vichy France and the Catholic press in England: contrasting attitudes to a moral problem'. *Recusant History*, 21, 1992.

1322 Greenslade, Roy. *Maxwell's fall.* London: Simon & Schuster, 1992.
Close-up biography – 'the appalling legacy of a corrupt man' – by a former editor of the *Daily Mirror.*

1323 – – –. 'The unpopular press'. *The Guardian (Media Guardian)*, 19 Oct 1992.
An investigation into the all-round and increasing decline in newspaper sales.

1324 – – –. 'Soft centres and hard hearts on quality street'. *The Guardian (Media Guardian)*, 6 Sep 1993.
Economic forces have led to a new price war – cuts for *The Times* (in particular) have caused an uproar ... but, remarks Greenslade, 'Britain's newspapers are in historical decline'.

1325   – – –. 'Fond memories of monochrome'. *British Journalism Review*, 4, 3, 1993.
Meanwhile, colour is not the be-all and end-all of the modern newspaper.

1326   Greenwall, Harry James. *Scoops: being leaves from the diary of a special correspondent*. London: Stanley Paul, 1923. 287pp. New York: 1923.
The author was Paris correspondent for the *Daily Express* etc.

1327   – – –. *Round the world for news*. London: Hutchinson, [1935]. 286pp.
Post-World War I, Greenwall reported for the *Daily Express* and *Continental Daily Mail*.

1328   – – –. *I hate to-morrow: an autobiographical experiment*. London: J. Gifford, 1939; Book Club, 1940. ix + 314pp.
Re the *Daily Express*, Beaverbrook etc.

1329   – – –. 'War reporting – to-day and yesterday'. *The Strand Magazine*, Jun 1940.
Looks back from World War II to World War I, and beyond to W.H. Russell and other pioneers.

1330   – – –. *Northcliffe: Napoleon of Fleet Street*. London: Allan Wingate, 1957. vii + 240pp.
Considers what might have happened had Northcliffe lived on with his full powers into the 1930s and 1940s. The first biography to inject a critical note.

1331   Greenwood, George A. 'A matter of modern opinion: Mr J.L. Garvin and *The Observer*'. In *Great thoughts from master minds*. London: Bailey Bros, 1935. (A Langham Booklet.)

1332   Gregory, Alfred Thomas. *Recollections of a country editor, by a Devon journalist*. Tiverton (Devon), [1932]. 126 + viiipp.
By the proprietor/editor of the *Tiverton Gazette*, 1877–1931. (Established 1858, this still appears weekly as one of the Northcliffe Newspapers group.)

1333   Gregory, Kenneth, ed. *The first cuckoo: a selection of witty, amusing and memorable letters to The Times, 1900–1980*. London: Allen & Unwin/Times Books, 1981; Unwin Paperbacks, 1983. 359pp. Publ in France as *Le premier coucou*; and in Canada and the USA as *Your obedient servant*.

1334   – – –. *The last cuckoo: the very best letters to The Times since 1920*. London: Unwin Hyman, 1987. viii + 343pp.
The third and sixth of a fascinating series – in itself a commentary on current news and topics. Gregory provided introductions to each volume.

1335   – – –. *From Grace to Botham*. London: Times Books, 1989.
The achievements of fifty great cricketers as recorded in *The Times*.

1336   Grey, Anthony. *Hostage in Peking*. London: Michael Joseph, 1970. 343pp.

1337   – – –. *A man alone*. London: Michael Joseph, 1971. 128pp.

1338 – – –. *Some put their trust in chariots*. London: Michael Joseph, 1973. 184pp. New English Library, 1975. 159pp.

Remembers when, as Reuters correspondent, the author was imprisoned by the Red Guards in Peking.

1339 Grey, Elizabeth. *The story of journalism*. London: Longman, 1968. 88pp. (Young Books series.)

1340, 1341 No entries.

1342 Griffiths, Dennis (Morgan). *Plant here The Standard*. Basingstoke (Hants): Macmillan, 1994.

No 1 of the original evening daily, which was founded by Charles Baldwin in 1827, carried the slogan 'Plant here THE STANDARD: here we shall best remain', hence the title of this authoritative history. (*The Standard* became a morning paper in 1857. The *Evening Standard* (q.v.) began as such in 1860, and has survived; but the (morning) *Standard* was a wartime casualty, ceasing in 1916. Pearson owned both from 1904 to 1910, and Davison Dalziel from 1910 to 1915.)

1343 – – – 'A woman's work'. *British Journalism Review*, Spring 1991.
Traces the role of women as editors.

1344 – – – 'Satellite technology and newspapers'. *British Library Newspaper Library Newsletter*, 13, Autumn/Winter 1991.
Includes 'the UK scene', summarizing the installation of satellite printing systems by every national newspaper group.

– – –, ed. *The encyclopedia of the British press, 1422–1992: see Reference Works section*.

1345 Grigg, John (Edward Poynder). 'Profile of *The Times*'. *The Political Quarterly*, Jul–Sep 1955.

1346 Grimsditch, Herbert B. 'Berry, William Ewert, Viscount Camrose'. *In Dictionary of national biography, 1951–1960*. Oxford: Oxford University Press, 1971.

1347 Grose, Roslyn. *The Sun-sation*. London: Angus & Robertson, 1980. 128pp.
Celebrating twenty years of *The Sun* – 'Britain's bestselling daily newspaper'.

1348 Gross, John. *The rise and fall of the man of letters: aspects of English literary life since 1800*. London: Weidenfeld, 1969. Harmondsworth (Middx): Penguin, 1991 (with new foreword and afterword).

A major survey that covers most nineteenth- and twentieth-century belletrists and journalists.

1349 Grove, Valerie. 'A polemical perfectionist foresees fine time at The Thunderer'. *The Sunday Times*, 18 Mar 1990.
Interview with Simon Jenkins, newly appointed editor of *The Times*.

1350 Grünbeck, Max. *Das Werden der modernen britischen Presse*. Leipzig: 1936. 31pp.

1351 – – –. *Die Presse Grossbritanniens, ihr geistiger und wirtschaftlicher Auf-bau.* Leipzig: Noske, 1936. 2 vols. Supplement, 1936–8. Leipzig: Meiner, 1939. This ranks as the most complete (and authoritative) survey of the British press published outside the UK; in fact, it is among the very best, up to World War II, even when measured against Britain's own major treatises.

1352 – – –. 'Organisation und Persönlichkeit des Reuter-Büros'. *Zeitungs-wissenschaft*, 1 Jul 1934.

1353 – – –. '*The Times*: ein geschichtlicher Rückblick'. *Zeitungswissenschaft*, 1 Jan 1935.

1354 Guardian, The. *The bedside Guardian: a selection from The Guardian.* Annual. London: Collins, 1952–89; from no 39 (1990), Fourth Estate. Eds: nos 1–36, William Leslie Webb; no 37, Hugh Hebert; nos 38–9, Nicholas de Jongh; nos 40, 41 and 42, John Course.

1355 – – –. *The story of The Guardian.* London: 1964.
The pedigree of *The Guardian* (retitled as such in 1959, and printed in London also from 1961) dates back to the launch in 1821 of *The Manchester Guardian* (q.v.). It remains, with the *Manchester Evening News* and *The Observer* (and its own *Guardian Weekly* and *Guardian Europe*), the product of an independent trust.

1356 *Guardian, The.* 150th anniversary supplement. 5 May 1971.

1357 – – –. '*The Guardian* moves to 119 Farringdon Road'. London (supple-ment). 15 Sep 1976.

1358 – – –. 25th anniversary of first printing in London: supplement. 11 Sep 1986.

1359 Guardian, The. *Guardian book of the Spanish Civil War, The.* Aldershot (Hants): Gower Press (Wildwood), 1987. xx + 332pp. Eds R.H. Haigh, D.S. Morris and A.R. Peters.
Based on *The Manchester Guardian* of the time, with latter-day commentary.

1360 – – –. *Guardian book of the General Strike, The.* Same publishers and eds, 1988. xxvi + 175pp. Anthology from 1926.

1361 – – –. *Guardian book of Munich, The.* Same publishers and eds, 1986. xxvi + 316pp.
Extracts from 1938.

Guardian index, The: see Reference Works section.

1362 *Guardian Journal.* Centenary supplement. Nottingham: 1 Jul 1961.
One of the two ancestors of the *Guardian Journal* – the *Nottingham Journal* – was founded in 1710; it was the *Nottingham (Daily) Guardian* that first appeared in 1861. Both were suitably celebrated in this commemorative publication. The *Guardian Journal* ceased publication in 1973.

1363 Guild of British Newspaper Editors. *Officially secret*. London: GBNE, 1988. 24pp.
'How the role of the nation's newspapers as public watchdogs is being severely blunted by a pervasive, almost institutionalised secrecy in our society'. Produced by the Guild's Parliamentary and Legal Committee.

1364 Guthrie, Diana. *The first fifty years of the Sheffield Daily Telegraph: an experiment in provincial journalism*. Sheffield: University of Sheffield, 1970 (MA thesis).
The period covered is 1855–1905.

1365 Gwynne, H[owell] A[rthur]. 'The press in war'. *Journal of the Royal United Services Institute*, 58, 1913. Reprinted from a lecture at the RUSI, 5 Nov 1913.
Gwynne (1865–1950) was Reuters' representative in the Boer War, editor extraordinary, and major 'backroom' political figure of his time. He edited *The Standard* (the morning paper) from 1904 to 1911, and then *The Morning Post* to its end in 1937.

1366 – – –. 'Farewell and hail!'. *The Morning Post*, 30 Sep 1937.
Valediction in the last issue of his paper on its merger with *The Daily Telegraph*. Unlike some similar occasions, he comments: 'The utmost consideration has been given to the staff.'

1367 *Hackney Gazette*. 125th anniversary number. London: May 1989.
Special issue to celebrate 1864–1989.

1368 Hadley, W[illiam] W[aite]. *The bi-centenary record of the Northampton Mercury, 1720–1920*. Northampton: 1920. 60pp.
A youthful new editor looks back over the long story of his paper.

1369 – – –. *Munich: before and after*. London: Cassell, 1944. 184pp.
By then near the middle of his long editorship of *The Sunday Times*, Hadley deals authoritatively with the Munich agreement of 1939 and its outcome.

1370 – – –. 'Northamptonshire memories'. *Northamptonshire Past and Present*, 2, 1956.

1371 Haines, Joe [Joseph Thomas William]. *The politics of power*. London: Jonathan Cape, 1977. xi + 228pp.
The author was for seven years press secretary to Harold Wilson when the latter was Prime Minister, and later returned to political journalism with the *Daily Mirror*.

1372 – – –. *Maxwell*. London: Macdonald; Futura, 1988. ix + 525pp; publ in France as *L'incroyable Mons. Maxwell: histoire d'un empire*. Paris: Odile Jacob, 1988.
'The definitive biography' – but very much the authorized version. Serialized in the *Daily Mirror*, Feb–Mar 1988.

1373 Haldane, Charlotte. *Russian newsreel*. London: Secker & Warburg, 1942.
Into battle with the Red Army for the *Daily Sketch*.

1374 – – –. *Truth will out*. London: Weidenfeld & Nicolson, 1949.
Mainly later memories from her days with the *Daily* and *Sunday Express*.

1375 Hale, Oron James. *Publicity and diplomacy, with special reference to England and Germany, 1890–1914*. New York: Appleton-Century, 1940. xi + 486pp.

1376 Hales, Alfred Greenwood. *Campaign pictures of the war in South Africa, 1899–1902*. London: 1900.
An Australian, Hales was a graphic correspondent with that country's forces for *The Daily News* in the Boer War.

1377 – – –. *Broken trails: the revelations of a wandering life*. London: John Leng, 1931. 320pp; Wright & Brown, [1937]. 287pp.

1378 – – –. *My life of adventure*. London: Wright & Brown, [1937]. 288pp.

1379 – – –. 'The life of a war correspondent'. *The Pall Mall Gazette*, 13 Feb 1901.

1380 Haley, *Sir* William (John). *The public influence of broadcasting and the press*. Manchester: 1954. Clayton Memorial Lecture.
Haley, born in 1901, went from the director-generalship of the BBC to a very successful editorship of *The Times* (1952–66); this is one of his few public pronouncements. He died in 1967.

1381 – – –. '*The Times*'. *The Times House Journal*, Jan–Feb 1965.

1382 – – –. 'Jones, Sir (George) Roderick'. *In Dictionary of national biography, 1961–1970*. Oxford: Oxford University Press, 1981.
After receiving an OBE in 1918, Jones – says his biographer – 'naturally authoritative, became imperial'.

1383 – – –. '*Guardian years*, by Alastair Hetherington'. Book review in *The Sunday Times*, 1 Nov 1981.
A long and informative notice by this former editor of the *Manchester Evening News* and *Guardian* director.

1384 Hall, Norman, ed. *Press pictures of a decade*. London: Photography (magazine), 1950.
A collection of 154 plates, selected from ten British Press Pictures of the Year exhibitions.

1385 Hall, Richard. *My life with Tiny*. London: Faber, 1987. xiii + 257pp.
Disaffected employee's view of R.W. Rowland of *The Observer* etc.

1386 Hall, Stuart. 'The social eye of *Picture Post*'. In *Working papers in cultural studies*, 2. Birmingham: University of Birmingham, 1972.

1387 – – –. 'The determination of news photographs'. In *Working papers in cultural studies*, 3. Birmingham: University of Birmingham, 1972.

1388   Hall, Valerie J. *Women in journalism: a sociological account of the entry of women into the profession of journalism in Great Britain until 1930.* Colchester: University of Essex, 1978 (PhD thesis). 372pp.

1389   Halle, Kay, ed. *Randolph Churchill: the young unpretender.* London: Heinemann, 1971.
Essays in tribute by his friends, many of whom were working journalists too.

1390   Hambro, Carl Joachim. *Newspaper lords in British politics.* London: Macdonald, 1958. 63pp.
Largely a sketchy, inconsequential biography of Beaverbrook with passing references to Northcliffe and Rothermere.

1391   Hamilton, Alan. 'All the pictures fit to print'. *The Times* 22 Oct 1981.
Marking the 7,000th issue of *The Illustrated London News.*

1392   Hamilton, *Sir* [Charles] Denis. *Who is to own the British press?* London: University of London (Birkbeck College), 1976. 20pp. Haldane Memorial Lecture.
By the then editor-in-chief of Times Newspapers (and former editor of *The Sunday Times* from 1961 to 1967).

1393   – – –.   *Editor-in-chief: the Fleet Street memoirs of Sir Denis Hamilton.* London: Hamish Hamilton, 1989. xii + 208pp.
Posthumous memoirs concentrating particularly on his years (1967–81) in quiet but sure command of Times Newspapers; also a close-up view of Kemsley Newspapers in earlier post-war years. There are no penetrating revelations.

1394   – – –.   'Fleet Street in the eighties'. *In* D. Campbell, ed. *The British press.* London: CPU, 1978.

1395   Hamilton, Geoffrey E. *Satisfying researchers' needs for access to newspapers.* London: British Library (for IFLA), 1993. Paper read at the Barcelona Conference of the International Federation of Library Associations and Institutions. 'Are there new solutions to an old problem?'

1396   – – –.   'Newspaper preservation and access: development and possibilities'. *Interlending and Document Supply,* 20, Apr 1992.
By the head of the British Library Newspaper Library.

1397   Hamilton, J.A.B. 'Progress of provincial newspapers'. *Admap,* Feb 1968.
Explains the functions of the Evening Newspaper Advertising Bureau and Weekly Newspaper Advertising Bureau – then both in operation.

1398   Hamilton, Mary Agnes. 'The woman newspaper reader'. In *Sell's Dictionary of the World's Press, 1919.* London: Sell, 1919.

1399   *Hamilton Advertiser: a century of service, 1856–1956.* Hamilton (then Lanarkshire): 1956. 32pp.

1400   Hamilton-Tweedale, B. *The British press and Northern Ireland*. Sheffield: University of Sheffield, 1988 (MPhil thesis).
Surveys the situation since 1969.

1401   Hamlavi, A.I.H. 'The British press'. *Asiatic Review*, 43, 156, Oct 1947.
An Iranian view.

1402   Hammerton, *Sir* John Alexander. *With Northcliffe in Fleet Street: a personal record*. London: Hutchinson, [1932]. 288pp.
A nerve-racking association with the mercurial press lord, recollected in tranquillity. (After Northcliffe's death, Hammerton continued the editing of educational books and partworks for the Amalgamated Press.)

1403   Hammond, John Lawrence Le Breton. *C.P. Scott and the Manchester Guardian*. London: Bell; New York: Harcourt, 1934. xv + 365pp.
Deals at length with Scott's – and *The Guardian*'s – attitude towards party politics, World War I, Ireland, and foreign policy generally. There is a fascinating chapter by W.P. Crozier on 'C.P.S. in the office'.

1404   Hammond, Lawrence (Victor) Francis. *W.H. Smith, a story that began in 1792*. London: W.H. Smith, 1979. 28pp.
A brief illustrated history of the company.

1405   *Hampshire Advertiser*. Centenary number. Southampton: 28 Jul 1923.

1406   *Hampshire Chronicle*. 'Our 150th anniversary'. Winchester: 26 Aug 1922.

1407   – – –.   '*Hampshire Chronicle* and its readers'. 6 Apr 1957.

1408   – – –.   '*Hampshire Chronicle*: 1772–1959'. 31 Oct 1959.

1409   – – –.   '190 years of history'. 12 May 1962.

1410   Hampshire Chronicle. *Hampshire Chronicle, 1792–1972: a bicentenary publication*. 18 Aug 1972.
Booklet commemorating 'Hampshire's first newspaper'.

1411   *Hampstead and Highgate Express*. Centenary number. London: 21 Oct 1960.
The '*Ham and High*' is a north London weekly in the Home Counties group.

1412   Hand, Charles. *I was after money*. London: Partridge Publications, 1949. 223pp. 56 illus, and 20 sketches by Adam Horne.
By a leading theatre columnist, who was also a well-known Fleet Street 'character' with a most sensitive 'nose' for news.

1413   *Handlist of selected newspaper holdings both national and regional in London's public libraries ('Hosnill')*. 3rd edn, prepared by Hammersmith L.B. London: 1977. 4th edn, by Croydon L.B. London: 1982.

1414   Handover, Phyllis Margaret. *A history of The London Gazette, 1665–1965*. London: HMSO, 1965. vii + 95pp.

A brief official 'tricentenary' celebration of the world's oldest surviving periodical, founded (because of the plague in London) as *The Oxford Gazette* on 16 November 1665; when the Court moved back, it became (with no 24, 5 February 1966) *The London Gazette* – still 'published by authority'. Almost the only news medium of its time, it was later restricted to official announcements, as remains the case today.

1415   *Handy Newspaper List*. London: Charles & Edwin Layton, [1890–] 1915. Annual. The final edition is described as '25th year'.

1416   Hanley, Gerald (Anthony). *Monsoon victory*. London: Collins, 1946. 256pp.
The author reported from Burma for *The Spectator*.

1417   Hannan, Patrick (David). *The first rough draft: history and journalism*. Aberystwyth (Dyfed): National Library of Wales, 1993. Welsh Political Archive Lecture, 1992.
Hannan takes his title from the aphorism of Ben Bradlee of *Washington Post* fame: 'Journalism is the first draft of history.' He pays tribute to the success of journalists such as the Berry and Cudlipp brothers from modest south Wales origins, but comments that many talented Welsh people are now preferring to become historians. He avers that indeed 'history is what you might call an improved version of journalism'.

1418   Hansard, B.M. *In and out of Fleet Street, and some personalities I have met*. Gosport (Hants): Hansard Publishing Co, 1935. 308pp.
Includes a close-up of Edgar Wallace, who edited a racing paper published by Hansard, and of the *Evening Standard*.

1419   Hansen, Ferdinand. *The unrepentant Northcliffe: a reply to the London Times of October 19, 1920*. Hamburg: Overseas Publishing Co, 1921. 47pp.
The 'reply' is to *The Times*'s review of the author's 'An open letter to an English officer' and incidentally 'to the English people on British policy during and after the European war'. A German riposte to the anti-German sentiments perpetuated in *The Times* under Northcliffe.

1420   Harborough Mail. *125 years of newspaper publishing: souvenir supplement, 1854–1979*. Market Harborough (Leics): 18 Oct 1979.
Today this paper is the *Market Harborough Advertiser*, in the EMAP group.

1421   Hardman, Thomas H., comp. *A parliament of the press: the first Imperial Press Conference*. With a preface by the Earl of Rosebery. London: Horace Marshall, 1909. xii + 249pp.
An official report of the conference in London that led to the formation of the Empire Press Union. These proceedings include speeches on literature and journalism by Lord Morley, Augustine Birrell, Winston Churchill, Lord Milner, Sir Edward Russell, W.L. Courtney, and T.P. O'Connor.

1422   Hardy, Bert. *Bert Hardy, photojournalist*. London: Gordon Fraser, 1975. 86pp. Introduction by Tom Hopkinson.
Outstanding award-winning contributions to *Picture Post*.

1423 – – –. *Bert Hardy: my life*. London: Gordon Fraser, 1985. 224pp.
Retrospect, after half a century, with more than three hundred dramatic shots, notably from wartime London, in Europe after the Allied invasion, and the Korean War. In the last-named, he accompanied James Cameron on behalf of *Picture Post*.

1424 Hargreave, Mary. 'Women's newspapers in the past'. *The Englishwoman*, 21 Jan/Mar 1914.

1425 Hargreaves, Ian, and Bernard Simon. 'Black magic at work around the world'. *Financial Times*, 21 Oct 1992.
On Conrad Black and his newspaper interests.

1426 Harling, Robert. *The paper palace*. London: Chatto & Windus, 1955; Reprint Society, 1952. 317pp.
'A triangle of which the Columnist, the Editor and the Baron-proprietor are the characters and the newspaper office is the scene'.

1427 – – –. *The enormous shadow*. London: Chatto & Windus, 1955; Reprint Society, 1956.
Another novel with a newspaper setting. Harling was a notable typographical expert, an adviser for example to Kemsley Newspapers.

1428 Harper, Edith Katherine. *Stead the man: personal reminiscences*. London: W. Rider, 1914. xiv + 263pp.

1429 Harper, Harry. *My fifty years in flying*. London: Associated Newspapers, 1956. 256pp.
It was fitting that the *Daily Mail* themselves published this final memoir by their pioneer air correspondent.

1430 Harriman, Ed. *Hack: home truths about foreign news*. London: Zed Books, 1987. 202pp.
The author draws on his own experience as a foreign correspondent to complain how the reality often does not appear in print.

1431 Harris, Brian. *The courts, the press and the public*. Chichester (W Sussex): Barry Rose, 1976.
Quick reference tool by a clerk to justices.

1432 Harris, [David] Kenneth. *Kenneth Harris talking to . . .* London: Weidenfeld and Nicolson, 1971.
With *The Observer* since 1950, he has achieved particular fame as its chief interviewer.

1433 Harris, Frank [born James Thomas]. *My life and loves*. 4 vols. Paris: (privately) 1922–7; New York: 1925; Paris: Obelisk Press, 1945; New York: Grove Press, 1963; London: W.H. Allen, 1964. Ed John F. Gallagher. 5 vols; Transworld (Corgi), 1966. xvi + 1070pp. Abridged as *Frank Harris: his life and adventures*. London: Richards Press, 1952. 387pp; intro Grant Richards; and *Frank Harris: my life and adventures*. London: Paul Elek, 1958. 383pp.

Intended from the start as a sensational money-spinner, this notorious work finally destroyed the professional career of a gifted journalist. (Harris's only major newspaper role was as editor of the *Evening News* in the 1880s.)

1434 Harris, Geoffrey, and David Spark. *Practical newspaper reporting*. London: Heinemann (for NCTJ), 1966. 390pp. Revised by F.W. Hodgson. Oxford: Butterworth-Heinemann (Focal Press), 1993. 280pp.
'A down-to-earth guide to reporting techniques', produced for the National Council for the Training of Journalists.

1435 Harris, [Henry] Wilson. *The daily press*. Cambridge: Cambridge University Press, 1943. x + 146pp. Rptd 1946. (In the Current Problems series.)
Sprightly, well-written 'backgrounder' for the general reader in wartime Britain. It stresses the public service side of newspaper journalism, and deplores any contemporary lapses into sensationalism as 'hangovers from the devil's decade of the 1930s'.

1436 – – –. *J.A. Spender*. London: Cassell, 1946. viii + 246pp.
For long the only individual biography of a major political journalist. Spender was born into journalism, his uncle Edward having founded the *Western Morning News* (Plymouth) and *Eastern Morning News* (Hull). He started his own career as an editor with the latter. His enduring fame rests with his editorship of *The Westminster Gazette*. Harris describes Spender as 'the very mould and pattern of the highest type of journalist, alike in competence and in character'; but also makes clear that these very attributes militated against his understanding of the business pressures on management.

1437 – – –. *Life so far*. London: Jonathan Cape, 1954. 321pp.
Harris (born in 1883) died the year after publication of this autobiography – which is important not only on the personal and professional level, but also as analysis of the report of the (1949) Royal Commission on the Press.
  Although Harris's name is indelibly linked with *The Spectator* (of which he was editor from 1932 to 1943), he had also worked previously in daily journalism, including reporting for *The Daily News* in immediate post-World War I Geneva, where he was accredited to the League of Nations, and became the first president of the International Association of Journalists.

1438 Harris, Martyn. 'Snapping at her heels'. *The Daily Telegraph*, 3 Apr 1993.
The 'ratpack' of Royal photographers, currently dogging the footsteps of the Princess of Wales.

1439 Harris, Michael, Jeremy Black, and Nicholas Hiley. *A history of English newspapers*. London: Routledge (in preparation).
Dr Hiley is writing the section spanning 1850 to 1990.

1440 Harris, Nigel G.E. *Professional codes of conduct in the United Kingdom: a directory*. London: Mansell, 1989.
Includes the code of the Institute of Journalists as it then stood.

1441 – – –. 'Codes of conduct for journalists'. *In* A. Belsey and R. Chadwicks, eds. *Ethical issues in journalism and the media*. London: Routledge, 1992.

1442   Harris, Paul. *Somebody else's war: frontline reports from the Balkan Wars, 1991–92*. Stevenage (Herts): Spa Books, 1992. 164pp.
The author includes several extracts from his own reports in *The Scotsman, Scotland on Sunday*, the *Sunday Mail* (Glasgow), and the *Daily Express*. But this is by no means a self-centred work. It portrays the growing horror of the conflicts in the former Yugoslavia, and how the press and broadcasting have striven to report them.

1443   Harris, Robert. *Gotcha!: the media, the government and the Falklands crisis*. London: Faber, 1983. 158pp.
An excellent summary of all the facts that were then publicly available.

1444   – – –.   *The good and faithful servant: the unauthorised biography of Bernard Ingham*. London: Faber, 1990. 202pp.
Critical study of the career of Mrs Thatcher's press secretary.
   In 1994, Faber published *The media trilogy*, combining these two books and *Selling Hitler* (Harris's 1986 story of the fake Hitler diaries which duped Times Newspapers).

1445   – – –.   'Rupert Murdoch: news tycoon, strike-breaker and citizen of the world.' *The Listener*, 22 Jan 1987.

1446   Harris, Walter Burton. *Morocco that was*. Edinburgh: Blackwood, 1921. viii + 333pp.
Part of the prolific and impressive literary output of a pioneer *Times* foreign representative: officially 'Our Special Correspondent in Morocco' from 1906.

1447   Harrison, John Fletcher Clews, and Dorothy Thompson. *Bibliography of the Chartist movement, 1837–1976*. Hassocks (W Sussex): Harvester Press; Atlantic Highlands (NJ): Humanities Press, 1978.
Lists ninety-three Chartist periodicals and newspapers, mostly those that were news-oriented as well as political, which serve as an eloquent testimony to Chartist literacy.

1448   Harrison, Stanley. *Poor men's guardians: a record of the struggles for a democratic newspaper press, 1763–1973*. London: Lawrence & Wishart, 1974. 256pp + xvipp of plates.
A survey in popular style, 'from Wilkes through the Chartist papers to *The Labour Weekly*'. Useful bibliography.

1449   Hart, Andrew. *Understanding the media: a practical guide*. London: Routledge, 1991. 267pp.
For teachers in the media field.

1450   Hart, James Allee. 'Electoral campaign coverage in English and United States daily newspapers'. *Journalism Quarterly*, 42, 1965.

1451   – – –.   'Foreign news in United States and English daily newspapers: a comparison'. *Journalism Quarterly*, 43, 1966.

1452   Hart-Davis, Duff. *Behind the scenes on a newspaper*. London: Phoenix House, 1964. (In Behind the Scenes series.)

1453 – – –. *Peter Fleming: a biography*. London: Jonathan Cape, 1974. 419pp.
An affectionate study of the talented elder Fleming, who wrote 'fourth leaders' and much special correspondence for *The Times*, the notable Strix column for *The Spectator*, as well as several classic travel books.

1454 – – –. *The house the Berrys built*. London: Hodder & Stoughton, 1990. 368pp; Coronet, 1991, 476pp.
'In the *Telegraph* 1928–1986'. The author began his association with *The Sunday Telegraph* on its launch in 1961, and traces the success story of *The Daily Telegraph*, in particular from the time that William Berry (1st Lord Camrose) acquired it, followed after his death in 1954 by his son Michael (Baron Hartwell). The problems encountered in the 1980s and eventual sale of both papers to Conrad Black, the Canadian entrepreneur, are recounted in vivid detail.

1455 *Hartlepool Mail*. Centenary supplement. Hartlepool (Cleveland): 14 May 1977.
Formerly *Northern Evening Mail* – and still an evening title, in the Portsmouth and Sunderland group.

1456 Hartmann, Paul. 'Industrial relations in the mass media'. *Industrial Relations*, 6, 1976.

1457 – – –. 'News and public perceptions in industrial relations'. *Media, Culture and Society*, 1, 3, 1979.

1458 Hartmann, Paul, and Charles Husband. *Racism and the mass media*. London: Davis-Poynter, 1974.
'A study of the role of the mass media in the practice of white beliefs and attitudes in Britain'.

1459 Hartmann, Paul, Charles Husband, and John Clark. 'British national press'. In *Race as news*. Paris: Unesco Press, 1974.

1460 Hartwell, [William] Michael Berry, *Baron*. *William Camrose: giant of Fleet Street*. London: Weidenfeld & Nicolson, 1992. xxii + 362pp.
The great press proprietor, by his second son. A major work in every respect.

1461 – – –. 'How newspapers have changed in my lifetime'. *The Sunday Telegraph*, 23 Aug 1987.
Contributed in the month of his retirement as editor-in-chief of the *Daily* as well as the *Sunday Telegraph*, after fifty-four years in journalism.

1462 Harvey, P., and P. Roberts. '*The Sheffield Independent and Commercial Register*'. *Morning Telegraph* (Sheffield), 11 Dec 1969.
Kemsley Newspapers amalgamated the *Independent* with the *Sheffield Telegraph* in 1938.

1463 Harwood, Elaine, and Andrew Saint. 'The *Daily Express* building'. In *London*. London: HMSO, 1992. (Exploring England's Heritage series, vol 1.)

One of two hundred London buildings selected for individual treatment: 'the first major Modern Movement front in London'.

1464   Haselden, W(illiam) K(erridge). *Daily Mirror reflections*. London: Pictorial Newspaper Co/Daily Mirror, from 1908.
'Being 100 cartoons (and a few more) culled from the pages of the *Daily Mirror*'. This series, reflecting the current British scene in humorous vein, continued for some twenty years; Haselden was the *Mirror*'s leading cartoonist from 1904 to 1940, and as such the first regular British newspaper strip artist.

1465   Haslam, James. *The press and the people: an estimate of reading in working-class districts*. Manchester: Manchester City News, 1906. 20pp. Rpd from the *Manchester City News*.

1466   Haste, Cate. *Keep the home fires burning: propaganda in the First World War*. London: Allen Lane, 1977. x + 230pp.

1467   Hastings, Macdonald. 'The men who send the front line news'. *Picture Post*, 14 Oct 1944.
In this illustrated feature, Hastings – father of Max Hastings and a leading contributor to *Picture Post* in its great days – gives statistics: '800 war correspondents are accredited to Supreme HQ Allied Expeditionary Force: of these 35 represent British national newspapers and agencies – perhaps 25 are the real British war correspondents'.

1468   Hastings, Max (Macdonald). 'New era of scepticism lays Torygraph to rest'. *UK Press Gazette*, 27 Oct 1986.
Extracted from speech, as editor of *The Daily Telegraph*, to the International Federation of Newspaper Publishers (Brussels, 1986).

1469   Hastings, Max, and Peter Jenkins. *The battle for the Falklands*. London: Michael Joseph, 1983. xii + 372pp.
Hastings reported the Falklands War of 1982 for the London evening paper, then *The Standard*, from the front line. He became editor of *The Daily Telegraph* in 1986. Jenkins, then political correspondent of *The Economist*, largely confines himself to the diplomatic side of the episode in this successful example of journalistic collaboration.

1470   Hattenstone, Simon. 'Never mind the Pollock'. *Newspaper Focus*, Apr 1993.
Interview with David Pollock, director of the Newspaper Publishers Association.

1471   Hattersley, Roy (Sydney George). *Press gang*. London: Robson Books, 1983. 192pp.
'Media' contributions to *Punch* etc by the Labour politician.

1472   Havighurst, Alfred Freeman. *Radical journalist: H.W. Massingham (1860–1924)*. London: Cambridge University Press, 1974. xv + 350pp.
A worthy but dull biography of a liberal giant.

1473   Hawke, Edward G. 'A brief history of the British newspaper press'. *Bulletin of the International Committee of Historical Sciences*, 7, 3, 28 Sep 1935. (Paris: Presses Universitaires de France.)

1474 Hayward, D.W. *The British press and Anglo-American relations, with reference to the Irish problem, 1916–22.* Manchester: University of Manchester, 1960 (MA thesis).

1475 Hayward, F.H., and B.N. Langdon-Davies. *Democracy and the press.* Manchester: National Labour Press, [1919]. 76pp.
In the ILP Library. Urges a Truthful Press Act, enforced throughout 'national guilds of journalists ... serious matters on the front page, cultural affairs on the back'.

1476 Headlam, Cecil. *An argument against the abolition of the daily press.* Oxford: Blackwell, 1904. 16pp.

1477 *Headline.* London: Headline Publications, [1973–4]; Malmö: K.G. Best-mark, [1975].
Collections of news stories from the British press of the previous year.

1478 Heald, Tim. 'Lies, damn lies and news ...' *The Listener* (Press issue), 24 Apr 1986.
On the receiving end of press attention.

1479 Healey, Tim. *Strange but true: the world's weirdest newspaper stories.* London: Octopus, 1983. 192pp.

1480 Healy, Christopher. *The confessions of a journalist.* London: Chatto & Windus, 1904. xv + 383pp.
Dedicated to W.T. Stead.

1481 Heath, J.E. 'Derbyshire newspapers'. *Derbyshire Miscellany*, 7, 1974.

1482 Heath, Michael. *The complete Heath.* London: John Murray, 1990.
The development of a political cartoonist's remarkable talent.

1483 Heath, Ray Brian. *Newspapers.* London: The Bodley Head, 1968. (In The Mass Media series.)

1484 Heaton, David, and John Higgins, eds. *Lives remembered: The Times obituaries of 1991.* Pangbourne (Berks): Blewbury Press, 1992. 357pp.
One hundred and eighty assessments selected from the nine hundred-plus published in *The Times* during the year. Includes John Leese (editor-in-chief, *Evening Standard*), Gerald Priestland, Cyril Ray, Jean Rook, Walter Terry (political editor, *Daily Mail* and *Daily Express*), Robert Maxwell. Foreword by Lord Annan. The first book of *Times* obituaries to appear for thirteen years (for earlier volumes, *see under Times, The*).

1485 *Hebden Bridge Times.* Centenary supplement. Hebden Bridge (W Yorks): 12 Aug 1981.
Weekly now owned by Johnston Press.

1486 Hedley, Peter, and Cyril Aynsley. *The D Notice affair.* London: Michael Joseph, 1967. 144pp.
How Chapman Pincher's disclosures in the *Daily Express* set in motion a major parliamentary row.

1487   Heenan, Patrick. 'News Corporation Limited'. In *International Directory of Company Histories*, Vol 4. Chicago and London: St James Press, 1991.

1488   Heide, Walther, *et al. Handbuch der Zeitungswissenschaft*. Vol 1. Leipzig: Hiersemann, 1940.
This was the only volume of this massive textbook on 'newspaper science' to appear before it was overtaken by the outbreak of World War II. But the British Library holds a copy of a supplement, Lieferung 5 (G–H), published in Leipzig in 1941, and compiled by E.H. Lehmann *et al*; this includes 'Grossbritannien' as a major article; and one of Lieferung 7 (J–K) (Leipzig, 1943).

1489   Heighway, Arthur J. *My inky way through life*. London (Bromley): 1979. 101pp.
Privately published autobiography of the former proprietor/editor of *World's Press News*, *WPN Inky Way Annual* etc.

1490   Heindel, Richard Heathcote. 'Press citations in British documents'. *Journalism Quarterly*, 14, Sep 1937.
On the origins of World War I.

1491   – – –.   'British diplomats and the press'. *Public Opinion Quarterly*, 2, 3, Jul 1938.
Publicity during World War I.

1492   Helm, William Henry. *Memories of W.H. Helm*. London: Richards, 1937. xiii + 102pp.
Memories especially of *The Morning Post*, of which Helm was in turn parliamentary reporter and literary editor.

1493   Henderson, Alexander. *Eyewitness in Czecho-Slovakia*. London: Harrap, 1939. 335pp.
Henderson was then European correspondent for the *Daily Herald*.

1494   *Hendon Times*. Centenary supplement. Hendon (London): May 1975.
Weekly in Westminster Press ownership.

1495   Hennessy, Brendan. *Writing feature articles: a practical guide to methods and markets*. London: Heinemann, 1991; revised edn, Oxford: Butterworth-Heinemann (Focal Press) (in preparation). 360pp.

1496   Hennessy, Peter (John). *What the papers never said*. Redhill (Surrey): Portcullis Press (for Politics Association), 1985.
Comparison of contemporary press reporting (as published) with the official files of the Public Record Office.

1497   – – –.   'Why journalists should breach the wall of political secrecy'. *The Independent*, 1 Apr 1987.

1498   – – –.   'The quality of political journalism'. *Journal of the Royal Society of Arts*, Nov 1987.
Lecture to the Society, 1 Apr 1987.

1499 Henry, Georgina. 'The white knuckle editor'. *The Guardian*, 6 Apr 1992. On Andrew Neil, editor of *The Sunday Times*, and his relationship with the proprietor, Rupert Murdoch.

1500 Henry, Georgina, and Nigel Willmott. 'The battle for Sunday'. *The Guardian*, 11 Sep 1980.
Assessing the market for national Sundays on the occasion of the launching of *The Sunday Correspondent*.

1501 Henry, Harry. *The dynamics of the British press, 1961–1984: patterns of circulations and cover prices*. London: Advertising Association, 1986. 178pp.
Tables, charts and commentary.

1502 – – –. *Key regional newspaper trends*. Henley-on-Thames (Oxon): NTC Publications (for Newspaper Society), 1990. 130pp.
One hundred and sixty-seven tables, seventy-eight charts.

1503 – – –. 'Balance sheet of the press'. *Planning*, 21, 1955.

1504 – – –. 'Some observations on the effect of newspaper rationing (1939–1959) on the advertising medium'. *Journal of Advertising History*, 1, Dec 1977.

1505 – – –. 'Classified advertising: the staple of the press'. *Admap*, May 1978.

1506 – – –. 'Patterns and trends of the national newspaper press'. *Admap*, Sep 1982.

1507 – – –. 'Newspaper circulations and price changes: the background pattern'. *Admap*, May 1986.

1508 – – –. 'Twenty years in the life of the nationals'. *Admap*, May 1993.

1509 Henry, Harry, ed. *Behind the headlines: the business of the British press*. London: Associated Business Press, 1978. viii + 240pp.
'Readings in the economics of the press': twenty-seven contributions on finance, technology, Fleet Street, regionals, consumer magazines, trade and technicals – much of it now dated. Edited by a pioneer market researcher turned professor of marketing communications.

1510 – – –, ed. 'Press economics: Part One: Regional newspapers; Part Two: Fleet Street'. *Admap*, Sep/Oct 1977.

1511 *'Henry Sell' Collection of historic newspapers dating from 1626, The*. London: Sell, [n.d.]. 37pp.
The core of this booklet is a descriptive catalogue of the Sell Collection, the greatest of its kind. Then in private hands, it was later (in 1931) given to the Press Club (London) as a major extension of the club's historic newspaper collection. This catalogue is preceded by 'The origin of the newspaper press' and followed by 'The press of the past', by H.W. Peet (then editor of *Sell's World's Press*). This article was reprinted from the *Stock Exchange Christmas Annual*.

1512   Herbert, (*Sir*) A(lan) P(atrick). 'Newspapers and the Bar'. *The Guardian*, 15 Oct 1963.
A.P.H. of *Punch* etc in expansive vein: 'These two fine callings . . . have the same fine purpose, the assertion of truth and justice.'

1513   Herbert, [Dennis] Nicholas (*3rd Baron* Hemingford). 'Freedom fight on all fronts'. *The Media Reporter*, Winter 1984.
The editorial director of Westminster Press speaks at a police-press seminar in Sheffield, ventilating the current problems.

1514   Herd, Harold. *The making of modern journalism*. London: Allen & Unwin, 1927. 119pp.
A popular 'tuppence-coloured' history of the rise of the mass press of Britain, in capsule biographical form: Beaverbrook, the Berry brothers, Edward Cook, Dawson, Garvin, Hulton, Kennedy Jones, Newnes, Northcliffe, O'Connor, Pearson, Rothermere, Spender, Charles Starmer, Stead are all featured.

1515   – – –.   *Press days and other days*. London: Fleet Publications, 1936. 216pp.

1516   *The march of journalism: the story of the British press, 1622 to the present day*. London: Allen & Unwin, 1952. 352pp.
A readable popular condensation of a mass of newspaper and periodical history which omits most references to sources but has limited use as a connected narrative.

1517   *Hereford Times*. Centenary supplement, 1832–1932. 15 Oct 1932.
Still published weekly, in the Reed Midland group.

1518   – – –.   150th anniversary supplement. 2 Jul 1982.

1519   Heren, Louis (Philip). *Growing up on The Times*. London: Hamish Hamilton, 1978. 319pp.
An autobiographical 'log cabin to White House'-style narrative by the East End lad who rose from copy-boy to become *The Times*'s correspondent in Washington, foreign editor, and finally deputy editor; written while the skies were still Thomson 'holiday blue' over Printing House Square and Gray's Inn Road.

1520   – – –.   *The power of the press?* London: Orbis, 1985. 208pp.
A general survey of both the British and the US scene, observed by Heren in his retirement. The question-mark in the title is significant.

1521   – – –.   *Memories of Times past*. London: Hamish Hamilton, 1988. 313pp.
A further slice of autobiography to the end of his long and distinguished career with *The Times*. Deputy editor under William Rees-Mogg, and associate editor under the latter's successor, Harold Evans, Heren clearly preferred the former's style; however, he expresses approval of Rupert Murdoch's management and results.

1522   *Herne Bay Gazette*. Centenary issue. Herne Bay (Kent): 2 Jul 1982.
In Kent Messenger group.

1523   Heron, Robert. *The death of the Fourth Estate*. London: 1985. 13pp.
Reprint of a lecture given at the Stationers' Hall, London, to the Wynkyn de Worde
Society. Noting how the bicentenary of *The Times* was being celebrated, Heron believes
that both the principles and the practices of the national press have deteriorated in the
twentieth century.

1524   Herries, J.W. *I came, I saw*. Edinburgh: 1937. 306pp.
Reminiscences of a senior reporter for *The Scotsman*. Notable events covered include
the surrender of the German fleet in 1918 and the Versailles Peace Conference the
following year.

1525   *Herts and Essex Observer*. Centenary supplement. Bishop's Stortford
(Herts): 28 Apr 1961.
Founded as the *Bishop's Stortford Observer*.

1526   Hetherington, [Hector] Alastair. *Guardian years*. London: Chatto &
Windus, 1981. x + 382pp.
Written some years after he stepped down as editor – Hetherington's time in office
(1956–75) spanned the paper's change of title and move of head office to London – this
is a riveting account of a 'make or break' transitional period in the long life of Britain's
only liberal-left newspaper. Hetherington, who had recently become research professor
of media studies at Stirling University, reveals how he had to struggle for its very life
when tax debts seemed about to absorb every penny.

1527   – – –. *Press, police and public interest*. Chichester (W Sussex): Barry
Rose, 1984. 20pp. Frank Newsam Memorial Lecture.

1528   – – –. *News, newspapers and television*. London: Macmillan, 1985.
ix + 329pp.
An independent close-up study of contemporary editing at national level, in particular
the decision-makers at the *Daily Mail*, *Daily Mirror*, *Guardian*, *Times*, and on the television newsdesks. One chapter, by Innis Macbeath, is devoted to the newspaper coverage
of the 1984–5 coal dispute. Comments Hetherington: 'Some of the best newspapers in
the world are published in Britain – and some of the worst.'

1529   – – –. *News in the regions*. London: Macmillan, 1989. 283pp.
A major study of current regional journalism – in both newspapers and television.
Media in the Midlands, Yorkshire, South West England, and Central Scotland are
covered.

1530   Hetherington, Peter. 'Cock of the North takes wing'. *The Guardian* (*Media
Guardian*), 8 Jun 1992.
'The *Glasgow Herald* dropped the "Glasgow" but is more Scottish than ever' . . . The
new management's drive to become a truly national newspaper.

1531   *Hey daily diddle*. London: T. Werner Laurie, 1928.
'A brilliant and amusing burlesque of the daily press, compiled by members of the
Granta staff at the University of Cambridge'.

1532 Hicks, J.C. *Newspaper finance.* London: London General Press, 1929.

1533 Hicks, Wynford. *English for journalists.* London: Routledge, 1993. 84pp.
Up-to-the-minute style manual for students etc.

1534 Higginbottom, Frederick James. *The vivid life: a journalist's career.*
London: Simpkin, Marshall, 1934. 262pp.
The author's long career is mainly notable for his editorship of *The Pall Mall Gazette*
in immediate pre-World War I days. After the war he served *The Daily Chronicle* as
political and parliamentary correspondent. Higginbottom was a founder member of the
Institute of Journalists.

1535 Hildick, Edmund Wallace. *A close look at newspapers.* London: Faber,
1966, 1969. 141pp.

1536 Hiley, Nicholas (Peter). *Making war: British news media and government,*
1914–1916. Thesis for Open University, deposited at Imperial War Museum,
London, 1984. 725pp (2 vols).
Includes reportage and photography from all the major fronts.

1537 – – –. 'Sir Hedley Le Bas and the origins of domestic propaganda in
Britain, 1914–1917'. *Journal of Advertising History*, 10, 2, 1987.
Le Bas, a successful mass-market publisher, launched the first of several large-scale
recruiting campaigns well before the outbreak of war.

1538 – – –. ' "Lord Kitchener resigns": the suppression of *The Globe* in
1915'. *Journal of Newspaper and Periodical History*, 8, 2, 1992.
How the influential – but small-circulation – London evening, *The Globe*, was suspended
by Government order for two weeks. It had published prematurely the intention of
Kitchener to resign as secretary of war.

1539 – – –. ' "Enough glory for all": Ellis Ashmead-Bartlett and Sir Ian
Hamilton at the Dardanelles'. *Journal of Strategic Studies*, 12, 2, Jun 1993.
How Ashmead-Bartlett brought about the dismissal of Hamilton from command.

1540 – – –. 'The candid camera in the Edwardian tabloids'. *History Today*,
Aug 1993.
The first flowering of photojournalism.

1541 Hill, Arthur. 'The Government's newspaper'. *The Strand Magazine*, Jul
1903.
On *The London Gazette*.

1542 Hill, Dave. 'Major's knight editor'. *The Guardian (Media Guardian)*, 9 Mar
1992.
On Sir David English, then editor-in-chief of the *Daily Mail* and deputy chairman of
Associated Newspapers.

1543 – – –. 'Parting notes of the labour reporter'. *The Guardian (Media*
Guardian), 6 Sep 1993.

In the days of wildcat strikes and other industrial disputes, labour correspondents were thick on the ground; now they are a small body rarely with anything dramatic to report.

1544 Hill, Douglas, ed. *Tribune 40: the first forty years of a socialist newspaper.* London: Quartet Books, 1977. viii + 214pp.
A symposium in celebration of a child of socialism with a somewhat chequered career. A leading contributor is Michael Foot, former editor of *Tribune* as well as Labour Party leader.

1545 Hill, Maureen A. *Daily Mail: women in the twentieth century.* London: Chapmans Publishers, 1991. 224pp.
Selection from the *Daily Mail*'s women's page, with text that 'counterpoints' the wealth of visual material.

1546 Hill, Timothy H. *Daily Mail: The Seventies.* London: Chapmans Publishers, 1991.
The decade through *Daily Mail* eyes: a large-format publication.

1547 Hillebrandt, Bela. *Typen englischer Zeitschriften; ihre Struktur mit besonderer Berücksichtigung ihrer Haltung bis zum Weltkrieg.* (Types of English magazines; their structure, and consideration of their attitude up to the World War). Dresden: M. Dittert, 1941. Originally a Berlin dissertation.

1548 Hills, Jean R. 'The British press on "the Yanks" '. *The New Republic* (Washington), 23 Aug 1954.
About British press treatment of the USA.

1549 *Hinckley Times, The.* Centenary supplement. Hinckley (Leics): Jan 1989.
Independent weekly, founded by Thomas Baxter, and still owned by that family.

1550 Hindle, Wilfrid Hope. *The Morning Post, 1772–1937: portrait of a newspaper.* London: Routledge, 1937. xi + 260pp. Westport (CT): Greenwood Press, 1974.
Ironically, this was published in what turned out to be the year in which the paper was acquired by *The Daily Telegraph*. Hence it has a definitive status, although brief and somewhat uncritical in vein: 'staunch and strong, upright and downright, scorning wrong'.

1551 – – –, ed. *Foreign correspondent: personal adventures in search of the news, by 12 British journalists.* London: Harrap, 1939. 268pp. Publ in the USA as *We were there.* New York: 1939.
The twelve are: O.D. Gallagher, Ian S. Munro, Arthur Koestler, Alexander Henderson, Douglas Reed, Darsie Gillie, Vernon Bartlett, F.A. Voigt, H.D. (Hubert) Harrison, George L. Steer, Sir Alfred Watson, Karl Robson.

1552 Hird, Christopher. 'How Maxwell got the *Mirror*'. *The New Statesman*, 17 May 1985.

1553 Hird, Christopher, and Richard Belfield. 'The global giant who overstretched'. *The Guardian*, 5 Nov 1991.
On Rupert Murdoch . . . wishful thinking at that juncture?

1554   Hirsch, Fred, and David Gordon. *Newspaper money: Fleet Street and the search for the affluent reader.* London: Hutchinson, 1975. 146pp.
A study of the British quality press, and its reliance on advertising; some interesting European comparisons.

1555   Hirst, Francis Wrigley. 'English newspapers and their authority'. In *The six panics: and other essays.* London: Methuen 1913.
By the radical editor of *The Economist*, which until his dismissal in 1916 opposed the war.

1556   Hobson, *Sir* Harold. *Theatre in Britain: a personal view.* London: Phaidon, 1984.
Distillation of a unique career as dramatic critic (*The Sunday Times*, 1947–76).

1557   Hobson, *Sir* Harold, Phillip Knightley, and Leonard Russell. *The pearl of days: an intimate memoir of The Sunday Times, 1822–1972.* London: Hamish Hamilton, 1972. xxxiv + 506pp.
This is authoritative and unfailingly interesting, especially on the array of journalists and specialist critics at the disposal of *The Sunday Times* over the years. The principal twentieth-century personalities are considered in depth: Kemsley, Roy Thomson, Denis Hamilton, Harold Evans etc. The three *Sunday Times* authors are headed by the distinguished dramatic critic, Harold Hobson.

1558   Hobson, *Sir* Oscar (Rudolf). *How the City works.* London: News Chronicle, [1938]. 149pp; Dickens Press, 1966.
Before becoming financial editor of the *News Chronicle*, Hobson had made his name in a similar capacity with *The Manchester Guardian* and as editor of *The Financial News*. This authoritative work long stood the test of time.

1559   Hodgson, F(rederick) W(est). *Modern newspaper practice: a primer on the press.* London: Heinemann, 1984; revised Oxford: Butterworth-Heinemann (Focal Press), 1992. 188pp.
Intended as a first easy-to-use background and reference for students. Appendix: 'A career in journalism'.

1560   – – –.   *Modern newspaper editing and production.* London: Heinemann, 1987. Revised as *Subediting: a handbook of modern newspaper editing and production.* Oxford: Butterworth-Heinemann (Focal Press), 1992. 284pp.

1561   Hodgson, Godfrey. *Truth, journalism and the Gulf.* London: City University, 1991.
The Fifth James Cameron Memorial Lecture, by the foreign editor of *The Independent*, who is critical of relations between the 'minders' and the press.

1562   – – –.   'Private power and the public interest: the case of Times Newspapers'. *Political Quarterly*, Oct-Dec 1981.

1563   – – –.   'Dateline Britain: the revolt of the press barons'. *Columbia Journalism Review*, Sep/Oct 1986.

1564   – – –.   'Resident experts to flying dashmen'. *British Journalism Review*, 2, 4, 1991.

Traces the reduced role and style of the foreign correspondent since the end of World War II.

1565   Hodson, James Lansdale. *Thunder in the heavens: . . . in England and elsewhere between April 3rd 1947 and March 29th 1949*. London and New York: Wingate, 1950.

J.L. Hodson was a correspondent successively for the *Daily Mail, News Chronicle* and *Sunday Times*. This was the last of several contemporary chronicles straddling the period of World War II; Hodson also turned his hand to fiction with success.

1566   Hogarth, Paul. *The artist as reporter*. London: Gordon Fraser, 1986. 192pp. Earlier short version publ London: Studio Vista; and New York: Reinhold, [1967]. 96pp.

A wide-ranging work, itself an example of fine art, which gives due credit (in chapters entitled 'The special artist' and 'The death and glory boys') to the pioneers.

1567   Hoggart, P.R. 'Edward Lloyd, "the father of the cheap press"'. *The Dickensian*, Spring 1984.

Relates how the famous name survived in *Lloyd's Sunday News* until 1923 – thirty-three years after Edward Lloyd's death.

1568   Holden, Anthony. *Of presidents, prime ministers and princes: a decade in Fleet Street*. London: Weidenfeld & Nicolson, 1984. ix + 325pp.

Includes a preface by Harold Evans, the author's editor when he was 'Atticus' of *The Sunday Times*; his extracts from other journalism also include work for *The Observer* (for which he was US correspondent), *Punch* etc.

1569   – – –, ed. *The last paragraph: a collection of David Blundy's journalism*. London: Heinemann, 1990.

A tribute to an outstanding war reporter, killed in San Salvador in the course of duty for *The Sunday Times*. He also wrote for *The Sunday Telegraph* and *The Sunday Correspondent*.

1570   Holland, Patricia. 'In these times when men walk tall: the popular press and the Falklands conflict'. *Cencrastus*, 17, 1984.

1571   Holland, Steve. 'Lord Northcliffe and the Amalgamated Press'. *Book and Magazine Collector*, Aug 1992.

A good summary, bringing in Alfred Harmsworth's purchase of the *Evening News* (1894) and launch of the *Daily Mail* (1896) and *Daily Mirror* (1904) etc.

1572   Hollingsworth, Mark. *The press and political dissent: a question of censorship*. London: Pluto, 1986. viii + 367pp.

A hefty chunk of left-wing polemic, with a misleading title. But factually valuable for its up-to-date appendix: 'Ownership and commercial interests of Britain's national press'.

1573   Hollingworth, Clare (Mrs Geoffrey Hoare). *The three-week war in Poland*. London: Duckworth, 1940.

No 2 under Hugh (Carleton) Greene for *The Daily Telegraph* at the outbreak of World War II.

1574   – – –.   *There's a German just behind me*. London: Secker & Warburg, 1942. 300pp.
German invasion of the Balkans, 1941–2, when correspondent for the *Daily Express*.

1575   – – –.   *Mao and the men against him*. London: Jonathan Cape, 1985. 372pp.
Correspondent for *The Daily Telegraph* in China in the 1970s, with much eye-witnessed material.

1576   – – –.   *Front line*. London: Jonathan Cape, 1990. x + 301pp.
This autobiography carries a fully justifiable title.

1577   Holloway, David, ed. *The Fifties: a unique chronicle of the decade*. London: Simon & Schuster, 1991.
Culled from the archives of *The Daily Telegraph* and presented in large format.

1578   – – –.   *The Sixties: a chronicle of the decade*. London: Simon & Schuster, 1992. 176pp.
Another *Daily Telegraph* anthology, with perceptive foreword by W.F. Deedes.

1579   – – –.   *The Thirties*. London: Simon & Schuster (in preparation).
Another in the series.

1580   Holroyd, J.E. 'Press palace'. In *The Penrose Annual, 1962*.
On the then new *Daily Mirror* building in Holborn Circus, London – its design and equipment.

1581   Holton, Robert J. '*Daily Herald* v *Daily Citizen*, 1912–15; the struggle for a labour daily in relation to the labour unrest'. *International Review of Social History*, 19, 1974.

1582   Home Counties Newspapers. *Family group*. Luton: Home Counties Press, 1952.
A history of one of the larger newspaper publishing groups in Greater London and to the north of the capital.

1583   Hooper, Alan. *The military and the media*. Aldershot (Hants): Gower, 1982. xv + 247pp.
A fair defence of censorship in wartime from the point of view of a serving officer in the Royal Marines who is more fearful of the dangers of press ignorance and suggestibility than of public ignorance.

1584   Hooper, David. *Public scandal, odium and contempt*. London: Secker & Warburg, 1984.
'An investigation of recent libel cases', with a summary of press coverage.

1585   – – –.   *Official secrets: the use and abuse of the Act*. London: Secker & Warburg, 1987; Sevenoaks (Kent): Coronet, 1988. ix + 348pp.

1586   Hopkin, Deian (Rhys). *The newspapers of the Independent Labour Party, 1893-1906*. Aberystwyth: University College of Wales, 1980 (PhD thesis).

1587   – – –.   'Domestic censorship in World War I'. *Journal of Contemporary History*, 1970.

1588   – – –.   'The local newspapers of the Independent Labour Party, 1893-1906'. *Bulletin of the Study of Labour History*, 8/29, Spring/Autumn 1974.

1589   – – –.   'The socialist press in Britain, 1890-1910'. *In* [D.]G. Boyce *et al.* (eds.), *Newspaper history* . . . (q.v.).

1590   – – –.   'The Edwardian labour press'. *In* Kenneth D. Brown, ed. *The first Labour Party, 1906-1914*. London (Beckenham): Croom Helm, 1985.

1591   – – –.   'Riddell, George Allardice, 1st Lord Riddell'. *In* David J. Jeremy, ed. *Dictionary of business biography*, Vol 4. London: Butterworth, 1985. Although a successful newspaperman before the turn of the century, it was after he became chairman of the *News of the World* in 1903 that Riddell made an indelible mark on press history.

1592   Hopkinson, *Sir* [Henry] Tom. *Of this our time: a journalist's story, 1905-1950*. London: Hutchinson, 1982. 317pp.
The first volume of a remarkable self-portrait that reads more like a novel than a report. Hopkinson progressed from comfortable childhood in Edwardian Manchester to initial stagnation as a young man in Fleet Street until he found his true *métier* on the editorial side of news picture magazines. He spent four formative years with (*Weekly*) *Illustrated* before joining Hulton, taking over from Stefan Lorant as editor of *Picture Post* in 1940. Although modest in expression, Hopkinson narrates a saga of solid editorial achievement. The volume culminates in his resignation in dispute with his proprietor ten years later.

1593   – – –.   *Under the tropic*. London: Hutchinson, 1984. 307pp.
This second volume of memoirs is centred on his life and work in Africa (especially as founder-editor of *Drum Magazine*).

1594   – – –.   'My life and times'. Series in *The Media Reporter*, Mar, Jun, Sep, Dec 1979; Spring, Summer 1980.
After *Picture Post*, and before the African episode, Hopkinson was features editor of the *News Chronicle*. Later he became the first director of the Centre for Journalism Studies in Cardiff (1970-5), a postgraduate centre for the study of journalism techniques.

1595   – – –.   'Closing ranks to say: farewell Cameron'. *UK Press Gazette*, 4 Feb 1985.
An obituary tribute to James Cameron.

1596   – – –.   'When Britain armed itself with a camera'. *The Guardian (Weekend Guardian)*, 11-12 Feb 1989.
How the 35mm Leica transformed photojournalism, and led to the pre-eminence as a news medium of *Picture Post*, particularly in 1939-40.

1597 – – –, ed. *Picture Post, 1938–50.* Harmondsworth (Middx): Allen Lane
The Penguin Press, 1970. 288pp. Rptd, Penguin, 1979; also, with new foreword, London: Chatto & Windus, 1984.
Picture Post – 'Hulton's national weekly' – was the most successful magazine of its era,
with a circulation rising from 750,000 at its launch to 1,300,000-plus, maintained even
in the early post-war days. It eventually died in 1957. Stefan Lorant, the Hungarian-born
founder-editor, and Hopkinson who succeeded him, have left – with the aid of a brilliant
team of reporters and photographers – a remarkable illustrated legacy as a commentary
on the contemporary news and social scene.

1598 *Horncastle News.* Centenary supplement. Horncastle (Lincs): 5 Sep 1985.
A weekly in the Mortons group.

1599 *Hornsey Journal.* Centenary supplement. Hornsey (London): 23 Nov 1979.
One of the Capital Newspapers group.

1600 Hoskins, Percy. *They almost escaped.* London: Hutchinson, [1938].
The then young Hoskins of the *Daily Express* tells the story of murderers caught by
their hunters.

1601 – – –. *No hiding place!: the full and authentic story of Scotland Yard in
action.* London: Daily Express, [1951].

1602 – – –. *The sound of murder.* London: Long, 1973.

1603 – – –. *Two men were acquitted: the trial and acquittal of Doctor Bodkin
Adams.* London: Secker & Warburg, 1984.
The title of this fascinating and instructive tale by the doyen of Fleet Street crime
reporters about the trial of Dr Adams for mass murder is taken from what Lord Beaverbrook said to the author (his *Daily Express* employee). The 'two men acquitted' were
of course Adams – and Hoskins, whose staunch belief in Adams's innocence had been
vindicated.

1604 Hoskins, William George. *Local history in England.* London: Longman,
1959. xi + 196pp; 1972. xiii + 268pp.
Includes chapters on 'Old newspapers' and 'Indexing of old newspapers' – a standard
work.

1605 Houfe, Simon. *The dictionary of British book illustrators and caricaturists,
1800–1914.* Woodbridge (Suffolk): Antique Collectors' Club, 1978, 1981. 520pp.
Includes a chapter on 'The special artists' (mainly those contributing to newspapers and
magazines).

1606 House of Commons Defence Committee. *The handling of press and public
information during the Falklands conflict.* London: HMSO, 1982. 2 vols:
HC17-1. Report and minutes of proceedings; HC17-2. Minutes of evidence.
8 + 493pp.
The report is often openly critical of the Ministry's media relations. *See also* Ministry
of Defence.

1607 *House of Menzies, The.* Edinburgh: Menzies, 1958. 76pp.
Marking the 125th anniversary of the foundation of John Menzies & Co, the Scottish
booksellers and newsagents, and the centenary of the opening of their first three railway
bookstalls.

1608 Houston, Henry James. *The real Horatio Bottomley.* London: Hurst &
Blackett, 1923. 287pp.
Published when Bottomley was safely behind bars. His former secretary here relates how
the launch of the *Sunday Pictorial* in 1915 was bolstered by weekly sermonizing articles
by the plausible rogue.

1609 'How good is *The Guardian?*: a symposium'. *Delta*, 31–2, 1963–4.

1610 'How Reuters was sold for £65,000'. *Reuters World*, Jul 1981.
A house journal article on the acquisition of the historic papers formerly held by the
family of Sir Roderick Jones (former Reuters chief executive).

1611 'How the PA gets its news'. *World's Press News*, 13 Jun 1929. (In the Pillars
of the Press series.)
In 1929, as now, the Press Association was of national significance, and concerned solely
with the collection and distribution of domestic news throughout the UK.

1612 'How the press covered Hitler's Austrian coup'. *World's Press News*, 17 Mar
1938.

1613 Howard, Anthony (Michell), ed. *The Crossman diaries: selections from the
diaries of a Cabinet Minister, 1964–1970.* London: Jonathan Cape/Hamish
Hamilton, 1979. 188pp.
The introduction is also by Howard, who followed Crossman as editor of *The New
Statesman.* Howard was the first – if short-lived – Whitehall correspondent of *The
Sunday Times*; then Washington correspondent of *The Observer*, later editor of *The
Listener*, eventually returning to *The Observer* as deputy editor.

1614 – – –. 'The role of the lobby correspondents'. *The Listener*, 21 Jan 1965.

1615 – – –. 'The tycoon who was captured by *The Times*'. *The Observer*, 18
Aug 1976.
On Lord Thomson of Fleet.

1616 – – –. 'Decline and fall of the political weekly'. *Journalism Studies
Review*, 1978. Similar article in *The Times*, 22 Jul 1978.

1617 – – –. 'Historians at work'. *Contemporary Record*, 1, 1987.
In the process, surveys his own journalistic career, harking back to *The New Statesman*.

1618 Howard, Anthony (Michell), and Richard West. *The making of the Prime
Minister.* London: Jonathan Cape, 1965. 239pp.
'The events leading up to the appointment of the Right Hon. James Harold Wilson as
Prime Minister'. Both authors received friendly co-operation from their subject.

1619 Howard, Peter Dunsmore. *Beaverbrook: a study of Max the unknown.*
London: Hutchinson, 1964. 164pp.

Howard, a leading *Evening Standard* journalist and aide to Beaverbrook, was a founder of the Oxford Group (Moral Re-Armament). The biography was intended to counter-balance Driberg's *Beaverbrook*.

1620   Howard, Philip (Nicholas Charles). *We thundered out: 200 years of The Times 1785–1985*. Research by Jack Lonsdale. London: Times Books, 1985. 176pp; Maplewood (NJ): Hammond, 1985.
The then literary editor of *The Times* tells the bicentenary story, making extensive use (on a 275 × 375 mm format) of facsimiles of historic pages and copious other illustrations, many hitherto unpublished. It is a model of editorial selection, with admirably well-balanced comment.

1621   – – –.   'Times remembered from 189 years at Printing House Square'. *The Times*, 22 Jun 1974.
On the last day before the move to Gray's Inn Road.

1622   – – –.   'No scoop like an old scoop'. *The Times*, 9 Feb 1987.
Re the (Belfast) *News-Letter* and other claimants to longevity among British newspapers.

1623   – – –, ed. *The Times bedside book*. London: HarperCollins (for The Times), 1991. ix + 278pp.

1624   Howe, Ellic (Paul), and H.E. Waite. *The London Society of Compositors: a centenary history*. London: Cassell, 1948.
This trade union was merged into the London Typographical Society in 1955.

1625   Howe, Stephen, ed. *Lines of dissent: writing from The New Statesman, 1907–1988*. London: Verso, 1988. 376pp.

1626   Hubback, David F. *No ordinary press baron: a life of Walter Layton*. London: Weidenfeld & Nicolson, 1985. ix + 271pp.
Lord Layton (1884–1966) first made his mark as a quietly effective editor of *The Economist* (1922–38), and rose to be executive head of *The Daily News* and its successor the *News Chronicle* – with its London evening partner *The Star*.

1627   *Huddersfield Daily Examiner*. Centenary supplement. 1 Sep 1951.
This evening paper began life in 1851 as the *Huddersfield and Holmfirth Examiner*. Trinity International acquired it in 1993.

1628   Huddleston, Sisley. *In my time: an observer's record of war and peace*. London: Jonathan Cape; New York: Dutton, 1938. ix + 411pp.
An English contributor to several British and US newspapers in the 1920s and 1930s, including (briefly) Paris correspondent of *The Times*. The book gives a close-up of Paris in World War I and thereafter, and of Northcliffe etc. Later Huddleston sided with the Fascist dictators, and on the fall of France in World War II remained in Vichy territory.

1629   Hudlestone, F.J. *Use of newspapers to the enemy intelligence service*. London: (unpubl) War Office, for the Directorate of Military Intelligence, 1917.
A justification of censorship, and an argument for *not* accepting self-censorship by working journalists as an alternative.

1630 Hudson, Derek (Rommel). *British journalists and newspapers*. London: Collins, 1945. 48pp. (In the Britain in Pictures series.)
An attractive booklet giving a brief survey of 'recent' press history enhanced by illustrations (many in colour) of memorable personalities, and memorable features such as the remarkably accurate forecast of World War II air raid defence published in *The Illustrated London News* in 1924.

1631 – – –. *Writing between the lines: an autobiography*. London: High Hill Books, 1965. 214pp.
Includes chapters on three editors of *The Times*: Dawson, Barrington-Ward, Casey.

1632 – – –. 'Newspapers'. *In* S. Nowell-Smith, ed. *Edwardian England, 1901–1914*. London: Oxford University Press, 1964.

1633 Hudson, Richard L., Patrick M. Reilly, and Meg Cox. 'Bloated empire'. *The Wall Street Journal*, 13 Sep 1991.
The subheading of this article read 'Media mogul Maxwell revelled in growth: must now scale back' – a warning ignored.

1634 Huggett, Frank Edward. *The true book about newspapers*. London: Muller, 1955. 144pp.
Includes an outline of newspaper history.

1635 – – –. *The newspapers*. London: Heinemann, 1968. 116pp. (In the Liberal Studies series.)
A sharply considered and very well-informed study of the press in the 1960s by a former *Daily Telegraph* subeditor, who was also one of the most effective teachers of journalistic skills at Britain's first officially recognized post-war journalism school, at the then Polytechnic of Central London.

1636 – – –. *Cartoonists at war*. Leicester: Windward; and London: Book Club Associates, 1981. 192pp.
Covers from 1793 to 1945.

1637 Hughes, Catherine. 'Imperialism, illustration and the *Daily Mail*, 1896–1904'. *In* M. Harris and A.J. Lee, eds. *The press in English society from the 17th to the 19th centuries*. Cranbury (NJ) and London: Associated Universities Presses, 1986.
Featuring in particular the Boer War, with many illustrations including cartoons.

1638 Hughes, Herbert. *Chronicle of Chester: the 200 years, 1775–1975*. London: Macdonald & Jane's, 1975. xiv + 274pp.
The history of the *Chester Chronicle*, still published weekly. Hughes was a former editor.

1639 Hughes, Richard. *Foreign devil: thirty years of reporting from the Far East*. London: André Deutsch, 1972. 320pp; Century, 1984. (In the Lives and Letters series.)
By a *Sunday Times* correspondent, who was a notable personality as well as journalist.

1640 Hughes, Spencer Leigh. *Press, platform and Parliament.* London: Nisbet, 1918, 1921. xi + 320pp.

By a parliamentary correspondent (as 'Sub Rosa' on e.g. *The Morning Leader* and *The Star*) who became a Member of Parliament.

1641 *Hull Daily Mail, 1787–1926.* Hull: 1926. 39pp.

It was the *Hull Packet* that was founded in 1787, being incorporated with the *Hull Daily Mail* in 1886; although the latter is today an evening in the Northcliffe Newspapers group, it pre-dated its famous national namesake by eleven years.

1642 *Hull Daily Mail.* Jubilee supplement, 1885–1935. 20 Sep 1935.

1643 – – –. Centenary supplement. 30 Sep 1985.

1644 Hulton, *(Sir)* Edward George Warris. *Conflicts.* London: Neville Spearman, 1966. 223pp.

This Edward Hulton (1906–88) explains how he followed his father, also Sir Edward (1869–1925), as a publisher. But unlike Sir Edward Hulton I (a major newspaper owner), he achieved success only in the magazine field. His most notorious 'conflict' was with Tom Hopkinson, editor of *Picture Post*, who resigned on policy grounds in 1950. Hulton sold out to Odhams in 1959.

1645 – – –. 'The future of *Picture Post*'. In *The Penrose Annual, 1940.*

By the proprietor at the outset of his magazine's most famous decade: 'The Government will at once inform a newspaper proprietor that he is one of the principal persons helping to win the war; but it will do everything in its power to hamper his work.'

1646 Hulton Press. *Hulton Readership Survey.* Eds J.W. Hobson and Harry Henry. London: 1947–55. Annual.

'An analysis, for advertiser, of the readers of newspapers . . . by region, sex, age, social class'.

1647 Humpherys, Anne. 'G.W.M. Reynolds: popular literature and popular politics'. *Victorian Periodicals Review*, Fall/Winter 1983.

George William MacArthur Reynolds (1814–79), a Chartist lawyer, played a remarkable part in popular journalism in mid-Victorian times. His name survived in the national Sunday paper, *Reynolds News*, right up to 1962 (when it was absorbed with the *Sunday Dispatch* into the *Sunday Citizen*); this began as *Reynolds's Weekly Newspaper* in 1850.

1648 Humphreys, Edward Morgan. *Y wasg Gymraeg.* Liverpool: H. Evans, 1945. 62pp.

Brief – but worthy – history of the Welsh press.

1649 Hunt, H. Cecil. *There's fun in Fleet Street.* Glasgow: Blackie, [1938]. x + 194pp.

1650 – – –. *Ink in my veins: literary reminiscences.* London: Robert Hale, 1948. 149pp.

1651 Hunt, J.R. *Pictorial journalism.* London: Pitman, 1937. 112pp.

The author describes his work for the *Yorkshire Post* etc.

1652   Hunter, Fred(eric) (Newlands). *Grub Street and academia: the relationship between journalism and education, 1880–1940*. London: City University, 1982 (PhD thesis). 444pp.
'With special reference to the London University diploma for journalism, 1919–1939'.

1653   – – –. 'Women in British journalism'. *In* Dennis Griffiths, ed. *The encyclopedia of the British press, 1422–1992*. Basingstoke (Hants): Macmillan, 1992.

1654   Hunter, Ian. *Malcolm Muggeridge: a life*. Glasgow: Collins, 1980; London: Fontana, 1981. 270pp.

1655   Hunting, Penelope, ed. *Ludgate*. London: Broadgate Properties, 1993.
The history of the area – embracing Fleet Street and what is now Ludgate Circus as the centre for printers and press – leading up to its redevelopment. Superbly illustrated.

1656   Hurley, Alfred J. *Days that have gone: milestones I have passed in south-west London*. London: [1947].
The author's journalism was largely on the *Tooting and Balham Gazette*.

1657   Husni, S.A. *A content analysis of press coverage of the 1975–1976 Lebanese Civil War by the New York Times and The Times of London*. Ann Arbor (MI): University Microfilms, 1980.

1658   Hutcheon, William. *Gentlemen of the press: memories and friendships of forty years*. London: John Murray, 1933. 239pp.
From the provinces to *The Morning Post*, at which Hutcheon spent twenty years as night editor.

1659   Hutcheson, John A. *Leopold Maxse and the National Review, 1893–1914: right-wing politics and journalism in the Edwardian era*. New York: Garland, 1989. xix + 508pp.

1660   Hutchison, David. 'The press in Scotland: articulating a national identity'. *In* D. McCrone, ed. *The Scottish Government Yearbook, 1987*. Edinburgh: Unit for the Society of Government in Scotland, 1987.

1661   – – –, ed. *Headlines – the media in Scotland*. Edinburgh: EUSPB, 1978. 112pp.
A collection of essays, including Myra Macdonald on 'The press in Scotland' – with due note of D.C. Thomson's massive-circulation *Sunday Post*.

1662   Hutt, [George] Allen. *An outline of newspaper technology*. London: National Union of Journalists, 1950. 47pp.
A reprint of six articles from the *Journalist*.

1663   – – –. *Newspaper design*. London: Oxford University Press, 1960, 1967. xvi + 307pp.
This was the first full-scale textbook to appear in Britain on a much-neglected subject. *See also* Hutt and James *below*.

1664 – – –. *The changing newspaper: typographic trends in Britain and America, 1622–1972.* London: Gordon Fraser, 1973. 224pp.
Hutt, whose eminence was recognized by his appointment as a Royal Designer for Industry, had just finished his record service as editor of the National Union of Journalists' *Journalist* when this invaluable survey appeared.

1665 – – –. 'The front page'. *Typography*, 3, 1937.

1666 – – –. 'A forgotten campaign of *The Times* against trade unions'. *Modern Quarterly*, 2, 1, Jan 1939.

1667 – – –. 'A Gothic titlepiece and the English newspaper'. *Alphabet and Image*, 3, Dec 1940.

1668 – – –. 'A new face for newspaper text'. In *The Penrose Annual, 1955.* Introducing Jubilee.

1669 – – –. 'Newspaper format: broadsheet into tabloid'. In *The Penrose Annual, 1960.* Trends then current.

1670 – – –. 'The future of newspaper design'. In *The Penrose Annual, 1964.*

1671 – – –. 'The *"Mirror"* monarch'. *Daily Worker*, 8 Feb 1967.
An appraisal of Cecil King, then chairman of IPC, from a left-wing standpoint.

1672 Hutt, [George] Allen, and Bob James. *Newspaper design today: a manual for professionals.* London: Lund Humphries, 1989. 192pp.
An updated version of Hutt's original (1960/1967) work. A further revision is in preparation.

1673 Hyams, Edward Solomon. *The New Statesman: the history of the first fifty years, 1913–1963.* With an introduction by John Freeman. London: Longman, 1963. xiii + 326pp.

1674 Hyde, (Harford) Montgomery, ed. *Privacy and the press: the Daily Mirror press photographer libel action.* London: Thornton Butterworth, 1947. v + 250pp.
The action referred to in the title is now a classic case: Thomas Lea v. Justice of the Peace Ltd and R.J. Acford Ltd, concerning wedding photos.

1675 Hyndman, Henry Mayers. *The record of an adventurous life.* London: Macmillan, 1911. x + 460pp.

1676 – – –. *Further reminiscences.* London: Macmillan, 1912. ix + 545pp.
Hyndman became a leading socialist propagandist as reflected in what his obituarist in the *Dictionary of national biography* described as 'two fascinating and provocative books'. But in his younger days, he worked for *The Pall Mall Gazette.*

1677 Ichikawa, Tomoko. *The Daily Citizen, 1912–1915: a study of the first Labour daily newspaper in Britain.* Aberystwyth: University College of Wales, 1985 (MA thesis).
Remains the only national daily to have been owned by the Labour Party.

1678   Iddon, Don. *Don Iddon's diary*. London: Falcon Press, 1951.
Largely about Iddon's time as *Daily Mail* correspondent in the USA. He had previously represented the *Daily Express* in New York.

1679   Iles, Lawrence Irvin. *Charles Masterman: halfway between Labour and Liberal?*
Biography of a notable politician, public servant – and journalist. (In preparation.)

1680   Illert, Helmut. *Die deutschen Rechte der Weimarer Republik im Urteil der englischen Presse, 1928–1932.* (German rights in the Weimar Republic in the opinion of the English press, 1928–1932). Cologne: Gouder & Hansen, 1966. iv + 384pp.

1681   Illustrated London News, The. *Great centenary: story of The Illustrated London News.* London: 1942.
Contributions from, *inter alia*, Sir Arthur Bryant and Sir John Squire. Bryant claimed, with reason, that the 118 six-month folio volumes covering the Victorian period were 'probably the most important and comprehensive single historical document ever compiled'.

1682   *Illustrated London News, The.* 125th anniversary issue: 1842–1967. 13 May 1967. 112pp. Includes 'An era of growth and revolution through the eyes of the *ILN*' (an article on its own history by Peter Biddlecombe).
On 14 May 1842, 189 Strand was the focus of one of the most exciting events in British press history: publication of the first issue of *The Illustrated London News*. It was primarily the brainchild of Herbert Ingram, and its instant success was developed by his son (Sir) William and grandson (Sir) Bruce – the latter's editorship (from 1900 until his death in 1963) being an all-time long-service record. (In 1985, the magazine, now monthly, was sold by Thomson to the Sea Containers group.)

1683   – – –.   Anniversary issue. (14 May) 2, 1992. 218pp.
A splendid 150th birthday souvenir, including a potted history of the *ILN* itself by its editor, James Bishop.

1684   *Images of war: the real story of World War II*. London: Marshall Cavendish, 1988–9; reissued 1994. In fortnightly parts, each covering a major campaign. With complete facsimile newspapers from the John Frost Collection.

1685   'Imperial Press Conference and its limitations, The'. *Blackwood's Magazine*, 186, Jul 1909.

1686   Incorporated Society of British Advertisers. *The readership of newspapers and periodicals in Great Britain, 1936.* Ed W.N. Coglan. London: ISBA, 1936. xxx + 387pp.
Valuable analysis; although concentrated on urban areas only, the result of 82,613 interviews.

1687   Independent, The. *The best of The Independent, 1989–1990*. London, 1990.
Compilation selected from the newspaper's columns.

Independent, The, Index to: see Reference Works section.

1688 Independent Labour Party. *The capitalist press: who owns it and why.* London: [1924?].

1689 'Influence of Marconi on ships' newspapers, The'. *Shipbuilding and Shipping Record*, 9, 16, Sep 1943.
Refers to the special collection of such papers assembled by the Press Club (London).

1690 *Infringement of privacy: consultation paper.* London: Central Office of Information, for Lord Chancellor's Department and the Scottish Office, 1993. 89pp.
Argues that the right to privacy should be recognized in law, as the redressing of a general civil wrong.

1691 Ingelhart, Louis Edward. *Press freedom: a descriptive calendar of concepts, interpretations, events, and court actions, from 4000 B.C. to the present.* Westport (CT): Greenwood, 1987. xix + 430pp.
A tour-de-force, although the British element is mainly concentrated on early history.

1692 Ingham, (*Sir*) Bernard. *The reporter: an endangered species.* London: Stationers' Company, 1986. Reprint of the Annual Livery Lecture to the Company (1986); also in *UK Press Gazette*, 17 Feb 1986.

1693 – – –. *Kill the messenger.* London: HarperCollins, 1991. 408pp.
By the Prime Minister's press secretary for eleven years, after her (and his) retirement. Ingham writes of 'a steady deterioration over the 1980s in standards of journalism'. Many readers find special value in his early days as a cub reporter on the *Hebden Bridge Times*.

1694 Inglis, Brian (St John). *The press.* London: Blond Educational, 1964. 56pp. (In the Today is History series.)

1695 – – –. 'The influence of *The Times*'. *Historical Studies*, 3, 1961. Paper read to the Fourth Irish Conference of Historians (Cork, 1959).

1696 Ingram, Derek. 'Gemini covers the world'. *The Media Reporter*, Autumn 1980.
The story, by its editor, of the foundation and development of the independent Gemini News Service, specializing in Third World and Commonwealth affairs.

1697 Ingrams, Richard Reid. 'Cockburn, (Francis) Claud.' In *Dictionary of national biography, 1981–1985*. Oxford: Oxford University Press, 1990.
By the co-founder of *Private Eye*.

1698 Innis, Harold Adams. *The press: a neglected factor in the economic history of the twentieth century.* London: Oxford University Press, 1949; Constable (Athlone Press), 1951. 48pp. Stamp Memorial Lecture.
This most perceptive account of the industrialization of the Anglo-American news business was given by a Canadian economist whose importance as a media historian was duly recognized by Marshall McLuhan.

1699 – – –. 'The newspaper in economic development'. *Journal of Economic History*, 2, Supplement, Dec 1942.

1700 Institute of Incorporated Practitioners in Advertising. *Investigated press circulations and markets*. London: 1932–.
The 1932 publication reported on a national basis; that dated 1933 covered Manchester.

1701 – – –. *Survey of press readership*. London: IIPA, 1939. 3 vols.
The fieldwork for this pioneer survey consisted of 45,000 interviews as to readership of more than a hundred newspapers. It was followed after World War II by another, more sophisticated, survey (1947).

1702 Institute of Journalists, The. *The grey book*. London: National Association of Journalists, 1886–. (In 1890, was granted a Royal Charter and became the Institute of Journalists, and in 1990 its professional wing the Chartered Institute of Journalists.) Constitution; organisation; roll of members.
The 1st edition has a preface by Algernon Borthwick, president, 'inviting the notice of all the classes of Pressmen to an Association with the probability of large and increasing benefits to Journalism and to Journalists'.

1703 – – –. *Freelances*. London: IOJ; latest edn 1989–90 (new edn in preparation).
Directory of specialist writers, photographers, artists and broadcasters in membership of the Institute.

– – –. *Journal, The*: see Reference Works section.

1704 *International Press and Printing Exhibition (Crystal Palace, London, 1902)* – official catalogue, comp and ed William A. Lawton. London: 1902.

1705 International Press Foundation. *As we see you/Comme nous vous voyons*. London and Paris: IPF, 1992. 68pp.
The result of research (October-December 1990) and a 1991 conference arranged by the Foundation, distilling the views of France expressed in seven British newspapers and those of Britain in eight French publications. The leader of the research on the British side was Linda Christmas.

1706 International Press Institute. *The flow of the news*. Zürich: IPI, 1953. 266pp.
The first major publication from the IPI (set up in 1951), this is a factual account of the handling of news in and out of Western Europe, the USA and India.

1707 – – –. *As others see us*. Zürich: IPI, 1954. 85pp.
Contains ten studies in press relations between the USA and five other countries including the UK. Correspondents report on coverage of their own countries in those to which they are assigned, and vice versa.

1708 – – –. *The active newsroom: IPI manual on techniques of news editing,*

sub-editing and photo-editing, ed Harold Evans. Zürich: IPI, 1961.
Based on experience in IPI 'workshops' in Asia.

1709 – – –. *Professional secrecy and the journalist*, comp R.W. Desmond. Zürich: IPI, 1962.
Covers twenty-one countries and the result of an IPI inquiry.

1710 – – –. *Press councils and press codes.* 4th edn. Zürich: IPI, 1966. 134pp.
Includes Britain's Press Council.

– – –. *IPI Report: see Reference Works section.*

1711 International Press Institute and 'Justice'. *The law and the press.* London: 1965.
Report of a joint working party from the organization 'Justice' and the British committee of IPI, chaired by Lord Shawcross; many recommendations were made for changes in British law.

1712 *Into the nineties: the future for the regional and local press.* London: Newspaper Society, 1988.
Study commissioned by the Society, through the Henley Centre for Forecasting; booklet summarizing the report also published.

1713 *Inverness and Highland News.* Centenary edition. Inverness: 27 Oct 1983.
Founded as *Highland News* in 1883.

1714 Inverness Courier. *A Highland newspaper: the first 150 years of the Inverness Courier, 1817–1967.* Inverness: Robert Carruthers, 1969.
Now in Scottish Provincial Press group.

1715 Inwood, Stephen. *The role of the press in English politics during the First World War, with special reference to the period 1914–16.* Oxford: University of Oxford, 1971 (PhD thesis).

1716 *Irish News.* Centenary. Belfast: 1955.
An independent morning paper.

1717 Ironside, Virginia. *Problems! Problems!: confessions of an agony aunt.* London: Robson, 1991.
Running the 'agony' column in the *Sunday Mirror*.

1718 Irving, Clive. 'Can newspapers move from the Stone Age to the Space Age?'. In *The Penrose Annual, 1967.*

1719 Isaacs, George A. *The story of the newspaper printing press.* London: Co-operative Printing Society, 1931. 287pp.
A reprint of articles from *Society* journal. The author was general secretary of NATSOPA, the printing trade union, and a Member of Parliament.

1720 *Isle of Man Examiner.* Centenary number. Douglas (IOM): 11 Jul 1980.

1721   Isle of Man Times. *The jubilee of the Isle of Man Times: the story of its first half century.* Douglas: 1911.

1722   *Isle of Wight County Press.* Centenary supplement. Newport (IOW): 30 Nov 1984.

1723   'It flourisheth by circulation'. *The Newspaper World*, 3 Jun 1939. (In The Oldest Newspapers series.)
On the history of the *Northampton Mercury*.

1724   Izatt, Janet. 'Behind our own lines at the MoD'. *PR Week*, 30 Aug 1990.
How the Ministry of Defence information staff work as a link between the press, other media and the public.

1725   Jack, Ian. *Before the oil ran out: Britain 1977–86.* London: Secker & Warburg, 1987. 283pp.
Selected journalism, largely from *The Sunday Times*. The author's view is jaundiced in the extreme – especially on the News International policy (and practice) on the move to Wapping.

1726   Jackson, Harold. 'The journalist and the library'. *In* Selwyn Eagle, ed. *Information sources for the press and broadcast media.* Sevenoaks (Kent): Bowker-Saur, 1991.
A senior *Guardian* staffer explains how the journalist's information needs can now be met by in-house libraries using an online database as well as conventional resources.

1727   Jackson, Ian. *The provincial press and the community.* Manchester: Manchester University Press, 1971.
Functions and historical background are both covered.

1728   Jackson, R.A. *Jak on parade.* London: Express Books, 1967–. Annual.
The stinging Jak cartoons from the *Daily Express* and (*London/Evening*) *Standard* in annual form.

1729   Jacob, Alaric. *A traveller's war: a journey to the wars in Africa, India and Russia.* London: Collins, 1944. 448pp.
Initially a correspondent for Reuters; a convinced Marxist, Jacob came into his own when (in 1944) he was appointed the *Daily Express* correspondent with the Red Army.

1730   Jacobs, Eric. *Stop press: the inside story of the Times dispute.* London: André Deutsch, 1980. x + 166pp.
A first-hand report of the year (in fact, eleven months) when there was a lock-out or suspension of labour by the management of Times Newspapers, involving *The Times*, *The Sunday Times*, and the Times Supplements. Written by a principal labour editor of *The Times* soon after this energy-wasting and financially exhausting period (1978–9).

1731   Jaffa, Sam. *Maxwell stories.* London: Robson, 1992.
A loosely written collection of anecdotes on Robert Maxwell.

1732   James, Anthony. *Media and the law*. Sale (Cheshire): Brennan Publications, 1977. (Media Guide No 1.)

1733   James, Barbara. 'Indexing *The Times*'. *The Indexer*, 11, 4, 1979.

1734   James, Bob. 'Face value: design sense'. *Journalist's Week*, 9 Feb 1990.
The typefaces currently used in the nationals.

1735   – – –.   'Climbing in Lakeland'. *UK Press Gazette*, 31 May 1993.
Marking the 175th birthday of *The Westmorland Gazette*, published from Kendal and today a Westminster Press title.

1736   James, (*Colonel*) Lionel. *On the heels of De Wet*. Edinburgh: Blackwood, 1902. v + 346pp.
'By the Intelligence Officer' – but in truth James had joined *The Times* as special correspondent in 1899, and covered the Boer War for that paper. Later he turned his knowledge to good use in helping to edit *The Times history of the war in South Africa*.

1737   – – –.   *With the conquered Turk: the story of a latter-day adventurer*. London: Nelson, [1913]. 370pp.

1738   – – –.   *High pressure: being some record of activities in the service of 'The Times' newspaper*. London: John Murray, 1929. xi + 314pp.

1739   – – –.   *Times of stress*. London: John Murray, 1929. vi + 320pp.
'A record of activities as a war correspondent of *The Times*'.

1740   – – –.   '*The Times* and wireless war correspondence'. (Report from Wei-hai-wei, 26 Jun 1904). *The Times*, 27 Aug 1904.
James was then doubling up as correspondent for Reuters.

1741   Jameson, Derek. *Touched by angels*. London: Ebury Press, 1988; Harmondsworth (Middx): Penguin, 1989. 304pp.
This first volume of his memoirs takes Jameson through his early years and his always eventful career in journalism up to his move from the *Daily Mirror* to editorship of the *Daily Express* in 1977. He was later the first editor-in-chief of the *Daily Star*, and then edited the *News of the World*.

1742   – – –.   *Last of the hot metal men: from Fleet Street to showbiz*. London: Ebury Press, 1990; Harmondsworth (Middx): Penguin, 1991. 224pp.
Sequel to *Touched by angels*. Jameson's love affair with 'the Street' survives: 'the most exciting place on earth'.

1743   Janes, A.W. *The Bedfordshire Times, 1845–1969*. Bedford: Bedford County Press, 1969.
By an ex-editor of the *Bedfordshire Times*, which is now a weekly in the EMAP group.

1744   Jarché, James. *James Jarché, 1891–1965*. London: Popperfoto, 1980. 32pp.
Derek Smith wrote the text of this tribute to the top photographer of both the *Daily Herald* and (*Weekly*) *Illustrated*. Jarché had earlier served the *Daily Sketch*.

1745 Jeans, William. *Parliamentary reminiscences*. London: Chapman & Hall, 1912. 325pp.
Brother of (Sir) Alexander Jeans (the paper's managing director), William Jeans was parliamentary correspondent of the *Liverpool Daily Post* – and the *Dundee Advertiser* – for forty-five years.

1746 Jeffrey, Ian. *Bill Brandt: photographs, 1928–1983*. London: Thames & Hudson, 1993. 192pp.
Although Brandt's work did not appear in newspapers, the breadth and unique quality of his social and pictorial coverage in *Weekly Illustrated* and then in the two Hulton magazines, *Picture Post* and *Lilliput,* make the inclusion of this volume imperative. Jeffrey contributes a long and informed commentary to coincide with a major retrospective exhibition at The Barbican, London.

1747 Jeffries, J[oseph] M[ary] N[agle]. *Front everywhere*. London: Hutchinson, 1935. 298pp.
The author was war correspondent for the *Daily Mail* from 1914 until 1933.

1748 Jeffs, Harry. *Press, preachers and politicians: reminiscences, 1874 to 1932*. London: Independent Press, 1933. 251pp.
The author wrote for the *Evening Star* (Wolverhampton) etc.

1749 Jenkins, David. 'Newspapers of the historian'. *Welsh Bibliographical Society Journal,* 11, 1–2, 1973–4.

1750 Jenkins, David. *Financial Times Print Works*. London: Architectural Design Technology Press, 1991.
Monograph on the outstanding building designed by Nicholas Grimshaw & Partners and erected in London's Docklands in 1988.

1750A Jenkins, Peter (George James). *The battle of Downing Street*. London: Charles Knight, 1970. xiv + 171pp.
By a leading political columnist successively with *The Guardian* (for whom he wrote for twenty-five years), *The Sunday Times,* and finally *The Independent.* The essence of the book is a narrative of the Labour Party's attempts at trade union reform.

1751 Jenkins, Roy Harris (*Baron* Jenkins of Hillhead). 'How free should the press be?'. *The Listener,* 93, 1974.
At that time the Labour Party's home secretary.

1752 Jenkins, Simon (David). *Newspapers: the power and the money*. London: Faber, 1979. 125pp. New York: Faber. 130pp.

1752A – – –. *Newspapers through the looking-glass*. Manchester: Manchester Statistical Society, [1981].
A paper delivered to the Society.

1753 – – –. *Market for glory: Fleet Street ownership in the twentieth century*. London: Faber, 1986. 247pp.

1754 – – –. 'Why the *Times* and *Sunday Times* vanished'. *Encounter*, Aug 1979.
This article was published towards the end of the eleven months when the two papers mentioned in its title were suspended.

1755 – – –. 'Where Fleet Street fears to tread'. *The Sunday Times*, 25 Jan 1987.
Jenkins, having been editor of the *Evening Standard* and political editor of *The Economist*, became a columnist for *The Sunday Times* 1986–90, and was then appointed editor of *The Times*. He retired as such in 1992, but continued to contribute to the paper.

1756 – – –, ed. *The Times guide to English style and usage*. London: Times Books, 1992. 190pp.

1757 Jenkins, Tudor. *The Londoner*. London: MacGibbon & Kee, 1962. 239pp.
The author had edited The Londoner's Diary in the *Evening Standard* for twenty years when this anthology appeared.

1758 Jenkinson, Norman. 'Normality still reigns'. *UK Press Gazette*, 29 Mar 1993.
Writes of his twenty-two years as news editor of *The Belfast Telegraph*: 'At one time, we had a three-man team of reporters on riot duty.'

1759 Jensen, John. ' "Curious! I seem to hear a child weeping!": Will Dyson, 1880–1938'. In *Politics in cartoon and caricature:* special issue of *20th Century Studies*, 13/14, Dec 1975.
Jensen (political cartoonist of *The Sunday Telegraph* and social cartoonist of *The Spectator*) repeats the title of Dyson's sadly prescient cartoon (in the *Daily Herald*) on the fate of the next generation.

1760 Jeremy, David J. 'Pearson, Weetman Dickinson, 1st Viscount Cowdray'. *In* D.J. Jeremy, ed. *Dictionary of business biography*, Vol 4. London: Butterworth, for the Business History Unit, London School of Economics, 1985.

1761 *Jewish Chronicle, The, 1841–1941: a century of newspaper history*, comp Cecil Roth. London: Jewish Chronicle, 1949. xv + 187pp.

1762 *Jewish Chronicle*. 150th anniversary number. 15 Nov 1991.

1763 *Jewish Chronicle*. Index. Years from foundation in 1841 progressively indexed by the publishers; partially – and fully from 1985 – available in microfilm from Reading: Research Publications (International).

1764 Johansson, Eve. 'The British Library Newspaper Library: looking ahead'. *Journal of Newspaper and Periodical History*, Summer 1986.
By the then head of the Newspaper Library.

1765 John, Alun. *Newspaper photography: a professional view of photojournalism*

today. Marlborough (Wilts): Crowood Press, 1988. 160pp.
By the picture editor of *The Independent*.

1766 John Rylands University Library of Manchester. *The Labour Party news-paper cuttings collection*, ed J.F. Laidlar. Vol 1. Manchester: John Rylands Library, 1983. vii + 197pp.
This first volume covers 25,000 cuttings from papers published between 1909 and 1978. Volume 2 is in preparation.

1767 Johnson, Frank. *Out of order*. London: Robson, 1982. 256pp.

1768 – – –. *Frank Johnson's election year*. London: Robson, 1983.
Johnson writes as a political commentator, formerly with *The Daily Telegraph*, then the short-lived magazine *Now!*, and latterly with *The Times*; his light touch is well in evidence here.

1769 Johnson, Paul (Bede). *The pick of Paul Johnson*. London: Harrap, 1985. 277pp.
Anthology selected by Johnson himself, in two groups. First are comments on the media, including notable pieces on Malcolm Muggeridge, especially as editor of *Punch*, and on Harold Evans and his ill-starred editorship of *The Times*. All the articles in this section are from *The Spectator*, except a tribute to William Deedes as editor of *The Daily Telegraph*. The second group are some of his 'weekend essays' from the last-named; they afford an unrivalled close-up (as his successor) of Crossman's equally short-lived editorship of *The New Statesman*. Johnson, by then a regular contributor to the *Daily Mail*, was singled out by Alan Rusbridger in the *Media Guardian* anniversary issue of 20 June 1994 as 'the columnist's columnist'.

1770 – – –. 'Monsieur Sam, the king of Paris'. *Evening Standard*, 5 Sep 1988.
Obituary tribute to Sam White, the *Standard*'s long-serving Paris correspondent.

1771 Johnson, Peter. 'Braving the pickets – the real refuseniks'. *The Sunday Times*, 25 Jan 1987.
'Front-line' view of the Wapping confrontation.

1772 Johnson, Priscilla A. *The United States in the British press from 1914 to 1939*. Oxford: University of Oxford, 1952 (BLitt thesis).

1773 Johnston, A.R, ed. *Wigtown Free Press newspaper: a local index to the Galloway Advertiser and Wigtownshire Free Press newspaper*. Vol 3: Personal names, 1915–1925. Dumfries and Galloway Regional Council, 1986. 565pp.

1774 Johnston, Christopher N. 'A great newspaper: *The Scotsman*'. *The Nineteenth Century and After*, Mar 1924.

1775 Johnston, Fred. 'The press in Scotland'. In D. Campbell, ed. *The British press*. London: CPU, 1978.
By the chairman of the Johnston Press group.

1776   Jones, Aled (Gruffydd). *Press, politics and society: a history of journalism in Wales.* Cardiff: University of Wales Press, 1993. xii + 317pp.
The first major historical study of the origins, production and social impact of newspaper journalism in Wales.

1777   Jones, David, Julian Petley, Mick Power, and Lesley Wood. *Media hits the pits.* London: Campaign for Press and Broadcasting Freedom, 1985.
A broadside alleging a collective and deliberate policy by the national mass media against the National Union of Mineworkers during the 1984–5 strike.

1778   Jones, *Sir* [George] Roderick. *A life in Reuters.* London: Hodder & Stoughton, 1951. 496pp.
Jones (1877–1962) to all intents and purposes personified Reuters from the time he came from setting up the service in South Africa to take over the managing directorship in London (1915). 'I tell of events in the last fifty years falling within my own knowledge and participation. In several I was the principal actor, and alone know the whole story . . .' He explains in this valuable, if verbose, autobiography how in 1917 he was offered by Beaverbrook the simultaneous government appointment of director of propaganda, but accepted only on the understanding that the two responsibilities (and their finances) were to be kept quite separate. After World War I, he chaired Reuters until 1941, by which time his close ties with government were clearly seen by his fellow-directors as an increasing embarrassment. In his account, he passes abruptly but in a dignified way over the circumstances of his sudden resignation.

1779   Jones, Ifano. *A history of printers and printing in Wales to 1810, and of successive and related printers to 1923.* Cardiff: 1925.
Contains considerable detail on the early history of *The Cambrian*, established in Swansea as the first English-language newspaper in Wales (1804). Its first printer, publisher and editor was Thomas Jenkins; he espoused no particular cause except 'the spirit of enterprise', but his paper was briefly popular in London coffee-houses with a 'Jacobin' clientele.

1780   Jones, J. Clement. *Mass media codes of ethics and councils: a comparative international study on professional standards.* Paris: Unesco, 1980.
Now inevitably dated.

1781   Jones, James A(lfred). *Courts day by day.* London: Sampson Low, [1946]. 370pp.
A selection from one of the most popular and long-running features of the *Evening News*.

1782   Jones, Kennedy. *Fleet Street and Downing Street.* London: Hutchinson, 1920. 363pp.
Important on several levels. Jones begins with a survey of press history, then proceeds to a more detailed coverage of Fleet Street in the 1890s and early 1900s. From the start a close associate of Northcliffe, he later felt that 'the Chief' had not sufficiently recognized his services. His account – so long after – of the purchase of the *Evening News*, launch of the *Daily Mail* and *Daily Mirror*, and take-over of *The Times*, is biased

towards his own part in the saga of success. Jones writes as if his style of bluster and blackmail were quite normal, generalizing cynically: 'the political line is the proprietor's own affair – Conservative'. He eventually left journalism for politics.

1783   – – –.   'Press and platform'. *In Sell's World's Press, 1921*. London: Sell, 1921.

1784   Jones, Marjorie. *Justice and journalism*. Chichester (W Sussex): Barry Rose, 1974.
'A study of the influence of newspaper reporting upon the administration of justice by magistrates'.

1785   Jones, Mark. 'Newspaper man of destiny'. *Media Week*, 12 Jun 1992.
On Conrad Black.

1786   Jones, Mervyn. *Michael Foot*. London: Gollancz, 1994.
Major biography which covers *inter alia* Foot's extensive career in journalism.

1787   Jones, Nicholas. *Strikes and the media: communication and conflict*. Oxford: Basil Blackwell, 1986. iv + 220pp.
By the labour correspondent of BBC radio.

1788   Jones, Philip Henry. *A bibliography of the history of Wales*. Cardiff: University of Wales, 3rd edn 1989. Microfiche + 75pp booklet.
Lists writings about the Welsh press – and publications themselves – from 1780 to the present.

1789   Jones, (*Sir*) Thomas Artemus. 'Our network of news: the Press Association and Reuter'. *Windsor Magazine*, 1906.
In 1906, as now, the Press Association and Reuters covered national and international news respectively.

1790   Jones, Victor Pierce. *Saint or sensationalist?: the story of W.T. Stead*. East Wittering (W Sussex): Gooday Publishers, 1988. 116pp.

1791   Jordan, Philip (Dillon). *Russian glory*. London: Cresset Press, 1942. 181pp.

1791A   – – –.   *Jordan's diary*. London: Collins, 1944. 256pp.
A leading war correspondent for the *News Chronicle*.

1792   Joseph, Joe. *The Japanese: strange, but not strangers*. London: Viking, 1993. ix + 276pp.
By a *Times* staff journalist, with a few episodes adapted from that newspaper.

1793   Joseph, Michael, ed. *The autobiography of a journalist*. London: Hutchinson, [1929]. 286pp.

1794   *Journal of Advertising History*. London: Admap, for The History of Advertising Trust, 1977–84; Bradford: MCB University Press, 1986–9. Varying frequency.

1795   *Journal of Commerce and Shipping Telegraph.* Centenary souvenir. Liverpool: Jan 1926.
Founded in 1825 as *Liverpool Commercial Chronicle*, and for much of its long history titled *Liverpool Journal of Commerce*, this paper later became a daily *Journal of Commerce and Freighting World*. It ceased publication in 1985.

1796   *Journalism, by some masters of the craft.* London: Pitman, 1932.
'A series of lectures on the technique of modern journalism delivered under the auspices of the Institute of Journalists'. Accompanied by photo portraits of twelve of the twenty-three contributors.

1797   *Journalism Today.* London: Institute of Journalists, 1967–72. 2 per year.

1798   *Journalist in the making, The.* London: 1925.
Record of lectures at the University of London journalism course: reprinted from *The Newspaper World*.

1799   'Journalists and the South African War'. In *Sell's Dictionary of the World's Press, 1901.* London: Sell, 1901.
A fifty-nine-page treatment.

1800   Jouvenel, Henry de, *et al. The educational role of the press.* Paris: International Institute for International Co-operation, 1934. 90pp.
There was one British contributor to this international study: Kingsley Martin.

1801   Junor, *Sir* John (Donald Brown). *The best of J.J.* London: Sidgwick & Jackson, 1981.
From Junor's Current Events column in the *Sunday Express* – of which in 1986 he ended his thirty-two years as editor. He is an idiosyncratic but shrewd observer of the passing scene, and a worthy successor of his fellow-Scots colleague John Gordon. (The *Sunday Express* was founded by Beaverbrook in 1918, and has remained in parallel with the *Daily Express*.)

1802   – – –.   *Listening for a midnight tram: memoirs.* London: Chapmans Publishers, 1990; Pan. 341pp.
Effective on his early years in the profession; less so when he recounts, in gossipy vein, his later contacts in society and the political world.

1803   – – –.   'For Queen and Country – and proud of it!'. *In* D. Campbell, ed. *The British press.* London: CPU, 1978.

1804   Kaldor, Nicholas (*Baron*), and Rodney Silverman. *A statistical analysis of advertising expenditure and of the revenue of the press.* Cambridge: Cambridge University Press, 1948. xiii + 199pp. (In the National Institute of Economic and Social Research's Economic and Social Studies series.)

1805   Karpf, Anna. *Doctoring the media: the reporting of health and medicine.* London: Routledge, 1988.

1806 Kay, Anne. 'British newspaper reporting of the Yugoslav resistance, 1941–1945'. *Storia delle Relazioni Internationali*, 6, 1990.

1807 Keane, John. *The media and democracy.* Oxford: Polity Press/Basil Blackwell, 1991. xiii + 202pp.
The opening chapter, 'Liberty of the press', parades great names and pronouncements in the vanguard of press freedom.

1808 Keating, Frank. *Half-time whistle: an autobiography.* London: Robson Books; Warner, 1994.
Sports journalism, especially for *The Guardian.*

1809 Keay, Douglas. *Royal pursuit: the Palace, the press and the people.* London: Severn House (Enigma Books), 1983. 253pp; New York: Dodd, Mead, 1984.

1810 Kee, Robert. *The world we left behind: a chronicle of the year 1939.* London: Weidenfeld & Nicolson, 1984; Sphere, 1985. 395pp.

1811 – – –.   *1945: the world we fought for.* London: Hamish Hamilton, 1985; Sphere, 1986. 371pp.
Kee, a notable reporter first making his name on *Picture Post* and then a television personality, in a new guise as social historian. He makes copious use of contemporary press coverage.

1812 – – –.   *The Picture Post album: a 50th anniversary collection.* London: Barrie & Jenkins, 1989. 176pp. Foreword by Sir Tom Hopkinson.
Picture Post was in fact launched on 1 October 1938. Many of the illustrations – both individual shots and series – remain the most vivid of images; but its often equally effective text is missing here.

1813 Keefe, H.J. '*The Morning Post* in retrospect'. *The Listener*, 18, 1937.
A tribute on the demise of the famous daily.

1814 Keenan, Mary. 'Paper mill's hard grind'. *The Guardian*, 3 Apr 1989.
Feature on Ireland's only Irish-language daily: *Lá* (Day), published from a former flax mill on Belfast's Falls Road.

1815 Keene, Martin. *Practical photojournalism: a professional guide.* Oxford: Butterworth-Heinemann (Focal Press), 1993. xii + 245pp.
Based on fourteen years' experience, mainly with the *Herald Express* (Torquay) and the Press Association.

1816 Kehoe, Barbara Benge. *The British press and Nazi Germany.* Chicago: University of Illinois, 1981 (PhD dissertation). 327pp. Available on microform from University Microfilms International (Ann Arbor, MI).

1817 Keir, David. *Newspapers.* London: Edward Arnold, 1948. (Merlin Books series.)

1818   Kelly, Mary. 'Power, control and media coverage of the Northern Ireland conflict'. *In* Patrick Clancy *et al.*, eds. *Ireland: a sociological profile*. Dublin: Institute of Public Administration and Sociological Association, 1986.

1819   Kemsley, [James] Gomer Berry, *1st Viscount*. 'Journalism as a career'. *The Welsh Anvil/Yr Finion*, 1, Apr 1949.
Advice in his native Wales.

1820   Kemsley Newspapers. *Reference book*. London: [c. 1947].
A staff manual, privately printed and distributed, and compiled by Ian Fleming when the future novelist was foreign manager and special writer for *The Sunday Times*.

1821   – – –.   *The Kemsley manual of journalism*. London: Cassell, 1950, 1954. xiii + 424pp.
'A detailed guide to the entire range of newspaper work and the careers it offers . . .': as such, unique among the publications from Britain's national newspaper groups. Has an introduction by (the 1st) Viscount Kemsley; contributions are largely from then staff members of the group. They include 'The editor' and 'The British press: a survey', both by W.W. Hadley, recently retired from the editorship of *The Sunday Times*; 'The making of a newspaper' (the *Daily Graphic*), by Denis Hamilton (then personal assistant to Lord Kemsley); and 'Newspaper make-up and typography', by Robert Harling.

1822   Kennedy, Aubrey Leo. 'Geoffrey Dawson'. *The Quarterly Review*, 294, 1956.
An estimate of the significance of Dawson's editorship of *The Times*.

1823   Kennedy, Dennis. *The widening gulf: northern attitudes to the independent Irish state, 1919–1949*. Belfast: Blackstaff, 1988.
History based on detailed study of Northern Ireland newspapers.

1824   Kennedy, Douglas. 'The quiet man'. *GQ*, May 1994.
Full-length profile of Peter Preston, editor of *The Guardian*.

1825   Kennedy, Henry. *The Irish News and Belfast Morning News, 1885–1935*. Belfast: Irish News, 1935.

1826   Kennett, M. 'A century of the *News*'. *Hampshire*, 17, Jul 1977.
History of the *Evening News* (now *The News*) and *Southern Standard* (Portsmouth).

1827   *Kensington News and West London Times*. Centenary issue: 1869–1969. London: 10 Jun 1969.
One of the London Newspaper group (Adscene ownership).

1828   Kent, Ray, ed. *Measuring media audiences*. London: Routledge (in preparation). 224pp.
Current techniques in exact analysis of audiences – and readership.

1829   *Kent and Sussex Courier*. Centenary edition, 1872–1972. Tunbridge Wells (Kent): 6 Oct 1972.
A weekly with several editions, in the Associated Newspapers group.

1830 *Kent Messenger.* 75th birthday supplement. Maidstone (Kent): 30 Dec 1933.

1831 — — —. Centenary number, ed H.R. Pratt Boorman. 2 Jan 1959.
The *Maidstone Telegraph* was founded in 1859, the title *Kent Messenger* being introduced in 1871. The Kent Messenger group, still centred at Maidstone, now covers a series of county weeklies and *Kent Today,* a daily evening paper.

1832 *Kent Messenger Gazette.* 150th anniversary number. Maidstone: 5 Jan 1965.
First published as the *Maidstone Gazette* in 1815.

1833 *Kentish Express.* Jubilee number. Ashford (Kent): 15 Jul 1905.
This weekly, today in the Kent Messenger group, was founded in 1855.

1834 Kentish Gazette. *Bridging three centuries: the story of the Kentish Gazette, the oldest Kent newspaper.* Canterbury: Jul 1929. 12pp.

1835 — — —. *250th anniversary: a pictorial souvenir, 1717–1967.* 20 Oct 1967.
The 1717 date actually applies to *The Kentish Post, or Canterbury Newsletter,* which was published until 1768. The title then disappeared on the acquisition of the paper by its newly launched rival, *The Kentish Gazette,* which is today a weekly in the Kent Messenger group.

1836 *Kentish Independent.* Centenary number. London (Woolwich): 1 Jan 1943.
This Greater London weekly ceased publication in 1984.

1837 *Kentish Mercury.* Centenary supplement, 1833–1933. London (Deptford): South East London & Kentish Mercury, 20 Oct 1933.

1838 Kentish Mercury. *Mercury, 1833–1983: 150 years' service to the community.* Written by John Freeman. 1983.
On the cover is reproduced the front page of no 1 of the *Greenwich, Woolwich, and Deptford Gazette, and West Kent Advertiser.* The *Mercury* series continues to serve a large area of south-east London.

1839 *Kentish Observer.* Centenary issue. Canterbury (Kent): 7 Jul 1932.
This weekly ceased publication in 1977.

1840 Kersh, Cyril. *A few gross words: the Street of Shame, and my part in it.* London: Simon & Schuster, 1990. x + 206pp.
The funny side of Fleet Street – mainly from a ringside seat at *The People* and the *Sunday Mirror.*

1841 Kessler, Sidney, and Fred Bayliss. *Contemporary British industrial relations.* Basingstoke (Hants): Macmillan, 1992.
Copious references to the disputes involving the Messenger Group (Warrington) and News International (Wapping).

1842 Kidd, Janet (Gladys) Aitken. *The Beaverbrook girl.* London: Collins, 1987. 240pp.

Notable, in a gossipy way, not only about the author's father (Lord Beaverbrook) in his heyday, but also on such stars in the *Express* firmament as his close confidant and gossip-writer, Lord Castlerosse.

1843   Kiernan, Thomas. *Citizen Murdoch.* New York: Dodd, Mead & Co, 1986; London: Robert Hale, 1989.

1844   Kieser, Rolf. *Englands Appeasementpolitik und der Aufstieg des Dritten Reiches im Spiegel der britischen Presse.* Winterthur (Switzerland): Keller, 1964. 140pp.

1845   Kieve, Jeffrey L. *The electric telegraph: a social and economic history.* Newton Abbot (Devon): David & Charles; and New York: Harper & Row, 1973. 310pp.
Important in a press context, giving an outline of the development of the national news agencies and their impact on news writing.

1846   *Kilburn Times, The.* Centenary number, 1868–1968. London: 15 Mar 1968.
In the Capital Newspapers group.

1847   *Kilmarnock Standard, The.* Centenary supplement, 1863–1963. Kilmarnock (now Strathclyde): 22 Jun 1963.
In Trinity International ownership.

1848   Kimble, P. *Newspaper reading in the third year of the war.* London: Allen & Unwin, 1942. 24pp.

1849   King, Cecil Harmsworth. *The future of the press.* London: MacGibbon & Kee, 1967. 117pp.
A reprint of Granada Northern Lectures (1966). In view of the author's eventual downfall, there are remarkably few signs of delusions of grandeur here: 'The limitations of so-called power are painfully obvious to the publishers of all newspapers . . . what they cannot do is to reverse public opinion.'

1850   – – –. *Strictly personal: some memoirs of Cecil H. King.* London: Weidenfeld & Nicolson, 1969. viii + 232pp.
Although published soon after King's removal from the chairmanship of the International Publishing Corporation, this is cool and unrancorous in tone. Born into newspapers (being Northcliffe's nephew), King became a director of the *Daily Mirror* at the age of twenty-eight, and chairman of its publishers twenty-two years later.

1851   – – –. *With malice toward none: a war diary,* ed William Armstrong. London: Sidgwick & Jackson, 1970. vi + 343pp.

1852   – – –. *Without fear or favour.* London: Sidgwick & Jackson, 1971. 247pp.

1853   – – –. *The Cecil King diary, 1965–1970.* London: Jonathan Cape, 1972. 353pp.

1854 – – –. *The Cecil King diary, 1970–1974*. London: Jonathan Cape, 1975. 415pp.

1855 Kingsford-Smith, Dimity, and Dawn Oliver, eds. *Economical with the truth: the law and the media in a democratic society*. Oxford: ESC, 1990.

1856 Kingswell, Elma. *Kingswell, war correspondent*. London: Cassell, 1938. xv + 278pp.
On George Herbert Kingswell, co-founder of the *Johannesburg Sunday Times*.

1857 Kinnear, A. 'Parliamentary reporting'. *The Contemporary Review*, 87, 1905.

1858 Kipling, [Joseph] Rudyard. 'The press'. In *A diversity of creatures*. London: Macmillan, 1917.
Five-stanza poem. The last reads:

> The Pope may launch his Interdict,
>   The Union its decree,
> But the bubble is blown, and the bubble is pricked
>   By Us and such as We,
> Remember the battle and stand aside
>   While Thrones and Powers confess
> That King over all the children of pride
>   Is the Press – the Press – the Press!

1859 *Kirkintilloch Herald*. Centenary souvenir, 1883–1983. Kirkintilloch (Strathclyde): 22 Jan 1983.
A Johnston Press weekly.

1860 Kitchin, (Frederick) Harcourt. *Moberly Bell and his Times: an unofficial narrative*. London: Philip Allan, 1925. viii + 298pp. Publ in the USA as *The London Times under the management of Moberly Bell*. New York: Putnam, 1925.
Valuable for the very reason that it *is* unofficial, for Kitchin (who also wrote as Bennet Copplestone) was Bell's immediate editorial assistant in the critical *Times* days of the early twentieth century.

1861 – – –. 'Adventures in Printing House Square'. *Cornhill Magazine*, Mar–Aug 1924.
Kitchin eventually left to become editor of the *Glasgow Herald*.

1862 Klein, Edward. 'The sinking of Cap'n Bob'. *Vanity Fair*, Mar 1992.
The end of Maxwell.

1863 – – –. 'Black mischief'. *Vanity Fair*, Nov 1992.
On Conrad Black.

1864 Klein, R. 'The powers of the press'. *Political Quarterly*, 154, 1973.

1865 Knight, Edward Frederick. *Reminiscences: the wanderings of a yachtsman and war correspondent*. London: Hutchinson, 1923. 320pp.

Knight was severely wounded when serving as the *Morning Post* correspondent in South Africa.

1866   Knightley, Phillip. *The first casualty: the war correspondent as hero, propagandist, and myth maker from the Crimea to Vietnam.* London: André Deutsch, 1975; New York: Harvest Books, 1976. Rptd as *The first casualty: from the Crimea to Vietnam: the war correspondent as hero, propagandist, and myth maker.* London: Quartet Books, 1978. 465pp; and with the sub-title *from the Crimea to the Falklands.* London: Pan, 1989. 478pp.

A special correspondent himself for *The Sunday Times*, Knightley asserts that our attitude towards history is moulded by what we read in wartime, and that what we read too often bears little resemblance to reality. He is particularly convincing on the coverage in the Western press of the Russian Revolution, and the reporting of the bombing of Guernica in 1937. Unquestionably this is the best-written as well as best-researched history since World War II of modern war reporting. (The phrase 'The first casualty when war comes is truth' is ascribed to Senator Hiram Johnson (1917).)

1867   – – –.   'The Falklands: how Britannia ruled the news'. *Columbia Journalism Review*, Sep–Oct 1982.

1868   – – –.   'A cold hard eye on history'. *The Sunday Times Magazine*, 5 Mar 1989.

Ethical considerations for the photojournalist confronted by war or other human disaster.

1869   – – –.   'Don't swallow without a pinch of salt'. *The Times*, 21 Jan 1991.

At the outset of the Gulf conflict, draws uneasy parallels with British propaganda in World War I.

1870   – – –.   'Here is the patriotically censored news'. *Index on Censorship*, 20, 4/5, Apr/May 1991.

1871   Knowles, Ron. 'Behind the union's *Journalist*'. *The Media Reporter*, 2, 2, 1978.

The *Journalist* is the publication of the National Union of Journalists.

1872   Knox, Collie. 'The guardian of the radio listener'. In *The press, 1898–1948* (*The Newspaper* World Golden Jubilee). London: Benn, 1948.

Knox contributed his pioneer Radio Page to the *Daily Mail* for seven pre-war years, alternating with weekly general comment; after the war, he continued a Radio Column and wrote much other journalism elsewhere.

1873   Knox-Peebles, Brian P. 'The regional press in Western Europe: perceptions and conceptions. Part One: UK.' *Admap*, Nov 1974; 'Part Four: The UK regional press – the men who shaped it, and the future before it'. *Admap*, Jan 1975.

1874   – – –.   'National newspapers: the significance of present initiatives'. *Admap*, Feb 1987.

1875 Koestler, Arthur. *Spanish testament*. London: Gollancz, 1937. 384pp.
Incorporates a translation of *Menschenopfer unerhört*, written in Koestler's first working language and published in Paris by Editions Carrefour in 1937. It covers Koestler's hundred days' imprisonment by Franco during the Spanish Civil War when he was a correspondent for the *News Chronicle*.

1876 – – –. *Dialogue with death*, translated by Phyllis and Trevor Blewitt. London: Macmillan, 1942; Collins/Hamish Hamilton, 1954. 222pp; Arrow, 1961. 223pp; Hutchinson, 1966, 1973. 207pp; Macmillan, 1983. 206pp; Harmondsworth (Middx): Penguin, 1942. 175pp; New York: Macmillan, 1942, 1960, 1967.
An abridged version of *Spanish testament*. It has been published in numerous other languages.

1877 – – –. *Bricks to Babel*. London: Hutchinson, 1980. 697pp.
An anthology described by Koestler (1905–83) himself as 'reducing 9,000 pages to 700'; in both scale and presentation, a worthy memorial to a major literary (and journalistic) figure. Among his many powerful writings were his regular contributions to *The Observer* after World War II. The title of Book Two of *Bricks to Babel*, 'In search of a synthesis', indicates his change of direction from political affairs to science and the paranormal.

1878 Koss, Stephen (Edward). *Fleet Street radical: A.G. Gardiner and the Daily News*. London: Allen Lane; Hamden (CT): Archon Books, 1973. x + 339pp.
A most accomplished biography offering fresh insights on Liberal politics, the workings of the press generally during Gardiner's years as editor of *The Daily News* (1902–19), and the social and intellectual life of that now remote Edwardian 'sunset' period.

1879 – – –. *The rise and fall of the political press in Britain*. London: Hamish Hamilton; Chapel Hill (NC): University of North Carolina Press. 2 vols. Vol 2: *The twentieth century*. 1984. x + 718pp. Single-vol pbk: London: Fontana, 1990.
There are at least two conflicting myths about the British press: that it is, and always has been, a Tory-led capitalistic swindle; and that it has never had much political influence. Both these myths get sharp if not short shrift from Koss (professor of history at Columbia University, New York) in this over-long but exceedingly well-researched and authoritative study, with references right up to mid-1983. There are few references to the regional or local press.

1880 – – –, ed. *The pro-Boers: the anatomy of an anti-war movement*. Chicago: University of Chicago Press, 1973. xl + 280pp. Introduction also by Koss.
Includes material reprinted from the daily press.

1881 Kurian, George Thomas, ed. *World press encyclopedia*. New York: Facts On File; London: Mansell, 1982. 2 vols: total 1,228pp.
A major global compendium, with individual contributions on seventy countries preceded by the editor's 'The world press: a statistical profile', and by other 'international' articles. Volume 2 contains a good, factually accurate, contribution on the UK by James

W. Welke of the University of Wyoming. Includes 'The world's élite newspapers', by
John C. Merrill. Now inevitably dated.

1882   Kynaston, David. *The Financial Times: a centenary history.* London:
Viking, 1988. x + 543pp.
Traces the competitive development of *The Financial News* (founded 1884) and *Financial
Times* (from 1888), and the single paper's great strides from 1945 on. The contribution
of (Sir) Gordon Newton as editor from 1949 to 1972 is shown to have been crucial.

1883   – – –.   *A short history of the Financial Times.* London: Financial Times,
1988. 8pp.

1884   – – –.   'Telling the story of a century of news'. *Financial Times,* 11 Feb
1988.
How the centenary volume was compiled.

1885   – – –.   'The first 100 years'. 15 Feb 1988.
On the *FT* itself: three pages out of a sixty-four-page special report.

1886   Kyte, Colin H.J. '*The Times* index'. *The Indexer,* Spring 1967.
Summarizes the history of the various indexes to the newspaper, official and unofficial,
the most notable of the latter being *Palmer's,* which for long had the field to itself.

1887   – – –.   'Indexing *The Times*'. *Library Association Record,* 71, 1, 1969.

1888   Labour Party Study Group. *The people and the media.* London: 1974.
This report, on the relationships between the general population, the press and broadcasting, spelt out criticism aimed at the then imminent Royal Commission on the Press.

1889   Labour Research Department. *The press.* London: 1922.

1890   – – –.   *The millionaire press.* [1946]. 20pp. Foreword by Gordon
Schaffer.

1890A   – – –.   *Who owns the press?* [1961]. 20pp.
'After the deals and mergers'.

1891   Lake, Brian. *British newspapers: a history and a guide for collectors.* With
an introduction by John Frost, including illustrations from his Historical
Newspaper Service. London: Sheppard Press, 1984. 213pp.
A lavishly illustrated but small-format handbook for newspaper collectors, especially
those new to the activity.

1892   Lamb, *Sir* [Albert] Larry. *Sunrise.* London: Macmillan (Papermac), 1989.
x + 260pp.
'The remarkable rise and rise of the best-selling soaraway *Sun*' – by its first editor
(1969–72) after revival by Murdoch (Lamb returned 1975–81, and later moved to edit
the *Daily Express*).

1893   – – –.   'How the *Sun* overtook the *Mirror*'. *Admap,* Oct 1986.

1894   Lambert, Derek. *Don't quote me . . . but: my adventures as a cub reporter.* London: Arlington Books, 1979. 221pp.

1895   – – –. *And I quote: my country adventures as a reporter.* London: Arlington Books, 1980. 224pp.

1896   – – –. *Unquote.* London: Arlington Books, 1981. 224pp.

1897   – – –. *Just like the Blitz: a reporter's notebook.* London: Hodder & Stoughton, 1987. vii + 158pp.
As it was on the *Daily Express*, 1962–5.

1898   *Lancashire Evening Post.* Centenary. Preston: 18 Oct 1986.
For a long period (1893–1949) the *Lancashire Daily Post*; today it is in the United Provincial Newspapers group.

1899   *Lancashire Evening Post – a history resource.* Preston: 1992.
Developed by Paul Cross, headmaster of a Preston primary school, for the Newspaper Society's Newspapers in Education scheme. Front pages are reproduced covering more than a hundred years.

1900   *Lancashire Evening Telegraph.* Centenary supplements. Blackburn: Mar–Oct 1986.
Began in 1886 as the *Northern Daily Telegraph*; it was a Kemsley Newspapers title from 1945 to 1959, then with Thomson Regional Newspapers until 1991, when it was acquired by Reed Regional Newspapers.

1901   Lancaster, (*Sir*) Osbert. *The life and times of Maudie Littlehampton.* Cartoons 1939–80, selected by Geraldine Cook. With an introduction by John Julius Norwich. London: John Murray; Harmondsworth (Middx): Penguin, 1982. 111pp.
These are sharp social cartoon comments published in the *Daily Express* over two generations. (Lancaster was also notable as an architectural writer and stage designer.)

1902   *Lancaster Guardian.* Centenary supplement, 1837–1937. 29 Jan 1937.
Today a weekly in the United Provincial Newspapers group.

1903   Landon, Perceval. *Lhasa: an account of the country and people of Central Tibet and the progress of the mission sent there by the English Government in the year 1903–4.* London: Hurst & Blackett, 1905. 2 vols.
On-the-spot reportage by a notable *Times* war correspondent – and later a long-service *Daily Telegraph* man in both war and peace.

1904   Lane, Margaret. *Edgar Wallace: the biography of a phenomenon.* London: Heinemann, 1938. xii + 423pp; New York: Doubleday, Doran, 1939; revised edn, London: Hamish Hamilton, 1964. xiv + 338pp. With an introduction by Graham Greene.
Wallace (1875–1932) is one of the only four journalists commemorated in Fleet Street. He is also remembered via the Edgar Wallace Reading Room in the Press

Club nearby; and in the 'Edgar Wallace' public house in Essex Street off The Strand. He was a Boer War correspondent for Reuters and then the *Daily Mail*. Returning to London as the latter's crime correspondent, he was also appointed acting editor of *The Evening News*, drama critic for *The Morning Post*, editor of *Lloyd's Sunday News*, and so on before embarking on his brilliant career as popular novelist and playwright. This suitably fast-moving biography is by his daughter-in-law (later the Countess of Huntingdon).

1905 Langdon, Julia. 'High noon at the Holborn oasis'. *The Guardian (Media Guardian)*, 29 Mar 1993.
Leading political commentator considers the case of Paul Foot, on the brink of leaving the *Daily Mirror* after writing his own left-wing campaigning column for thirteen years.

1906 Langdon, R. 'End of an era for the county's oldest paper'. *Blackcountryman*, 12, 1980.
A tribute to the *Wolverhampton Chronicle*, founded in 1789.

1907 Langdon-Davies, John. *Behind the Spanish barricades*. London: Martin Secker & Warburg, 1936. 302pp. Abridged version 1937. 241pp.
A very full, well-illustrated, and heartfelt report from the front line in the government cause in the Spanish Civil War: 'one side is right, the other criminally wrong.' So, he declares, are Garvin and the Conservative press, 'both dignified and gutter'. The author had been sent out by the *News Chronicle*; later, during World War II, he was to be science editor of several publications.

1908 Lansbury, George. *Miracle of Fleet Street: the story of the Daily Herald*. London: Labour Publishing Co (Victoria House), 1925. 66pp.
In retrospect, the 'miracle' was Lansbury's own achievement in his fifties when invited to edit the paper.

1909 – – –. *My life*. London: Constable, 1928. 293pp.
Before becoming leader of the Labour Party, Lansbury (1859–1940) was co-founder and editor of (*The*) *Daily Herald* for ten years (from 1912).

1910 *Largs and Millport Weekly News*. Centenary supplement. Ardrossan (Strathclyde): 8 Apr 1977.
A Clyde and Forth Newspapers weekly.

1911 Larsen, Egon (pseudonym of Egon Lehrburger). *First with the truth: newspapermen in action*. London: John Baker, 1968. 198pp.
Relates 'case histories' where campaigning journalists have uncovered criminal or other secret activities, including Stead and 'the Maiden Tribute'; Duncan Webb and the Messina brothers; C.P. Scott and the 'troubles' in Ireland; P.P. Graves and 'the plot that never was'; and the work of the *Sunday Times* Insight Team.

1912 'Last edition, The.' *The Times*, 18 Oct 1960.
A leader on the death of the *News Chronicle*.

1913 Laugharne, Elfrida. 'Spain, Nancy'. *In* Janet Todd, ed. *Dictionary of British women writers*. London: Routledge, 1989.
Nancy Spain was a high-profile writer on the *Daily Express* and later *News of the World*.

1914 Laughton, George Ebenezer, and Lorna Rutherford Stephen. *Yorkshire newspapers: a bibliography with locations*. London: Library Association, for its Yorkshire Branch, 1960. 61pp.
Contains 446 entries.

1915 Laurence, Ben. 'Piling up a profit on paper'. *The Guardian (Media Guardian)*, 22 Jan 1992.
On Conrad Black, as his Hollinger combine prepared to launch The Telegraph Group as a public company.

1916 – – –. 'Cracks in the mirror'. *The Guardian (Media Guardian)*, 26 Oct 1992.
On the appointment – anathema to many of the staff – of David Montgomery as chief executive of Mirror Group Newspapers.

1917 'Law, William' [William Dixon]. *Our Hansard, or the true mirror of Parliament*. London: Pitman, 1950. xi + 80pp.
'A full account of the Official Report'.

1918 Lawrence, Anthony. *Foreign correspondent*. London: Allen & Unwin, 1972. 201pp.

1919 Lawrence, Arthur, ed. *Journalism as a profession*. London: Hodder & Stoughton, 1903. x + 189pp. (In Start in Life series.)
Includes article by Alfred Harmsworth, 'The making of a newspaper', and preface by W. Robertson Nicoll.

1920 Lawrence, Rachel. 'Lloyd, Frank'. *In* David J. Jeremy, ed. *Dictionary of business biography*, Vol 3. London: Butterworth, for the Business History Unit, London School of Economics, 1985.
About Edward Lloyd's son, who took over and extended his father's thriving newspaper and papermaking enterprise.

1921 Lawrenson, John Ralph, and Lionel Barber. *The price of truth: the story of the Reuters millions*. Edinburgh: Mainstream Publishing, 1985; London: Sphere, 1986. vi + 177pp.
An updated history of the Reuters news agency, but – more important – hitherto unpublished material on Reuters' relationship with the British Government in World War II, and the full story of the more recent flotation of the agency as a public company.

1922 Layton, Walter Thomas (*1st Baron*). *Newsprint*. London: [O'Donoghue], 1946.
A pamphlet explaining the procedure of the wartime Newsprint Supply Company, signed by Layton (then Sir Walter) as its chairman.

1923   Le Sage (formerly Sage), *Sir* John Merry. 'Fifty years of journalism'. *In*
Sell's World's Press, 1914. London: Sell, 1914.
In fact, Le Sage served *The Daily Telegraph* for sixty years, nearly forty of them as
nominal managing editor. His main claim to fame as a foreign correspondent in his
earlier years was to report from within Paris during the Prussian occupation in 1871.

1924   Leach, Henry. 'Newspaper London'. *In* George R. Sims, ed. *Living*
London, Vol 2. London: Cassell, 1906. Originally in monthly parts.
'In Newspaper-land there is no time for sleep.'

1925   Leapman, Michael. *Barefaced cheek: the apotheosis of Rupert Murdoch.*
London: Hodder & Stoughton, 1983. 269pp; (Coronet), 1984. Publ in the USA
as *Arrogant Aussie: the Rupert Murdoch story*. Secaucus (NJ): Lyle Stuart, 1985.
288pp.
By a former *Times* journalist, who expresses grudging admiration for the material (if
not ethical) achievements of the outstanding Australian (born in 1931) who, by the age
of fifty, had spread his publishing net across the world, and in Britain – through News
International – bought control of *The Sun*, the *News of the World*, *The Times*, and *The*
Sunday Times.

1926   – – –.   *Treacherous estate: the press after Fleet Street*. London: Hodder
& Stoughton, 1992. 304pp.
Bearing a title deliberately evocative of Francis Williams's benchmark *Dangerous estate*;
a thoughtful latter-day analysis.

1927   – – –.   'An entertaining end to a shooting star'. *The Independent*, 18 Feb
1987.
Looking back over the twenty-six years since *The Sunday Times Magazine* was founded
as the first of the Sunday 'colour supplements'.

1928   – – –.   'No accounting for taste'. *UK Press Gazette*, 7 Sep 1987. (The
Tabloids series).
An introductory 'setting the scene' article.

1929   LeBor, Adam. 'Times past, times future'. *The Sunday Times Magazine*, 2
Jul 1989.
'The new Fleet Street. It survived the Blitz but not the new technology. As the money
men move in, Whitefriars rises from its ashes.' With brief illustrated reports on the
moves of the major nationals.

1930   Lee, Alan John. *The origins of the popular press in England, 1855–1914*.
London (Beckenham): Croom Helm; Totowa (NJ): Rowman & Littlefield, 1976.
310pp.
Lee, who died suddenly in his thirties, was one of the very few press historians to pay
serious attention to recent history. His thesis here is that the gulf between the ideal concept of the press (as represented by *The Times* under Delane) and its less exalted reality
(on e.g. *The Daily News*) was widened greatly by the industrialization in the 1890s

of what had been largely family businesses concerned more with public service than exploitation. Hence, the phenomenon of newspapers as 'chewing gum' for the idle mind rather than as providers of functional information for the caring citizen.

1931 – – –. 'Franklin Thomasson and *The Tribune*'. *Historical Journal*, 16, 1973.
This *Tribune* was the short-lived Liberal daily founded by Thomasson and immortalized in fiction by Gibbs in *The street of adventure*.

1932 – – –. 'The radical press'. *In Edwardian radicalism, 1900–1914*, ed A.J.A. Morris. London: Routledge & Kegan Paul, 1974.

1933 – – –. 'The structure, ownership and control of the press, 1855–1914'. *In* [D.]G. Boyce *et al*, eds. *Newspaper history* . . . (q.v.).

1934 – – –. 'The British press and its historians'. *Journalism Studies Review*, 3, 1978.
An informed appraisal up to that date.

1935 Lee, F. *The City page*. London: Nelson, 1939. 228pp. (In the Discussion Books series.)

1936 '*Leeds Intelligencer – Yorkshire Post*'. *The Newspaper World*, 19 Aug 1939. (In The Oldest Newspapers series.)

1937 *Leicester Mercury*. Royal opening souvenir. Leicester: 12 Jan 1967.
Includes a history of what was originally the *Leicester Daily Mercury* and of other papers published in the city.

1938 – – –. Centenary souvenir issue, 1874–1974. 31 Jan 1974.
The *Mercury* of today (an evening title) is in the Associated Newspapers group.

1939 Leigh, David. *The frontiers of secrecy: closed government in Britain*. London: Junction Books, 1980. x + 291pp.
'Don't trust the Government an inch', warns *The Observer*'s man in the aftermath of a general election with a large majority for one party.

1940 Leigh, J.G. 'What do the masses read?. *Economic Review*, 1904.

1941 Leinster-Mackay, Donald, and Elizabeth Sarfaty. *Education and The Times: an index of letters to 1910*. London: Mansell, 1994.
The index ends at 1910 because *The Times Educational Supplement* began as a separate publication in the following year.

1942 Leitch, David. *Deadline: collected journalism*. London: Harrap, 1984. x + 245pp.
Largely comprising Leitch's feature-length reportage from various parts of the world to *The Sunday Times* (from the 1960s on), and to the *New Statesman* from France in the 1970s. Contains outstanding photos by Don McCullin and others.

1943   Lejeune, Anthony. 'The Press Club'. In his *The Gentlemen's Clubs of London*. London: Macdonald & Jane's, 1979. Photos by Malcolm Lewis.
Features, notably, the Edgar Wallace Room and Chair. The latter is preserved by the present-day London Press Club.

1944   Lejeune, C[aroline] A[lice] (Mrs E. Roffe Thompson). *Chestnuts in her lap, 1936–1946*. London: Phoenix House, 1947. 192pp.
A selection of film reviews etc from the author's long and distinguished career with *The Observer* (1928–60).

1945   Lennon, Peter. 'The orphaned journalist'. *The Listener*, Press issue, 24 Apr 1986.
The dilemma of the professional journalist looking for a vocation.

1946   – – –.   'Tabloid man is back to basics'. *The Guardian*, 5 Feb 1990.
Profile of Roy Greenslade; moving from managing editor (news), *The Sunday Times*, to editor, *Daily Mirror*.

1947   Leslie, Anita. *Cousin Randolph: the lift of Randolph Churchill*. London: Hutchinson, 1985. 216pp.
The turbulent career of Winston's son Randolph included much professional journalism, for example in the Korean War for *The Daily Telegraph* and wide-ranging reporting for the *Evening Standard*. This sympathetic biography also describes Randolph Churchill's famous (and successful) libel action against *The People*.

1948   Leslie, Ann (Elizabeth Mary) [Mrs Michael Fletcher]. 'Woman in Fleet Street'. *In* V. Brodzky *et al*, eds. *Fleet Street: the inside story of journalism*. London: Macdonald, 1966.
The author joined the *Daily Express* as a columnist at the age of twenty-three, and had to make her way in a man's world. She later became a star contributor to the *Daily Mail*.

1949   Lessle, Manfred. *Englands Weg zum Appeasement, 1932–1936*. Karlsruhe: Berenz, [1969]. 278pp.
A thesis for Heidelberg University, 'a consideration of the press' in England during the mid-1930s.

1950   Letham, G.H. 'The National Union of Journalists: what it is and what it is doing'. In *Sell's Dictionary of the World's Press, 1910*. London: Sell, 1910.

1951   Leventhal, F[red] M[arc]. *The last dissenter: H.N. Brailsford and his world*. Oxford: Clarendon Press, 1985. viii + 326pp.
Brailsford was a prominent novelist, foreign correspondent and leader-writer (e.g. for the *Daily Herald*), but his editorship of the Independent Labour Party's *New Leader* (1922–6) was particularly noteworthy.

1952   Levin, [Henry] Bernard. *Taking sides*. London: Jonathan Cape, 1979.
A first selection of Levin's journalism: this has been followed by a series of anthologies, all published by Cape.

1953 – – –. 'Profit and dishonour in Fleet Street'. *The Times*, 19 Mar 1971.

A literary rather than news journalist, Levin himself made the headlines after publication of this article shortly after he joined *The Times* as chief columnist. It led to a long-drawn-out libel action by his former employers (Lord Rothermere and Associated Newspapers, publishers of the *Daily Mail*).

1954 – – –. 'Fleet Street: now the truth can be told'. *The Times*, 3 Feb 1986.

'For many years now, newspapers have been produced in conditions which combined a protection racket with a lunatic asylum.' Written a few days after *The Times* and the other News International titles had moved overnight to Wapping.

1955 – – –. 'A life stranger than fiction'. *The Times*, 1 Jan 1992.

On Robert Maxwell.

1956 Levy, Geoffrey. *The Daily Mail is its own best story*. London: Associated Newspapers, 1989. 15pp.

Historical summary for staff on moving to Kensington, August 1989.

1957 Levy, [Herman] Phillip. *The Press Council: history, procedure and cases*. London: Macmillan, 1967. 500pp.

A detailed record of the first fourteen years of the Press Council (which was founded as the General Council of the Press). Following the forcibly expressed opinion of the 1961–2 Royal Commission on the Press, the Council was reconstituted in 1963 to include lay members.

1958 Lewinski, Jorge. *The camera at war: a history of war photography from 1848 to the present day*. London: W.H. Allen, 1978; Octopus Books, 1986, 240pp.

Among the classics illustrated (and described) are those of Bert Hardy of *Picture Post* and Don McCullin of more recent times.

1959 Lewis, Jon E., ed. *The mammoth book of true war stories*. London: Robinson, 1992. 565pp.

Contains outstanding war reportage from W.H. Russell to Max Hastings and, *en route*, a brief Boer War report by Kipling (then on the staff of the British Army newspaper *The Friend (of the Free State)*.

1960 Lewis, Norman. *A view of the world: selected journalism*. London: Eland Books, 1986. 296pp.

Although Lewis is a distinguished travel writer, and most of the twenty articles here illustrate his descriptive powers, some, like the now-famous 'Genocide' (originally in *The Sunday Times*) about the Brazilian Indians, have had an international impact of an altogether different dimension.

1961 *Lewisham Mercury*. 150 years of service to the community. London: 20 Oct 1983.

A Westminster Press title.

1962   *Leyton, Leytonstone and Waltham Forest Guardian.* Centenary supplement. London: 7 May 1976.
Now in Reed ownership.

1963   Liddell Hart, (*Sir*) Basil (Henry). *The real war.* London: Faber, 1930.
A close and authoritative analysis of World War I, still of value today.

1964   – – –.   *The memoirs of Captain Liddell Hart.* London: Cassell, 1965. 2 vols. Publ in the USA as *The Liddell Hart memoirs.* New York: 1965–6.
Liddell Hart was the most influential military correspondent of modern times, notably in the columns of *The Daily Telegraph* (1925–35) and *The Times* (1935–9). Unusual in being a long-term strategist rather than a front-line reporter, he espoused the use of air and mechanized forces – developed in practice by the Germans in World War II.

1965   *Lincolnshire, Boston and Spalding Free Press.* Centenary number. Spalding (Lincs): 6 Oct 1947.
Founded as the *Spalding Free Press,* today the *Lincolnshire Free Press* and part of the EMAP group.

1966   *Lincolnshire Chronicle.* 'One hundred years'. Lincoln: Apr 1933.
Began publication in Stamford.

1967   – – –.   Anniversary souvenir, 1833–1983. 27 Jun 1983.

1968   *Lincolnshire Echo.* Centenary. Lincoln: 31 Jan 1993.
First in a series, cumulated as *Centenary Echo,* 23 September 1993. The *Lincolnshire Echo* is one of Northcliffe Newspapers' evenings.

1969   *Lincolnshire Standard.* (Boston edition) 75th anniversary supplement. Boston (Lincs): 6 Jul 1987.
Now an Adscene free weekly.

1970   Lind, Harold. *The future of evening newspapers in London and the regions: a forecast to 1985.* London: Admap (monograph), 1981.

1971   – – –.   *The evening newspaper market: how bad is it, and can it get worse?* *Admap* (monograph), 1984.

1972   – – –.   *The 24-hour newspaper: can it work in Britain?* *Admap* (monograph), 1985.
Published nearly two years before Maxwell's abortive attempt with *The London Daily News.*

1973   – – –.   'The next 200 years: can the paper's books be balanced?'. *Campaign,* 14 Dec 1984.
An assessment by a leading analyst of the likely performance of *The Times* after its bicentenary.

1974   Lindop, Audrey (Beatrice Noel) Erskine. *The tall headlines.* London: Heinemann, 1950; Pan.
A newspaper novel.

1975 Lindsay, T(homas) F(anshawe). *Parliament from the Press Gallery*. London: Macmillan, 1967. ix + 176pp.
By a leading *Daily Telegraph* sketch-writer.

1976 Linklater, Magnus (Duncan). 'Don't rely on what they say'. *UK Press Gazette*, 14 Sep 1987. (The Tabloids series.)
Includes profiles of eleven current editors of tabloids. This was written by Linklater soon after his editorship of the short-lived *London Daily News* and before he became editor of *The Scotsman*. He had previously held senior appointments with the *Evening Standard*, *The Sunday Times*, and *The Observer*.

1977 — — —. 'Observing the rules'. *The Guardian*, 3 May 1993.
A critical view of *The Observer*'s drift, especially in management, as it moved to acquisition by *The Guardian*.

1978 — — —. 'An insight into Insight'. *British Journalism Review*, 4, 2, 1993.
Linklater was on the staff of *The Sunday Times* for fourteen years, and so writes with inside knowledge of the important work of the Insight Team.

1979 Linton, [George] David [Hough]. 'Mr Mitchell's "national work" '. *Journal of Advertising History*, 2, 1979.
A brief survey of the unique history of *The Newspaper Press Directory*, from its foundation by London advertising agent Charles Mitchell in 1846 to its development with the Benn name from 1978. *See under Reference Works section.*

1980 — — —. 'Sell's publications: a hundred years and more'. In *Sell's Directory: Products and Services, 1985* (centenary edition).
Features the history of *Sell's Dictionary of the Work's Press* (later *Sell's World's Press*), and the Henry Sell Collection of Historic Newspapers, absorbed into the Press Club's collection in 1931. Sell, like Mitchell, began in Fleet Street as an advertising agent.

1981 — — —. 'Mitchell's, May's and Sell's: newspaper directories of the Victorian era'. *Journal of Newspaper and Periodical History*, Spring 1987.
Mitchell's *Newspaper Press Directory* survives as *Benn's Media*, and May's as *Willings Press Guide*. *See Reference Works section.*

1982 — — —. 'Chancellor turns editor: the eight days of *The British Gazette*'. *Churchill Tales* (International Churchill Society), 2, 1, Jun 1991.
Although Winston Churchill was chancellor of the exchequer when the General Strike was called in May 1926, he moved swiftly to mastermind the Government's own newspaper for the duration: *The British Gazette*. It was printed on the commandeered presses of *The Morning Post*.

1983 — — —. 'Fleet Street in fiction'. *Newspaper Focus*, Sep 1992.

1984 — — —. 'Journalism's own journalism'. *In* Dennis Griffiths, ed. *The encyclopedia of the British press, 1422–1992*. Basingstoke (Hants): Macmillan, 1992.
The trade press – periodicals, directories and other reference works.

Linton, [George] David [Hough], and Raymond (Jack) Boston. *The newspaper press in Britain: an annotated bibiography: see Reference Works section.*

1985   No entry.

1986   Linton, Tony. 'Extel – the next hundred years'. *In* D. Campbell, ed. *The British press*, London: CPU, 1978.
Looking ahead for the former Exchange Telegraph group.

1987   Littleton, Suellen M. *The Wapping dispute.* Aldershot (Hants): Ashgate (Avebury); Brookfield (VT): Ashgate, 1992. xiii + 223pp.
'An examination of the conflict and its impact on the national newspaper industry'.

1988   *Liverpool Courier.* Centenary number. Liverpool: 6 Jan 1908.

1989   *Liverpool Daily Post.* Jubilee number. 13 Jun 1905.

1990   Liverpool Daily Post. *The centenary of the Liverpool Post and Mercury: a record of the progress of Liverpool and its leading newspaper.* Liverpool: 1911.
The *Liverpool Mercury* was founded in 1811.

1991   *Liverpool Daily Post.* Centenary supplement. 11 Jun 1955.
Established in 1855 as the *Daily Post*, a title to which this leading independent provincial daily has now reverted. Its current publishers are the Trinity International group.

1992   '*Liverpool Daily Post*'. *Caxton Magazine*, 2, 1901–2. (In the Great Provincial Newspapers series.)

1993   *Liverpool Echo.* 'Ourselves: the *Daily Post*'. *Liverpool Echo*, 14 Nov 1904.
An early pronouncement from the evening partner of the (*Liverpool*) *Daily Post.*

1994   – – –.   Centenary edition. 27 Oct 1979.

1995   – – –.   35,000th edition. 3 Dec 1992.

1996   'Liverpool's only morning newspaper: its 80 years of public service'. *Liverpolitan*, 4, 1935.
On the *Liverpool Daily Post.*

1997   'Liverpool's shipping daily'. *The Newspaper World*, 11 Mar 1939. (In The Oldest Newspapers series.)
Features the *Journal of Commerce.*

1998   Lloyd, H.J. 'The *Denbighshire Free Press*'. *Transactions of the Denbighshire Historical Society*, 22, 1973.

1999   Lloyd, Herbert. *The legal limits of journalism.* Oxford: Pergamon, 1968.

2000   Lloyd, John. 'The Senate and the IRA'. *Financial Times* (a leader); 'No compromise, no surrender'. *Financial Times*; both rptd *UK Press Gazette*, 4 Jan 1988 (Classics of Journalism series).
Contributed as industrial editor.

2001   Lloyd, John, and Helen Hague. 'The Wapping time-bomb: how the fuse was lit'. *UK Press Gazette*, 3 Feb 1986. Rptd from the *Financial Times*.
An instant report on the overnight move of News International's four national titles to the new plant at Wapping, bypassing the 'traditional' printing unions.

2002   *Lloyd's List.* 'Daily publication for 100 years'. London: 1 Jul 1937.

2003   *Lloyd's Weekly News.* Diamond Jubilee number. London: 30 Nov 1902.

2004   Lloyd's Weekly News. *The story of the making of Lloyd's Weekly News ('from forest to fireside').* London: 1909.
Edward Lloyd (1815–90) was the most successful as well as the most prolific publisher of popular newspapers in the Victorian era. After *Lloyd's Penny Sunday Times* came *Lloyd's Illustrated London Newspaper*, which (as *Lloyd's Weekly Newspaper*) was the first in the world to reach a circulation first of 100,000 and later of 1,000,000.

2005   Locks, Ian. 'A great future for the frees'. *AFN News* (newsletter of the Association of Free Newspapers), Autumn 1983. Rptd in *The Media Reporter*, Autumn 1983.

2006   Lofts, W(illiam) O(liver) G(uillemont), and Derek (John) Adley. *The British bibliography of Edgar Wallace.* London: Howard Baker, 1969. 361pp.
Wallace wrote about one hundred and seventy books, numerous plays – and copious daily journalism.

2007   Loizou, Andreas. 'United Newspapers PLC'. *In International directory of company histories*, Vol 4, Chicago and London: St James Press, 1991.

2008   *London Press Club Newsletter.* 1986–. Occasional.
Primarily for members of the club (established 1986) that carries on the traditions – including the newsletter itself – of the original Press Club (established 1882).

2009   *London, Provincial and Colonial Press News.* London: weekly, 1866–1912.

2010   London Research and Information Bureau. *Press circulations analysed.* London: LRIB, 1928.
Probably the first general readership survey, based on a sample of twenty thousand homes.

2011   London Research Bureau. *The nation's newspaper.* London: LRB (for Daily Mail), 1924.
A collection of unstandardized market reports – the first known readership survey.

2012   *Long Eaton Advertiser.* Centenary issue. Long Eaton (Notts): 5 Aug 1982.

2013   Longhurst, Henry (Carpenter). *The best of Henry Longhurst – golf and life.* Comp and ed Mark Wilson and Ken Bowden. London: Collins, 1979; Fontana, 1980.
Anthology of *The Sunday Times's* golf correspondent – from 1932, for forty-five years.

2014   Loosley, Arthur Ernest. *The business of photojournalism*. London: Focal Press, 1970.

2015   Lord, Shirley (*née* Williamson). *Small beer at Claridge's*. London: Michael Joseph, 1968.
The author presents a gossipy tale of working journalism for a long list of publications: mainly women's magazines, but also the *Daily Mirror, Evening Standard*, and *Evening News*.

2016   Loshak, David. 'Medical journalists and society'. *THS Health Summary*, Feb 1986.
By a leading medical editor and correspondent.

2017   *Loughborough Echo*. '*Echo* 90 years young – still going strong'. Loughborough (Leics): 7 Nov 1981.

2018   Lovelace, Colin J. *Control and censorship of the press in Britain during the First World War*. London: University of London (King's College), 1982 (PhD thesis). 224pp.

2019   – – –.   'British press censorship during the First World War'. *In* [D.]G. Boyce *et al*, eds. *Newspaper history* . . . (q.v.).

2020   Loven, Basil. *The making of a newspaper*. London: Newspaper Society, 1987.
For students etc.

2021   Lovesey, John. 'Pressing ahead to the high-tech newspaper'. *The Sunday Times*, 28 Oct 1984.
The success story of the *Express and Star*, based at Wolverhampton, and its switch to new production technology.

2022   Low, Bob, ed. *The Observer book of profiles*. London: W.H. Allen, 1991.
To mark the newspaper's two hundredth anniversary.

2023   Low, (*Sir*) David (Alexander Cecil). *Sketches by Low*. Supplement to *The New Statesman*, 16 Jan–17 Jul 1926: a series of 20 portraits; these were rptd with 16 new portraits in *Lions and lambs*. London: Cape, 1928. 156pp. Interpretation by 'Lynx' (Rebecca West). Second series, supplement to *New Statesman and Nation*, 21 Oct 1933–6 Jan 1934; 12 more portraits. Selection from both series rptd in *New Statesman*, 1981.
These form a unique gallery of personalities of the 1920s and 1930s.

2024   – – –.   *Years of wrath: a cartoon history, 1931–1945*. New York: Simon & Schuster, 1946. Text by Quincy Howe. Publ in the UK as *Years of wrath: a cartoon history, 1932–1945*. London: Gollancz, 1949. Text of this edition by Low himself, including a notable commentary on the Nuremberg war trials. Rptd Gollancz, 1986. Introduction by Michael Foot.
Among his vast output, this is commonly held to be Low's literary masterpiece.

2025 – – –. *Low's autobiography*. London: Michael Joseph, 1956; New York: Simon & Schuster, 1957. 387pp.

'I came from the outside world ... without respect for institutions and persons that have no right to respect.' Includes more than sixty drawings and photos, plus political history and commentary to accompany the author's own story. This New Zealander (1891–1963), first introduced to English newspaper readers (via *The Star*) in 1919, towers over everyone in an outstanding generation of political cartoonists. Low's genius had its full flowering when he was allowed remarkable latitude by Beaverbrook to express his political stance in *The Evening Standard* from 1927 to 1950. The *Daily Herald* and *Manchester Guardian* were later major vehicles for his art.

2026 Low, Frances H. *Press work for women: a textbook for the young woman journalist*. London: L. Upcott Gill; New York: Scribner, 1904.

2027 – – –. 'Journalism as an occupation for girls'. *The Girl's Realm*, Oct–Nov 1902.

'First let me warn any girl who is highly educated and has delicate literary taste ... that she should avoid journalism.'

2028 *Lowestoft Journal*. Centenary supplement. Lowestoft (Suffolk): 27 Jul 1973. Weekly in the Eastern Counties Newspapers group.

2029 Lowndes, Marie (Adelaide) Belloc (*née* Marie Belloc). 'Journalism as a profession for women'. *Leisure Hour*, 5, 1902.

2030 Lowther, Frederick L. *In Northcliffe's service*. London: 1927.

2031 Loynes, Tony. '20 things you didn't know about *The Sun*'. *UK Press Gazette*, 5 Oct 1987. (The Tabloids series.)

Interview by the editor with Patsy Chapman, then deputy editor of *The Sun*.

2032 – – –. 'How to put an end to the fear and loathing'. *UK Press Gazette*, 4 Jul 1988. (Cleaning up the 4th Estate series.)

On the journalist's instinctive aversion to legislation.

2033 Lucas, E[dward] V[errall]. *Reading, writing and remembering*. London: Methuen, 1932. xvi + 309pp.

These memoirs include evocative material on reporting for the evening *Globe* in his early days.

2034 Lucas, E[dward] V[errall], and Charles [Larcom] Graves. *Change for a halfpenny: being the prospectus of the Napolio Syndicate*. London: Alston Rivers, 1905. 64pp. Illus George Morrow.

'By the authors of *Wisdom while you wait*' – i.e. Lucas and Graves; they aimed to guy the ambitious Norrhclifte, whose monogram N was (no doubt intentionally) reminiscent of that of Napoleon.

2035 Lucas, Peter J. 'Local newspapers (sources for local history)'. *Local Historian*, 11, 6, May 1975.

2036   Lucas, Reginald J. *Lord Glenesk and the Morning Post.* London: Alston Rivers, 1910. ix + 443pp.
The author was commissioned by Lady Bathurst, the new owner, to write this biography of her father. Born Algernon Borthwick, Lord Glenesk was the first newspaper proprietor to enter the House of Lords.

2037   Lucy, *Sir* Henry William. *Sixty years in the wilderness: some passages by the way.* London: Smith, Elder, 1909. x + 450pp. First publ in *The Cornhill Magazine.*
Traces Lucy's career from humble beginnings in Lancashire to his journalism in London as parliamentary gallery correspondent. He was also Cross Bench columnist in *The Observer.* Most notable of all was his work for *Punch*, for which Lucy was destined to remain 'Toby, M.P.' until 1916, respected and appreciated by all parties.

2038   – – –. *Nearing Jordan: being the last volume of 'Sixty years in the wilderness'.* London: Smith, Elder, 1916. x + 453pp.

2039   – – –. *Men and manner in Parliament.* London: T. Fisher Unwin; New York: Dutton, 1919. 259pp. First publ anonymously in *The Gentleman's Magazine* in 1874.

2040   – – –. *The diary of a journalist.* London: John Murray, 1920–3. 3 vols. New York: Dutton.
Unedited extracts from his 'Toby, M.P.' diary in *Punch.*

2041   Lunn, Hugh. *Vietnam: a reporter's view.* St Lucia (Australia): University of Queensland Press, 1985.
At the time of the Vietnam War, a Reuters correspondent.

2042   Lyall, Gavin. 'Bringing colour to the British Sunday'. *The Sunday Times*, 23 Jan 1962.
Marking the launch of the first colour magazine with a British Sunday paper.

2043   Lynch, George. *Impressions of a war correspondent.* London: George Newnes, 1912. xix + 235pp.
Reporter for *The Morning Herald, The Echo*, and *The Illustrated London News*, Lynch became bored when cooped up in the Ladysmith siege, so ventured out to the Boer lines, and was naturally captured. This is just one of his anecdotes.

2044   Lynch, George, and Frederick Palmer, eds. *In many wars – by many warcorrespondents.* [Tokyo: 1904].
This collector's piece is a compendium of short contributions from no fewer than fortynine correspondents (twenty-two British, including Lynch, then of *The Daily Chronicle*), waiting in Tokyo to go to the front line in the Russo-Japanese War – proceeds to a Japanese Forces' relief fund.

2045   Lyons, A. Neil. *Robert Blatchford: the sketch of a personality: an estimate of some achievements.* London: Clarion Press, 1910. 189pp.
By a close friend and member of Blatchford's editorial staff on *The Clarion.*

2046 Lysaght, Charles Edward. *Brendan Bracken*. London: Allen Lane, 1979. 372pp.

Before World War II, Bracken founded *The Banker* and chaired the company that acquired *The Financial News, The Investor's Chronicle,* and a 50 per cent share in *The Economist*. Immediately after the war he became chairman of the *Financial Times* (with which its competitor had been merged). During it, he was Churchill's minister of information and close associate. This excellent biography, by a Dublin lawyer, gives a full picture of a many-sided man. Bracken House, the former City headquarters of the *Financial Times,* still bears his name.

2047 Lytton, *Hon* Neville Stephen. *The press and the General Staff*. London: Collins, [1921]. xvi + 231pp.

An elegant account by the British press officer attached for most of World War I to Allied Army HQ in France. The British press was permitted only five correspondents, but these were usually conducted into the war zone by men whom they could respect, such as C.E. Montague of *The Manchester Guardian*.

2048 McAleer, Joseph. 'Get me the boy from the age of six: D.C. Thomson & Co Ltd'. In his *Popular reading and publishing in Britain, 1914–1950*. Oxford: Oxford University Press, 1992.

Although this well-researched chapter on a notoriously difficult target (the D.C. Thomson publishing empire) is largely about boys' comics and women's magazines, it also charts the early success of Thomson and his family in publishing popular newspapers. The author gives detail of their development, e.g. *The (Dundee) Courier,* and the eventual pooling arrangement with John Leng & Co and their *Dundee Advertiser* and *(Dundee) Evening Telegraph*.

2049 McAllister, Bryan. *Little boxes: a selection of Bryan McAllister's cartoons from The Guardian*. With commentary by Simon Hoggart and McAllister; foreword by Richard Boston. London: The Guardian, 1977. 94pp.

The deserved fame of McAllister as a satirical cartoonist is based on frankly crude line drawings which prove just as effective as the captions in their awful suggestibility.

2050 – – –. *Look, no feet!* London: Gollancz, 1987. 96pp.

'The best of Bryan McAllister's cartoons from *The Guardian*'.

2051 MacArthur, Brian (Raymond). *Eddy Shah, Today, and the newspaper revolution*. Newton Abbot (Devon): David & Charles, 1988.

By the first editor-in-chief of *Today,* under the Shah aegis.

2052 – – –. *Deadline Sunday: a life in the week of The Sunday Times*. London: Hodder & Stoughton, 1991. 160pp.

MacArthur started his third stint at *The Sunday Times* in 1987, as executive editor.

2053 – – –. 'Underdog routs the Fleet Street giants'. *The Sunday Times,* 4 Oct 1987.

'*The Independent* celebrates its first anniversary this week.'

2054 – – –. 'Agency with the world as its oyster'. *The Sunday Times*, 27 May 1990.
Summary of the current operations of Reuters, now the world's biggest news organization.

2055 – – –. 'Silencing the critics'. *UK Press Gazette*, 12 Aug 1991.
The Press Association's newsroom in action: an expensive service, but seen by MacArthur as unrivalled.

2056 – – –. 'The catalyst, the lubricant and the internal revolution'. *UK Press Gazette*, 26 Aug 1991.
On Stuart Garner, recently appointed editorial director of Thomson Regional Newspapers.

2057 – – –. 'Variety and quality of the weekly press'. *UK Press Gazette*, 16 Sep 1991.
The current scene.

2058 MacArthur, Brian (Raymond), ed. *Despatches from the Gulf War*. London: Bloomsbury, 1991.
Includes such notable reportage as that from Robert Fisk, Simon Jenkins, Paul Foot, Hugo Young and Tim Kelsey.

2059 Macaulay, Sean. 'The devil and the deep blue tongue'. *The Guardian*, 12 Nov 1992.
Close-up of Kelvin MacKenzie, editor of *The Sun*.

2060 Macbeath, Innis. *Cloth cap and after*. London: Allen & Unwin, 1973. 225pp.
A *Times* labour editor's commentary.

2061 McCann, Eamonn. *The British press and Northern Ireland*. London: Pluto Press, for the Northern Ireland Socialist Research Centre, 1971.

2062 MacCarthy, *Sir* [Charles Otto] Desmond. *Desmond MacCarthy: the man and his writings*. With an introduction by Lord David Cecil [MacCarthy's son-in-law]. London: Constable, 1984. 313pp.
After a notable career with *The New Statesman*, MacCarthy (1877–1952) spent his last twenty-four years with *The Sunday Times*, becoming the acclaimed doyen of dramatic critics. This memoir reminds us that he was also an editor, notably of 'Life and Letters' during his early years at *The Sunday Times*.

2063 McClelland, William Douglas. *Readership profiles of mass media*. London: Institute of Practitioners in Advertising, 1963.

2064 – – –. *Printing and publishing: printing and publishing of newspapers and periodicals*. Oxford: Pergamon (for Royal Statistical Society and Economic and Social Research Council), 1987.
Review of *UK Statistical Sources*, Vol 22.

2065   MacColl, René (Marie). *A flying start: a memory of the nineteen twenties.* London: Jonathan Cape, 1939. 303pp.

2066   – – –.   *No idea!* London: Jonathan Cape, 1952. 255pp.

2067   – – –.   *Just back from Russia.* London: Daily Express, [1954], 224pp.
A report on seventy-seven days spent by the author in the Soviet Union.

2068   – – –.   *Deadline and dateline.* London: Oldbourne (Daily Express), 1956. 256pp.
The author was a long-serving, wide-ranging foreign correspondent–roving reporter – for the *Daily Express* (and in earlier years *The Daily Telegraph*).

2069   MoConnah, J.V. 'The Army and the press in war'. *Journal of the RUSI,* 98, 1953.

2070   McCoy, Jack, comp. *An index to the County Down Spectator, 1904–1964.* Ballynahinch: (Irish) South East Education and Library Board, 1983.

2071   – – –.   *An index to the Mourne Observer, 1949–1980.* Ballynahinch: 1984.

2072   McCullin, Don(ald). *The destruction business.* London: Macmillan (Open Gate Books)/Chatto & Windus, 1971. 95pp. Publ in the USA as *Is anyone taking any notice?* Cambridge (MA): MIT Press, [1973].
A selection from the early war images by one of the most realistic, uncompromising photographers of recent times. Many of the pictures were commissioned by *The Observer*.

2073   – – –.   *Unreasonable behaviour: an autobiography.* London: Jonathan Cape, 1990; Viking, 1992. 287pp. With Lewis Chester.
As outstanding for its honest self-critical narrative as for its classic photography.

2074   MacDonagh, Michael. *The Reporters' Gallery.* London: Hodder & Stoughton, [1913]. xii + 452pp.
Still widely regarded as a standard work on parliamentary journalism. It deals not only with the author's own view of the House of Commons for *The Times*, but also contains excellent historical material on such as Johnson, Coleridge, Dickens, Hansard.

2075   – – –.   *In London during the Great War (diary of a journalist).* London: Eyre & Spottiswoode, 1935. 336pp.
His description of the end of Zeppelin L-31 is particularly vivid.

2076   – – –.   'Our special correspondent'. In *The Newspaper Press Directory, 1903.* London: Mitchell, 1903.

2077   – – –.   'The wires and the newspapers'. In *Sell's Dictionary of the World's Press, 1906.* London: Sell, 1906.

2078   MacDonald, Barrie (Ian), comp. *The media.* London: Library Association, 1977. (In the Reader's Guide series.)
A selective bibliography, with some useful annotations.

2079 – – –. *Keyguide to information sources in media ethics*. London: Mansell (in preparation).
Coverage includes the printed media.

2080 MacDonald, Fiona. 'Over the sea to Skye'. *Journalist's Handbook*, Autumn 1986.
The story of the *West Highland Free Press*, published weekly in Skye since 1972 . . . 'the land, the language and the people'.

2081 – – –. 'The vicar of Pennington Street'. *The Journalist's Handbook*, Summer 1993.
On Ruth Gledhill, religious correspondent of *The Times*.

2082 – – –. 'King of the rat pack'. *The Journalist's Handbook*, Autumn 1993.
On James Whitaker, Royal correspondent of the *Daily Mirror*.

2083 Macdonald, Ian. *The Times*. Paisley (Strathclyde): Gleniffer Press, 1985.
A limited-edition bicentenary history in miniature format (35mm × 50mm).

2084 McDonald, Iverach. *A man of The Times: talks and travels in a disrupted world*. London: Hamish Hamilton, 1976. xv + 220pp.
A certain ambiguity underlines the author's choice of title: is he writing as a man of *The Times*, or a man of the times? A parallel ambiguity of aim runs through the book. It is partly a re-telling of history from 1932 to 1964, with many revealing footnotes, and partly the story of a newspaper during that period – or rather of *the* newspaper. McDonald had retired from *The Times* as associate editor in 1973.

2085 McDonough, Francis. '*The Times*, Norman Ebbutt and the Nazis, 1927–37'. *Journal of Contemporary History*, Jul 1992.

2086 – – –. 'Rethinking *The Times* and appeasement'. *Journal of Newspaper and Periodical History*, 8, 2, 1992.
The central figure in these articles in Norman Ebbutt, correspondent for *The Times* in Berlin from 1927. He complained, frequently and bitterly, how his reports were cut or watered down. He was in any case sufficiently a nuisance to be expelled in August 1937.

2087 McDougall, Ian. *Foreign correspondent*. London: Frederick Muller, 1980.

2088 Macdowall, [Charles] Ian, comp, and F(rederick) W(est) Hodgson, ed. *The Reuters handbook for journalists*. Oxford: Butterworth-Heinemann (Focal Press), 1992. 192pp. Foreword by Mark Wood.
Style guide for Reuters staff offered for public readership.

2089 McElvoy, Anne. *The saddled cow: East Germany's life and legacy*. London: Faber, 1992. xiii + 258pp.
By *The Times*'s correspondent in Berlin.

2090 McEwen, John M. 'The press and the fall of Asquith'. *Historical Journal*, 21, 1978.

2091 – – –. 'Northcliffe and Lloyd George at war, 1914–1918.' *Historical Journal*, 24, 1981.

2092 – – –. 'The national press during the First World War: ownership and circulation'. *Journal of Contemporary History*, Jul 1982.

2093 – – –. 'Lloyd George's acquisition of the *Daily Chronicle* in 1918'. *Journal of British Studies* (Chicago), 22, 1, Fall 1982.

2094 – – –. ' "Brass-hats" and the British press during the First World War'. *Canadian Journal of History*, 18, 1983.

2095 McGill, Angus. *The Evening Standard*. London: Associated Newspapers, 1989. 10pp.
Historical summary for staff on moving to Kensington.

2096 – – –. 'Goodbye Fleet Street . . . hello Kensington'. *Evening Standard*, 12 Dec 1988.
Chronicling the first stage of the move of Associated Newspapers' editorial offices, after one hundred and sixty-one years in and around Fleet Street.

2097 McGowan, Garry. *Industrial relations and Fleet Street – the Wapping dispute and the law*. London: City University, 1987 (MBA thesis).

2098 McGowan, Robert, and Jeremy Hands. *Don't cry for me, Sergeant-Major*. London: Futura, 1983. 317pp.

2099 – – –. *Try not to laugh, Sergeant-Major*. London: Macdonald, 1984; Futura, 1984. 233pp.
The authors represented the *Daily Express* and ITN respectively in the Falklands conflict, which they faithfully record from the ranker's point of view.

2100 McGrandle, Leith. 'Hello to the future'. *Sunday Express*, 9 Apr 1989.
Express Newspapers' group financial editor points out the significance of their short move to Blackfriars Road: occupying a new purpose-designed building, but remaining close to the major decision-making centres of the capital.

2101 McGregor of Durris, Oliver Ross, *Baron*. *A free press in a free society*.
The 1991 Tom Olsen Lecture (at St Bride's Church, London) by the first chairman of the Press Complaints Commission. He stresses the probationary nature of the Commission – the Government giving the press only eighteen months' grace to set their house in order.

2102 McGuigan, Jim. *Cultural populism*. London: Routledge, 1992. 304pp.
A thought-provoking work in the new discipline of cultural studies, featuring tabloid journalism – notably by analysing the various published analyses of *The Sun*.

2103 'Machiavelli, or the Prince?'. *UK Press Gazette*, 8 Jul 1991.
Profile of Sir David English, editor of the *Daily Mail* for twenty-one years (and rescuer of *The Mail on Sunday* after its fitful start).

2104 McIlvanney, Hugh. *McIlvanney on boxing: an anthology.* London: Stanley Paul, 1982. 189pp; 1990. 240pp.

In 1982, McIlvanney was already a leading sports journalist with *The Observer*, and was to win many awards in that role; in 1993, he moved to *The Sunday Times* as that paper's sports no 1.

2105 Macintyre, Donald John. *Talking about trade unions.* Hove (E Sussex): Wayland Press, 1979.

By the labour correspondent of *The Times*, who later became labour editor of *The Sunday Times*.

2106 Maciver, Iain. 'Wee paper, big voice'. *UK Press Gazette*, 19 Apr 1993.

On the twenty-first birthday of the *West Highland Free Press* – known in Gaelic as *Am paipear beag* ('The wee paper') because of its tabloid format.

2107 Mack, Louise (later Creed). *A woman's experience in the Great War.* London: T. Fisher Unwin, 1915. 297pp.

Australian-born writer – employed by Stead on his *Review of Reviews*, and then by Northcliffe on the *Daily Mail* and *Evening News*. She reported as the only Englishwoman in Antwerp after the German occupation.

2108 Mackay, Ian [John Cockburn Marshall]. *The real Mackay: being essays by Ian Mackay*, ed Stanley Baron. Illustrated by Vicky. London: News Chronicle, 1953. xiv + 146pp.

This selection suggests why Mackay's stint as industrial correspondent for the *News Chronicle* was followed by an unexpected but triumphant career as a columnist with a remarkably wide range, writing an estimated one million words. R.J. Cruikshank, in a profile, comments: 'The best newspaper diarist and essayist of our time was buttoned up inside the man who was so knowledgeable about trade union practice and labour relations.'

2109 McKay, Ron, and Brian Barr. *The story of the Scottish Daily News.* Edinburgh: Canongate Publications, 1976. vi + 170pp.

An account of the short-lived experiment of an independent daily which rose, phoenix-like, out of the ashes of the full-blown *Scottish Daily Express*.

2110 McKenzie, Frederick Arthur. *The rise and progress of the Harmsworth publications.* London: B.W. Young, 1897.

2111 – – –. *From Tokyo to Tiflis: uncensored letters of the war.* London: Hurst & Blackett, 1905. x + 340pp.

On the Russo-Japanese War.

2112 – – –. *The mystery of the Daily Mail, 1896–1921.* London: Associated Newspapers, 1921. 128pp.

A somewhat oddly titled celebration of the paper's twenty-fifth birthday.

2113 – – –. *Russia before dawn.* London: T. Fisher Unwin, 1923.

McKenzie, representing the *Daily Mail*, had been one of the first correspondents admitted to Moscow by the Soviet government.

2114 – – –. *Beaverbrook: an authentic biography of the Right Honourable Lord Beaverbrook*. London: Jarrolds, 1931. 296pp.
As may be judged from the title, an uncritical study – unsurprisingly, since Beaverbrook had secretly funded it.

2115 MacKenzie, John. *Country editor: relating sixty-seven years with weeklies on a Scottish island and the Canadian prairie, 1901–1968*. Rothesay (Bute): Bute Newspapers, 1968. 72pp.
By the editor of *The Buteman*.

2116 MacKenzie, John Macdonald. *Propaganda and Empire: the manipulation of British public opinion, 1880–1960*. Manchester: Manchester University Press, 1984. viii + 272pp.
Concentrates on the effects of 'imperial' propaganda on the public.

2117 – – –, ed. *Imperialism and popular culture*. Manchester: Manchester University Press, [1986]. 264pp.

2118 – – –. *Popular imperialism and the military*. Manchester: Manchester University Press, 1992.

2119 McKenzie, S.P. 'Vox populi: British Army newspapers of the Second World War'. *Journal of Contemporary History*, 24, 1989.

2120 Mackie, Alister. *The trade unionist and the tycoon*. Edinburgh: Mainstream, with The Herald (Glasgow), 1992. Foreword by Tony Benn; introduction by Arnold Kemp. 224pp.
The story – 'now it can be told' – of how Robert Maxwell (the tycoon) made false promises to Mackie (the trade unionist) at the time of the launch of the ill-fated *Scottish Daily News*.

2121 McKie, David. 'Shock! Horror!: *The Sun* puts the heat on Major'. *The Guardian*, 29 Mar 1993.
Comment on the change of stance of *The Sun* – pro-Tory at the last general election – and the *Daily Mirror* – then firmly pro- Labour, now under new management apparently with Tory sympathies.

2122 Mackintosh, *Sir* Alexander. *Echoes of Big Ben: a journalist's parliamentary diary, 1881–1940*. London: Hutchinson, 1945; Jarrolds, 1946. 176pp.

2123 – – –. 'Fifty-seven years in the Press Gallery'. *World's Press News*, 7 Apr 1938.
The author worked in the House of Commons press gallery for the *Aberdeen Free Press* etc.

2124 McKittrick, David. *Despatches from Belfast*. Belfast: Blackstaff, 1989.

2125   McLachlan, Donald Harvey. *In the chair: Barrington-Ward of The Times, 1927–1948*. London: Weidenfeld & Nicolson, 1971. xvi + 304pp.
Robert McGowan (known as Robin) Barrington-Ward died in harness as editor of *The Times*; he had taken over on Dawson's retirement in 1941, and unobtrusively led the paper through the remaining war years and beyond. McLachlan, the author of this admirable biography based on Barrington-Ward's diaries, was himself in senior posts at *The Times*; he moved to *The Daily Telegraph* as deputy editor (1954–61), and became the first editor of *The Sunday Telegraph*.

2126   – – –.   'The press and public opinion'. *British Journal of Sociology*, 6, 1955.

2127   McLaine, Ian. *Ministry of morale: Home Front morale and the Ministry of Information in World War II*. London: Allen & Unwin, 1979. ix + 325pp.
A detailed account (and critical assessment) of the 'two-way' activities of the wartime MOI etc.

2128   McLaughlin, Eve. *Family history from newspapers*. Birmingham: Federation of Family History Societies, 1986, 1989. 16pp.

2129   McLean, Jack. *The bedside urban Voltaire*. Moffat (Dumfries): Lochar, 1990.

2130   – – –.   *More bedside urban Voltaire*. Lochar, 1991.
From McLean's column in *The (Glasgow) Herald*.

2131   McLean, Ruari. 'The life and death of *Picture Post*'. *Antiquarian Book Monthly Review*, Sep 1985.
McLean was the magazine's typographical adviser in its later years.

2132   MacMahon, K.A. 'Local history and the newspaper'. *Amateur Historian*, 5, 1961–3.

2133   MacManus, James. 'Woman at war: the amazing life of Clare Hollingworth'. *The Sunday Telegraph (Review)*, 27 Aug 1989.
Over fifty years, *The Daily Telegraph*, *Daily Express*, *The Manchester Guardian*, and *The Observer* have all carried Clare Hollingworth's outstanding reports.

2134   McMillan, James. *The way we were: 1900–1914*. London: William Kimber, 1978.
Includes many fascinating press advertisements of the period, and an appendix on the ownership of the *Daily Express*.

2135   – – –.   *The way it was: 1914–1934*. Kimber, 1979.

2136   – – –.   *The way it happened: 1935–1950*. Kimber, 1980.

2137   – – –.   *The way it changed: 1951–1975*. Kimber, 1987.
This nostalgic series is all based on the files (and photo library) of the *Daily Express*, of which McMillan was at one time chief leader writer and then political adviser.

2138   Macmillan, Kate. 'Christopher Pole-Carew'. *Newspaper Focus*, Jun 1991. (Back Issues series.)
As managing director of T. Bailey Forman, Pole-Carew installed at *The Evening Post* (Nottingham) Britain's first direct-input editorial system. This led to manning cuts and bitter but eventually unsuccessful strikes. Pole-Carew later masterminded the installation of News International's equipment at Wapping.

2139   McNae, Leonard Cyril James, ed. *Pressman's guide to courts and local government*. London: National Union of Journalists, 1952.

2140   – – –.   *Essential law for journalists*. London: Staples, 1954, 1963. Revised and edited by R.M. Taylor: Staples, 1967, 1969, 1972; Crosby Lockwood Staples, 1975, (revised and edited by Walter Greenwood and Tom Welsh) 1979; Butterworth, 1982; 9th edn, under the title *McNae's essential law for journalists*, 1985. 185pp; 10th edn, 1988; 11th edn, 1990; 12th edn, 1992. x + 263pp.
A standard textbook for the National Council for the Training of Journalists on an increasingly complex subject, expanding on G.F.L. Bridgman's pre-war *The pressman and the law*.

2141   McNair, Brian. *Images of the enemy: reporting the new cold war*. London: Routledge, 1988. 216pp. (In the Communication and Society series).

2142   – – –.   *News and journalism in the UK*. London: Routledge, 1994. xi + 212pp. (In the Communication and Society series.)
Examines the recent fundamental changes, from the 'Wapping revolution' to the Calcutt Report. Incorporates much material from interviews, combining an academic and a professional approach.

2143   McNiven, Peter. 'The *Guardian* Archive in the John Rylands University Library of Manchester'. *Bulletin of the John Rylands University Library of Manchester*, 74, 2, 1992.

2144   McParland, Kelly. 'Gemini and the Commonwealth'. *Round Table*, 300, 1986.
On the Gemini News Service: founded by Derek Ingram in 1967, and especially geared to providing news across the Commonwealth and from developing countries.

2145   McQuail, Denis. *Review of sociological writing on the press*. London: HMSO, 1976. 86pp. (Royal Commission on the Press: Working Paper 2.)

2146   – – –.   *Analysis of newspaper content*. London: HMSO, 1977. (Royal Commission on the Press: Research Series 4, Cmnd 6810-4.)

2147   – – –.   *Mass communication theory: an introduction*. London and Beverly Hills (CA): Sage, 1983. 256pp; new edn, 1987. 336pp.

2148   MacShane, Dennis. *How to use the media*. London: Pluto Press, 1979. (A Worker's Handbook.)

2149   Maddox, Brenda. 'A byline by any other name'. *The Daily Telegraph*, 31 Oct 1990.
How the byline has been increasingly introduced, especially in Britain.

2150   Maddox, Bronwen. 'The big lie: inside Maxwell's empire'. *Financial Times (Weekend FT)*, 13–14 Jun 1992.
Part one of a series collating the interviews by a team of *Financial Times* journalists of more than one hundred and fifty people in thirteen countries, over seven months.

2151   Magee, Kathleen. 'Prince of the Province'. *UK Press Gazette*, 21–28 Dec 1992.
On Edmund Curran, award-winning first editor of the tabloid *Sunday Life* (Belfast) – a Thomson title – in 1988.

2152   Magistad, Mary. *The Ethiopian bandwagon: the relationship between news media coverage and British foreign policy toward the 1984/85 Ethiopian famine.* Brighton: University of Sussex, 1986 (LMA thesis).

2153   *Maidenhead Advertiser*. Centenary number, 1869–1969. Maidenhead (Berks): 28 Jul 1969.

2154   Maitland, Francis (Anthony) Hereward. *One hundred years of headlines, 1837–1937*. London: Wright & Brown, [1938]. 251pp.
A Coronation Year retrospect of news stories 'from the British Empire' over the century.

2155   Maitland, *Hon* Peter (Francis) (*17th Earl of* Lauderdale). *European dateline.* London: Quarto Press, 1946. 211pp.
Balkans and Danubian correspondent for *The Times*, 1938–41; in Washington and war correspondent for *News Chronicle*, 1941–3. Later edited *The Fleet Street Letter*.

2156   Majdalany, Fred. *The monastery*. London: The Bodley Head, 1945.
Not instant journalism, but an outstanding narrative by a journalist-turned-soldier who took part in the siege of Monte Cassino in May 1944. Majdalany, a dramatic critic pre-war (*Sunday Referee*), was film critic for the *Daily Mail* from 1946 to 1961.

2157   'Making money from socialism'. *The Sunday Telegraph*, 10 Nov 1991.
Profile of the *Daily Mirror* – looking both back, and forward to post-Maxwell days.

2158   Man, Felix H. (Hans Felix S. Baumann). *Feliex H. Man: reporting and portraits, 1923–76*. London: National Portrait Gallery, 1976. 19pp.
Catalogue of exhibition covering Man's work to that date.

2158A   – – –.   *Man with camera: photographs from seven decades*. London: Secker & Warburg, 1983.
The famous photographer intersperses this selection with autobiographical comment. Born (in Germany) in 1893, he was to die in 1985 when another retrospective exhibition, Felix H. Man: Photo-Reporter of London, was in preparation. He first came to London in 1934, and became a regular contributor of picture stories to *Weekly Illustrated*; with those for *Picture Post*, from its inception in 1938 through the war to 1945, and again briefly in 1948, these now rank as classics of their kind.

2159 *Man bites man: the scrapbook of an Edwardian eccentric, George Ives,* ed Paul Sieveking. With an introduction by Jeremy Brooks. London: Landesman, 1980; Harmondsworth (Middx): Penguin, 1981. 160pp.
A selection of 'press cuttings extraordinary' from forty-five volumes collected by Ives, covering a period from Edwardian times to 1950.

2160 'Man of judgment, The'. *New Society,* 19 May 1978.
A profile of William Rees-Mogg eleven years into his editorship of *The Times.*

2161 'Man who first showed Britain the news, The'. *The Times,* 26 Apr 1982.
An appreciation of (Sir) Tom Hopkinson on the occasion of the publication of the first volume of his autobiography.

2162 *Manchester Evening News.* Diamond jubilee number. Manchester: Oct 1928.

2163 – – –. Centenary supplement, 1868–1968. 9 Oct 1968. Includes John Alldridge: 'The *Evening News* story'.
The *MEN* is in the same ownership as *The Guardian,* having been bought in 1922 by C.P. Scott from his cousin Russell Allen. It has the largest circulation of any evening paper outside London.

2164 Manchester Evening News. *Greater Manchester – 125 years' images from the Manchester Evening News.* Manchester: 1993.
Three hundred illustrations, selected from the paper's archives.

2165 *Manchester Evening News.* 125 years of the Manchester Evening News. Supplement to *Manchester Evening News Magazine,* 13 Oct 1993.

2166 *Manchester Guardian, The.* Centenary number, 1821–1921. 5 May 1921.
Apart from its historical importance in tracing the first hundred years of the first national British newspaper to originate outside London, this 'commemorative' includes C.P. Scott's classic essay. *See also under* Mills, W.H.; Scott, C.P.

2167 Manchester Guardian. *The Manchester Guardian advertising review.* 16 Jul 1924. 32pp.

2168 *Manchester Guardian, The.* C.P. Scott, 1846–1932: memorial number. 5 Jan 1932.

2169 – – –. *C.P. Scott, 1846–1932: the making of The Manchester Guardian.* London: Muller, 1946. 252pp.
This celebration of the centenary of Scott's birth consists of contributions on *The Guardian* before Scott; on Scott himself; Scott as editor; *The Guardian* under Scott; some of Scott's own writing on journalism and other topics (*see also under* Scott); and *The Guardian* since Scott. The foreword was written, and the whole edited, by (Sir) William Haley, a former editor of the sister *Manchester Evening News* (and at the time of this publication director-general of the BBC). The book is a fitting tribute, in non-academic vein, to one man's unique influence as editor and success as proprietor without any pretensions to being a 'press baron'.

2170 – – –. Centenary supplement, 1855–1955. 2 Jul 1955 (the centenary of the *Guardian* as a daily).
For later publications, *see under Guardian, The* (the change of title took place in 1959). (The *(Manchester) Guardian* archives are in the John Rylands University Library of Manchester, and in *The Guardian*'s Manchester offices.)

2171 Manchester Press Club. *Fifty years of us: a jubilee retrospect of men and newspapers.* Manchester: CWS, 1922.
The club was in fact founded in 1870.

2172 – – –. *A hundred years of us*, ed Denys Ainsworth. Manchester: 1970.

2173 Mander, Michael. 'How Times Newspapers changed the game'. *Admap*, Dec 1979.
At the end of the eleven months without publication.

2174 Mann, Roderick. *The headliner*. London: Cassell, 1968. 233pp.

2175 Mansfield, Frederick J. *Sub-editing*. London: Pitman, 1932. xv + 248pp.

2176 – – –. *The complete journalist: a study of the principles and practice of newspaper-making.* London: Pitman, 1935. xviii + 389pp. Revised as *Mansfield's complete journalist*, ed Denis Weaver. Pitman, 1961. xii + 279pp.
Based largely on lectures given at the University of London. Chapters include 'Evolution of the British press' and 'Some of the stars'. This long-standard textbook by a former president of the National Union of Journalists and experienced *Times* man remains a delightful read and historical resource.

2177 – – –. *'Gentlemen, the press!': chronicles of a crusade.* London: W.H. Allen, 1943. 579pp.
The official history of the National Union of Journalists from 1906 to 1943.

2178 – – –. 'Social and personal'. *Journalist*, 20, 1937.
A contribution to the NUJ's own journal.

2179 – – –. 'Royal interest in the press'. *The Newspaper World*, 8 May 1937.

2180 Marchant, Hilde. *Women and children last: a woman reporter's account of the Battle of Britain.* London: Gollancz, 1941.
Critical report by a front-line woman war correspondent for the *Daily Express*, who later became a special writer for *Picture Post*. When reporting from Dover, described by an American journalist as 'a sort of Spitfire attached to the ground . . . passionate in her belief in the common people'.

2181 Margach, James (Dunbar). *The abuse of power: the war between Downing Street and the media from Lloyd George to Callaghan.* London: W.H. Allen, 1978. vi + 199pp.

2182 – – –. *The anatomy of power: an enquiry into the personality of leadership.* London: W.H. Allen, 1979; Star Books, 1981.

By the doyen of lobby correspondents at the end of his outstanding career for *The Sunday Times*. The titles of this book and the above indicate the unexpectedly critical view taken by Margach of the lobby system, which he describes as having 'corrupted all concerned with Whitehall'; he expresses anxiety about the future of democracy in Britain.

2183   Marnham, Patrick. *The Private Eye story: the first twenty-one years*. London: André Deutsch/Private Eye, 1982. 232pp.
An insider's but a detached view of a most unlikely story of journalistic success, despite the law-suits.

2184   Marriott, Charles. (A history of Reuters.) MS of 60,000 words written 1919–20 by a staff member, but not publ.

2185   Marshall, Alan. 'The revolution that never was'. *Newspaper Focus*, Feb 1992.
New technology has not brought in the anticipated radical changes in design. Says the author: 'It is possible to produce the dullest paper by the most advanced techniques.'

2186   Marshall-Fraser, W. 'A history of printing of the press and of publication in the Channel Islands'. *Société Guernesiaise Report and Transactions*, 15, 1, 1951.

2187   Martell, Edward (Drewett), and Ewan Butler. *The murder of the News Chronicle and the Star*. London: Christopher Johnson, 1960.
'Killed by trade union restrictive practices', assert these outspoken authors in the immediate aftermath of the closure; but theirs is too simple an explanation for such a long-drawn-out and complex marketing failure. Martell, incidentally, deserves at least a footnote to post-war British press history for having, in the same year, launched *The New Daily* as the 'only daily newspaper in Great Britain independent of combines and trade unions': it lasted five years in daily format.

2188   Martin, [Basil] Kingsley. *Fascism, democracy and the press*. London: New Statesman & Nation, 1938. 32pp.
A pamphlet from the early years of Kingsley Martin's editorship of *The New Statesman*, which began in 1931, the year in which *The Nation* was absorbed.

2189   – – –.   *The press the public wants*. London: Hogarth Press, 1947. 143pp.
Aniticipating Martin's evidence to the Royal Commission on the Press (1947–9). He argued that a consistent lack of news in Fleet Street's output was counter-productive and not at all what the public wanted *or* deserved.

2190   – – –.   *Father figures: a first volume of autobiography, 1897–1931*. London: Hutchinson, 1966. 219pp; Harmondsworth (Middx): Penguin, 1969. 224pp.
Covering the author's pre-*New Statesman* years, which included those as co-founder and co-editor of *The Political Quarterly*.

2191   – – –.   *Editor: a second volume of autobiography, 1931–45*. London: Hutchinson, 1968. xiii + 340pp; Harmondsworth (Middx): Penguin, 1969. 335pp.
Concerning the first years of Kingsley Martin's fame and influence.

2192 – – –. *Portrait and self-portrait*, ed Mervyn Jones. London: Barrie & Jenkins, 1969. 166pp.
Martin, born in 1897, died in the year that this revealing final book appeared.

2193 Martin, Roderick. *New technology and industrial relations in Fleet Street*. Oxford: Clarendon Press, 1981; New York: Oxford University Press, 1981. xii + 367pp.
Observe how the Joint Studies Council set up by the Trades Union Congress and National Graphical Association produced (in 1946) *Progress for action* – an abortive attempt before the first Royal Commission on the Press published its findings.

2194 – – –. *Bargaining power*. Oxford: Clarendon Press, 1992.
An important follow-up, in which (so far as the press is concerned) the spotlight moves from 'Fleet Street' to Wapping.

2195 Mason, Keith. *Front seat*. Derby: Brennan Publications, 1983.
Close encounters by an industrial correspondent on the *Daily Herald* (later *The Sun*).

2196 Mason, Tony. 'Sporting news, 1860–1914'. *In* Michael Harris and A.J. Lee, eds. *The press in English society from the 17th to 19th centuries*. Cranbury (NJ) and London: Associated University Presses, 1986.

2197 Mass Observation. *The press and its readers*, ed Charles Madge and Tom Harrisson. London: Art & Technics, for the Advertising Service Guild, 1949. 128pp.
A report by the first (established in 1937) and most famous of the primary social research organizations.

2198 Massingham, Henry William. *H.W.M.: a selection from the writings of H.W. Massingham*, ed Harold John Massingham (his eldest son). London: Butler & Tanner; New York: Harcourt, Brace, 1924. 368pp.
H.W. Massingham's thesis about the decline of the press during his lifetime (1860–1924), in changing from a paternalistic group of individual family businesses to a materialistic mass industry intent only on maximizing profits, appears in 'The Press and the people' originally written for *Co-operative News* and reprinted here.

2199 – – –. 'The ethics of editing'. *National Review*, 25, 1900.

2200 – – –. 'The independent editor'. In *Sell's World's Press, 1921*. London: Sell, 1921.

2201 – – –. 'The journalism of Lord Northcliffe'. *The Nation*, 31, 1922.

2202 Massingham, Hugh. 'Journalists and politicians'. *Aspect*, Feb 1963.
An article in which the youngest son of H.W. Massingham explains his approach as a political commentator, best exemplified in his work as a diarist for *The Observer*.

2203 Masterman, Lucy (*née* Lyttelton). *C.F.G. Masterman: a biography*. London: Nicholson & Watson, 1939. 400pp. Cass, 1968.

Although a prominent (Liberal) politician and one-time *Daily News* journalist, Masterman carries significance in any study of the press because of his direction throughout World War I of 'Wellington House', responsible for the dissemination of British propaganda worldwide. This outstanding biography is by his widow.

2204 Matheson, Ann. 'Scottish newspapers'. *Library Record*, 36, 1987. Summary of Scottish newspaper publishing.

2205 – – –. 'Scottish newspapers: acquisition and preservation.' *Scottish Local History*, 28, Jun 1993. Paper read at Dundee conference of the Scottish Local History Forum, by the keeper of printed books at the National Library of Scotland.
Makes the point that, while the best collections of the oldest Scottish newspapers are in Scottish libraries, the most complete holdings of (nineteenth- and) twentieth-century issues are in the British Library Newspaper Library (Colindale).

2206 Mathews, Joseph James. *Reporting the wars*. Minneapolis (MN): University of Minnesota Press; Oxford: Oxford University Press, [1957]. x + 322pp. A good general survey of war reporting worldwide.

2207 – – –. *George W. Smalley: forty years a foreign corresponent*. Chapel Hill (NC): University of North Carolina Press, [1973]. x + 229pp.
The unusual story of Smalley, who was an American journalist, the 'foreign commissioner' for the *New York Tribune* in London. He came to wear 'a second hat' as correspondent for *The Daily News* and was later *The Times*'s man in Washington.

2208 Matthews, Roy T., and Peter Mellini. *In Vanity Fair*. London: Scolar Press; Berkeley: University of California Press, 1982; Gloucester: Alan Sutton, 1984. 275pp.
This sumptuous volume, with its selection of the caricatures that appeared in *Vanity Fair* during its forty-six-year existence, includes a chapter on press personalities.

2209 Matthews, T(homas) S(tanley). *The sugar pill: an essay on newspapers*. London: Gollancz, 1957. 221pp; New York: Simon & Schuster, 1959.
Written in London by an ex-editor of *Time*, this book contrasts in idiosyncratic style the *Daily Mirror* and *Manchester Guardian*. Matthews analyses the 'confusing' personality of the latter while also confessing to a secret passion for the former. He illustrates how each 'sugared the pill of information' to suit its totally different readership during their common anti-Suez stand in 1956.

2210 Matthews, Virginia, and Mark Jones. 'Sunday bloody Sunday'. *Evening Standard*, 9 Dec 1992.
Media commentary on the 'war' between *The Mail on Sunday* (edited by Jonathan Holborow) and *Sunday Express* (edited by Eve Pollard).

2211 Matveyev, B.A. *Imperiya Flit Strit* (Empire of Fleet Street). Moscow: 1961. 303pp.

2212 Maurer, Hanspeter. *Die Entwicklung der englischen Zeitungsschlagzeile von der Mitte der zwanziger Jahre bis zur Gegenwart*. Berne: Francke, [1972]. 161pp.
The title translates as 'Development of the English newspaper headline from the middle of the 'twenties up to the present day'.

2213 Maxwell, *Sir* William. *From the Yalu to Port Arthur: a personal record*. London: Hutchinson, 1906. xvi + 407pp.
The author was an 'Edwardian gentleman' correspondent for *The Standard* reporting on the Russo-Japanese War.

2214 Mayne, Alan. *The imagined slum: newspaper representations in the English-speaking world, 1870–1914*. Leicester: Leicester University Press, 1993. 256pp.

2215 Mays, Isabella Fyvie. *Recollections*. London: 1910.
The author was one of Britain's earliest women journalists.

2216 Mazur, Janet. 'The exodus from Fleet Street'. *Editor and Publisher* (New York), 26 Sep 1987.

2217 Mead, Roper. *The Press Council*. Sale (Cheshire), later Derby: Brennan Publications, 1978. 32pp. (Media Guide no 2.)
A factual booklet by the former assistant secretary of the Council.

2218 Meaney, Joseph. *Scribble street*. London: Sands, [1945]. 144pp.
Concerning criminal trials etc.

2219 Medina, Peter. *Careers in journalism*. London: Kogan Page, 1981; 3rd edn, with Vivien Donald, 1988; 4th edn, 1989; 5th edn, 1992.

2220 Meech, Peter, and Richard Kilborn. 'Media and identity in a stateless nation: the case of Scotland'. *Media, Culture and Society*, 14, 2, Apr 1992.
A current overview.

2221 Mellini, Peter. 'Colonel Blimp's England'. *History Today*, Oct 1984.
A feature, suitably illustrated, on Low's famous cartoon figure and its impact.

2222 – – –. 'Gabriel's message'. *History Today*, Feb 1990.
On the career of the political cartoonist James Friell, who drew for the *Daily Worker* as 'Gabriel' pre-war and immmediately post-war, and briefly (and surprisingly) for the *Evening Standard* under his own name in the late 1950s.

2223 – – –. 'Why didn't they think?: political cartooning and British foreign policy, 1933–1940'. *Journal of Newspaper and Periodical History*, 6, 1990.
Featuring in particular Low, 'Vicky' and 'Gabriel'.

2224 Mellor, George R. 'History from newspapers'. *Amateur Historian*, 2, 4, 1955.

2225 Mellor, William. 'A paper for the people'. *Daily Herald*, 12 Nov 1929.
Mellor was editor of the *Daily Herald* from 1926 to 1930.

2226 Melvern, Linda. *The end of the Street*. London: Methuen, 1986. vi + 276pp.
An account, by a former member of the *Sunday Times* Insight Team, of the dramatic move by Rupert Murdoch's News International from Fleet Street to Wapping.

2227 Memory, Frederic William. *Memory's: the adventures of a newspaperman*. London: Cassell, 1932. 311pp.
The author was chief reporter for the *Daily Mail*.

2228 Mercer, Derrik, ed. *Chronicle of the 20th century*. London: Chronicle Communications, 1988.
British edition of a massive volume re-telling, as reportage by leading present-day journalists, the major news stories of the twentieth century.

2229 Mercer, Derrik, Geoff Mungham, and Kevin Williams. *The fog of war: the media and the battlefield*. London: Heinemann, 1987. xvi + 433pp. Foreword by Sir Tom Hopkinson.
Distillation of a study at the Centre for Journalism Studies, University College, Cardiff, into 'relations between government, the armed forces and the media in time of armed conflict', primarily concerning the Falklands War. The Vietnam War, US occupation of Grenada, and Israel's attacks on Lebanon are also discussed.

2230 Merrill, John Calhoun, and Harold A. Fisher. *The élite press: great newspapers of the world*. New York and London: Pitman, 1968, 1976. xiv + 336pp.
Following a most informative opening essay on the world's press as a whole, Merrill (from the College of Journalism of the University of Maryland) and Fisher (from Bowling Green State University) cover forty individual newspapers, including *The Times*, *The Guardian*, *The Scotsman*, and *The Yorkshire Post*.

2231 – – –. *The world's great dailies: profiles of fifty newspapers*. New York: Hastings House, 1980. (In the Communications Arts Books series.)
This second book adds *The Daily Telegraph*.

2232 *Merthyr Express*. Centenary number. Merthyr Tydfil (Mid Glamorgan): 7 Nov 1964; supplement, 13 Nov 1964.
A Celtic Press title (Thomson Regional Newspapers).

2233 Mervis, Joel. *The Fourth Estate: a newspaper story*. Johannesburg: Jonathan Bell Publisher, 1989.
An international survey.

2234 Messinger, Gary D. *British propaganda and the State in the First World War*. Manchester: Manchester University Press, 1992.

2235 Meyers, William H. 'Murdoch's global power play'. *The New York Times Magazine*, 12 Jun 1988.

2236 Middleton, Edgar Charles. *Beaverbrook: the statesman and the man*. London: Stanley Paul, 1934. 256pp.
The author was active in Beaverbrook's Empire Crusade.

2237   *Midhurst and Petworth Observer.* Centenary supplement. Portsmouth: 4 Feb 1982.
Began as *Midhurst Times*; today a Portsmouth and Sunderland weekly.

2238   Mildenhall, Donald A. 'Founder's name still in title'. *The Media Reporter*, 2, 12, 1978.
George Philip Rigney Pulman founded *Pulman's Weekly News* in Crewkerne in 1857; it has survived under the same title, being published today from Yeovil. It is also associated with the even older *Western Gazette* in the Bristol Evening Post group.

2239   Mildren, James. *125 years with the Western Morning News.* Bodmin (Cornwall): Bossiney Books, 1985. 120pp.
Celebrating, with excellent illustrations, the 125th anniversary of the *Western Morning News*, published daily in Plymouth.

2240   Millar, Peter. *Tomorrow will be my own.* London: Bloomsbury, 1993.
The final years of the German Democratic Republic by the resident man from Reuters.

2241   Miller, David *The struggle over, and impact of media portrayal of, Northern Ireland.* Glasgow: Glasgow University (in preparation).

2242   – – –. 'Official sources and "painting rainbows": the case of Northern Ireland'. *Media, Culture and Society,* Jul 1993.

2243   – – –. 'The Northern Ireland Information Service: aims, strategy, tactics'. *In* John Eldridge, ed. *Getting the message: news, truth and power.* London: Routledge, 1993.

2244   Miller, Jonathan. 'Raising the *Standard*, a capital investment'. *The Sunday Times*, 3 May 1992.
The recent success of London's only current evening paper.

2245   Miller, William L(ockley). *Testing the power of media consensus: a comparison of Scots and English media treatment of the Falklands campaign.* Glasgow: University of Strathclyde Press, [1985]. 29pp.
Stresses the comparative lack of impact of the war in Scotland as reflected in the Scottish press.

2246   – – –. *Media and voters: the audience, content and influence of press and television in the 1987 general election.* Oxford: Clarendon Press, 1993. xvii + 231pp.

2247   Millichip, Jane. 'Lord Thomson'. *Newspaper Focus*, Jul–Aug 1991. (Back Issues series.)
On Roy Thomson, 1st Lord Thomson of Fleet.

2248   – – –. 'Down but not out'. *Newspaper Focus*, Summer 1992.
Free newspapers' fight for survival; the current situation.

2249   Mills, G.H. Saxon. *There is a tide.* London: Heinemann, 1954. viii + 197pp.

About the career in advertising of Sir William Crawford; and British advertising as a whole from 1914. Mills had been copy director at Crawfords, and later masterminded the 'Top People' campaign for *The Times*.

2250 Mills, John Saxon. *Sir Edward Cook, K.B.E.: a biography*. London: Constable, 1921. viii + 304pp.
A barrister's biography of a leading editor (*Pall Mall Gazette*, *Westminster Gazette*, *Daily News*) of the 1890s who became joint director of the Official Press Bureau (the government's censorship organization) in World War I. The book contains much useful material on other leading journalists of the time, such as Morley, Spender, Stead.

2251 – – –. *The press and communications of the Empire*. London: Collins, 1924; New York: Holt. 289pp. (In the British Empire series.) Foreword by Lord Burnham.
Contains extensive information on the services of Reuters by Herbert Jeans, the chief editor.

2252 Mills, William Haslam. *The Manchester Guardian: a century of history*. With a preface by C.P. Scott. London: Chatto & Windus, 1921. 146pp. New York: Henry Holt, 1922. A reprint of the history given in the centenary number (*see under Manchester Guardian*).
Mills (chief reporter, 1890–1918) here writes a readable version for the scholarly reader.

2253 – – –. *Grey pastures*. London: Chatto & Windus, 1924.
Reprints of articles on unusual Manchester people and places.

2254 Milne, [John] Maurice. 'The historian and local newspapers'. *Local Studies Librarian*, 1, 1982.

2255 Milner, Violet Georgina Maxse, *Viscountess*. 'Fifty-five years: an historical note'. *The National Review*, Oct 1948.
Written at the end of the author's remarkable sixteen years' editorship of *The National Review*, which she took over from her brother Leo Maxse.

2256 Ministero degli Affari Esteri. *Il libre italiano nella stampa britannica* (The Italian book on the British press). Rome: 1980.

2257 Ministry of Defence. *The handling of press and public information during the Falklands conflict: observations on the first report presented by the Secretary of State for Defence*. London: HMSO, 1983. Cmd 8820. 6pp.
While initiating changes resulting from the Falklands experience, the Minister explains that operational requirements must be paramount.

2258 – – –. *The protection of military information: report of the Study Group on Censorship*. 1983. Cmd 9112.

2259 – – –. *The protection of military information: government responses to the report of the Study Group on Censorship*. 1985. Cmd 9499. *See also* House of Commons Defence Committee.

2260 – – –. *The Defence Advisory Notices: a review of the D Notice system.*
London: Ministry of Defence, 1993. (Open Government Document No 93/06.)
Announcing the change of D Notices to DA (for Defence Advisory) Notices – and
publicizing the remaining six (of eight) such Notices. The management of the system
is similarly re-styled the Defence, Press and Broadcasting Advisory Committee.

2261 Minney, R[ubeigh] J[ames]. *The journalist*. London: Bles, 1931. 191pp. (In
the Life and Work series.)

2262 – – –. *Viscount Southwood*. London: Odhams, 1954. 384pp.
Julius Salter Elias, born in 1873, is an outstanding example of a national newspaper
proprietor largely uninterested in journalism *per se*; Minney, long-time editor of *Everybody's Weekly*, recalls in this official biography: 'Political attitudes did not really concern
him. Printing was a job of work.' As chairman of Odhams (publishers of this biography)
Elias controlled the destinies of the *Daily Herald*, *The People*, and *John Bull* in their
great years between the world wars. He was created Baron Southwood in 1937, and
elevated to a viscountcy in the year of his death (1946).

2263 Mitchell, *Sir* Peter Chalmers. *My fill of days*. London: Faber, 1937.
Mitchell was scientific correspondent of *The Times Literary Supplement* and thereafter
leader-writer on *The Times* itself.

2264 Mitchell, W.A., ed. *Or was it yesterday?: glimpses of the way of life during
200 years obtained from the pages of The Press and Journal on the occasion of that
newspaper's bicentenary*. With a foreword by Viscount Kemsley. Aberdeen: Press
and Journal, 1947. 88pp.
Traces its history back to its foundation in 1748 as *The Aberdeen Journal*.

2265 Mitford, *(Hon)* Nancy (Freeman). *A talent to annoy: essays, articles and
reviews, 1929–1968*. New York: Beaufort House; London: Hamish Hamilton,
1986. Ed Charlotte Mosley.
Although primarily famous as a novelist of aristocratic society, she produced the significant newspaper journalism included in this collection (e.g. as columnist for *The Sunday
Times* from Paris).

2266 *Model behaviour*. London: Newspaper Society, 1992. 30pp.
The results of a detailed research study for the Society, carried out by the Henley Centre
for Forecasting, into the sales performance of paid-for regional newspapers, 1975–91.

2267 *Modern journalism: a guide for beginners*. London: Sidgwick & Jackson,
1909. 'By London editors'. Preface by George R. Sims.

2268 *Modern newspaper, The: how it is produced*. Manchester: Hulton, 1905.

2269 Mokken, R.J. 'The Times and Munich'. *Gazette*, 4, 2, 1958.

2270 Molloy, Michael (John). *The century*. London: Macdonald, 1990. 679pp;
Fontana, 1991. 896pp.
Written by the long-reigning editor-in-chief of Mirror Group Newspapers (previously

editor of the *Daily Mirror*). This enormous, portentous ('a brilliant saga of newspaper people') and obsessive exercise in faction-writing only just manages to sustain interest in its fictional characters over seventy-five years by drawing them from life and leaving the reader to guess their identity.

2271   – – –.   *Sweet sixteen*. London: Sinclair-Stevenson, 1992.

2272   – – –.   *Cat's paw*. London: Sinclair-Stevenson, 1993.

2273   – – –.   *Home before dark*. London: Sinclair-Stevenson (in preparation).
Novels with a woman crime reporter as the heroine.

2274   Moncrieff, Chris(topher). 'Conscience of the lobby'. *The House Magazine*, 5 Jun 1989.
Important manifesto by the lobby correspondent of the Press Association: 'For myself, I have never yet been able to locate a conscience even if I had wanted to struggle with it. If a story is on offer, it seems to me it doesn't matter how it is imparted so long as it is within the law.'

2275   Monks, Noel. *Eyewitness*. London: Muller, [1956]. 344pp.
An Australian, Monks reported first for the *Daily Express*, being based for most of the 1930s in Paris and covering the wars in Abyssinia and Spain. He then moved to the *Daily Mail* in World War II, and later covered the Korean War.

2276   *Monmouthshire Beacon*. 150th anniversary number. Monmouth (Gwent): 1987.
Now a Tindle group weekly.

2277   Monopolies and Mergers Commission. *Wholesaling of newspapers and periodicals*. London: HMSO, 1978. Cmnd 7214.
'A report on the wholesale supply of national newspapers and periodicals in England and Wales, and in Scotland . . .'.

2278   – – –.   *Lonrho Ltd and Scottish & Universal Investments Ltd and House of Fraser Ltd: a report on the proposed merger of Lonrho and Scottish & Universal Investments, and on the resulting merger situation between Lonrho and the House of Fraser*. London: HMSO, 1979. HC261.
Duly approved, this merger heralded a major change in Scottish newspaper ownership, SUITS (until 1992) controlling both George Outram (*Glasgow Herald* etc) and the S & UN group of weeklies.

2279   – – –.   *A report on the proposed transfer of The Observer, a newspaper of which Atlantic Richfield Co is the proprietor, to George Outram & Co Ltd, a subsidiary of Scottish & Universal Investments Ltd, whose parent company is Lonrho Ltd*. London: HMSO, 1981. HC378.
Another successful bid by Rowland's Lornho enterprise, this time securing *The Observer* from its (American) Atlantic Richfield owners.

2280   – – –.   *The Berrow's Organisation Ltd and Reed International Ltd*. London: HMSO, 1981. Cmnd 8337.

The Commission rejected Reed's application to acquire Berrow's on the grounds that the former already owned papers in an area near those of the latter based in Taunton (a ruling reversed by the Secretary of State for Trade).

2281 – – –.   *South Wales Argus and Express Newspapers.* London: HMSO, 1981. Cmnd 8385.
This Express bid was approved: 'The proposed transfer [is seen] as part of the continuing process of ownership of provincial newspapers by major groups.'

2282 – – –.   *Benham Newspapers, St Regis International and Reed International.* London: HMSO, 1982. HC402.
Reed's application for Benham (in Essex) and the UK publishing interests of St Regis was approved, but with two dissenters.

2283 – – –.   *United Newspapers Plc and Fleet Holdings Plc: a report on the proposed transfer of Fleet Holdings Plc to United Newspapers Plc.* London: HMSO, 1985. Cmnd 9610.
No objection was raised by the Commission to this major proposal.

2284 – – –.   *Birmingham Post and Mail Holdings Plc and Yattendon Investment Trust.* London: HMSO, 1985. Cmnd 9516.
Proposed transfer (duly approved) of Birmingham papers to Lord Iliffe's trust.

2285 – – –.   *Southern Newspapers Plc and EMAP Plc, Pearson Plc, Reed International Plc and Trinity International Holdings Plc: a report on the proposed transfer of controlling interests.* London: HMSO, 1991. Cm 1772.
Although approved, in the event none of the four companies made a bid.

2286 – – –.   *Trinity International Holdings Plc and Scottish and Universal Newspapers Ltd: a report on the proposed transfer of controlling interests.* London: HMSO, 1992. Cm 2013.
Also approved – and Trinity made their acquisition.

2287 – – –.   *EMAP Plc and United Newspapers Plc: a report on the proposed transfer of controlling interests . . . in three newspapers.* London: HMSO, 1992. Cm 2058.
The transaction being approved, three Welsh newspapers were transferred from EMAP to United Newspapers – and, in return, EMAP acquired the *Northampton Mercury* (weekly) and its daily stablemate, *Chronicle and Echo.*

2288 – – –.   *Argus Press Ltd and Trinity International Holdings Plc: a report on the proposed transfers.* London: HMSO, 1993. Cm 2373.
Favourable – and carried into effect.

2289 – – –.   *Trinity International Holdings Plc and Joseph Woodhead & Sons Ltd: a report on the proposed transfers of controlling interests.* London: HMSO, 1993. Cm 2374.
The same verdict – and result. The Woodhead family had long owned the *Huddersfield (Daily) Examiner.*

2290 – – –.   *The supply of national newspapers.* London: HMSO (for

Department of Trade and Industry), 1993. Cm 2422.
Covers England and Wales.

2291 Monopolies Commission. *Report on the proposed transfer to a newspaper proprietor of The Times and Sunday Times newspapers.* London: HMSO, 1966. HC273.
The first report of its kind following the Monopolies and Mergers Act 1965, concluding: 'The proposed transfer [to Thomson] . . . may be expected not to operate against the public interest.'

2292 Montague, C(harles) E(dward). *A hind let loose.* London: Methuen, 1910. 310pp; Penguin, 1936. 255pp.
'A wild morality farce', according to its author (1867–1928), who was with *The Manchester Guardian* for most of his working life. This first novel, dedicated to his father-in-law and editor, C.P. Scott, is indeed frank caricature, with plenty of wit and extravagant language. It concerns one Colum Fay, brilliant Irish journalist, who simultaneously writes Tory leaders for the *Halland Warder* (alias *The Times*) and Liberal leaders for the *Halland Stalwart* (or *Manchester Guardian*), 'thus producing a right merry verbal how-de-do!'. When, out of sheer laziness, he writes the same leader for both, he is dismissed by both editors. He then has to be re-employed almost immediately because the readers have expressed boredom with his dull successors – the editors themselves!

2293 – – –. *A writer's notes on his trade.* London: Chatto & Windus; and New York, 1930. 192pp; Harmondsworth (Middx): Penguin (Pelican Books), 1949.

2294 Montague, C(harles) E(dward), and *Sir* Muirhead Bone. *The Western Front.* London: Country Life, 1917. 2 vols.
Montague's front-line impressions as a commentary to Bone's drawings.

2295 Montgomery, John. *The twenties: an informal social history.* London: Allen & Unwin, 1957. 335pp.
Unabashed nostalgia. In the chapter 'Literature', there figures a brief summary of the newspapers of the 1920s. One episode of sideline interest is how the *Daily Mirror's* introduction of A.B. Payne's Pip, Squeak and Wilfred strip cartoon proved a winner.

2296 Montgomery, Louise Falls, ed. *Journalists on dangerous assignments: a guide for staying alive.* London: International Press Institute, 1986. 84pp.
Twenty-four contributions from correspondents 'in the field'; edited in the USA, but with some British content.

2297 *Montrose Review.* Centenary number. Montrose (Angus): 13 Jan 1911.

2298 – – –. 150th anniversary souvenir. 12 Jan 1961.

2299 – – –. 175th anniversary number (with supplement). 16 Jan 1986.
Celebrating Scotland's second oldest weekly with a continuous history.

2300 Mooney, Bel. *Differences of opinion.* London: Robson Books, 1984. 210pp.
Distilled from fifteen years' freelancing, mainly for national newspapers. In her introductory article, 'Hot metal v. cool mettle', Mooney deplores 'the rubbish competent

women have to take from the jolly but ill-educated office-boys and businessmen who rise to run Fleet Street . . . the woman's page as such must go.'

2301   Moonman, Eric, ed. *The press: a case for commitment.* London: Fabian Society, 1969. (A Fabian Tract.)
Contains articles by Richard Briginshaw and other trade unionists.

2302   Moore, Charles, and Christopher Hawtree, eds. *1936 as recorded by The Spectator.* London: Michael Joseph, 1986.
Fifty years on, Moore was the current editor of the magazine, and Hawtree a regular reviewer. Several leading writers add their comment.

2303   Moorehead, Alan (McCrae). *Afican trilogy.* With a foreword by Viscount Montgomery. London: Hamish Hamilton, 1944. 592pp. A reprint of *Mediterranean front, A year of battle,* and *The end in Africa.*

2304   – – –.   *Eclipse.* London: Hamish Hamilton; New York: 1945.
The campaigns in Europe, 1943–5.

2305   – – –.   *A late education: episodes in a life,* ed Lucy Milner (Mrs Moorehead). London: Hamish Hamilton, 1970. 175pp; Harmondsworth (Middx): Penguin, 1976. 185pp.
Based on reportage largely for the *Daily Express,* by the Australian who was arguably the leading war correspondent of his day.

2306   Moorhouse, Geoffrey. *The press.* London: Ward Lock (Educational), [1967]. 94pp.

2307   Moran, James Charles. *Printing presses: history and development from the fifteenth century to modern times.* London: Faber; Berkeley (CA): University of California Press, 1973. 263pp.
A standard work by the then editor of *Printing World.*

2308   – – –.   *NATSOPA – seventy-five years.* London: Heinemann, 1964.
The National Society of Operative Printers and Assistants (as it originally was), 1889–1964.

2309   – – –.   *Stanley Morison: his typographic achievement.* London: Lund Humphries, 1971. 184pp.

2310   – – –.   'The newspaper in Britain today'. In *The Penrose Annual, 1967.*
A nineteen-page treatment.

2311   Morgan, Charles (Langbridge). *Reflections in a mirror.* London: Macmillan, 1942. 225pp; second ser, 1946. 229pp.
Dramatic critic for *The Times* (1926–39) as well as distinguished novelist, Morgan later contributed a series of unsigned essays to *The Times Literary Supplement.* He was revealed as the author when these selections were published.

2312   Morgan, *Prebendary* Dewi. *Phoenix of Fleet Street: 2,000 years of St Bride's.* London: Charles Knight, 1973. vii + 290pp.

A history of the church regarded as the 'cathedral of Fleet Street', with close ties with press and printing. The last two chapters deal particularly with that aspect.

2313 – – –, ed. *Faith in Fleet Street*. London: Mowbray, 1967. 153pp.
Contains contributions from fifteen prominent journalists, edited by the rector of St Bride's who retired in 1985.

2314 Morgan, James. 'A free for all future'. *Journalism Studies Review*, 1982.
An account of the growth of 'freesheets' in Britain between 1975 and 1982.

2315 Morgan, Jean. 'Winning – the Welsh way'. *UK Press Gazette*, 19 Sep 1988.
On the revival of the *Western Mail* under the editorship of John Humphries.

2316 – – –. 'Reuters shapes up'. *UK Press Gazette*, 13 Mar 1989.
Interview with Mark Wood, editor-in-chief-designate.

2317 – – –. 'A distinctly Scottish spirit'. *UK Press Gazette*, 5 Aug 1991.
Feature on Thomson Newspapers' *Scotland on Sunday*, three years after its launch.

2318 – – –. 'Andrew's war: 10 years fighting the Establishment'. *UK Press Gazette*, 22 Feb 1993.
Andrew Neil's near-decade – the last seven years at Wapping – as editor of *The Sunday Times*.

2319 – – –. 'Heading for happy ever after'. *UK Press Gazette*, 2 Aug 1993.
Interview with Peter Hollinson, editor of *Wales on Sunday*.

2320 Morgan, Kenneth. 'A system more sinned against than sinning'. *UK Press Gazette*, 6 Jun 1988. (In Cleaning Up the 4th Estate series.)
On the role of the Press Council, by its director.

2321 – – –. 'The Press Council: an epitaph'. *UK Press Gazette*, 3 Dec 1990.

2322 – – –. 'Press freedom – public rights'. *Concord* (English–Speaking Union), May 1993.

2323 Morgan, Kenneth O(wen). *Keir Hardie: radical and socialist*. London: Weidenfeld & Nicolson, 1975. xii + 343pp.
Covers Hardie's editorship (1891–1904) of *The Labour Leader* – a paper serious in intent, but with many popular features.

2324 Morgan, Robin, and Brian Whitaker. *The Rainbow Warrior: the French attempt to sink Greenpeace*. London: Century Hutchinson (Arrow), 1986. 302pp.
A *Sunday Times* Insight Team investigation into the French underground action in New Zealand against the Greenpeace anti-nuclear movement.

Morison, Stanley [Edward]. *The English newspaper: some account of the physical development of journals printed in London between 1622 and the present day: see Reference Works section.*

2325   – – –.   'The making of newspapers'. *Alphabet and Image*, 1, Spring 1946.
Deals with English papers, from the seventeenth century on.

2326   – – –.   'The bibliography of newspapers and the writing of history'. *Library*, 5th ser, 9, 13, Sep 1954.
A reprint of a lecture to the Bibliographical Society given on 16 February 1952. A particularly authoritative review.

2327   Morley, David. 'Industrial conflict and the mass media'. *Sociological Review*, 24, 1976.

2328   Morning Advertiser, The. *The oldest newspaper in Fleet Street: a brief sketch of the history of the daily newspaper of the Incorporated Society of Licensed Victuallers*. London: 1925; rptd 1949. 16pp. With a facsimile of no 1 (8 Feb 1794).
The original (1925) edition marked the 110th anniversary of the move to Fleet Street itself. Although its long history was as the voice of the licensed trade, *The Morning Advertiser* was a leading general newspaper in its early years.

2329   – – –.   *The Morning Advertiser, established 1794*. 20pp.
Historical pamphlet, published after the return in 1956 to St Andrew St, London EC.

2330   *Morning Advertiser*. Bicentenary special. Slough (Berks): 8 Feb 1994.
(Thereafter the twice-weekly *Licensee and Morning Advertiser*.)

2331   'Morning and evening at Liverpool'. *The Newspaper World*, 25 Feb 1939. (In The Oldest Newspapers series.)
In 1939, as now, the (*Liverpool*) *Daily Post* and *Liverpool Echo* were in harness as the principal newspapers published on Merseyside.

2332   *Morning Post, The*. 150th anniversary number (1772–1922). 2 Nov 1922.

2333   – – –.   50,000th number. 19 Sep 1932.
Founded in 1772 by a syndicate and originally scurrilous in nature, *The Morning Post* failed to make any impact, but its purchase by Daniel Stuart in 1795 saved it from oblivion. When Stuart sold out in 1803, it had achieved the highest circulation of its day. As the voice of the Tories, it also achieved lasting political influence; its eventual merger into *The Daily Telegraph* in 1937 caused widespread regret among traditionalists.

2334   *Morning Post Building, The, Inveresk House, 1 Aldwych*. London: McKenna & Co, 1978. 32pp.
Authoritative accounts, embracing not only the *Morning Post's* office from 1907 to 1927 (later that of Illustrated Newspapers), but also the development of the newspaper in that locality by the Borthwick family. Algernon Borthwick (Baron Glenesk) was sole proprietor from 1876 to his death in 1908.

2335   *Morning Telegraph*. 125th anniversary supplement. Sheffield: 6 Jun 1980.

2336 – – –. 40,000th issue. Jun 1984. With facsimiles of the early days.

The *Sheffield Telegraph* (founded as the *Sheffield Daily Telegraph* in 1855) was retitled *Morning Telegraph* by United Newspapers in 1966.

2337 – – –. Final issue. 8 Feb 1986.

Included an eight-page souvenir.

2338 Morris, Albert. *Scotland's paper: The Scotsman, 1817-1992*. Edinburgh: Scotsman, 1992. 64pp.

Scanning its 175-year history.

2339 Morris, Anthony J.A. *The scaremongers: the advocacy of war and rearmament, 1896–1914*. London: Routledge & Kegan Paul, 1984. xi + 494pp.

An academic view of 'the owners, editors and correspondents who, for different reasons, at different times, insisted that Germany and Britain were set on a collision course, and whose doom-laden prophecies became dreadful reality on 4 August 1914'.

2340 Morris, Barry. *The roots of appeasement: the British weekly press and Nazi Germany during the 1930s*. London: Frank Cass, 1991. 220pp.

Based on PhD thesis at the University of Cambridge, 1977.

2341 Morris, Claud. *I bought a newspaper*. London: Arthur Barker, [1963]. 224pp.

The story of what happened when a Fleet Street journalist left his well-paid job to pit his wits against adversity in the form of a nearly bankrupt newspaper in South Wales. Somehow he was able to rebuild the fortune of the *South Wales Voice* and to launch his *Voice* magazines for industry in various areas so that he could resell at a small profit; he returned to London a sadder but wiser man.

2342 Morris, James Humphrey (later Jan). *Coronation Everest*. London: Faber, 1958 etc. 145pp. Rptd with new introduction, London: Boxtree, 1992.

Morris accompanied the successful Everest Expedition of 1953 as *The Times*'s correspondent, his reports (some sent in code) achieving classic status as well as being a world exclusive. He was five years on *The Times* staff, five with *The Guardian*.

2343 Morrison, David E., and Howard Tumber. *Journalists at war: the dynamics of news reporting during the Falklands conflict*. London: Sage, 1988. xiv + 370pp. Publ in association with the Broadcasting Research Unit.

The strength of this extensive study lies in the remarkably frank verbatim interviews with every correspondent who went to the Falklands. Should be required reading for anyone who may be involved in any future military action.

2344 – – –. 'The foreign correspondent: date-line London'. *Media, Culture and Society*, Oct 1985.

Stress how their research shows that correspondents based in London set great store on the interpretation of the news in Britain's own 'quality' press.

2345   Morrison, Doreen. 'Indexes to *The Times* of London: an evaluation and comparative analysis'. *The Serials Librarian*, 13, 1, Sep 1987. Abridged version in *Journal of Documentation*, 42, 3, Sep 1986.
The most complete comparison yet of the official indexes and the independently published *Palmer's*.

2346   Morrison, George Ernest. *The correspondence of G.E. Morrison*, ed Lo Hui-min. Cambridge: Cambridge University Press, 1976. 2 vols: Vol 1, 1895–1912. xiv + 848pp. Vol 2, 1912–1920. xi + 905pp.
'Chinese' Morrison of *The Times*, as revealed in his own words; these letter are also of considerable historical significance. Despite Morrison's 'Chinese' sobriquet and long service in China, he was Australian born and bred. Strangely, he read his own obituary in *The Times* in 1900; head office in London had thought him killed in the Boxer uprising. In fact, he served with *The Times* until 1912, and survived until 1920.

2347   Morrison, Ian F.M. *This war against Japan*. London: Faber, 1943.

2348   – – –.   *Malayan postscript*. Sydney: Angus & Robertson; London: Faber, 1943. 196pp.
Ian followed in the footsteps of his famous father, G.E. Morrison, as *The Times*'s correspondent in the Far East. He was killed in the front line in Korea when only thirty-seven.

2349   Mortimer, F(rancis) J(ames). *Photography for the press*. London: Amateur Photographer, 1905.

2350   – – –.   'Photography's part in the war'. *Photographic Journal* (series), Apr 1941–Apr 1944.
By the journal's then veteran editor.

2351   Morton, H[enry] [Canova] V[ollam]. *H.V. Morton's London*. London: Methuen, 1940; New York, 1941.
Reprint of the first three collections of Morton's 'London' essays for the *Daily Express*. They were originally published in 1925–6, and in 1931 – already the most successful travel writer of his time – he moved to the *Daily Herald* in a similar capacity.

2352   – – –.   *Atlantic meeting*. London: Methuen, 1943.
At the request of the Ministry of Information, Morton attended the secret mid-Atlantic rendezvous between Churchill and Roosevelt which preceded the entry of the USA into World War II – a 'one-off' in the long catalogue of his works.

2353   Morton, J[ohn] [Cameron Andrieu] B[ingham] [Michael]. *The bumper Beachcomber*. London: Bloomsbury, 1991. Ed Richard Ingrams. Illustrated by Jeff Fisher.
One of the recent anthologies of the third – and most famous – 'Beachcomber', responsible for the 'By the way' column in the *Daily Express* for over fifty years. He aimed his humorous shafts at every conceivable target with genius, and invented an unforgettable string of characters.

2354   Moseley, Sydney Alexander. *The truth about the Dardanelles*. London: Cassell, 1916.

2355   – – –.   *The truth about a journalist*. London: Pitman, 1935. xvi + 352pp.

2356   – – –.   *The private diaries of Sydney Moseley*. London: Parris, 1960. xvi + 565pp.
By a special correspondent for the *Daily Express* during World War I (one of the first to get a byline in the paper). Later he became editor of the *Daily Herald* and was also a pioneer radio critic. This is an outspoken book, cynical on the author's battles with officialdom; Moseley also devotes much space to the issues of spiritualism.

2357   Mosley, Leonard (Oswald). *Down stream: the uncensored story of 1936–39*. London: Michael Joseph, 1939. 300pp.

2358   – – –.   *Report from Germany*. London: Gollancz, 1945. 125pp.
As *The Daily Telegraph*'s front-line correspondent, dropped with the parachute troops into Normandy. Mosley had earlier represented the *Daily Sketch* and Allied (later Kemsley) Newspapers.

2359   – – –.   *Castlerosse*. London: Arthur Barker, 1956.
A close-up study of a larger-than-life Irish peer who made his name as a society gossip columnist for the *Sunday Express* in the inter-war years.

2360   Mosley, Paul. *The British economy as represented by the popular press*. Glasgow: University of Strathclyde (Centre for the Study of Public Policy), 1982.

2361   Moss, Louis, and Kathleen L. Box. *Newspapers: an inquiry into newspaper reading amongst the civilian population*. London: Ministry of Information, 1943. (Wartime Social Survey.)

2362   *Moston, Middleton and Blackley Guardian*. Centenary special supplement. Rochdale (Lancs): 2 Dec 1977.

2363   Mowat, John. 'Romance of the Orkney and Shetland press'. *Orkney Antiquarian Society Proceedings*, 16, 1937.

2364   Moynihan, Michael. *War correspondent*. Barnsley (S Yorks): Pen & Sword Books (Leo Cooper), 1994.
Serving the *News Chronicle* from the Normandy invasion to the Japanese surrender.

2365   Muggeridge, [Thomas] Malcolm. *Picture palace*. London: Eyre & Spottiswoode, 1934. Rptd Weidenfeld & Nicolson, 1987. 206pp. Introduction by Richard Ingrams.
A novel with a thinly veiled *Manchester Guardian* setting – including a splenetic portrait ('old Savoury') clearly representing its guiding spirit, C.P. Scott – which that newspaper succeeded in suppressing for fifty-three years. The paramount reason?: 'Savoury's' high

moral tone for his morning paper is utterly contradicted by the contents of its evening stablemate . . . as in reality, *The Manchester Guardian* was 'carried' by the profits made by its carefree partner, the *Manchester Evening News.*

2366   – – –.   *The thirties: 1930–1940 in Great Britain.* London: Hamish Hamilton, 1940. 326pp; Collins, 1967. 351pp; Fontana, 1971. 318pp.
Muggeridge worked on the Londoner's Diary of the *Evening Standard* in this period, and finished the book while on Army service. Unblinkered reportage.
    Pre-war, Muggeridge had also worked in Calcutta (for *The Statesman*) as well as in London and Moscow, and immediately post-war he reported for *The Daily Telegraph* in Washington and London. He edited *Punch* from 1953 to 1957 (not it would seem his most congenial assignment), and was also a frequent and effective broadcaster.

2367   Mulchrone, Vincent. *The best of Vincent Mulchrone.* London: Associated Newspapers, [1978].
'A lifetime of wit and observation of the folly and splendour of his fellow humans by the *Daily Mail*'s finest reporter'.

2368   Mullin, Chris. *Error of judgement: the Birmingham bombing.* London: Chatto & Windus, 1986.
Crusading MP's (eventually successful) campaign, with the aid of the press, to free the six Irishmen found guilty of the pub bombing in Birmingham.

2369   Munford, Anthony Peter, comp. *South Yorkshire newspapers, 1754–1976.* Barnsley: South Yorkshire County Council, 1976. 19pp.
A well-researched monograph.

2370   Munro, Donald J. '175 years of the *Montrose Review*: Scotland's second oldest weekly newspaper'. *Journal of Newspaper and Periodical History*, Summer 1986.

2371   Munster, George. *A paper prince.* Ringwood (Australia): Viking, 1985. 291pp.
An Australian journalist's detailed business life of Rupert Murdoch, dissecting his Australian origins as son of press magnate Sir Keith Murdoch and his fulfilment of unremitting ambition.

2372   Murphy, David. *The silent watchdog: the press in local politics.* London: Constable, 1976. 186pp. (In the Communication and Society series.)
The provincial press, rarely studied by academics, is here treated with searching scrutiny by a Manchester-based journalist, dealing with two fictional newspapers as 'case studies'. He shows how the present trend towards ever greater ownership concentration operates not merely against the interests of individual editorial departments but also against the free flow of ideas and access to functional information.

2373   – – –.   *The Stalker affair and the press.* London: Unwin Hyman, 1991. [254pp].
On the press treatment of the 1984 investigation led by John Stalker (formerly deputy

chief constable of Manchester) into allegations of a 'shoot to kill' policy by the British Army in Northern Ireland.

2374   – – –.   'The built-in line of deference that rings British journalists'. *Journalism Studies Review*, 1981.
However, Murphy bemoans the expense and time involved in true investigative journalism.

2375   Murphy, Michael John. *Newspapers and local history*. Chichester (W Sussex): Phillimore, for British Association for Local History, 1991. 24pp.
A good basic guide.

2376   Murray, Alex. 'Reuters – Fleet Street's own success story'. *The Sunday Telegraph*, 19 Sep 1982.
A City-page summary of the financial 'bonanza' first enjoyed by Reuters in the late 1970s, largely through its computer-based information services; these emerged as its strength when it was floated as a public company in 1984.

2377   Murray, George McIntosh. *The press and the public: the story of the British Press Council*. With a foreword by Howard Rusk Long. London: Feffer & Simons; Carbondale and Edwardsville (IL): University Press of Southern Illinois, [1972]. xi + 243pp. (In the New Horizons in Journalism series.)
After forty years with the *Daily Mail* as leader-writer etc, Murray became chairman of the Press Council.

2378   Murray, Margaret (Leonora). 'Parliament's own newspaper'. *The Strand Magazine*, Mar 1944.
A well-documented (and illustrated) record of the *Parliamentary Debates – Hansard*.

2379   Murray, Nancy. 'Reporting the riots'. *Sage Race Relations Abstracts*, 11, 1986.
The so-called race riots in Britain's inner cities are covered.

2380   Musson, Albert Edward. *The Typographical Association: progress and history up to 1949*. Oxford: Oxford University Press, 1954. viii + 550pp.
The TA and the London Typographical Society (LTS) joined forces as the National Graphical Association (NGA) in 1964.

2381   Myers, Robin. 'The records of the Worshipful Company of Stationers and Newspaper Makers'. *Publishing History*, 13, 1983.
The Company of Newspaper Makers, founded 1931, joined the Stationers' Company officially in 1937.

2382   – – –, ed. *Records of the Stationers' Company, 1554–1920*. Cambridge, and Teaneck (NJ): Chadwyck-Healey, 1985–. On microfilm (115 reels), with printed guide.
All the relevant records in the archives at Stationers' Hall, London – the single most important source for the history of the English book trade. Myers is the archivist of the Stationers' Company.

2383   – – –.   *The archive of the Stationers' Company, 1554–1984: an account of the records.* Winchester: St Paul's Bibliographies, 1990. 500pp.

2384   – – –.   *The History of the Stationers' Company.* (In preparation.) From 1800 to the present day.

2385   Myson, William, comp. *Surrey newspapers: a handlist and tentative bibliography.* London: Merton LBC, 1961. ix + 36pp.

2386   Mytton-Davies, Cynric. *Journalist alone: the story of the freelance and the Freelance Section of the Institute of Journalists.* Newtown: Clifton Press (for IOJ), [1968]. 88pp.
Mytton-Davies later became president of the IOJ.

2387   Nally, Michael. 'The last call of the *Clarion*'. *The Guardian (Media Guardian)*, 16 Dec 1991.
Marking the centenary of Blatchford's radical newspaper, which first came off the presses of the Co-operative Society in Manchester in 1891; it lasted in a comparatively pallid form until 1935.

2388   Napoli, James, and Luanna Napoli. 'The ethnic voice: heard, even seen – but only rarely read'. *British Journalism Review*, Winter 1990.

2389   Narracott, Arthur (Henson). *War news had wings: a record of the RAF in France.* London: Frederick Muller, 1941. 224pp.
The author served in World War II, first as a press officer with the Royal Air Force, then as air correspondent of *The Times* (which he remained until his death in 1967).

2390   National Board for Prices and Incomes. *Costs and revenues of national daily newspapers.* London: HMSO, 1967. Cmnd 3435 (PIB Report no 43); and 1970. Cmnd 4277 (PIB Report no 141).

2391   – – –.   *Journalists' pay.* London: HMSO, 1969. Cmnd 4077 (PIB Report no 115).

2392   National Council for the Training of Journalists. Handbooks: *Training in journalism.* Epping (Essex): NCTJ, 1952; 7th edn, 1975; *How journalists are trained.* Epping: 1988, 1989; *Journalist training and assessment.* Harlow (Essex): 1993.
'A quick reference to all aspects of the national training scheme'. A page on 'the 40-year history' harks back to the foundation in 1952 of the National Advisory Council for the Training and Education of Junior Journalists; the title was changed to the present one in 1955.

2393   – – –.   *The practice of journalism.* London: NCTJ, 1963.
Professionalism, or the occupational prestige of journalism, as defined by former provincial practitioners.

2394   – – –.   *Daily English.* London: 1964. Comp F.E. Pardoe and G. Liddle.
Examples of good newspaper writing.

2395 National Heritage Select Committee. *Fourth report: privacy and media intrusion.* London: HMSO, 1993. HC 294. Vol I, Report and minutes of proceedings. liiipp; Vol II, Minutes of evidence. viii + 264pp; Vol III, Appendices to the minutes. viii + pp 265–394.

The all-party select committee, chaired by Gerald Kaufman, here recommends the replacement of the Press Complaints Commission by a Press Commission, with 'more teeth', and the appointment of a statutory Press Ombudsman.

2396 *National Readership Survey.* London: Institute of Practitioners in Advertising, 1954, 1956–67; Joint Industry Committee for National Readership Surveys (JICNARS), 1968–91; National Readership Surveys, 1992–. Now 3 vols a year.

Extensive statistical analysis, including all national and some regional newspapers.

2397 National Union of Journalists. *NUJ rule book.* London: NUJ: revised 1986.

A code of professional conduct first appeared as an appendix in 1936.

2398 – – –. *Freelance directory.* London: NUJ, 1957–. Every two years; latest edn, 1993–4.

Lists the members of the Freelance Branch of the NUJ, with their specialities.

2399 – – –. *Journalists and new technology.* London: NUJ, 1977; revised 1980, and 1987, with sub-title: *avoiding the hazards.* By Alison Simpson and Jacob Ecclestone.

2400 – – –. 'Who owns what'. Chart, rptd from *Journalist*, 20 Sep 1988.

– – –. *Journalist: see Reference Works section.*

2401 No entry.

2402 Naughtie, James, ed. *Playing the Palace: a Westminster collection.* Edinburgh: Mainstream Publishing, 1985. 209pp.

An anthology of some of the best of parliamentary writing (and speaking) over more than two centuries. Naughtie was then chief political correspondent for *The Scotsman.*

2403 Naylor, Thomas Ellis. *The principles and practice of newspaper make-up.* Leicester: Raithby, Lawrence, 1918. 79pp. Preface by Lord Burnham.

'A text-book for journalists and printers'.

2404 Needham, Leslie William (Bill). *Fifty years of Fleet Street.* London: Michael Joseph, 1973. 165pp.

By the recently retired advertisement director of Beaverbrook Newspapers.

2405 Negrine, Ralph. *Politics and the mass media in Britain.* London: Routledge, 1989, 1994.

2406 – – –. 'The press and the Suez crisis: a myth re-examined'. *Historical Journal,* 25, 1982.

2407 Neilly, J. Emerson. *Besieged with B.P.: a full and complete record of the siege.* London: Pearson, 1900. 296pp.

About Colonel (later Lord) Baden-Powell, at Mafeking in the Boer War. By the correspondent for *The Pall Mall Gazette*.

2408 Neustatter, Angela. 'The first ladies of Fleet Street'. *The Independent*, 28 Jan 1987.

The possibility of a woman becoming editor of a national newspaper (later in the year, Wendy Henry was appointed at the *News of the World*, and Eve Pollard at the *Sunday Mirror*).

2409 Nevett, Terry R. *Advertising in Britain: a history.* London: Heinemann, for History of Advertising Trust, 1982.

A general historical survey, stronger on the nineteenth century than the twentieth.

2410 Nevinson, Henry Woodd. *Ladysmith: the diary of a siege.* London: Methuen, 1900. xii + 306pp.

Despatches to *The Daily Chronicle*.

2411 – – –. *The Dardanelles campaign.* London: Nisbet, 1918. xx +429pp.

Nevinson (1856–1941) wrote this critical eyewitness report for *The Manchester Guardian* soon after the disastrous Dardanelles episode in World War I.

2412 – – –. *Changes and chances.* London: Nisbet; New York: Harcourt Brace, 1923. xiii + 360pp.

The author here looks back to the period 1897–1900, when he made his name as a correspondent for *The Daily Chronicle* in the Greco-Turkish and Boer Wars.

2413 – – –. *More changes, more chances.* London: Nisbet; New York: Harcourt Brace, 1925. xvi + 427pp.

Nevison's personal story – via *The Daily News* etc – continues to World War I.

2414 – – –. *Last changes, last chances.* London: Nisbet; New York: Harcourt Brace, 1928. xv + 361pp.

From 1914 to the mid-1920s: World War I, the Washington Disarmament Conference, post-war Germany.

2415 'New *Daily Herald*, The'. *The Times*, 17 Mar 1930.

Marks the first issue of the revamped product of Daily Herald (1929) Ltd.

2416 'New *Hansard*, The'. In *Sell's Dictionary of the World's Press, 1909*. London: Sell, 1909.

'The world-famous century-old record of the debates in Parliament becomes a Government publication.'

2417 New Statesman. *New Statesmanship: survey of readership of The New Statesman and Nation.* London, [1956]. 35pp.

Revealing documentation from the independent political weekly.

2418 *New Statesman.* 50th birthday number, 1913–1963. London: Apr 1963.
Now incorporates *New Society* (combined title *New Statesman and Society*).

2419 *Newcastle Journal, The.* Centenary number. Newcastle upon Tyne: 12 May 1932.
Founded as a weekly in 1832, it became a morning daily in 1861; with the (*Newcastle*) *Evening Chronicle* and *Sunday Sun*, it was acquired by Allied (later) Kemsley Newspapers in 1924. The three papers later became Thomson Regional titles; the current title of the morning is simply *The Journal*.

2420 Newkey-Burden, George. 'The *Telegraph* reaches number 1'. *Quaynotes*, Apr 1992.
An illustrated feature in *The Daily Telegraph*'s staff journal, on the historic progress of the newspaper from 253 Strand (in 1855) to 1 Canada Square (in 1992).

2421 Newman, Henry. *A roving commssion.* London: Bell, 1937. 328pp.
The author was a Reuters correspondent in the East.

2422 Newman, Peter C. *The establishment man: a portrait of power.* Toronto: McClelland & Stewart, 1982.
An early biography of Conrad Black.

2423 *News, The.* Centenary supplement. Portsmouth: 23, 25, 26, 27 Apr 1977.
Formerly the *Evening News*, today *The News* is in the Portsmouth and Sunderland Newspapers group.

2424 *News, The.* London: News International, 1986–. Monthly.
The group's house journal.

2425 News Chronicle. *News Chronicle story of twenty-five years*, comp W.J. Makin. London, 1935.
Celebrating the Royal Silver Jubilee.

2426 *News Chronicle.* Centenary number. London: 21 Jan 1946.
Marking in fact the centenary of the foundation of the senior parent, *The Daily News*; the other was *The Daily Chronicle*. The combined paper was the national voice for the Liberal cause from its foundation on 2 June 1930 until its sudden and still mourned demise on 17 October 1960, when Associated Newspapers purchased the *News Chronicle* and its evening partner (*The Star*) from the Cadbury interests, and killed both immediately. Although never a circulation leader, it was a popular newspaper with justified pretensions to first-class journalism in every sphere.

2427 '*News Chronicle* centenary, The: heir to a great political and literary tradition'. *The Newspaper World*, 19 Jan 1946.

2428 News International. *Fact files.* London: [1990].
Series of data sheets for *The Times, The Sunday Times, News of the World, The Sun*, and production of the group at Wapping.

2429   News Letter. *The News Letter: a history of the oldest British daily newspaper.*
Belfast: 1987.
The facts supporting the paper's valid claims of two hundred and fifty years' unbroken
history (although a weekly until 1855). *See also Belfast News-Letter.*

2430   News of the World. *Through four reigns: the romance of a great newspaper.*
[1928]. 88pp.

2431   *News of the World.* Centenary number. 3 Oct 1943.
Founded by John Browne Bell in 1843 as a Sunday paper for the mass market, the *News
of the World*'s formula for success soon proved irresistible; passing the 1 million circulation mark in 1906, it was destined to surpass 8 million – the world's highest – in the
heady post-World War II years. Sold by the Carrs to News International under Murdoch
in 1969, it remains the most popular Sunday.

2432   – – –.   150th birthday special. *Sunday (News of the World Magazine),*
3 Oct 1993.
With facsimile of issue no 1 (1843).

2433   *News/Post.* Centenary number. Blyth (Northumberland): 9 May 1974.
Harking back to the *Blyth Evening News* and *Wansbeck Telegraph.* Today a Portsmouth
and Sunderland title.

2434   *Newspaper Finance Annual,* ed Roy Hopkins. London: 1930, 1931.

2435   'Newspaper make-up'. *World's Press News* (series). 9 Jun–1 Dec 1932.

2436   *Newspaper publishers.* 10th edn. Hampton (Middx): ICC Financial Surveys,
1993.
Business Ratio Report.

2437   *Newspaper Publishers' Handbook.* Norwich: Eastern Counties Newspapers
Group (Adprint), 1981–91. Annual.
Had brief introductory articles on various topical aspects of the newspaper industry as
well as a directory section concentrating largely on production and technology.

2438   *Newspaper Publishing Plc: offer for subscription.* London: 1986. 44pp.
Prospectus for the launch of *The Independent* – then the largest sum sought in the City
of London as start-up capital.

2439   Newspaper Society. *Newspaper Society, 1836–1936: a centenary retrospect.*
London: NS, 1936. 71pp. By E.W. D[avies].
The first hundred years of the national body for the regional press.

2440   – – –.   *Free newspaper review.* NS, 1989, 1992.
An occasional survey carried out by the Society of those of its members publishing free
titles. By 1992, the great majority were tabloid weeklies published by groups, with an
average circulation of 55,000.

2441   – – –.   *Britain's press: in defence of self-regulation.* 1992. The Society's
evidence to Sir David Calcutt for his review of press behaviour.

2442 – – –. *The making of a newspaper.* [n.d].
A small booklet for schools etc.
See also Headlines and *Newstime* in *Reference Works section.*

2443 Newspaper World, The. *Silver Jubilee review of the press.* London: 1935.
Marking the twenty-fifth anniversary of King George V's accession.

2444 *Newspaper World, The.* 'The Oldest Newspapers' (series). 18 Mar to 28 Oct 1939.
See also Reference Works section.

2445 *Newspapers.* London: Key Note Publications, 1978; later Hampton (Middx): 10th edn, 1991.
Key Note Reports: detailed analyses of the British newspaper industry.

2446 'Newspapers'. In *Publishing in the UK.* London: Key Note Publications, 1989; later Hampton (Middx): 3rd edn, 1993.
A Key Note Marketing Review.

2447 *Newspapers in Wales: a directory.* Caerphilly (Mid Glamorgan): Community Work Information Centre for Wales, 1975.

2448 Newsprint Supply Company. *Newsprint 1939–1949: the crisis of the British press.* London: News Chronicle, 1948. 42pp.
Minutes of evidence to the Royal Commission on the Press (1947–8), plus an account of negotiations for the newsprint budget for 1949.

2449 Newton, David. *Mercury story: a brief record of the Lincoln, Rutland and Stamford Mercury.* Stamford (Lincs): EMAP, 1962.
An attractive promotion booklet, albeit claiming the now-discredited 1695 foundation date.

2450 – – –. *Men of mark: makers of East Midland Allied Press.* Peterborough (Northants): EMAP, 1977. xii + 238pp.
The EMAP group has developed from a series of local East Midlands weeklies.

2451 Nichols, [John] Beverley. *The unforgiving minute.* London: W.H. Allen, 1978. vii + 311pp.
Autobiography after retirement of one of the most prolific of columnists in the era between the two World Wars. Nichols contributed his Page Two column to the *Sunday Chronicle* from 1932 to 1947.

2452 Nickell, James Merle. *The British press and the Ethiopian crisis, 1935–1936.* Lexington : University of Kentucky, 1978 (PhD dissertation). 369pp. Available in microform from University Microfilms International (Ann Arbor, MI).

2453 Nisbet-Smith, Dugal. 'The Newspaper Society'. *In* Dennis Griffiths, ed. *The encyclopedia of the British press, 1422-1992.* Basingstoke (Hants): Macmillan, 1992.
By the director of the society.

2454   Nobbs, David. *Pratt of the Argus*. London: Methuen, 1988. 384pp.
Novel – based on personal experience – on a 1950s' reporter with the fictitious *Thurmarsh Evening Argus*.

2455   ' "Noble engine of freedom": the *Reading Mercury*'. *The Newspaper World*, 17 Jun 1939. (In The Oldest Newspapers series.)

2456   Noon, M.A. *New technology and industrial relations in provincial newspapers: computerization and buying power of journalists*. London: Imperial College of Science and Technology, 1989 (PhD thesis).

2457   *Norfolk News and Weekly Press*. Centenary number. Norwich: 6 Jan 1945.

2458   Norling, Bernard. 'The Soviet disorders, 1919–25, and the English press'. *Lithara*, 3, 2, 1964.

2459   Norris, William. *One from seven hundred: a year in the life of Parliament*. Oxford: Pergamon, 1966.
By a *Times* parliamentary reporter.

2460   *Northampton and County Independent*. Press special. Northampton: Apr 1978.
The history of the press in the area.

2461   *Northampton Mercury*. Bicentenary number. 7 May 1920.

2462   – – –.   250th anniversary supplement. 30 Apr 1970.
'The men who have shaped the destiny of the *Mercury*: 13 editors in the span of 250 years'. The *Northampton Mercury* of today is a weekly in EMAP ownership.

2463   '*Northampton Mercury*, 1720–1920'. In *Sell's World's Press, 1921*. London: Sell, 1921.

2464   *Northamptonshire Evening Telegraph*. 75 years of news, 1897–1972: souvenir supplement. Kettering: 4 Oct 1972.
Now an EMAP title.

2465   *Northavon Gazette*. Centenary issue: 100 years of progress. Dursley (Glos): 29 Jan 1984.
In Bailey Newspaper group.

2466   Northcliffe, Alfred Charles William Harmsworth, *Viscount*. *The romance of the Daily Mail*. London: 1903.

2467   – – –.   *The rise of the Daily Mail*. 1916. 50pp.
Northcliffe (1865–1922) expressed himself through the columns of his periodicals – starting with *Answers* in 1888 – and newspapers rather than in books. But these early promotions for the *Daily Mail* (which he had founded in 1896) have the authentic flavour.

2468 – – –. *At the war*. London: Hodder & Stoughton; New York: George H. Doran, 1916. viii + 355pp. Rptd as *A la guerre*. Paris: Payot, 1917. Publ in aid of the Red Cross and Order of St John.

2469 – – –. *Lord Northcliffe's war book*. New York: A.L. Burt, 1917. 283pp. Includes chapters on America at war. This and the previous entry were best-sellers. Northcliffe had already precipitated the fall of the Asquith Government in favour of Lloyd George before heading the British Mission to the USA in 1917. In the last year of the war, he was the director of propaganda in enemy countries.

2470 – – –. *Newspapers and their millionaires . . . with some meditations about us*. London: 1922. 24pp.
Fleet Street, at least, sat up and took notice of this mordant pamphlet.

2471 – – –. *My journey round the world (16th July 1921–26th February 1922)*, ed Cecil and St John Harmsworth. London: John Lane; Philadelphia: Lippincott, 1923. xii + 326pp.
A disconnected swansong, published posthumously.

2472 – – –. 'How I dropped £100,000 on the *Mirror*'. *Daily Mirror*, 27 Feb 1904.
A remarkably frank leader by the then Sir Alfred Harmsworth, less than two months after re-launching the *Daily Mirror* as a fully pictorial paper.

2472A – – –. 'The making of the modern newspaper'. *The World Today*, Dec 1905.

2473 – – –. 'The daily newspaper of today'. In *The Newspaper Press Directory, 1905*. London: Mitchell, 1905.

2474 – – –. 'Birthday of newspapers: 300 years of English journalism'. *The Times*, 2 Dec 1920.
One of Northcliffe's few signed leaders in *The Times*, this marked the publication of the *Tercentenary handlist of . . . newspapers*. He controlled *The Times* from 1908 to 1922.

2475 – – –. 'Some functions of a newspaper'. In *Sell's World's Press, 1921*. London: Sell, 1921.

2476 Northcliffe Newspapers Group. *Scanning the provinces*. London: Associated Newspapers, 1978. 59pp. 1979. 52pp.
An informative brochure on the modern Northcliffe regional group.

2477 Northern Echo, The. *The Northern Echo, the great North Country morning newspaper*. Darlington (Co Durham): 1928.

2478 *Northern Echo, The*. Centenary number. 1 Jan 1970.

2479 – – –. Centenary supplement. 1 Jul 1970.
This first halfpenny morning daily is today in the Westminster Press group. When edited by W.T. Stead in the 1870s, it was described as 'the most influential paper in Britain',

notwithstanding its circulation of only 13,000. Nearly one hundred years later, Harold Evans first made a national name for himself as a campaigning editor of *The Northern Echo*.

2480   *Northern Ireland political literature on microfiche: catalogue and indexes.* Phase 1: Periodicals, 1966–1987. Belfast: Linen Hall Library, 1989.
The Political Ephemera collection in this library includes many newspapers.

2481   Norton, J., and Leslie Willcocks. *Managing a multinational: financial and business strategy at News International, 1980–87.* Cranfield (Beds): Cranfield Institute of Technology, 1988.

2482   'Norwich Mercury'. *The Newspaper World*, 13 May 1939. (In The Oldest Newspapers series.)
The *Mercury* dates back to 1726, and continues weekly as an Eastern Counties Newspapers title.

2483   *Norwich Post, The, its contemporaries and successors.* Norwich: Norfolk News, 1951.
Celebrates '250 years of Norwich newspapers'. The foundation – by the printer Francis Burges – of *The Norwich Post* is generally dated as 1701, and it thus ranks as the very first regular provincial newspaper.

2484   *Nottingham Journal.* Souvenir supplement, 1710–1920. 18 Jan 1922.
The *Nottingham Journal* was a historic title, acquired by Westminster Press in that year (1922).

2485   *Notts Free Press.* Centenary supplement, 1885–1985. Sutton-in-Ashfield (Notts): 5 Sep 1985.
Was *Nottinghamshire Free Press and Derbyshire Chronicle*.

2486   Novion, François. *La presse anglaise contemporaire et ses grands quotidiens.* Paris: 1923.

2487   Nulty, Geoffrey, ed. *Guardian country: being the first 125 years of Cheshire County Newspapers.* Chester: 1978. 190pp.

2488   'Nursery of journalists, A'. *The Newspaper World*, 1 Jul 1939. (In The Oldest Newspapers series.)
Re the *Chester Courant*.

2489   Oakeshott, Arthur. *Arctic convoy to Russia.* London: 1941.
Reuters correspondent with Royal Navy on no fewer than thirty Arctic convoys.

2490   O'Brien, Conor Cruise. *The press and the world.* London: University of London (Birkbeck College), 1980. 12pp. Haldane Memorial Lecture.

2491   – – –.   *Passion and cunning and other essays.* London: Weidenfeld & Nicolson, 1988. 293pp.
Mainly from *The Observer*, of which O'Brien (a former Irish diplomat and minister) became editor-in-chief.

2492   — — —.   'The expanding *Observer*'. *In* D. Campbell, ed. *The British press*. London: CPU, 1979.

2493   Observer, The. *The Observer, 1791–1921: a short record of one hundred and thirty years*. With a foreword by J.L. Garvin; illustrated by Fred Pegram. London: The Observer, [1921]. 24pp.
Something of a collector's piece, especially the Pegram drawings and reproductions from the Guildhall Library. The warning leader 'Peace and dragons' teeth' published on 11 May 1919 is reprinted; it is a typical example of *The Observer*'s unwaveringly independent stance.

2494   — — —.   *The Observer: its book, 1791–1925*. 1925. 16pp.

2495   — — —.   *150 years of The Observer*. 30 Nov 1941.
A necessarily sparse celebration during the dark and newsprint-rationed days with Britain in the severest grip of war, this harked back to the foundation of *The Observer* in 1791; its eighteenth-century survival; and its steady rise in sales and influence thereafter under first Northcliffe (from 1905) and then the Astors (from 1911).

2496   — — —.   *Observer profiles*. With an introduction by Ivor Brown. London: Allan Wingate, 1948.
Brown completed in 1948 his service as the first editor since the Garvin era.

2497   Observer, The. 175th anniversary supplement. 4 Dec 1966.

2498   — — —.   *Read all about it!* 1979. [12pp.]
A brief illustrated history.

2499   — — —.   'Blowing our own trumpet'. *Observer* (magazine), with the 10,000th edn of the newspaper, 8 May 1983.
Largely on personalities in the paper's long history – it is the senior British Sunday – and about remaining an independent and influential voice even after its acquisition by Atlantic Richfield (1976) and subsequent sale to Lonrho (1981).

2500   — — —.   (*Observer* magazine). 21st birthday number. 8 Sep 1985.

2501   — — —.   'Our double century'. 1 Dec 1991.
Editorial marking the bicentenary: 'perhaps the most remarkable aspect of the *Observer*'s survival has been its stand-alone position. For this we have to thank Lonrho, whose tenth anniversary as owners is also marked this year.' Facsimile of 4 December 1791 included in magazine; also historical article by Janet Watts (q.v.). The paper was sold again, in 1993 (to the Guardian Media group).

2502   O'Connor, T[homas] P[ower]. *Memoirs of an old parliamentarian*. London: Benn, 1929. 2 vols.
Written late in his career, this contains regrettably little on T.P.'s turbulent time in journalism.

2503   — — —.   'The Lloyds'. *The Sunday Times*, 29 May 1927.

A tribute to Edward Lloyd and his son Frank (who had just died), pioneers of the popular Sunday paper. As to the author – on a memorial at Chronicle House, Fleet Street, appears: 'T.P. O'Connor . . . journalist, parliamentarian, 1848–1992 . . . his pen could lay bare the bones of a book or the soul of a statesman in a few vivid lines.'

2504   Odhams, William James Baird. *The business and I*. London: Martin Secker, 1935. 194pp.
Written during the heyday of the *Daily Herald* by the son of William Odhams, founder (1847) of the printing and publishing giant.

2505   O'Donovan, Patrick. *For fear of weeping*. London: MacGibbon & Kee, 1950. 232pp.
Reports for *The Observer* from South-East Asia; in an interlude between wars, these are more upbeat than might be assumed from the title. From first-hand observation: 'There exists a profound difference between American and British correspondents. The Americans seem more nearly politicians; the British more purely technicians.'

2506   – – –.   *A journalist's odyssey*. London: Esmonde, 1985. 109pp.
An anthology of *Observer* and other pieces forming a fitting memorial for O'Donovan's range and quality.

2507   O'Hagan, Henry Osborne. *Leaves from my life*. London: John Lane, 1929. 2 vols: 545, 427pp.
Memoir by a City financier which contains a chapter on 'Financial newspapers'. This describes the author's part in the launch of both *The Financial News* (1884) and *Financial Times* (1888).

2508   O'Higgins, Paul. *Censorship in Britain*. London: Nelson, 1972. 232pp.
A readable narrative of wartime press censorship from the closing months of the Crimean War to the Suez landings.

2509   'Oldest evening paper, The'. *The Newspaper World*, 1 Apr 1939. (In The Oldest Newspapers series.)
The *Shields Gazette*'s claim is unassailable. It was founded in 1849 and is still in existence.

2510   'Oldest provincial daily, The: the *Nottingham Journal*'. *The Newspaper World*, 8 Apr 1939. (In The Oldest Newspapers series.)
The *Nottingham Journal* based its claim to 'oldest' on an unconfirmed foundation date of 1710. Eventually it merged with the *Nottingham(shire) Guardian* as the *Guardian Journal*, which has since disappeared too.

2511   *Oldham Chronicle*. Centenary supplement. Oldham (Lancs): 8 May 1954.
Like many other morning papers, this survives only as a weekly free-distribution title.

2512   *Oldham Evening Chronicle*. Centenary special. 17 Mar 1980.
Still a thriving paid-for daily.

2513   Olins, Rufus. 'The last tycoon'. *The Sunday Times*, 19 Jul 1992.
How the 3rd Viscount Rothermere – unlike the heads of the other Fleet Street

dynasties – has not merely survived but also prospered, combining 'obsession with the past and ambition for the future'. Illustrated by a family tree showing the relationship of the parent Daily Mail and General Trust, Associated Newspapers, and its subsidiaries.

2514 Olson, Kenneth Eugene. *The history makers: the press of Europe from its beginnings through 1965*. Baton Rouge (LA): Louisiana State University Press, 1966. xiii + 471pp.
Has nearly thirty pages on the British Isles.

2515 O'Malley, Pat. ' "The invisible censor": civil law and the state delegation of press control, 1890–1952'. *Media, Culture and Society*, Oct 1982.

2516 O'Malley, William. *Glancing back: 70 years' experiences of press men, sportsmen and Members of Parliament*. London: Wright & Brown, 1933. 293pp.
The author was a notable staff man for *The Star* etc.

2517 'Once you smile, he's gotcha'. *The Sunday Telegraph*, 28 Jul 1992.
Profile of Kelvin MacKenzie, editor of *The Sun* 1981–94.

2518 *One hundred headlines: stories from the Belfast Telegraph*. Dundonald (Northern Ireland): Blackstaff Press, 1983.
The *Belfast Telegragh* is an evening paper established in 1870, with Northern Ireland's largest circulation; it is in the Thomson Regional group.

2519 'Opening up Fleet Street'. *Building Design*, 5 Feb 1988.

2520 Oram, Hugh. *The newspaper book: a history of newspapers in Ireland, 1649–1983*. Dublin: MO Books, 1983. 356pp; Boston: G.K. Hall, 1989.
Poorly indexed, anecdotal and occasionally unreliable, but nevertheless a readable and pictorially attractive survey of the Irish press over the centuries.

2521 – – –. *The advertising book: the history of advertising in Ireland*. Dublin: MO Books, 1986.
Includes Northern Ireland newspapers – but only marginally.

2522 – – –. *Paper tigers*. Belfast: Appletree Press, 1993. 192pp.
'The story of Irish newspapers by the people who made them'.

2523 Orbell, John. 'Pearson Plc'. In *International Directory of Company Histories*, Vol 4. Chicago and London: St James Press, 1991.
The Pearson enterprise includes the *Financial Times*, Westminster Press group etc.

2524 Orme, Edward B. '*The Illustrated London News*'. *Book and Magazine Collector*, 7, Sep 1984.
First-class summary of the magazine's history.

2525 Orwell, George (pseudonym of Eric Arthur Blair). *The road to Wigan Pier*. London: Gollancz, for the Left Book Club, 1937, 1965; Secker & Warburg, 1959; Harmondsworth (Middx): Penguin, 1962; New York: 1958.
A penetrating analysis of industrial England and its future, based on eyewitness reporting during the Depression.

2526 – – –.   *Homage to Catalonia*. London: Secker & Warburg, 1938, 1951; Harmondsworth (Middx): Penguin, 1962; New York: 1952, 1958.
Orwell served in the Catalan (Republican) militia, the experience clearly causing a drastic revision of his beliefs: 'It was above all things a political war.' In his short life (1903–50), Orwell was a prolific journalist in a great variety of media; these included (1943–6) regular contributions to the Forum feature of *The Observer* and reviews in *The New Statesman*, and the literary editorship of *Tribune* during the same period.

2527   Osman, Colin. 'The colour supplements'. *Creative Camera*, Mar 1984.
About the origins of the *Sunday Times, Observer, Sunday Telegraph* and *Sunday Express* magazines, *Sunday* (the *News of the World*'s magazine), *You* (with the *Mail on Sunday*), and other less successful national 'supplements'.

2528   *Oswestry and Border Counties Advertizer*. Centenary of *Border Counties Advertizer*. Oswestry (Shropshire): 1949.
In North Wales Newspapers group.

2529   Outram, George, & Co. *Scottish newspapers in the making: the Outram press*. Glasgow: Outram, 1931. 34pp.
Covers the *Glasgow Herald*, the *Evening Times*, the *Bulletin*, the *Glasgow Weekly Herald*. (In 1992, *The Herald* and *Evening Times* went to new ownership; the remaining Outram titles came under the control of Trinity International.)

2530   Owen, [Humphrey] Frank. *Tempestuous journey: Lloyd George, his life and times*. London: Hutchinson, 1954; New York: McGraw-Hill, 1955. 784pp.
Now supplanted overall by less unswervingly admiring assessments, Owen, as a practising journalist, gives useful chapter and verse on Lloyd George's participation in the affairs of United Newspapers between 1919 and 1926, but omits any mention of his other manipulations of the press in the party interest. This biography was commissioned (and edited behind the scenes) by Beaverbrook.

2531   – – –, ed. *SEAC souvenir: a South-East Asia Command account of the Burma Front*. Calcutta: SEAC, 1945. 2 parts.
Former MP and editor of the *Evening Standard*, and later to edit the *Daily Mail*, Owen went out to South-East Asia from 1944 to 1946 to edit the highly successful *SEAC Magazine* for the 'forgotten' Fourteenth Army and its allies in that particular Asian theatre.

2532   Owen, Louise. *The real Lord Northcliffe: some personal recollections of a private secretary, 1902–1922*. London: [1922]. 52pp.

2533   – – –.   *Northcliffe: the facts*. [Privately printed, 1931]. 334pp.
By an embittered secretary who 'went public' after Northcliffe's death. The book includes his will *in extenso*, including the revealing codicils.

2534   'Ownership of the press'. *Planning*, 21, 1955.

2535   *Oxford Times*. Centenary number. 7 Sep 1962.
Now a weekly in the Westminster Press group.

2536 Padev, Michael. *Escape from the Balkans*. London: Cassell, 1943. 256pp; Indianapolis: Bobbs-Merrill. 311pp.
The Times's man in Bulgaria, 1940.

2537 Page, Bruce, David Leitch, and Phillip Knightley. *Philby: the spy who betrayed a generation*. With an introduction by John le Carré. London: André Deutsch, 1968.
Three members of the original *Sunday Times* Insight Team probe the public-school background and ultimate treachery of the infamous Soviet spy recruited in the 1930s. He was a foreign correspondent for *The Observer* at the time of his defection.

2538 Page, Gordon. *Early days: a short history of the Guild of British Newspaper Editors*. London: GBNE, 1991.
The Guild was founded in 1946. (Its title has since been abbreviated to Guild of Editors.)

2539 Page, John Robert. *Darlington newspapers*. Darlington (Co Durham): Darlington Borough Council, 1972. viii + 31pp.

2540 Page, Tim. *Page after page*. London: Sidgwick & Jackson, 1988; New York: Atheneum, 1989. 241pp.
A harrowing photographic (and personal) record of the Vietnam War. Page is a Londoner, but his work was largely for the US press.

2541 *Paisley Daily Express*. Centenary souvenir, 1874–1974. Paisley (Strathclyde): 2 Sep 1974.
Today in the Trinity International group.

2542 *Pall Mall Gazette, The*. Last number. 27 Oct 1923.
Established in 1865 as a Liberal evening (the title was taken from Thackeray's *Pendennis*), *The Pall Mall Gazette* passed through various owners; for example, it was W.W. Astor's first British purchase (1892). Eventually it was absorbed into the *Evening Standard*, in 1923. But it was W.T. Stead in the 1880s whose professional skill and campaigning ardour made the *Gazette* a national institution.

2543 Palmer, Alasdair. 'The history of the D-Notice Committee'. *In* C.M. Andrew and D.N. Dilks, eds. *The missing dimension: governments and intelligence communities in the 20th century*. London: Macmillan, 1984. xi + 300pp.

2544 Palmer, Frederick. *With my own eyes: a personal story of battle years*. London: Jarrolds, 1934. 350pp.

2545 No entry.

2546 Palmer, Jay D. 'The selling of Reuters'. *Time*, 11 Jun 1984.
'A news agency makes news, stirs concern, and creates fortunes.' This is a long but readable feature on the latest developments in the long story of Reuters.

2547 Palmer, Michael (Beaussenat). *Des petits journaux aux grands agences: naissance de journalisme moderne, 1863–1914*. Paris: Aubier, 1963. 330pp.
Covers not only Reuters etc, but also less famous news agencies such as Dalziel's.

2548   Palmer, Michael (Beaussenat), and Jeremy Tunstall. *Liberating commu-nications: policy-making in France and Britain.* Oxford: Blackwell, 1990. 342pp.
Comparison of media development.

2549   Papas, [William]. *The press.* London: Oxford University Press, 1964.
Large-format 'tongue-in-cheek' treatment of Fleet Street in cartoon style. Papas, South African-born, became a cartoonist with *The Guardian* and *Sunday Times*.

2550   *Papers of C.P. Scott, The, 1846–1932.* Marlborough (Wilts): Adam Matthew Publications, 1991. From the John Rylands University Library of Manchester. Journalism and Politics, Series One. Part One: Political diaries, 1911–1928; and correspondence, 1870–1932. Listings and guides accompanying microfilm collections.
The first publication in full of these valuable records of the editor/proprietor of *The Manchester Guardian*, documenting his major role in both national and international affairs.

2551   'Papers of the firing-line'. *The Strand Magazine*, Nov 1916.
About trench papers, regimental and naval journals – shot through with humour even in the darkest days of World War I.

2552   Pardey, Hans. *Das Recht der englischen Presse.* Hamburg: 1928.

2553   Parisi, Frank Joseph. *From Main Street to Fleet Street: R.D. Blumenfeld and the London Daily Express, 1887–1932.* Washington (DC): Washington University Press, 1985. 401pp.
Originally a PhD dissertation.

2554   Parker, Ralph. *Moscow correspondent.* London: Muller, 1949. 304pp.
The Times's man in early post-World War II days.

2555   Parkinson, Stephen. 'Reminiscences of a chief reporter: forty years of newspaper work in the provinces'. In *Sell's Dictionary of the World's Press, 1907.* London: Sell, 1907.
  Re *The Yorkshire Post* etc.

2556   Parliamentary Press Gallery. *The story of the Press Gallery in the British Parliament.* London: Kemsley Newspapers, [1950]. 32pp.

2557   − − −. *Partners in Parliament.* London: Mercury, 1964. 76pp.
The Parliamentary Lobby Journalists and the Parliamentary Association of Overseas Correspondents are both based on the Press Gallery, which has its own secretariat. This pamphlet was the report of an enquiry into the status and working conditions of parliamentary journalists, the recommendations of which were largely accepted.

2558   Parmentier, Guillaume. 'The British press in the Suez crisis'. *Historical Journal*, 23, 1980.

2559 Parris, Matthew (Francis). *So far so good*. London: Weidenfeld & Nicolson, 1991. 279pp.
A collection of his highly regarded parliamentary sketches for *The Times*.

2560 – – –. *Look behind you!: sketches and follies from the Commons*. London: Robson Books, 1993. 216pp.

2561 Parry, D.R. *The British attitude to the second Hague Conference: a study of newspaper opinion in England, 1906–7*. Cardiff: University of Wales, 1937 (MA thesis).

2562 Parsons, [D.] Wayne. *The power of the financial press: journalism and economic opinion in Britain and America*. Aldershot (Hants): Edward Elgar, 1989. 288pp.
The first in-depth study of economic journalism and economic policy.

2563 Pate, C.W. *Strategies for survival: industrial relations aspects of new technology and restructuring in the British and Swedish newspaper industries*. Brighton: University of Sussex, 1989 (PhD thesis).

2564 Patmore, Angela. *Marje: the guilt and the gingerbread*. London: Little, Brown, 1992; revised edn, with afterword by Marjorie Proops, Warner, 1993. vi + 346pp.
The deliberate – indeed shocking – baring of her own private life by the most famous of 'agony aunts', after nearly forty years as doyenne of *Daily Mirror* columnists.

2565 Patmore, Derek (Coventry Deighton). *Balkan correspondent*. New York and London: Harper, 1941. xii + 319pp.
The author was writing for the *News Chronicle* and Exchange Telegraph in the first years of World War II.

2566 Paton, Maureen. 'The last to leave'. *UK Press Gazette*, 10 Apr 1989.
A *Daily Express* journalist marks the move of Express Newspapers' editorial departments out of Fleet Street.

2567 Patrick, Stuart. *Law for journalists*. Reading (Berks): Media Law Tutors, 1976; revised edn, on libel and contempt of court, 1988.

2568 Paul, Noël Strange, ed. *Principles for the press: a digest of Press Council decisions, 1953–84*. London: Press Council, 1985. 218pp.
A distillation under 108 subject headings of case law and press ethics. Paul was the secretary (later director) of the Council from 1968 to 1979.

2569 – – –. 'Why the British Press Council works'. *Columbia Journalism Review*, Mar–Apr 1972.

2570 Pawley, Martin. 'The star with the stripes'. *The Guardian*, 6 Feb 1989.
On Ludgate House, the future editorial office for United Newspapers (*Daily Express* etc):

'perhaps by accident – the best piece of architecture the new newspaper revolution has produced to date'.

2571   Payne, *Major* Charles T. 'England and propaganda in the Great War: Home Front myths versus trench realities'. *British Army Review*, 104, 1993.

2572   Peacocke, Emilie Hawkes (*née* Marshall). *Writing for women.* London: A. & C. Black, 1936. x + 135pp. (In Writers' and Artists' Library.)
'The story of modern journalism is that of the rise of the woman's story', claims Mrs Peacocke . . . As the climax of nearly forty years as a newspaper journalist, she became head of the woman's department of *The Daily Telegraph* in the following year.

2573   Pearce, Edward. *The senate of Lilliput.* London: Faber, 1983. 176pp.
A parliamentary sketch-writer of *The Daily Telegraph* dissects Britain's current rulers.

2574   – – –.   *Hummingbirds and hyenas.* London: Faber, 1985. 198pp.
Parliament again – and beyond, including a tilt at media people.

2575   – – –.   *Looking down on Mrs Thatcher.* London: Hamish Hamilton, 1987.
Distilling eight years in the Press Gallery for *The Daily Telegraph*.

2576   – – –.   *Election rides.* London: Faber, 1992.
As a latter-day 'Cobbett', Pearce moves round with the political circus during the 1992 general election campaign.

2577   Pearl, Cyril. *Morrison of Peking.* Sydney: Angus & Robertson, 1967. vi + 431pp.
On the remarkable 'Chinese' Morrison, the *Times* man in Peking from 1897 to 1912, and later political adviser to the Chinese Government. He advised the dissolute Empress Dowager Cixi (who died in 1908) on her dealings with the British Foreign Office – also President Sun Yat-Sen.

2578   Pearman, Hugh. 'Parallel turns'. *The Sunday Times*, 11 Apr 1993.
Architectural comparison between Nicholas Grimshaw's award-winning 'flagship' for the *Western Morning News* in Plymouth – 'you have to go back to Fleet Street in the 1930s to find a newspaper building of equivalent power' – and classical styles elsewhere.

2579   Pears, *Sir* Edwin. *Forty years in Constantinople: the recollections of Sir Edwin Pears, 1873–1915.* London: Herbert Jenkins, 1916. ciii + 390pp.
A British barrister practising in Turkey, Pears became regular (and controversial) correspondent for *The Daily News*.

2580   Pearse, Henry H.S. *Four months besieged: the story of Ladysmith.* London: Macmillan, 1900. xiv + 244pp.
The siege and relief of Ladysmith, where Pearse – a veteran of several wars – represented *The Daily News*, and also produced the *Ladysmith Bombshell* in cartoon style for the troops.

2581 Pearson, [Edward] Hesketh [Gibbons]. *Labby: the life and character of Henry Labouchere.* London: Hamish Hamilton, 1936. 318pp.

2582 Pearson, Evan. 'Focus on Fleet Street'. *Tribune,* 21 Nov 1958.

2583 Pearson, John George. *The life of Ian Fleming.* London: Jonathan Cape, 1966; Hodder & Stoughton (Coronet), 1989. 476pp.
The second of the Fleming brothers was a world best-selling novelist through the Bond books; but he had previously found material through service with Reuters (including Moscow 1933–5) and the Kemsley group (including foreign manager and the 'Atticus' column in *The Sunday Times*) as well as naval intelligence.

2584 Pearson, Kenneth, ed. *Drawn and quartered: the world of the British newspaper cartoon, 1720–1970.* London: Times Newspapers (for Newspaper Publishers Association and British Cartoonists' Association), 1970. Extended catalogue for exhibition at the National Portrait Gallery (London). Introduction by Osbert Lancaster; preface by Giles.

2585 Peattie, Charles, and Russell Taylor. *The Alex omnibus.* Harmondsworth (Middx): Penguin, 1993.
Their own strip cartoons from *The Independent,* 1987–92.

2586 Peck, David. 'How people read newspapers'. *Admap,* Apr 1974.
Informed comment by the advertisement manager of the *Daily Mail.*

2587 No entry.

2588 Peet, Hubert William. 'Changing Fleet Street'. *Sell's World's Press, 1914.*
'The coming year will witness the completion of the rebuilding of Fleet Street' . . . meaning the south side; unhappily of course the cataclysm of World War I was imminent.

– – –. *A bibliography of journalism: a guide to the books about the press and pressmen: see Reference Works section.*

2589 Peet, John. *Long engagement: memoirs of a Cold War legend.* London: Fourth Estate, 1989. 242pp.
A communist reporter whose career with Reuters ended spectacularly with an openly declared crossing to East Germany in 1950.

2590 Pegg, William E. 'The conductors of the *Western Mail*'. *Wales,* May–Dec 1911.

2591 Peirce, Gareth. 'Unleashing an uncritical press'. *The Guardian,* 15 Mar 1982.
Published crime figures attacked by a solicitor.

2592 Pemberton, *Sir* Max. *Lord Northcliffe: a memoir.* London: Hodder & Stoughton, [1922]. 250pp.
Described by Northcliffe himself as 'frivolous'.

2593   – – –.   *Sixty years ago and after*. London: Hutchinson, 1936. 282pp.
Pemberton (1863–1950) is best remembered as a popular novelist, but he also started the
London School of Journalism in 1920, and became a director of Northcliffe Newspapers.

2594   'Pendennis'. 'The honourable tradition of muckraking'. *The Observer*, 3
May 1964.
A long and interesting flashback from accounts of contemporary football scandals to
1885: child prostitution and the heyday of W.T. Stead.

2595   Pendleton, John. *How to succeed as a journalist*. London: Grant Richards,
1902.

2596   *People's Journal, The*. Centenary number. Dundee: 4 Jan 1958.
The John Leng organization founded *The People's Journal* as a national Scottish medium
alongside its newspapers serving largely Dundee. It is now published by D.C. Thomson
(weekly) from three cities.

2597   Perkin, Harold. 'The origins of the popular press'. *History Today*, Jul
1957; rptd as one chapter in his *The structured crowd: essays in English social
history*. Brighton: Harvester Press; Totowa (NJ): Barnes & Noble, 1981. x +
238pp.
The author was formerly professor of social history at Lancaster University, and his
essay sums up the conventional thinking on this subject.

2598   Perrot, Patty, ed. *Reporter: being the records of events and scenes and reflections in the London of George V from the writings of Francis Perrot*. London:
Hutchinson, 1938. 287pp.
Francis Perrot, a prominent *Manchester Guardian* journalist in the inter-war years –
quoted extensively in Ayerst's *Guardian: biography of a newspaper* – provides a first-hand
account of his life in British journalism.

2599   Perry, George. 'Pioneer of the picture scoop'. *The Sunday Times Magazine*,
7 May 1967.
A tribute on the occasion of the 125th anniversary of *The Illustrated London News*.

2600   Perry, Roland. *The exile: Burchett, reporter of conflict*. London: Heinemann,
1988. x + 258pp.
Technically, Wilfred Burchett won the libel action he took out against an Australian
senator who alleged that he was a KGB agent. But the Court also found that the article
was privileged, and Burchett – an outstanding reporter of international status – was
financially ruined and forced into exile.

2601   *Perthshire Advertiser*. Centenary number. Perth: 12 Aug 1929.

2602   – – –.   1829–1979 supplement. 7 Aug 1979.
Published today as one of Trinity International's Scottish titles.

2603   Pethick-Lawrence, Frederick Lawrence, *Baron*. *Fate has been kind*. London:
Hutchinson, 1943. 219pp.

As well as being a prominent socialist (and pro-suffragette) politician, Lawrence was owner and editor of *The Echo* from 1902 to 1905.

2604 Pethybridge, Roger William, ed. *Witnesses to the Russian Revolution.* London: Allen & Unwin, 1964. 308pp.

2605 Pettifer, James, ed. *Cockburn in Spain: despatches from the Spanish Civil War.* London: Lawrence & Wishart, 1987.
From the *Daily Mirror*, and Cockburn's own *The Week*.

2606 Petty, M. *Cambridge newspapers and the local researcher.* Cambridge: Cambridgeshire CC (Cambridgeshire Collection), 1966.

2607 Philby, Kim [Harold Adrian Russell]. *My silent war.* London: MacGibbon & Kee, 1969. xxv + 164pp; Panther, 1969, 1973, 1979. 189pp.
The journalist-traitor's own version of his double-dealing career (later reprinted in the *Sunday Express*); it has a curiously un-English ring.

2608 Phillips, Alastair. *Glasgow's Herald, 1783–1983: 200 years of a newspaper.* Glasgow: Richard Drew, 1982.
A full-scale history commissioned by the publishers.

2609 Phillips, [John] Gordon [Picton]. 'The archives of *The Times*'. *Business Archives*, Jan 1976.

2610 – – –. 'Advertising and *The Times*'. *Journal of Advertising History*, 1, Dec 1977.

2611 – – –. 'Some publications of *The Times*, 1785–1935'. *Antiquarian Book Monthly Review*, May 1978.
Three authoritative articles by the then archivist of *The Times*.

2612 Phillips, John Searles Ragland. 'British pressmen in Germany'. In *Sell's Dictionary of the World's Press, 1908.* London: Sell, 1908.
Phillips was editor of *The Yorkshire Post* (1903–19).

2613 No entry.

2614 Phillips, *Sir* Percival. *The 'red' dragon and the Black Shirts: a study of the Fascisti movement.* London: [Daily Mail], [1923].
The American-born Phillips was first a 'special' for *The Daily Telegraph* with the Greek Army in Turkey in 1897, and then covered the Spanish–American War in Cuba. One of the first group of correspondents accredited to the Western Front in World War I, he was then in the middle period of his service for the *Daily Express*; finally came twelve years as a foreign correspondent for the *Daily Mail*. This particular publication resulted from his having been sent by that newspaper to conduct an enquiry into Mussolini's Fascists in Italy. He contrasted them with the 'dragon' revolutionaries in China.

2615 Phillips, William. 'Selling *The Times*' (Part 1 to 1966; Part 2 to 1980). *Admap*, Feb–Mar 1981.

2616   – – –.   'What's in the paper' (3 parts: Fleet Street dailies; 'Shadows of the evening'; and 'The Nottingham revolution' (Christopher Pole-Carew versus the unions at the Nottingham *Evening Post*).) *Admap*, Apr–Jun 1985.

2616A   – – –.   'The Shah goes to war'. *Investors Chronicle*, 7–13 Jun 1985.
About the financial aspects of Eddy Shah's plans for his new national newspaper, suggesting plenty of backing for the project.

2617   – – –.   'What makes Rupert run?'. *Admap*, Oct 1986–Apr 1987 (series of seven).
On Rupert Murdoch's operations.

2618   – – –.   'After the exodus: newspapers' "new world" '. *Admap*, Oct–Dec 1987.

2619   – – –.   'Rupert's rocky road'. *Admap*, Apr–May 1992.
Further instalments on Murdoch and News International.

2620   Philo, Greg. 'Political advertising: popular belief and the 1982 British general election'. *Media, Culture and Society*, Jul 1993.

2621   Pickering, (*Sir*) Edward (Davies). 'Barnetson, William Denholm, Baron Barnetson'. In *Dictionary of national biography, 1981–1985*. Oxford: Oxford University Press, 1990.
An admirable summary of the remarkable career of a Scot who first came to prominence as the administrator who re-founded the German press after World War II, and (among forty-two organizations with which he was at one time concerned) rose to be chairman of United Newspapers and Reuters.

2622   – – –.   'Evans, Sir Trevor Maldwyn'. In *Dictionary of national biography, 1981–1985*. Oxford: Oxford University Press, 1990.
Evans made his name as industrial editor of the *Daily Express* and later a director of Express Newspapers.

2623   Picture Post. *The half decade; a picture history*. London: Hulton, 1950. 54pp.
A special issue, dated 7 January 1950, of 'Hulton's national weekly'. Founded in 1938 by Stefan Lorant, *Picture Post* was edited by Tom Hopkinson during its most famous decade, 1940–50. It folded in 1957.

2624   Pierce, Robert N. 'How the tabloid was born'. *Journalism Studies Review*, 2, 1973.
Northcliffe is revealed as more of an imitator of an American idea than an innovator who showed America how.

2625   – – –.   'Lord Northcliffe: transatlantic influences'. *Journalism Monographs*, 40, 1975.

2626 Pierce-Goulding, *Lieutenant-Colonel* Terence, comp. *The 11th Commonwealth Press Conference (UK), 1970.* London: Commonwealth Press Union, [1971]. xi + 168pp.
The papers delivered at this meeting, based at Gleneagles – and reprinted here – include W.D. Barnetson on 'Free sheets'; Lord Shawcross on 'Press freedom and private rights'; (Sir) Thomas Blackburn on 'Parliament, press and freedom of expression'; H.J.C. Stevens on 'Newspaper economics'; and Denis Hamilton on 'The problems of running a newspaper of record [*The Times*]'.

2627 – – –. *The 12th Commonwealth Press Conference (Hong Kong), 1974.* London: Commonwealth Press Union, [1975]. 152pp.
Contributions include Lord Shawcross on 'Pressures on the press' (with a discussion paper by J. Clement Jones); and Eric W. Cheadle: 'Newsprint: problems and prospects'.
(The proceedings of the CPU's later major conferences have not been published in book form.)

2628 Pile, Stephen. 'Hot gossip about a long-gone Hickey'. *The Sunday Times*, 22 Feb 1987.
Marking the end of the latter-day William Hickey column in the *Daily Express* with some episodes in its chequered history.

2629 Pilger, John. *Heroes.* London: Jonathan Cape, 1986. xi + 591pp; Pan, 1987.
The Australian-born Pilger made his name as a world-ranging reporter for the *Daily Mirror*, investing his stark power of description (e.g. of the Vietnam War) with utterly uncompromising and independent views (notably anti-American). The 'heroes' of Pilger's title are in the main unknown men and women, but also others, like some journalists, who have risked their jobs or even lives rather than toe the line. He is on the other hand fiercely critical of the current wave of internationally oriented newspaper proprietors.

2630 – – –. *Distant voices.* London: Vintage, 1992; Virago, 1994.
A stinging indictment: ' "Normalisation" is carried out not with tanks, but illusions, notably that of free expression.'

2631 – – –. 'Wanted: journalists who go too far'. *Journalism Studies Review*, 1982.
An impassioned anti-Establishment plea: 'Among thinking journalists, objectivity has become a dirty word.'

2632 Pilton, Patrick. *Page 3 girls.* London: The Sun, [n.d.].
Approve or not: Page 3 has long been the paper's centre of titillation.

2633 Pincher, [Harry] Chapman. *The secret offensive: a saga of deception, disinformation, subversions, terrorism, sabotage and assassination.* London: Sidgwick & Jackson, 1985.

2634 – – –. 'Press freedom and national security'. *Journalism Today* (Proceedings of the Institute of Journalists), Spring 1968.

With the *Daily Express* from 1946 as defence and science correspondent, Pincher soon earned a national reputation for important as well as exclusive exposés. It was the 'D' Notice imbroglio of 1966 that gave rise to his strongly worded lecture to the IOJ (reprinted as above).

2635   'Pioneer of all the Welsh newspapers'. *Herald of Wales*, 30 Jan 1954.
On *The Cambrian* (founded in Swansea in 1804).

2636   Plimmer, Martyn. 'Fair game – fair play'. *UK Press Gazette*, 21 Sep 1987. (In The Tabloids series.)
On the tabloids' role in investigative journalism.

2637   Plouman, S.J. *Developments in the newspaper press of Northumberland and Durham, 1906 to 1939*. Newcastle upon Tyne: University of Newcastle upon Tyne, 1980 (PhD thesis). 294pp.

2638   Pocklington, Geoffrey Richard. *The story of W.H. Smith & Son, 1820– 1920*. London: W.H. Smith, 1921; revised by F.E. Foat, 1932, 1937; rewritten by Gwen Clear, 1949, 1955.
Recounts how the first W.H. Smith bookstall was opened at Euston in 1848, and how national newspaper distribution, directed from headquarters in The Strand (London), kept pace with that of other technical developments.

2639   Pocock, Tom. *1945: the dawn came up like thunder*. London: Collins, 1983. 256pp.
In 1945, Pocock (aged nineteen) was the youngest correspondent, representing Hulton's *Leader* magazine.

2640   – – –.   *East and west of Suez: the retreat from empire*. London: Bodley Head, 1986. 208pp.
Not only Suez, but also Cyprus, Arabia and South-East Asia: the British (and French) withdrawal seen through the front-line experience of a *Times* and (London) *Standard* correspondent.

2641   – – –.   *Alan Moorehead*. London: Bodley Head, 1990; Pimlico, 1991. iii + 311pp.
A major biography of a war correspondent in the highest class, his early post-war success, and sad later years. It throws new light on the close friendship, forged on the battlefront, between Moorehead of the *Daily Express*, Alexander Clifford of the *Daily Mail*, and Christopher Buckley of *The Daily Telegraph* – known as The Trio; and on his marriage to Lucy Milner, women's pages editor of the *Express*.

2642   – – –.   'Alan Moorehead's polaroid journalism'. *Despatches* (Ministry of Defence), 4, Autumn 1993.
Moorehead's biographer spells out the resentment felt (and expressed) by the general body of war correspondents on active service towards the privileges enjoyed by the élite 'stars', exemplified by Moorehead.

2643 Political and Economic Planning (PEP). *Report on the British press.* London: PEP, 1938. 333pp. Rptd 1946. Ed (anon) Gerald Barry [then editor, *News Chronicle*].
'A survey of its current operations and problems, with special reference to national newspapers and their part in public affairs'. This is the result of three years' research by the PEP Press Group, covering production, finance, structure, personnel, law etc; it still ranks as a landmark in the field.

2644 – – –. 'Population and the press: the Royal Commission Reports'. *Planning*, 16, 301, 8 Aug 1949; followed by 'Balance sheet of the press . . .', 21, 384, 8 Aug 1955; 'Ownership of the press . . .', 21, 388, 14 Nov 1955; 'Performance of the press . . .', 22, 397, 18 June 1956; 'The work of newspaper trusts . . .', 25, 435, 24 Aug 1959.

2645 Pollock, David. 'Newspaper Publishers Association'. *In* Dennis Griffiths, ed. *The encyclopedia of the British press, 1422–1992.* Basingstoke (Hants): Macmillan, 1992.
By the director of the Association.

2646 Ponsonby, Arthur. *Falsehood in war-time.* New York: Dutton, 1929.
Although published in the USA, contains much material from the British press, with gross propaganda on German 'atrocities' in World War I.

2647 Pope, T. Michael, ed. *The book of Fleet Street.* London: Cassell, 1930. xii + 306pp.
Thirty contributed articles, and eight illustrations, on the current scene.

2648 *Popular newspapers during World War I.* Marlborough (Wilts): Adam Matthew Publications, 1993.
Listing and guide accompanying microform collection. Three parts, covering complete runs of the *Daily Express, Daily Mail, News of the World, The People,* and *Sunday Express.*

2649 *Popular newspapers during World War II.* Marlborough (Wilts): Adam Matthew Publications, 1993. Five parts, covering the same newspapers as previous entry.

2650 Porritt, Edward. 'A history of the Press Gallery'. In *Sell's Dictionary of the World's Press, 1903.* London: Sell, 1903.

2651 – – –. 'The value of political editorials'. In *Sell's Dictionary of the World's Press, 1910.* London: Sell, 1910.
Porritt is notable in having served with success on newspapers in both England – including six years in the Press Gallery – and the USA. He was an associate editor of *Sell's* for twenty-two years.

2652 Porter, Dilwyn. 'A newspaper owner in politics: Arthur Pearson and the Tariff Reform League, 1903–1905'. *Moirae* (Journal of the School of Politics, Philosophy and History, Ulster Polytechnic), 5, 1980.

2653   – – –.   'Journalist, financier, "dishonest rogue", "scoundrel": the life and times of Harry Marks, M.P.'. *Moirae*, 8, 1984.
About the adventurous career of the founder of *The Financial News*.

2654   – – –.   'Marks, Harry Hananel'. *In* David J. Jeremy, ed. *Dictionary of business biography*. London: Butterworth, for the Business History Unit, 1985.

2655   – – –.   'Pearson, Sir (Cyril) Arthur'. *In* David J. Jeremy, ed. *Dictionary of business biography*, Vol 4. London: Butterworth, for the Business History Unit, 1985.

2656   – – –.   ' "A trusted guide of the investing public": Harry Marks and the *Financial Times*, 1884–1916'. *Business History*, Jan 1986.

2657   Porter, Henry. *Lies, damned lies – and some exclusives*. London: Chatto & Windus/Hogarth Press, 1984. 211pp; Coronet, 1985. 266pp.
A *Sunday Times* man's arraignment of the Fleet Street of 1983 – a detailed study of the errors and sheer falsehoods perpetrated by the national press during that year; entertaining but with serious intent. Has a useful appendix: 'The men who run Fleet Street'.

2658   – – –.   'We lead, the rest follow'. *The Guardian (Media Guardian)*, 25 Jan 1993.
On the superior ways of *The Economist*.

2659   – – –.   'Thunderer versus the blunderer'. *The Guardian (Media Guardian)*, 28 Jun 1993.
On Peter Stothard, a new editor of *The Times* highly critical from the start of the new Conservative Government.

2660   – – –.   'Lording it from a slippery perch'. *The Guardian (Media Guardian)*, 22 Jul 1993.
'As chairman of United Newspapers, Baron Stevens of Ludgate has exhibited a steely grip and a short fuse.'

2661   Portsmouth and Sunderland Newspapers. *Getting to know Portsmouth and Sunderland Newspapers Ltd*. Sunderland: 1980.
This promotion booklet explains how Samuel Storey founded the *Sunderland Daily Echo* (1873) and what became the *Northern Daily Mail* (1877); and acquired (*inter alia*) the *Hampshire Telegraph* and *Portsmouth Evening News*. Today the *Sunderland Echo* and *The News* (Portsmouth) – both evenings – are the principal titles of the group.

2662   *Portsmouth Times, The*. Final issue. Portsmouth: 30 Mar 1928.
An unusual tribute: 1850–1928.

2663   'Posh papers, The, 1970–80'. *Political Quarterly*, Jan–Feb 1980.

2664   Postgate, Raymond William. *The life of George Lansbury*. London: Longman, 1951. xiii + 332pp.

Covers Lansbury's editorship of the *Daily Herald* and *Lansbury's Labour Weekly* in depth. Lansbury was born in 1859, and died in 1940.

2665 Postgate, Raymond William, and Aylmer Vallance. *Those foreigners: the English people's opinion on foreign affairs as reflected in their newspapers since Waterloo (1815–1937)*. London: Harrap, 1937. 295pp. Publ in the USA as *England goes to press: . . .* Indianapolis: Bobbs-Merrill, 1937. 337pp.
Wars, social and economic matters, and personalities are among the topics covered.

2666 Pound, Reginald, and (*Sir* Arthur) Geoffrey (Annesley) Harmsworth. *Northcliffe*. London: Cassell, 1959; New York: Praeger, 1960. xvi + 933pp.
A massive biography written with full family co-operation (the co-author being North-cliffe's nephew). Overall, an admirably balanced portrait.

2667 Powell, [Elizabeth] Dilys. *The Dilys Powell film reader*. London: Carcanet, 1990; Oxford: Oxford University Press, 1993. xiv + 453pp. Ed C. Cook.
An omnibus collection of some of her reviews for *The Sunday Times* from her start in 1939; the treatment is thematic. She was the paper's leading film critic for forty years, and has long ranked as Britain's senior working woman journalist.

2668 Powell, Kenneth. 'Farewell to Fleet Street'. *The Daily Telegraph*, 7 Aug 1987.
By an architectural correspondent.

2669 Power, William. 'Grub Street'. *Library Review*, 7, 55, Autumn 1943.

2670 'Power players'. *Newspaper Focus*, 1993–4 (12-part ser).
'Profiles of the 200 most influential people in British newspapers'.

2671 Prager, Arthur. *The mahogany tree: an informal history of 'Punch'*. New York: Hawthorn Books, 1979. xx + 306pp.
Contrives to be both informal and informative. Thackeray used the term 'the mahogany tree' for the famous '*Punch* table' – in fact, it is made of deal.

2672 Prebble, John (Edward Curtis). 'Britain's fabulous Fleet Street'. *Holiday* (Philadelphia), Jun 1957.

2673 *Press, The*. London: 1899–1902. Monthly.
'An independent journal for pressmen, proprietor, printer, publisher and stationer'.

2674 'Press, advertising and trade under war conditions'. *The Advertising World*, Oct 1940.

2675 Press Association. *News is our business*. London: PA, [1968].
The PA was founded, under the chairmanship of J.E. Taylor of *The Manchester Guardian*, in 1868.

2676 – – –. *The album of a nation: the many faces of Britain*. New York and London: Paddington Press, 1979.
Reproducing some 350 of the 1½ million pictures in the PA library. The agency first

transmitted photos as long ago as 1890. PA-Reuter Photos was set up as a separate enterprise in 1944; Reuters pulled out in 1965, and PA Photos once more became a department of the Press Association.

2677   Press Club. *Coming of age souvenir of the Press Club.* London: 1903. 32pp. The illustrations especially are evocative of the late Victorian era: G.A. Sala, of course, as principal founder of the club in 1882, is well featured.

2678   – – –.   *The once only.* (40th anniversary). 1922. [4pp].

2679   – – –.   *The Press Club: what it was and what it is.* [1927]. 34pp. Illustrated brochure.

2680   – – –.   *Catalogue of an exhibition illustrating the history of the English newspaper through three centuries,* comp Andrew Stewart [Club hon librarian, and later archivist]. London: Bumpus, for the Press Club, 1932. viii + 64pp. The exhibition, at Bumpus's the London booksellers, was described in *The Times* (25 May 1932) as 'fully representative', most of the exhibits coming from the club's own unique collection.

2681   – – –.   *Catalogue of an exhibition illustrating the evolution of the newspaper in England from its origins to the present day.* London: Press Club, 1935. vi + 161pp. A later display, staged at the conference of the Institute of Journalists.

2682   – – –.   *Catalogue of the Press Club Library on journalism,* comp Andrew Stewart. 3 vols. London: Press Club. Vol 1, *The evolution of the English newspaper from its origins to the present day.* 1935. v + 161pp. The 540 items in this volume are arranged in 11 parts, the majority with annotations. Vol 2, *Bibliography (histories of the press, biographies and memoirs).* 1946. iii + 78pp. Vol 3, *The wartime press.* 'Collections of newspapers, magazines, news bulletins, wall newspapers etc, printed, typed or handwritten by or for the Forces serving at home and overseas during the 1939–45 War, with explanatory notes'. 1949. iv + 63pp.

2683   – – –.   *Press Club, 1882–1942: a diamond jubilee souvenir.* London: 1942. 13pp.

2684   – – –.   *Life has its own larks: history of the Press Club, London,* comp Horace Sanders [hon librarian]. [1956]. 2 vols (unpubl MS). Private (illustrated) record. Includes a chapter on 'The early English newspaper'.

2685   'Press Club newspaper collection, The'. *The Times Literary Supplement,* 3 Oct 1935.

2686   *Press Complaints Commission: first annual report 1991.* London: PCC, 1992. 16pp. With upbeat foreword by the Commission's first chairman, Lord McGregor of Durris, stressing the small number of complaints (up to that time) against the popular national newspapers.

2687 – – –. *Submission to the review of press self-regulation.* 1992. 31pp.

2688 – – –. *Annual report 1992.* 1993.

2689 – – –. *How to complain.* 1993. 12pp.

Press Council, The. *The press and the people* (Annual reports): *see Reference Works section.*

2690 – – –. *The Aberfan inquiry and contempt of court: a statement by the Press Council.* Booklet 1. London: 1967.

2691 – – –. *Privacy, press and public: a memorandum by the Press Council.* Booklet 2. 1971.

2692 – – –. *The Press Council: outline of practice and principles.* Booklet 3. 1973.

2693 – – –. *Reforming the law of defamation: a memorandum by the Press Council.* Booklet 4. 1973.

2694 – – –. *Press conduct in the Lambton affair: a report by the Press Council.* Booklet 5. 1974.

2695 – – –. *Press conduct in the Thorpe affair: a report by the Press Council.* Booklet 6. 1980.

2696 – – –. *Press conduct in the Sutcliffe case: a report by the Press Council.* Booklet 7. 1983.

2697 – – –. *Principles for the press: a digest of Press Council decisions, 1957–1984.* 1986.

2698 – – –. *The Hillsborough inquiry: press coverage of the disaster at Hillsborough Stadium, Sheffield, on 15 April 1989.* 1989.

2699 – – –. *Report to the Council of the committee reviewing its role and function.* 1989. 119pp.

2700 – – –. *Press at the prison gates.* 1991. 210pp.
'Report of the inquiry of the Press Council into press coverage of the Strangeways Prison riot and related matters'. A detailed – and critical – survey.

2701 'Press freedom'. *Crossbow*, Spring 1977.

2702 'Press in war time, The'. In *The Newspaper Press Directory, 1945*. London: Mitchell, 1945.
This first post-war issue not surprisingly lacked an overseas section; but that lack was made up for by this very exhaustive review, compiled from a variety of sources.

2703 *Presswoman, The.* London: Women's Press Club, 1956–67.
Members' magazine (previously, and later, entitled *News Letter*).

2704   Preston, Peter (John). 'The rise and rise of a qualipop'. *In 100 years of Fleet Street*. London: Press Club, 1982.
A short but perceptive comment on the recent development of *The Guardian*, by its editor (from 1975).

2705   – – –.   'Fleet Street in the bingo age'. *Admap*, Jan 1985.

2706   – – –.   'How *The Guardian* decided to take a lesson from its Spanish pupil'. *The Guardian*, 11 Feb 1988.
On the re-design of the paper.

2707   Price, Eric. *Boy in the bath, or how to work on 13 newspapers and survive*. Bristol: Abson Books, 1982.
Memoirs of a former editor of the *Western Daily Press* etc.

2708   – – –.   'The Guild of Editors – guardians of a free press'. *Newstime*, 150th anniversary issue, Apr–May 1986.
A brief history of the Guild of British Newspaper Editors, contributed on the Newspaper Society's 150th anniversary. (The title has since been officially abbreviated to Guild of Editors.)

2709   Price, George Ward. *Extra-special correspondent*. London: Harrap, 1957. 346pp.
Recording fifty years as the *Daily Mail*'s (and *Sunday Dispatch*'s) foreign, and war, correspondent.

2710   – – –.   *Fifty years of the Daily Mail, 1896–1946*. 456pp.
Major, but unhappily unpublished, history.

2711   – – –.   'Journalism's greatest jester'. *Inky Way Annual*, Book II (1946).
On Charles Hands: from *Birmingham Daily Mail* to *The Star*, *Pall Mall Gazette*, and especially *Daily Mail* (foundation in 1896 to 1921). Hands was a serious enough character to become a director of Associated Newspapers.

2712   Price, Julius Mendes. *Six months on the Italian Front*. London: Chapman & Hall, 1917.

2713   – – –.   *On the path of adventure: the Italian Front, 1914*. London: John Lane, 1919.

2714   Price, Morgan Philips. *The truth about Allied intervention in Russia*. Moscow: 1918. 16pp.
Fifty thousand reprints of this on-the-spot exposé of 'Allied folly' by *The Manchester Guardian*'s correspondent were distributed by the Bolshevik revolutionaries: 'Let the workers of England know the truth about this great cause.' Some reached the British troops sent by Lloyd George to support the White Russians; all were condemned by the *Times* correspondent, Robert Wilton, as 'propaganda' even though he was elsewhere for most of the relevant time.

2715   – – –.   *My three revolutions*. London: Allen & Unwin, 1969. 310pp.

The revolutions of the title are the Russian revolution (*see above*); 'the first German revolution and the republic that failed' – observed by Price when *Daily Herald* correspondent in Berlin; and 'the British revolution' – he had become a Labour Member of Parliament, and used this epithet as wishful thinking.

2716 Price, R(ichard) G(eoffrey) G(eorge). *A history of Punch.* London: Collins, 1957. 384pp.
Generously illustrated with some outstanding cartoons from 1841 to 1957, this is overall the best as well as the most readable history of the magazine. It is also without any spurious sociological hindsights in the separate chapters devoted to the various editors, from dramatist and essayist Mark Lemon to television pundit Malcolm Muggeridge.

2717 Priestland, Gerald. *The dilemmas of a journalist.* Guildford (Surrey): Lutterworth Press, 1979.
'Speaking for myself', and primarily based on the author's broadcasting career, but 'a journalist is a journalist is a journalist'.

2718 – – –. *Journalism as I see it.* Guildford: Lutterworth Press, 1979.
An engaging polemic on the 'sticky-tricky' world of Fleet Street values by one of the BBC's outstanding 'explainers', who clearly prefers Lord Reith to Lord Rothermere, and puts over several 'sermons' about journalistic malpractices.

2719 – – –. *Something understood.* London: André Deutsch, 1986.

2720 Priestley, J[ohn] B[oynton]. *Instead of the trees: a final chapter of autobiogaphy.* London: Heinemann, 1977. 152pp.
Priestley (1894–1984) had published his first volume of memoirs forty years previously. His obituary in *The Times* averred: 'It is possible to say that he never wrote a dull sentence.' Recognized internationally as a truly English novelist, playwright and broadcaster, Priestley was a journalist for *The Daily News* etc early in his career.

2721 – – –. 'The value of a local press'. In *Advertisers' Aid, 1935.* London: Newspaper Society, [1935].

2722 Pringle, John (Martin) Douglas. *Have pen: will travel.* London: Chatto & Windus, 1973. x + 192pp.
First impressions by a special writer with *The Times*, 1948–52: 'The subeditors looked up in hostility from their crosswords if you dared to tiptoe into their room. The reporters were tucked up out of sight in some remote part of the building . . . gradually however I discovered that Printing House Square was full of brilliant, charming and eccentric people.' Pringle later had two periods as editor of the *Sydney Morning Herald*, but had started two stints at *The Manchester Guardian* as long before as 1934.

2723 *Printers' Register, The.* London: 1867–1956. Monthly.
Recorded *inter alia* newspaper circulation etc.

2724 Printing and Kindred Trades Federation. *National newspaper industry: a survey conducted for the Federation by the Labour Research Department.* London: 1972.
Contains a very detailed 'diary of events' during the eventful 1960s.

2725 Printing and Publishing Industry Training Board. *The compleat subeditor.* London: PPITB, 1974; 2nd edn, 1982. 2 vols.
Training package, by Bob James and Ted Bottomley.

2726 – – –.   *The compleat reporter.* London: PPITB, [1981]. Consultant eds, Alec Newman and Bob James.
Package for 'journalist trainers and their trainees'; special edition for Scotland.
  The Board was set up under the Industrial Training Act in 1968, but was wound up in 1982.

2727 Printing World. *A century in print* (Centenary supplement). London: Benn Publications, 22 Mar 1979.
Celebrating the 100-years-plus since the foundation of *British and Colonial Printer and Stationer and Newspaper Press Record* (established Dec 1878). Includes Bob James on 'Newspaper design'; and a very comprehensive chronology of printing over the century.

2728 Prior, Melton. *Campaigns of a war correspondent,* ed Samuel Levy Bensusan. London: Edward Arnold, 1912.
The absorbing memoirs of a prolific figure in the history of reporting – not only through the printed word but also through draughtsmanship. Prior (1845–1910) covered no fewer than thirteen campaigns in the front line, and has an individual memorial in St Paul's Cathedral (London). His name and fame are indelibly linked with *The Illustrated London News.*

2729 Prittie, (*Hon*) Terence (Cornelius Farmer). *Through Irish eyes.* London: Bachman & Turner, 1977. 309pp.
A former foreign and diplomatic correspondent with *The Manchester Guardian* writes in retirement about 'the view [of Europe] from the West'.

2730 Private Eye. *Private Eye's bumper book of boobs.* London: Private Eye/ André Deutsch, 1977. 192pp.
Press howlers – illustrated by Larry, Ralph Steadman and Bill Tidy.

2731 – – –.   *Rock bottom: the Gibraltar killings – government and press cover-up.* London: Pressdram, 1989.
The controversial SAS action in Gibraltar (March 1988), with its climax the shooting of three IRA terrorists, and the subsequent handling of the media.

2732 Procter, Harry. *The street of disillusion.* London: Allan Wingate, 1958. 219pp.
The autobiography of a reporter whose experience successively with the *Daily Mirror, Daily Mail* and *Sunday Pictorial* led to his discovery of the 'boomerang' effect of highly paid but needlessly sensational reporting – which can 'bounce back' most damagingly.

2733 *Production Journal.* London: Newspaper Society, 1958–. 6 per year.
For those concerned with newspaper management and production, new equipment etc.

2734 Proops, Marjorie (*née* Rebecca Marjorie Israel, later Rayle). *Dear Marje* . . . London: André Deutsch, 1976.
Culled from the famous Proops 'agony' column in the *Daily Mirror* (but *see* Patmore, Angela).

2735 'Proprietors for 143 years'. *The Newspaper World*, 7 Jan 1939. (In The Oldest Newspapers series.)
About the Henderson family's long connection with the *Belfast News-Letter* – now a free paper alongside the paid-for *Ulster News Letter*.

2736 Prosser, David Russell. *The British press in mid-century*. Cardiff: 1957.
By the editor of the *Western Mail*, 1947–56.

2737 *Protection of military information, The: government response to the Report of the Study Group on censorship*. London: HMSO (White Paper), 1985. Cmnd 9499.
The guiding principle for journalists in the case of any future war operations should, in this considered view of the Thatcher Government, be supportive co-operation.

2738 *Provincial press, The: report of a Productivity Team representing the British provincial press which visited the United States of America in 1951*. London: Anglo-American Council on Productivity (for the Productivity Team), 1952.

2739 *Public Ledger, The.* Bicentenary supplement. London: 12 Jan 1960. 32pp. With a partial reprint of no 1 (12 Jan 1760).
Founded by John Newbery – already a notable publisher – and others, *The Public Ledger* has appeared ever since, without interruption. It is therefore the oldest surviving English-language daily publication with a continuous history. Giants like Goldsmith, Sterne and Thackeray contributed in its early days as a 'literary' newspaper; today it is a trade and commercial periodical sold by subscription only.

2740 *Publishing History*. Cambridge, and Teaneck (NJ) (later Alexandria (VA)): Chadwyck-Healey, 1977–. 2 per year.
On the 'social, economic and literary history of book, newspaper and magazine publishing'.

2741 Punch. *Mr Punch: an interesting talk about himself and his renowned contributors*. London: [1910]. 52pp. 'Price one penny'.
An early – and most effective – promotion piece.

2742 Punch. '*Punch* is now one hundred years old'. 16 Jul 1941.
Celebration, in the newsprint-starved days of World War II, was somewhat muted. But this issue contains a facsimile of the cover of no 1, and a splendid cartoon by E.H. Shepard: 'Looking backward: here's to you all, and to those who have followed you' . . . nine of the greatest men being toasted by Mr Punch at the *Punch* Table.

2743 – – –. 125th anniversary number. 13 Jul 1966.
Contains a complete reprint of the first issue of 1841; and contributions by major current *Punch* writers (notably A.P. Herbert) and cartoonists.

2744 Punch. *Cartoon history*. (Ser) 11, 18, 25 Mar, 1, 8 Apr 1987.

2745   − − −.   *The Punch cartoon album: 150 years of classic cartoons*, ed Amanda-Jane Doran: with a foreword by Miles Kington. London: Collins/ Grafton, 1990. 228pp.
Three hundred selected from the half a million of so published in the magazine over the century and a half.

2746   − − −.   *Still crazy after all these years!: Punch at 150*. 1991. 34pp.
Illustrated promotion booklet.

2747   *Punch*. 150th anniversary edition. 17 Jul 1991.
But that for 8 April 1992 was sadly the last issue.

2748   Purves, Libby. 'Brave fronts, front women and front lines'. *The Times*, 21 Jan 1991.
On women war correspondents: harks back to *The Times*'s own Flora Shaw (later Lady Lugard), who rose to be the paper's first Colonial editor.

2749   − − −.   'How the PCC took the sting out of my fury'. *The Times*, 6 Apr 1994.
Admiration for the Press Complaints Commission and their sympathetic (and eventual upholding) of her personal complaint against *Today* of misrepresentation.

2750   Rabinovitch, Dina. 'Birthday greetings . . . *The Observer Mag* comes of age'. *UK Press Gazette*, 9 Sep 1985.
Marking the twenty-first anniversary of *Observer* (the newspaper's magazine), and reviewing the 'state of the art'.

2751   *Race and the press: four essays*. London: Runnymede Trust, [1971]. 60pp.
By Clement Jones, Peter Harland, Hugo Young, and Harold Evans. With an introduction by Lord Devlin.

2752   Rafferty, Ken. *That's what they said about the press*. New York: Vantage Books, 1975. 137pp.
Contains more than five hundred quotations, some of them British.

2753   Raleigh, *Sir* Walter Alexander. *The war and the press*. Oxford: Clarendon Press, 1918. 19pp.
A reprint of a lecture given at Eton College by a notable literary scholar who was then engaged on the official history of the RAF.

2754   Ralph, Julian. *War's brighter side*. London: Pearson, 1901; New York: Appleton, 1901.
By an American-born 'special' for the *Daily Mail* writing about the South African War.

2755   Randall, Michael (Bennett). *The funny side of the Street*. London: Bloomsbury, 1988. 192pp.
By a former editor of the *Daily Mail* (1963–6) – with a close-up of the (2nd) Lord Rothermere, among others. Later he held senior editorial appointments at *The Sunday Times*.

2756 Ransome, Arthur (Michell). *Bohemia in London*. Illustrated by Fred Taylor. London: Chapman & Hall, 1907. x + 284pp; Stephen Swift, 1912. xii + 293pp.
About the author's early days in Fleet Street and off duty in the Press Club.

2757 – – –. *Six weeks in Russia in 1919*. London: Allen & Unwin, 1919. Rptd London: RedWords, 1992. With an introduction by Paul Foot. Publ in the USA as *Russia in 1919*. New York: 1919.

2758 – – –. *The crisis in Russia*. London: Allen & Unwin, 1921. Rptd London: RedWords, 1992. With an introduction by Paul Foot.
Ransome's service as *Daily News* correspondent in Russia (1913–19) was latterly alongside the Bolsheviks. He later served *The Manchester Guardian* in the Middle and Far East, and then wrote a regular weekly column before turning to his famous stories for children.

2759 – – –. *The autobiography of Arthur Ransome*. With a prologue and epilogue by Rupert Hart-Davis. London: Jonathan Cape, 1976. 368pp; Century, 1985.
An unfinished memoir of an eventful life.

2760 Raphael, Adam. *M'learned friends*. London: W.H. Allen, 1990. Publ in pbk as *Grotesque libels*. London: Corgi, 1993.
On libel, by the executive editor of *The Observer*.

2761 Rappaport, Armin. *The British press and Wilsonian neutrality*. London: Oxford University Press; Stanford (CA): Stanford University Press, 1951. 162pp.

2762 *Rare radical and labour periodicals of Great Britain*. Brighton: Harvester Microform; later Reading: Research Publications (International).
Two series, incorporating several esoteric newspaper titles, from both the nineteenth and the twentieth centuries.

2763 Rawling, Gerald. 'Swindler of the century'. *History Today*, Jul 1993.
On Horatio Bottomley, 'journalist, publisher, MP and con-man'.

2764 Raymond, E.T. (pseudonym of Edward Raymond Thompson). *Uncensored celebrities*. London: T. Fisher Unwin, 1918. 244pp.
Those covered include Northcliffe; *The Morning Post* and H.A. Gwynne; and Beaverbrook.

2765 – – –. *Portraits of the new century: the first ten years*. London: Benn, 1928. 336pp.
Including 'Press magnates' and 'Five editors': J.A. Spender, Gardiner, Garvin, Strachey, H.W. Massingham. E.R. Thompson was Beaverbrook's first editor of the *Evening Standard*, from 1923 until his death in 1928.

2766 Rayner, J. 'Features for two million'. *Typography*, 2, 1936.
Daily Express make-up.

2767　Read, Donald. *The power of news: the history of Reuters, 1849–1989*. Oxford: Oxford University Press, 1992. xv + 431pp; pbk, 1994.
A major work of scholarship, produced with the aid of an in-house team.

2768　– – –. 'Sir Roderick Jones and Reuters: rise and fall of a news emperor'. *In* Derek Fraser, ed. *Cities, class and communication: essays in honour of Asa Briggs*. London: Harvester Wheatsheaf, 1990.

2769　– – –. 'War news from Reuters: Victorian and Edwardian reporting', *Despatches* (Ministry of Defence), 4, 1993.

2770　– – –. 'Chancellor, Sir Christopher John Howard'. In *Dictionary of national biography, 1985–1990*. Oxford: Oxford University Press (in preparation).

2771　'Read all about it'. *Which?*, Aug 1988.
'A consumer's guide to the national daily newspapers': an analysis over September–October 1987 by Glasgow University Media Group.

2772　Reading, Bryan. *Cruel Britannia: town and country cartoons*. London: Park/McDonald, 1993.
From the *Daily Mail, The Guardian* etc.

2773　*Reading Mercury, The*. Bicentenary (historical supplement). Reading: 7 Jul 1923.
The history of *The Reading Mercury* (established in 1723) is indelibly linked with the name of John Newbery, who began his unique career as a publisher by acquiring and editing the paper. It later became *The Berkshire Mercury*, and finally a weekly simply titled *The Mercury*.

2774　Readings, Reginald. 'The indexing of *The Times*'. *British Library Newspaper Library Newsletter*, 7, Apr 1987.

2775　'Reconversion of the *Daily News*, The'. *The Review of Reviews*, 23, 1901.
Probably the work of W.T. Stead (owner and editor of *The Review of Reviews*).

2776　Reddaway, W.B. 'The economics of newspapers'. *The Economic Journal*, Jun 1963.

2777　Redden, Richard. 'Untying the web of weekly ownership'. *The Media Reporter*, Summer 1981.
Notably concerned with the complexities of the British Electric Traction (BET) group.

2778　Redpath, William. *The war of the newspaper giants*. Close-up by the editor-designate in Newcastle upon Tyne for Allied Newspapers (controlled by the Berry brothers) on the sales war instigated in 1929 by Lord Rothermere and his newly established Northcliffe Newspapers. The latter launched, as the first of a projected series, the *Newcastle Evening World* in head-to-head rivalry to Allied's well-established *Evening Chronicle*. The upshot within three years was

Rothermere's defeat and the take-over of the *Evening World*; only its sister-paper in Bristol survived, under joint ownership.

2779   Redwood, [William Arthur] Hugh. *Bristol fashion*. London: Latimer House, 1948. 281pp.
Memoirs of a journalist well known both in Bristol and in London.

2780   Reed, Douglas. *Insanity fair*. London: Jonathan Cape; and (with subtitle *A European cavalcade*) New York: Random House, 1938. 420pp.
About Europe in the 1930s, as seen and reported on by *The Times*'s assistant correspondent in Berlin and (1935–8) Central European chief in Vienna. Reed's highly charged anti-appeasement opinions caused his abrupt move to the *News Chronicle*, although his base remained in Europe.

2781   – – –.   *Disgrace abounding*. London: Jonathan Cape, 1939. 447pp.
A warning sequel.

2782   – – –.   *From smoke to smother, 1939–1948*. London: Jonathan Cape, 1948. 317pp.

2783   – – –.   *Far and wide*. London: Jonathan Cape, 1951. 398pp.
On the post-war scene.

2784   Reed, Frederick William. *The Queen Mother and her family*. London: W.H. Allen, 1980.
As chief photographer of the *Daily Mirror*, Reed accompanied many Royal tours worldwide.

2785   – – –.   *Freddie Reed's Royal tours: 50 years of Royal photographs*. Newton Abbot (Devon): David & Charles, 1989. 128pp.
Distilled from sixty-four Royal tours on behalf of the *Daily Mirror*.

2786   Reed, Jane. 'Ethel to Elysium: "drop dead" '. *British Journalism Review*, 3, 1, 1992.
As former managing director of *Today*, as well as editor of leading women's magazines, stoutly defends the content as well as the massive circulation (the highest in Europe) of Britain's national tabloids: 'campaigning and investigative, as well as entertaining'.

2787   Rees, Nigel. *The newsmakers*. London: Headline, 1987. 380pp.
A novel.

2788   – – –.   *'The Daily Telegraph'*. *The Listener*, 27 Feb 1986.
'A reassuring raft on the wild sea of events' . . . adapted from Rees's broadcast in the BBC Pillars of Society series, which included several interviews with present and immediate past management and staff.

2789   Rees-Mogg, William (*Baron*). *Picnics on Vesuvius: stops towards the millennium*. London: Sidgwick & Jackson, 1993.
A collection of Rees-Mogg's columns in *The Independent* over six years. He has since returned to *The Times* as a regular commentator on issues of the day.

2790 — — —. 'The political journalist'. In *Inside journalism*, ed R. Bennett-England. London: Peter Owen, 1967.
Written when Rees-Mogg was taking up his long and distinguished period (to 1981) as editor of *The Times*. He had previously held senior positions at the *Financial Times* and *The Sunday Times*.

2791 — — —. 'Changing times at the helm of the Thunderer'. *The Independent*, 27 Jul 1992; rptd under title 'The changing face of the British broadsheet newspapers'. *CPU News*, Sep 1992.
Written when Peter Stothard had just taken over the editorship of *The Times*.

2792 *Referee, The.* Jubilee number. 21 Aug 1927.
Founded by Ashton Dilke and Henry Sampson in 1877 in association with *The Weekly Dispatch*, initially to cover sport and the theatre. They built up a notable staff who preserved an independent standpoint. It eventually became the *Sunday Referee*, and was incorporated into the *Sunday Chronicle* in 1939.

2793 Regan, Simon. *Rupert Murdoch: a business biography*. Sydney and London: Angus & Robertson, 1976.
Disappointingly thin – even on Murdoch's early Australian enterprises – and now outdated.

2794 *Regional Extra.* London: Regional Newspaper Advertising Bureau. 1980–8.
The main periodical of the RNAB during its eight-year existence: the Bureau was then absorbed into the Newspaper Society.

2795 Regional Newspaper Advertising Bureau. *Where?*: *regional press marketing handbook*. London: RNAB, 1985. xxi + 1,166pp. Supplement, 1986.
Detailed information on virtually all the paid-for and more than half the free-distribution titles in the UK.

2796 — — —. *Front page news*. London: RNAB, 1986. 2 parts, total 80pp. Souvenir exhibition catalogue.
'Significant happenings as recorded in the pages of Britain's regional newspapers 1783–1986': a broadsheet-format celebration of the foundation in 1962 of the Evening Newspaper Advertising Bureau (a predecessor of the RNAB) and of the Newspaper Society's 150th anniversary.

2797 Reid, Fred(erick). 'Keir Hardie and the *Labour Leader*, 1893–1903'. *In* Jay Winter, ed. *The working class in modern British history: essays in honour of Henry Pelling*. Cambridge: Cambridge University Press, 1983. xi + 365pp.

2798 Repington, *Lieutenant-Colonel* Charles à Court (formerly à Court, Charles). *The soul of a nation*. London: 1904.
Published at the outset of the author's long commitment as military (as opposed to war) correspondent for *The Times*, this work (a reprint) concerned Japanese Bushido militarism, as demonstrated in the Russo-Japanese War.

2799 – – –. *The war in the Far East, 1904–1905*. London: John Murray, 1905. xvi + 656pp.
A detailed volume of observational reportage.

2800 – – –. *Vestigia*. London: Constable, 1919; New York. vi + 373pp.
'A book of reminiscences from schooldays to the eve of the European War'. It is significant that Repington, in the words of *The Times's* official historian, 'in many ways the most influential, and certainly the most controversial, of the writers on the paper's staff', was described by another commentator as 'the twenty-third member of the Cabinet'. There was an outcry in Parliament because he was appointed simultaneously editor of *The Army Review* – an arrangement quickly dropped.

2801 – – –. *The First World War, 1914–1918: a diary*. London: Constable, 1920. 2 vols.
Deals exclusively with Repington's *Times* service, even though early in 1918 continual disagreement with Dawson, the editor, had led to Repington's resignation and move to *The Morning Post*.

2802 – – –. *After the war: a diary*. London: Constable, [1922]. xv + 480pp.
'London–Paris–Rome–Athens–Prague–Vienna–Budapest–Bucharest–Berlin–Sofia–Coblenz–New York–Washington'.

2803 *Report from Select Committee on Parliamentary Debates*. London: Houses of Parliament, 1907. HC 239.
As a result of this report, the *Official Report (House of Commons)* was established (January 1909), with staff appointed by the House itself. The name 'Hansard' was returned to the title-page in 1943. There is a separate *Hansard* for the House of Lords.

2804 *Report of the trial of Sir Edward Russell at the Liverpool Assizes for criminal libel in the Liverpool Post and Mercury, A*. Liverpool: 1905 . . . plus the proceedings on the application for a rule before the Divisional Court.
Russell, at the height of his fame as editor of the *Liverpool Post and Mercury*, was arraigned for libel against the Liverpool magistrates.

2805 Reporters Sans Frontières. *Freedom of the press throughout the world*. London: John Libbey & Co. Annual report.
An independent source, the latest (1994) report covering attacks on press freedom in one hundred and forty-nine countries.

2806 Reuters. *Reuters in Aachen*. Aachen (Germany): Oct 1962.
Facsimile typescript (plus set of photos and press cuttings) commemorating the first meeting of the Reuters Board outside the UK since the company's foundation in Aachen in 1850.

2807 'Reuters' centenary'. *World's Press News*, 13 Jul 1951.
As full a tribute as could be managed under the strict newsprint restrictions of the day.

2808   *Reuters Holdings Plc: offer by sale by tender by S.G. Warburg & Co. Ltd,
and N.M. Rothschild & Sons Limited.* London: (May) 1984.
This prospectus, widely published both in the financial press and as a separate document,
contained historical background to the company as well as detailed financial information.

2809   *Review of press self-regulation.* Report by Sir David Calcutt. London:
HMSO (for Department of National Heritage), 1993. Cm 2135. xiv + 88pp.
The main conclusion of this second Calcutt inquiry into press conduct was in fact that
the Press Complaints Commission (set up after the first Calcutt Report) had failed in
its purpose, and should be replaced by a statutory press tribunal. This was not accepted,
but the other principal recommendations – to make specific examples of 'physical intrusion' and 'covert surveillance' criminal offences – were approved by the Government as
desirable.

2810   Review of Reviews, The. *His Majesty's Public Councillors: the editors of the
London daily papers.* London: Nov 1904.

2811   *Review of Reviews, The.* 500th number. 81, 1931.
After leaving *The Pall Mall Gazette* in 1890, the indefatigable W.T. Stead soon started
(with George Newnes) *The Review of Reviews.* Its editorial 'mix' of news digest with
original material proved a most successful venture ('200,000 per month – the most widely
circulated political and literary periodical in the world'). It also had European, US and
Australasian editions. The London edition survived until 1936.

2812   Reynolds, Frank. *Humorous drawings for the press.* London: Methuen,
1947. 85pp.
The distinctive Reynolds characters first appeared in *Punch* in 1906, and continued to
entertain throughout both world wars.

2813   Reynolds, Michael. 'The war correspondent's job'. *Army Quarterly*, Jan
1950.

2814   *Reynolds's Weekly Newspaper.* Centenary supplement, 1850–1950. London:
Reynolds News, 7 May 1950.
References to G.W.M. Reynolds and his famous paper include that in *The London
Journal* (which he had edited), 29 November 1845; his obituary in *The Bookseller*, 2 July
1879; an entry by F. Boase in the *Dictionary of national biography*; and by M. Summers,
in *The Times Literary Supplement*, 4 July 1942.

2815   Rhodes, Peter. *The loaded hour: a history of the Express & Star.* Hanley
Swan (Hereford & Worcester): SPA (with Express & Star), 1992.
Brings up to date the success story of the newspaper and its sisters in the Midland News
Association group, still under the control of the founding Graham family. The 'loaded
hour' in the title is taken from Kipling's poem 'The press' (1917).

2816   Richards, Anthony. *Law for journalists.* Plymouth (Devon): Macdonald &
Evans, 1977.
Now inevitably dated.

2817 Richards, Huw. *Constraint, conformity and control: the taming of the Daily Herald, 1921-1930*. Milton Keynes (Bucks): Open University, 1993 (PhD thesis).

2818 – – –. 'The *Daily Herald*, 1912-64'. *History Today*, Dec 1981.

2819 – – –. 'News coverage – or bingo?'. *Journalism Studies Review*, 1983. Deals with the pre-war circulation battle of the *Daily Herald*.

2820 Richardson, Joseph Hall. *From the City to Fleet Street: some journalistic experiences*. London: Stanley Paul, 1927. 302pp. By a crime journalist who worked on *The Daily Telegraph* for forty years – a mine of information on that newspaper.

2821 Richmond, Lesley, and Bridget Stockford, comps. 'The Press Association'. In *Company archives*. Aldershot (Hants): Gower, 1985. Notable among the records are those on the Spanish Civil War, the 1936 Abdication crisis, and 'D' Notices.

2822 *Richmond and Twickenham Times*. Special centenary issue. Twickenham (Middx): 15 May 1973. Weekly owned by the Dimbleby family.

2823 Rickard, Graham. *Great press barons*. Hove (E Sussex): Wayland, 1981. Featuring Hearst, Beaverbrook, Axel Springer, Rupert Murdoch.

2824 Riddell, George Allardice Riddell, *1st Baron. The story of the Western Mail*. Cardiff: Western Mail, [1929]. The *Western Mail* was founded by the (3rd) Marquess of Bute in 1869, Riddell being instrumental in securing its future shortly afterwards. He had relinquished his interests long before writing this pamphlet.

2825 – – –. *Lord Riddell's war diary, 1914-1918*. London: Nicholson & Watson, 1933. xi + 387pp. Significant material on government/press relations; Riddell was a persistent critic of the Official Press Bureau.

2826 – – –. *Lord Riddell's intimate diary of the Press Conference and after, 1918-1923*. London: Gollancz, 1933. xii + 435pp; New York: 1934. A close associate of Lloyd George, then Prime Minister, Riddell explains his role as the Government's press liaison officer; in effect, poacher turned gamekeeper.

2827 – – –. *More pages from my diary, 1908-1914*. London: Country Life, 1934. xii + 238pp. In pre-World War I days, Riddell (1865-1934) directed the fortunes of two famous papers: not only the *Western Mail* but the *News of the World* as well; and also became chairman of the Newnes and Pearson publishing companies. This last of his three valuable diaries harks back to that period.

2828 – – –. *The Riddell diaries: a selection, 1908–23*, ed John M. McEwan. London: Athlone Press, 1986. xviii + 430pp.
Extra material here, notably on press censorship in World War I, and on Lloyd George's acquisition of *The Daily Chronicle*.

2829 Riddell, H.G. *The English press and the Moroccan crisis of 1911*. Liverpool: University of Liverpool, 1949 (MA thesis).

2830 Riddell, Peter. 'Lobby uncertain on threshold of its second century'. *Financial Times*, 17 Jan 1984.

2831 Righter, Rosemary. *IPI – the undivided word: a history of the International Press Institute*. Zürich: IPI, 1976. 155pp.
The author was then with *The Sunday Times*.

2832 – – –. *Whose news?: politics, the press and the Third World*. London: Burnett Books/André Deutsch, for IPI, 1978. 272pp.
Discusses at length (and critically) the role of Unesco, while also dissecting the Third World activities of Reuters and the other world agencies.

2833 Righyni, S.L. 'Typography of the provincial press'. *Typography*, 6, 1938.

2834 – – –. 'Provincial newspapers in transition'. *Alphabet and Image*, Jan 1946.

2835 Ritchie, Jean. *150 years of true crime: stories from the News of the World*. London: Michael O'Mara Books, 1993.
Highlights the cases covered by such famous crime reporters as Norman Rae (over two thousand stories in his thirty years with the paper).

2836 'Ritchie, Findlay and Law'. *The Newspaper World*, 28 Jan 1939. (In The Oldest Newspapers series.)
William Ritchie was a founder of *The Scotsman* in 1817; his brother John and then members of the Findlay and Law families were the paper's owners over the next century and beyond.

2837 Road, Alan, ed. *Newspaper dragon*. Swansea: C. Davies, 1977. 194pp.
'Extracts from newspapers covering three decades of Welsh life'.

2838 Robb, John (pseudonym of Norman Robson). *Front page story: the drama of newspapers*. London: Hutchinson, 1960. 124pp.

2839 Robbins, Alan Pitt. *Newspapers to-day*. London: Oxford University Press, 1956. 142pp. (In the Pageant of Progress series.)

2840 – – –. 'The lobby correspondent'. In *Journalism, by some members of the craft*. London: Pitman, 1932, for the Institute of Journalists.
Alan Pitt Robbins (1888–1967), younger son of Sir Alfred, made his name as parliamen-

tary correspondent of *The Times*; he later became foreign news editor, and is also remembered as first secretary (1953–60) of the General Council of the Press (later Press Council), and as president of the Institute of Journalists.

2841 – – –. 'Newspaper'. Entry in *Encyclopaedia Britannica*, 14th edn, revised, 1973.

2842 Robbins, *Sir* Alfred (Farthing). *The press*. London: Benn, 1928. 80pp. (In Benn's Six-Penny Library.)

2843 – – –. 'Evening papers: their evolution'. *Notes and Queries*, 14 Apr 1917.

2844 Robbins, [Alfred] Gordon. *Fleet Street Blitzkrieg diary*. London: Benn, 1944. 64pp.
Gordon Robbins (1883–1944), elder son of Sir Alfred, preceded his younger brother Alan as parliamentary correspondent of *The Times*, and later became chairman of Benn Brothers, the publishers.

2845 Robbins, Harry C. 'The Press Association and its work'. *The Nineteenth Century and After*, Jan 1925.
H.C. Robbins, who had joined the PA in 1894, succeeded his father Sir Edmund as general manager in 1917; he remained in that position until 1938.

2846 Robbins, Jan C. 'The paradox of press freedom: a study of British experience'. *Journalism Quarterly*, 44, 1967.

2847 Robbins, Keith. 'Public opinion, the press and pressure groups'. *In British foreign policy under Sir Edward Grey*, ed F.H. Hinsley. Cambridge: Cambridge University Press, 1977.

2848 'Robert Maxwell: the authorised life'. *The Media Reporter*, Autumn 1984.
A brief factual biography of Maxwell, culminating in the gaining of control by his company (Pergamon) of Mirror Group Newspapers in 1984.

2849 Roberts, Glenys. *Metropolitan myths: foibles and fetishes of Londoners based on popular articles in the London Standard*. London: Gollancz, 1982. xxi + 116pp.
The paper from which these articles are taken, the *Evening Standard* (q.v.), first reverted to its old title of *The Standard* in 1981, after the merger in the previous year with the *Evening News*, under the joint ownership of Associated Newspapers and the Trafalgar House group.

2850 – – –. *Hard pressed*. London: Quartet Books, 1989. 286pp.
'A comic novel in which an unlettered girl reporter is appointed editor of England's oldest newspaper' ... based (loosely) on the author's first-hand experience with the *Sunday Express* and other nationals.

2851   Robertson, Geoffrey. *People against the press: an enquiry into the Press Council.* London: Quartet Books, 1983. 182pp.
An indictment resulting from an enquiry (set up on behalf of the Campaign for Press and Broadcasting Freedom) by a group of journalists, academics, lawyers and trade unionists. Robertson presents a detailed case for giving the Press Council legal powers and on the need for a Press Ombudsman.

2852   Robertson, Geoffrey, and Alexander Surtees Chancellor. 'Reuters: the price of greed'. *The Spectator*, 22 Oct 1983.
An article warning of the obstacles confronting a public flotation of Reuters; in the event, these were overcome. Chancellor writes as editor of *The Spectator* and son of Sir Christopher Chancellor, former general manager of Reuters.

2853   Robertson, Geoffrey, and Andrew G.L. Nicol. *Media law: the rights of journalists and broadcasters.* London: Oyez Longman, 1984. xxxvi + 403pp. 3rd edn, Harmondsworth (Middx): Penguin, 1992. With amended sub-title: *the rights of journalists, broadcasters and publishers.* Sage, 1985. 448pp.
A comprehensive reference source which is also full of press history: 'The blind Goddess of Justice seems to raise her sword against investigative journalism while her other hand fondles the Sunday muck-raker.'

2854   Robertson, Grace. *Grace Robertson: photojournalist of the 1950s.* London: Virago, 1989. 127pp.
Outstanding work for *Picture Post* for eight years, in its heyday.

2855   Robertson-Glasgow, R(aymond) C(harles). *Crusoe on cricket: the collected cricket writings of R.C. Robertson-Glasgow.* London: Alan Ross, 1966. 321pp; Michael Joseph (Pavilion Books), 1985. 328pp. Introduction by Alan Ross.
The author was cricket correspondent of *The Observer* for eighteen years.

2856   Robertson Scott, John William. *Faith and works in Fleet Street: an editor's convictions after sixty-five years in journalism.* London: Hodder & Stoughton, 1947. xviii + 143pp.

2857   – – –.   *'We' and me: memories of four eminent editors I worked with, a discussion by editors of the function of editing, and a candid account of the founding and the editing, for twenty-one years, of my own magazine.* London: W.H. Allen, 1956. 239pp.
The four editors are Alfred Spender of *The Westminster Gazette*, Edmund Garrett of *The Pall Mall Gazette* and *The Westminster Gazette*, H.W. Massingham ('Boanerges') of *The Star* and *The Daily Chronicle*, and Ernest Parke of *The Star*. Accounts of the relations between them and their employers are particularly valuable elements in the narrative. Robertson Scott's own brainchild was *The Countryman*.

2858   Robinson, Gertrude. *News agencies and world news.* Fribourg (Switzerland): University Press of Fribourg, 1981.

2859 Robinson, *Sir* Harry Perry. *The turning point: the Battle of the Somme.* London: Heinemann, 1917. ix + 291pp.
A leading *Times* correspondent on the Western Front and elsewhere.

2860 Robinson, Jeffrey. *The risk takers: portraits of money, ego and power.* London: Allen & Unwin, 1985; Unwin Paperbacks, 1986. viii + 311pp.
Gossipy profiles, including Rowland and Maxwell.

2861 – – –. *The risk takers – five years on.* London: Mandarin, 1990. viii + 470pp.
The same subjects – plus a few new ones.

2862 Robinson, Lionel. *Boston's newspapers.* Boston (Lincs): Richard Kay Publications, 1974. vi + 65pp. (In the History of Boston series.)

2863 Roby, Kinley. *The King, the press and the people: a study of Edward VIII.* London: Barrie & Jenkins, 1975. 335pp.

2864 *Rochdale Observer.* Jubilee number. Rochdale (Lancs): 17 Feb 1906.

2865 – – –. Centenary supplement. 18 Feb 1956.

2866 Rogers, Edmund Dawson. *The life and experiences of Edmund Dawson Rogers.* [1911].
Rogers was editor of the *Eastern Daily Press* (established in Norwich in 1870), and later first manager of the National Press Agency. This autobiography was reprinted from the magazine *Light*.

2867 Rogers, (*Sir*) Frank. 'The provincial press and its future'. *UK Press Gazette*: souvenir issue, 3 Jun 1985.
Highlights the current activities of the author's own group in the overall regional context (chairman of EMAP and previously a managing director in the national sphere).

2868 Rolph, C.H. (pseudonym of Cecil Rolph Hewitt). *Kingsley: the life, letters and diaries of Kingsley Martin.* London: Gollancz, 1973; Harmondsworth (Middx): Penguin, 1978.
A very readable 'warts and all' biography, by a former close colleague, of one of the most effective editors of a political weekly – *The New Statesman* – in the history of British journalism. It is a useful key to some obscure passages in Martin's own autobiography.

2869 Rolston, Bill, ed. *The media and Northern Ireland: covering the Troubles.* Basingstoke (Hants): Macmillan, 1991. xi + 229pp.

2870 'Romance of the *Daily Mirror*, The'. *Advertising News*, 2 Jun 1905.
Interesting in being an assessment nineteen months after the *Mirror's* initial disastrous launch.

2871 Rook, Jean. *Rook's eye view.* London: Express Books, 1979.
Popularly known as 'the first lady of Fleet Street', Rook arrived at the *Daily Express* via *The Sun*, the *Daily Sketch*, and the *Daily Mail*.

2872   − − −.   *The cowardly lioness*. London: Sidgwick & Jackson, 1989; Pan, 1990. 199pp.
Autobiography, ten years on.

2873   − − −.   'We're the 21st century *Express*'. *Daily Express*, 8 Apr 1989.
Express Newspapers' senior woman journalist reports from her new desk in Ludgate House: 'Technically, I'm still the First Lady of Fleet Street. Hi-technically, I suppose I'm now the Bitch of Blackfriars.'

2874   − − −.   'Farewell to Fleet Street'. *Daily Express* (special souvenir front page), 17 Nov 1989.
Marking the last edition of any newspaper printed in Fleet Street itself. No 121 had been the home of Express Newspapers for nearly ninety years.

2875   Rose, Kenneth. 'The growth of freedom in the reporting of parliamentary debates'. *Gazette*, 2, 4, 1957.
A paper read at a Journalism Convention in Trieste by a senior *Daily Telegraph* representative.

2876   Rosen, Murray. *The Sunday Times thalidomide case: contempt of court and the freedom of the press*. With a foreword by Lord Scarman. London: Writers & Scholars Educational Trust, for the British Institute of Human Rights, 1979. 130pp.
An outside view of the highly successful investigative campaign by *The Sunday Times* on behalf of the children who had suffered as a result of their mothers taking the drug thalidomide during pregnancy.

2877   Rosie, George. 'The secret life of the comic kings'. *The Sunday Times Magazine*, 29 Jul 1973.
Hard-hitting exposé of the D.C. Thomson publishing house, for long rigorously non-union and 'non-ABC' (Audit Bureau of Circulations).

2878   − − −.   'The warlocks of British publishing'. In *The D.C. Thomson bumper fun book*. Edinburgh: Paul Harris Publishing, 1977.
Again, the lid off the D.C. Thomson empire – newspapers included.

2879   − − −.   'A splash in black and white'. *The Independent*, 19 Aug 1987.
On the many community newspapers flourishing in the Scottish Highlands and Islands.

2880   Ross, Betty. *Reporter in petticoats*. London: Hurst & Blackett, [1947].

2881   Rosselli, John. 'How *The Guardian* is printed'. *The Guardian*, 11 Sep 1961.
To mark the start of simultaneous typesetting in London and Manchester.

2882   *Ross-shire Journal*. Centenary edition, 1875–1975. Dingwall (Highland): 21 Feb 1975.
Now in Scottish Provincial Press ownership.

2883 Rotha, Paul. 'Making *The Times* film (1939–40)'. In his *Documentary diary: an informal history of British documentary film, 1928–39*. London: Secker & Warburg, 1973.

Fourth Estate, filmed largely in Printing House Square in 1939 and edited after the outbreak of war, is described by Rotha (its director and producer) as 'the most technically complicated documentary to be attempted to that date'. He provides telling pen-portraits of *Times* people: e.g. Geoffrey Dawson, the editor, originally remote but in the event insistent on appearing; Stanley Morison: 'his tall crow-like figure, always clad from head to feet in black'; Charles Morgan, dramatic critic; Peter Fleming, appointed liaison officer. A tranquil picture emerges of Britain – indeed the world – with *The Times* in a pivotal role; but it was decided not to proceed as it was considered 'not suitable for wartime propaganda'. The film was not shown publicly until 1970, under the auspices of Lord Thomson as the paper's proprietor.

2884 Rothenberg, Ignaz. *The newspaper: a study in the workings of the daily press and its laws*. London: Staples, 1946. xvi + 351pp.

Well documented: mainly on Britain, France, Germany.

2885 Rothermere, Harold Sidney Harmsworth, *1st Viscount. My fight to re-arm Britain*. London: Eyre & Spottiswoode, 1939.

2886 – – –. *Warnings and predictions*. London: Eyre & Spottiswoode, 1939.

Mainly through the *Daily Mail* (of which he was proprietor), Rothermere espoused Chamberlain and his policy of appeasement with the dictators: simultaneously, he promoted a stronger Royal Air Force.

2887 – – –. 'Northcliffe Newspapers'. *Daily Mail* and *Daily Mirror*, 13 Feb 1928.

This marked an earlier significant episode in the first Rothermere's career as Harmsworth supremo after Northcliffe's death. Running to two thousand words, it announced the foundation of a new company primarily geared to publish a new chain of evening papers (*Evening Worlds*) in provincial centres. This was in direct competition with the Berrys' Allied (later Kemsley) Newspapers; in the event only the *Newcastle Evening World* and *Bristol Evening World* ever appeared, and neither lasted long.

2888 Rowland, Roland Walter ('Tiny') (*né* Furhop). 'All's well that ends well'. *The Observer*, 23 May 1993.

A lengthy farewell life-story as his company's (Lonrho's) ownership of the paper came to an end: 'Ours was a one-sided love affair.'

2889 Rowland, Tom. 'The fourth estate'. *The Daily Telegraph*, 20 Sep 1989.

'On the architectural follies of press barons'.

2890 Rowlands, Don(ald) G.H. *The development of the Thomson Foundation Editorial Study Centre, 1963–1979*. Cardiff: University of Wales, 1983 (MEd thesis).

2891 Roy, Kenneth. 'The year in Metroland'. *The Journalist's Handbook*, Summer 1986.

On the battle in Birmingham between the old-established (and paid-for) *Birmingham Post* and the new (and free) *Daily News*.

2892   − − −.   'A toothless watchdog'. *The Journalist's Handbook*, Winter 1988. Interview with Kenneth Morgan, director of the Press Council.

2893   − − −.   'Charles Garside: saviour of *The European*'. *The Journalist's Handbook*, Summer 1993. Interview with the editor who, with the Barclay brothers as the new owners, took over this Maxwell enterprise.

2894   Royal Household. *History of the Office of Press Secretary to the Sovereign.* London: Buckingham Palace (Press Office). Handout from the Palace tracing this latter-day public relations appointment back to the Court Newsman for George III, one of whose duties was daily distribution of the *Court Circular* to the principal London papers. The first modern-style press secretary was appointed during the reign of George V, in 1918; the office lapsed in the 1930s but resumed in 1944.

2895   *Royal papers.* London: HarperCollins (Fontana), 1992. Introduction by Nigel Dempster. A large-format book recording 'the reign of HM Queen Elizabeth II' [forty years] told through newspaper front pages' – all from the John Frost Collection.

2896   *Royal papers, The.* London: Marshall Cavendish, 1977. Weekly parts. Ed Lynn Picknett. 'Produced with the co-operation of today's British newspapers', this similar work marked the Queen's twenty-five years on the throne.

2897   Royle, Edward. *Radicals, secularists and republicans: popular freethought in Britain, 1866–1915.* Manchester: Manchester University Press; Totowa (NJ): Rowman & Littlefield, 1980. xii + 380pp. This and previous work by Royle contain considerable material on the press promoting the cause.

2898   Royle, Trevor. *War report: the war correspondent's view of battle from the Crimea to the Falklands.* Edinburgh: Mainstream, 1987; London: Graphic Paperbacks, 1989. 240pp. Narrative on war reporting, featuring G.W. Steevens, Edgar Wallace, C. à C. Repington, Claud Cockburn, Chester Wilmot (Australian-born broadcaster), James Cameron.

2899   Rusbridger, Alan. 'A revolution that tore heavy industry from capital's heart'. *The Guardian*, 8 Feb 1988. Commenting on, and illustrating, the 'Farewell to Fleet Street' exhibition staged at the Museum of London: '. . . [in Fleet Street] Filofaxes outnumber the flongs.'

2900   − − −.   'Moving into a wider European orbit'. *The Guardian*, 11 Feb 1988. On the newly re-designed *Guardian*.

2901 Russell, *Sir* Edward Richard (later *1st Baron* Russell). *That reminds me.* London: 1899.

Published around halfway through Russell's remarkable fifty-one years as editor of the *Liverpool Daily Post.* Born in 1834, Russell was ennobled in 1919 and died still in editorial harness the following year.

2902 Russell, Thomas. 'The curious side of advertising' (ser). *Evening News,* Nov 1910.

Russell is notable in the history of advertising as advertisement manager of *The Times,* and later the first independent 'advertising consultant'.

2903 Rust, William. *The inside story of the Daily Worker: 10 years of working class journalism.* London: Daily Worker, 1939.

2904 – – –. *The Daily Worker reborn.* London: 1943. 16pp.

Celebrating the return of the paper after its suppression under wartime Defence Regulations.

2905 – – –. *The story of the Daily Worker.* With a foreword by J.R. Campbell. London: People's Press Printing Society, 1949. 128pp.

This history, written by a former editor, of Britain's communist daily (established 1930, suppressed 1941–2) was completed after Rust's death by Allen Hutt. The paper's title was changed to *Morning Star* in 1966.

2906 *Rutherglen Reformer.* Centenary special. Glasgow: 3 Dec 1975.

Weekly now owned by Trinity International.

2907 Ryan, Albert P. *Lord Northcliffe.* London: Collins, 1953. 158pp. (In the Brief Lives series.)

A elegant essay by an accomplished stylist of the old 'quality Liberal daily' school.

2908, 2909 No entries.

2910 Ryan, Cornelius. *The longest day.* London: Gollancz, 1960.

D-Day (1944) by an author 'who was there' for *The Daily Telegraph.*

2911 Ryan, W.M. *Lt-Col à Court Repington: a study in the interaction of personality, the press and power.* New York: Garland, 1987.

On Repington, a military correspondent of *The Times.*

2912 Rye, George. *Norwich Mercury, 1714–1947.* Unpubl MS in the Colman Library, Norwich.

2913 *Salisbury and Winchester Journal.* 1729–1929 bicentenary supplement. Salisbury (Wilts): 7 Jun 1929.

2914 Salisbury and Winchester Journal. *The story of the Salisbury and Winchester Journal, 1729 to 1939.* 7 Jun 1939.

Today's weekly *Salisbury Journal* is part of the Berrows group (Reed International).

2915 'Salisbury and Winchester Journal'. *The Newspaper World.* 24 Jun 1939. (In The Oldest Newspapers series.)

2916   *Salisbury Journal*. 250th anniversary supplement. 7 Jun 1979.

2917   Salmon, Lucy Maynard. *The newspaper and the historian*. London and New York: Oxford University Press, 1923. xviii + 566pp; Octagon Books, 1976.
'For students of history' – but not itself a history, urging research and reflecting 1920s America. Valuable too for its wide-ranging social history approach, and its extensive footnotes, which create a partial bibliography of US and British works and journalists.

2918   – – –.   *The newspaper and society*. New York: Oxford University Press, 1923. xxviii + 505pp.
A companion volume to the previous entry.

2919   Salmond, James Bell. *Andrew Lang and journalism*. Edinburgh: Nelson, 1951. 35pp. Andrew Lang Lecture.
Lang (1844–1912) was a leader-writer for *The Daily News*, and an astonishingly prolific freelance writer, who considered himself a 'gentlemanly belletrist' rather than a professional journalist.

2920   Salter, Cedric (Stephen). *Flight from Poland*. London: Faber, 1940. 226pp.
By the *Daily Mail* correspondent on the spot.

2921   Sampson, Anthony (Terrell Seward). *The changing anatomy of Britain*. London: Hodder & Stoughton, 1982.
Includes a chapter on 'The press and tycoons: the threat to diversity'. This is the fourth of Sampson's *Anatomy of Britain* series.

2922   Sanders, Michael L., and Philip M. Taylor. *British propaganda during the First World War, 1914–18*. London: Macmillan, 1982. x + 320pp.
A useful examination of an over-guarded secret.

2923   Sari, H.K. *The Arab image in the British press*. Bradford (W Yorks): University of Bradford, 1986 (PhD thesis). 313pp.

2924   Saunders, George. *The last of the Huns*. London: Routledge, [1914]. vii + 192pp.
Saunders was the first correspondent in Berlin for *The Morning Post* and then *The Times*. He continued his warnings about Germany's intentions when transferred to Paris, where he wrote this polemic about Kaiser Wilhelm II.

2925   Savage, Jon. *Picture Post idols*. London: Collins & Brown, 1992.
Some of the famous of the mid-century as captured by the cameramen of *Picture Post*.

2926   Sayle, Murray. 'Rupert Murdoch's Gallipoli'. *The Spectator*, 10 Oct 1981.
The role of Rupert's father, Sir Keith Murdoch, in uncovering the 'shameful' cover-up of the 1915 Gallipoli story is the centrepiece of this biographical sketch. The author, ex-*Sunday Times*, writes as literary editor of *The Age* (Melbourne).

2927   *Scarborough Evening News*. Centenary supplement. Scarborough (N Yorks): 23 Feb 1976.
Formerly called the *Scarborough Daily Post*.

2928   *Scarborough Mercury*. Jubilee number. 21 Jul 1905.
This weekly – now *The Mercury* – was founded in 1855.

2929   Scarfe, Gerald. *Scarfe: line of attack*. London: Hamish Hamilton, 1988.
A selection of nearly four hundred cartoons for *The Sunday Times*, contributed over twenty-one years by one of the most biting as well as diamond-sharp draughtsmen of modern times.

2930   Schillinger, Elisabeth Hupp. 'British and United States newspaper coverage of the Bolshevik revolution'. *Journalism Quarterly*, Spring 1966.

2931   Schlesinger, Philip. *The Scott Trust*. Manchester: The Guardian, [1986]. 14pp.
The Scott Trust, founded in 1936, was re-constituted in 1948; it controls *The Guardian, Manchester Evening News*, and (from 1993) *The Observer*.

2932   Schmuhl, Robert, ed. *The responsibilities of journalism*. Notre Dame (IN): Notre Dame Press, 1984. 138pp.
An important collection of papers from a 1982 conference in the USA, exploring 'the moral dimensions of Anglo-American journalism'.

2933   Schofield, [Edward] Guy. *The men that carry the news: a history of United Newspapers Limited*. London: Cranford Press, 1976. x + 201pp.
Non-controversial, and mainly useful in outlining the early tortuous years – with potted histories – of the Yorkshire and Lancashire papers in the group as at 1975, consisting of United (Provincial) Newspapers and several major periodicals, then including *Punch*. The author was himself Yorkshire-born, and had risen to national editor status: *Evening News* (1942–50) and *Daily Mail* (1950–5).

2934   Schüssler, W. *Die Daily-Telegraph-Affaire: Fürst Bulow, Kaiser Wilhelm und die Krise des zweites Reiches, 1908*. Göttingen (Germany): Göttinger Bausteine, 1952. 126pp.
This treatise was the result of research carried out at the University of Berlin in 1943. It begins with the Second Reich under the Kaiser (Wilhelm II), and describes its unstoppable slide into World War I. It then relates how, in the early days of the century, when Prince Bulow was state chancellor, he was forced to resign because of an interview with *The Daily Telegraph*, which made him seem too bellicose towards the alliance of England, France and Russia.

2935   Schwartz, George Leopold. *Bread and circuses, 1945–1958*. London: Sunday Times, [1959]. 220pp.
Reprints of a selection of the author's influential writing in *The Sunday Times*, of which he was then deputy City editor, on the national economy. Schwartz was also economic adviser to the Kemsley group.

2936   *Scope*. Cardiff (intermittently London): The Thomson Foundation, 1964–. Twice per annum; latterly annual.
Newspaper-format chronicle of the Foundation's courses in the UK and overseas, and the staff and students involved.

2937 Scotsman, The. *The centenary of The Scotsman, 1817–1917.* 25 Jan 1917. 47pp.
The Scotsman first appeared in 1817 as a weekly paper, getting into its stride as a Scottish national daily when stamp duty was withdrawn in 1855.

2938 *Scotsman, The.* Centenary supplement (*Daily Scotsman*). 29 Jan 1955.
By the time that this appeared, Lord Thomson had acquired *The Scotsman* (1953); ten years later, the *Evening News* (Edinburgh) also joined the Thomson group.

2939 *Scotsman, The, 1817–1955: Scotland's national newspaper.* Edinburgh: Scotsman, 1955.

2940 *Scotsman, The.* 150th anniversary supplement. 24 Jan 1967.

2941 Scotsman, The. *The glorious privilege: the history of The Scotsman,* ed Magnus Magnusson *et al.* With an introduction by Lord Thomson. London: Nelson, for The Scotsman, 1967. 196pp.
The title harks back to Burns's phrase 'the glorious privilege of being independent', which *The Scotsman* was – in ownership terms – until Thomson's take-over.

– – –. *Index to The Scotsman: see Reference Works section.*

2942 Scott, Brough. *Front runners.* London: Gollancz, 1991.
Horse racing, for *The Sunday Times* etc.

2943 Scott, Charles Prestwich. 'Press and government'. *The Manchester Guardian,* 12 Mar 1918.

2944 – – –. 'The Manchester Guardian's first hundred years'. 5 May 1921 (centenary number). Rptd as *Newspaper ideals.* New York: Halcyon-Commonwealth Foundation (Halcyon Booklet), 1964. Rptd again in *The Media Reporter,* Autumn 1976.
Incorporates the famous phrase: 'Comment is free, but facts are sacred.'

2945 – – –. 'An independent press'. *The Manchester Guardian,* 5 Apr 1928.

2946 – – –. 'The function of the press'. *Political Quarterly,* Jan–Mar 1931.
One of the most influential editor/proprietors in the history of British journalism, Scott (1846–1932) published very little under his own name but played *éminence grise* to Lloyd George and the Liberal Party in the pre-1914 period.

2947 Scott, David. *Once a week is enough.* Birmingham: D.B. Scott, 1987.
'For the thousands of people who are thinking of becoming a journalist' – by the chief executive of the *Daily News* (Birmingham), Britain's first free daily. The message of his title is that paid-for weekly papers are a dying breed. (In 1991, however, the paper was renamed *Metro News,* and became weekly.)

2948 Scott, George (Edwin). *Reporter anonymous: the story of the Press Association.* London: Hutchinson, 1968. 307pp.
The official history of Britain's only national newsgathering agency, from its formation

as a national syndicate in 1868 to its quietly responsible return to its original monopoly status when Extel ceased its competitive general news service in 1965. The author turned up some interesting archival facts on the pay and working conditions of reporters in the pioneer days, and is very readable on the men who fashioned the Press Association – led by the formidable (Sir) Edmund Robbins.

2949 Scott, James Maurice. *Extel 100: centenary history of the Exchange Telegraph*. London: Benn, 1972. ix + 239pp.
Relates how Extel, founded 1872, set up a foreign service, but emerged as a more considerable competitor on the home front.

2950 Scott, Noll, and Derek Jones, eds. *Bloody Bosnia: a European tragedy*. London: Guardian Books/Channel 4 Television, 1993. 52pp.
Published initially as accompaniment in print to Channel 4's series on the war in Bosnia. Eyewitness accounts from Ian Traynor, Ed Vulliamy, and Maggie O'Kane; endpiece by Mark Woollacott – all of *The Guardian*.

2951 Scott-James, Anne Eleanor (Mrs Macdonald Hastings, later Lady Lancaster). *In the mink*. London: Michael Joseph, 1953.

2952 – – –. *Sketches from a life*. London: Michael Joseph, 1993. x + 198pp.
Wartime woman's editor of *Picture Post* – and post-war, filled a similar role at the *Sunday Express* and later (1960–8) columnist with the *Daily Mail*.

2953 Scott-James, R[olfe] A[rnold]. *The influence of the press*. London: S.W. Partridge, [1913, 1926]. 319pp.
An analysis of the British and United States press, notably the Northcliffe revival of *The Times*; partly a history, partly critique.

2954 *Scottish Press Directory and Advertiser's Guide*. Glasgow: D.C. Cuthbertson, [1924].

2955 'Scottish takeover, The: Lonrho, SUITS and Outram'. In *The press and the people, 1977/1978* (Press Council Annual Report).
In the event, Lonrho's application to the Monopolies and Mergers Commission to acquire SUITS and (through them) Outram was not approved until March 1979.

2956 Seale, Patrick, and Maureen McConville. *Philby, the long road to Moscow*. London: Hamish Hamilton, 1973.
Two *Observer* writers consider the career of one of their more notorious colleagues, who was representing the paper in Beirut just before he defected to Moscow.

2957 Searle, Chris. *Your daily dose: racism and The Sun*. London: Campaign for Press and Broadcasting Freedom, 1989.
'*The Sun*'s racism examined, analysed and exposed'.

2958 Searle, Ronald (William Fordham). *Ronald Searle's golden oldies, 1941–1961*. London: Pavilion Books, 1985. 145pp.

One of the artist's own selections of his mordantly witty (and in some cases deadly serious) drawings; his talent has been seen to advantage in such publications as the *News Chronicle*, the *Sunday Express*, *Punch*, *Tribune* and *Lilliput*.

2959   Seaton, Jean, and Ben Pimlott, eds. *The media in British politics*. Aldershot (Hants): Gower (Avebury), 1987. 266pp.
Essays from fourteen, including the two editors. The others include 'Goodbye to *The Times*', by Peter Kellner, and 'Local press', by David Murphy.

2960   Seaton, Ray. *Malcolm Graham: sixty years in the news*. Wolverhampton: Express and Star, 1983. 64pp.
A tribute 'to the chairman from the editorial staff of the *Express and Star*', in the form of a history in particular of the genesis of the *Evening Star* in 1880 by local businessman Thomas Graham and famed philanthropist Andrew Carnegie. It recounts how the latter, originally intent on setting up a newspaper empire as a vehicle for his republican views, eventually withdrew, leaving Graham and his descendants to develop the enterprise which became the Midland News Association.

2961   Sebba, Anne. *Battling for news: the rise of the woman reporter*. London: Hodder Headline (John Curtis), 1994.
Covers the subject internationally, and in all ages. Includes a chapter on 'The remarkable Flora Shaw' – whose service with *The Times* just entered the twentieth century (she retired in September 1900).

2962   Seligman, E.R.A., ed. 'The Walter family'. In *Encyclopedia of social sciences*, Vol 15. London: Macmillan, 1935.
Sorting out the dynasty who founded and controlled *The Times* for more than a century.

2963   Sellers, Leslie. *Doing it in style: a manual for journalists, PR men and copy-writers*. Oxford: Pergamon, 1968.
By the then production editor of the *Daily Mail*: a dictionary with its own attractive style.

2964   – – –.   *The simple subs book*. Oxford: Pergamon, 1968; revised 1985.
Another standard teaching – and learning – aid, this one for the subeditor's desk.

2965   – – –.   *Keeping up the style*. London: Pitman, 1975.
An updated version of *Doing it in style*.

2966   Seppings Wright, Henry Charles. *Two years under the Crescent*. London: James Nisbet, 1913. xiii + 508pp.
An *Illustrated London News* 'special' in several campaigns, of which the Balkans was only one.

2967   Sergeant, (*Sir*) Patrick (John Rushton). 'Tip for tap in the City'. In *100 years of Fleet Street*. London: Press Club, 1982.
By the City editor of the *Daily Mail*, 1960–84.

2968   Settle, Edith. *My editor says* ... London: Pitman, 1937. xi + 104pp.

2969 Sewell, Gordon. *Echoes of a century: the centenary history of Southern Newspapers Ltd, 1864–1964*. Southampton: Southern Newspapers, 1964. 159pp.
The principal titles of this group today are the *Southern Daily Echos* published in Southampton, Bournemouth and Weymouth.

2970 Seymour-Ure, Colin [Knowlton]. *The press, politics and the public: an essay on the role of the national press in the British political system*. London: Methuen, 1968. 328pp.
Economic, organizational and legal functions are discussed with statistical evidence. Special attention is given to the lobby system.

2971 – – –. *The political impact of the mass media*. London: Constable; Beverly Hills (CA): Sage, 1974. 296pp. (In the Communication and Society series.)
Covers *inter alia* political communication and the effects of the mass media. It provides detailed case studies, e.g. on *The Times* and appeasement of Hitler; *Private Eye* etc.

2972 – – –. *The British press and broadcasting since 1945*. Oxford: Basil Blackwell, 1991. xii + 269pp. (In Making Contemporary Britain series.)
An up-to-date students' manual, with an especially useful chapter on prime ministers and parties.

2973 – – –. 'Policymaking in the press'. *Government and Opposition*, 4, 4, 1969 – a special number.

2974 – – –. 'Parliament and mass communications in the twentieth century'. *In* S.A. Walkland, ed. *The House of Commons in the twentieth century*. Oxford: Clarendon Press, 1969.

2975 – – –. 'The press and the party system between the wars'. *In* G. Peela and C. Cook, eds. *The politics of re-appraisal, 1918–1939*. London: Macmillan, 1975.

2976 – – –. 'Press barons and press power in Britain'. *Book Forum*, 1, 1974.

2977 – – –. 'Media policy in Britain: now you see it, now you don't'. *European Journal of Communication*, 2, 3, Sep 1987.

2978 – – –, joint ed. *Studies on the press*. Royal Commission on the Press Report, Working Paper 3. London: HMSO, 1977.

2979 Seymour-Ure, Colin [Knowlton], and Jim Schoff, eds. *David Low*. London: Secker & Warburg, 1985. xii + 180pp.
Contains more than 250 examples of Low's cartoons, drawing widely on archives and personal sketchbooks. Schoff (first director of the Centre for the Study of Cartoons and Caricature, University of Kent) carried out the initial selection and research; Seymour-Ure comments knowledgeably and fluently.

2980   Shah, Eddy. 'Launching a national newspaper'. *Journal of the Royal Society of Arts,* Jun 1986.
The pioneer-in-the-news lectured in upbeat fashion to the Society on 22 January 1986. *Today* was launched on 4 March – but by June it was failing, and sold to Lonrho in that month.

2981   Shamsuddin, M. *British press coverage and the role of the Pakistan press from independence to the emergence of Bangla Desh.* London: City University, 1986 (PhD thesis).

2982   Shane, T. *Passed for press.* London: Association of the Correctors of the Press, 1954.
A centenary history. The ACP was a trade union for proofreaders working within fifteen miles of central London. It was merged into the National Graphical Association in 1965.

2983   Shard, K.C. 'Readership differences in the quality daily press'. *Admap,* Feb 1968.
The author was a marketing man with *The Daily Telegraph.*

2984   Sharf, Andrew. *The British press and Jews under Nazi rule.* London and New York: Oxford University Press, for the Institute of Race Relations, 1964. vi + 228pp.
An analysis of the muted British press coverage of the persecution of the Jews by the Nazis, especially in the run-up to World War II, but also including reaction to events in Palestine and the Nuremberg trials.

2985   – – –.   *Nazi racialism and the British press, 1933–1945.* London: World Jewish Congress, [1965]. 14pp.
A reprint of the Noah Barou Memorial Lecture, 1963.

2986   Shattock, Joanne. 'General histories of the press'. *In* J. Don Vann and R. VanArsdel, eds. *Victorian periodicals: a guide to research.* New York: MLA, 1978.

2987   Shaw, Christine. Various entries in David J. Jeremy, ed. *Dictionary of business biography.* London: Butterworth, for the Business History Unit, London School of Economics, 1984–5.
Entries in Vol 1 provided by this author include those on Berry, James Gomer, 1st Viscount Kemsley; Berry, William Ewert, 1st Viscount Camrose; Bottomley, Horatio; Cadbury, George; Cadbury, Laurence John; Chancellor, Sir Christopher John Howard (Chancellor was general manager of Reuters from 1944 to 1959 and later briefly chairman of Odhams); and Crowther, Geoffrey, Lord Crowther of Headingley (in the press context, principally remembered as editor of *The Economist,* but also an acting editor of *The Observer* immediately post-Garvin).
     Contributions in Vol 3 include those on Harmsworth, Alfred Charles William, Viscount Northcliffe; and Harmsworth, Harold Sidney, 1st Viscount Rothermere; Iliffe, Edward Mauger, 1st Lord Iliffe; Lawson, Edward Levy, 1st Lord Burnham; and (written with R.P.T. Davenport-Hines) Hulton, Sir Edward.

Contributions in Vol 4 include that on Newnes, Sir George; and in Vol 5 Reuter, Paul Julius, 1st Baron de Reuter.

2988 Shawcross, William. *Rupert Murdoch: ringmaster of the information circus.* London: Chatto & Windus, 1992. xiv + 616pp; Pan, 1993.
Not an 'authorized' biography; but Murdoch allowed an interview, and the treatment is on balance sympathetic.

2989 Shearman, Hugh. *News Letter: 1737–1987.* Belfast: Century Newspapers, [1987]. 64pp.
To quote Captain O.W.J. Henderson, then chairman of its proprietors, 'truly the Belfast *News Letter* has mirrored the Northern Irish community with a continuing identity of interest over its unique 250 years of publication.'

2990 *Sheffield Daily Telegraph.* Jubilee, 1855–1905. Sheffield: 1905.

2991 Sheffield Daily Telegraph. *A record of seventy years: June 8th 1855–June 8th 1925.* 1925. 96pp.
Founded in the year (1855) when the newspaper tax was abolished, but its great days began nine years later, when Frederick Clifford and (Sir) William Leng acquired it. Allied Newspapers became the owners in 1925.

2992 *Sheffield Telegraph.* Centenary number. 8 Jun 1955.
By 1955, the paper had not only a new title, but a new owner: Thomson. It later moved to United Newspapers, and underwent a final change of title, to *Morning Telegraph.*

2993 Sheldon-Williams, Douglas. 'The war correspondents: then and now'. *The Sphere*, 20 Nov 1917.
Sheldon-Williams was a special artist for *The Sphere* in both the South African War and the Russo-Japanese War. In the First World War, he was an official artist accredited to the Canadian Expeditionary Force.

2994 Shepherd, C(ecil) W(illiam). *Let's walk down Fleet Street.* London: Gerald G. Swan, 1947. 190pp.
Gossipy, but quite useful.

2995 Shepherd, William G. 'Confessions of a censor-fighter'. *The Strand Magazine*, Sep 1917.
On the trials and tribulations of the front-line war reporter.

2996 Sheppard, Major E.W. 'The military correspondent'. *Army Quarterly*, 53, 2, Jun 1952.

2997 Sheppard, S.T. 'The genesis of a profession'. *United Service Magazine*, 9, 40, Mar 1907.
The profession in question is that of war correspondent.

2998 *Shetland Times, The.* Centenary supplement, 1872–1972. Lerwick (Shetland Islands): 16 Jun 1972.

2999   Shields Gazette. *Centenary: 100 Years of the Shields Gazette, 1849–1949.*
[1949].
The *North and South Shields Gazette* was founded as a weekly, and became the first provincial daily evening when the newspaper tax was lifted in 1855. The *Shields Gazette*,
which it became under new management in 1884, survives today, ranking as the oldest
English evening.

3000   *Shields Gazette.* Centenary of first publication as an evening. 2 Jul 1955.

3001   'Shooting from the hype'. *The Guardian (Media Guardian)*, 20 Sep
1993.
Assessment by ten 'friends and foes' of the record of Andrew Neil after ten years as editor
of *The Sunday Times.*

3002   Shorter, C(lement) K(ing). *C.K.S.: an autobiography: a fragment of himself*,
ed J.M. Bulloch. London: 1927. xxiii + 176pp.
Second only to the Ingram dynasty in the early history of illustrated journalism, Shorter
was editor of their *Illustrated London News* (1890), founded *The Sketch* with William
Ingram (1893), then founded *The Sphere* (1900) and the latter-day *Tatler* (1901). This
book is essential reading.

3003   *Shrewsbury Chronicle.* 150th anniversary supplement. Shrewsbury: 8 Dec
1922.

3004   – – –.   175th anniversary. Nov 1947.

3005   Shrewsbury Chronicle. *Through nine reigns: 200 years of the Shrewsbury
Chronicle, 1772–1972.* 23 Nov 1972.
Today a weekly in the Midland News Association group.

3006   '*Shrewsbury Chronicle* – Salop's first newspaper'. *The Newspaper World*, 7
Oct 1939. (In The Oldest Newspapers series.)

3007   Shulman, Alexander. 'Paper mate'. *Tatler*, Jan 1986.
On Lord Stevens of Ludgate, in the early days of his chairmanship of Express
Newspapers.

3008   Sibbald, Raymond. *The war correspondents: The Boer War.* Stroud (Glos):
Alan Sutton, 1994. ix + 244pp.
A selection of the reports from the 'specials' for *The Times* on the spot, plus a few extracts
from the newspaper in London. Being *The Times*, none of the reports are bylined. The
long introduction discusses coverage only in that newspaper.

3009   Sidebotham, Herbert. *Pillars of the State.* London: Nisbet, 1921. viii +
256pp. Publ in the USA as *Political profiles from British public life.* Boston:
Houghton Mifflin, 1921.
These evocative profiles were originally published in *The Times*, bylined 'Student of
Politics'.

3010 — — —. *The sense of things*. London: Hodder & Stoughton, 1938. 247pp.
Sidebotham wrote these articles as 'Candidus' in the *Daily Sketch*; simultaneously he achieved an even more influential readership as 'Scrutator' in *The Sunday Times*.

3011 Siebert, Fredrick Seaton, Theodore Peterson, and Wilbur Schramm. *Four theories of the press*. Urbana (IL): University of Illinois Press, 1956. 153pp; New York: Books for Libraries Press, 1973.
Siebert, doyen, writes on the authoritarian and libertarian concepts of what the press 'should be and do'; ex-dean Peterson writes on the social responsibility concept; and Schramm considers the Soviet communist concept of an 'agit-prop' press.

3012 Silvester, Christopher. 'Paper boys'. *ES (Evening Standard Magazine)*, Oct 1991.
The situation at *The Independent* (and *Independent on Sunday*), critical of all three founders: Andreas Whittam Smith, Matthew Symonds, and Stephen Glover.

3013 — — —, ed. *The Penguin book of interviews*. London: Viking, 1993. xvii + 632pp.
The first interview selected dates from 1859 (in the USA); but later comes an impressive parade of profiles in the twentieth-century British newspaper press. These range from Harold Williams's 1905 interview of Tolstoy in *The Manchester Guardian* to Terry Coleman confronting Margaret Thatcher in *The Guardian*, 1971. The only British journalist represented by two interviews is Henry Brandon of *The Sunday Times*: of Frank Lloyd Wright in 1957, and J.F. Kennedy in 1960. The editor provides a well-researched and valuable introduction.

3014 Simonis, Henry. *The street of ink: an intimate history of journalism*. London: Cassell; New York: Funk & Wagnall, 1917. xx + 372pp.
A gossipy account of Fleet Street newspaper politics and personalities by an author who was advertisement manager of *The Morning Leader* for many years before becoming a director of *The Daily News*. The material was published originally in *The Newspaper World* as a series of articles.

3015 Simpson, Donald Herbert. *Commercialisation of the regional press: the development of monopoly, profit and control*. Aldershot (Hants): Gower, 1981. xv + 224pp.
Deals with economic and social aspects, not with individual cases. The author decries the decline of editorial content in the face of advertising pressures.

3016 Simpson, Paul. 'Lord Northcliffe' (Jan 1991); 'Lord Beaverbrook' (Feb 1991); 'Cecil King' (May 1991); 'Harold Evans' (Nov–Dec 1991). *Newspaper Focus*. (Back Issues series).
The assessment, both personal and professional, of Evans is particularly perceptive.

3017 — — —. 'Richard the Lionheart'. Jan 1992.
Interview with Sir Richard Storey, chairman of Portsmouth and Sunderland Newspapers.

3018 – – –.   'A man of substance'. Jun 1992.
Interview with Simon Jenkins, editor of *The Times* (which he left later in the year).

3019 – – –.   'Rich man, Boorman'. Summer 1992.
Edwin Pratt Boorman, third-generation chairman of the Kent Messenger group.

3020 – – –.   'The last resort'. Sep 1992.
Examination of the new-style *Evening Argus* (Brighton).

3021 – – –.   'Association football'. Nov 1992.
On Robert Simpson, new chief executive of the Press Association at a critical time in its relations with its newspaper customers.

3022 – – –.   'Alexander the great'. Dec 1992.
On the editor-in-chief of the *Leicester Mercury*, Alex Leys.

3023 – – –.   'The quite man'. Jan 1993.
Richard Palmer, editor of the *Financial Times*.

3024 – – –.   'The words of the Lord'. Mar 1993.
On Lord McGregor, beleaguered chairman of the Press Complaints Commission.

3025 – – –.   'The seven column itch'. Apr 1993.
Review of the re-design of *The Independent*, from issue no 2,000; the page grid then changed from eight to seven columns.

3026 – – –.   'Mail model'. Apr 1993.
Report on the Westminster Press's *Oxford Mail*, fastest-growing evening paper, and its editor, Eddie Duller.

3027 – – –.   'South almighty'. Jun 1993.
On James Sexton, chief executive of the growing Southern Newspapers group.

3028 – – –.   'The thrill of it all'. Aug 1993.
Interview with Chris Oakley, group managing director of the newly formed Midland Independent Newspapers (based in Birmingham).

3029 – – –.   'Leads United'. Nov 1993.
Interview with Michael Toulmin, chairman of United Provincial Newspapers.

3030 – – –.   'Simply the best'. Dec 1993.
The Newspaper Design Awards in 1953 (when they began), in 1993 (just announced) – and a look ahead to 2003.

3031 – – –, ed. *European newspaper industry*. Leatherhead (Surrey): Pira International, 1994. 260pp.
Major detailed survey, with the United Kingdom among the country profiles and several British publishing houses featured in an analysis of top European companies. Daily, weekly, paid-for and free segments are all covered.

3032 Sims, George R. *My life: sixty years' recollections of Bohemian London*. London: Eveleigh Nash, 1917.

Sims ('Dagonet') is thought to have written some two thousand articles for *The Referee* alone.

3033 Sinclair, David. *Dynasty: the Astors and their times*. London: Dent, 1984. vi + 426pp.
Gives very full coverage of the Astors' place in newspaper history, with a useful family tree.

3034 Sinclair, Keith. 'British prestige press editorial on leadership during the 1979 campaign'. *Journalism Quarterly*, Summer 1982.

3035 – – –. ' "Horse-race" vs. substance in coverage of the election by the British prestige press'. *Journalism Quarterly*, Winter 1982.

3036 Sinclair, Robert. *The British press: the journalist and his conscience*. London: Home & Van Thal, 1949. 271 pp.
Written after Sinclair had left Fleet Street, where during World War II he was news editor of *The Star*. An extract on the recruitment of journalists was reprinted in *The Media Reporter*, Autumn 1984.

3037 Singleton, Frank. *Tillotsons 1850–1950: a centenary of a family business*. Bolton: Bolton Evening News, 1950. x + 94pp.
A history of enterprise in the newspaper and the associated paper and packaging industries from late-Victorian times, notably the foundation by William Frederic Tillotson in 1867 of the subscription and syndication pioneer, the *Bolton Evening News*, of which Singleton himself was editor until his retirement in 1960. Singleton wrote extensively and exquisitely, both fiction and non-fiction.

3038 – – –. 'The provincial press: the weeklies'. *The Author*, 65, 1956.

3039 Sington, Derrick. *Freedom of communication*. London: Ampersand, 1963. 126pp.
A philosophical consideration of the British people's 'right to know' by a distinguished ex-foreign correspondent and leader-writer of *The Manchester Guardian*.

3040 'Sir Emsley Carr: fifty years as editor'. *World's Press News*, 1 May 1941.
An obituary tribute to Emsley Carr, installed by his uncle Lascelles Carr as editor of the *News of the World* in 1891, and later to become joint proprietor himself.

3041 *Sir William Bailey: an album of remembrance*. [1949].
Tribute to a leading figure of the Westminster Press for more than fifty years, becoming joint managing director. Bailey was also post-war chairman of the Newsprint Supply Co and long-serving president of the Newspaper Society.

3042 'Sir William Haley: enemy of moral compromise in the press'. *The Times*, 8 Sep 1987.
Obituary of the former editor (1952–66), who died 6 September 1987.

3043 'Sir William Haley: head of his profession'. *The New Statesman*, 6 Feb 1954. Rptd in *New Statesman profiles*. London: Phoenix House, 1957.

3044 Sisson, Keith. *Industrial relations in Fleet Street: a study in pay structure.* Oxford: Blackwell, 1975. xvi + 185pp.
Now superseded and of academic interest only.

3045 Slade, J.J., and Mrs Herbert [Norah] Richardson. 'Wiltshire newspapers past and present'. *Wiltshire Archaeological and Natural History Magazine*, 40, 1917–22.

3046 Slattery, Jon. 'Putting it all on the line'. *UK Press Gazette*, 25 Nov 1991.
Interview with Chris Oakley, leading the management buy-out of the Birmingham Post and Mail group (including *Birmingham Post, Birmingham Evening Mail, Sunday Mercury, Coventry Evening Telegraph*).

3047 Slaven, Anthony, and Marian Quigley. 'David Couper Thomson'. *In* Anthony Slaven and Sydney Checkland, eds. *Dictionary of Scottish business biography*, Vol 2. Aberdeen: Aberdeen University Press, 1990.

3048 Slocombe, George Edward. *The tumult and the shouting: the memoirs of George Slocombe.* London and New York: Heinemann, 1936. 437pp.
Covers the period 1912–37, and deals especially with Slocombe's career as, for many years, the only (but highly regarded) foreign correspondent for the *Daily Herald*. Later he was correspondent for the *Evening Standard*.

3049 *Slough, Eton and Windsor Observer.* Centenary souvenir. Slough (Berks): 6 May 1983.

3050 Smail, H.M. 'A hundred and fifty years of newspaper production'. *Berwickshire Naturalists Club History*, 31, 2, 1949.
The origins of the Tweeddale Press group.

3051 Smalley, George Washburn. *Anglo-American memories.* New York and London: Putnam, 1911. ix + 441pp.
An important figure in US journalism history, Smalley came to London in 1866 as 'foreign commissioner' for the *New York Tribune*, sharing the new transatlantic cable in a syndicate with *The Daily News*; later he served *The Times* (London) in Washington. These 'memories' cover more than fifty years in both countries.

3052 Smith, A. *Working together: a study of the collective behaviour of general reporters in pursuit of 'hard news' stories.* Bristol: Bristol Polytechnic, 1984 (MPhil thesis).

3053 Smith, A.M. *The New Statesman, 1913–1931: a study of intellectual attitudes.* Canterbury: University of Kent, 1980 (thesis). 432pp.

3054 Smith, Adrian. 'Low and Lord Beaverbrook: cartoonist and proprietor'. *Encounter*, Dec 1985.

3055 Smith, Alan, and 'John Callendar'. 'Media fingerposts – the quality dailies'. *Admap*, Jun 1983.

3056 Smith, A[nthony] C[harles] H. *Paper voices: the popular press and social change, 1933–1965*. London: Chatto & Windus; Totowa (NJ): Rowman & Littlefield, 1975. 265pp.
A superficial if academic study, with Elizabeth Immirzi and Trevor Blackwell, comparing the *Daily Express* and *Daily Mirror* over a thirty-year span. Especially valuable in analysing coverage of general elections.

3057 – – –. 'Gossip columns'. *New Society*, 27 Dec 1967.

3058 Smith, Anthony (David). *The newspaper: an international history*. London: Thames & Hudson, 1979. 192pp.
With 111 illustrations, this is a book to be displayed as much as read. It contrives to survey a large and complex canvas, once over lightly but elegantly.

3059 – – –. 'State intervention and the management of the press'. *In* J. Curran, ed. *The British press*. London: Macmillan, 1978.

3060 – – –, ed. *The British press since the war*. Newton Abbot (Devon): David & Charles; Totowa (NJ): Rowman & Littlefield, 1974. 320pp. (In the Sources for Contemporary Issues series.)
A compendium of current material, documenting newspaper finance, amalgamation and production; social and governmental restraints; and changing relationships between owner, editor, journalist and reader.

3061 – – –. *Newspapers and democracy: international essays on a changing medium*. Cambridge (MA): MIT Press, 1980. xiv + 368pp.
British contributors are James Curran, Angus Douglas, Gary Whannel, David J. Hunt, Ben Pimlott, Jane Seaton, and Pauline Wingate.

3062 Smith, C.G. *The Reporter, 1856–1966*. Gravesend (Kent): 1966.
A history of the *Gravesend Reporter*, now in the Westminster Press group.

3063 Smith, Ernest. *Fields of adventure: some reflections of forty years of newspaper life*. London: Hutchinson, 1923; Boston: Small, Maynard, 1924. ix + 319pp.
The author's adventurous career took in Paris for *The Daily News* at the time of the Dreyfus scandal, and then the South African War.

3064 Smith, Ernest Anthony. *A history of the press*. London: Ginn, [1970]. 112pp.
'Aspects of social and economic history', illustrated in colour.

3065 Smith, Geoffrey. *Local government for journalists*. London: LGC Communications (for National Council for the Training of Journalists), 1983–92; 5th edn, under title *Essential local government*, by Geoffrey Smith, Derrick Hender, and David Kett. LGC (for NCTJ), 1993.
A standard textbook.

3066 Smith, Godfrey. 'We had a ball'. *The Sunday Times Magazine*, 29 Mar 1987.
By the second editor of the magazine.

3067 Smith, Laura (Alex). 'Women's work in the press: editorial and journalistic'. In *The Newspaper Press Directory, 1900*. London: Mitchell, 1900.
The last in a series of articles for the directory by a pioneer woman journalist.

3068 Smith, Lorna. *Devon newspapers: a finding list*. Exeter: Torbay Borough Council (for the Standing Conference on Devon History), 1973. 33pp; revised edn, 1975. Amendments publ in *Devon Historian*, 14, Spring 1977.
Comprehensive, but lacking in accuracy.

3069 Smith, P.G. 'Early days of *Newspaper World*'. *The Newspaper World*, 3 Jan 1948.
Marking this trade journal's Golden Jubilee year.

3070 Smith, Wareham. *Spilt ink*. London: Benn, 1932. 281pp.
The author was a long-service advertisement manager (later director) for the *Daily Mail*; he joined Northcliffe in 1896. One of the best sources on the early twentieth-century history of newspaper advertising.

3071 Smyly, Robert. *The Berry brothers*. Privately published, 1982.
Booklet by a grandson of Seymour Berry (Viscount Buckland).

3072 Snider, Paul B. *The British Press Council: a study of its role and performance, 1953–1965*. Iowa City: University of Iowa, 1968 (PhD dissertation).

3073 Snoddy, Raymond. *The good, the bad and the unacceptable: the hard news about the British press today*. London: Faber, 1992. xiv + 210pp.
Sound and well-informed survey for the general reader by the *Financial Times* media correspondent.

3074 – – –. 'Read all about him'. *Financial Times*, 1 Feb 1988.
Interview with Rupert Murdoch: 'You're a hero one day, a menace the next'; re *The Sun*: 'It laughs, it knows what it's doing, it's non-pretentious – healthily anti-Establishment'; on editorials in *The Times*: 'It's all I can do to read them, let alone contemplate writing them'.

3075 – – –. 'Newspaper magnate in the making'. *Financial Times*, 8 Apr 1989.
On Lord Stevens.

3076 – – –. 'Robert Maxwell: contrasts and complexity'. *Financial Times*, 6 Nov 1991.
An instant obituary – before all the facts and figures emerged.

3077 – – –. 'Out of the red and into the Black'. *Financial Times* (Weekend), 22–23 Feb 1992.

On how Conrad Black had turned round the fortunes of *The Daily Telegraph*.

3078 Snowden, (James) Keighley. *Barbara West*. London: John Long, 1901.

3079 – – –. *The free marriage*. London: Stanley Paul, [1911].
This and the above entry are novels with a press setting.

3080 Snyder, Louis Leo, ed. *Masterpieces of great reporting: the great moments of World War II*. New York: Messner, 1962. xviii + 555pp.

3081 Snyder, Louis Leo, and Richard B. Morris, eds. *A treasury of great reporting: 'literature under pressure' from the sixteenth century to our own time*. New York: Simon & Schuster, 1949; new edn, 1962. xxxv + 795pp; Stuttgart: Steingruber, 1953.
From the Fugger newsletters to the date of publication, including (from the twentieth century) Kaiser Wilhelm profiled in *The Daily Telegraph*; H.G. Wells in the columns of *The Daily Chronicle*; and a report of the Reichstag fire in *The Times*.

3082 Soames, Jane. *The English press: newspapers and news*. London: Stanley Nott, 1936. 178pp. Revised edn Drummond, 1938. 181pp.
'The freedom of the press is essential [to democracy]' . . . but 'in Britain, it is controlled by a very small ring, which is universally accepted and believed'.

3083 Society of Women Writers and Journalists. *Centenary 1894–1994*, by Jean Bowden and Joan Livermore. London: SWWJ, 1994. 24pp.
Illustrated history of the Society. The words 'Writers and' were added to the title of the Society in 1952.

3084 'Soldiers of the press'. *Editor and Publisher*, 23, 30 Dec 1944.
Lists US and British war correspondents killed, to that date.

3085 Somerfield, Stafford. *Banner headlines*. Shoreham-by-Sea (W Sussex): Scan Books, 1979. 203pp.
The only personal story published by an ex-editor of the *News of the World*. Somerfield, following ten years in the job, left soon after Murdoch's News International acquired the paper. His story is both readable and important in the context of press politics.

3086 *Somerset County Gazette*. Centenary supplement, 1836–1936. Taunton (Somerset): 2 Jan 1937.
Today a weekly in the Berrows group (Reed International).

3087 Somerset County Gazette. *The story of a community and a newspaper*. 9 Jan 1987.
150th anniversary booklet.

3088 *Somerset Standard*. Centenary supplement. Frome: 1986.
A Westminster Press weekly.

3089 Sones, Mike, and Liz Sones, comps. *An introduction to Robert Blatchford and the Clarion newspaper*. London (Harrow): Clarion Workshop Press, 1986.

3090   Soutar, Andrew. *With Ironside in North Russia*. London: Hutchinson, 1940; Lawrence & Wishart, 1961.
By *The Times*'s correspondent on the British expedition against the Bolsheviks in 1918.

3091   *South Eastern Gazette*. Centenary number. Maidstone (Kent): 5 Jan 1915.

3092   – – –.   120th birthday number. Jan 1935.
Originally entitled *Maidstone Gazette*.

3093   *South Wales Argus*. Centenary issue. Newport (Gwent): 30 May 1992.
Founded in 1892 by Sir Garrod Thomas in the Liberal Party cause, the *Argus* is today a politically independent evening paper in the United Provincial Newspapers group.

3094   *South Wales Echo*. Centenary number. Cardiff: 13 Oct 1984.
In the Thomson Regional Newspapers group.

3095   *South Western Star*. Centenary edition. London (Tooting): 26 Oct 1977.
Then a weekly in the Argus group; now in Trinity International ownership.

3096   *South Yorkshire Times*. Centenary supplement. Mexborough (S Yorks): 23 Jul 1977.
Started as *Mexborough and Swinton Times*; now a Johnston Press title.

3097   Southern Daily Echo. *Newspaper history from 126 years ago*. Southampton: 18 Apr 1956.

3098   *Southern Evening Echo*. 25,000th issue, 1888–1969. Southampton: 23 Oct 1969.
The *Southern Daily Echo* – to which the title has since reverted – remains the principal publication of the Southern Newspapers group.

3099   *Southport Visiter*. Centenary number. Southport (then Lancs): 6 May 1944.
The story of an independent weekly with a long and fascinating history. (The spelling '*Visiter*' is correct!)

3100   Sparks, Colin. 'The working-class press: radical and revolutionary alternatives'. *Media, Culture and Society*, Apr 1985.

3101   – – –.   'The popular press and political democracy'. *Media, Culture and Society*, Apr 1988.

3102   Spencer, J.H. 'Preston's early newspapers'. *Preston Herald*, 30 Dec 1949, 18 Aug 1950.

3103   Spender, Dale. 'West, Rebecca'. *In* Janet Todd, ed. *Dictionary of British women writers*. London: Routledge, 1989.
Potted but useful biography.

3104   Spender, [Edward] Harold. *The fire of life: a book of memories*. London: Hodder & Stoughton, [1926].
Spender's 'Parliamentary Notes' (often illustrated by F.C. Gould) in *The Westminster Gazette* were – and still are – particularly appreciated.

3105   Spender, John Alfred. *The public life*. London and New York: Cassell, 1925. 2 vols: Vol 2 covers 'The press and public life'.
Spender (1862–1942) was unusual in being a busy national newspaper editor – in his case, of the Liberal evening *The Westminster Gazette* from 1896 to 1922 – who later wrote widely for publication.

3106   – – –.   *Life, journalism and politics*. London: Cassell; New York: F.A. Stokes, 1927. 2 vols: 471pp total.
This *apologia pro vita sua* is Spender's very full personal testament. He admits that the pursuit of the latest news was not his ambition with the *Westminster*, preferring 'a proper sense of perspective and value'.

3107   – – –.   *Weetman Pearson, First Viscount Cowdray, 1856–1927*. London: Cassell, 1930. xi + 315pp.
A close-up biography of one of the most significant, but least known, of the press financiers of the early twentieth century. In 1908, Pearson acquired *The Westminster Gazette* (and was thus Spender's proprietor), and thereby laid the foundation of what later became the Pearson Longman group (today Pearson Plc).

3108   – – –.   'The press and the State'. In *4th Annual Imperial Press Conference, 1939*. London: Empire Press Union, 1939.

3109   'Sphinx, A'. *Journalism – a career for women*. London: Newnes, [1918]. 30pp.

3110   Spiegl, Fritz. *Keep taking the tabloids!: what the papers say and how they say it*. London: Pan, 1983. 181pp.
'Fleet Street language and lunacy'.

3111   – – –.   *MediaSpeak: MediaWrite*. London: Elm Tree Books, 1989. 85 + 94pp (printed *tête-bêche*).

3112   Spillman, Ronald. *How to take photographs that editors will buy*. London: Focal Press, [1956].

3113   Spillus, Alex. 'From riches to rags . . .'. *Evening Standard*, 18 Jan 1993.
On the future of London's local newspapers, many of them deliberately going down-market to bolster sales.

3114   Spring, [Robert] Howard. *Hard facts*. London: Collins, 1944. 288pp; Fontana, 1956. 259pp.
Novel centred on a Manchester weekly paper with the same title, and based on the author's long service as a *Manchester Guardian* reporter. He became a very successful full-time novelist.

3115   – – –.   *The autobiography of Howard Spring*. London: Collins, 1972.
Combined, posthumously, the three volumes of memoirs published by Spring in his lifetime.

3116   – – –.   'The pedlar of dreams'. *The Manchester Guardian*, 1931.
On Beaverbrook – who was so impressed that he recruited Spring for the *Evening Standard*; he soon became book critic in place of Arnold Bennett.

3117   Springfield, Lincoln. *Some piquant people*. London: T. Fisher Unwin, 1924. 287pp.
Springfield was the first news editor of the infant *Daily Mail* (1896–1902). He was engaged by Alfred Harmsworth: 'a fresh-looking, straw-coloured, rather handsome, very eager young man'. He also recounts his role in recruiting, in turn, Charles E. Hands, who became special correspondent for the *Mail* in Cuba, South Africa and Manchuria . . . eventually: 'a world-wide institution, and probably the best-known Londoner in the globe apart from professional showmen'; and G.W. Steevens, another *Mail* special in South Africa, who died at Ladysmith. Springfield later purchased and edited *London Opinion*.

3118   Stacey, Tom. *Deadline*. London: Heinemann, 1988; New York: St Martin's Press, 1989. 122pp.
A veteran correspondent's reaction to his successors: a fictional sequel to *The Sunday Times*'s former chief foreign correspondent's real-life experience.

3119   Stack, Neville. *Editing for the nineties*. Wolfson College, University of Cambridge, 1989. Unpubl essays.
On the ethics of journalism and current newspaper practice.

3120   *Staffordshire Advertiser*. 150th anniversary number. Stafford: 6 Jan 1945.

3121   – – –.   175th anniversary souvenir supplement, 1795–1970. 16 Apr 1970.

3122   Staffordshire Sentinel. *The Sentinel: Staffordshire's great daily newspaper*. Hanley (Staffs): 1913.

3123   – – –.   *Rendezvous with the past: Sentinel centenary, 1854–1954*. Stoke-on-Trent: 1954.
'100 years' history of North Staffordshire . . . as reflected in the columns of the *Sentinel* . . . founded on January 7, 1854'. The title on foundation was in fact *Staffordshire Daily Sentinel*. Today its direct descendant is the *Staffordshire Weekly Sentinel*, which with the *Evening Sentinel* (established in 1873) is another title in the Northcliffe Newspapers group. (*See also* Bennett, Arnold: *Hilda Lessways*; *The card*.)

3124   Stanhope, Aubrey. *On the track of the great: recollections of a 'special correspondent'*. London: Eveleigh Nash, 1914. xii + 309pp.

3125   Stanhope, Henry. 'Local funerals in the rain'. *Despatches* (Ministry of Defence), 4, Autumn 1993.
Former defence correspondent of *The Times* reviews the current scene, and concludes that 'the younger generation of journalists are in grave danger of taking themselves too seriously' . . . Local training, he avers, is still a good basis.

3126 Stannard, Russell. *With the dictators of Fleet Street: the autobiography of an ignorant journalist*. London: Hutchinson, 1934. 287pp.
Covering 1914–34, and in particular Beaverbrook's 'empire'. The 'ignorant' author became news editor of the *Sunday Express*.

3127 Stapleton, Laetitia. 'Lt. Col. Charles à Court Repington, C.M.G., 1859–1925'. *Army Quarterly*, Apr 1975.
A controversial *Times* military correspondent under the microscope, in an article by his daughter.

3128 Star, The. *The story of The Star (1888–1938): 50 years' progress and achievement*. London: 1938. 111pp.
Part I, by William Pope (editor from 1920 to 1930), takes the story in outline to the latter year. He highlights the talents of his predecessors: T.P. O'Connor, H.W. Massingham, Ernest Parke, James Douglas.
    This most notable of the London newspapers named *The Star* was founded by a syndicate in 1888 as an evening in the Liberal cause, with O'Connor in charge. Typographically novel and with its staff and contributors leaders in 'the new journalism', it prospered, and eventually (1910) came under the control of the Cadbury family interests. It ceased publication, with its morning counterpart, the *News Chronicle*, in 1960.

3129 *Star, The.* 20th birthday number. 19 Feb 1908.

3130 – – –. 'Our 10,000th number'. 6 May 1920.

3131 – – –. Jubilee number. 17 Jan 1938.
Includes an article by G.B. Shaw entitled 'When we were very young'. His famous 'Corno di Bassetto' music criticism appeared in *The Star* during 1888 and 1889. 'The romance of *The Star*' was an insert.

3132 *Star, The.* Centenary 1887–1987: 100 years of local news. Sheffield: Jun 1987 (supplement).
An evening paper in the United Provincial Newspapers group.

3133 Stark, Malcolm. *The pulse of the world: Fleet Street memories*. London: Skeffington, 1915. 243pp.
By a London representative of the *Glasgow Herald*.

3134 Starmer, *Sir* Charles. 'The story of the *Birmingham Gazette*'. *World's Press News*, 17 Oct 1929.

3135 – – –. 'The importance of the provincial press'. *World's Press News*, 12, 8, 1930.
By the chairman of the former Starmer group.

3136 Startt, James D. *Journalists for Empire: the imperial debate in the Edwardian stately press, 1902–1913*. New York: Greenwood, 1991. xii + 275pp.

3137 – – –. 'Good journalism in the era of the new journalism: the British press, 1902–1914'. *In* J.H. Wiener, ed. *Papers for the millions.* Westport (CT): Greenwood Press, 1988.

3138 – – –. 'Northcliffe the imperialist: the lesser-known years, 1902–1914'. *The Historian*, 57, 1989.

3139 – – –. 'G.E. Buckle, Lord Northcliffe, and the Conservative revolution at *The Times*'. *Journal of Newspaper and Periodical History*, 7, 1, 1991.
George Earle Buckle was editor of *The Times* from 1884 to 1912.

3140 – – –, ed. *Exploring media sources in British and Commonwealth history.* (In preparation.)

3141 Stead, William Thomas. *The truth about the war.* London: The Review of Reviews, [1900]. 63pp.
About the Boer War, published as a 'special' from the offices of Stead's then new publishing venture.

3142 – – –. 'Then and now'. *In The Newspaper Press Directory, 1912.* London: Mitchell, 1912.
A nostalgic survey of the period covered by the directory from its start in 1846. Stead himself started his editorial career with *The Northern Echo* in 1871, aged twenty-two.

3143 Steed, (Henry) Wickham. *The making of a newspaper.* London: 1921. 12pp.
The inaugural address to journalism students at the University of London, 11 October 1921.

3144 – – –. *Through thirty years, 1892–1922: a personal narrative.* London: Heinemann; Garden City (NY): Doubleday, Page, 1924. 2 vols: 830pp total.
Steed (1871–1956), a first-class journalist by any standards, reached prominence as *The Times*'s man in Berlin, Rome and Vienna. During World War I, he directed propaganda against Austria-Hungary. Later, as foreign editor, he proved himself particularly well versed in European affairs. He was appointed editor in 1919. In the words of a historian, he was 'an arresting personality, with wit, panache and style'. But Steed was unfortunate in being in charge during Northcliffe's terminal illness, and a combination of circumstances led to his dismissal late in 1922. His memoirs are also important in their close-up view of the 1919 Peace Conference.

3145 – – –. *The press.* Harmondsworth (Middx): Penguin, 1938. 250pp. (Penguin Special, no 20.)
An authoritative survey that can still be read with profit today. Steed appended a two-page postscript in angry vein. The principles he sets out for the ideal newspaper will endure.

3146 – – –. *The fifth arm.* London: Constable, 1940. 162pp.
An important treatise, with historical notes on the author's work with government propaganda under Northcliffe in World War I.

3147 − − −. 'Thoughts on *The Times*'. *The Fortnightly Review*, new ser, 133, 1933.
After leaving *The Times*, Steed acquired and edited *The Review of Reviews*.

3148 Steel, Donald John, ed. 'Births, marriages and deaths from newspapers'. *In* his *National index to parish registers*, Vol 1. London: Society of Genealogists, 1968.

3149 Steele, Henry J.B. 'The censorship: what it is − and has been − and how it works'. In *Sell's World's Press, 1915*. London: Sell, 1915.
With fascinating illustrations of the Press Bureau (London) in action.

3150 Steer, George Lowther. *Caesar in Abyssinia*. London: Hodder & Stoughton, 1936. 411pp; Boston, 1937.

3151 − − −. *Tree of Gernika: a field study of modern war*. London: Hodder & Stoughton, 1938. 400pp.
The despatches by Steer to *The Times* on the Italian invasion of Abyssinia, then on the German bombing of Gernika (Guernica) in the Spanish Civil War, had a marked influence on British and international public opinion.

3152 − − −. *Sealed and delivered: a book on the Abyssinian campaign*. London: Hodder & Stoughton, 1942. 256pp.
More reports from Africa − and from Abyssinia; but this time the author was working for *The Daily Telegraph*. The book recounts a then rare success story for British arms.

3153 Steevens, George Warrington. *From Capetown to Ladysmith: an unfinished record of the South African War*, edited (with a concluding chapter) by Vernon Blackburn. Edinburgh: Blackwood, 1900. viii + 180pp.

3154 − − −. *Things seen: impressions of men, cities and books*, ed G.S. Street, with a memoir by W.E. Henley. Indianapolis: Bobbs-Merrill, 1900. xxvi + 326pp.
By then a famous front-line correspondent for the *Daily Mail* in the Boer War, Steevens died at Ladysmith when only thirty. His last words are said to have been: 'This is a sideways ending to it all.' Steevens was described by Churchill 'as the most brilliant man in journalism I have ever met'.

3155 Stephenson, Hugh. 'The void in the paper package'. *UK Press Gazette*, 30 May 1988. (In Cleaning Up the 4th Estate series.)
The professor of journalism at City University (London) asserts that the craft is under attack from marketing interests, e.g. in the Sunday magazines.

3156 Stephenson, Hugh, and Pierre Mory, eds. *Journalism training in Europe*. [Brussels]: European Community, 1990. 367pp.
Comprehensive survey − partly in English, partly in French − of current courses. Edited by the professors of journalism at City University and Mons (Belgium).

3157   Stephenson, William Henry. *Alfred Frederick Stephenson, Knight Bachelor: a Lancashire newspaper man.* Manchester: Sherratt & Hughes, 1937. 125pp.
The subject was locally famed as proprietor of the *Southport Visiter* [q.v.]; he was later a director of *The Observer*.

3158   Stevens, Christopher. *In black and white.* Bristol: 1991.
Newspaper novel in newspaper format.

3159   Stewart, Margaret. 'The night the blow fell'. *The New Statesman*, 22 Oct 1960.
Notable as a pioneer woman industrial correspondent, Stewart was at her desk on the paper when the *News Chronicle* was summarily closed down.

3160   Stewart, *Major* Oliver. 'Newspaper English'. *The Strand Magazine*, Jun 1948.
By a leading aviation journalist who held strong views on 'journalese'. One of Christiansen's daily bulletins to his editorial staff at the *Daily Express* is appended.

3161   Stirling Observer. *Ninety years' progress, 1836–1926.* Stirling: Jamieson & Munro, 1926.

3162   *Stirling Observer.* Centenary number, 1836–1936. 15 Sep 1936.

3163   – – –.   150th anniversary issue. Sep 1986.
Today published twice weekly; in Trinity International ownership.

3164   *Stockport Advertiser.* Centenary supplement, 1822–1922. Stockport (then Cheshire): Mar 1922.

3165   – – –.   150th anniversary supplement. Mar 1972.
Later merged into the *Stockport Express Advertiser*, serving a large area of Greater Manchester.

3166   *Stockport Express Advertiser.* Supplement to celebrate the centenary of *Stockport Express.* Oct 1989.

3167   Stokes, Penelope. '. . . *No apology is needed . . .': the story of the Newbury Weekly News, 1867–1992.* Newbury (Berks): Blacket Turner, 1992. xii + 160pp.
125th anniversary history of a newspaper still under the original family ownership (Turner).

3168   Stoppard, Tom (formerly Tomas Straussler). *Night and day.* London: Faber, 1978. 94pp.
A stage play, set in a fictitious African republic but peopled by British journalists covering a rebellion. Stoppard's sure touch on press ethics and trade union practices is based on first-hand experience: 'I'm with you on the free press. It's the newspapers I can't stand.'

3169   Storey, Graham. *Reuters' century, 1851–1951.* With a foreword by Lord Layton. London: Max Parrish, 1951. Publ in the USA as *Reuters: the story of a century of news-gathering.* New York: Crown, 1951. xii + 276pp.

A centenary history of the famous British-based international news agency, commissioned officially and largely based on the archives.

3170 Storey, *(Hon) Sir* Richard. 'Techno could have saved lost papers'. Paper given at the Press '84 Conference, Berlin. Rptd in *UK Press Gazette*, 16 Apr 1984.

3171 – – –. 'Regional newspapers: the changing future'. *Admap*, May 1986.
By the chairman of Portsmouth and Sunderland Newspapers – greatgrandson of Samuel Storey (1841–1925), one of the most significant figures in the history of the regional press as well as MP for Sunderland. Sir Richard himself has held a succession of other top appointments in the newspaper industry.

3172 Storry, T. *The local press: two case studies in the production of news.* Leicester: University of Leicester, 1977 (MPhil thesis).

3173 'Story of another kind, A'. In *Sell's Dictionary of the World's Press, 1905*. London: Sell, 1905.
Re the amalgamation of the *Liverpool Daily Post* and *Liverpool Mercury* (Nov 1904).

3174 *Story of the Press Gallery in the British Parliament, The.* London: Kemsley Newspapers (for Parliamentary Press Gallery), [1950].
With six contributing authors.

3175 Stott, Mary (*née* Waddington). *Forgetting's no excuse: the autobiography of Mary Stott, journalist, campaigner and feminist.* London: Faber, 1973. 194pp. Quartet, for Virago, 1975.

3176 – – –. *Before I go: reflections on my life and times.* London: Virago, 1985. x + 246pp.
Another plain-speaking memoir: 'The state of the British newspaper press is parlous. The national dailies and Sundays are practically all in the hands of very wealthy tycoons.' By the remarkable women's page editor of *The (Manchester) Guardian* (1957–72) and co-founder of Women in Media.

3177 – – –. 'Why women must have their own voice'. *Journalism Studies Review*, 1982.
The function and role of the women's page, based on more than fifty years' experience.

3178 – – –, ed. *Women talking: an anthology from the Guardian women's page, 1922–35 and 1957–71.* London: Pandora Press, 1987. 274pp.

3179 Stovall, James Glen. *The Scottish press and nationalism: a content analysis of newspaper attention to nationalism, 1966–1976.* Knoxville (TN): University of Tennessee, 1979 (PhD dissertation). 230pp. Available in microform from University Microfilms International (Ann Arbor, MI).

3180 Strachey, [John] St Loe. *The adventure of living: a subjective autobiography, 1860–1922.* London and New York: Putnam, 1922. 500pp; London: Nelson, 1925. 441pp.

Includes discussion of the ethics and status of journalism. Strachey was owner–editor of the latter-day *Spectator* from 1898 to 1925.

3181   Straw, Jack. *The declining standards in press reporting of Parliament.* London: Labour Party, 1993. Research by Benjamin Wegg-Prosser.
Contrasts, with statistics, the coverage of parliamentary proceedings in *The Times, The (Manchester) Guardian, The Daily Telegraph* and the *Daily Mirror* in 1973 and in later decades. *Hansard,* while giving verbatim reports, has become, says this survey, prohibitively expensive for most individuals.

3182   Street, P. 'War correspondents: South Africa, 1899–1902'. *Orders and Medals Research Society,* Summer 1986.

3183   *Street's Newspaper Directory for Great Britain and Ireland.* London: Street, 1898–1917, 1920. A successor to *Street's List of Newspapers Published in Great Britain and Ireland,* 1872 on.

3184   Strick, H.C. *British newspaper journalism, 1900–56: a study in industrial relations.* London: University of London, 1957 (PhD thesis).
By the first director of the National Council for the Training of Journalists.

3185   Stuart, *Sir* Campbell (Arthur). *Opportunity knocks once.* London: Collins, 1952. 248pp.
The autobiography of Stuart, a Canadian (1885–1972), whose association with Northcliffe began as his deputy in the Directorate of Propaganda in Enemy Countries in World War I. It continued with Stuart's appointment as managing director of *The Times* – a unique role – and managing editor of the *Daily Mail.* He masterminded the sale of *The Times* after Northcliffe's death.

3186   Stubbs, Jean. *Northern correspondent.* London: Macmillan, 1984. 288pp. Vol 4 of *Brief chronicles.*
A novel centred on provincial newspapers and the development of the railways.

3187   Stubbs, John O. 'Appearance and reality; a case study of *The Observer* and J.L. Garvin, 1914–42'. *In* [D.]G. Boyce *et al,* eds. *Newspaper history . . .* (q.v.).

    Studies in Newspaper and Periodical History: see Reference Works section, under Journal of Newspaper and Periodical History.

3188   *Study Group on Censorship report: the protection of military information.* London: HMSO. 1983. Cmnd 9112. 92pp.
This report was produced by the British Government after the Falklands War.

3189   Stutterheim, Kurt von. *The press in England,* trans W.H. Johnston. London: Allen & Unwin, 1934. 223pp. Originally publ in Berlin: 1933.
A deceptively relaxed essay, intended to give the 'average German reader' a general idea of the subject. But the inclusion by the author – who lived and worked in London in the 1920s – of much original research made it worthy of later publication in England.

3190   *Suffolk newspapers, 1717–1988.* Ipswich: Suffolk Record Office, [1991].
xi + 19pp.
Still described as an 'interim' finding list.

3191   'Suffragette newspapers in the Newspaper Library'. *British Library Newspaper Library Newsletter*, 15, Spring 1993.
The first of the high-profile publications promoting the cause of woman's suffrage was
Votes for Women, started in 1907 under the editorship of Emmeline and Frederick
Pethick-Lawrence. The other two significant titles were *The Suffragette* (founded in 1912
by Christabel Pankhurst in a split from the Pethick-Lawrences) and *The Woman's Dreadnought* (established 1914; editor Christabel's sister Sylvia).

3192   *SULIS: Suffolk Union list of serials*, ed R.T.M. Wilson. Ipswich: Suffolk
College of Higher and Further Education, 1981 etc.

3193   Sullivan, A.E. 'Getting the story: some facts about war correspondents'.
Army Quarterly, 21 Jan 1961.

3194   *Sun, The.* 'Good morning! Yes, it's time for a new newspaper'. London:
15 Jun 1964.
The former *Daily Herald* was noisily re-launched as *The Sun* by Hugh Cudlipp and the
International Publishing Corporation. But it proved to be a damp squib and sales soon
languished.

3195   Sun, The. *Page two: a selection of editorials from The Sun, 1969–1977.*
London: News International, 1977. 99pp.
Some brief, punchy leaders from the face-lifted *Sun*. It was 'sold for a song' by IPC to
Murdoch's News International in 1969, and was quickly transformed into the most
popular contemporary daily, with a formula of sex, crime and (initially) Tory politics.

3196   – – –.   *The public view: a look at how the public view some key issues confronting Britain today.* London: News International, 1977. 36pp.
The results of research, largely by *The Sun*.

3197   – – –.   *The New Establishment: an inquiry into who really governs Britain
in 1978.* London: News International, 1978.
By Anthony Shrimsley, then assistant editor of *The Sun*.

3198   – – –.   *The Sun book of royalty.* London: Invincible Press/The Sun,
[1983].
Royal front pages from the newspaper during the fourteen years since its re-launch.

3199   *Sunday Chronicle.* 50th anniversary number. Manchester: 1 Sep 1935.
Established in 1885 by Hulton in Manchester, with notable contributions from leading
journalists such as Blatchford, it added a London printing and achieved semi-national
status when transferred to the Kemsley group. The *Sunday Referee* was incorporated in
1939, but itself disappeared on merger into the *Empire News* in 1955.

3200   *Sunday Dispatch.* 150th anniversary number. London: 27 Sep 1951.

By the 1950s, the days of the former (and long-lived) *Weekly Dispatch* were numbered: it was closed in 1961.

3201   Sunday Sport. *The best of Sunday Sport: bus found buried at South Pole.* London: Macdonald (Sphere Books), 1989.
The subtitle derives from one of the 'news' headlines perpetrated in what can politely be termed a 'phenomenon' of current British journalism.

3202   *Sunday Telegraph, The* (editorial). London: 5 Feb 1961.
A statement by the editor in the first issue, concerning the aims and style of this partner to *The Daily Telegraph* – the first new national Sunday for forty-three years.

3203   Sunday Telegraph, The. *Faces of our time, 64–85.* (Special section to mark the twenty-first anniversary of the launching of what was initially *Weekend Telegraph.*) *Telegraph Sunday Magazine*, 29 Sep 1985.

3204   *Sunday Telegraph, The.* 25th anniversary. *The Telegraph Sunday Magazine*, 11 May 1986.
Celebrating the 'jubilee' of *The Sunday Telegraph* with a selection of articles from the first twenty-five years of the newspaper itself.

3205   – – –.   'Not quite right on the night'. *The Sunday Telegraph*, 3 Feb 1991.
Looking back to the first – very tentative – issue.

3206   Sunday Times, The. *100 years of history.* London: 1920.
Tracing the paper's antecedents back to *The New Observer* (1821), *The Sunday Times* first appeared as such in 1822. Its great days began with its acquisition in 1915 by William and Gomer Berry, the latter (as Lord Kemsley) becoming sole owner from 1937. It moved in 1959 to Thomson ownership, and – with *The Times* – to News International in 1981.

3207   – – –.   *Leonard Rees.* 1932. 27pp.
Collected obituaries, in tribute to the editor for thirty-one years.

3208   – – –.   *The Sunday Times: a pictorial biography of one of the world's great newspapers.* 1961.
Particularly valuable for the photos of leading personalities at that time.

3209   – – –.   *Encore: the Sunday Times book*, ed Leonard Russell. With an introduction by Denis Hamilton. London: Michael Joseph, 1962, 1963.
Largely made up of articles from the then newly launched *Sunday Times* (colour) *Magazine*.

3210   – – –.   *The Sunday Times bedside book: the best of contemporary writing from one of the world's great newspapers*, ed George Darby. London: André Deutsch, 1978. 232pp. 1980. 256pp.

3211   – – –.   *The Sunday Times Magazine.* 1,001st edn. 30 May 1982.

Also celebrating the twentieth anniversary of the launch (as *The Sunday Times Colour Section*) of the first British Sunday 'colour supplement'. The theme is 'who were the greatest?' over the twenty-year period.

3212 *Sunday Times, The.* 'The future of Fleet Street'. 19 Jan 1986.
A twelve-page 'Innovation Special' marking the paper's first (record-breaking) issue to total 112pp, resulting from the utilization of News International's new presses at Wapping in London's Docklands. It is introduced by a leader entitled 'Putting our house in order', which expresses the sentiment that 'the affairs of Fleet Street have been a national disgrace for at least four decades'. It also includes an interview with Rupert Murdoch, the company's chairman.

3213 – – –. 'Our special Silver Anniversary edition'. *The Sunday Times Magazine* (25th birthday number), 22 Feb 1987.

3214 *Sunday Times* (Insight Team). *Ulster.* London: André Deutsch; Harmondsworth (Middx): Penguin, 1972. 316pp; New York: Random House, 1972.

3215 – – –. *The thalidomide children and the law.* London: André Deutsch, 1973. 156pp.
Documents and texts.

3216 – – –. *Insight on the Middle East War.* London: André Deutsch, 1974. 256pp.

3217 – – –. *The Yom Kippur War.* London: André Deutsch, 1975. xi + 514pp.

3218 – – –. *Suffer the children: the story of thalidomide.* London: André Deutsch, New York: Viking Press, 1979. ix + 309pp.

3219 – – –. *Siege!* London: Hamlyn, 1980.
The story of the siege of the Iranian Embassy in London.

3220 – – –. 'Arthur Scargill's Libyan connection'. *The Sunday Times,* 29 Oct 1984, rptd *UK Press Gazette,* 23 Nov 1987 (Classics of Journalism series).
For other books by the Insight Team, *see under* individual authors.

3221 '*Sunday Times, The*'. *The Newspaper World,* 16 Apr 1938.

3222 'Sunderland and Portsmouth'. *The Newspaper World,* 11 Feb 1939. (In The Oldest Newspapers series.)
Outlines the genesis of the Portsmouth and Sunderland Newspapers group.

3223 *Sunderland Echo.* Centenary supplement. Sunderland: 22 Dec 1973.
Founded by Samuel Storey and others in 1873 as the *Sunderland Daily Echo.*

3224 *Surrey Comet.* Centenary number. Kingston upon Thames (Surrey): 7 Aug 1954.

This paper remains a leading Home Counties weekly, and was acquired from Argus Press by Reed Regional Newspapers in 1993 (moving offices to Twickenham).

3225 *Surrey Herald.* Centenary supplement. Chertsey (Surrey): Dec 1992.
Another former Argus title, acquired in 1993 by Southnews group.

3226 'Survivor's guide to free newspapers, A'. *Journalist's Week,* 28 Sep 1990.
The current state of a fluctuating market.

3227 *Surrey Mirror.* Centenary edition. Reigate: 27 Jul 1979.
Another ex-Argus weekly, transferred to Trinity International ownership.

3228 Susanto-Sunario, Astrid S. *Die politische Kräfte durch die Entstehung des britischen Presserätes* (Political forces during the setting up of Britain's Press Council). Berlin: 1965 (DPhil thesis).

3229 *Sussex Express.* Centenary supplement. Lewes (E Sussex): 11 Jun 1937.
Founded in 1837 as *Sussex Agricultural Express,* it is today a weekly in the EMAP group.

3230 Sutherland, Douglas. *Portrait of a decade: London life, 1945–1955.* London: Harrap, 1988. 239pp.
Students of journalism in that decade immediately after World War II will find entertaining material in its frank and gossipy portrayal of the Fleet Street scene: on duty with e.g. The Londoner's Diary in the *Evening Standard* and *Picture Post,* off duty in bars and clubs galore.

3231 *Sutton and Cheam Herald.* Centenary souvenir, 1878–1978. Sutton (Surrey, now Greater London): 2 Aug 1978.
Formerly belonging to the Argus group, now part of Trinity International.

3232 Swaebe, A.W. *Photographer royal.* London: Frewin, 1967.

3233 Swaffer, [Frederick Charles] Hannen. *Northcliffe's return.* London: Hutchinson, 1925; Psychic Press, 1939. xiii + 286pp. Foreword by Lord Beaverbrook.
The consuming interest outside journalism of Swaffer – greatest personality among journalists of his era – was spiritualism. This book reports 'comment' of Northcliffe, his former chief, from beyond the grave.

3234 – – –. *Hannen Swaffer's who's who.* London: Hutchinson, 1929. 255pp. Foreword by Edgar Wallace.
A gallery of pen-portraits.

3235 – – –. 'Meet cameraman Jarché: officialdom v. the press'. *Illustrated,* 1946.
Tribute by Swaffer, then editor of the *Daily Herald,* to that paper's leading press photographer of the time.

3236 Swan, Annie S. (later Burnett-Smith). *An American woman*. London: Hutchinson, 1902.
Romantic novel with a journalist as heroine.

3237 Swanton, E[rnest] W[illiam], ed. *Back page cricket*. London: Queen Anne Press, 1987.
Wide-ranging press anthology, with commentary. His own writing has been most notably for *The Daily Telegraph*.

3238 Sweeney, John. 'Gotcha!: the *first* profile of Kelvin MacKenzie, the elusive editor of the oafish *Sun*'. *The Tatler*, Oct 1986.

3239 – – –. 'The *Sun* and the *Star*'. *The Independent Magazine*, 11 Feb 1989.
The *Star* in question is the *Daily Star*.

3240 Swift, Graham. *Out of this world*. London: Viking, 1988.
Novel with photojournalism as a central theme.

3241 Swinnerton, Frank Arthur. *Figures in the foreground: literary reminiscences, 1917–40*. London: Hutchinson, 1963; Garden City (NY): Doubleday, 1964. 272pp.
Valuable comment from an author and critic closely concerned with the world of the literary periodical over two later decades and more. There is a chapter on 'four journalists': Robert Lynd, James Bone, H.M. Tomlinson, Philip Gibbs; and another on the *Evening News*, where Swinnerton was brought in as book critic and became a friendly rival of Arnold Bennett, whose Books and Persons column in the *Evening Standard* was, as Swinnerton admits, 'one of the sensations of the day'. Discussing great editors of his day – J.A. Spender, Gardiner, H.W. Massingham, Donald, Garvin – he comments: 'In office, they wielded unlimited power; out of it, they were lost.'

3242 Swinton, Sir Ernest (Dunlop). *Eyewitness*. London: Hodder & Stoughton, 1932. 321pp.
'Being personal reminiscences of certain phases of the Great War, including the genesis of the tank'. In a press context, recounts how (September 1914–July 1915) he was installed as 'Eye-Witness' to feed HQ, and hence the press at home, with official news – before accredited correspondents were allowed at the Front. Swinton had had experience with the *Continental Daily Mail* before the war.

3243 *Swinton and Pendlebury Journal*. Centenary supplement, 1875–1975. Swinton (Greater Manchester): 3 Sep 1975.
Founded as *Pendlebury and Swinton Journal*.

3244 Sykes, Christopher. *Evelyn Waugh: a biography*. London: Collins, 1975. xii + 468pp. Revised edn, Harmondsworth (Middx): Penguin, 1977 etc. 619pp.
A masterly portrait of a master stylist, novelist – and journalist.

3245 Symon, James David. *The press and its story*. London: Seeley, Service, 1914. xii + 328pp.

'An account of the birth and development of journalism up to the present day, with the history of all the leading newspapers, daily, weekly, or monthly, secular and religious, past and present' by the 'sometime assistant editor' of *The Illustrated London News*. In popular vein, but accurate within its limits; the pictorial press is featured effectively, and there is a long section on the distribution operations of W.H. Smith & Son.

3246   'Tabloids, The'. *UK Press Gazette*, 7 Sep–5 Oct 1987 (series). *See also* Askew, Barry; Leapman, Michael; Linklater, Magnus; Loynes, Tony; Plimmer, Martyn.

3247   *Tamworth Herald, The*. 125th anniversary supplement. Tamworth (Staffs): 6 Aug 1993.

3248   Tausk, Petr. *A short history of press photography*. Prague: International Organization of Journalists, 1988. 232pp.
A global survey, celebrating one hundred and fifty years of photography, and covering 'press' in the widest sense – including for example magazine covers and advertising as well as news shots. Britain is among the countries represented among the selection of two hundred photos.

3249   Taylor, A[lan] J[ohn] P[ercivale]. *Beaverbrook*. London: Hamish Hamilton; New York: Simon & Schuster, 1972. xvii + 712pp; Harmondsworth (Middx): Penguin, 1974. 896pp.
A massive, fully documented work with an extensive bibliography, by one who was a close friend of Beaverbrook as well as an outstanding historian. This is the most generous biography in the extensive literature about Beaverbrook, whose methods of remote but direct control of his newspapers and their policies are graphically described. Taylor was a frequent leader-writer for Beaverbrook's *Sunday Express*.

3250   – – –.   'The Beaverbrook Library'. *History*, 69, Feb 1974.
Contributed by Taylor as director of the Beaverbrook Library, then housed in St Bride St (London EC) behind the *Daily Express* offices. In the following year, the library was closed, and most of the contents were deposited by the First Beaverbrook Foundation in the House of Lords Record Office.

3251   – – –, ed. *Off the record: political interviews, 1933–1943, by W.P. Crozier*. London: Hutchinson, 1973. xxi + 397pp.
Having joined *The Manchester Guardian* in 1904, William Percival Crozier took over 'brilliantly' as editor in 1932, when C.P. Scott's son Edward was drowned in a boating accident; Crozier continued as editor until 1944, the year of his death.

3252   Taylor, Allan K. *From a Glasgow slum to Fleet Street*. London: Alvin Redman, [1949]. xiii + 245pp.

3253   Taylor, Geoffrey, ed. *Changing faces: a history of The Guardian, 1956–88*. London: Fourth Estate, 1993. xiii + 354pp.
An insider's view, by a former foreign editor, Northern editor, assistant editor, and chief leader-writer. It begins when the editorship passed to Alastair Hetherington, and of

course spans the period when the paper became a truly national organ: with the title abbreviated to *The Guardian* in 1959, first London issue in 1961, and editorial move in 1964. The only editor since Hetherington, Peter Preston, took over in 1975. Its stance has remained left of centre.

3254 Taylor, H(enry) A(rchibald). *Robert Donald: being the authorised biography of Sir Robert Donald, G.B.E., LL.D., journalist, editor and friend of statesmen.* London: Stanley Paul, [1934]. 288pp.
Donald (1860–1933) was editor of *The Daily Chronicle* from 1904 to 1918, when he resigned (on the change of ownership); there is a complete chapter here entitled 'The tragedy of the *Daily Chronicle*', following its fortunes beyond the Donald era up to its merger into the *News Chronicle* in 1930. Taylor also gives details of the early years of United Newspapers, publishers of *The Daily Chronicle, Lloyd's Sunday News* etc during those twelve years.

3255 – – –. *Freedom number one: liberty of expression and the British press.* London: Signpost Press, 1944. 29pp.

3256 – – –. *The British press: a critical survey.* London: Arthur Barker, 1961. 176pp.
One of the best of the occasional essays on the subject by a concerned senior journalist with experience of both the provinces and Fleet Street (where he served under Donald on *The Daily Chronicle*). Taylor was likewise president of the Institute of Journalists (twenty-five years after Donald), a Member of Parliament during World War II, and chairman of the Newspaper Features agency for nearly forty years.

3257 – – –. 'Through fifty years: an outline of the history of the Institute of Journalists'. *Journal*, Jubilee supplement, 28, 1940.

3258 – – –. 'The British concept of the freedom of the press'. *Gazette*, 21, 1965.

3259 Taylor, John. *War photography: realism in the press.* London: Routledge (Comedia), 1991. 199pp.
A well-documented arraignment of the lack of objectivity often practised by newspapers in the national (and/or their own) interest. The chapters on the Falklands campaign and 'Northern Ireland and terrorism' are particularly valuable.

3260 Taylor, Justine. 'Reuters Holdings Plc'. In *International directory of company histories*, Vol 4. Chicago and London: St James Press, 1991.

3261 – – –. 'Reuters'. *In* Dennis Griffiths, ed. *The encyclopedia of the British press, 1422–1992.* Basingstoke (Hants): Macmillan, 1992.
A good summary history.

3262 Taylor, Neville. 'Behind the Whitehall curtain'. *British Journalism Review*, Autumn 1989.
'The only commodity which the Government Information Service trades in is professional integrity.' As a former director-general of the Central Office of Information and

head of information in five Whitehall departments, the author is well placed to voice his disquiet.

3263   Taylor, Philip M. *The projection of Britain: British overseas publicity and propaganda, 1919–1939.* Cambridge: Cambridge University Press, 1981. xv + 363pp.

3264   – – –. *War and the media: propaganda and persuasion in the Gulf War.* Manchester: Manchester University Press, 1992. xii + 338pp.
More material on television than on newspapers.

3265   – – –. 'Publicity and diplomacy: the impact of the First World War upon Foreign Office attitudes to the press'. *In* D. Dilks, ed. *Retreat from power.* London: Macmillan, 1981.

3266   Taylor, S(ally) J. *Shock! Horror!: the tabloids in action.* London: Bantam Press, 1991. xiv + 354pp.
An American journalist's generally enthusiastic endorsement of the present-day popular tabloids both in her own country and in Britain.

3267   – – –. History of the *Daily Mail.* (In preparation for the centenary of the newspaper in 1996.)

3268   Tchikawa, Tomoko. *The Daily Citizen, 1912–15.* Cardiff: University of Wales, 1984 (MA thesis).

3269   Telen, Elmira Federovna. *Sotsialnaia mimikrlia burzhuaznykh massovykh gazet Veliko-Britanii* (Social mimicry of the bourgeois mass newspapers of Great Britain). Moscow: 1978.

3270   Terraine, John (Alfred). *Images of war: 1914 and 1918.* London: Hutchinson, 1970. ix + 267pp.

3271   Terrington, Derek. *The British newspaper industry: market overview.* London: Jordan & Sons (Surveys), 1981.

3272   Tetlow, Edwin. *As it happened: a journalist looks back.* London: Peter Owen, 1990. 189pp.
War correspondent for the *Daily Mail* (Eighth Army etc) and in peace for *The Daily Telegraph* (1950–65, including in New York).

3273   Thatcher, Margaret (Hilda), *Baroness. The Downing Street years.* London: HarperCollins, 1993. 862pp.
Relations between Prime Minister and the media, with Bernard Ingham as ever-vigilant press secretary, are discussed.

3273A   Thayer, Frank. *Newspaper management.* New York: Appleton, 1926. Revised edn, Appleton-Century, 1938.

3274   *Thetford and Watton Times.* Centenary supplement. Thetford (Norfolk): 22 Feb 1980.
Originally *People's Weekly Journal*; today in Eastern Counties group.

3275 'Third degree, The: Drew Robertson and the *Sunday Sport*'. *Company Magazine*, Sep 1986.
The London editor of this maverick paper in close-up.

3276 Thomas, Denis John Roy. *Challenge in Fleet Street: a candid commentary on today's national newspapers*. London: Truth Publishing Co (Staples), 1957. 60pp.
A pamphlet that contains a contemporary description of the *News Chronicle*, highlighting its traditional style.

3277 – – –. *The story of newspapers*. London: Methuen, 1965. 94pp. (Oxford Pamphlet on Home Affairs.)

3278 Thomas, Donald. *A long time burning: the history of literary censorship in England*. London: Routledge, 1969. xii + 546pp.
Includes a twenty-page bibliography.

3279 Thomas, Frederick Moy, ed. *Fifty years of Fleet Street: being the life and recollections of Sir John R. Robinson*. London: Macmillan, 1904. xiii + 404pp.
Robinson was managing editor of *The Daily News* from 1868 to 1901.

3280 Thomas, Harford. *Newspaper crisis*. Zürich: IPI, 1967.
Concerning developments in the British press in 1966–7, with implications at that time for the industry elsewhere in Europe.

3281 Thomas, Ian. *The newspaper*. London: Oxford University Press, 1943. 32pp. (Oxford Pamphlet on Home Affairs.)

3282 Thomas, Leslie (John). *In my wildest dreams*. London: Arlington Books, 1984.
Autobiography of the bestselling novelist – who gravitated via local papers and the (London) *Evening News*.

3283 Thomas, Robbie. *The Advertiser family: a story of North Wales Newspapers Ltd*. Oswestry (Shropshire): 1988. 99pp.

3284 Thomas, *Sir* William Beach. *A traveller in news*. London: Chapman & Hall, 1925. xii + 306pp.
Most valuable in its close-up glimpses of Northcliffe, who sent the author on an Empire tour in 1922 for the *Daily Mail* and *The Times*.

3285 Thompson, A.M. *Newspaper crisis presentation*. Manchester: University of Manchester Institute of Science and Technology, 1978 (PhD thesis).

3286 Thompson, Alexander Mattock ('Dangle'). *Here I lie: the memorial of an old journalist*. London: Routledge, 1937. xii + 324pp. Introduction by Lord Snell.
By the joint founder-editor, with Robert Blatchford, of *The Clarion*. Later Thompson was a labour writer for the *Daily Mail*.

3287   Thompson, C[ecil] V[incent] R[aymond]. *I lost my English accent*. London: Nicholson, 1939. 306pp; New York, 1939.
By a US correspondent for the *Daily Express*.

3288   Thompson, Denys. *Reading between the lines: or how to read a newspaper*. London: Muller, 1949.

3289   Thompson, E[dward] P[almer]. *The struggle for a free press*. London: People's Press Printing Society, 1952. 22pp.

3290   – – –. *The making of the English working class*. London: Gollancz, 1963, 1980. 958pp; Harmondsworth (Middx): Penguin, 1968. 848pp.
On his death in 1993, Thompson was described as a 'thoroughly English dissident' in *The Guardian*, where his radical views were often vividly expressed.

3291   No entry.

3292   Thompson, J[ohn] W[illiam] M[cWean]. 'Sturdy growth of *The Sunday Telegraph*'. *In* D. Campbell, ed. *The British press*. London: CPU, 1978.
Thompson, appointed editor of *The Sunday Telegraph* in 1976, had previously written essays under the pseudonym of 'Peter Quince'.

3293   Thompson, Peter, and Anthony Delano. *Maxwell: a portrait of power*. London: Bantam, 1988. 240pp. Revised pbk edn, London: Corgi, 1991.

3294   Thompson, R(eginald) W(illiam). *Men under fire*. London: Macdonald, [1946]. x + 160pp.
A collection of despatches for the Kemsley group and *The Sunday Times* from the European Front, November 1944 to March 1945. The author estimates that he filed 200,000 words in twelve weeks.

3295   – – –. *Cry Korea*. London: Macdonald, 1951. 303pp; Panther, 1956; London and New York: White Lion, 1974.
The author was in the front line for *The Daily Telegraph*. His sad summing-up: 'There was no safety, no life, no living room, for the people of Korea any more.'

3296   Thomson, Alex. *Smokescreen: the media, the censors and the Gulf*. Tunbridge Wells (Kent): Spellmount, 1992.
A fierce attack, from first-hand experience, of the censorship imposed in the Gulf War.

3297   Thomson, George Malcolm. *Lord Castlerosse: his life and times*. London: Weidenfeld & Nicolson, [1973]. 176pp.
A colleague's close-up of a larger-than-life Anglo-Irish gossip writer for the *Sunday Express* and confidant of Beaverbrook.

3298   – – –. 'The young men who make them'. *Daily Express*, 12 Jul 1933.
Refers to the *Daily Express* and *Sunday Express*: 'The eaglets are tumbling about in the nest, stretching their wings and opening their beaks . . . near by, an older bird watches them.'

3299 Thomson, *Rear Admiral (Sir)* George Pirie. *Blue pencil admiral: the inside story of press censorship (1939–1945)*. London: Sampson Low, 1947. viii + 216pp.
The author was chief press censor at the Ministry of Information almost throughout World War II. The book is valuable in going to the limit in what could be divulged so soon by an 'insider'.

3300 Thomson, Roy Herbert, *1st Baron* Thomson of Fleet. *After I was sixty: a chapter of autobiography*. London: Hamish Hamilton, 1975. x + 224pp.
The straightforward and modestly written story of the Canadian who came to Britain at the age of fifty-nine to bid – successfully – for *The Scotsman*, proceeded to set up Scottish Television, and then (in addition to making various acquisitions outside the media) bought the Kemsley group (including *The Sunday Times*), formed Thomson Publications (periodicals and books), and in 1966 acquired *The Times*. Thomson died in 1976, and has a memorial in St Paul's Cathedral (London). The Thomson Corporation remains based in Toronto.

3301 – – –. 'The next ten years'. *In* V. Brodzky, ed. *Fleet Street: the inside story of journalism*. London: Macdonald, 1966.
Thomson's fascinating forecast when he was on the brink of purchasing *The Times*.

3302 Thomson, William, and David Couper Thomson. *The Dundee Courier and the Dundee Weekly News: their progress and development*. [Dundee]: [1889]. 31pp.
An early promotion booklet from the founders (in 1905) of the giant D.C. Thomson group in Dundee.

3303 Thomson Foundation, The. *The news machine: a guide to advanced techniques in journalism*. 2nd edn, Cardiff: 1972; 3rd edn, London: 1985. Two parts: Part 1: Getting the news; Part 2: Getting to press.
Spiral-bound manual, produced with the particular requirements in mind of the Foundation's students from overseas, but of practical value generally.

3304 Thorn, Arthur F. *Journalism today*. London: Foyle, 1924. v + 166pp. Revised by Llywelyn W. Maddock – publ 1928.

3305 'Threats come in many guises'. *The Sunday Times*, 25 Jun 1987.
Threats to the freedom of the press – from the print unions, or from the Government by censorship etc.

3306 'Three and a quarter centuries of illustrated journalism'. *World's Press News*, 14 Jul 1932.

3307 'Three generations at Trowbridge'. *The Newspaper World*, 25 Apr 1939. (In the Pillars of the Press series.)
The story of the *Trowbridge and Wiltshire Advertiser*, founded in 1855.

3308 'Thribb, E.J.' 'Lines on the 20th anniversary of the *Sun* newspaper'. *Private Eye*, 15 Mar 1989.
By *Private Eye*'s 'poet-in-residence' . . . fifteen lines, ending:

Unfortunately,
Like everything
Else in the *Sun,*
This is
Not true.
    E.J. Thribb (17½–34½–17½)

3309   *Thurrock Gazette.* Centenary supplement. Basildon (Essex): 25 May 1984.
Now a free newspaper in the Westminster Press group.

3310   Thwaite, Mary Florence, comp. *Hertfordshire newspapers, 1772–1955.* Hertford: Hertfordshire Local History Council, 1956. 42pp.

3311   Times, The. *The history of The Times.* London: *The Times*; New York: Macmillan. Reprints of Vols 1–4, Nendeln (Liechtenstein): Kraus Reprint, 1971. 5 vols. Vol 3: *The twentieth century test, 1884–1912.* Publ 1947. xvi + 862pp. Vol 4 (2 parts): *The 150th anniversary and beyond, 1921–1948.* Publ 1952. xvi and viii + 1,182pp (total). Vol 5: *Struggles in war and peace, 1939–1966.* By Iverach McDonald; with an appendix to 1982, by E.C. Hodgkin. Publ 1984. ii + 514pp. Vol 6: *The Thomson years, 1966–1981.* By John Grigg. Publ 1993. xv + 632pp.

These volumes are among the most important – and best-balanced – histories published by any British newspaper. In accord with the then tradition of the paper, the first four volumes carry no evidence of authorship, but it is known that the editor and in large part author and designer was Stanley Morison. Technical and visual development are deliberately excluded, but Morison – leading typographer of the era – himself filled the gap with other authoritative works, some likewise anonymous.

Volume 1 was published to mark the 150th anniversary, and Vol 5 timed to coincide with the bicentenary. The latter broke precedent in bearing McDonald's name as author, and in giving extensive (and welcome) biographical notes on individual history-makers.

John Walter I – first of the founding dynasty – launched *The Daily Universal Register* on 1 January 1785, changing its title to *The Times* exactly three years later. It swiftly became a national campaigning voice. The great years of Delane's editorship (he succeeded Barnes in 1841) saw the circulation rise to a level more than treble that of the other London dailies combined.

But eventually cheaper and more popular competitors meant that *The Times* became increasingly isolated. In 1908, Northcliffe stepped in as the new owner, with John Walter IV retained as chairman. The next major change came after Northcliffe's death in 1922, when J.J. Astor took over as chairman. Two further changes in ownership have reflected further financial strains: to Lord Thomson in 1966, and – with *The Sunday Times* – to Rupert Murdoch (News International) in 1981.

(In 1991, The Times Archives were installed in News International's Wapping offices.)

Note: the publisher of all publications listed below is London: The Times (or latterly Times Publishing or Times Books), unless otherwise stated.

– – –.   *The Times Index: see Reference Works section.*

3312   – – –.   *A selection of types for display advertisements.* [1910]. 34pp.

3313   – – –.   *The Times on advertising.*
Reprint of a series in 1904–5 of in-depth articles now known to have been contributed by Thomas Russell, the paper's advertisement manager.

3314   – – –.   *Printing number* (No 40,000). 10 Sep 1912. 44pp.
Includes 'Origin and growth of the British newspaper, 1622–1714'; and A.W. Pollard on 'The story of printing since Gutenberg'. Largely the handiwork of Stanley Morison (whose role, as then customary with *The Times,* is unacknowledged), this has been described as 'the most impressive supplement ever put out by a daily paper'. Reprinted in book form: 1912. viii + 220pp + 72pp of advertisements.

3315   – – –.   *The press of the world and The Times printing number (40,000th issue).* 1913. v + 165pp.
'Appreciations by the newspapers of many countries'.

3316   – – –.   *Readers of The Times.* 1913.
Sepia reproductions by contemporary artists, with linking text – an early (and superior) example of newspaper publicity.

3317   – – –.   *Printing number.* 6 Oct 1919.
Includes 'Illustration of newspapers', by Ulric van den Bogaerde. He had been art editor and photographer for *The Times history of the war,* but it was May 1922 – shortly before Northcliffe's death – before Bogaerde took charge of the paper's first page of news photos.

– – –.   *Tercentenary handlist: see Reference Works section.*

3318   – – –.   *Strike nights in Printing House Square: an episode in the history of The Times.* 1926. xiii + 48pp.
Printed for private circulation to staff and voluntary workers during the General Strike (May 1926); devotes special attention to issue no 44, 263 – 'Little Sister', published on the second day of the strike. There was no break in daily publication of the paper.

3319   – – –.   *Printing in the twentieth-century: a survey.* 1930. xvi + 300pp + xx. A survey rptd from *The Times printing number,* 29 Oct 1929.
Covers Western Europe and the USA as well as the UK, and includes 'Newspaper types: a study of *The Times*', by Stanley Morison. Has four pages in full colour.

3320   – – –.   *Printing The Times: a record of the changes introduced in the issue for 3 October, 1932.* 1932. 38pp.
Times New Roman, painstakingly evolved by Morison in his capacity of typographical adviser, represented a completely new typeface and a landmark in newspaper design. It was adopted widely elsewhere, although criticized later as suitable only for 'a dignified newspaper to be read by people with some leisure'.

3321   – – –.   *Fifty years, 1882–1932: memories and contrasts*. London: Thornton Butterworth, 1932. 224pp. Foreword by G.M. Trevelyan.
'A composite picture of the period by twenty-seven contributors to *The Times*' . . . who are all, in this special instance, named. Both text and rotogravure photos are valuable elements in this fascinating evocation of a changing Britain, reprinted from a series in the paper; the popular press is loftily blamed for some of the less admirable changes.

3322   – – –.   *The Times: past, present, future*. 1932. 47pp; 1935. Ed Harold Child.

3323   *Times, The*. 150th anniversary supplement: 1785–1935. 1 Jan 1935.

3324   Times, The. *A newspaper history, 1785–1935*. 1935. vii + 213pp. Rptd from 150th anniversary no.
Hartley Withers contributes the articles on *The Times* itself and the City; but there is much authoritative, if brief, coverage of wider subjects, e.g. 'London newspapers', 'Scotland and the provinces', 'Sunday newspapers' (all by Andrew Stewart); 'The religious press' (H.W. Peet); 'Weekly journals' (J.D. Newth); 'The growth of the agencies' (Sir Roderick Jones); 'The Post Office and newspapers' (J.H. Brebner); 'The London scene in 1785' (Percy Lovell).

3325   – – –.   *Europe under the Nazi scourge – a picture and an indictment*. 1940. viii + 146pp.
Appeasement forgotten: a reprint of recent articles on conditions in German-occupied Europe.

3326   – – –.   *The Times and the Post Office*. 1946. 12pp.
On revenue stamps etc.

3327   – – –.   *When the sirens sounded: an account of air raid precautions in Printing House Square, 1937 to 1945*. 1949. 99pp.
The worst bombing 'incidents' were on 24 September 1940, with two direct hits, but production continued almost uninterrupted.

3328   – – –.   *Printing The Times since 1785: some account of the means of production and changes of dress of the newspaper*. 1953. xii + 198pp (incl appendix). 'Upwards of 50 facsimiles of pages'.
Restricted to two limited editions totalling 750 copies, this large-folio book, with text in 24-point Times New Roman, is itself universally regarded as a classic in newspaper typography. It was planned, edited and largely written by Stanley Morison – who under *Times* tradition had to remain anonymous. By this time the first four volumes of *The Times*'s official *History*, edited by Morison, had all appeared.

3329   – – –.   *The history from 1276 to 1956 of the site in Blackfriars consisting of Printing House Square*, 'with later accretions along Glasshouse and Playhouse Yards, Huish Court, and other thoroughfares, the whole now being the freehold property of The Times Publishing Company, Limited', comp Phyllis M. Handover. 1956. xiii + 140pp.

One hundred copies were made on handmade paper with private distribution. (*The Times* moved to Gray's Inn Road in 1974, after 189 years, and to Wapping in 1986.)

3330 – – –. *Red and black: the duty and postage stamps impressed on newspapers, 1712–1870, and on The Times or its postal wrappers from 1785 to 1962*, ed Stanley Morison and Phyllis Handover. London: *The Times*, 1962; and special edn: Oxford University Press. Rptd in part, 1980.

3331 – – –. *The European press: special report*. Supplement, 16 Feb 1972. 8pp.
Country by country, with a short commentary on the situation in Britain.

3332 – – –. *The world's press: special report*. Supplement, 23 Jul 1973. 12pp.
With introductory discussion of the current international – and British – scene. This follows a similar report, with the same title, publ 17 Dec 1970.

3333 – – –. *The Times reports the National Government, 1931: extracts from The Times, January to October 1931*, ed and with an introduction by Colin Bell. 1975. xxxi + 209pp.
Bell pulls no punches: 'Dawson was a complicated man, of great ability; a first-class brain who lent all his professional weight to the maintenance of the role of the second-rate, the exclusion of the best, during his second Editorship.'

3334 – – –. *Obituaries from The Times*, comp Frank C. Roberts. Reading: Newspaper Archive Developments. 3 vols. Part I: selection of obituaries; Part II: index to all obituaries and tributes. All are rptd as publ in the paper.
1951–1960, publ 1979. 896pp; 1,450 entries.
1961–1970, publ 1975. 952pp; 1,500 entries.
1971–1975, publ 1978. 648pp; 1,000 entries.
'Newspapers' is a classification in the subject index of the latter two volumes. All the volumes are of course especially full and authoritative on former *Times* people. *See also under* Heaton, David.

3335 *Times, The.* Bicentenary edn, 2 Jan 1985. Facsimile of the issue of 1 Jan 1785 as insert. Includes a leader: 'The next two hundred'.

3336 Times, The. *The Times: past – present – future*, ed George Darby. 7 Jan 1985. 166pp.
A colour magazine for the bicentenary. Signed contributions: 'All in a day's work', by Raymond Mortimer; 'The voice of The Thunderer', Roy Jenkins; 'Momentous times: triumphs and tribulations', Alan Hamilton; 'Our men out there: frontline reporting', Phillip Knightley; 'The picture man', Dirk Bogarde (about Ulric van den Bogaerde, the first art editor – his father); 'The agony column', Miles Kington; 'The *Times* crossword', Edmund Akenhead; 'Obituaries', Colin Watson; 'The Fourth Leader', E.C. Hodgkin; 'Reporting Parliament', David Wood; 'Letters to the editor', Geoffrey Woolley; also '*Times* past' (chronology of two hundred years) and '*Times* future', Charles Douglas-Home (then editor).

3337 – – –. 'The regional press'. 6 May 1986. 'Focus' special report to mark the 150th anniversary of the Newspaper Society.

3338 – – –. 'One year at Wapping'. 26 Jan 1987.

3339 *'Times, The*, and its New Roman type'. *The Monotype Recorder*, 31, Sep–Oct 1932.
Special issue itself printed in the newly introduced Times New Roman; four (anonymous) contributions by Stanley Morison.

3340 *'Times, The*, and the Bolshevik Revolution'. *Journalism Quarterly*, 56, 1979.
This commentary should be read as a belated warning against wishful thinking by editors about Bolshevism.

3341 *'Times, The:* from Delane to Northcliffe'. *The Quarterly Review*, 239, 1923.

3342 *Times House Journal, The.*
Monthly magazine (1924–66) for the newspaper's staff, established (London) in 1921 as *The Times AAA Journal*; later *Times News*, 1967–1978; *TNL News*, 1981–85; *The News*, 1986–.

3343 No entry.

3344 *Times Literary Supplement, The.* Printing number. London: 13 Oct 1927.
With woodcuts and samples of type.

3345 Timpson, John. *Paper trail.* London, Muller, 1989. 235pp.
Novel about young newspaperman in 1950s Norfolk.

3346 Tindle, (*Sir*) Ray(mond) (Stanley). *The press today and tomorrow.* London: Stationers' Company, 1975. Annual Livery Lecture.
Tindle, whose Tindle Newspaper group has been a major force in the regional newspaper scene, was later master of the Stationers' Company, as well as president of the Newspaper Society.

3347 Tomalin, Nicholas. *Nicholas Tomalin reporting*, ed Ron Hall. London: André Deutsch, 1975. 317pp.
Some of the outstanding writing by a *Sunday Times* correspondent who was killed in the Yom Kippur War in 1972. The excerpts include a long article on *Private Eye* (from *The Sunday Times Magazine*, 27 March 1966), and 'Stop the press, I want to get on' (*The Sunday Times Magazine*, 26 October 1969): 'The only qualities essential for real success in journalism are ratlike cunning, a plausible manner, and a little literary ability.'

3348 Toner, Michael. 'Farewell Fleet Street'. *Sunday Express*, 9 Apr 1989.
Comment on his newspaper's move across Blackfriars Bridge from Fleet Street to Ludgate House.

3349 Topolski, Feliks. *Russia in war.* London: Methuen, 1942. 128pp.
A remarkable portfolio from the Polish-born artist who made an enduring journalistic mark in *Picture Post*. He was the only foreign artist to report from the Soviet Union during World War II.

3350 'Top 250 European daily newspapers, The'. *Newspaper Focus*, Oct 1993.
Features *Today* (no 27 in terms of circulation) and the *Manchester Evening News* (no 107).

3351 Tory, Peter. *Giles: a life in cartoons*. London: Headline, 1992. 192pp.
The first in-depth study (profusely illustrated) of Carl Giles and his unique career as
cartoonist for the *Daily Express* and *Sunday Express* since 1943. He had made his name
with *Reynolds News*.

3352 – – –. *The Giles family: the illustrated history of Britain's best-loved
family*. London: Headline, 1993. 192pp.
Follow-up, with one hundred and fifty more cartoons, all featuring the famous 'family'
launched by Giles in the *Sunday* (then *Daily*) *Express* immediately after World War II.

3353 – – –. *Giles at war*. London: Headline, 1994.
To complete a trilogy on Giles's unique portfolio.

3354 Tracey, Herbert, ed. *The British press: a survey, a newspaper directory, and
a who's who in journalism*. London: Europa, [1929]. 139pp. (A Parchment
Guide.)

3355 Tracy, Walter. *Letters of credit: a view of type design*. London: Gordon
Fraser, 1986.
By a leading authority on the subject.

3356 Trelford, Donald (Gilchrist). 'The new deal that newspapers need'. *The
Observer*, 10 Jul 1977.
The editor's manifesto during *The Observer*'s Atlantic Richfield regime.

3357 – – –. 'Heeding our ancestral voices'. *The Observer*, 10,000th edn.
8 May 1983.
The editor's salute to his predecessors.

3358 – – –. 'The survival of the Street'. *Campaign*, 30 Mar 1984.
'Newspapers will only survive if they continue to serve a fundamental need in our society.'

3359 – – –. 'How trivialisation is killing our claims to a free press'. *UK Press
Gazette*, 18 Mar 1985.
'Too many of our newspapers have given up the primordial battle to find things out.'

3360 – – –. 'The rights and wrongs of a fettered press'. *UK Press Gazette*,
20 Jun 1988. (In Cleaning Up the 4th Estate series.)

3361 – – –. 'The dogs that fail to bark'. *The Guardian (Media Guardian)*,
6 Apr 1992.
On the poor defence offered by the press in general against its detractors – and, in
Trelford's opinion, the weak stance taken by the Press Complaints Commission.

3362 – – –, ed. *Sunday best*. London: Observer/Gollancz, 1981. *Sunday best
2*. London: Observer/Gollancz, 1982. 215pp. *Sunday best 3*. London: Observer/
Gollancz, 1983. 249pp.

Annual selections made by Trelford, the editor of *The Observer* from 1976 to 1993; the standard of much of the material is such that it is difficult to believe that it originated in a newspaper.

3363 – – –, ed. *The Observer at 200*. London: Quartet Books, 1992.
Selection of items from the newspaper during its bicentenary year.

3364 Trewin, John Courtenay, and Evelyn Mansfield King. *Printer to the House: the story of Hansard*. London: Methuen, 1952. xv + 272pp.
The *Official Report of Parliamentary Debates* – published daily by HMSO for both Lords and Commons when in session – still carries the name Hansard on its title-page in honour of Luke Hansard and his son Thomas Curson Hansard, the latter being its printer (from 1807) and also proprietor (from 1812). The name was added to the title itself in 1829, but dropped again long afterwards. King contributes here from the stand-point of a Member of Parliament.

3365 'Trimbles of Enniskillen, The'. *The Newspaper World*, 2 Sep 1939. (In The Oldest Newspapers series.)
The story of *The Impartial Reporter*, established in 1825 and still in the Trimble family ownership today.

3366 Trotter, Stuart. 'Sex, money and God'. *The Journalist's Handbook*, Autumn 1993.
Summary view of the current religious press.

3367 Tuccille, Jerome. *Rupert Murdoch*. New York: Donald I. Fine, 1989. Publ in the UK as *Murdoch: a biography*. London: Piatkus Books, 1990. xvi + 284pp.

3368 Tudorov, Dafin. *Freedom press: development of the progressive press in Western Europe and the USA*. Prague: International Organization of Journalists, [n.d.].
Includes section on Britain.

3369 Tulloch, John. 'Policing the public sphere: the British machinery of news management'. *Media, Culture and Society*, Jul 1993.
The Government Information Service under a critical microscope.

3370 Tumber, Howard. ' "Selling scandal": business and the media'. *Media, Culture and Society*, Jul 1993.

3371 Tunstall, [C.] Jeremy. *The Westminster lobby correspondents: a sociological study of national political journalism*. London: Routledge & Kegan Paul, 1970. vii + 142pp.
Includes the first revelation of the lobby 'rules' system.

3372 – – –. *Journalists at work: specialist correspondents, their news organisations, news sources and competitor-colleagues*. London: Constable; Beverly Hills (CA): Sage, 1971. 304pp. (In the Communication and Society series.)
A distillation of data from more than two hundred interviews and returns from individual journalists covering many fields.

3373 – – –. *The media are American: Anglo-American media in the world.* London: Constable; New York: Columbia University Press, 1977. 352pp. (In the Communication and Society series.)
Maintains that American leadership of the world's mass media was permitted by the weakness of the British Empire and the English language, and by a complete lack of dynamism from the Empire's centre in Britain.

3374 – – –. *The media in Britain.* London: Constable; New York: Columbia University Press, 1983. xiv + 304pp. (In the Communication and Society series [which Tunstall, professor of sociology at City University (London), edited throughout its period of publication from 1971 to 1984].)
This important book is notably full of well-documented facts and figures, adding weight to the author's criticism of British media policy. Has an extensive annotated bibliography.

3375 – – –. 'Research for the Royal Commission on the Press, 1974–7'. *In* M. Bulmer, ed. *Social research for Royal Commissions.* London: Allen & Unwin, 1980.

3376 – – –, joint ed. *Studies on the press.* Royal Commission on the Press report, Working Paper 3. London: HMSO, 1977.

3377 Tunstall, Jeremy, and Michael (Beaussenat) Palmer. *The media moguls.* London: Routledge, 1991. 258pp. (In the Communication and Society series.)
Current international assessment, but with specific relevant chapters: 'Media moguls in Britain' (mainly Murdoch – also Maxwell, whose malpractices are hidden); and 'News agencies and the data business' (notably Reuters).

3378 Turner, E(rnest) S(ackville). *The shocking history of advertising!* London: Michael Joseph, 1952; revd edn, Harmondsworth (Middx): Penguin, 1965.
Something of a minor classic in its neat combination of hard fact and entertainment.

3379 Turner, Graham. 'What the editors say'. *The Sunday Telegraph,* 7 Nov 1993.
'With leading politicians falling over themselves to win their support, today's newspaper editors command more power than ever before.' Profiles of interviews with the following editors: Peter Stothard (*The Times*), Andreas Whittam Smith (*The Independent*), David Banks (*Daily Mirror*), Kelvin MacKenzie (*The Sun*), Andrew Neil (*The Sunday Times*), Max Hastings (*The Daily Telegraph*), Sir Nicholas Lloyd (*Daily Express*), Paul Dacre (*Daily Mail*), Peter Preston (*The Guardian*).

3380 Turner, (*Sir*) Henry Ernest, comp. *The Imperial Press Conference in Australia, 1925.* With a foreword by Viscount Burnham. London: Empire Press Union. xix + 321pp.
Report of the EPU's third conference, centred in Melbourne.

3381 – – –. *The fourth Imperial Press Conference (Britain), 1930.* With a foreword by Major the Hon J.J. Astor. London: Empire Press Union. xii + 378pp.
Report of the EPU's second meeting in London.

3382 – – –. *The fifth Imperial Press Conference (South Africa), 1935.* With a foreword by T.E. Mackenzie. London: Empire Press Union. vii + 319pp.

3383 – – –. *The sixth Imperial Press Conference (Britain), 1946.* With a foreword by Colonel the Hon J.J. Astor. London: Empire Press Union. ix + 165pp. Papers include one by Francis Williams on 'Freedom of the press'; with a contribution to the debate from Brendan Bracken.

3384 – – –. *The 7th Imperial Press Conference (Canada), 1950.* London: Commonwealth Press Union, 1951. vi + 154pp.
The EPU had become the CPU between the conference and the publication of its proceedings.

3385 – – –. *The Commonwealth Press Conference (8th), in Australia and New Zealand.* London: CPU, 1955. iv + 80pp.
The conference, as well as the organization, now bore the 'Commonwealth' title. This was the last of the six reports that (Sir) Henry Turner compiled as the Union's general secretary.

3386 Turner, John R. *What the press artist should know.* London: Pitman, 1936.

3387 Turner, Michael L. 'Tillotson's Fiction Bureau: agreements with authors'. *In* R.W. Hunt, I.G. Philip and R.J. Robert, eds. *Studies in the book trade in honour of Graham Pollard.* Oxford: Oxford Bibliographical Society, 1975.
The Tillotson family directed the Bureau (syndicating to newspapers etc) until 1935.

3388 Twigg, John. 'Neville Cardus: a review essay'. *British Journal of Sports History*, 3, 1986.

3389 '222 years in Canterbury: the *Kentish Post* and the *Kentish Gazette*'. *The Newspaper World*, 20 May 1939. (In The Oldest Newspapers series.)
Covers two historic weeklies: *The Kentish Post or Canterbury News Letter* was published from 1717 to 1768; the *Kentish Gazette*, launched in the latter year, is still published today.

3390 '228 years on Tyneside: *The Newcastle Journal and Courant*'. *The Newspaper World*, 15 Apr 1939. (In The Oldest Newspapers series.)
The Newcastle Journal remains a major provincial daily, as *The Journal*; the *Newcastle Courant* was founded in 1711, but merged into the *Journal* in 1902.

3391 '244 years old: the story of the *Stamford Mercury*'. *The Newspaper World*, 25 Mar 1939. (In The Oldest Newspapers series.)
Old . . . but as is now generally agreed, not *that* old.

3392 Twyman, Michael. *Printing, 1770–1970: an illustrated history of its development and use in England.* London: Eyre & Spottiswoode, 1970.
Marking the bicentenary of its publishers; a superb production.

3393 Tynan, Kathleen. *The life of Kenneth Tynan.* London: Weidenfeld & Nicolson, 1987; Methuen, 1988.

Arguably the most influential voice in the British theatre in the 1950s and 1960s, Tynan then had the ideal platform as dramatic critic of *The Observer*.

3394 Tytler, David. 'It's a funny old chess game'. *The Guardian (Media Guardian)*, 13 Jul 1992.
On the latest changes in 'Fleet Street' editors: *inter alia*, David English, Paul Dacre, and to come (and in the event, fleetingly) Simon Jenkins.

3395 UK Press Gazette. *UK Press Gazette law for journalists*. Cockfosters (Herts): Maclean Hunter, 1991.
In loose-leaf form, with updates. Principal author, David Newell.

3396 *Union Jack: a scrapbook: British forces newspapers in the Second World War*. London: HMSO, 1989. 256pp.
Incorporates many facsimile pages, with a brief introductory essay by Dr Gwyn Bayliss of the Imperial War Museum.
   The volume takes its title from one of the most notable of the genre. *Union Jack* was first published by the British Army Newspaper Unit in Algiers thrice weekly in March 1943, and eventually appeared daily for the forces invading Southern Europe. The editor-in-chief was Lieutenant Colonel Hugh Cudlipp.

3397 *Union list of London local newspapers*, comp E.A. Willats. London: British Library, 1984.
Limited edition in microfiche. It is under constant revision.

3398 'United Newspapers: a story of fast growth'. In *The press and the people, 1969–1970*. (Press Council Annual Report.)
Tracing the group's development from its foundation in 1918. (There has been further major expansion in the last few years, notably the acquisition of Fleet Holdings – the *Daily Express* etc – in 1985.)

3399 Unwin, Philip (Soundby). *The Stationers' Company, 1918–1977: a livery company in the modern world*. London: Benn, 1978. 144pp.
Bringing the historic story of the Stationers' Company up to date.

3400 Unwin, Philip (Soundby), and George Unwin. 'Newspaper publishing', and part of 'Publishing, history of'. In *Encyclopaedia Britannica*, 15th edn. Chicago, revised 1985–6.
A lengthy historical exposition by British publishers writing for a standard reference work now American-owned.

3401 Ure Smith, J. 'The communist press in Britain, 1920–24'. *Media, Culture and Society*, Apr 1985.
Details the little-known story of *The Communist, Workers' Weekly, Sunday Worker* etc, in the early post-World War I years.

3402 Urquhart, James. *A local index of the Dumfries and Galloway Standard and Advertiser and its predecessors over 200 years*. [Dumfries: J. Urquhart]. 3 vols.

Vols 1 and 2: *The Dumfries Weekly Journal*, publ 1980, 1981; Vol 3: *The Dumfries Courier* etc, publ 1981.
The Dumfries and Galloway Standard of today is a weekly in the Trinity International Group.

3403   *Uttoxeter Advertiser and Ashbourne Times*. Centenary souvenir. Uttoxeter (Staffs): 19 May 1982.

3404   Valdar, Colin. 'How it all began'. In *UK Press Gazette: souvenir issue*. 3 Jun 1985.
The founder-publisher of the *UK Press Gazette* relates the beginnings of 'journalism's newspaper'.

3405   Vallance, Aylmer. *Control of the press*. London: Bureau of Current Affairs, 1946. 20pp.
A polemical tract by a former (pre-war) editor of the *News Chronicle*.

3406   Valliappan, S.M. *Marketing of newspapers: a comparative study of the sales promotion practices in the United Kingdom and Malaysia*. Glasgow: Strathclyde University, 1985 (MCom thesis).

3407   Vanstone, Alan R. *'Cory's Chronicle': the story of the world's strangest newspaper*. Hartland (Devon): A.R. Vanstone, 1981.
How Thomas Cory Burrows founded the weekly *Hartland Chronicle* in 1896, and ran it almost single-handed until 1940.

3408   Veljanovski, Cento. *The media in Britain today: the facts and figures*. London: Collins (for News International), 1990. 91pp. Foreword by Sir Alan Peacock.

3409   Vernon, Anne. *Three generations: the fortunes of a Yorkshire family*. London: Jarrolds, 1966.
Outstanding in the third of the three generations of the Morrell family recorded here was John Bowes Morrell (1873–1963); originally purchasing *The Northern Echo* in 1903, he built up with (Sir) Charles Starmer and Arnold Rowntree what became in 1921 the Westminster Press and thus the nucleus of today's major group. In the opinion of his biographer: 'If a history of the provincial newspaper comes to be written, John Bowes [Morrell] will figure largely in it.'

3410   *Vickers's Newspaper Gazetteer*. London: J.W. Vickers, 1900–16. Annual.
'An annual reference book of the press for the United Kingdom' – and latterly the Colonies etc also.

3411   'View from the goldfish bowl'. *The Guardian*, 22 Oct 1983.
Profile of Andrew Neil, editor of *The Sunday Times*.

3412   Villiers, Frederic. *Pictures of many wars*. London: Cassell, 1902. xii + 238pp.
By the famous war artist/correspondent for *The Graphic* and *The Illustrated London News*

and published soon after his return from the Boer War. Bombastic in tone, but essential source material for his day and age. Villiers promises 'no fiction in its pages', but *The Times* in his obituary was unusually scathing: 'In energy and personality he made up for his lack of talents.'

3413   Viner, George. *All-media survey of journalists' training*. London: Printing & Publishing Training Board, [*c.* 1977]. 2 vols.

3414   – – –. 'On the road to NUJ–IOJ merger'. *The Media Reporter*, 1, 4, 1977.
A former training officer for the National Union of Journalists writing on the proposed (but in 1994 still unconsummated) merger between that union and the Institute of Journalists.

3415   Vines, Colin M. *A little nut-brown man: my three years with Lord Beaverbrook*. London: Leslie Frewin, 1968. 276pp.
An unintentionally entertaining account of Beaverbrook as 'chief' in his last years, by his secretary.

3416   Viollis, Andrée (Mme de Tizac). *Lord Northcliffe*. Paris: Librairie Bernard Grasser, 1919. 63pp.

3417   – – –. 'Lord Northcliffe: a character study of the man who is more fiercely attacked than any other personality'. *The London Magazine*, 62, 1919.

3418   Vizetelly, Edward Henry. *From Cyprus to Zanzibar by the Egyptian Delta: the adventures of a journalist*. London: Pearson, 1901. xx + 480pp.
This Vizetelly (pseudonym 'Bertie Clere') served *The Daily News*.

3419   Vizetelly, Ernest Alfred. *In seven lands: Germany – Austria – Hungary – Bohemia – Spain – Portugal – Italy*. London: Chatto & Windus, 1916. xiii + 393pp.
E.A. Vizetelly (1853–1922) was the son of Henry (R.), the co-founder of *The Illustrated London News*, and is thought to have been the youngest of all war correspondents when in Paris in 1870.

3420   Voigt, Frederick Augustus. *Combed out*. London: Swarthmore Press, 1920. vi + 162pp, Jonathan Cape, 1929 (Travellers' Library).
In the year that Voigt published these front-line reminiscences of the Western Front, he was appointed *The Manchester Guardian*'s representative in Germany: he later moved to Paris.

3421   Vulliamy, Ed. 'This war changed my life'. *British Journalism Review*, 4/2, 1993.
The Guardian's correspondent on the front line in what used to be Yugoslavia.

3422   Wade, Nigel, ed. *A professional stranger: how to handle a foreign news assignment*. London: Daily Telegraph, 1989.
Distils the experience of more than twenty *Telegraph* journalists.

3423 Wadsworth, A(lfred) P(owell). *Newspaper circulations, 1800–1954.* Manchester: Manchester Statistical Society Transactions, 1955. 41pp.
Reprint of a paper read on 9 March 1955 (marking the centenary of the abolition of the duty on newspapers) by the then editor of *The Manchester Guardian.* It is still a standard reference, although the circulations are given in round figures rather than exact. Wadsworth, born in 1891, was with *The Guardian* from 1917 until shortly before his death in 1956.

3424 Wainwright, David. *Journalism made simple.* London: W.H. Allen, 1972, 1982. xiii + 221pp. (In Made Simple Books series.)
Designed for new entrants.

3425 Wainwright, Martin. 'Brum gets its papers back'. *The Guardian (Media Guardian),* 25 Nov 1991.
On the buy-out from Ingersoll by Chris Oakley and others of the Birmingham Post and Mail group.

3426 Waitman, R. *'Daily News – News Chronicle* completes 100 years in the service of Liberalism'. *World's Press News,* 17 Jan 1946.
Saluting the *Daily News* centenary, perpetuated by its offspring, the *News Chronicle.*

3427 *Wakefield Express.* Jubilee number: 1852–1902. Wakefield (W Yorkshire): 8 Mar 1902.

3428 – – –. Centenary supplement, 1852–1952. 15 Mar 1952.
The centenary was also marked by the production of an appealing documentary film, depicting the role of the *Express* as a continuing chronicle of the local community. Today it is a weekly in the Yorkshire Weekly Newspapers group.

3429 Walker, David (Esdaile). *Death at my heels.* London: Chapman & Hall, 1942. 256pp.

3430 – – –. *I go where I'm sent.* London: Chapman & Hall, 1952.
Foreign correspondent for the *Daily Mirror* etc.

3431 Walker, Martin. *Daily sketches: a cartoon history of British twentieth-century politics.* London: Muller; St Albans (Herts): Granada (Paladin), 1978. 207pp.
An illustrated survey that deserves to be better known.

3432 – – –. *Powers of the press: the world's great newspapers.* London: Quartet Books, 1982. ix + 401pp.
An excellent study of twelve famous papers of the time, preceded by a perceptive twenty-eight-page introductory essay. Walker does not include his own paper, *The Guardian,* although he considers it 'the finest in the world'. But the results of his three years of research into *The Times* – the only British paper selected – typify the high quality and value of his judgements generally.

3433 – – –. 'Logs in the intellectual pulp mill'. *The Guardian,* 4 Feb 1982.

3434   Wallace, Marjorie. *Campaign and be damned!: the place of crusading journalism – past and present – in a secretive society*. London: The Guardian, 1991. Guardian Research Fellowship Lecture at Nuffield College, Oxford, February 1991.
Wallace was formerly an investigative journalist with the Insight Team etc at *The Sunday Times*. She traces campaigns for causes back to the nineteenth-century 'golden years' of the press.

3435   Wallace, [Richard Horatio] Edgar. *Unofficial dispatches*. London: Hutchinson, [1901]. 327pp.
A selection of Boer War reports reprinted from the *Daily Mail*.

3436   – – –. *People: a short autobiography*. London: Hodder & Stoughton, [1926]. 253pp; rptd as *Edgar Wallace: a short autobiography*. 1929. Publ in the USA as *Edgar Wallace: by himself*. 1932.
The last-named edition was published to mark Wallace's death, at the age of only fifty-seven.

3437   Waller, Ian. 'The "lobby" and beyond'. *Encounter*, 25 Jun 1965.
A perceptive assessment of the parliamentary lobby system by *The Sunday Telegraph*'s representative.

3438   Wallis, Lawrence W. *The devil's background*. Privately published, 1992.
The craft of printing over the ages, from the 'printer's devil' to 'post-Wapping' technology.

3439   – – –. *Typomania: selected essays on typesetting and related subjects*. Upton-upon-Severn (Worcs): Severnside Printers, 1993. xiii + 161pp.
Includes: 'From frame to desktop: a century of typesetting', originally published in *British Printer*, January 1988; and 'Forty years on', reprinted from a retrospective lecture relating, *inter alia*, the first British direct input at the *Evening Post* (Nottingham), followed by the *Express and Star* (Wolverhampton).

3440   Walter, John, 'IV'. *Notes on the history of The Times*. London: The Times, [1932]. 20pp.
This John Walter (1873–1968) was the last in the family dynasty with an active interest in *The Times*. He was the son of Arthur Fraser Walter and grandson of John Walter III.

3441   Walters, John Cuming. *Knight of the pen*. Manchester: Sherratt & Hughes, 1933. 253pp.
Journalism from the *Manchester City News*.

3442   *War despatches, The: 1939–1945:* London: Marshall Cavendish, 1977. 160pp.
'World War II as it happened': pages from the *Daily Mail*, provided from the John Frost Collection.

3443   *War papers*. London: Collins/Fontana, 1989. Introduction by Ludovic Kennedy.

A large-format book, 'presenting a fascinating collection of historic newspaper front pages, 1939–45', from the John Frost Collection.

3444 *War papers, The.* London: Marshall Cavendish, 1976–8. In 90 weekly parts; illustrated from originals in the John Frost Collection.

3445 Ward, Edward (Henry Harold), *7th Viscount* Bangor. *I've lived like a lord.* London: Michael Joseph, 1970. 190pp.
By one who was a foreign correspondent from 1946 to 1960, both in print and on radio, and widely travelled.

3446 Ward, Mrs Humphry (Mary Augusta), and C(harles) E(dward) Montague. *William Thomas Arnold, journalist and historian.* Manchester: Manchester University Press, 1907. 136pp.
Commemorates Arnold's long service as C.P. Scott's chief leader-writer at *The Manchester Guardian.*

3447 Ward, Ken. *Mass communication and the modern world.* Basingstoke (Hants): Macmillan, 1989. 214pp.
A media primer.

3448 Ward, *Sir* Leslie. *Forty years of 'Spy'.* London: Chatto & Windus, 1915. xii + 351pp.
Ward in fact produced his immortal caricatures of late Victorian and Edwardian personalities as 'Spy' for *Vanity Fair* between 1873 and 1909. His own book includes two hundred examples.

3449 Warde, Beatrice L. *Stanley Morison.* Pasadena (CA): 1967. 16pp. Paul A. Bennett Memorial Lecture.

3450 Warren, Low. *Journalism.* London: Cecil Palmer, [1923]. xx + 352pp; revised as *Journalism from A to Z.* London: Herbert Joseph, 1931; Banner Books, 1947. 255pp. Introduction by Alan Pitt Robbins; foreword by Geoffrey L. Butler.

3451 *Warrington Guardian.* Centenary supplement. Warrington (then Lancs): 9 Apr 1953.

3452 *Warwick and Warwickshire Advertiser.* 150th anniversary supplement. Warwick: 6 Jan 1956.
First published in 1806, the *Warwick Advertiser* is today a weekly in the Heart of England Newspapers group.

3453 Waterfield, Lina. *Castle in Italy: an autobiography.* London: John Murray, 1961.
The author was dismissed as *The Observer*'s Italian correspondent because of her openly declared lack of sympathy for the Fascists. This was a sad end to a long and fruitful association with her editor, Garvin, who was simultaneously strongly anti-Nazi.

3454 Waterhouse, Keith (Spencer). *The Mirror's way with words.* London: Mirror Books, 1981.
Daily Mirror style – from within. 'A polemic against shoddy or tired writing and a plea for fresh and workmanlike writing'.

3455 – – –. *English our English.* London: Viking, 1990.
A sequel on style, equally to the point.

3456 – – –. *Sharon and Tracy and the rest.* London: Hodder & Stoughton, 1992. 245pp.
Selection of pieces from the *Daily Mail.*

3457 – – –. *Waterhouse on newspaper style.* Harmondsworth (Middx): Penguin, 1993. 250pp. Illustrated by 'Trog'.
From the author's latest introduction: 'Expanded, revised and updated, what started as the *Mirror*'s in-house style book now blossoms forth as a manual . . . for the general reader as well as for journalists, trainee journalists, teachers and students of English.' Waterhouse established a new reputation as a columnist for the *Daily Mail.*

3458 – – –. 'Standfirst'. *British Journalism Review*, Autumn 1989.
Introductory excerpts from *Waterhouse on newspaper style.*

3459 Waters, Ivor. *Chepstow printers and newspapers.* Chepstow (Gwent): Moss Rose Press (for Chepstow Society), [1970]. 40pp. Revised 1977, 1981. 86pp.

3460 Waterson, Michael J., and Stephen Haq. *Boom or bust?: free newspapers, 1990–1992.* Henley-on-Thames (Oxon): Allied Information Technologies (for Newspaper Society), 1990.
Prospects for the hitherto booming free newspaper business.

3461 Watkins, Alan [Rhun]. *Brief lives: with some memoirs.* Illustrated by Marc. London: Hamish Hamilton, 1982. xiii + 222pp.
Pen-portraits of twenty-eight personalities, including Beaverbrook and many contemporary 'communicators', chosen from personal knowledge and appreciation by a notable *Observer* political commentator.

3462 – – –. *A slight case of libel: Meacher v. Trelford and others.* London: Duckworth, 1990.
Detailed account of the action (which, unusually among such cases, failed) by Michael Meacher MP against *The Observer* and its editor, Donald Trelford.

3463 – – –. 'My days with Beaverbrook'. *The New Statesman*, 1 Sep 1972.
Watkins was at one time 'Cross-Bencher' in the *Sunday Express*, one of the sharpest political gossip columns in any national newspaper.

3464 – – –. 'The political columnist's craft'. *The New Statesman*, 16 Jan 1976.
Largely a tribute to the iconoclastic Hugh Massingham (a predecessor of Watkins at *The Observer*) and also to Henry Fairlie.

3465   Watling, Cyril. *Ink in my blood*. Cape Town: Russell, 1966.
Although published in South Africa, this contains much Fleet Street material.

3466   Watson, Aaron. *A newspaper man's memories*. London: Hutchinson, [1925].
324pp.
The author had a varied career, first in Newcastle upon Tyne, where he worked on the
Newcastle Chronicle during the redoubtable Joseph Cowen's day, then edited the *Shields
Gazette*. Later he worked in Fleet Street with *The Echo* etc. (His son, Arthur E. Watson,
became managing editor of *The Daily Telegraph* in 1924.)

3467   Watson, Edmund Henry Lacon. *I look back seventy years*. London: Eyre
& Spottiswoode, 1938. vii + 312pp.
'Author and journalist': *inter alia*, served Reuters in World War I on several European
fronts.

3468   Watson, John. 'Thomas Russell and British advertising in the early days
of this century'. *Business Archives*, Dec 1973.
Russell was advertisement manager of *The Times* (1905–8), and later the first (self-styled)
advertisement consultant. His influence in establishing clear principles and honest working practices was immense.

3469   Watt, David. *The inquiring eye: a selection of the writings of David Watt*.
Harmondsworth (Middx): Penguin, 1988. Ed Ferdinand Mount.
'Published in memory of one of the outstanding political journalists of his generation'.
Watt was Washington correspondent and then political editor back in London for the
Financial Times; *The Times* later published his contributions regularly.

3470   Watts, Janet. 'Published, and often damned'. *The Observer*, 1 Dec 1991.
Brief chronicle for the bicentenary: 'By a typical oversight, *The Observer*, the oldest
Sunday newspaper in the country, has never seen its own history into print.'

3471   Waugh, Auberon (Alexander). *The diaries of Auberon Waugh: a turbulent
decade, 1976–1985*. Illustrated by William Rushton. London: André Deutsch,
for Private Eye, 1985.

3472   – – –.   'Press freedom: how the latest threat can, with luck, be avoided'.
The Spectator, 25 May 1991.
Bemoans the non-smoking vote of the journalists at the *Daily* and *Sunday Telegraphs*
buttressing the rule imposed by Murdoch on his News International staff at Wapping.
    Evelyn Waugh's son has made his own journalistic mark, notably as political correspon-
dent on *The Spectator*, and regular columnist for *The New Statesman* and later *The Sunday Telegraph*; he was also (1970–85) a *Private Eye* familiar.

3473   Waugh, Evelyn (Arthur St John). *Waugh in Abyssinia*. London and New
York; Longman, 1936. 253pp; Methuen, 1984; Harmondsworth (Middx):
Penguin, 1985. 169pp. (In the Penguin Travel Library.)
First-hand (largely pro-Italian) despatches for the *Daily Mail*.

3474 − − −. *Scoop: a novel about journalists.* London: Chapman & Hall, 1938. 308pp. Reset (without subtitle) 1964. 247pp; Harmondsworth (Middx): Penguin, 1951, 1987. 222pp; London: Eyre Methuen, 1978. 254pp; London: Folio Society, 1982. Illustrated by Quentin Blake. 229pp. First publ (in part) in *The Strand Magazine.*
Probably the most entertaining comic novel about the press, and derived from the lighter side of Waugh's own experiences in Abyssinia etc. The anti-hero Boot, a nature writer with Lord Copper's *Daily Beast,* is mistakenly chosen to become a most bewildered but ultimately successful war correspondent.

3475 − − −. *A little learning: the first volume of an autobiography.* London: Chapman & Hall, 1964. 234pp; Sidgwick & Jackson, 1973; Methuen, 1983; Harmondsworth (Middx): Penguin, 1983.

3476 − − −. *A little order: a selection from his journalism,* ed Donat Gallagher. London: Eyre Methuen, 1977. xv + 192pp.
Ranges wide in Waugh's work: not only that for the *Daily Mail,* but also for *The Spectator, Harper's Bazaar* etc.

3477 − − −. *The essays, articles and reviews of Evelyn Waugh,* ed Donat Gallagher. London: Methuen, 1983; Harmondsworth (Middx): Penguin, 1986. 662pp.
Contains much pure gold among the dross: 'Every piece was, to some extent, a performance . . . versatility was Waugh's most obvious distinction.' Born in 1903, he died in 1966.

3478 Wavell, Stuart. 'The lord of the frees'. *The Guardian,* 6 Mar 1989.
On Ian Fletcher, whose rapidly growing Yellow Advertiser Newspaper group currently owned 142 free papers in the Home Counties.

3479 − − −. 'Calcutt: curse or cure?'. *The Sunday Times,* 17 Jan 1993.
'Does Britain want a free press or a lapdog?' . . . in-depth analysis after the publication of the Calcutt Report.

3480 Weaver, Denis. *On Hitler's doorstep.* London: Hodder & Stoughton, 1942. 263pp.
The author was based in neutral Sweden during World War II.

3481 − − −. *Front page Europe.* London: Cresset Press, 1943. 256pp.
Weaver was a leading correspondent for the *News Chronicle* (and with that paper for thirty-three years in all).

3482 Weaver, Maurice. 'Hunting the ghosts of Grub Street'. *The Daily Telegraph,* 5 Jan 1987.
'As the national press leaves [Fleet Street], the historians are moving in.'

3483 − − −. 'D-Day on the D-Notice deal'. *The Daily Telegraph,* 12 Jan 1988.
'The Government has been given an ultimatum by the press's own security "censors".'

3484   – – –.   'Dignity is restored as the *Mirror* reflects demise of daily Max-well'. *The Daily Telegraph*, 6 Dec 1991.
With the future of Mirror Group Newspapers in doubt, a useful brief retrospect of some of the great events (and larger-than-life people) in the history of the *Daily Mirror*.

3485   Webb, Colin. 'Press Association'. *In* D.M. Griffiths, ed. *The encyclopedia of the British press, 1422–1992*. Basingstoke (Hants): Macmillan, 1992.
Webb writes this brief résumé as the agency's editor-in-chief.

3486   Webb, [Thomas] Duncan. *Crime is my business*. London: Muller, 1953. 224pp.

3487   – – –.   *Deadline for crime*. London: Muller, 1955. 237pp.

3488   – – –.   *Line-up for crime*. London: Muller, [1956]. 234pp.
Cases of the 1950s, as reported by Webb, an investigative reporter for *The People*, in that paper's individual muckracking tradition.

3489   Webber (later Wells), Rosemary, comp. *World list of national newspapers: a union list of national newspapers in the British Isles*. London: Butterworth, 1976. viii + 95pp.
Contains 1,500 entries for papers in more than fifty British libraries. This work was prepared under the auspices of the Standing Conference of National and University Libraries (SCONUL), with the Social Science Research Council. Supplement 1 (1984), of revised entries compiled by J. Westmancoat, was published in the *British Library Newspaper Library Newsletter*, 1985.

3490   Webster, [Andrew] Drew. 'There's nothing to beat the lobby élite!' *UK Press Gazette*: souvenir issue, 3 Jun 1985.
By a former chairman of the parliamentary press lobby and London editor of United Newspapers, drawing on a lifetime's experience of parliamentary reporting.

3491   Webster, Jack. *A grain of truth: a Scottish journalist remembers*. Edinburgh: Paul Harris, 1981. viii + 200pp; London: Fontana, 1987.

3492   – – –.   *Another grain of truth*. London: Fontana, 1989.

3493   Wedell, George, Georg-Michael Luyken, and Rosemary Leonard, eds. *Mass communications in Western Europe: an annotated bibliography* (*Communication de masse en Europe occidentale*). Manchester: European Institute for the Media, 1985. 326pp. (Media Monograph no 6.)
Compiled under Unesco contract, and covering publications largely from the period 1980–5. It is arranged in country sections. In the UK section, twenty-nine entries have a 'press' classification out of seventy-nine in total.

3494   Weekes, Gareth. 'There's no news like the old news'. *Hendon Times*, 16 Sep 1982.
The celebration of the fiftieth anniversary of the establishment of the British Museum's (now British Library's) Newspaper Library at Colindale. This extensive report is illus-

trated by reproductions of some of the Library's historic mastheads and a photo of its devastation in a 1940 air raid.

3495 'Weekly that became a national daily, The'. In *The press and the people, 1975/1976*. (Press Council Annual Report).
An examination of *The (Manchester) Guardian* – for so long bolstered financially by the *Manchester Evening News*.

3496 Weightman, Gavin. *Picture Post Britain*. London: Collins & Brown, 1990.
How the country looked to the photographers of *Picture Post* during the magazine's coverage of the mid-century.

3497 '*Wellington Journal*: advertising and literature'. *The Newspaper World*, 10 Jun 1939.
On the *Wellington Journal* (published in Wellington, Shropshire), founded in 1854.

3498 Wells, Charles. *History of the Bristol Times and Mirror, 1713–1913*. Bristol: [1913]. 16pp.
Traces, briefly but with reproductions of several historic mastheads, a complex of family trees back to *Sam. Farley's Bristol Post Man* (established in 1713) and William Bonny's *Bristol Post-Boy*, of which the oldest extant copy is dated even earlier: 1704. (Eventually, in 1932, the *Bristol Times and Mirror* was merged into the *Western Daily Press*.)

3499 Wells, H[erbert] G[eorge]. *Journalism and prophecy, 1893–1946*, comp and ed W. Warren Wagar. Boston: Houghton Mifflin, 1964. xxvi + 447pp; London: Bodley Head, 1965. xxi + 330pp.
A varied collection of Wells's prophetic newspaper and magazine writings, including his famous description of warfare being brought to Britain from the air (written in the 1920s), and his revealing comments, based on personal knowledge, on Shaw, several Roosevelts, Lenin and Churchill.

3500 Wells, Ronald: 'The voice of Empire: the *Daily Mail* and British emigration to North America'. *The Historian*, 43, 1981.
Covers the period 1896–1912.

3501 Werth, Alexander. *France in ferment*. London: Jarrolds, 1934. 309pp.

3502 – – –. *The twilight of France, 1933–1940: a journalist's chronicle*. London: Hamish Hamilton, 1942. xxiv + 394pp.

3503 – – –. *Moscow '41*. London: Hamish Hamilton, 1942. 268pp. Publ in the USA as *Moscow war diary*. New York: 1942.

3504 – – –. *The year of Stalingrad: an historic record and a study of Russian mentality, methods and policies*. London: Hamish Hamilton, 1946. xviii + 478pp; New York: Knopf, 1947.

3505 – – –. *France, 1940–1955*. London: Robert Hale, 1956. xxxii + 764pp.

3506 – – –. *Russia at war, 1941–1945*. London: Barrie & Rockliff, 1964.

xxv + 1,100pp; New York: Dutton; Toronto: Smithers & Bonnellie, 1964; London: Pan, 1965. 984pp.

Russian-born, and for long periods Moscow-based, Werth was a foreign correspondent for *The Manchester Guardian*, Reuters and – most notably – *The Sunday Times*.

3507   Wesker, Arnold. *The journalists, a triptych*. London: Jonathan Cape, 1979. 288pp. Contains: (i) *The journalists*. First publ in the Polish arts magazine *Dialog*; then London: Writers and Readers Cooperative, 1975; (ii) *A journal of the writing of The journalists*. Rptd from *Theatre Quarterly*, 26, 1977; (iii) *Journey into journalism*. London: Writers and Readers Cooperative, 1977.

This last is a pretentious piece of 'imaginative recreation' full of misinterpretations and misunderstandings, by 'a frustrated journalist turned playwright', based on notes made in the offices of *The Sunday Times* five years previously.

3508   West, John. *Town records*. Chichester (W Sussex): Phillimore, 1983. xviii + 366pp.

Includes a chapter: 'Provincial newspapers from 1690', plus 'Gazetteer of English and Welsh newspapers, 1690–1981'. This latter is an entirely new collation, under towns of publication, of (*The Times*) *Tercentenary handlist of English and Welsh newspapers . . .* (1920) and the *Catalogue of the Newspaper Library* (BL, 1975), with revisions.

3509   West, (*Dame*) Rebecca (pseudonym of Cicily Isabel Andrews, *née* Fairfield). *The meaning of treason*. New York: Viking, 1947; London: Macmillan 1949, 1952, revised with additions 1965; with new preface, Virago, 1982; also publ with revisions in the USA as *The new meaning of treason*. New York: Viking, 1964.

Vivid, indeed classic, reporting of some of the dramatic trials, immediately post-war, of individuals accused of spying or other treasonable activity against the State.

3510   – – –. *A train of powder*. New York: Viking, 1955. 310pp; London: Macmillan, 1955. vii + 331pp; Virago, 1984.

More criminal cases – the central scene being the 1946 Nuremberg war trials, which West had covered for *The Daily Telegraph*.

3511   – – –. *The Vassall affair*. London: Sunday Telegraph, [1963].

Vassall was the defendant in a sensational Admiralty spy trial.

3512   – – –. *Rebecca West: a celebration: selected from her writings*. New York: Viking, 1977. xix + 789pp; London: Macmillan, 1978. With an introduction by Samuel Hynes. Rptd as *The essential Rebecca West*. Harmondsworth (Middx): Penguin, 1979.

This selection 'by her publishers with her help' is a massive but rewarding work, including excerpts from *Black lamb and grey falcon*, a series of travel reports developed into a two-volume study of Yugoslavia.

3513   – – –. *The young Rebecca: writings of Rebecca West 1911–17*. With an introduction by Jane Marcus. London: Macmillan, 1982; Virago, 1983. x + 402pp.

West first made her journalistic mark in Blatchford's *Clarion*, in pre-World War I days, then (as highlighted in this selection) in the *The Daily News* at the height of the war. During her distinguished career she contributed to many other periodicals and newspapers, notably the *Evening Standard*. Dame Rebecca died in 1983 at the age of ninety, reviewing regularly for *The Sunday Telegraph* up to the end.

3514 *West Briton (and Royal Cornwall Gazette)*. 150th anniversary supplement: 1810–1960. Truro (Cornwall): 21 Jul 1960.
Today a weekly in the Northcliffe Newspapers group.

3515 *West Herts and Watford Observer*. Centenary: 1863–1963. Watford: 1963.
Today a weekly in the Westminster Press group.

3516 *West Lothian Courier*. Centenary edition. Bathgate (then W Lothian): 21 Jul 1972.
Now *Lothian Courier*, a Trinity International weekly.

3517 *West Somerset Free Press*. 125th anniversary souvenir issue. Williton (Somerset): 1985.
Marking unbroken publication since 1860. Now in the Tindle Newspapers group.

3518 *West Sussex Gazette*. Centenary supplement, 1853–1953. Arundel: 28 May 1953.
Today a weekly in the Portsmouth and Sunderland Newspapers group.

3519 *Western Daily Mercury*. Diamond Jubilee number. Plymouth: 2 Jan 1920.
Founded in 1860 as the *Daily Western Mercury*, it has since ceased publication.

3520 *Western Daily Press*. Centenary supplement. Bristol: 2 Jun 1958.
Today a Bristol United Press title – as is the *Bristol Evening Post* (established in 1932).

3521 – – –. Special souvenir supplement. 1 Jun 1983.
'Champion of the West for 125 years'.

3522 '*Western Daily Press*'. *Caxton Magazine*, Oct 1901. (In the Great Provincial Newspapers series.)
The *Western Daily Press* was founded in Bristol by J. Stuart Macliver in 1858.

3523 *Western Gazette: two hundred years of local news*. Yeovil (Somerset): 1937.
Reprinted from the *Western Gazette* of 18 December 1936, tracing its history back to the *Sherborne Mercury* (established in 1737 by William Bettinson). Today the *Gazette* is in the Bristol Evening Post group.

3524 *Western Gazette*. 250th anniversary number. 20 Feb 1987.

3524A – – –. 250th anniversary magazine. Sep 1987.

3525 *Western Independent*. Centenary supplement, 1833–1933. Plymouth: 19 Feb 1933.
Today the *Sunday Independent*, owned by Yattendon, ranks as the third oldest Sunday paper in Britain.

3526   *Western Mail*. Jubilee number. 1869–1919. Cardiff: 1 May 1919.

3527   Western Mail. *Western Mail Ltd: a brief history of the company*. 1920.

3528   – – –.   *Western Mail and its progress: a record of development and expansion*. 1924.

3529   *Western Mail*. Centenary number. 1 May 1969.
Now the only morning paper in Wales, with former rival *South Wales Echo* as its evening partner in the Thomson Regional group. It passed from its original owner, the Marquess of Bute, to Lord Riddell and his partner Lascelles Carr, thence to the Berry brothers as a leading title in the Allied (later Kemsley) group before sale to Thomson in 1959.

3530   *Western Morning News*. 50th anniversary supplement. Plymouth: 23 Jan 1910.

3531   Western Morning News. *Western Morning News company: a brief history*. 31 Aug 1963.
The founders of the *Western Morning News* (in 1860) were William Saunders and Edward Spender; the latter set up an editorial office in London, and pioneered the 'London Letter'. Purchased in 1920 by Leicester Harmsworth, a younger brother of Northcliffe, the paper is today a daily in the Northcliffe Newspapers group.

3532   *Western Morning News*. 125th anniversary number. 3 Jan 1985.
Includes Crispin Gill: 'part of the West Country's way of life for 125 years'.

3533   Western Morning News. *Western morning views*, comp Crispin Gill and James Mildren. With a foreword by Charles Causley. Dartmouth (Devon): Harbour Books, 1985.
A 1984–5 anthology.

3534   '*Western Morning News*'. *Caxton Magazine*, Dec 1901. (In the Great Provincial Newspapers series.)

3535   *Western Times*. Centenary number. Exeter: 7 Oct 1927.
Originally, when it began in 1827, this paper was called the *Exeter Weekly Times*. Today it is in the Northcliffe Newspapers group.

3536   Westmancoat, [Keith] John. *Newspapers*. London: British Library, 1985. 64pp.
An introductory booklet 'for the general reader' by the British Library Newspaper Library's information officer, with sixty illustrations. (Reflecting the holdings at Colindale, many of the publications featured are not news media.)

3537   – – –.   'Newspapers and periodicals'. *In* Michael Deare, ed. *Local studies collections: a manual*, Vol 2. Aldershot (Hants): Gower, 1991.

3538   – – –.   *All at sea: ships' newspapers*. Unpubl MS, held at British Library Newspaper Library.
Publications for the passengers of the ocean liners in the days when there was time to imbibe the news of the day.

3539 *Westmorland Gazette*. 175th anniversary. Kendal (Cumbria): 23 May 1993.
Today a Westminster Press weekly.

3540 'W.H. Smith bicentenary'. *The Times* (special report), 24 Jan 1992.
Contains articles by Derek Harris and Alan Hamilton on the 'newswalk' origin in 1792, and the role of newspapers in the later history of what is today W.H. Smith Group Plc.

3541 Whale, John. *Journalism and government*. London: Macmillan, 1972.
Valuable in its time, but now dated.

3542 – – –. *The politics of the media*. Manchester: Manchester University Press, 1980.
Government–media relations from the end of World War II.

3543 *Wharfedale and Airedale Observer*. Special centenary edition. Bradford (W Yorks): 6 Jun 1980.

3544 Wharton, Michael (Bernard). *A dubious codicil*. London: Chatto & Windus, 1991. 261pp. Rptd with its predecessor as *The missing will and a dubious codicil*. London: Hogarth Press, 1992.
The second volume of the autobiography of 'Peter Simple' of *The Daily Telegraph*: with much close-up, no-holds-barred hilarity on the paper's management and his colleagues.

3545 Whates, Harold Richard Grace. *The Birmingham Post, 1857–1957: a centenary retrospect*. Birmingham: Birmingham Post & Mail, 1957. xv + 255pp.
Published on 4 December 1957 simultaneously with the centenary supplement and incorporating facsimiles of that and of the issue of 4 December 1857. This is a straightforward history by a former staffer who later became editor of the sister paper, the *Birmingham Evening Mail*; it has abundant biographical material on J.F. Feeney, founder of the *Post*.

3546 Whatmore, Geoffrey. *The modern news library: documentation of current affairs in newspaper and broadcasting libraries*. London: Library Association; Syracuse (NJ): Gaylord, 1978. ix + 157pp.
A standard work.

3547 – – –. *The Daily Herald*. Reprint of a lecture given at Meisei University, Japan, in 1974.

3548 – – –. 'News libraries and collections'. In *Encyclopedia of Library and Information Science*. New York: Dekker, 1976.

3549 – – –. 'Newspapers and other material on recent events'. In *Printed reference material*, ed G. Higgens. London: Library Association, 1980, 1984.

3550 Wheeler, David. *Mould*. London: André Deutsch, 1967.
A survey by a BBC journalist and presenter of his early newspaper life.

3551 Wheeler, Katharine V. *A guide to the political papers, 1874–1970, deposited by the First Beaverbrook Foundation*. London: House of Lords (Record Office), 1975.

Summarizes the important collection, now housed in the House of Lords, that was formerly in the Beaverbrook Library. It includes the Beaverbrook, Blumenfeld, Donald and Strachey Papers, as well as those of two Prime Ministers: Lloyd George and Bonar Law.

3552   Wheen, Francis. *Tom Driberg: his life and indiscretions*. London: Chatto & Windus, 1990. 452pp.
The life-story – public and private. Wheen pays full tribute to Driberg's undoubted skills as William Hickey in the *Daily Express*.

3553   Whicker, Alan (Donald). *Within Whicker's world*. London: Elm Tree Books, 1982. ix + 390pp.
The famous broadcaster 'cut his teeth' journalistically as an Army photographer/editor in World War II, and afterwards as a correspondent for Extel in Korea.

3554   Whitaker, Brian. *News Ltd: why you can't read all about it*. With a preface by (Sir) Tom Hopkinson. London: Minority Press Group (later Comedia), 1981. 176pp.
Contrasts the newsgathering practices of the conventional and the 'alternative' press, supported by the detailed story of the five-year life (in the 1970s) of the *Liverpool Free Press*. With an appendix by Crispin Aubrey: 'Beyond the free press'.

3555   Whitaker, James. *Diana v. Charles*. London: Signet, 1993.
The *Daily Mirror*'s royal reporter – with previous experience on four other nationals – gives his own 'inside' version of the breakdown of the marriage of the Prince and Princess of Wales.

3556   Whitcomb, Noel (Bernard). *A particular kind of fool*. London: Quartet Books, 1990. xviii + 382pp.
Diary writing for the *Daily Mirror* – highly entertaining. Whitcomb took his title from Evelyn Waugh: 'Most fools can get a book published, but it takes a particular kind of fool to hold down a job on a daily newspaper.'

3557   White, Michael. 'A hundred years of seductive secrecy'. *The Guardian*, 18 Jan 1984.
Tracing the evolution of the parliamentary lobby system.

3558   White, R.F., & Son. *A list of newspapers published in the United Kingdom, newly arranged and classified*. London: 1878–1912. Intermittent.
From one of the largest advertising agents of the time.

3559   White, Sam. *Sam White's Paris: the collected despatches of a newspaper legend*. London: New English Library, 1983. 336pp.
Records most of the forty-one years during which White was Paris correspondent for the (*Evening*) *Standard*. A Russian Jew by birth, he emigrated to Australia, but joined the British Army in World War II. He served as a war correspondent, and after a brief return to Australia was recruited by Beaverbrook to the Paris assignment which made him famous.

3560 Whitehorn, Katharine (Elizabeth) (Mrs Lyall). *View from a column.* London: Eyre Methuen, 1981.
One of a long series of selections from her regular contributions to *The Observer*, for which she first started writing in 1960.

3561 – – –. *Ethics and the media.* Guildford: University of Surrey, 1988. 17pp.

3562 Whitley, Edward. 'A very private person'. *The Spectator*, 26 Oct 1991.
On the 3rd Viscount Rothermere, and his success – quiet in contrast to his contemporaries – with the fortunes of Associated Newspapers.

3563 Whittam Smith, Andreas. 'A new golden age?'. *British Journalism Review*, Autumn 1989.
The founder of *The Independent* warns of the dangers posed to the freedom of newspapers, however responsible, by the excesses of the minority in the invasion of privacy.

3564 'Who is Rupert Murdoch?'. *M* (magazine), Feb 1991.

3565 'Who's who in British journalism'. In *The Media Yearbook, 1992.* Ayr: Carrick Publishing, 1992.
A latter-day revival of *Who's Who in the Press (see below)*, with two hundred-plus current biographies in potted style.

3566 *Who's Who in Financial Journalism.* London: Dewe Rogerson, 1978 etc.
Photos as well as biographical data.

3567 *Who's Who in the Press: a biographical guide to British journalism.* Ayr: Carrick Publishing, 1984. 192pp; 1986. 133pp.

3568 *Whose news?: ownership and control of the news media.* Manchester: Development Education Project, 1988.
Designed for GCSE-level students.

3569 Whyte, *Sir* Frederic. *The life of W.T. Stead.* London: Jonathan Cape; Boston: Houghton Mifflin, 1925. 2 vols: 713pp total; New York: Garland, 1971.
Remains the standard biography of a remarkable editor whose death was as dramatic as his life: he drowned in the *Titanic* disaster. But Stead is honoured to this day by a memorial, on London's Embankment facing the site of his *Review of Review* offices, 'in recognition of his many gifts, generous spirit and devotion to the service of his fellow men'.

3570 *Widnes Weekly News.* Centenary supplement. Widnes (Cheshire): 25 Jun 1976.
Today in Thomson Regional Newspapers.

3571 Wiener, Joel (Howard), ed. *Papers for the millions: the new journalism in Britain, 1850s to 1914.* Westport (CT): Greenwood Press, 1988. xix + 328pp.

Largely the proceedings of a conference at the City University of New York in 1986, plus a valuable bibliographical essay by the editor.

3572   Wignall, Trevor C. *I knew them all.* London: Hutchinson, 1938. 340pp.
Beaverbrook's no 1 sports writer on the *Daily Express*, following a long stint at the *Daily Mail.*

3573   Wile, Frederick William. *News is where you find it: forty years' reporting at home and abroad.* Indianapolis: Bobbs-Merrill, 1939.
Wile was a well-connected American who became a highly paid correspondent for the *Daily Mail* in Berlin during the run-up to World War I.

3574   Wilkerson, Marjorie. *News and newspapers.* London: Batsford, 1970.

3575   Wilkinson, Glenn R. ' "There is no more stirring story": the press depiction and images of war during the Tibet expedition, 1903–1904'. *War and Society* (University of New South Wales, Canberra), 9, 2, Oct 1991.
On the British Army's foray into Tibet under Younghusband, and how the reporters on the spot – Henry Newman of Reuters (quoted in the title), Perceval Landon of *The Times*, and Edmund Candler of the *Daily Mail* – particularly embellished the glory of war against ill-equipped natives.

3576   – – –.   ' "Soldiers by instinct, slayers by training": the *Daily Mail* and the image of the warrior, 1899–1914'. *Journal of Newspaper and Periodical History*, 8, 2, 1992.

3577   Wilkinson, [Henry] Spenser. *Thirty-five-years, 1874–1909.* London: Constable, 1933. ix + 325pp.
Autobiography of a military correspondent and leader-writer first for *The Manchester Guardian* and then *The Morning Post.*

3578   Willcocks, Leslie. *Corporate strategy and Fleet Street industrial relations: the case of Times Newspapers.* Cranfield (Beds): Cranfield Institute of Technology, 1985.

3579   Willcox, Temple. 'Projection or propaganda?: rival concepts in the pre-war planning of the Ministry of Information'. *Journal of Contemporary History*, 18, 1, Jan 1983.

3580   *Willesden and Brent Chronicle.* Centenary supplement. London: 4 Mar 1977.
Today in Capital Newspapers group.

3581   Williams, Betty. *Know about newspapers.* London: Blackie, 1963.
For junior readers.

3582   Williams, David Glyndwr Tudor. *Not in the public interest: the problem of security in democracy.* London: Hutchinson, 1965. 224pp.
Remains a standard treatise in its field.

3583 Williams, [Edward] Francis (*Baron* Francis-Williams). *Press, Parliament and people.* London: Heinemann, 1946. 254pp.

Williams (1903–70: created life peer as Baron Francis-Williams) was editor of the *Daily Herald* from 1936 to 1940; he was controller of news and censorship at the Ministry of Information from 1941 to 1945, and adviser on public relations to the Prime Minister (Attlee) from 1945 to 1947. This, his first post-war book, distilled his experience to date.

3584 – – –. *Dangerous estate: the anatomy of newspapers.* London and New York: Longman, 1957. 304pp; London: Arrow, 1959. 255pp. Rptd Wellingborough (Northants): Patrick Stephens, 1984. [304pp]. With a foreword by Michael Foot. (In the Classics of 20th Century Journalism series.)

This still ranks as the most readable history-with-commentary of the British press since World War II. Williams was then editing the Labour weekly *Forward*.

3585 – – –. *The right to know: the rise of the world press.* Harlow (Essex): Longman, 1969. vii + 336pp.

An outstanding work, covering historically the 1820s to 1960s worldwide, and including a critical appraisal of the Anglo-American concept of journalism.

3586 – – –. *Nothing so strange: an autobiography.* London: Cassell, 1970. ix + 354pp.

Includes a first-hand account of the free-gifts war of the 1930s, led by the *Daily Herald* when Williams was editor.

3587 – – –. 'Government facilities affecting the press and the supply of government information'. In *The fourth annual Imperial Press Conference, 1939.* London: Empire Press Union, 1939.

3588 – – –. 'Freedom of the press'. In *The sixth Imperial Press Conference (Britain), 1946.* London: Empire Press Union.

3589 – – –. 'On serving two masters'. In *The editor and the publisher: a many-sided relationship.* Zürich: IPI, 1957.

Reprint of an article written when Williams was editor of the *Daily Herald*; his 'masters' were Odhams Press and the Labour Party.

3590 – – –. 'The murder of the *News Chronicle*'. *The New Statesman*, 22 Oct 1960.

Williams commented weekly on the press in *The New Statesman* for ten years.

3591 – – –. 'The age of Hearst and Northcliffe'. *Purnell's history of the 20th century*, 6, 1968.

3592 – – –. Foreword to *The British press: an historical survey*, by Claude-Jean Bertrand. Paris: OCDL, 1969.

3593 – – –. 'Northcliffe, Alfred Charles William Harmsworth, Viscount'. Entry in *Encyclopaedia Britannica* (Chicago, 14th edn, final revision, 1973).

3594 Williams, Frederic Condé. *From journalist to judge: an autobiography.* Edinburgh: George A. Morton, 1903. ix + 319pp.
An account of journalism in Birmingham – Williams was editor of the *Birmingham Daily Gazette* – and Paris.

3595 Williams, Griffiths John. *Y wasg Gymraeg ddoe a heddiw.* Bala (Gwynedd): Llyfrau'r Faner, 1970. 27pp.
The Welsh-language press.

3596 Williams, Gron. *Firebrand: the Frank Owen story.* Worcester: Square One Publications, 1993. 175pp.
A biography of Owen (1905–79) – considered by many the best journalist of his generation – was long overdue. His was an eventful and eventually fruitful career, in both peace and war.

3597 Williams, Ian, ed. *Newspapers of the First World War.* Newton Abbot (Devon): David & Charles, 1970. [160pp].
Comprises facsimile pages reprinted from outstanding British and American papers from 1914 to 1919. From the John Frost Collection.

3598 Williams, John Ringer. *Whitehaven News centenary: an outline of 100 years.* Whitehaven (then Cumberland): 1952.
Established in 1852, the *Whitehaven News* is today in the Cumbrian Newspapers group.

3599 Williams, Marcus. 'James Bourchier: forgotten man of *The Times*'. *Stamps and Foreign Stamps*, Aug 1985.
J.D. Bourchier, Balkan correspondent of *The Times*, was a national hero of Bulgaria, and appeared on a series of stamps from that country in 1921.

3600 – – –, ed. *Double century: 200 years of cricket in The Times.* London: Collins Willow, 1985. xi + 621pp.
Match reports, profiles, leading articles etc; many famous contributors.

3601 Williams, Nicola. 'Ahead of its (financial) times'. *Newstime*, Jul–Aug 1985.
Marking the latest step in the development of the *Financial Times*: publication in New York.

3602 Williams, Paul. *The computerized newspaper: a practical guide for systems users.* London: Butterworth-Heinemann, 1990. 380pp.

3603 Williams, Raymond (Henry). *Culture and society, 1780–1950.* London: Chatto & Windus; New York: Columbia University Press, 1958. 363pp; Harmondsworth (Middx): Penguin (Pelican Books), 1984.

3604 – – –. *The long revolution.* London: Chatto & Windus; New York: Columbia University Press, 1961. 396pp; Harmondsworth (Middx): Penguin (Pelican Books), 1965, 399pp.
Planned as a mature restatement of *Culture and society* from a more considered Marxist standpoint, this intense study contains several useful essays on such functional informa-

tion topics as education and the press. See especially the chapter: 'The growth of the popular press'.

3605 – – –. *Britain in the sixties: communications.* Harmondsworth (Middx): Penguin (Pelican Books), 1962. 134pp. Revised as *Communications.* London: Chatto & Windus, 1966. 196pp; Harmondsworth (Middx): Penguin, 1966, 1976. 192pp.
This volume of 'required reading' discusses the sociopolitical role of the mass media in Britain; many parallels with the USA emerge, particularly the concentration of ownership in ever fewer hands.

3606 – – –. *Towards 2000.* London: Chatto & Windus (Hogarth Press), 1983; Harmondsworth (Middx): Penguin (Pelican Books), 1985. 273pp.
The analysis of 'Britain in the sixties' originally propounded in *The Long revolution* is reconsidered and extended.

3607 – – –. *Resources of hope.* London: Verso, 1989.
A posthumous anthology of his work.

3608 Williams, Valentine. *World of action: autobiography.* London: Hamish Hamilton; Boston: Houghton Mifflin, 1938. vii + 479pp.
A wide canvas, covering Reuters pre- and post-World War I, the Tutankhamen excavation in Egypt 1923–4, and the author's work for Northcliffe, e.g. for the *Daily Mail* in World War I (when he resigned in disgust at censorship).

3609 Willis, Peter. 'Life on the Mersey beat – the best of both worlds'. *UK Press Gazette,* 19 Mar 1984.
About the *Daily Post* (Liverpool) and its editor, Jim Mansell. The first of a series on 'The editors'.

3610 Willox, *Sir* John Archibald. 'The press of Liverpool: Sir John Willox's reminiscences'. *Liverpool Courier,* 6 Jan 1908.
The Courier's proprietor/editor had died in 1905, after becoming a Member of Parliament as well as achieving national prominence in the press (as president of the Institute of Journalists, for example).

3611 Wilmott, R.H. *Reporting the century.* Oxford: Blackwell, [1971]. 77pp. (A 20th Century Topic book.)

3612 Wilson, *Sir* Angus (Frank Johnstone). *The strange ride of Rudyard Kipling: his life and works.* London: Secker & Warburg, 1977. xiv + 370pp; Panther, 1979. 492pp.

3613 Wilson, Brian. 'Voice of the people'. *The Guardian (Media Guardian),* 12 Apr 1993.
One of the founders celebrates the twenty-first birthday of the *West Highland Free Press,* published in Skye – probably Britain's only left-wing local weekly.

3614 – – –, ed. 'This is the face of Fleet Street 1977'. *Journalism Studies Review,* 1977.

A series of profiles of the then current editors of the nationals: nine dailies, seven Sundays.

3615   Wilson, Charles Henry. *First with the news: the story of W.H. Smith since 1792.* London: Jonathan Cape, 1985. 510pp; Garden City (NY): Doubleday, 1986.

Professor Wilson recounts the success story of the W.H. Smith business, starting with the 'newswalk' founded in Grosvenor Street, London, by Henry Walton Smith in 1792. The author's account of the early-nineteenth-century newspaper scene, and in particular of the 'taxes on knowledge' and their eventual abolition, comes from a novel viewpoint. The last period covered (1949–72) is given summary treatment.

3616   Wilson, Derek. *The Astors: landscape with millionaires.* London: Weidenfeld & Nicolson, 1993. xix + 439pp.

The English members of the Astor dynasty became major – and wholly beneficial – players in the saga of twentieth-century British newspapers, with the purchase by William Waldorf (later 1st Viscount) Astor of *The Observer* in 1911, and by his second son John Jacob (later 1st Baron Astor of Hever) of *The Times* in 1922. Both papers eventually went to other owners, but the Astor influence is very well documented in this major family history.

3617   Wilson, Des[mond]. *The secrets file: the case for freedom of information in Britain today.* London: Heinemann, 1984. 166pp.

3618   Wilson, H[enry] W[rigley]. *Convicted out of her own mouth: the record of German crimes.* London: Hodder & Stoughton, 1917. 32pp. Rptd from *The National Review.*

By a military and naval historian of considerable stature. Wilson served forty years in all on Northcliffe's publications, notably as assistant editor (and chief leader-writer) of the *Daily Mail,* and wrote the article on Northcliffe in the first edition of the *Encyclopaedia Britannica* after the latter's death.

3619   Wilson, Keith M(alcolm). *A study in the history and politics of the Morning Post, 1905–1926.* Lampeter (Dyfed): Edwin Mellen Press, 1990. viii + 294pp. (In Studies in History series.)

3620   – – –.   'Sir John French's resignation over the Curragh affair: the role of the editor of the *Morning Post*'. *English Historical Review,* 99, 1984.

The editor concerned is H.A. Gwynne (appointed in 1911, and remaining in office until the paper was merged into *The Daily Telegraph* in 1937).

3621   – – –.   'The fate of a young Churchillian conceit: "The War on the Nile" letters and the *Morning Post*'. *Victorian Periodicals Review,* Winter 1985.

3622   – – –.   'Spenser Wilkinson at bay: calling the tune at the *Morning Post,* 1908–1909'. *Publishing History,* 19, 1986.

Wilkinson in fact served *The Morning Post* as leader-writer etc from 1896 to 1914.

3623 – – –. 'The *Yorkshire Post*, Conservative Central Office, and the negotiations for the purchase of the *Morning Post*, 1923–24'. *Publishing History*, 33, 1993.
In the event, Lady Bathurst (owner since the death of her father, Lord Glenesk, in 1908) sold to a Conservative syndicate of which the Duke of Northumberland was chairman.

3624 – – –, ed. *The rasp of war: the letters of H.A. Gwynne to The Countess Bathurst, 1914–1918*. London: Sidgwick & Jackson, 1988. xix + 346pp. Foreword by W.F. Deedes.
From editor to proprietor under the stress of war. Some of Her Ladyship's correspondence carries its own message of astringency.

3625 Wilson, Peter. *The man they couldn't gag*. London: Stanley Paul, 1977. 386pp.
Sports – and especially boxing and tennis – writer for the *Daily Mirror* (over twenty years), *Daily Express* and *Sunday Pictorial*, Wilson specialized in highly-coloured, self-dramatizing reporting.

3626 Wilson, Robin. 'Shell-shocked'. *The Journalist's Handbook*, Summer 1993.
The editor of the Irish weekly *Fortnight* decries the dwindling impact of the newspapers available in Northern Ireland; the leading Sunday is now *The Sunday World*, Dublin-based but with a northern edition from Belfast.

3627 Wilson, Trevor, ed. *The political diaries of C.P. Scott, 1911–28*. London: Collins; Ithaca (NY): Cornell University Press, 1970.
Scott, like another great editor of the early 1900s – Garvin of *The Observer* – was a major political figure behind the scenes.

3628 Wilton, Robert. *Russia's agony*. London: Edward Arnold, 1918. xii + 356pp.
Wilton was resident *Times* correspondent in Petrograd, and spent fourteen years in Russia. His dedication 'to my gallant friends, the Cossacks', and the terms of his final chapter (completed in December 1917): 'the agony of a living, breathing organism struggling to find expression, wrestling against . . . Bolshevism' – not to mention his assertion: 'The day of Lenin and destruction draws to a close' – caused a considerable, if temporary, stir, largely because he was elsewhere during the first months of revolution but refused to admit it.

3629 – – –. *The last days of the Romanovs, from 15th March 1917*. London: Thornton Butterworth, 1920. 320pp. Rptd Paris, [1921]. Pt 1, The narrative, by Wilton; Pt 2, The depositions of eye-witnesses.

3630 *Wilts and Gloucestershire Standard*. Centenary supplement. Cirencester (Glos): 30 Jan 1937.
A history of the paper with a facsimile of no 1. Founded in Malmesbury (Wiltshire) in 1837, the *Standard* is still published weekly. Today it is in the Bailey group.

3631 – – –. 150th anniversary supplement. 28 Jan 1987.

3632   Winchester, Simon. *In holy terror: reporting the Ulster troubles*. London: Faber, 1974.
Winchester was a *Guardian* reporter at the time this book appeared.

3633   – – –. *Prison diary, Argentina: a Falklands story*. London: Chatto & Windus (Hogarth), 1983. 217pp.
By then a *Sunday Times* reporter, the author was imprisoned at the start of the Falklands War and held for two months on the Argentine mainland.

3634   *Windsor, Slough and Eton Express*. 150th anniversary supplement. Windsor (Berks): Aug 1962.
Founded as the *Windsor and Eton Express* in 1812. Acquired in 1993 by Southnews group.

3635   Winkworth, Stephen, ed. *Amazing times!: a selection of the most amusing and amazing articles from The Times, 1945–1981*. Illustrated by ffolkes. London: Allen & Unwin, 1982. 252pp; Unwin Paperbacks, 1983.

3636   – – –. *More amazing times!* Illustrated by ffolkes. London: Allen & Unwin, 1985. 267pp.

3637   – – –. *Room two more guns: the intriguing history of the personal column of The Times*. London: Allen & Unwin, 1986. 280pp.

3638   Winn, Godfrey [Herbert]. *A month of Sundays*. London: Cassell, 1938. ix + 243pp.
From the author's gossipy diary in the *Sunday Express* in the immediate pre-World War II days.

3639   – – –. *The infirm glory*. London: Michael Joseph, 1967. 396pp.
The first volume of his autobiography. Winn relates how Cudlipp hired him for the *Daily Mirror* in 1936, and how his Personality Parade brought him immediate fame and the highest freelance pay in Fleet Street.

3640   – – –. *The positive hour*. London: Michael Joseph, 1970.
Autobiography continued, with service as a war correspondent (for the *Daily Express* in France etc), then in the Royal Navy, as the high points.

3641   Winnington, Alan. *Breakfast with Mao: memoirs of a foreign correspondent*. With an introduction by Neal Ascherson. London: Lawrence & Wishart, 1986.
Retails the unique experiences of a *Daily Worker* reporter disowned by his native Britain and, ultimately, by the People's Republic of China after he had spent twelve years as official representative of the British Communist Party.

3642   Winnington, Richard. *Film criticism and caricatures, 1943–53*. London: Paul Elek, 1975. Introduced and selected by Paul Rotha.
Influential critic for the *News Chronicle*, working closely with Vicky.

3643   Winsbury, Rex. *Government and the press*. London: Fabian Society, 1968. (A Fabian Tract.)

3644 – – –. *New technology and the press*. London: HMSO, 1975. Royal Commission on the Press: Working Paper 1. The Acton Society Press Group were co-authors with Winsbury.

3645 – – –. *The electronic newsroom*. Epping (Essex): National Council for the Training of Journalists, 1985.
A brief but authoritative guide for students.

3646 – – –. 'Electronic publishing – what's in it for regional and local newspapers?'. *Newstime* (Newspaper Society), Apr 1984.

3647 Wintour, Charles (Vere). *Pressures on the press: an editor looks at Fleet Street*. London: André Deutsch, 1972. xi + 276pp.
Wintour had already been editor of the *Evening Standard* (London) for thirteen years when this was published; it is still essential reading both for 'state-of-the-art' information and for balanced professional comment. Hidden pressures, such as 'D' Notices, are considered as well as overt pressures, such as misuse of the defamation laws.

3648 – – –. *The rise and fall of Fleet Street*. London: Hutchinson, 1989. xxi + 271pp.
Covers the major British press 'dynasties', from the Harmsworths onwards.

3649 – – –. 'Nought for Fleet Street's comfort'. *The Observer*, 28 Oct 1982.

3650 – – –. 'The world newspaper has arrived'. *The Sunday Times*, 27 Jan 1985.
Of the international papers already in being, Wintour points to the *Financial Times* and its Frankfurt edition, and to its plans to print in the USA. He regards the British press as 'running the race with one hand tied behind its back' an allusion to the insistence by some of Britain's printing unions on their members handling all typesetting.

3651 – – –. 'A world of turmoil and change'. *UK Press Gazette: souvenir issue*. 3 Jun 1985.
Wintour writes as editor, surveying the twenty years since the *UKPG* was started.

3652 – – –. 'Rupert Murdoch shows us his Dockland plant'. *UK Press Gazette*, 3 Feb 1986.

3653 Wintour, Charles (Vere), and Graham Serjeant. '*Telegraph* control goes to Black'. *UK Press Gazette*, 16 Dec 1985.
Informed background to the news that the majority holding in the Telegraph group (the *Daily* and *Sunday Telegraph*) had been passed by Lord Hartwell (of the Berry family) to Conrad Black, the Canadian businessman.

3654 *Wipers Times, The*. London: Herbert Jenkins, 1918; Eveleigh Nash & Grayson, 1930; rptd Peter Davies, 1973. 377pp. This edn with introduction, notes and glossary by Patrick Beaver. Foreword by Henry Williamson.
A complete facsimile of a World War I trench newspaper, which thrived on parody in the most unlikely circumstances. *The Wipers Times* was founded and edited by Lieute-

nant Colonel F.J. Roberts, initially from a disused printing press near Ypres in Feb 1916; it continued as *The 'New Church' Times, The Kemmel Times, The Somme-Times, The B.E.F. Times* and *The 'Better Times'* until December 1918 (after the Armistice).

3655   Witherow, John. 'The publishing battle.' *Journalism Studies Review*, 1983. Written in the aftermath of the Falklands War by the *Times* correspondent with Britain's Task Force.

3656   Withey, Richard, and Elizabeth Huggett. 'Fleet Street's second revolution: online technology in information gathering for newspapers'. *In* Selwyn Eagle, ed. *Information sources for the press and broadcast media*. Sevenoaks (Kent): Bowker-Saur, 1991.
By two senior editorial database staff of News International.

3657   Wolfe, Humbert. *The uncelestial city*. London: Gollancz, 1930. In this book of poetry appears, in Book 1: Over the fire, the famous aphorism:

> You cannot hope
>   to bribe or twist,
> thank God! the
>   British journalist.
> But, seeing what
>   the man will do
> unbribed, there's
>   no occasion to.

3658   *Wolverhampton and its press*. Wolverhampton: Express and Star, 1950.

3659   'Wolverhampton's evening paper'. *The Newspaper World*, 24 Dec 1938.
This feature on *The Express and Star* – established in 1874, and still in the control of the founding family, the Grahams – brings the story up to immediate pre-war days. But it is in later years through enterprise, both technically and in marketing, that it has become an outstanding success among provincial evenings.

3660   *Woman Journalist, The*. Society of Women (Writers and) Journalists, 1910–. Now quarterly.
The organization itself was founded (as Society of Women Journalists) in 1894.

3661   'Women in journalism'. *The Writer*, Jun 1926.

3662   Wood, Alan. *The true history of Lord Beaverbrook*. London: Heinemann, 1965. xiii + 359pp.
A one-time Beaverbrook journalist, Wood finished his narrative at 1952, fearing a libel action. There is an 'epilogue' by Sir John Elliot.

3663   Wood, David. 'The reporting of Westminster politics'. *The Times*, 6 Feb 1981.

3664   – – –.   'Why public ministers leak like sieves'. *The Times*, 16 Mar 1981.

3665 – – –. 'The sources of political information'. *The Times*, 30 Mar 1981.
By a much respected *Times* parliamentary man.

3666 Woodhead, Henry George Wandesford. *A journalist in China*. London:
Hurst & Blackett, 1934. 281pp. Publ in Japan as *Adventures in Far Eastern
journalism*. Tokyo: Hokuseido Press, 1935. ix + 266p.
'A record of thirty-three years' experience', of which sixteen were spent as editor of
the *Peking and Tientsin Times*, and even longer editing the *China Year Book*. Woodhead
was also a long-service stringer in China for Reuters, Associated Press, and various
newspapers.

3667 Woods, Frederick, ed. *Young Winston's wars: the original despatches of
Winston S. Churchill, war correspondent, 1897–1900*. London: Leo Cooper, 1972.
xviii + 350pp; Sphere, 1972. 437pp.
About Churchill's despatches from the North-West Frontier (1897), Sudan (1898),
and South Africa (1899–1900). The editor, in his introduction, points out that only
those from the last-named theatre of war were reprinted unchanged in the books
published at the time. Those from Sudan were sent under 'personal' cover to Lord
Glenesk, proprietor of *The Morning Post*, to bypass the military and other objections
to Churchill's self-appointed role as a war correspondent.

3668 – – –. *Winston Churchill: war correspondent, 1895–1900*. London:
Brassey's, 1991.

3669 Woods, Oliver Frederick John Bradley, and James Drew Bishop. *The story
of The Times*. London: Michael Joseph, 1983. 392pp. Revised (bicentenary)
edn, 1985. 398pp.
Woods, an assistant editor of *The Times*, died before finishing this book; it was completed
by Bishop, by then editor of *The Illustrated London News*. Acceptable as a comparatively
brief popular work, it does not measure up to the official history.

3670 Woodthorpe, A.J. *Education and the national daily press, 1945–1975*. Leeds:
University of Leeds, 1980 (PhD thesis).

3671 Woodville, R(ichard) Caton. *Random recollections*. London: Eveleigh Nash,
1913. 267pp.
Woodville – son of a noted American artist of the same name – became the public's (and
Queen Victoria's) favourite war artist by specializing in the large set-piece battle scene;
he was a major contributor to *The Illustrated London News*.

3672 Woodward, David. *Front line and front page*. London: Eyre & Spottiswoode,
1943. 232pp.
News Chronicle war correspondent.

3673 Wooldridge, Ian (Edmund). *The best of Wooldridge*. London: Everest, 1978.
192pp.
From the *Daily Mail*'s sports pages.

3674 – – –. *Sports in the '80s: a personal view*. London: Centurion, 1989. 176pp.
A collection from Wooldridge's columns and articles in the *Daily Mail*.

3675 – – –, ed. *Great sporting headlines*. London: Collins, 1984.
A large-format book with a parade of facsimile pages.

3676 Woollan, J.C. 'The Lord Glenesk'. *Caxton Magazine*, 2, 1902.
Published when the Borthwick family (with the 1st Baron Glenesk at its head) was controlling the fortunes of *The Morning Post*.

3677 – – –. 'The men of *The Times*'. *Caxton Magazine*, 3, 1902.
Features A.F. Walter, Buckle, Moberly Bell.

3678 'Workaday Northcliffe, The – by one who worked with him'. *The Manchester Guardian*, 15 Aug 1922.

3679 *Working in journalism*. Sheffield: Careers and Occupational Information Centre, 1989, 1992. 25pp.
Guide with profiles of typical careers.

3680 World's Press News. *Who's Who in Press, Publicity, Printing*. London: Cosmopolitan Press, 1932.

3681 – – –. *(WPN) Inky Way Annual*, ed A.J. Heighway. London: 1947–52 (6 issues).
Special Christmas publications, with largely original contributions.

3682 – – –. *Newspaper and Magazine Personnel and Data*. From 1952 (annual, with quarterly supplements); continued (as *Directory of Newspaper and Magazine Personnel and Data)* to 1968; superseded by *Who's Who in Journalism* (*see under* Campaign).
See also Reference Works section.

3683 *Worshipful Company of Stationers and Newspaper Makers, The: a short account of its history and hall*. Written by James Moran. London: Stationers' Company, 1978. 32pp; revised edition, 1989. 24pp.

3684 Worsthorne, (*Sir*) Peregrine (Gerard). *Peregrinations*. London: Weidenfeld & Nicolson, 1980. 277pp.
A selection of political commentary, in a highly individual style, by the associate editor (from 1986 to 1989 editor) of *The Sunday Telegraph*. (This paper was launched as the partner of *The Daily Telegraph* in 1961; a colour magazine was added in 1964.)

3685 – – –. *By the right*. Dublin: Brophy Books, 1987. 192pp.

3686 – – –. *Tricks of memory*. London: Weidenfeld & Nicolson, 1993. ix + 290pp.
This engaging and well-written autobiography contrives to be not merely self-searching but also frank to a fault. It suggests that life on the *Daily* (and *Sunday*) *Telegraph* could on occasion be rollicking fun.

3687 Wrench, Sir (John) Evelyn (Leslie). *Uphill: the first stage in a strenuous life.* London: Nicholson & Watson, 1934. x + 316pp.
Autobiography to 1913.

3688 – – –. *Struggle, 1914–1920.* London: Nicholson & Watson, 1935. 504pp.
Covers the author's life during World War I, and the post-war empire unity campaign. Wrench founded both the Over-Seas League and the English-Speaking Union, but it is his eventful career in the press that is our concern. In charge of the *Continental Daily Mail* as early as 1907, he joined Beaverbrook at the Ministry of Information near the end of the war; long after, he owned and edited *The Spectator*.

3689 – – –. *Geoffrey Dawson and our Times.* With a foreword by Lord Halifax. London: Hutchinson, 1955. 487pp.
Dawson (born Geoffrey Robinson in 1874, died 1944) was editor of *The Times* under Northcliffe from 1912 to 1919, and again (after the latter's death) from 1922 to 1941. This biography, based largely on Dawson's diaries, is especially valuable on his controversial role in the Abdication crisis of 1936, and in pursuing a strong appeasement policy in the run-up to World War II. Dawson's eminence at this time owed something to the fact of his editorship being a 'second coming'. Calling on a consummate mastery of journalism (anonymous, of course, according to contemporary *Times* custom), he showed a confidence stemming from his wide contacts in the governing Establishment and in international circles.

3690 Wright, Charles, and C(harles) Ernest Fayle. *A history of Lloyd's, from the founding of Lloyd's Coffee House to the present day.* London: Macmillan, 1928. xxi + 475pp.
The name of Edward Lloyd is immortalized in the world-famous Lloyd's marine insurance corporation. But it is also perpetuated in *Lloyd's List*, a specialized daily newspaper dating back indirectly to 1734. There were for a short period two rival Lloyd's Coffee Houses, each publishing a *Lloyd's List*; the survivor was the New Lloyd's, set up in Pope's Head Alley in 1769.

3691 Wright, Frederick Victor. *A hundred years of the West Sussex Gazette, 1853–1953.* Arundel (W Sussex): 1953. 42pp.
Today a weekly in the Portsmouth and Sunderland newspaper group.

3692 Wright, Jeffrey A. *The origins and development of British press photography, 1884–1914.* Swansea: University College (University of Wales), 1982 (MSc Econ thesis).
Very fully researched documentation on a subject which, as the author points out, hitherto has been 'somewhat ephemeral'.

3693 – – –. 'If you really want to know – look into the Victorian *Mirror*'. *Journalism Studies Review*, 1982.
A reminder of the early, struggling days of the *Daily Mirror* when it was an illustrated paper mainly for 'gentlewomen'.

3694   Wright, Patrick. 'The bottle thrower'. *The Guardian (Media Guardian)*, 2 Feb 1993.
Profile of *Sun* columnist Richard Littlejohn – declared 'Irritant of the Year'.

3695   Wyatt, Woodrow (Lyle) (later *Baron* Wyatt of Weedon). *The confessions of an optimist*. London: Collins, 1985.
The outspoken autobiography of the politician/printer/publisher/columnist on the *Daily Mirror* and *The Times*/broadcaster etc.

3696   – – –.   'Lord Beaverbrook'; 'Mr Hugh Cudlipp'. In his *Distinguished for talent: some men of influence and enterprise*. London: Hutchinson, 1955.

3697   Wynn Jones, Michael. *The cartoon history of Britain*. London: Tom Stacey, 1971; New York: Macmillan. Foreword by (Michael) Cummings.

3698   – – –.   *A newspaper history of the world*. Newton Abbot (Devon): David & Charles, 1974. 192pp; New York: William Morrow, 1974.
'An anthology of famous news stories from 1850 to the present day, and a collection of great scoops, leaks, exposures, crusades, triumphs and disasters from the pages of the British and American press'.

3699   – – –.   *Deadline disaster: a newspaper history*. Newton Abbot: David & Charles, 1976. 192pp.
Large-format coverage of events from 1870 to 1976, with press items from the John Frost Collection.

3700   Yates, Ian. 'PA today – and tomorrow'. *In* D. Campbell, ed. *The British press*. London: CPU, 1978.
The author takes stock as general manager of the Press Association.

3701   *Yorkshire Evening Press*. Centenary souvenir supplement. York: 2 Oct 1982.
In the Westminster Press group.

3702   *Yorkshire Herald*. Jubilee number. York: 2 Jan 1905.

3703   – – –.   20,000th number. 18 May 1915.
Now titled *Yorkshire Gazette and Herald*, this is a Westminster Press group weekly. Its evening associate is *The Yorkshire Evening Press*, a former Kemsley group paper.

3704   '*Yorkshire Journal–Doncaster Gazette*'. *The Newspaper World*, 28 Oct 1939. (In The Oldest Newspapers series.)
The *Doncaster Gazette* was established in 1786; it ceased publication in 1981.

3705   *Yorkshire Observer*. '75 years' retrospect.' Bradford (Yorks): 6 Feb 1909.
The seventy-five years are the period since the foundation of the *Bradford Observer*.

3706   – – –.   Diamond Jubilee number. 5 Oct 1928.
Celebrating sixty years as a daily.

3707 – – –. Centenary supplement. 6 Feb 1934.

3708 – – –. '120 years of progress: the *Yorkshire Observer*'s long service to the community'. 6 Feb 1934.
It has since ceased publication, leaving the Westminster Press group's *Telegraph and Argus*, an evening paper, as Bradford's only daily.

3709 Yorkshire Post, The. *The Yorkshire Post and the General Strike.* Leeds, [1927]. 42pp.

3710 *Yorkshire Post, The.* Centenary supplement, 1866–1966. Leeds: 4 Jul 1966.
The *Leeds Intelligencer* was founded as a weekly by Griffith Wright in 1754. It became the (daily) *Yorkshire Post* in 1866, and in November 1939 enhanced its already independent influence and wide circulation by incorporating the *Leeds Mercury*. With the *Yorkshire Evening Post*, acquired by United Newspapers in 1969, it remains that group's most significant regional title.

3711 Young, [Alexander Bell] Filson. *The relief of Mafeking.* London: Methuen, 1900.
The author was a youthful special correspondent for *The Manchester Guardian* in South Africa. (He served as an Army war correspondent once more in World War I, and became an adviser to the BBC in the early days of radio.)

3712 Young, [Charles] Kenneth. *The press and the universities.* Hull: University of Hull, 1964. Reprint of a lecture.

3713 – – –. *Churchill and Beaverbrook: a study in friendship and politics.* London: Eyre & Spottiswoode, 1966. 349pp.
Calls on Churchill and Beaverbrook's extensive correspondence.

3714 – – –. *The bed post: a miscellany of the Yorkshire Post.* London: Macdonald, for the *Yorkshire Post*, 1962.

3715 – – –. *The second bed post.* London: Macdonald, 1964.
Young was editor of the *Yorkshire Post* itself from 1960 to 1964, then political and literary adviser to Beaverbrook Newspapers.

3716 Young, Gavin. *Worlds apart: travels in war and peace.* London: Hutchinson, 1987. 343pp; Harmondsworth (Middx): Penguin, 1988. 400pp.
Anthology of the author's journalism, largely for *The Observer*; reports distilled from fifteen wars and wide-ranging foreign travel.

3717 Young, [George] Gordon [Fussell]. *Outposts of war.* London: Hodder & Stoughton, 1941. 251pp.
By a Reuters correspondent (including a period in Finland): the first of three *Outposts* memoirs.

3718 Young, Hugo (John Smelter). *The Crossman affair.* Hamish Hamilton/ Jonathan Cape, for The Sunday Times, 1976. 224pp.

A *Sunday Times* political writer (for eighteen years) gives a detailed account of the legal furore caused by the publication in 1975 of *The diaries of a Cabinet minister* by Richard Crossman.

3719   – – –.   *One of us*. London: Macmillan, 1989; Pan, 1990.
Fascinating account of Margaret Thatcher and her Government, with considerable use of press coverage.

3720   – – –.   'The press we don't deserve'. *The Sunday Times*, 18 Mar 1984.

3721   – – –.   'Rupert Murdoch and the *Sunday Times*: a lamp goes out'. *The Political Quarterly*, 55, Oct–Dec 1984.

3722   – – –.   'Two centuries of The Thunderer: do top people still take *The Times*?'. *The Listener*, 3 Jan 1985.
As the presenter of the BBC television documentary *The Times at 200* (2 January 1985), Young takes a realistic look at its current status: 'With Murdoch, the paper could be said to have returned to its origins. It is in the hands of a man driven by commercial ambition.'

3723   – – –.   'The Marxist myth that made the Tories misread Arthur'. *The Guardian*, 7 Jan 1985.
By then Young had resigned from *The Sunday Times* and joined *The Guardian*.

3724   – – –.   'Maxwell the megaphone'. *The Guardian*, 5 Mar 1990.
Interview of the *Mirror* (etc) proprietor in his penthouse office.

3725   Younghusband, *Sir* Francis Edward. 'The first fifty years'. *The Nineteenth Century and After*, Mar 1927.
'Soldier, diplomatist, explorer, geographer and mystic' . . . the entry in the *DNB* could well have added 'journalist', because before leading the controversial British expedition into Tibet in 1902 Younghusband had, as correspondent for *The Times*, accompanied his brother George on the expedition to relieve Chitral and also visited South Africa for a brief but eventful tour of duty.

3726   Zaghlami, R. *Media coverage of industrial relations issues and audience perception, with particular reference to the Wapping dispute*. Guildford: University of Surrey, 1988 (MPhil thesis).

3727   Zimmermann, Walter. *Die englische Presse bis zum Ausbruch des Weltkrieges* (The English press up to the outbreak of the World War [I]). Charlottenburg (Germany): Hochschule nach Ausland, 1928.

3728   Zvavich, Isaak Semenovich. *Angliiskaia pressa*. Moscow: 1946. 21pp.
A reprinted lecture on the English press.

LATE ENTRIES

Reference Work

3729 *Media Pocket Book, The.* Henley-on-Thames (Oxon): NTC Publications (for Advertising Association), 1991–. Annual.
Statistics, including national and selected regional newspapers.

The Bibliography

3730 Balfour, Michael. *Propaganda in war, 1939–1945: organisations, policies and publics in Britain and Germany.* London: Routledge & Kegan Paul, 1979. xvi + 520pp.
Shows how Germany's early successes in this field paled before the combined efforts of British and US propagandists.

3731 Barrett, Norman, ed. The *Daily Telegraph chronicle of cricket.* Enfield: Guinness, 1994.

3732 Brivati, Brian, ed. *Owners and image makers: essays on British newspapers in the 20th century.* London: Cass (for Institute of Contemporary British History, in preparation).
Distilled from proceedings from the 1993 ICBH Summer School. Includes Peter Catterall: 'Local press and politics in Bolton and Bradford after World War I'.

3733 Bromley, Michael. *Teach yourself journalism.* London: Hodder & Stoughton (in preparation).

3734 Buckingham, Lisa. 'The Pink Panther's new teeth'. *The Guardian (Media Guardian),* 13 Jun 1994.
On Frank Barlow, managing director of Pearson (*Financial Times,* Westminster Press etc).

3735 Butler, David, and Gareth Butler. 'The press'. *In* their *British political facts, 1900–85* (6th edn). London: Macmillan, 1986. *1900–1994* (7th edn), in preparation.
Valuable data on proprietors, editors, etc – historical as well as current.

3736 Crosland, Susan. *The magnates.* London: Orion, 1993. 325pp.
The overpowering press magnate in this further novel has many near-Maxwell attributes.

3737 *D.C. Thomson & Co Ltd: a Scottish success story.* London: D.C. Thomson, 1993. 34pp.
Promotion brochure. Retails the claim of *The Sunday Post* to be 'Britain's best-read newspaper': it is estimated, by six of every ten Scottish adults.

3738 Deppa, Joan, *et al. The media and disasters: Pan Am 103.* London: David Fulton Publishers, 1993.
Cities the case of the Lockerbie terrorist bomb in 1988 as a major example of massive media investigation.

3739 di Giovanni, Janine. *Bosnia.* London: Phoenix (in preparation).
Covering the harrowing war in Bosnia for *The Sunday Times* from late in 1992: 'The images never leave me. I keep my flak jackets, my helmets, my press passes and my lucky torch.'

3740 El Sharkawi, B. *The Arab press in London.* Salford (Lancs): University of Salford, 1992 (MPhil thesis).

3741 Fry, Richard. *The role of a financial journalist.* Manchester: Manchester Statistical Society, 1945. 21pp.
Paper by *The Manchester Guardian's* financial editor.

3742 Gollancz, Victor. *In darkest Germany.* London: Gollancz, 1947.
The prominent left-wing publisher visited occupied Germany in October–November 1946; his critical reports appeared *inter alia* in *The Times, The Manchester Guardian* and *The Observer.*

3743 Grant Duff, Shiela. *The parting of ways: a personal account of the Thirties.* London: Peter Owen, 1982; Unwin, 1984. 223pp.
Her troubled times as correspondent for *The Observer* in Central Europe. She ultimately resigned in protest at the paper's pro-Nazi stance.

3744 Greene, Graham. *Mornings in the dark: the Graham Greene film reader.* London: Carcanet, 1993. 737pp. Ed David Parkinson.
Reviews and essays.

3745 *Guardian, The. 1984–1994–2014*: 10th anniversary edition. *Media Guardian,* 20 Jun 1994.
Twenty contributors include Peter Fiddick (original editor), Roy Greenslade ('before Wapping – after Wapping'), Alan Rusbridger (on the long-serving columnists of the nationals), Michael McNay (new technology in newspaper design).

3746 Haines, Joe, and Peter Donnelly, eds. *Malice in wonderland: Robert Maxwell v. Private Eye.* London: Macdonald, 1986. 191pp. Reported by John Jackson.
Transcript of the High Court trial in which Maxwell won extensive damages. Lists the so-called 'litany of lies' – fifty-three cases over the previous decade when *Private Eye* had agreed to publish an apology.

3747 Harcup, Tony. *A northern star: Leeds Other Paper and the alternative press, 1974–1994.* Upton (W Yorks): Campaign for Press and Broadcasting Freedom, 1994. 32pp.

The chequered history of the 'alternatives' – massing more than seventy local titles in their heyday in the early 1980s – is the background to this close-up of a leading example.

3748 Heaton, David, and John Higgins, eds. *Lives remembered: The Times obituaries of 1992*. Pangbourne (Berks): Blewbury Press, 1993. Foreword by Alistair Cooke. Series continued: Anthony Howard and David Heaton, eds . . . *The Times obituaries of 1993*. Blewbury (Berks): Blewbury Press, 1994. Foreword by Roy Hattersley.

3749 Holman, Gordon. *Stand by to beach!* London: Hodder & Stoughton, 1994. 224pp.
'Ringside' view of the D-Day landings by the *Evening Standard*'s correspondent.

3750 Howard, Philip (Nicholas Charles). '65,000 rolls of thunder'. *The Times*, 7 Jul 1994.
Retrospect from issue no 65,000 through the generations in leaps of 10,000.

3751 Inman, Colin, comp. *Financial Times style guide*. London: Financial Times, 1993.

3752 Keeble, Richard, ed. *The newspapers handbook*. London: Routledge, 1994. 368pp.
The editor and other contributors write from the Department of Journalism at City University (London).

3753 Kent Messenger Group Newspapers. *Colour impressions*. Maidstone: 1992. 40pp.
To mark inauguration of new printing plant at group headquarters (Larkfield). Incorporates historical and other background information.

3754 Lamb, Ted, and Dick Chennell, eds. *Guidelines for correspondents*. Cheltenham (Glos): Edict Publications, 1990; revd edn, Harlow (Essex): National Council for the Training of Journalists, 1993.
The essentials of print journalism for local correspondents.

3755 Leppard, David. *On the trail of terror: the inside story of the Lockerbie investigation*. London: Jonathan Cape, 1991.
One of the *Sunday Times* Insight Team makes his assessment of the explosive crash on Lockerbie on 21 December 1988.

3756 Lovesey, John, ed. *Great moments in British sport: legendary triumphs and dramas relived*. London: Witherby, 1993. 192pp.
The editor was sports editor of *The Sunday Times* for fourteen years.

3757 Macmillan, Kate, and Paul Simpson. 'TRN: the inside story'. *Newspaper Focus*, May 1994.
Stuart Garner, about to become chief executive of Thomson Regional Newspapers, building on the transformation set on course by Gordon Paul.

3758 Marnham, Patrick. *Crime and the Académie Française: despatches from Paris*. London: Viking, 1994.

Fine writing by *The Independent*'s man in Paris.

3759   Mirror Group Newspapers. 'Canary Wharf special: going for gold'. London: 14 Mar 1994. Adapted as supplement in *UK Press Gazette*, 14 Mar 1994.
Publ the day after the *Daily Mirror*, having moved from Holborn Circus, produced its first issue from the new offices at Canary Wharf.

3760   Monopolies and Mergers Commission. *Guardian and Manchester Evening News Plc and Thames Valley Newspapers: a report on the proposed transfer of newspapers*. London: HMSO, 1993. Cm 2438.
Another successful bid.

3761   – – –. *Johnston Press Plc and Halifax Courier Holdings Ltd: a report*. London: HMSO, 1994. Cm 2596.
Also approved.

3762   Morgan, John. *John Morgan's Wales: a personal anthology*. Swansea: Christopher Davies, 1993.
Fitting legacy from a born communicator, whose journalism has appeared in e.g. The *Western Mail* and *The New Statesman*.

3762A   Morsley, Clifford. *News from the English countryside, 1851–1950*. London: Harrap, 1983.
A second pleasing anthology.

3763   Northmore, David. *Lifting the lid: the guide to investigative journalism*. London: Cassell (in preparation).

3764   Ogilvy-Webb, Marjorie. *The Government explains: a study of the Information Services*. London: Allen & Unwin, 1965. 239pp. Foreword by Sir Kenneth Grubb.
A report for the Royal Institute of Public Administration, this is one of the few in-depth studies of the development of the Government's public relations machinery.

3765   O'Kane, Brian. *Essential finance for journalists*. Dublin: Oak Tree Press (for Price Waterhouse), 1993.

3765A   Pitcher, Harvey. *Witnesses of the Russian Revolution*. London: John Murray, 1994.
First-hand accounts, some by leading British correspondents: Morgan Philips Price (*The Manchester Guardian*), Arthur Ransome (*The Daily News*), and Harold Williams (by 1917, *The Daily Chronicle*).

3766   Pragnell, Anthony, ed. *Opening up the media 1983–1993*. London: John Libbey (for European Institute for the Media), 1993. 218pp. (Media Monograph no 17). Ed Per Egil Hogge.
The Institute – founded in Manchester – moved to Düsseldorf in 1992.

3767   Press Complaints Commission. *Review*. 1994.
Statement – with Code of Practice as a supplement.

3768 *Presswatch Quarterly, The.* Great Bardfield (Essex), latterly London, 1992–.
Monitors and evaluates national press coverage of British companies.

3769 Prichard, Craig. *The changing vision.* Preston: University of Central Lancashire, 1993. 50pp.
Research report into changes in the regional newspaper industry and their implications for the training and development of journalists and managers.

3770 Schlesinger, Philip, and Howard Tumber. *Reporting crime: the media politics of criminal justice.* Oxford: Oxford University Press, 1994.

3771 Simpson, Paul. 'Deadlier than the Mail'. *Newspaper Focus.* Feb 1994.
On Eve Pollard and her battle as editor of the *Sunday Express* against *The Mail on Sunday*.

3772 – – –. 'Top 50 UK newspaper publishers'. *Newspaper Focus,* Jan 1994.
Detailed analysis of current performance.

3773 Spain, Nancy (Brooker). *Why I'm not a millionaire: an autobiography.* London: Hutchinson, 1956. 356pp.
Light-hearted, frothy – but fascinating in its penetrating insights, reflecting on her long and successful career as a *Daily Expres* writer.

3774 Tweedie, Jill (Sheila). *Eating children.* London: Viking, 1993; with an unfinished additional memoir, *Frightening people.* Harmondsworth (Middx): Penguin, 1994. 404pp.
Jill Tweedie was a regular and highly acclaimed columnist with *The Guardian* from 1969 to 1984. This is explained in an afterword by Alan Brien.

3775 Vulliamy, Ed. *Seasons in hell: understanding Bosnia's war.* London: Simon & Schuster, 1993. 370pp.
Written with passion by an outstanding front-line *Guardian* correspondent, who later joined *The Observer*.

3776 Waterhouse, Keith (Spencer). *City lights: a street life.* London: Hodder & Stoughton, 1994.
In the early pages fondly recalls his days as a young reporter on the *Yorkshire Evening Post*.

3777 Wiener, Joel (Howard). *The Americanization of the British press, 1830–1914.* (in preparation).
A *magnum opus*, resulting from many years' research.

3778 Williams, Granville. *Britain's media: how they are related.* London: Campaign for Press and Broadcasting Freedom, 1994.
Analysis of the evidence of the multi-media revolution, and presentation of the case for more democratic control. An A2 wall chart was published simultaneously to illustrate the current pattern of cross-media ownership.

3779 Worcester, Robert (Milton). *Demographics and values.* London: 1994.
Paper, with graphic illustrations, delivered at City University conference, February 1994, by the founder of Market and Opinion Research International (MORI): 'what the British public read and what they think about their newspapers'.

CHRONOLOGY OF BRITISH NEWSPAPER HISTORY, 1900–1994

The listing of a title without additional comment indicates its year of foundation.

1900	Reuters achieved a historic 'beat' by announcing the relief of Mafeking in a telegram smuggled out to London
	Daily Mail started its Northern edition in Manchester, and with a highest recorded circulation of 1,320,373 claimed the largest sale in the world
	Lloyd's Weekly News had also reached a million circulation, and was the best-selling Sunday paper
	C. Arthur Pearson purchased *Morning Herald*, retitled *Daily Express and Morning Herald*
	The Hultons founded *Daily Dispatch* (also in Manchester)
1901	George Cadbury and associates acquired *The Daily News*
1903	*Daily Mirror*, started by Alfred Harmsworth as a women's daily in Nov 1903, transformed into a successful general readership picture paper in Jan 1904
	St James's Gazette to Pearson
1904	*The Standard* and *Evening Standard* to Pearson
	W.K. Haselden, first regular British popular newspaper cartoonist, began his long career at *Daily Mirror*
1905	Harmsworth (by then Northcliffe) purchased *The Observer* and grouped his *Daily Mail*, *The Evening News* and *Weekly Dispatch* into Associated Newspapers
	The final *Echo*
	St James's Gazette absorbed into *Evening Standard*
1906	Newspaper Proprietors' Association
1907	National Union of Journalists
	C.P. Scott purchased *The Manchester Guardian* (also editor, 1872–1929)
1908	*The Times* acquired by Northcliffe and revived
	Pearson took over *The Westminster Gazette*
	J.L. Garvin editor of *The Observer* (until 1942)
1909	London staged first Imperial Press Conference; foundation of the Empire (later Commonwealth) Press Union

Daily Sketch started by Hulton (initially in Manchester)

HMSO became publisher of *Hansard* as daily official report of Parliament

1910   Pearson sold *The Standard* to Davison Dalziel (later 1st Baron Dalziel of Wooler)

1911   Control of *The Observer* passed to William Waldorf (later 1st Viscount) Astor

New Copyright Act, which laid down the basis of present-day legal deposit in certain libraries

1912   *Daily Herald* launched – a printers' lock-out sheet

1913   *The New Statesman*

1914   Price of *The Times* reduced to 1*d*

Press Bureau set up to censor press

Harold Harmsworth (Rothermere) gained majority control of *Daily Mirror*

1915   Rothermere launched *Sunday Pictorial* (later *Sunday Mirror*)

William and Gomer Berry acquired *The Sunday Times*

Illustrated Sunday Herald launched by Hulton

Evening Standard sold to Hulton

'Teddy Tail' – first British comic strip, by Charles Folkard – in *Daily Mail*

1916   Max Aitken (later Beaverbrook) acquired control of *Daily Express*

1917   *The Standard* (morning paper) ceased general publication

1918   *Sunday Express* started by Beaverbrook

Lloyd George Fund with syndicate under Henry Dalziel (later Baron Dalziel of Kirkcaldy) financed United Newspapers, controlling *The Daily Chronicle, Lloyd's Weekly Newspaper* etc

1919   William Berry acquired *Financial Times* and *The Daily Graphic*

1921   *The Globe* absorbed into *The Pall Mall Gazette*

The Westminster Gazette became a morning paper

1922   Death of Northcliffe; Associated Newspapers and Amalgamated Press passed to Rothermere; J.J. Astor (later 1st Baron Astor of Hever) secured control of *The Times*, with Geoffrey Dawson reinstated as editor

Labour Party and Trades Union Congress took over *Daily Herald* as official Party newspaper

1923   Hulton chain (including *Daily Sketch* and *Daily Dispatch*) acquired by Rothermere

Workers' Weekly (later *Daily Worker*)

Evening Standard absorbed *The Pall Mall Gazette* (controlling interest to Beaverbrook)

1924   William and Gomer Berry and Edward Iliffe formed Allied Newspapers, consisting of most of former Hulton chain and *The Sunday Times*

Woking Offers (later *Woking Review*) – 'the oldest free in the country'

Sunday Express published first crossword puzzle

1925	Odhams, under Julius Elias (later Lord Southwood), acquired *The People*
	Press Association took majority holding in Reuters
1926	General Strike: public rivalry between the Government's *British Gazette* and the TUC's riposte, *The British Worker*
1927	Berry brothers and Iliffe purchased *Daily Sketch* and *Illustrated Sunday Herald* (later *Sunday Graphic*) from Rothermere
1928	Berry brothers and Iliffe acquired *The Daily Telegraph*
	Westminster Gazette merged into *The Daily News*
	Northcliffe Newspapers set up by Rothermere as provincial subsidiary of Associated Newspapers
	Provincial Newspapers set up as subsidiary of United Newspapers
1929	Odhams acquired controlling interest in *Daily Herald*, the Labour Party retaining minority interest
	Reynolds's (Illustrated) News transferred to Co-operative interests
1930s	Circulation war among the popular dailies during 'devil's decade'
1930	*The Daily Chronicle* merged with *The Daily News* to form *News Chronicle*
	Daily Worker (later *Morning Star*)
1931	Audit Bureau of Circulations
	Sunday Graphic absorbed *Lloyd's Sunday News*
	Company of Newspaper Makers (later incorporated into Worshipful Company of Stationers and Newspaper Makers)
1932	British Museum Newspaper Library opened at Colindale
1933	Beaverbrook secured full control of *Daily Express*, *Sunday Express* and *Evening Standard*
1934	*Daily Mirror*, edited by Bartholomew, started again as a tabloid 'picture paper with news', directed by Cecil Harmsworth King
	Odhams started *Weekly Illustrated* (later *Illustrated*)
1936	First British colour newspaper advertisement (in *Daily Record*, Glasgow)
1937	Break-up of Allied Newspapers: Camrose (formerly William Berry) took over *The Daily Telegraph* and retained Amalgamated Press and *Financial Times*; Kemsley (Gomer Berry) retained *Daily Sketch*, *The Sunday Times*, three other Sundays, and provincial chain (later Kemsley Newspapers)
	The Daily Telegraph absorbed *The Morning Post*
1938	*Picture Post* created by Stefan Lorant and financed by Edward Hulton II
1939	Ministry of Information set up for duration of World War II
1940	Newsprint rationing imposed
1941	Suppression of *Daily Worker* and *The Week* as subversive; *Daily Mirror* spared
	Press Association and Newspaper Proprietors' (later Publishers) Asso-

	ciation became equal proprietors of Reuters
1942	Establishment of John Hilton Bureau for advice to readers of the *News of the World*
1944	Iliffe acquired BPM Holdings (*Birmingham Post* etc)
1945	Reverse take-over of *Financial Times* by Financial News Ltd, Bracken as chairman
1946	*Daily Mail* Golden Jubllee
	Some newsprint restrictions removed
	Guild of British Newspaper Editors
	Kemsley changed *Daily Sketch* to *Daily Graphic*
1947	First Royal Commission on the Press (Ross Report published 1949)
1950	*News of the World* circulation approached 8,500,000
1951	King and Hugh Cudlipp in full control of Mirror Group
1952	Rothermere interests, through Associated Newspapers, reacquired *Daily Graphic* (the title of which later reverted to *Daily Sketch*)
1953	General Council of the Press
	Coronation Day issue of *Daily Mirror* sold 7,161,704 – record for a British daily
	Roy Thomson acquired *The Scotsman*
1955	*Daily Telegraph* centenary
	Month-long national press strike (*The Manchester Guardian* excepted)
	Daily Record (Glasgow) acquired by Mirror Group
	News Chronicle absorbed *Daily Dispatch* (Manchester)
1957	*Picture Post* closed
	Financial Times became part of the Pearson group
1958	Mirror group acquired Amalgamated Press (renamed Fleetway Press)
	End of newsprint rationing
1959	*The Manchester Guardian* became *The Guardian*
	Thomson acquired Kemsley Group (including *The Sunday Times*)
	Six-week printing strike on provincial newspapers
	Odhams acquired the Hulton and then Newnes groups
1960s	Photocomposition and web-offset printing progressively introduced into press production
1960	*News Chronicle* ceased publication; also *Sunday Graphic, Empire News*, and *The Star* (London evening)
1961	*The Sunday Telegraph*
	Second Royal Commission on the Press (Shawcross Report published 1962)
	Sunday Dispatch absorbed into *Sunday Express*
	Mirror Group acquired Odhams (including *Daily Herald*)
	The Guardian started printing in London as well as Manchester
1962	Launch of *Sunday Times Magazine* (as *Sunday Times Colour Section*)
	Reynolds News merged into *Sunday Citizen*
1963	International Publishing Corporation (IPC)

Thomson took over Edinburgh Evening News; in exchange, United Newspapers acquired Sheffield newspapers

End of boom-time for local evenings, with six titles closing

1964   *The Sun* launched by IPC, replacing *Daily Herald*

Death of Beaverbrook – and birth of the era of the conglomerates

General Council of the Press re-formed as The Press Council

The Guardian editorial office moved to London

The Observer Magazine; and *Weekend Telegraph*

1966   *The Times* carried news on the front page for the first time

Thomson bought *The Times* and its supplements

1967   *Sunday Citizen* closed

Cowdray companies – Financial News, Financial Times, Westminster Press etc – combined as S. Pearson Publishers

1968   King ousted from chairmanship of IPC

1969   Rupert Murdoch's News International acquired *The Sun* and *News of the World*, the former changing to tabloid format

United Newspapers purchased *Yorkshire Post* and *Punch*

1970   Reed International formed from Reed Group and IPC

Trial of *Sunday Telegraph* editor and reporter under Official Secrets Act (both acquitted)

1971   *Daily Mail*, having absorbed *Daily Sketch*, became a tabloid

Daily Jang launched London edition

1974   *The Times* moved out of Printing House Square into Gray's Inn Road

Third Royal Commission on the Press (final McGregor Report published 1977)

1975   Reed International formed two subsidiaries: Mirror Group Newspapers and IPC (periodicals etc)

1976   Atlantic Richfield took majority holding in *The Observer*

The Evening Post (Nottingham) became the first British newspaper to introduce direct input by journalists

1977   Trafalgar House acquired Beaverbrook Newspapers (renamed Express Newspapers) and Morgan-Grampian (periodicals)

Al Arab

1978   *Daily Star* – first new national for 75 years – launched from Manchester by Express Newspapers

Publication of *The Times* and *The Sunday Times* suspended for eleven months (1978–9)

1979   Lonrho acquired Outram (*The Glasgow Herald* and *The Evening Times*) and the S&UN chain of local Scottish newspapers

Financial Times launched first international edition, from Frankfurt

1980   *Daily Star* printed simultaneously by facsimile in London and Manchester

The Evening News (London) ceased publication; *Evening Standard* (retitled *New Standard* and later *The Standard*) under joint ownership

	(to 1988) Regional Newspaper Advertising Bureau

(to 1988) Regional Newspaper Advertising Bureau
(to 1991) Association of Free Newspapers

1981   News International acquired *The Times* and *The Sunday Times*
The Observer bought by Lonrho
Sunday Standard launched by Lonrho from Glasgow (ceased 1983)
Sunday Express Magazine; *Sunday* (also a colour magazine) with *News of the World*

1982   Trafalgar House publishing interests (except *The Standard*) 'hived off' as Fleet Holdings
The Mail on Sunday (Associated Newspapers) – first photocomposed national
National Graphical Association absorbed SLADE (union); Society of Graphical and Allied Trades absorbed NATSOPA, and became SOGAT '82

1983   *Glasgow Herald* bicentenary
Protracted industrial dispute at the Warrington plant of Eddy Shah's Messenger group

1984   Mirror Group sold by Reed to Robert Maxwell
Reuters floated as a public company
The (Birmingham) Daily News – initially free, five days a week

1985   *The Times* bicentenary
Association of British Editors
Fleet Holdings (*Daily* and *Sunday Express*, *Daily Star* etc) acquired by United Newspapers
The Standard became *The London Standard* (with full ownership to Associated Newspapers)
Conrad Black (Hollinger) secured controlling interest in *The Daily Telegraph* and *The Sunday Telegraph*

1986   News International moved all their national titles (*The Times*, *The Sunday Times*, *The Sun*, *News of the World*) to a new plant at Wapping
Sunday People reverted to the title *The People*
Shah's News (UK) launched *Today*, the first colour national; controlling interest later acquired by Lonrho, and (in 1987) by News International
The Independent initiated by Andreas Whittam Smith (Newspaper Publishing)
Sunday Sport

1987   Launch by Maxwell of *London Daily News* (lasted five months); simultaneous revival by Associated Newspapers of *Evening News* (closed later)
News Letter (Belfast): 250th anniversary
News on Sunday (seven months' existence)
Women took over editorship of two nationals: Wendy Henry at *News of the World*, Eve Pollard at *Sunday Mirror*

	Move out of Fleet Street area by editorial offices of the *Daily* and *Sunday Telegraphs*
1988	Moves also by *The Observer* and *Evening Standard* – latter followed (in 1989) by remainder of Associated Newspapers
	Daily Mirror became the first mass-market tabloid to use colour regularly
	Financial Times centenary
	Scotland on Sunday and *Sunday Life*, Belfast (both Thomson)
1989	Express Newspapers (*Daily* and *Sunday Express, Daily Star*) and *Financial Times* joined the 'diaspora'
	Wales on Sunday (Thomson)
	Official Secrets Act (covering defence, intelligence, international relations, security) re-cast
	The Sunday Correspondent – soon lost out to:
1990	*The Independent on Sunday*
	The European (Maxwell)
	First Calcutt Report (on 'privacy and related matters')
1991	As a result of the report, Press Complaints Commission replaced Press Council
	Two printing trade unions (NGA and SOGAT) merged as Graphical, Paper and Media Union
	Daily Sport
	The Observer bicentenary; *Punch* 150th anniversary
	Death of Robert Maxwell, followed by investigation of all his enterprises (including Mirror Group Newspapers)
	Management buyout of *The Birmingham Post* and associated titles; foundation of Midland Independent Newspapers
1992	Caledonian Newspaper Publishing acquired the Lonrho titles produced in Glasgow – *The Herald* and *Evening Times* – in another management buyout
	The remainder of Lonrho's Scottish papers sold to Trinity International
	Illustrated London News 150th anniversary
	Flotation of the Telegraph Plc
	Yorkshire on Sunday – the first Sunday title from Westminster Press
1993	Second Calcutt Report (into 'press self-regulation')
	The Observer acquired by the Guardian Media group
	News of the World 150th anniversary
	The Press Association's status as the national agency for home news affected by the launch of the rival UK News
	News International initiated sales war in the national arena, by cutting price of *The Times* and *The Sun*

1994   Mirror Group Newspapers moved to Canary Wharf
National Heritage Select Committee reported on 'privacy and media intrusion'
Mirror Group secured controlling interest in Newspaper Publishing (*The Independent, Independent on Sunday*)
Privacy Commissioner appointed by Press Complaints Commission

INDEX

Since the entries in the bibliography are alphabetical by author, this index is largely a source of complementary cross-references. The numbers listed refer to entry numbers.

'The' and 'A(n)' are here omitted from the titles of all publications. Honours such as peerages and knighthoods eventually bestowed are included in the entries for those concerned.

ABC: *see* Audit Bureau of Circulations
'ABC Trial' 178
Abdication crisis 3689
Aberdeen 702, 1148
Aberdeen Free Press 2122-3
Abyssinia: *see* Ethiopia
Adams, J.R.R. 68
Adley, D.J. 2006
Adscene 1827, 1969
advertising 1-4, 19, 64, 78, 83, 94-5, 109-12, 227, 459, 460, 473, 612, 762, 765, 843, 847, 967, 1060, 1084, 1199, 1304, 1397, 1504-5, 1554, 1686, 1700-1, 1794, 1804, 1873-4, 1970-3, 1979-81, 2134, 2167, 2409, 2521, 2586, 2610, 2615, 3342-3, 3378, 3558, 3729
   personalities 1068, 2249, 2404, 2902, 3034, 3070, 3468
Advertizer 2528, 3283
Africa 98, 287, 606, 1593; *see also* wars: Boer War; World War II
agencies: *see* news agencies
agony columns 1717, 2564, 2734, 3336, 3637
air: *see* aviation
Aitken 264, 593, 1842
Akerman, J. 2-4
'Alex' 2585
Alldridge, J. 2163
Allen, P.E. 15
Allied Newspapers 328, 526, 2358, 2419, 2778, 2887, 2991, 3529
alternative press 81, 179, 678, 3554, 3748
America: *see* Central America; United States
appeasement 500, 650, 653, 1186, 1211, 1361, 1369, 1695, 1949, 2085-6, 2269, 2340, 2780, 2886, 3325, 3689, 3743
Arab 2923, 3740

architecture 238, 1463, 1580, 1750, 1901, 2100, 2334, 2519, 2570, 2578, 2668, 2889, 2899
archives 55, 66, 85, 690, 2143, 2170, 2383, 2609, 3311
Argus Press 2288, 3224-5, 3231
Aris, S. 575
Army: *see* Service newspapers; Services (armed); wars
Arnold, H. 298
Arnold, W.T. 3446
artists: *see* cartoons and caricature; illustrated press
Ascherson, N. 3641
Ashmead-Bartlett, E. 1539
Asia 1063-4, 1181, 1639, 1903, 2505, 2639-40, 2758-9, 2798-800, 3575, 3725; *see also individual countries; and under* wars: World War II
Associated Newspapers 121, 784, 786, 793, 1022, 1542, 1829, 1938, 1953, 1956, 2096, 2426, 2513, 2711, 3562
Association of British Editors 13
Association of Free Newspapers 113, 193, 1038
Astor family 1206, 2495, 3033, 3616
Astor, *Hon* D. 651
Astor, J.J. (*1st Baron* Astor of Hever) 3311, 3381, 3383, 3616
Astor, W.W. (*1st Visct* Astor) 2542, 3616
Atlantic Richfield 2279, 2499
'Atticus' 1568, 2583
Aubrey, C. 3554
Audit Bureau of Circulations 290, 612, 759
Austin, A.B. 221
aviation 261, 707, 955, 1429, 2389, 2886, 3160, 3739, 3756
Aynsley, C. 1486

Western Morning News 1247, 2238, 2578
Westmancoat, J. 3489
Westminster Gazette 343, 801, 914, 917, 1165, 1290, 1436, 2250, 2857, 3104, 3105-7
Westminster Press 275, 276, 325, 424, 714, 917, 927, 1013, 1017, 1494, 1513, 1735, 1961, 2479, 2484, 2523, 2535, 3026, 3041, 3062, 3087, 3309, 3409, 3515, 3539, 3701, 3703, 3708, 3734
Westmorland Gazette 1735
Whannel, G. 3061
Whitaker 11
Whitaker, B. 2324
Whitaker, J. 298, 2082
White, C. 81
White, S. 1770
Whitehaven News 3598
Whittam Smith, A. 741, 1084, 3012, 3379
'Who's whos' 184, 517, 565-7, 3354, 3680, 3682
Whyman, J. 8
Wigtown Free Press 1773
Wilhoit, F. 10
Wilkinson, S. 3622
Willcocks, L. 2481
'William Hickey': *see* 'Hickey (William)'
Williams, F. (*Baron* Francis-Williams) 320, 3383
Williams, H. 3013, 3765A
'Williams, J.B.' 313
Williams, K. 2229
Willings Press Guide 1981
Willmott, N. 1500
Wilson, P. 749
Wilson, R. 289
Wilton, R. 2714
Wiltshire 3045
Wingate, P. 401, 770, 3061
Winsbury, R. 81, 631
Wintour, C. 90
Wintour, P. 1279

Witherow, J. 348
Withers, H. 3324
Withey, R. 3656
Wolverhampton Chronicle 1906
Woman's Dreadnought 3191
women editors 130, 543, 873, 1342, 1388, 1653, 2408, 2951-2, 3191, 3771
women journalists (pioneer) 215, 244, 329-30, 848, 1165, 1228, 1284, 1388, 1653, 1944, 1948, 2015, 2026-7, 2029, 2107, 2133, 2215, 2572, 2667, 2748, 2871-2, 3067, 3083, 3109, 3159, 3175-8, 3191, 3660, 3773
women's press 81, 127, 130, 318, 329-30, 360, 728, 797, 907, 931, 948, 1398, 1424, 1545, 1653, 2300, 2961, 3660
Women's Press Club 848, 2703
Wood, M. 2088, 2316
Woodhead 2289
Wooldridge, I. 1311
Woollacott, M. 2950
Woolley, R. 65
Woolven, G.B. 92
World Wars I and II: *see under* wars
World's Press News 5, 20, 1489
Worsthorne, *Sir* P. 297

Yattendon 2284, 3525
Yellow Advertiser 3478
Yorkshire 66, 695, 1914, 2369, 2933
Yorkshire Evening Post 3710, 3776
Yorkshire Post 143, 563, 650, 1224, 1651, 1936, 2230-1, 2555, 2612, 3623, 3714-15
Yorkshire Weekly Newspapers 3428
Young, G. 533
Young, H. 2058, 2751
Young, J. 657
Younghusband, *Sir* F. 3575
Yugoslavia 1806, 3512; *see also* wars: Balkans (1990s)